Anselm

The Complete Treatises

*with Selected Letters and Prayers
and the Meditation on Human Redemption*

Anselm

The Complete Treatises

with Selected Letters and Prayers
and the Meditation on Human Redemption

Edited and Translated by Thomas Williams

Hackett Publishing Company, Inc.
Indianapolis/Cambridge

25 24 23 22   1 2 3 4 5 6 7

For further information, please address
   Hackett Publishing Company, Inc.
   P.O. Box 44937
   Indianapolis, Indiana 46244-0937

   www.hackettpublishing.com

Cover design by Listenberger Design & Associates
Composition by Aptara, Inc.
Interior design by E. L. Wilson

Library of Congress Control Number: 2022934039

ISBN-13: 978-1-64792-080-7 (pbk.)
ISBN-13: 978-1-64792-083-8 (cloth)
ISBN-13: 978-1-64792-084-5 (PDF ebook)

The paper used in this publication meets the minimum requirements of American National Standard for Information Sciences—Permanence of Paper for Printed Library Materials, ANSI Z39.48–1984.

♾

CONTENTS

INTRODUCTION

In 1056 the twenty-three-year-old Anselm left his native Aosta, in what is now northern Italy, to escape his increasingly hostile father. At the time, he could hardly have foreseen that he would become the person we know as Saint Anselm, a man of striking spiritual depth and the greatest philosopher-theologian of Western Christianity in the eight hundred years between Augustine and Thomas Aquinas. Apart from a short-lived bout of religious fervor in his teens, Anselm had not at that point shown any great yearning for the monastic life. After leaving home, he wandered more or less aimlessly through Burgundy and France, probably trying out the teaching available from the entrepreneurial teacher-scholars who were so much a feature of that place and time.

In 1059 Anselm arrived in Normandy, where his interest was captured by the Benedictine abbey at Bec, whose famous school was under the direction of Lanfranc, the abbey's prior. Lanfranc was a scholar and teacher of wide reputation, and under his leadership the school at Bec had become an important center of learning, especially in dialectic. In 1060 Anselm decided to become a monk himself. He threw himself into monastic life with his whole heart, excelling not only as a teacher, but also as a spiritual guide. His intellectual and spiritual gifts brought him rapid advancement, and when Lanfranc was appointed abbot of Caen in 1063, Anselm was elected to succeed him as prior.

It was probably during his time as prior that Anselm first composed his dialogue *De grammatico*, although he may not have circulated the work until after he became abbot in 1078. *De grammatico* reflects the teaching of the trivium—grammar, rhetoric, and logic—in the school at Bec both as the foundation of the liberal arts and as preparation for the study of Scripture. It was also during his time as prior that Anselm began to compose his earliest prayers and meditations, which reflect an intense and highly affective spirituality that Anselm helped make popular.

Anselm's earliest major work, the *Monologion* (1075–1076),[1] reflects his concern for the spiritual and intellectual development of the monks in his charge. It is, as he explains in the prologue, a guide or template for his monks to follow in reflecting on what Anselm calls "the reason of faith." By "the reason of faith" (*ratio fidei*) Anselm means the intrinsically rational character of Christian doctrines in virtue of which they form a coherent and rationally defensible system. The

---

1. The dates of Anselm's works, which are to some extent conjectural, are taken from R. W. Southern, *Anselm: A Portrait in Landscape* (Cambridge: Cambridge University Press, 1991).

doctrines of the Christian faith are intrinsically rational, Anselm believes, because they concern the nature and activity of God, who is himself supreme reason and exemplifies supreme wisdom in everything he does. And because human beings are rational by nature, we can grasp the reason of faith.

Anselm's monks had insisted that this guide to the reason of faith be *purely* rational. In other words, Anselm was not to rely on scriptural or other authority but on argument alone. When Anselm submitted the *Monologion* for the approval of his old master Lanfranc, by then the archbishop of Canterbury, Lanfranc complained about the lack of any appeals to authority. Anselm assured his former superior that there was nothing in the *Monologion* that could not be found in Scripture or in Augustine, but he made no changes in the work itself, and he never submitted another work for Lanfranc's approval. Anselm never wavered in his belief that it is legitimate for Christians to explore the reason of faith without relying on authority.

When Anselm looked back over the *Monologion*, he was struck by how complicated a chain of argument it involved. So he began to look for an easier way to reach the conclusions he had argued for in the *Monologion*: a "single argument" (really, a single form or pattern of argument) that would prove everything he wanted to prove. Anselm's search for this master argument became something of an obsession with him; in fact, he tells us that he began to see it as a temptation and tried (unsuccessfully, as it turned out) to stop thinking about it.

The master argument finally came to him, and in the *Proslogion* (1077–1078) he wrote up the argument and showed how it could be used to generate a wide range of conclusions about God. Unlike the *Monologion*, in which Anselm adopted the role of someone trying to figure out by reason what he should believe, the *Proslogion* is written from the perspective of someone who already believes in God and is seeking to understand what he believes. The style of the two works is also quite different. The *Monologion* is straightforward, unadorned argumentation; the *Proslogion* is a passionate address to God in the style of Anselm's prayers and meditations. In spite of these differences in perspective and style, however, Anselm assures us that the *Monologion* and the *Proslogion* have the same aim: he wrote them both "mainly so that what we hold by faith concerning the divine nature and persons, leaving aside the Incarnation, could be proved by necessary reasons, independently of the authority of Scripture" (*On the Incarnation of the Word*, p. 234).

The central argument of the *Proslogion* is found in Chapters 2 through 4, in which Anselm attempts to show that the Psalmist's "fool," who has "said in his heart, 'There is no God'" (pp. 100–101), can be convinced by reason alone that God does indeed exist. Almost immediately, Anselm's argument found a sharp critic in an otherwise unknown monk named Gaunilo of Marmoutiers. Anselm was so pleased with Gaunilo's "Reply on Behalf of the Fool," and with the opportunity it gave him to clarify and extend his reasoning in the *Proslogion*, that he wrote a reply to Gaunilo and insisted that the exchange with Gaunilo be included whenever anyone copied the *Proslogion*.

In 1078 Anselm was elected abbot upon the death of Herluin, the founder and first abbot of Bec. Even though he found his new duties as abbot even more burdensome than the old ones, he did at least manage to keep writing. From 1080 to 1086 he composed three philosophical dialogues: *On Truth*, *On Freedom of Choice*, and *On the Fall of the Devil*. Anselm described them in his preface as "treatises pertaining to the study of Holy Scripture," but they are not scriptural commentaries in the usual sense. Instead, they are devoted to elucidating scriptural language through rational argument.

For example, *On Truth* begins by noticing that we speak of God as Truth. We derive such language from Scripture: Jesus identifies himself as the Truth in John 14:6, and 1 John 5:6 identifies the Spirit as Truth.[2] If we are to understand this scriptural language, we have to figure out what it could mean to speak of God as Truth. Is this our ordinary use of 'truth,' as when we speak of the truth of a statement or an opinion? And if it is, how can the Truth that is God be connected with the truth that statements and opinions have? Furthermore, Jesus speaks of "doing the truth" in John 3:21, so there must also be truth in actions. But what could that be? And how is it connected to the truth of statements, on the one hand, and the Truth that is God, on the other? In the same vein, one important line of argument in *On Freedom of Choice* is intended to elucidate the scriptural claim that "one who commits sin is a slave to sin" (John 8:34). For it would seem that if we can be enslaved by sin, we are weaker than sin or somehow subject to its power. And then what becomes of freedom and moral responsibility? Here again, in order to understand what Scripture is saying, we are driven to ask philosophical questions.

The three dialogues were Anselm's last major works as abbot of Bec. He continued to serve as abbot until 1093, when he was enthroned as archbishop of Canterbury over his own vehement objections. Though some observers at the time thought his professions of reluctance were insincere (a suspicion that has been shared by a handful of scholars in more recent years), it seems altogether plausible that he genuinely did not want to be archbishop. The position would mean even more administrative responsibility, which he greatly disliked; it would take him even further away from the normal monastic life that he had come to love so fervently; and—worst of all—it would mean contending with England's venal and ruthless king, William II. Anselm's struggles with the king proved to be as vexatious as he must have feared.

Around this time Anselm was drawn into a theological controversy over Trinitarian doctrine. Roscelin of Compiègne, a renowned teacher who would later

---

2. In Anselm's translation of the Bible, however, this verse says that the Spirit testifies that *Christ* is the Truth.

tangle with Peter Abelard as well, had raised a problem for the doctrine of the Trinity. He argued that either the three Persons of the Trinity are three distinct things, like three human beings, or else the Father and the Holy Spirit were incarnate along with the Son. Roscelin chose the first option; worse yet, he claimed that Anselm and Lanfranc had taught the same thing. To refute Roscelin's position Anselm wrote a letter, *On the Incarnation of the Word*. The first version, included here among Anselm's letters, was an open letter addressed to the whole Christian world. Anselm tells us that he left that version unfinished because he had heard that Roscelin recanted his position. But then Roscelin recanted his recantation, and Anselm revised and extended his earlier attack. The final version of the letter (1094), which I have included among the treatises, was addressed to Pope Urban II. Both versions include a discussion of the proper approach to theological disputation; the final version offers a revised and extended reply to Roscelin along with arguments about why it was fitting for the Son to become incarnate, rather than the Father or the Holy Spirit.

Not long after Anselm became archbishop, he began a work that would explore the reason of the one central part of the Christian faith he had yet to investigate: the Incarnation. His aim was to show that even if we knew nothing of a historical Christ, we would be able to show by reason alone that in order to heal the breach that sin has made between God and humanity, God would have to become incarnate and offer his own life. So he called the work *Cur Deus Homo:* "Why God Became a Human Being" or "Why a God-Man?"

The argument of *Cur Deus Homo* takes off from the objection that the Christian account of redemption represents God as acting in an irrational and unseemly way. The arguments by which Anselm seeks to defuse this objection are quite complicated and touch on a number of different issues, but there are two main threads that run through all of them. First, if we human beings fall, God has to offer us reconciliation. Having made us for the sake of happiness, God cannot simply abandon us to wretchedness and sin; to do so would be to allow us to thwart his plan for us. It would make it look as though either God had changed his mind about his purposes for human nature (thus impugning God's wisdom) or he was unable to bring those purposes to fulfillment (thus impugning God's power). And second, the only way for God to offer this reconciliation is through the voluntary self-offering of a God-man. In other words, far from being irrational, the death of God Incarnate is the only rationally acceptable way for God to effect a reconciliation between himself and us.

Anselm notes in his preface that he was forced to complete *Cur Deus Homo* in haste: "If I had been allowed freedom from distractions and enough time to work on it, I would have included and added quite a few things that I have left unsaid" (p. 246). Two other works translated here may well represent what was missing from *Cur Deus Homo*. Anselm's editor, F. S. Schmitt, believed that Anselm would have "included" (or interpolated) the discussions "of power, of necessity, of will, and of certain other things" to which he refers in *Cur Deus Homo* 1.1 and "added" (or appended) the treatment of original sin he postponed in *Cur Deus Homo* 2.17.[3] Anselm never put his thoughts on power, necessity, and will in final form, but sketches of a discussion of those topics are preserved in the Lambeth Fragments. He did, however, supply the missing appendix, a work *On the Virginal Conception, and On Original Sin* (1099). He also composed a summary of the argument of *Cur Deus Homo* in the form of a meditation, the *Meditation on Human Redemption*.

Though Anselm had begun *Cur Deus Homo* in England, he finished it abroad in 1098, having been forced into exile in November 1097 as a result of various disputes with the king. Anselm had asked permission three times to go see the pope and seek his advice. The king refused, and when Anselm left anyway, William refused to let him return to England.

William died in 1100, and the new king, Henry I, invited Anselm to return to England. Yet it was not long before Henry and Anselm were at odds, and Anselm found himself in exile again, from 1103 to 1106. Anselm did not manage to do any significant writing during his second exile, but after his return he completed one more work: *De concordia* (1107–1108), in which he reconciled human free choice with divine foreknowledge, predestination, and grace. By this time Anselm had become seriously ill and was so weak that he had to be carried around on a litter. It was becoming clear that he would not live to write a treatise on the origin of the soul, as he had hoped. On Wednesday of Holy Week, 21 April 1109, Anselm died peacefully, surrounded by the monks of Canterbury.

---

3. See the Schmitt text cited in the Lambeth Fragments.

Suggestions for Further Reading

Davies, Brian, and Brian Leftow, eds. *The Cambridge Companion to Anselm.* Cambridge: Cambridge University Press, 2004.

Holopainen, Toivo. *Dialectic and Theology in the Eleventh Century.* Leiden: E. J. Brill, 1996.

Plantinga, Alvin, ed. *The Ontological Argument.* Garden City, NY: Anchor Books, 1965.

Southern, R. W. *Anselm: A Portrait in Landscape.* Cambridge: Cambridge University Press, 1991.

Sweeney, Eileen C. *Anselm of Canterbury and the Desire for the Word.* Washington, DC: Catholic University of America Press, 2016.

Vaughn, Sally N. *Anselm of Bec and Robert of Meulan: The Innocence of the Dove and the Wisdom of the Serpent.* Berkeley: University of California Press, 1987.

Visser, Sandra, and Thomas Williams. *Anselm.* Great Medieval Thinkers. Oxford: Oxford University Press, 2008.

Williams, Thomas. *Anselm: A Very Short Introduction.* Oxford: Oxford University Press, 2022.

A Note on the Translation

With the exception of the letters Anselm wrote during his years at Bec, the Latin text translated here is the critical edition of F. S. Schmitt in *S. Anselmi Cantuariensis Archiepiscopi Opera Omnia* (Stuttgart-Bad Canstatt: Friedrich Fromann Verlag, 1968) and "Ein neues unvollendetes Werk des hl. Anselm von Canterbury," *Beiträge zur Geschichte der Philosophie und Theologie des Mittelalters* Band 33, Heft 3 (1936), 22–43. I have noted any departures from Schmitt's text in the footnotes. Anselm's letters as prior and then abbot of Bec are translated from the new edition of Samu Niskanen, *Letters of Anselm, Archbishop of Canterbury, Volume I: The Bec Letters* (Oxford: Oxford University Press, 2019). For those letters I first give the more familiar numbering from Schmitt's edition and then, in parentheses, Niskanen's numbering.

An asterisk in the text indicates that the word so marked is explained in the Glossary. I have generally marked such terms only on their first occurrence in a chapter and in passages where their use seems especially likely to cause misunderstanding.

Occasionally the same speaker who ends one chapter begins the next. In such cases, the new chapter begins without an indication of the speaker.

When Anselm speaks of "the Apostle," without a proper name, he is referring to Saint Paul.

Biblical citations are given according to the New Revised Standard Version of the Bible. In the case of quotations from the Psalms, a citation to the Latin Vulgate is also given in parentheses.

The Complete Treatises

De grammatico
(How Expert Is a Substance and a Quality)

1 STUDENT: I am asking you to make it clear to me whether expert[1] is a substance or a quality so that by knowing this, I will recognize how I ought to think about other terms that are likewise said denominatively.*

TEACHER: First, say why you are unsure.

S: Because it seems that both can be proved by compelling arguments—I mean, both that it is and that it is not [a substance, and that it is and that it is not a quality].

T: Then go ahead and prove it.

S: Then don't be in a hurry to object to what I say. Instead, let me state my argument in full, and then either approve it or correct it.

T: As you wish.

S: To prove that expert is a substance, it is enough to point out that every expert is a human being, and every human being is a substance. For whatever an expert has from which it follows that he is a substance, he has it precisely in virtue of the

---

1. "expert": *grammaticus*. The Latin word actually means "grammatical" (as an adjective) or "grammarian" (as a noun). To make the dialogue work in English, we need a word that has the same form as both an adjective and a noun, so I have settled on 'expert,' which can serve as either, and which is close enough in meaning to *grammaticus* that Anselm's examples and arguments still work as intended.

fact that he is a human being. Granted, then, that he is a human being, whatever follows from human being also follows from expert.

On the other hand, the philosophers who have considered this question acknowledge explicitly that expert is a quality. It is sheer effrontery to reject their authority on these matters.

Moreover, since it is necessary that expert is either a substance or a quality in such a way that whichever it is, it is not the other, and whichever it is not, it must be the other, any consideration that serves to support one alternative destroys the other, and whatever undermines one alternative reinforces the other. Since, therefore, one of these alternatives is true and the other false, I am asking you to uncover the truth for me by exposing the falsehood.

2   T: The arguments you put forward for both alternatives are compelling, except for when you said that if one is true, the other cannot be true. So you should not demand that I show one alternative is false—that's something no one can do—but rather that I explain how the two alternatives do not contradict each other, if that is something I can manage to do. But first I'd like to hear from you what objections you think could be offered against your arguments.

S: What you're asking of me is precisely what I was eagerly hoping to hear from you. But since you say that those arguments are irrefutable, my task, as the one who is uncertain, is to explain what is troubling me, and yours is to show that both alternatives are well established and that they are consistent with each other.

T: Then say what you are thinking, and I will try to do what you are asking.

S: I think the claim that an expert is a human being can be rebutted like this: no expert can be understood to lack expertise, and any human being can be understood to lack expertise. Moreover, any expert can be more or less, and no human being can be more or less. From each of these sets of two premises, a single conclusion follows: no expert is a human being.

3   T: That doesn't follow.

S: Why not?

T: Do you think the name 'animal' signifies anything other than 'animate substance capable of sensation'?

S: Certainly 'animal' is nothing other than 'animate substance capable of sensation' and 'animate substance capable of sensation' is nothing other than 'animal.'

T: That's right. But say also whether everything that is not other than an animate substance capable of sensation can be understood to be without rationality, and is not rational by necessity.

S: I can't deny it.

T: Therefore, every animal can be understood to be without rationality, and no animal is rational by necessity.

S: I can't deny that that does follow from the points I've conceded, but I am very much afraid of where I suspect you're headed with this.

T: Now no human being can be understood to be without rationality, and, necessarily, every human being is rational.

S: I am hemmed in on both sides.[2] If I concede this, you will draw the conclusion that no human being is an animal; if I reject it, you will say that not only can I be *understood* to be without rationality, I can truly *be* without rationality.

T: Don't worry. What you think follows, doesn't.

S: If what you are promising is really the case, I freely concede any premises you have put forward; but if not, I do so unwillingly.

T: Put together the four last propositions that I made into two syllogisms.

S: They can be arranged in this order:

    (1)   Every animal can be understood to be without rationality.

    (2)   But no human being can be understood to be without rationality.

Moreover,

    (3)   No animal is rational by necessity.

    (4)   But every human being is rational by necessity.

From both pairs of premises arranged in this order, this conclusion seems to follow:

    (5)   Therefore, no human being is an animal—

which is as false as any conclusion could be, though I do not see how the premises are shaky in any way. The two that have 'human being' as their subject term are so self-evident that it seems foolish to prove them, and the two that have 'animal' as their subject term are so well proved that it seems foolish to deny them. But I see that the logic of these two syllogisms is in every respect like the two I put forward myself just a little while ago. So I strongly suspect you offered your arguments precisely so that when I realized that their conclusion is obviously false, I would make the same judgment about the similar arguments I had made.

T: That's right.

---

2. Cf. Daniel 13:22 (Susanna 1:22): "I am hemmed in on every side."

S: Then identify the respect in which both sets of arguments are misleading, so that although they apparently have true premises and are constructed according to the rules of syllogisms, truth does not uphold their conclusions.

4   T: I will do that for your syllogisms; you, if you like, examine mine.

S: Let's proceed as you think best.

T: Repeat and construct the syllogisms that you made.

S: Every human being can be understood without expertise.

T: What do you say a human being can be understood to be without expertise?

S: A human being.

T: Then state that premise as you understand it.

S: Every human being can be understood to be a human being without expertise.

T: I grant that premise; take it as given.

S: No expert can be understood without expertise.

T: What can an expert not be understood to be without expertise?

S: Expert.

T: Then state what you mean.

S: No expert can be understood to be expert without expertise.

T: Combine these two complete premises as you have just now expressed them.

S: Every human being can be understood to be a human being without expertise. No expert can be understood to be expert without expertise.

T: Now examine whether they have a common term, since without a common term they do not entail any conclusion.

S: I see that they do not have a common term, and therefore nothing follows from them.

T: Construct the other syllogism.

S: There is no longer any need for you to take the trouble to expound it, because I detect the fallacy. I was understanding the premises to mean that no human being is any more or less a human being and that every expert is more or less expert. And since these two premises have no common term, they do not entail any conclusion.

T: And so do you think that no conclusion can be drawn from these sets of premises?

S: I certainly was thinking so, but this question of yours makes me wonder whether there is some hidden entailment after all. But how can they entail anything without a common term?

T: The common term of a syllogism has to be found more in the meaning than in the expression. In the same way that there is no entailment if the term is common in words but not in meaning, there is likewise nothing to prevent there being an entailment if the term is common in meaning but not in words. It's the meaning that holds a syllogism together, not the words.

5   S: I'm waiting for you to draw the conclusion from my premises.

T: They do indeed entail a conclusion, but it's not what you're expecting.

S: Whatever it might be, I will receive it gratefully.

T: Suppose someone says, "Every human being can be understood to be a human being without expertise" and "No expert can be understood to be expert without expertise." Doesn't that signify the same as "Being human does not require expertise" and "Being expert requires expertise"?

S: Nothing could be truer.

T: Do these two premises, which I just said are signified by those other two premises, have a common term?

S: They do.

T: Therefore, they establish that being expert is not the same as being human: that is, the two do not have the same definition.

S: That follows and is the case; I see that beyond any doubt.

T: And yet it does not follow, as you were thinking, that an expert is not a human being. But if you understand "An expert is not a human being" as meaning "Expert is not the same as human"—that is, they don't have the same definition—that conclusion is true.

6   S: I understand what you're saying.

T: So if you really understand what I have said, tell me how you would destroy this syllogism if someone were to construct it:

(6)   Every expert is so called on the basis of a quality.*
(7)   No human being is so called on the basis of a quality.
(8)   Therefore, no human being is an expert.

S: I think this is the same sort of thing as saying

5

(9) Everything rational is so called on the basis of a quality.

(10) But no human being is so called on the basis of a quality.

(11) Therefore, no human being is rational.

But in fact no proof can make it true that 'rational' is not predicated of any human being. Similarly, the syllogism that you put forward just now does not necessarily conclude that 'expert' is not predicated of a human being. For if we understand its premises in a way that accords with the truth, it is as if we were to say

(12) Every expert is called expert on the basis of a quality.

(13) No human being is called a human being on the basis of a quality.

It by no means follows from these two premises that 'expert' is not predicated of any human being, because there is no common term that is affirmed of expert and denied of human being. Now there would be a common term in these two premises, and they would necessarily entail a conclusion, if the second premise were kept the same and another premise, "No human being is called expert in virtue of a quality," were true, or the first premise were kept the same and another premise, "Every expert is called a human being in virtue of a quality," were true. For from either of those combinations it would follow that 'expert' is not predicated of any human being.

Now suppose someone means to understand "A human being is not expert" as "Human being is not the same thing as expert"—as if I were to say "Lightning is brightness" or "Lightning is not brightness" to mean "Lightning is the same thing as brightness" or "Lightning is not the same thing as brightness." If that is how someone understands "A human being is not expert," then on that understanding it follows from those premises, if one attends carefully to what they mean, that no human being is expert. For the purpose of proving that the essence* of human being is not the essence of expert, the signification of those premises has a common term.

7   T: You have rightly understood what I have said, but you have perhaps not rightly examined why I said it.

S: How is it that I have rightly understood but not rightly examined?

T: Tell me: What would follow if someone argued like this: "No human being can be understood without rationality, but every stone can be understood without rationality"?

S: Surely, "Therefore, no stone is a human being."

T: How do you understand this claim? Is it that a stone is in no way a human being, or is it that stone is not the same thing as human being?

S: It's that a stone is in no way a human being.

T: Then tell me how this syllogism differs from your syllogism, in which you say that an expert cannot be understood without expertise, whereas a human being can, and so an expert is not a human being.

S: As far as the force of the argumentation goes, I don't see how one differs from the other. In my syllogism, we are to understand that an expert cannot be understood to be expert without expertise, and a human being can be understood to be a human being without expertise. Similarly, in your syllogism, we are to understand that a human being cannot be understood to be a human being without rationality, and a stone can be understood to be a stone without rationality. Consequently, since the conclusion of your syllogism—that a stone is in no way a human being—is established, you seem to me to have destroyed the conclusion of my syllogism, which is exactly like yours, by your shrewd arguments. So now I understand why you said that I had understood correctly but not examined correctly: I correctly understood the meaning of the words you were using, but I did not correctly examine the point you were making, because I didn't realize how what you said was leading me astray.

T: No, in fact you didn't examine correctly because you didn't realize how it *wasn't* leading you astray.

S: How is that?

T: Clearly, if the syllogism that I proposed just now is expounded in the way I expounded yours—as "No human being can be understood to be a human being without rationality, but every stone can be understood to be a stone without rationality"—it will have exactly the same rational force that I said yours has. But because my syllogism can be understood in another way, in which yours cannot be understood, it has the conclusion that a stone can in no way be a human being. For when I say

> (14) No human being can be understood without rationality, and
> (15) Every stone can be understood without rationality,

this can, and indeed should, be interpreted as

> (16) No human being can in any way be understood without rationality, whereas
> (17) Every stone can in any way be understood without rationality.

From this we derive the conclusion

> (18) Therefore, no stone is in any way a human being.

In the case of your premises, however, truth by no means allows a similar interpretation. For it cannot be said that no expert can in any way be understood without expertise or that every human being can in every way be understood without expertise. For everyone who is expert can be understood to be a human being without expertise, and no human being can be understood to be expert without expertise. Hence we cannot derive the conclusion that an expert can in no way be a human being.

8   S: I don't have any objection to raise against your view. But because you have implicitly warned me not to be satisfied with understanding what you say, but to examine the significance of what you say, I think the conclusion that you showed to follow from my syllogism—"Being expert is not the same as being human"—requires further examination. For if that is true, then someone who has the essence of expert does not therefore necessarily have the essence of human being. But if human being follows from expert, the essence of human being follows from the essence of expert. But in fact the essence of human being does not follow from the essence of expert; therefore, human being does not follow from expert. Therefore, not every expert is a human being. And since in all who are expert there is one reason why they are human beings, either every expert is a human being, or no expert is a human being. Therefore, no expert is a human being. And so it seems that the conclusion you so skillfully took away from my syllogism, you have now even more skillfully restored.

T: Although my warning that you should examine carefully what you hear was merely implicit, it was not, apparently, useless. For although you sophistically prove that no expert is a human being, using the premise that being expert is not being human, it will nonetheless be useful for you when you see this sophism, which deceives you under the cover of genuine truth, in its naked fallaciousness.

S: Then show me in what respect, and at what point, this proof I just gave about the expert deceives me.

T: Let's go back to animal and human being, in which we can so "feel" the truth that no sophism would persuade us to believe something false, even if it seems to compel us to believe something false. Tell me: is the being of any given thing captured by its definition?

S: Yes.

T: Is the definition of human being the definition of animal?

S: Not at all. For if 'rational, mortal animal,' which is the definition of human being, were the definition of animal, 'rational, mortal' would apply to anything to which 'animal' applied, which is false.

T: So the being of a human being is not the being of an animal.

S: That follows.

T: So you can prove from this that no human being is an animal, using the same argument by which you just proved that no expert is a human being. Hence, if you see that your pattern of reasoning produces an obviously false conclusion in this case, you should not believe that it produces an obviously true conclusion in the case that has confused you.

S: You have now shown me *that* my argument is misleading. Now show me *where*.

T: Do you not remember what I said, and you agreed with, just a short time ago: that "The being of expert is not the being of human being" means the same as "The definition of expert is not the same as the definition of human being": that is, expert and human being are not in every respect the same? After all, just as 'human being' should not be defined using 'expertise,' 'expert' cannot be defined *without* using 'expertise.' Accordingly, this is how your argument ought to be understood: "Given that being expert is not unqualifiedly* being human, it does not follow that someone who has the essence of expert has unqualifiedly the essence of being human." Likewise, it should be understood that unqualifiedly human does not follow from expert: that is, if someone is expert, it does not follow that he is unqualifiedly human. And so in fact all that follows is this: "No expert is unqualifiedly human."

S: Nothing could be clearer.

9   T: But if it were to be proved (as I believe it easily could) that the being of expert is not the being of human being in the same way that the being of white is not the being of human being—after all, human being can exist without white and white without human being—then it would truly follow that some expert can be not a human being.

S: Then why are we in difficulties about this, if it can be proved? Prove it, and let this inquiry come to an end.

T: You should not demand this of me. For what we are hashing out in this inquiry is not whether some expert *can be* not a human being, but whether some expert *is* not a human being, which you see cannot be proved.

S: I don't yet see that, because I still have an objection to raise.

T: Go ahead.

S: Aristotle shows that expert is among the things that exist in a subject, and no human being exists in a subject.[3] Therefore, no expert is a human being.

---

3. Aristotle, *Categories* 2. See also Boethius's commentary, *In Categorias Aristotelis* I.1, 5.

9

T: Aristotle did not intend for that to follow from what he said. For Aristotle also says that a particular human being, and human being, and animal are expert.

S: Then how is this syllogism refuted?

T: Tell me: when you speak to me of expert, what shall I understand you to be speaking of: the word, or the things that it signifies?

S: The things.

T: Very well. What things does it signify?

S: Human being and expertise.

T: Then when I hear this word, I will understand human being or expertise, and if I speak of expert, I will be speaking of human being or of expertise.

S: That has to be right.

T: Well, then, is human being a substance, or in a subject?

S: Human being is not in a subject; it is a substance.

T: Is expertise a quality, and in a subject?

S: Yes, both.

T: Then how is it surprising if someone says that with respect to human being, expert is a substance and is not in a subject, and also that with respect to expertise, expert is a quality and is in a subject?

10   S: I can't deny that. But I still have one reason to offer why expert is not a substance: every substance is either primary substance or secondary substance, but expert is neither primary nor secondary.

T: Remember the words of Aristotle that I spoke just a short time ago. He says that expert is both primary and secondary substance, because, as the text shows, he says that expert is a particular human being, and human being, and animal. Still, on what basis do you prove that expert is neither primary nor secondary substance?

S: Because it is in a subject, which no substance is; and it is said of many, which is not true of primary substance; and it is neither genus nor species, nor is it said on the basis of quiddity,* as secondary substance is.

T: If you correctly remember what we have already said, none of these means that expert is not a substance, because in a certain respect expert is not in a subject, and it is a genus and species, and it is said on the basis of quiddity. For expert is both human being, which is species, and animal, which is genus, and these are said on the basis of quiddity. Expert is also individual in the same way that human being and animal are, because just as a particular human being and a particular animal are individual, so too a particular expert is individual. For Socrates is a human being and an animal and an expert.

S: I cannot deny what you are saying.

11   T: If you have no other arguments to prove that expert is not human being, now prove that expert is not expertise.

S: I can prove this more easily by pointing than by arguing. For you shattered all my arguments when you made it clear that 'expert' has various significations and we should speak and think about it on the basis of those significations. I can't deny that—yet it doesn't put my mind at ease, as if I had really found what I was looking for. In fact, it seems to me as if you don't care about teaching me, but just about destroying my arguments. But just as it was my task to explain what leads me into doubt about both alternatives, it was your task either to refute one of the alternatives or else to show how they do not contradict each other.

T: It has been shown that we should speak and think of expert sometimes with respect to human being and sometimes with respect to expertise; that is why it is not contradictory for expert to be a substance and to be a quality. Why do you not find this proof sufficient?

S: Because no one who understands the word 'expert' is unaware that it signifies human being and expertise. And yet if I counted on this understanding and went out in public and said "Expert is a useful field of study" or "This fellow knows expert really well," not only would experts be appalled, but even the uneducated would laugh. So I simply will not believe that the expositors of dialectic had no other reason to write so often and so deliberately in their books something that they themselves would be ashamed to say in conversation. Again and again, when they want to explain quality or accident, they say, "such as expert and the like," even though the actual practice of all speakers shows that expert is a substance rather than a quality. And when they want to teach something about substance, nowhere do they write, "such as expert or something else like that." And on top of that, if expert should be called both a substance and a quality because it signifies human being and expertise, why isn't human being likewise a quality and a substance? For 'human being' signifies a substance along with all the differences that are in human being, such as mortality and the capacity for sensation. But nowhere in any discussion of quality is 'human being' offered as an example.

12   T: You reject the explanation I gave for why expert is substance and quality, on the grounds that it doesn't work for the name 'human being.' The reason you do this is, I think, that you are not paying attention to how differently the name 'human being' signifies the things of which a human being consists, compared to how 'expert' signifies human being and expertise. Of course, the name 'human being' signifies directly (*per se*), and as one, the things of which a human being

consists, among which substance has the foremost place, because it is the cause of the others and possesses them, not in the sense that it needs them but in the sense that they need it. For there is no difference of a substance without which the substance cannot be found, and none of its differences can exist without it. Accordingly, although all these things [substance and differences] together as one whole are appellated[4] by the one name 'human being,' with one signification, nonetheless, this name chiefly signifies and appellates the substance. Thus, although it is correct to say "A substance is a human being" or "Human being is a substance," no one says "Rationality is a human being" or "A human being is rationality"—rather, one says "A human being possesses rationality."

By contrast, 'expert' does not signify human being and expertise as one; rather, it signifies expertise directly (*per se*) and human being indirectly (*per aliud*). And although this word appellates human being, it is not properly said to signify human being; and although it signifies expertise, it nonetheless does not appellate expertise. A word that appellates something (in the sense I am talking about now) is a word by which that thing is appellated in the ordinary way of speaking. In ordinary speech no one says "Expertise is expert" or "An expert is expertise," but rather "A human being is expert" and "An expert is a human being."

13   S: I don't see your point that 'expert' signifies expertise directly and human being indirectly, or how it merely signifies [but does not appellate] expertise. For human being consists of animal and rationality and mortality, and that is why 'human being' signifies these three; in the same way, expert consists of human being and expertise, and for that reason this name signifies both. After all, neither a human being without expertise nor expertise without a human being is ever called 'expert.'

T: If you're right, the definition and being of expert is this: human being possessing expertise.

S: It can't be anything else.

T: Therefore, since expertise distinguishes expert human being from non-expert, it brings an expert into being, and it is a part of its being, and it cannot be present in or absent from an expert without destroying the subject.

S: So?

T: Then expertise is not an accident, but a substantial difference, and human being is a genus and expert a species. And a similar argument would work for whiteness

---

4. "Appellated" translates *appellentur*, which often is simply "called" but here is used as a technical term; its meaning will emerge as the dialogue continues.

and similar accidents. But the content of the whole art [of dialectic] shows that this is false.

S: I can't deny what you're saying, but I'm not yet persuaded that 'expert' does not signify human being.

T: Let's suppose that there is some rational animal—but not a human being—who has expertise in the way that a human being has.

S: It's easy to imagine that.

T: Then there is a non–human being possessing expertise.

S: That follows.

T: And everyone who possesses expertise is expert.

S: Granted.

T: Then there is a non-human expert.

S: That follows.

T: But you say that human being is understood in expert.

S: I do.

T: Then some non-human is a human being, which is false.

S: That's where the argument goes.

T: So don't you see that the only reason 'expert' seems to signify human being more than 'white' does is that that expertise belongs (*accidit*) only to human beings, whereas white does not belong only to human beings?

S: That does follow from our thought experiment, but I want you to show it without any thought experiment.

T: If human being is included in expert, it is not predicated of anything at the same time along with human being, in the same way that animal is not predicated along with human being, because it is included in human being. For example, "Socrates is a human being animal" is not an apt expression.

S: There's no disputing that.

T: But "Socrates is a human expert" is a suitable expression.

S: Yes, it is.

T: So human being is not included in expert.

S: That does seem to follow.

T: Likewise, if expert is human being having expertise, one can appropriately substitute 'human being having expertise' wherever 'expert' appears.

S: Yes.

T: So if "Socrates is a human expert" is a suitable expression, "Socrates is a human human being having expertise" is also an appropriate expression.

S: That follows.

T: But every human being having expertise is a human expert.

S: Yes.

T: Then Socrates, who is a human human being having expertise, is a human human expert. And since expert is human being having expertise, it follows that Socrates is a human human human being having expertise, and so on to infinity.

S: I cannot resist these clear implications.

T: Moreover, if in 'expert' human being is to be understood along with expertise, in all similar denominatives* that which is denominated is to be understood along with that from which it is denominated.

S: I was figuring that out.

T: Therefore, 'today's' signifies what is called today's and today.

S: Where are you going with this?

T: 'Today's' therefore signifies something with time.

S: That must be the case.

T: Therefore, 'today's' is not a name but a verb, because it is an utterance that co-signifies time, and it is not a statement.[5]

14 S: You have sufficiently proved to me that 'expert' does not signify human being.

T: Then do you understand my point that 'expert' does not signify human being?

S: I do, and I'm looking forward to your showing that 'expert' signifies expertise.

T: Were you not saying yourself just a short while ago that 'expert' signifies 'human being possessing expertise'?

S: And I believed it.

---

5. Boethius, *In De interpretatione Aristotelis* 3: "A verb is something that co-signifies time, and no part of which has signification on its own"; 4: "A statement is an utterance that has a signification, some part of which has a signification of its own."

T: But by now it has already been quite thoroughly proved that it does not signify human being.

S: Quite.

T: So what's left?

S: That it signifies precisely 'possessing expertise.'

T: So it signifies expertise.

S: It has been sufficiently proved that 'expert' appellates human being, not expertise, and that it signifies expertise, not human being. But you said that 'expert' signifies expertise directly and human being indirectly, so I am asking you to distinguish these two significations clearly for me, so that I may understand how 'expert' signifies what in one way it doesn't signify, or how it appellates something it doesn't signify.

T: Suppose, unbeknownst to you, there is a white horse shut up in a building, and someone says to you, "In this building there is someone or something white," would you thereby know that there is a horse there?

S: No. For whether he says "something white" or "whiteness" or "something in which there is whiteness," I do not mentally conceive the essence of any definite thing except this color.

T: Even if you do understand something other than that color, it is clear that you do not understand by means of that name the essence of that in which the color exists.

S: That's clear. For even if body or surface comes to mind—which would happen only because I know from experience that whiteness is generally in bodies or on surfaces—the name 'white' by itself does not signify any of these, as was proved in the case of 'expert.' But I am still waiting for you to show what it does signify.

T: What if you see a white horse and a black cow standing next to each other, and someone says to you, "Strike it"—meaning the horse, but not showing by any sign which one he is talking about. Do you know that he is talking about the horse?

S: No.

T: But if you do not know and so you ask him, "Which one?" and he replies "The white one," do you understand which he is talking about?

S: By the name 'white' I understand the horse.

T: So the name 'white' signifies the horse to you.

S: Indeed it does.

T: Don't you see that it does this in a different way from the name 'horse'?

S: I do. Clearly, even before I know the horse is white, the name 'horse' directly, not indirectly, signifies to me the substance of horse. By contrast, the name 'white' does not signify the substance of horse directly, but only indirectly, in virtue of the fact that I know the horse is white. For since the name 'white' has exactly the same signification as the expression 'possessing whiteness,' just as the latter expression directly establishes for me an understanding of whiteness, and not of the thing that possesses whiteness, the same is true of the name 'white.' But because I know that whiteness is in the horse through something other than[6] the name 'white'—in this case, through sight—when I understand whiteness through that name, I understand the horse in virtue of the fact that I know whiteness is in the horse, that is, through something other than the name 'white,' by which, nonetheless, the horse is appellated.

15 T: Do you understand, therefore, how 'white' does not signify what it in some way signifies, and how it appellates something it does not signify?

S: Yes, I understand this too. After all, 'white' both does and does not signify the horse, because it does not signify it directly, but indirectly, and yet the horse is appellated white. And what I see in the case of 'white' I understand also in the case of 'expert' and similar denominatives. Hence it seems to me that the signification of names and verbs can be divided in this way: some signification is direct, and some is indirect.

T: Note also that of these two significations, direct signification by these significant utterances is substantial, whereas indirect signification is accidental. For when the definition of name or verb includes "significant utterance," we must understand only direct signification. For if indirect signification were to be understood in the definition of a name or verb, 'today's' would no longer be a name, but a verb. For as I said earlier, it sometimes signifies something indirectly along with time, and that is the function of a verb, not of a name.

16 S: What you say is clearly true. But the mind does not accept without hesitation that expert is a quality, even though it signifies expertise, or that human being alone (that is, without expertise) is expert, even though it has been proved that human being and expertise together are not expert—from which it follows that human being alone is expert, because human being can be expert in only one of two ways: alone or with expertise. For although the name 'expert' signifies expertise, if someone were to ask you what an expert is, "expertise" or "a quality" would

---

6. "through something other than": *per aliquid aliud quam*. This language makes it clear that Anselm is explaining what I have been translating as "indirect (*per aliud*) signification."

not be an apt reply. And if no one is expert otherwise than by sharing in expertise, it follows that human being is not expert except with expertise.

T: As far as answering your question goes, the statement "A human being alone, that is, without expertise, is expert" can be understood in two ways, one true and one false. Of course a human being alone, without expertise, is expert, because a human being alone has expertise. After all, neither expertise alone nor expertise with a human being has expertise. But a human being alone, that is, without expertise, is not expert, because no one can be expert in the absence of expertise. It is like the case of someone who leads another by going in front of him. He alone is the leader, because the one who follows is not the leader, neither separately nor as the two together form a pair; and alone he is not the leader, because he cannot be the leader unless there is someone who follows him. But the claim that expert is a quality is correct only in the sense that accords with Aristotle's treatise *On the Categories*.

17 S: Does that treatise contain anything beyond "Everything that exists is either substance or quantity or quality" and so forth? Therefore, if human being alone is expert, a substance alone is expert. So how, according to that treatise, is expert a quality rather than a substance?

T: Even if you are right in understanding this passage to mean that everything that exists is one of these, Aristotle's primary aim in that book was not to prove that, but to show that every name or verb signifies one of these. It was not his aim to show what individual things are, or which individual utterances appellate which things, but just to show what they signify. Now since utterances signify things, in the course of saying what utterances signify, he had to say what things are. To take just one example, the division that he makes at the beginning of the treatise *On the Categories* is sufficient evidence that this was his aim. He does not say "Each of the things that exist is either a substance or a quantity" and so forth; nor does he say "Each of the things that are spoken of using a non-composite expression is appellated either a substance or a quantity." No, he says, "Each of the things that are spoken of using a non-composite expression signifies either a substance or a quantity."

S: Reason convinces me of what you're saying.

T: So when Aristotle says, "Each of the things that are spoken of using a non-composite expression signifies either a substance or a quality" and so forth, which signification do you think he is talking about: what those expressions signify directly and substantially, or what they signify indirectly and accidentally?

S: He is talking only about direct signification, which he himself, in defining 'name' and 'verb,' said was present in those expressions.

T: Do you think he proceeded differently in his treatise from what he put forward in this division, or that any of those who followed him in writing about dialectic intended to take a different view from Aristotle's own view?

S: Their writings in no way allow anyone to think so, since we nowhere find any of them putting forward an expression in order to show what it signifies indirectly, but always in order to show what it signifies directly. After all, no one who wants to point out a substance offers the expression 'white' or 'expert,' whereas someone teaching about quality will offer 'white' and 'expert' and similar words.

18   T: Suppose, having put forward the division stated above, I ask you, "What is 'expert' according to this division and according to those who follow it in writing about dialectic?" What am I asking you, and what will your answer be?

S: Undoubtedly the question here can only be about either the expression or the thing it signifies. Accordingly, since it is uncontroversial that according to this division 'expert' does not signify human being, but expertise, I would unhesitatingly reply, "If you're asking about the expression, it is an expression signifying a quality; but if you're asking about the thing, it is a quality."

T: I'm sure you're aware that in that book Aristotle calls words by the name of the things they signify, and not by the name of the things they merely appellate. For example, he says "Every substance"—that is, every utterance signifying a substance—"evidently signifies something particular." Likewise, he names (or, as you put it a short time ago, points out) things by just the expressions that signify them and (often) do not appellate them.

S: I cannot fail to be aware of this. Consequently, when someone asks what expert is according to Aristotle's treatise and according to his followers, the right answer is the same whether the question is about the expression or about the thing: "It is a quality." And yet in terms of what the expression appellates, it is truly a substance.

T: Quite right. Even grammarians say one thing in accordance with the form of words and something else in accordance with the nature of things, so it should not bother us that dialecticians write about expressions in one way in accordance with what they signify, but use them in another way in speaking in accordance with what they appellate. Indeed, they say that *lapis* is masculine in gender, *petra* feminine, and *mancipium* neuter, and that *timere* is active and *timeri* passive; but no one says that a stone (*lapis*) is masculine or a rock (*petra*) feminine, or that a slave (*mancipium*) is neither masculine nor feminine, or that fearing (*timere*) is actively doing something whereas being feared (*timeri*) is passively undergoing something.

19   S: Your lucid reasoning leaves me no room to doubt any of what you've said. But there is still something left in this inquiry that I wish to learn. If expert is a quality because it signifies a quality, I don't see why armed is not a substance

because it signifies a substance. And if armed is a having because it signifies a having, I can't figure out why expert is not a having because it signifies a having. For in exactly the same way that 'expert' is proved to signify a quality because it signifies something that has a quality, 'armed' signifies a substance because it signifies something that has a substance, namely, weapons (*arma*). And just as 'armed' is shown to signify a having, because it signifies someone having weapons, so too 'expert' signifies a having, since it signifies someone having education.

T: Having examined this argument, I can by no means deny either that armed is a substance or that expert is a having.

S: Then I want you to teach me whether a single something can belong to different categories.

T: I certainly don't think one and the same *thing* can be classified under different categories, although there are some questionable cases that I think require a longer and deeper discussion than we have undertaken in this brief conversation of ours. But I don't see anything to prevent one *word* that signifies many things, not as one, from being sometimes included under more than one category—for example, if 'white' is called a quality and a having. For 'white' does not signify the quality and the having as one, in the way that 'human being' signifies as one the substance and qualities of which a human being consists. For the thing that is appellated 'human being' is something one, consisting of the things I have said, whereas the thing that is appellated 'white' is not something one consisting of the quality and the having, since nothing is appellated white except a thing that has whiteness, which by no means consists of a having and a quality. Hence, if someone says "Human being is a substance and human being is a quality," one and the same thing that is signified and appellated by this name is said to be both a substance and a quality, which seems problematic. But when we say that white is a quality and a having, we are not saying that what is appellated by this name is a quality and a having, but rather that these two things are signified by this name, and nothing problematic follows.

S: But then why isn't human being both a substance and a quality according to Aristotle's division, since it signifies both, in the way that white is both a quality and a having because it signifies both?

T: For the purposes of this inquiry I think what I said earlier is enough: it's that 'human being' principally signifies substance and because that one item it signifies is a substance, and not a quality, but something with a quality. By contrast, 'white' does not signify anything principally; it equally signifies a quality and a having; nor does some one item come to be from these two, which would be more one or more the other, and which 'white' would signify.

20   S: I would like to have a clearer explanation of how it is not the case that some one item comes to be from the items that 'white' signifies.

T: If something consists of them, it is either a substance or something belonging to one of the other categories.

S: There is no other possibility.

T: But none of those consists of having and whiteness.

S: I can't dispute that.

T: Furthermore: some one item comes to be from more than one only by the composition of parts that belong to the same category, as animal consists of body and soul; or by the coming together of a genus and one or more differences, for example, body or human being; or from a species and a collection of individuating characteristics, such as Plato. But the items that 'white' signifies do not belong to one category, nor is one related to the other as genus or difference, or as species and a collection of individuating characteristics, nor are they differences of one genus. Instead, they are accidents of one and the same subject; but 'white' does not signify that subject, since it signifies nothing other than a having and a quality. For that reason there is not some one item that comes to be from the items that 'white' signifies.

S: Granted, it seems to me that reason backs up everything you say; but I would like to hear how you would respond if someone were to raise the following objection to your claim that 'white' signifies nothing other than a having and a quality: "Although white is the same as having-whiteness, it does not determinately signify this or that having whiteness (say, a body); rather, it signifies indeterminately something having whiteness. White, after all, is either something that has whiteness or something that does not have whiteness. But something that does not have whiteness is not white. Therefore, white is something that has whiteness. Accordingly, since everything that has whiteness is something, it must be the case that white is something that has whiteness, or something having whiteness. Finally, either 'white' signifies something having whiteness, or it signifies nothing at all. But nothing cannot be understood to have whiteness. Therefore, it must be the case that 'white' signifies something having whiteness."

21   T: The question is not whether everything that is white is something or is something that has whiteness, but whether the word 'white' contains, in its signification, what is said to be something, or what has it—in the way that human being contains animal—so that just as human being is rational, mortal animal, so too white is something having whiteness or what has whiteness. For inevitably any given thing is many things that are nonetheless not signified by the name of that thing. For, necessarily, every animal has a color, and every animal is either rational

or irrational, but the name 'animal' does not signify any of these. Hence, although white is nothing other than something having whiteness, or something that has whiteness, it need not be the case that 'white' signifies this. For let's suppose that 'white' signifies something having whiteness. Still, something having whiteness is nothing other than something white.

S: It can't be anything else.

T: So 'white' always signifies something white.

S: Right.

T: So when 'white' is uttered, it is always correct to understand 'white' as something white.

S: That follows.

T: So when it is said that something is white, it is also correct to say it twice: "something something white." And where it is correct to say it twice, it is correct to say it three times, and infinitely many times.

S: That follows—and it is absurd.

T: And let white be the very same as what has whiteness. Yet 'has' is nothing other than 'is having.'

S: Exactly.

T: Then white is nothing other than what is having whiteness.

S: Exactly that.

T: But when someone says 'having whiteness,' this expression signifies nothing other than 'white.'

S: Correct.

T: So then white is the very same as what is white.

S: That follows.

T: And so wherever 'white' occurs, we can correctly substitute 'what is white.'

S: I can't deny it.

T: So if white is what is white, it is also what is what is white. And if that is the case, it is also what is what is what is white, and so on to infinity.

S: This follows just as much—and is just as absurd—as saying that white is something something, many times over.

T: Yet suppose someone says that 'white' signifies either something having white-ness or nothing having whiteness. If this is understood as meaning "'White' either signifies something having whiteness or not-something having whiteness" (so that 'not-something' is an indefinite name), the division is neither exhaustive nor correct, and so it proves nothing. It would be like saying "A blind person either sees something or sees not-something." But if it is understood as meaning that 'white' either signifies something having whiteness or does not signify something having whiteness, the division is exhaustive and correct, and it does not contradict what has been said.

S: It is sufficiently clear that 'white' does not signify either something having whiteness or what has whiteness, but simply having whiteness, that is, a quality and a having; and from them alone no one something is constituted. And so white is both, because it signifies both equally. I see that this argument works for all non-composite expressions that likewise signify a plurality of items from which no one item comes to be; and I judge that no legitimate objection can be made against anything you have said in this discussion.

T: I agree. Still, since you know how much the dialecticians contend these days about the questions you have raised, I do not want you to cling to the things we have said in such a way that you stubbornly uphold them if someone turns out to be able to defeat our conclusions and establish others by stronger arguments. If that should happen, at least you will have to admit that this discussion has been useful for us in practicing disputation.

Monologion
Letter to Archbishop Lanfranc[1]

To HIS REVERED and beloved lord, father, and teacher Lanfranc, archbishop of Canterbury, primate of the English, worthy of the warm embrace of our mother, the Catholic Church, for his faithful service to her: brother Anselm of Bec, in life a sinner, in habit a monk.

Because everything should be done with advice, but not with just any advice— as Scripture says, "Do all things with advice," but "Let your adviser be one in a thousand"[2]—I have chosen one adviser, whom you know: one, not in a thousand, but from among all mortals, one whom I would prefer to all others as a guide in my perplexity and a teacher in my ignorance, to call me back to the right path when I have strayed and to give approval when I have done well. Although I cannot rely on him as much as I would like, I have been determined to rely on him as much as I can. For although there are very many others, besides Your Prudence, from whose learning I in my ignorance might learn much, and to whose judgment my ignorance would compel me to submit, I have not known even one to whose teaching and judgment I would submit as confidently and as willingly as I do to yours, not one who would show me such fatherly affection if the occasion required it or rejoice with me if the occasion called for it. Everything your fatherly heart bestows on me is carefully considered by wisdom, strengthened by authority, and seasoned with love; whenever I draw something from it, I take pleasure in its sweetness and rest content in the assurance of its truth. But I am speaking to one who knows all these things, so I shall say no more of them, and pass on instead to the reason that I am calling them to mind now.

Certain brethren, your servants and my fellow servants, at last compelled me to yield to their frequent and earnest requests that I write certain things for them, as you will be able to gather from the short preface to that writing. To my surprise, not only those at whose insistence I wrote it, but many others as well, wanted not only to read the work but to copy it. Uncertain, then, whether I should refuse their requests or grant them—for I do not want people to think that I am grudging and hate me, or to recognize that I am ignorant and mock me—I have recourse to my one and only adviser: I send you this work for you to examine, that by your authoritative judgment it might be either hidden from sight as a failure or offered, with your corrections, to those who want it.

---

1. This formal dedicatory letter, intended to be prefaced to the *Monologion*, was preceded by two other, less formal letters, which can be found on pp. 451–53.
2. Ecclesiasticus 6:6.

Prologue

SOME OF THE brethren have often eagerly entreated me to write down some of the things I have told them in our frequent discussions about how one ought to meditate on the divine essence, and about certain other things related to such a meditation, as a sort of pattern for meditating on these things. Having more regard to their own wishes than to the ease of the task or my ability to perform it, they prescribed the following form for me in writing this meditation: absolutely nothing in it would be established by the authority of Scripture; rather, whatever the conclusion of each individual investigation might assert, the necessity of reason would concisely prove, and the clarity of truth would manifestly show, that it is the case, by means of a plain style, unsophisticated arguments, and straightforward disputation. They also insisted that I not disdain to answer even the simple and almost foolish objections that would occur to me.

Now for a long time I was reluctant to attempt this, and comparing myself to the task at hand, I tried many arguments to excuse myself. For the more they wanted what they had asked of me to be easy for them to use, the more difficult they made it for me actually to accomplish it. Finally, however, I was overcome by the modest persistence of their entreaties as well as the true worth of their eagerness, which was not to be slighted. Unwilling to do so because of the difficulty of the task and the weakness of my own talent, I set out to do as they had entreated me; but gladly, because of their charity, I accomplished it according to their directions, as far as I was able.

I was induced to do so in the hope that whatever I did would be known only to those who had required it, and that they would soon afterwards despise it as worthless and throw it away with contempt. For I know that I could not so much satisfy those who had entreated me as put an end to the entreaties that were hounding me. But somehow—I am not sure how—things did not turn out as I had hoped. Not only the brethren but also many others took the trouble to commend this writing to long remembrance, each copying it out in full for himself.

After frequently reconsidering it, I could not find that I had said anything in it that was inconsistent with the writings of the Catholic fathers, and especially with those of blessed Augustine. Therefore, if it should seem to anyone that I put forth anything in this work that either is too novel or diverges from the truth, I ask that he not immediately condemn me as someone who either introduces novelties or asserts falsehoods. Rather, let him first look carefully at the books of the aforesaid teacher Augustine on the Trinity and then judge my work according to them. For in saying that the supreme Trinity can be said to be three substances, I have followed the Greeks, who confess three substances in one person by the same faith by which we confess three persons in one substance. For they signify by 'substance' in God what we signify by 'person.'[3]

Now whatever I said there is put forth in the role of someone who, by thought alone, disputes and investigates within himself things that he had not previously realized, just as I knew that they whose request I was aiming to fulfill wanted me to do.

But I entreat and eagerly beseech anyone who wishes to copy this work that he take care to put this preface at the beginning of the book before the chapter titles. For I think it is very helpful for understanding the things he will read there if someone first knows with what intention and in what way they are discussed. I also think that anyone who first sees this preface will not be quick to judge if he finds something asserted contrary to his own opinion.

Chapters

---

3. See the Glossary entry for substance* (sense 3).

Chapter 1

That there is something that is best and greatest and supreme among all existing things

If anyone does not know, either because he has not heard or because he does not believe, that there is one nature,* supreme among all existing things, who alone is self-sufficient in his eternal* happiness, who through his omnipotent goodness grants and brings it about that all other things exist or have any sort of well-being, and a great many other things that we must believe about God or his creation, I think he could at least convince himself of most of these things by reason alone, if he is even moderately intelligent.

There are many ways in which he could do this, but I shall set forth the one that I think would be easiest for him. After all, everyone desires to enjoy only those things that he thinks good. It is therefore easy for him to turn the eye of his mind sometimes toward investigating the source of the goodness of those things that he desires only because he judges that they are good. Then, with reason leading and him following, he will rationally advance toward those things of which he is irrationally ignorant. But if in this I say anything that a greater authority does not teach, I wish to be understood in this way: even if I present a conclusion as necessary on the basis of arguments that seem compelling to me, I mean only that it can *seem* necessary for the time being, not that it is therefore in fact altogether necessary.

So, then, someone might easily speak silently within himself in this way: Since there are countless goods, whose great diversity we both experience through our bodily senses and discern through the reasoning of our mind, are we to believe that there is some one thing through which all goods whatsoever are good? Or are different goods good through different things? Indeed, to all who are willing to pay attention it is clear and quite certain that all things whatsoever that are said to be more or less or equally a certain way as compared to each other are said to be so through something that is not understood as different but rather as the same in diverse things, whether it is detected equally or unequally in them. For whatever just things are said to be equally or more or less just by comparison with other just things, they must be understood to be just through justice, which is not different in diverse things. Therefore, since it is certain that all goods, if they are compared to each other, are either equally or unequally good, it must be that they are all good through something that is understood to be the same in diverse good things, even though it seems that sometimes different goods are said to be good through different things.

For it seems that a horse is called good through one thing because it is strong and through another because it is fast. After all, though it seems that the horse is called good through its strength and good through its speed, it does not seem that strength is the same thing as speed. Yet if a horse is good because it is strong or fast, how is it that a strong and fast robber is bad? So instead, just as a strong and fast robber is bad because he is harmful, so too a strong and fast horse is good because it is useful. And indeed, nothing is ordinarily considered good except either because of some usefulness, as health and things that contribute to health are called good, or because of some intrinsic value, as beauty and things that contribute to beauty are regarded as good.

But since the argument we have already considered cannot be refuted in any way, it must also be the case that all useful or intrinsically valuable things, if they are genuinely good, are good through the very same thing—whatever that is—through which all goods must exist. Now who would doubt that this thing, through which all goods exist, is itself a great good? Therefore, he is good through himself, since every good exists through him. It follows, therefore, that all other things are good through something other than what they themselves are, and he alone is good through himself. Now no good that exists through another[4] is equal to or greater than that good who is good through himself. And so only he who

---

4. The expression "through another" appears frequently throughout the *Monologion*. Wherever it appears, it should be regarded as a shorthand form of "through something other than itself." Thus, when Anselm says that something "is good (or exists) through another," he means that the source of its goodness (or existence) is something other than itself. The contrast, sometimes merely implied but often expressed, is with God, who is whatever he is, not through another, but through himself.

alone is good through himself is supremely good. For something is supreme if it surpasses others in such a way that it has neither peer nor superior. Now that which is supremely good is also supremely great. There is, therefore, some one thing that is supremely good and supremely great—in other words, supreme among all existing things.

Chapter 2

On the same thing

Now just as it has been found that there is something supremely good, since all good things are good through some one thing that is good through itself, in the same way it is inferred with necessity that there is something supremely great, since whatever great things exist are great through some one thing that is great through itself. Now I do not mean great in size, as a given body* is great; rather, [I mean great in the sense] that the greater something is, the better or worthier it is, as wisdom is great. And since only what is supremely good can be supremely great, there must be something greatest and best, that is, supreme among all existing things.

Chapter 3

That there is a certain nature through whom all existing things exist, and who exists through himself and is supreme among all existing things

Furthermore, not only are all good things good through the same thing, and all great things great through the same thing, but it seems that all existing things exist through some one thing. For every existing thing exists either through something or through nothing. But nothing exists through nothing. For it is not so much as conceivable that any existing thing does not exist through something. So whatever exists, exists through something. Since this is so, either there is one thing, or there are several* things, through which all existing things exist.

Now if there are several, either they are traced back to some one thing through which they [all] exist, or each of them exists through itself, or they exist through each other. But if they exist through one thing, it is no longer true that all things exist through several things; rather, all things exist through that one thing through which the several things exist.

If, however, each of them exists through itself, there is surely some one power or nature of self-existing that they have in order to exist through themselves. And there is no doubt that they exist through this one thing through which they have self-existence. Therefore, all things exist more truly through that one thing than through the several things that cannot exist without that one thing.

Now no reasoning allows for several things to exist through each other, since it is irrational to think that something exists through that to which it gives existence. For not even relatives* exist through each other in this way. For when a master and a slave stand in relation to each other, the men who stand in relation do not in any way exist through each other, and the relations by which they are related do not in any way exist through each other, since they exist through their subjects.

And so, since truth altogether rules out the possibility that there are several things through which all things exist, there must be one thing through which all existing things exist. Therefore, since all existing things exist through that one thing, undoubtedly that one thing exists through himself. So all other existing things exist through another; he alone exists through himself. Now whatever exists through another is less than the one through whom all other things exist and who alone exists through himself. Therefore, he who exists through himself exists most greatly of all things. So there is some one thing that alone exists most greatly and supremely of all things. Now he who exists most greatly of all things, and through whom exists whatever is good or great and whatever is anything at all, must be supremely good, supremely great, and supreme among all existing things. Therefore, there is something (whether he is called an essence or a substance or a nature)[5] that is best and greatest and supreme among all existing things.

Chapter 4

On the same thing

Moreover, if someone considers the natures of things, he cannot help realizing that they are not all of equal dignity; rather, some of them are on different and unequal levels. For anyone who doubts that a horse is by its very nature better than wood, and that a human being is more excellent than a horse, should not even be called a human being. Therefore, since it is undeniable that some natures are better than others, reason makes it no less obvious that one of them is so preeminent that he has no superior. For if this difference of levels is infinite—so that there is no level so high that an even higher level cannot be found—reason is brought to the conclusion that there is no limit to the multitude of these natures. But everyone thinks this is absurd—except for someone who is quite absurd himself. Therefore, there must be some nature* that is so superior to any other thing or things that there is nothing to which he is inferior.

Now either the nature that is like this is the only one, or there are several* like him and equal to him. Suppose they are several and equals. They cannot be equals

---

5. Anselm is using these three words as synonyms. For a definition, see the Glossary entry for essence* (sense 1).

through different things, but rather through the same thing. Now that one thing through which they are equally so great is either the very thing that they are—that is, their essence*—or something other than what they are. Now if it is nothing other than their essence, then just as their essences are not several but one, so also the natures are not several but one. For I am here understanding nature to be the same as essence. On the other hand, if that through which those several natures are so great is other than that which they themselves are, they are certainly less than that through which they are great. For whatever is great through another is less than that through which it is great. Therefore, they are not so great that there is nothing else greater than they are. So if it is not possible either through that which they are or through something else for there to be several natures than which nothing is more excellent, there can in no way be several such natures. So the only remaining possibility is that there is one and only one nature that is so superior to the others that he is inferior to none.

Now whatever is like this is the greatest and best of all existing things. So a certain nature exists that is supreme among all existing things. But this cannot be the case unless he is through himself what he is and all existing things are through him what they are. For reason showed a little earlier that he who exists through himself, and through whom all other things exist, is supreme among all existing things. Therefore, either (conversely) he who is supreme exists through himself and all other things exist through him, or there will be several supreme beings. But it is evident that there are not several supreme beings. Therefore, there is a certain nature or substance or essence who through himself is good and great and through himself is what he is; through whom exists whatever truly is good or great or anything at all; and who is the supreme good, the supreme great thing, the supreme being or subsistent,* that is, supreme among all existing things.

Chapter 5

That, just as he exists through himself and other things exist through him, so he exists from himself and other things exist from him

And so, since what has been discovered is satisfactory, it is helpful to investigate whether this very nature, and all things that are anything, exist *from* him just as they exist *through* him. Now clearly it can be said that whatever exists *from* something also exists *through* that thing, and whatever exists *through* something also exists *from* that thing. For example, whatever exists from some matter and through a craftsman can also be said to exist through the matter and from the craftsman, since it has its existence through both and from both—that is, by both—although it does not exist through the matter and from the matter in the same way that it exists through the craftsman and from the craftsman. It follows, therefore, that just as all existing things are what they are through the supreme nature, and so he exists through himself, whereas other things exist through another, in the same way all existing things exist from that same supreme nature, and so he exists from himself, whereas other things exist from another.

Chapter 6

That he does not exist through the help of some other cause that brought him into existence, and yet neither does he exist through nothing or from nothing; and in what sense he can be understood to exist through himself and from himself

Therefore, since the expressions "to exist through something" and "to exist from something" do not always have the same meaning, we must more carefully investigate in what sense all existing things exist through or from the supreme nature. And since he who exists through himself and that which exists through another do not fit the same definition of existing, we shall first look separately at that supreme nature who exists through himself and then at those things that exist through another.

So, since it has been established that he is through himself whatever he is, and all other things are through him what they are, in what sense does he exist through himself? For whatever is said to exist through something seems to exist either through an efficient* cause or through some matter or through some other aid (for example, through a tool). Now whatever exists in any of these three ways exists through another and is both posterior* to and in some way less than that through which it has its existence. But the supreme nature in no way exists through another; nor is he posterior to or less than himself or any other thing. Therefore, the supreme nature could not come about either by his own agency or by that of some other thing, nor was he or anything else the matter from which he came about, nor did he or some other thing in any way help him to be what he was not already.

What then? Something that does not exist by the agency of something or from some matter, or come into existence by means of any aids, appears either to be nothing or, if it is something, to exist through nothing and from nothing. Now although on the basis of what has already been established by the light of reason about the supreme substance I think that these things can in no way apply to him, nonetheless, I shall not neglect to put together a proof of this. For since this meditation of mine has suddenly brought me to this important and interesting point, I do not wish to pass over any objection, however simple and almost foolish, that occurs to me in the course of my disputation. Thus, by leaving nothing doubtful in what went before, I can proceed with greater certainty to what follows; and further, if I should want to persuade anyone of what I have been thinking, even someone who is slow to understand can easily agree with what he has heard once every obstacle, however small, has been removed.

And so the claim that this nature,* apart from whom no nature at all exists, is nothing is as false as it would be absurd to say that whatever exists is nothing. Now he does not exist *through* nothing, since there is no intelligible sense in which what is something exists through nothing. But if in some sense he exists *from* nothing, he exists from nothing either through himself or through another or through nothing.

Now it has been established that in no way does something exist through nothing. Therefore, if he exists from nothing in any sense, he exists from nothing either through himself or through another. Now nothing can exist from nothing through itself, since if something exists from nothing through something, that through which it exists must exist beforehand. So, since this essence* does not exist before himself, he does not in any way exist from nothing through himself.

On the other hand, if it is said that he came to exist from nothing through some other nature, then he is not supreme among all things but inferior to at least one; moreover, he is what he is, not through himself but through another. Likewise, if he exists from nothing through something, that through which he exists was a great good, since it was the cause of so great a good. But no good thing can be understood [as existing] before that good without whom nothing is good. Now it is quite clear that this good, without whom no good thing exists, is the supreme nature that is under discussion. Therefore, it is not even conceivable that something preceded him through which he came to exist from nothing.

Finally, if this very nature is something either through nothing or from nothing, then undoubtedly either he is not through himself and from himself whatever he is, or he is himself said to be nothing. And there is no need to explain how false either of these alternatives is. Therefore, although the supreme substance does not exist through some efficient cause or from some matter, and although he was not helped by any causes in order that he might be brought into being, nonetheless, he does not in any sense exist through nothing or from nothing, since he is through himself and from himself whatever he is.

In what sense, then, are we to understand that he exists through himself and from himself, if he neither made himself, nor provided matter for himself, nor in any way helped himself to be what he was not already? It seems that perhaps this can be understood only in the same sense in which it is said that light shines, or is shining, through itself and from itself. For 'light' and 'to shine' and 'shining' are related to each other in just the same way as 'essence' and 'to be' and 'being,' that is, existing or subsisting.* Therefore, 'supreme essence' and 'supremely to be' and 'supremely being,' that is, supremely existing or supremely subsisting, are related to each other not unlike 'light' and 'to shine' and 'shining.'[6]

Chapter 7

In what way all other things exist through him and from him

It now remains for us to discuss the sense in which all those things that exist through another exist through the supreme substance, whether because he made them all, or because he was the matter of them all. For there is no need to ask whether they all exist through him merely because he in some way helped all things to exist, whereas some other thing made them or some other matter existed, since it is inconsistent with what became evident above if all existing things exist through him only in some secondary way and not principally.

And so I think I should first ask whether all things that exist through another exist from some matter. Now I have no doubt that the whole mass of this world with its parts, as we see it formed, consists of earth, air, fire, and water. These four elements can in some way be understood apart from the forms that we observe in formed things, in such a way that the unformed or even confused nature of the elements is seen to be the matter of all the bodies* that are made distinct by their own forms.[7] As I say, I have no doubt about that. But I ask where this thing of which I have spoken, the matter of the mass of the world, *comes from*. For if it in turn comes from some other matter, then that is more truly the matter of the physical universe.

If, then, the totality of things, whether visible or invisible, exists from some matter, it cannot exist—more than that, it cannot even be *said* to exist—from any matter other than the supreme nature, or from itself, or from some third essence that is neither. But of course nothing at all can even be thought to exist other than he who is supreme among all things, who exists through himself, and the totality of those things that do not exist through themselves but through that same supreme being. Therefore, that which is in no way something is not the matter of anything. But the totality of things, which does not exist through itself, cannot exist from its own nature. For if it did, it would in some way exist through

---

6. The Latin words for 'light,' 'to shine,' and 'shining' (*lux, lucere,* and *lucens*) are a noun, an infinitive, and a participle from the same stem. The same relation holds among the Latin words for 'essence,' 'to be,' and 'being' (*essentia, esse,* and *ens*).

7. In other words, what makes one body different from another is the particular form or configuration that the elements have in that body. But you can conceive of the elements by themselves, in isolation from this or that particular configuration. When you do, you realize that the elements in this unformed state are the building blocks of all bodies.

itself, and through something other than the one through whom all things exist, and he would not be the only thing through which all things exist—all of which is false. Moreover, everything that exists from matter exists from another thing and is posterior* to that thing. And since nothing is other than itself or posterior to itself, it follows that nothing exists from itself materially.

But if something less than the supreme nature can exist from the matter of the supreme nature, the supreme good can be changed and corrupted—which it is impious to say. Therefore, since everything that is other than the supreme good is less than he is, it is impossible for anything else to be from him in this way. Furthermore, anything through which the supreme good is changed or corrupted is, without a doubt, in no way good. Now if any lesser nature exists from the matter of the supreme good, the supreme good is changed or corrupted through himself, since nothing exists from any source other than the supreme essence. Therefore, the supreme essence, who is himself the supreme good, is in no way good—which is a contradiction. So no lesser nature exists materially from the supreme nature. Since, therefore, it has been established that the essence of those things that exist through another does not exist from the supreme essence as its matter, nor from itself, nor from some other thing, it is evident that it exists from no matter.

Therefore, since all existing things exist through the supreme essence, and nothing can exist through him unless he either makes it or is the matter for it, it follows necessarily that nothing but him exists unless he makes it. And since nothing exists or has existed except him and the things made by him, he could not make anything at all through any instrument or assistance other than himself. Now whatever he made, he certainly made it either from something as its matter or from nothing. Therefore, since it is perfectly obvious that the essence of all things that exist, other than the supreme essence, was made by that same supreme essence, and that it does not exist from any matter, there is undoubtedly nothing more evident than this: the supreme essence alone, through himself, produced so great a mass of things—so numerous a multitude, so beautifully formed, so orderly in its variety, so fitting in its diversity—from nothing.

Chapter 8

In what sense it is to be understood that he made everything from nothing

But something occurs to me about this "nothing." Whatever a thing is made from is a cause of the thing that is made from it, and, necessarily, every cause contributes some help toward the existence of the effect. This fact is so obvious to everyone from experience that no one can be talked out of it in debate, and hardly anyone can be tricked out of it through deception. Therefore, if something was made from nothing, then nothing itself was a cause of the thing that was made from nothing. But how could that which had no existence help bring something into existence? And if, on the contrary, nothing did not help bring anything into existence, who could be persuaded—and in what way—that something is brought about from nothing?

Furthermore, 'nothing' either signifies something or does not signify anything. Now if nothing is something, whatever was made from nothing was made from something. On the other hand, if nothing is not anything, then, since it is inconceivable that something is made from what does not exist at all, nothing is made from nothing—as the saying goes, "Nothing comes from nothing." From this it seems to follow that whatever exists was made from something, since it was made either from something or from nothing. Therefore, whether nothing is something or is not something, it seems to follow that whatever was made was made from something. But if this is admitted to be true, it contradicts everything that was settled above. Hence, since what was nothing will be something, what was in the greatest degree something will be nothing. After all, having found that there is a substance existing most greatly of all things, I proceeded by argument to the claim that all things were made by him in such a way that there was nothing from which they were made. Therefore, if that from which they are made—which I had thought was nothing—is in fact something, then whatever I thought I had discovered about the supreme being is nothing.

So then how is this 'nothing' to be understood? For I have already undertaken not to neglect any possible objection, foolish though it may be, in this meditation. And so it seems to me that if a substance is said to have been made from nothing, there are three ways of explaining this that would suffice to remove this present obstacle. One way is that we mean that what is said to have been made from nothing has not in fact been made at all. It is like a case in which someone asks what a silent person is talking about. "About nothing," is the answer—that is, he is not talking at all. In this sense, if someone were to ask about the supreme essence himself, or about something that did not and does not exist at all, "What was it made from?" one could correctly answer, "From nothing"—that is, it was not made at all. This sense cannot be properly applied to anything that actually has been made.

There is another meaning that can indeed be expressed but cannot be true: if something is said to have been made from nothing in the sense that it was made from nothing itself, that is, from what does not at all exist—as if nothing itself were some existing thing from which something could be made. Now since this is always false, some absurd impossibility will follow whenever it is assumed.

The third sense in which something is said to have been made from nothing is when we understand that it has indeed been made, but there was not anything from which it was made. It seems we use a similar meaning when we say that someone who is upset for no reason is upset about nothing. So if we understand our earlier conclusion in this sense, that all existing things other than the supreme essence were made by him from nothing—that is, not from anything—then just as this conclusion follows logically from our previous conclusions, so nothing illogical will follow from it later on.

Nonetheless, it would also be logical and free from any absurdity to say that the things that were made by the creating substance were made *from* nothing in the sense in which we often say that someone has come *from* poverty to wealth or *from* sickness to health—that is, he who once was poor is now rich, which he was not before, and he who once was sick is now healthy, which he was not before. So if it is said that the creating essence made all things from nothing, or that all things were made by him from nothing, these statements can quite sensibly be understood in this sense—that is, the things that once were nothing are now something. And the expression "he made them" or "they were made" is understood to mean that when he made them, he made something, and that when they were made, they were indeed made to be something. For in the same way, when we see someone whom some man has raised from a very lowly state to great riches or honors, we say, "Look! That man made him from nothing," or "He was made from nothing by that man"—that is, he who once was regarded as nothing is now thought to be truly something, because that man has made him so.

Chapter 9

That with respect to the reason of their maker, the things that were made from nothing were not nothing before they were made

But I seem to see something that forces me to distinguish carefully the sense in which the things that were made can be said to have been nothing before they were made. After all, there is no way anyone could make something rationally unless something like a pattern (or, to put it more suitably, a form or likeness or rule) of the thing to be made already existed in the reason of the maker. And so it is clear that what they were going to be, and what sorts of things, and how they were going to be, was in the reason of the supreme nature before all things were made.

Therefore, it is clear that the things that were made were nothing before they were made, in the sense that they were not what they now are and there was not anything from which they were made. Nonetheless, they were not nothing with respect to the reason of their maker, through which and in accordance with which they were made.

Chapter 10

That this reason is an utterance of things, as a craftsman says within himself what he is going to make

Now what is that form of things that existed in his reason before the things to be created, other than an utterance of those things in his reason, just as, when a craftsman is going to make some work of his art, he first says it within himself by a conception of his mind? Now by an "utterance" of the mind or reason, I do not mean what happens when one thinks of the words that signify those things, but what happens when the things themselves (no matter whether they are yet to exist or already exist) are examined within the mind by the gaze of thought.

For we know from frequent experience that we can say one and the same thing in three ways. For either we say a thing by making perceptible use of perceptible signs, that is, signs that can be perceived by the bodily senses; or by thinking imperceptibly within ourselves the very same signs that are perceptible when they are outside ourselves; or by not using these signs at all, whether perceptibly or imperceptibly, but rather by saying the things themselves inwardly in our mind by either a corporeal image or an understanding of reason that corresponds to the diversity of the things themselves. For example, in one way I say a man when I signify him by the word 'man,' in another way when I think that same word silently, and in yet another way when my mind sees the man himself either through an image of a body (as when it imagines his sensible appearance) or through reason (as when it thinks his universal essence, which is rational, mortal animal).

Each of these three kinds of utterance corresponds to its own kind of word. But the words of the kind of utterance that I put third and last, when they are about things that are not unknown, are natural; they are the same among all peoples. Now all other words were invented on account of these natural words. Therefore, where there are natural words, no other word is necessary to know a thing; and where natural words are impossible, no other word will serve to make a thing known. And it makes good sense to say that words are truer the more similar they are to, and the more distinctly they signify, the things of which they are words. Now except for those things that we use as their own names in order to signify themselves (like certain sounds: for example, the vowel 'a')—except for those, I say, no other word seems as similar to the thing of which it is a word, or expresses it in the same way, as the likeness that is expressed in the gaze of the mind of someone who is thinking the thing itself.[8] And so that should by right be called the most proper and principal word for the thing.

---

8. Anselm's point here is that natural words resemble the things of which they are words, whereas conventional words do not. For example, the natural word (that is, the concept) of a lion actually resembles the lion, since it is simply the mind's conception of the lion itself.

So no utterance of anything whatsoever comes as close to the thing as that which consists of words of this sort. Furthermore, no other word in anyone's reason can be as similar to the thing, whether it is yet to exist or already exists. It therefore quite rightly seems that such an utterance of things not only existed in the supreme substance before the things existed, in order that through it they might be made, but also exists in him now that they have been made, in order that through it they might be known.

Chapter 11

That nonetheless there is much dissimilarity in this comparison

So it has been established that the supreme substance first said (as it were) all of creation in himself and then created it in accordance with and through that innermost utterance of his, in the way that a craftsman first conceives in his mind what he afterwards makes into a completed work in accordance with the conception of his mind. Nonetheless, I see much dissimilarity in this comparison. After all, the supreme substance collected nothing at all from any other source from which he would either assemble within himself the form of the things he was going to make or bring it about that the things themselves exist. The craftsman, by contrast, cannot even imagine a physical object and thus conceive it in his mind unless he has somehow already come to know the object, either as a whole all at once or part by part through various things; nor can he complete the work that he has conceived in his mind if he lacks either the material or something without which the planned work cannot be made. For although a man could invent an animal the likes of which never existed, either by thinking it or by painting it, he could do this only by putting together parts stored in his memory from things he knew at another time.

Therefore, the creating substance's inward utterance of the work he is going to make differs from that of the craftsman in this respect: the Creator's utterance was not collected from or assisted by some other source; rather, as the first and sole cause it was sufficient for its Artisan to bring his work to completion. By contrast, the craftsman's utterance is neither the first nor the sole cause, and it is

---

The word 'lion,' by contrast, does not resemble the lion much at all. It is only by convention that the word 'lion' calls up an image of a lion rather than of some other thing. There is one sort of case, however, in which conventional words do resemble the things of which they are words, and that is when we use a thing as its own name. To take Anselm's example, we use the letter 'a' as its own name. Obviously, the letter 'a' is like the letter 'a,' and so the word is like the thing. But this is a limited and fairly uninteresting class of exceptions to the general rule that it is natural words that most closely resemble and most distinctly express the things of which they are words.

not sufficient for him even to get his work started. So the things that are created through the Creator's utterance are nothing at all but what they are through his utterance, whereas the things that are made through the craftsman's utterance would not be anything at all unless they were something other than what they are through his utterance.

Chapter 12

That the utterance of the supreme essence is the supreme essence

Now since by the teaching of reason it is equally certain that, whatever the supreme substance made, he did not make it through anything other than himself, and that whatever he made, he made it through his innermost utterance (whether by saying individual things by means of individual words, or instead by saying all things at once by means of one word),[9] what could be seen to be any more necessary than this: the utterance of the supreme essence is nothing other than the supreme essence? And so I do not think we should carelessly neglect to consider this utterance. But before we can discuss it carefully, I think we must earnestly investigate certain properties of the supreme substance.[10]

Chapter 13

That, just as all things were made through the supreme essence, so also they remain in existence through him

Therefore, it has been established that whatever is not the same as the supreme nature was made through him. Now only an irrational mind could doubt that all created things remain and continue in existence, as long as they do exist, because they are sustained by the very same being who made them from nothing so that they exist in the first place. For by an exactly similar argument to the one that shows that all existing things exist through some one thing, and so he alone exists through himself and all other things exist through another—by a similar argument, I say, it can be proved that everything that remains in existence does so through some one thing, and so he alone remains in existence through himself and all other things remain in existence through another. Now since it can only

---

9. In Chapter 30 Anselm resolves this question, maintaining that this utterance consists of one word, not of many words.

10. Anselm discusses the properties of the supreme substance in Chapters 13–28 and then resumes discussion of his utterance in Chapter 29.

be the case that created things remain in existence through another, and he who created them remains in existence through himself, it must be the case that, just as nothing was made except through the presence of the creating essence, so nothing remains in existence except through his conserving presence.

Chapter 14

That he exists in all things and through all things, and all things exist from him and through him and in him

If this is the case—or rather, since this is necessarily the case—it follows that where he does not exist, nothing exists. Therefore, he exists everywhere, both through all things and in all things. Now no created thing can in any way pass beyond the immensity of the Creator and Sustainer,* but it would be absurd to claim that in the same way the Creator and Sustainer cannot in any way go beyond the totality of the things he made. It is therefore clear that he undergirds and transcends, that he encompasses and penetrates all other things. Therefore, if these conclusions are joined to the ones we discovered earlier, it is he who exists in all things and through all things, and from whom and through whom and in whom all things exist.[11]

Chapter 15

*What can or cannot be said of him substantially**

Now I am strongly and quite reasonably moved to inquire, as diligently as I can, which of all the things that can be said of something can be applied substantially to such an astounding nature. For I would be amazed if we could find any noun or verb that we apply to things made from nothing that could be appropriately said of the substance that creates all things. Nevertheless, we must try to see what conclusion reason will lead us to in our investigation.

And so with respect to relatives,* at least, no one doubts that none of them is said substantially of the thing of which it is said relatively.* Therefore, if something is said relatively of the supreme nature, it does not signify his substance. And so it is clear that whatever can be said of him relatively—the fact that he is supreme among all things, or that he is greater than all the things that he made, or anything else like these—does not designate his natural essence. For if none of those things in relation to which he is said to be supreme or greater had ever existed, he would

---

11. Cf. Romans 11:36: "For from him and through him and in him all things exist."

not be understood as supreme or greater; but he would not on that account be any less good, and his essential greatness would in no way be diminished. This is an obvious conclusion from the fact that he has whatever goodness or greatness he has, not through another but through himself. So given that the supreme nature can be understood as not supreme and yet as in no way greater or less than when he *is* understood as supreme among all things, it is clear that 'supreme' does not simply signify that essence, who is in every way greater and better than whatever is not what he is. And what reason shows us about 'supreme' is found to be similar in the case of similarly relative terms.

And so, having dismissed those things that are said relatively, since none of them simply refers to the essence of anything, let us turn our attention toward other things that must be discussed. And indeed, if one looks carefully at each of them, whatever there is (other than relatives) is either such that _____ is in every respect better than not-_____, or such that not-_____ is in some respect better than _____. By "_____" and "not-_____" here I simply mean true and not-true, body and not-body, and so on.[12]

Now [some things are such that] it is in every respect better to be _____ than not-_____, for example, wise than not-wise: that is, it is better to be wise than not-wise. For although a just person who is not wise seems to be better than a wise person who is not just,[13] it is not better in an unqualified* sense to be not-wise than to be wise. Indeed, whatever is not-wise in an unqualified sense, insofar as it is not-wise, is less than what is wise, since everything that is not-wise would be better if it were wise. Similarly, it is in every respect better to be true than not, that is, than not-true, and just than not-just, and living than not-living.

By contrast, [some things are such that] it is in some respect better to be not-_____ than to be _____: for example, not-gold than gold. For it is better for a human being to be not-gold than gold, even though perhaps it would be better for something—say, for lead—to be gold than not-gold. For although both a human being and lead are not-gold, a human being is better than gold in proportion as he would be of an inferior nature if he were gold, and lead is baser in proportion as it would be more precious if it were gold.

But many relatives do not fall under this division at all, as is evident from the fact that the supreme nature can be understood as not-supreme, in such a way that

---

12. Where I have a blank, Anselm has *ipsum,* "the very same thing." His point is that you must fill in both blanks with the same word and then apply the test that he explains. If _____ is in every respect better than not-_____, then _____ can be said substantially of God. But if not-_____ is in some respect better than _____, _____ cannot be said substantially of God. (I owe this device to Paul Vincent Spade, trans. and ed., *Five Texts on the Mediaeval Problem of Universals* [Indianapolis: Hackett Publishing Company, 1994], p. 42, where it appears in a somewhat different context.)
13. Bear in mind that "just" here means "morally upright."

supreme is not in every respect better than not-supreme, and not-supreme is not in some respect better than supreme. I shall not stop to ask whether some relatives do fall under it, since for our present purposes what is already known about them is enough: none of them designates the simple* substance of the supreme nature.

As for everything else, if each is considered individually, either _____ is better than not-_____, or not-_____ is in some respect better than _____. Therefore, just as it is impious to think that the substance of the supreme nature is something that it is in some way better not to be, so he must be whatever it is in every respect better to be than not to be. For he alone is that than which absolutely nothing else is better, and he alone is better than all things that are not what he is.

Therefore, he is not a body,* or any of the things that the bodily senses perceive. Indeed, there is something better than all of these things that is not what they are. For the rational mind (concerning which no bodily sense perceives what, or what sort of thing, or how great it is) is greater than any of those things that are in the domain of the bodily senses, in proportion as it would be less if it were one of them. For the supreme essence must not at all be said to be any of those things to which something that is not what they are is superior; and, as reason teaches, he absolutely must be said to be any of those things to which whatever is not what they are is inferior. He must therefore be living, wise, powerful and all-powerful, true, just, happy, eternal,* and whatever similarly it is absolutely better to be than not to be. Therefore, why should we seek any further for what that supreme nature is, since it is evident which of all things he is and which he is not?

Chapter 16

That for him, to be just is the same as to be justice, and the same thing holds for those things that can be said of him in a similar way, and that none of these designates what sort of thing or how great he is, but rather what he is[14]

But perhaps when he is said to be just or great or something like that, this does not reveal what he is, but rather what sort of thing he is or how great he is. For it seems that all these things are said through a quality or a quantity. After all, everything that is just is just through justice, and so on for similar things. Therefore, that supreme nature is just precisely through justice. So it seems that the supremely good substance is said to be just in virtue of his participation in a quality, namely justice. But if that is the case, he is just through another and not through himself.

---

14. For an explanation of Anselm's point in this chapter, see the Glossary entry for quality/quantity/quiddity.*

But that is contrary to the clearly discerned truth that whatever he is—whether good or great or subsistent*—he is through himself and not through another.[15] So given that he is not just except through justice, and he cannot be just except through himself, what is more obvious, what is more necessary, than that this same nature is justice itself; and that when he is said to be just "through justice," this is the same as "through himself"; and that when he is said to be just "through himself," this means nothing other than "through justice"? Therefore, if someone asks, "What is this supreme nature you are discussing?" what truer answer could be given than "Justice"?

So we must see what is meant when that nature, which is justice itself, is said to be just. Now a human being cannot *be* justice, but he can *have* justice. Consequently, a just human being is not understood as existent justice but rather as having justice. Now the supreme nature cannot properly be said to *have* justice but rather to *exist as* justice. Therefore, when he is said to be just, he is properly understood as existent justice, not as having justice. Now if, when he is said to be existent justice, this does not express what sort of thing he is but rather what he is, it follows that when he is said to be just, this too does not express what sort of thing he is but what he is. Further, since to say of that supreme essence that he is just, is the same as to say that he is existent justice, and to say that he is existent justice is no different from saying that he is justice, there is no difference between saying that he is just and saying that he is justice. Therefore, when someone asks what he is, "Just" is no less fitting an answer than "Justice."

Now reason constrains the intellect to recognize that what we have discovered to be certain in the case of justice applies to all the things that are said of the supreme nature in a similar way. So whichever of them is said of him designates neither what sort of thing he is nor how great he is but rather what he is. Now it is clear that whatever good thing the supreme nature is, he is that supremely. And so he is the supreme essence, supreme life, supreme reason, supreme salvation, supreme justice, supreme wisdom, supreme truth, supreme goodness, supreme greatness, supreme beauty, supreme immortality, supreme incorruptibility, supreme immutability, supreme beatitude, supreme eternity, supreme power, supreme unity, which is none other than supremely being, supremely living, and other similar things.

---

15. Anselm argues for this claim in Chapters 1–4.

Chapter 17

That he is simple* in such a way that all the things that can be said of his essence are one and the same thing in him, and none of them can be said substantially of him except with respect to what he is

What then? If that supreme nature is so many good things, will he not be composed of several* good things? Or are they in fact not several good things, but one good thing signified by several words? For every composite needs the things of which it is composed if it is to subsist, and it owes what it is to them, since whatever it is, it is through them, whereas those things are not through it what they are. And consequently a composite is absolutely not supreme. So then, if that nature is composed of several good things, all these features, which hold true of every composite, must apply to him.

But the whole necessity of truth, which became evident above, destroys and overwhelms such impious falsehood by a clear argument. Therefore, since that nature is in no way a composite and yet is in every way those many good things, it must be that all those things are not several but one. So each of them is the same as all the others, whether all at once or individually. Thus, when he is said to be justice or essence, those words signify the same thing that the others do, whether all at once or individually. And therefore, just as whatever is said essentially* of the supreme substance is one, so whatever he essentially is he is in one way and under one aspect. For when a human being is said to be body and rational and human, these three things are not said in one way or under one aspect. For he is body according to one, rational according to another, and neither of these individually is the whole of the fact that he is human. By contrast, the supreme essence is in no way like this. Whatever he is in any way, he is in every way and under every aspect. For whatever he in any way essentially is, that is the whole of what he is. Therefore, whatever is truly said of his essence is not understood as expressing what sort of thing or how great he is, but rather as expressing what he is. For whatever is a thing of a certain quality or quantity is something else with respect to what it is, and so it is not simple but composite.

Chapter 18

That he exists without beginning and without end

So from what time has this so simple nature, the Creator and Sustainer* of all things, existed? And until what time will he continue to exist? Or does he instead exist, not from some time and until some time, but rather without beginning and without end? For if he has a beginning, either he has it from himself or through himself, or he has it from another or through another, or he has it from nothing or through nothing. But through the truth that has already been clearly discerned, it has been established[16] that he in no way exists from another or from nothing, or through another or through nothing. So no beginning was in any way allotted to him through another or from another, or through nothing or from nothing. But he cannot have a beginning from himself or through himself, although he does exist from himself and through himself. For he exists from himself and through himself in such a way that the essence he is through himself and from himself is in no way different from the essence through which and from which he exists. By contrast, whatever begins to exist from something or through something is not in every respect the same as that from which or through which it begins to exist. Therefore, the supreme nature did not begin to exist through himself or from himself. Therefore, since he has no beginning through himself or from himself, or through another or from another, or through nothing or from nothing, he in no way has a beginning.

But neither will he have an end. For if he is going to have an end, he is not supremely immortal and supremely incorruptible. But it has been established that he is supremely both immortal and incorruptible.[17] Therefore, he will not have an end. Moreover, if he is going to have an end, he will perish either willingly or unwillingly. Now surely that by whose will the supreme good perishes is not an unqualified* good. But he himself is a true and unqualified good. Therefore, he who assuredly is the supreme good will not perish voluntarily. But if, on the other hand, he is going to perish unwillingly, then he is not supremely powerful or all-powerful. But the necessity of reason has declared that he is supremely powerful and all-powerful.[18] Therefore, he will not perish unwillingly. And so, if the supreme nature will not have an end either willingly or unwillingly, he will in no way have an end.

Moreover, if that supreme nature has a beginning or end, he is not true eternity, as he was irrefutably found to be above.[19] Further, let anyone who can do so think of this: When did it begin to be true, or when was it not true, that something was going to exist? Or when will it cease to be true, and no longer be true, that something existed in the past? But given that neither of these is conceivable, and both statements cannot be true apart from truth, then it is impossible even to think that truth has a beginning or end. Finally, if truth had a beginning or will have an end, before it came into being it was then true that there was no truth, and after it has ceased to exist, it will then be true that

---

16. In Chapters 3, 5, and 6.
17. In Chapter 16.
18. Ibid.
19. Ibid.

there is no truth. Now nothing can be true apart from truth. So truth existed before truth existed, and truth will exist after truth has ceased to exist—which is an absolute absurdity. So, whether truth is said to have a beginning or end or is understood not to have a beginning or end, truth cannot be confined by any beginning or end. Therefore, the same thing follows with respect to the supreme nature, since he is himself the supreme truth.

Chapter 19

How nothing existed before him and nothing will exist after him

But look how nothing once again arises to trouble us, and whatever reason has taught us thus far, supported by the harmonious testimony of truth and necessity, it declares to be nothing. For if the things that were set out earlier are fortified with the defenses of necessary truth, it is not the case that something existed before the supreme essence or that something will exist after him. Therefore, nothing existed before him and nothing will exist after him. For, necessarily, either something or nothing preceded him or will follow him.

Now whoever says that nothing existed before him and nothing will exist after him appears to be saying that there was a time before him when nothing existed, and that there will be a time after him when nothing will exist. Therefore, when nothing existed, he did not exist; and when nothing will exist, he will not exist. So how is it that he did not begin to exist from nothing, and how is it that he will not come to nothing, if he did not yet exist when nothing already existed, and if he will no longer exist when nothing will still exist? Why, then, have we wielded such a weight of arguments, if their work is so easily wrecked by nothing? For if it is concluded that the supreme being both comes after nothing, which preceded him, and gives way to nothing, which will follow him, that which was established above as necessarily true will be destroyed by a worthless nothing.

Do we not instead need to fight against nothing, lest so many constructions of necessary reason be besieged by nothing and the supreme good, who has been sought out and discovered by the light of truth, be lost for nothing? Therefore, rather than allowing a place for nothing either before or after the supreme essence, so that nothing itself reduces to nothing the being who through himself brought into existence that which once was nothing, let it instead be declared (if this is possible) that nothing did not exist before the supreme essence and will not exist after him. For the single expression, "Nothing existed before the supreme essence," gives rise to a twofold meaning. One sense is this: Before the supreme essence existed, there was a time when nothing existed. But there is a second meaning: Before the supreme essence there was not anything. Thus, if I were to say "Nothing has taught me to fly," I would interpret this either as meaning that nothing itself, which signifies not-anything, has taught me to fly, and so it would be false, or else as meaning that there is not anything that has taught me to fly, which is true.

And so it is the first meaning that generates the absurdity discussed above,[20] and reason utterly rejects it as false. It is the other meaning, by contrast, that is perfectly consistent with our earlier conclusions and is compelled to be true by its whole interconnection with them. Therefore, the statement that nothing existed before him is to be understood in accordance with the second meaning. It should not be interpreted as meaning that there was a time when nothing existed but he did not, but rather as meaning that before him, there was not anything. The same sort of twofold meaning applies to the statement that nothing is going to exist after him. Therefore, if this interpretation of 'nothing' that I have offered is carefully examined, it is most truly concluded that neither something nor nothing either preceded or will follow the supreme essence, and that nothing existed before it or will follow it. And nonetheless, the solidity of what has already been established is not shaken by any worthless nothing.

Chapter 20

That he exists in every place and time

Now it was concluded above that this creating nature exists everywhere and in all things and through all things,[21] and that, from the fact that he neither came into existence nor will cease to exist, it follows that he always was and is and will be.[22] Nevertheless, I feel the rumblings of a contradiction, which compels me to investigate more carefully where and when he exists. Now the supreme essence exists either everywhere and always, or merely somewhere and sometimes, or nowhere and never; or, as I put it, either in every place or time, or determinately in some, or in none.

But what seems more absurd than this: that he who exists supremely and most truly, exists nowhere and never? So it is false that he exists nowhere or never. Further, since no good thing—indeed, since nothing at all—exists without him, if he exists nowhere and never, then every good thing exists nowhere and never, and absolutely everything exists nowhere and never. Just how false that is, there is no need to say. Therefore, it is also false that he exists nowhere and never.

Therefore, he either exists determinately somewhere and sometimes, or everywhere and always. Now if he exists determinately in some place or time, it is only in that place and time, where and when he exists, that anything can exist. Absolutely

---

20. That is, in the first paragraph of this chapter.
21. Anselm argues for this claim in Chapter 14.
22. Anselm argues for this claim in Chapter 18.

no essence exists where and when he does not exist, since without him nothing exists. From this it follows that there is some place and some time where and when nothing at all exists. But since that is false (after all, that place and that time are themselves *something*), the supreme nature cannot exist determinately somewhere or sometimes. And if it is said that through himself he exists determinately at a certain time and place, but through his power he exists wherever and whenever anything exists, that is not true. For since it is evident that his power is nothing other than himself, his power in no way exists apart from him. Therefore, since he does not exist determinately somewhere and sometimes, he must exist everywhere and always—that is, in every place and time.

Chapter 21

That he exists in no place or time

Now if this is so, either he exists as a whole in every place or time, or only part of him does, so that another part exists outside every place and time. But if he partly exists and partly does not exist in every place or time, he has parts, which is false. Therefore, he does not partly exist everywhere and always.

But then how does he exist as a whole everywhere and always? This could be understood in two ways: either he exists as a whole all at once in all places and times and by parts in each individual place and time, or he exists as a whole even in each individual place and time. Now if he exists by parts in each individual place and time, he does not escape the composition and division of parts. And that, as we have found,[23] is altogether foreign to the supreme nature. Therefore, he does not exist as a whole in all places and times in such a way that he exists by parts in each individual place or time.

The other possibility remains to be discussed, namely, how the supreme nature exists as a whole *both* in all times and places *and* in each of them individually. This of course can only be the case either all at once or at different times. Now up to this point a single pursuit has been able at once to trail both the argument about place and that about time, since they have followed the same tracks. But at this point they part ways; they seem, as it were, to flee from disputation along disparate paths. They must therefore be investigated in separate discussions. Therefore, we shall first see whether the supreme nature can exist as a whole in individual places either all at once or at different times. Then we shall ask the same question about times.[24]

---

23. In Chapter 17.

24. That is, whether the supreme nature can exist as a whole at individual times either all at once or at different times.

So, if he exists as a whole in individual places, individual wholes exist in individual places. For just as one place is distinct from another place, in such a way that they are individual places, what exists as a whole in one place is distinct from what at the same time exists as a whole in another place, in such a way that they are individual wholes. For if something exists as a whole in a given place, there is nothing of that thing that does not exist in that place. Now if there is nothing of a thing that does not exist in a given place, then there is nothing of that thing that exists at the same time outside that place. Therefore, if something exists as a whole in a given place, there is nothing of it that exists at the same time outside that place. Now if there is nothing of a thing that exists outside some place, there is nothing of that thing that exists at the same time in some other place. Therefore, if something exists as a whole in a given place, there is nothing of it that exists at the same time in some other place. So if something exists as a whole in a given place, how can that whole exist at the same time in some other place, if nothing of it can exist in any other place?

Therefore, since one whole cannot exist as a whole all at once in individual places, it follows that if anything exists as a whole all at once in distinct places, it exists as individual wholes in individual places. And so if the supreme nature exists as a whole at one time in all individual places, there are as many individual supreme natures as there can be individual places, which is an irrational view to hold. Therefore, he does not exist as a whole at one time in individual places. On the other hand, if he exists as a whole in individual places at different times, then as long as he exists in one place, there is no good and no essence in the other places, since without him nothing at all exists. But the places themselves show that this is absurd, since they are not nothing, but something. And so the supreme nature does not exist as a whole in individual places at different times. So, if he does not exist as a whole in individual places either at the same time or at different times, it is clear that he in no way exists as a whole in all individual places.

Now we must investigate whether that same supreme nature exists as a whole at individual times, either all at once or distinctly at individual times. But how does something exist as a whole at individual times all at once if those times themselves do not exist all at once? On the other hand, if he exists as a whole separately and distinctly at individual times, in the way that a human being exists as a whole yesterday, today, and tomorrow, then it is correct to say that he existed and exists and will exist. Therefore, his life, which is nothing other than his eternity, does not exist as a whole all at once; instead, it is prolonged by parts through the parts of time.

Now his eternity is nothing other than himself. So it would follow that the supreme essence is divided into parts in accordance with the distinction of times. For if his life is produced by means of the flow of times, he has a past, present, and future along with those times. But what is his life, or the duration of his existence, other than his eternity? Therefore, since his eternity is nothing other than his essence (as the argument laid out above[25] proves beyond doubt), if his eternity has a past, present, and future, it follows that his essence also has a past, present, and future. Now what is past is not present or future, and what is present is not future or past, and what is future is not past or present. So how will our conclusion survive, which became clear above[26] by a rational and evident necessity—namely, that the supreme nature is in no way composite, but instead is supremely simple* and supremely unchangeable—if he is one thing at one time and something else at another, and if he has parts distributed through time? Or instead, if those earlier conclusions are true—rather, since they are quite clearly true—how are these later conclusions possible?

So neither the creating essence nor his life nor his eternity in any way has a past or a future. For how can it be that he has no present, if he truly exists? But "he existed" signifies the past, and "he will exist" signifies the future. So he never existed and never will exist.[27] Therefore, he does not exist as a whole at individual times either distinctly or all at once.

So if, as I have argued, he does not exist as a whole in all places and times in such a way that he exists as a whole in all of them at once and through his parts in each of them individually, or in such a way that he exists as a whole in each of them individually, it is evident that he in no way exists as a whole in every place or time. And since I have likewise discerned that he does not exist in every place or time in such a way that one part exists in every place and time and another part exists outside every place and time, it is impossible for him to exist everywhere and always. For he cannot at all be understood to exist everywhere and always unless he does so either as a whole or in part.

Now if he does not in any way exist everywhere and always, either he exists determinately in some place or time, or else he exists in no place and time. And I have already shown that he cannot exist determinately in some place or time.[28] Therefore, he exists in no place or time. In other words, he exists nowhere and never. For if he exists at all, he must exist either in every place and time, or in some place or time. And yet, once again, since it is irrefutably established not only that he exists through himself, without beginning and without end,[29] but also that

---

25. In Chapters 16 and 17.

26. In Chapter 17.

27. To put Anselm's point somewhat less boldly: "he existed" is never true of God, and "he will exist" is never true of him, since both of those expressions signify temporal categories that do not apply to God.

28. In Chapter 20.

29. In Chapter 18.

without him nothing exists anywhere or at any time,[30] he must exist everywhere and always.

Chapter 22

How he exists in every place and *time and in no place or time*

How, then, will these two conclusions, which are presented as so contrary but proved as so necessary, be reconciled? Perhaps the supreme nature exists in place or time in a way that does not prevent him from existing as a whole all at once in individual places or times, but so that there are not several* wholes, but only one whole, and so that his life, which is nothing other than true eternity, is not divided into past, present, and future. For this law of place and time seems to constrain only those things that exist in place or time in such a way that they do not transcend the expanse of space or the duration of time. Of such things, therefore, it is most truthfully asserted that one and the same whole cannot exist as a whole all at once in different places and times; but that conclusion does not apply with any necessity to things that are not of that sort.

For it seems correct to say that a thing has a place only if its quantity is circumscribed by a place that contains it and contained by a place that circumscribes it, and a thing has a time only if its duration is somehow bounded by a time that measures it and measured by a time that bounds it. Therefore, if something is such that its size or duration is not set against any boundary, whether by place or by time, no place or time properly applies to it. For since no place does to it what place does, and no time does to it what time does, we may reasonably say that no place is its place and no time is its time. Now if something is seen to have no place or time, it is certainly shown to be in no way subject to any law of place or time. Therefore, no law of place or time in any way constrains a nature that no place or time encloses in any confinement.

Does not every reasonable way of looking at this utterly exclude the possibility that the creating substance, supreme among all things—who is necessarily alien to and free from the nature and law of all the things that he himself made from nothing—is enclosed in the confines of any place or time, since instead his power, which is nothing other than his essence, encloses all the things he made by containing them under himself? And how is it anything but shameless folly to say that any place circumscribes the size of the supreme truth, or that any time bounds his duration, since absolutely no greatness or smallness of extension in place or time applies to him?

---

30. In Chapter 20.

This, then, is the condition of place and time: whatever is enclosed within their boundaries does not escape being characterized by parts, whether the sort of parts its place receives with respect to size, or the sort its time suffers with respect to duration; nor can it in any way be contained as a whole all at once by different places or times. By contrast, if something is in no way constrained by confinement in a place or time, no law of places or times forces it into a multiplicity of parts or prevents it from being present as a whole all at once in several places or times. And so, since this is the condition of place and time, the supreme substance, who is not enclosed by any confinement of place or time, is undoubtedly not constrained by any of their laws.

Therefore, since an inescapable necessity demands that the supreme essence be present as a whole in every place and time, and since no characteristic of place and time prevents him from being present as a whole in every place and time, he must be present as a whole all at once in each and every place and time. For the fact that he is present in a given place or time does not prevent him from being simultaneously and similarly present in this or that other place or time. Nor does the fact that he existed or exists or will exist mean that something of his eternity has vanished from the present time with the past, which no longer exists; or passes away with the present, which barely exists;[31] or is yet to come with the future, which does not yet exist. For that which in no way confines its existence within place or time is not at all compelled or forbidden by the law of places or times to exist or not to exist anywhere or at any time.

For if that supreme essence is said to exist in a place or a time, even though the very same expression is used both of him and of localized or temporal natures because of our customary way of speaking, there is a different meaning because of the dissimilarity of the things themselves. When it comes to localized or temporal natures, this one expression signifies two things: that they are *present at* the times and places in which they are said to exist, and that they are *contained by* those times and places. But in the case of the supreme essence, only one of these meanings applies, namely, that he is present, not that he is contained by them.

Consequently, if our ordinary way of speaking permitted, it would seem more appropriate to say that he exists *with* a time or place rather than *in* a time or place. For saying that something exists *in* another thing implies more strongly that it is contained than does saying that it exists *with* that thing. And so he is properly said to exist in no place or time, since he is in no way contained by any other thing. And yet he can be said in his own way to exist in every place or time, since whatever else exists is sustained by his presence so that it does not fall into nothingness. He exists in every place and time because he is absent from none;

---

31. The present, as Anselm is thinking of it, exists only for a moment, and so it no sooner exists than it passes away.

he also exists in none, because he has no place or time. Nor does he receive in himself the distinctions of places or times, such as here or there or somewhere, or now or then or sometime. Nor is it the case that he exists in the fleeting present time that we experience, or that he has existed or will exist in the past or future, since these are proper to circumscribed and changeable things, which he is not. And yet they can in some sense be said of him, since he is present to all circumscribed and changeable things just as if he were circumscribed by the same places and changed by the same times.

And thus it is evident—enough so to dissolve the contradiction that arose earlier—how the supreme essence of all exists everywhere and always, as well as nowhere and never, that is, both in every place and time and in no place or time, according to a harmonious truth understood in different ways.

Chapter 23

How he can be better understood as existing everywhere, rather than as existing in every place

Indeed, since it has been established that the supreme nature does not exist in all places any more than in all existing things, not as if he were contained by them, but because he contains them all by pervading them all, why should he not be said to exist everywhere in the sense that he is understood as existing in all existing things, rather than merely as existing in all places? For the truth of the matter bears out this interpretation, and the proper way of speaking about place in no way prevents it. For we often quite properly use place-words for things that are not places and are not confined within any boundaries of place. For example, I might say, "Understanding is there in the soul, where rationality is." 'There' and 'where' are place-words, and yet the soul does not confine anything, and understanding and rationality are not confined, within any boundaries of place. Therefore, the truth of the matter is that the supreme nature would be more aptly said to exist everywhere according to this interpretation, so that he is understood as existing in all existing things rather than merely as existing in all places. And since, as the arguments laid out above show, this cannot be otherwise, he necessarily exists in all existing things in such a way that he exists completely as one and the same whole all at once in each of them individually.

Chapter 24

How he can be better understood as existing always, rather than as existing at every time

It has also been established that this supreme substance exists without beginning and without end,[32] and that he has no past or future, or even a temporal—that is, a fleeting—present such as we experience,[33] since his life or eternity, which is nothing other than himself, is unchangeable and without parts. So when 'always,' which seems to designate all of time, is said of him, is it not much more truly understood to signify eternity, which is never unlike itself, rather than the variation of times, which is always in some respect unlike itself?

Now for him, to exist is the same as to live. Therefore, if he is said to exist 'always,' this is best understood as meaning that he exists or lives eternally; in other words, that he enjoys illimitable life as a whole, perfectly, and all at once.[34] For his eternity appears to be an illimitable life existing as a whole all at once and perfectly. For, since it became perfectly clear earlier[35] that this same substance is nothing other than his own life and his own eternity, and that he is in no way limitable, nor exists otherwise than as a whole all at once and perfectly, what else is true eternity, which belongs to him alone, but an illimitable life existing as a whole all at once and perfectly? For by this alone is it evidently seen that true eternity exists in that substance alone, who alone has been found to be not made, but the Maker. For true eternity is understood as lacking the boundaries of a beginning and an end. But this is not true of any created thing, as is shown by the very fact that they were made from nothing.

Chapter 25

*That he cannot be changed by any accidents**

But that essence, who has been shown[36] to be in every respect the same as himself substantially: Is he not sometimes different from himself, at least accidentally? But then how is he supremely unchangeable if he can—I will not say, *be* changeable,

---

32. Anselm argues for this claim in Chapter 18.

33. Anselm argues for this claim in Chapters 21 and 22.

34. Anselm is here echoing the famous definition of eternity found in Boethius, *Consolation of Philosophy,* Book 5, prose 6: "Eternity is the whole and perfect possession of illimitable life all at once."

35. In Chapter 17.

36. Ibid.

but at least *be understood as* changeable through accidents? And on the other hand, how is he not subject to accidents, when the very fact that he is greater than all other natures, and that he is unlike them, seems to be accidental to him?

But why would susceptibility to certain of those things that are called accidents be inconsistent with natural immutability, if taking on those accidents causes no change in the substance? And in fact, among all the things that are called accidents, it is understood that some—all colors, for example—cannot be present or absent without some variation in the thing that participates in them. But there are others—some relations, for example—that are known to bring about no change at all in the thing of which they are said by beginning or ceasing to be present in it. For example, it is evident that I am not taller than, shorter than, equal to, or similar to a human being who will be born after this year. But once he has been born, I will be able—without any change on my part—to have and to lose all these relations with respect to him as he grows or is changed by various qualities. And so it becomes clear that among the things that are called accidents, some do imply a degree of mutability, whereas others in no way destroy immutability.

Therefore, just as the supreme nature never yields a place in his simplicity for accidents that bring about change, in the same way he does not reject being sometimes described in accordance with those accidents that in no way oppose his supreme immutability. And yet his essence is not subject to any accident by which it can be understood to be changeable. From this it can also be concluded that he is not susceptible of any accident. For surely those accidents that cause a change in something by beginning or ceasing to be present in it are judged, in virtue of that very effect, to be truly accidents of the thing they change; and by the same token, those that lack a similar effect are perceived to be improperly called accidents. Therefore, just as he is always in every respect the same as himself substantially, so he is never in any respect different from himself, even accidentally. But however things stand with the proper use of the word 'accident,' it is undoubtedly true that nothing can be said of the supremely unchangeable nature from which he could be understood to be changeable.

Chapter 26

In what sense he is to be called a substance, and that he is beyond every substance, and uniquely is whatever he is

But if what I have observed about the simplicity of this nature is certain, in what sense is he a substance? For although every substance is capable of taking on an admixture of differences or a change from accidents, his unchangeable purity is altogether inaccessible to admixture or change. Therefore, how will it be the case that he is a substance at all, unless 'substance' is used to mean 'essence,'[37] and he is just as much beyond as he is above every substance? For however great the difference is between the being who is through himself whatever he is and makes every other being from nothing, and a being that through another is made from nothing to be whatever it is, the difference is every bit as great between the supreme substance and those that are not the same thing that he is. And since he alone among all natures has from himself whatever existence he has, without the help of any other nature, is he not uniquely whatever he is, having nothing in common with his creatures? Accordingly, if any word is ever applied to him in common with others, it must undoubtedly be understood to have a very different signification.

Chapter 27

That he is not included in a common classification of substances, and yet he is a substance and an individual spirit

And so it is established that this substance is not included in any common classification of substances, since every other nature is excluded from having an essence in common with him. Indeed, every substance is classified as either universal or individual. A universal substance is essentially common to several* substances, as being-a-man is common to individual men; an individual substance has a universal essence in common with others, as individual men have in common with other individual men the fact that they are men. So how would someone understand the supreme nature as being included in this classification of other substances, since he is neither divided into several substances nor conjoined with any other through a common essence? Nevertheless, since he not only most assuredly exists but also exists in the highest way of all things, and the essence of any given thing is generally called a substance, surely, if he can be worthily called anything at all, there is nothing to prevent us from calling him a substance.

Now since we know of no worthier essence than spirit or body,* and of these, spirit is worthier than body, we must of course declare that he is a spirit and not a body. But since that spirit can have no parts, and there cannot be more than one spirit like him, he is necessarily an altogether individual spirit. For since (as was established earlier) he is not composed of parts,[38] and he cannot be understood as

---

37. Anselm's point here is that we cannot call God a substance in the sense in which a substance is distinguished from its accidents. But we can use the word 'substance' as interchangeable with 'essence,' in which case God is indeed a substance (that is, an essence or being) that is beyond and above all other substances.

38. Anselm argues for this claim in Chapter 17.

capable of being changed by any differences or accidents,[39] it is impossible for him to be divisible by any sort of division.

Chapter 28

That this spirit exists in an unqualified sense, and creatures do not exist at all compared to him*

It seems, therefore, to follow from our earlier conclusions that this spirit, who thus exists in his own wonderfully unique and uniquely wonderful way, is in a certain sense the only thing that exists, whereas all the other things that appear to exist do not exist at all compared to him. For if we look at this carefully, he alone will be seen to exist in an unqualified sense and perfectly and absolutely, whereas all other things nearly do not exist at all, and barely do exist. For because of his unchangeable eternity, it can in no way be said of that spirit because of any alteration that he existed or will exist; instead, he exists in an unqualified sense. Nor does he exist changeably, so that he is now something that at some time he was not or will not be. Nor does he fail to be now what at some other time he was or will be. Rather, whatever he is, he is once and for all, all at once, and illimitably. And since his existence is like this, he is rightly said to exist in an unqualified sense and absolutely and perfectly.

By contrast, all other things exist changeably in some respect, so that at some time they were or will be something that they are not now, or they are now something that at some time they were not or will not be. What they once were no longer exists, and what they will be does not yet exist, and what they are in the fleeting, utterly brief, and barely-existing present barely exists. Therefore, since they exist so changeably, it is not unreasonable to deny that they exist in an unqualified sense and perfectly and absolutely, and to assert that they nearly do not exist, and barely do exist.

Further, all things whatsoever that are different from him came from non-being to being, not through themselves but through another; and as far as their own power goes, they return to non-being unless they are sustained through another. How, then, can it be characteristic of them to exist in an unqualified sense or perfectly or absolutely, rather than barely to exist, or nearly not to exist? And only that ineffable spirit can in no way be understood to have begun from non-being, or to be capable of undergoing any degeneration from what he is into non-being; and whatever he is, he is not through anything other than himself, that is, through what he himself is. So is not his existence rightly understood to be the only unqualified, perfect, and absolute existence?

---

39. Anselm argues for this claim in Chapter 25.

Now surely that which is thus in an unqualified sense and in every respect the only perfect, unqualified, and absolute existence can in a certain sense rightly be said to be the only thing that exists. And on the other hand whatever is known through the above argument as not existing in an unqualified sense or perfectly or absolutely, but instead as barely existing or nearly not existing, is indeed in a certain sense rightly said not to exist. So according to this argument, only that Creator Spirit exists, and all created things do not exist. And yet it is not the case that they utterly do not exist, since they have been made from nothing by him who alone exists absolutely.

Chapter 29

That his utterance[40] *is the very same thing as himself; and yet they are not two spirits but one*

Now, having examined those things regarding the properties of the supreme nature that have occurred to me up to this point as I follow the guidance of reason, I think it is appropriate, if I can do so, to examine his utterance, by which all things were made.[41] And although everything I was able to ascertain about it above has the unbending rigor of reason, the fact that it is proved to be the very same thing as the supreme spirit himself especially compels me to discuss that utterance more carefully. For if the supreme spirit made nothing except through himself, and whatever was made by him was made through his utterance, how can that utterance be anything other than what he himself is?

Moreover, the things we have already discovered declare irrefutably that nothing at all ever could or can subsist* other than the creating spirit and what he creates.[42] Now it is impossible for the utterance of that spirit to be included among created things, since every subsistent created thing was made through it, and it could not have been made through itself. Indeed, nothing can be made through itself, since whatever is made is posterior* to that through which it was made, and nothing is posterior to itself. And so, since the utterance of the supreme spirit

---

40. His "utterance" is discussed in Chapters 10–12.

41. Anselm's discussion in Chapters 29–63 is meant to provide a philosophical explication of certain elements of the Christian understanding of God as a Trinity. Since some of Anselm's points, as well as much of the language that he uses, will not be fully clear unless the reader already has some knowledge of Trinitarian doctrine, I have provided the necessary explanations in the notes as well as in the Glossary. See the entries for consubstantial* and Word.*

42. Anselm argues for this claim in Chapter 7.

cannot be a creature, the only remaining possibility is that it is nothing other than the supreme spirit.

Finally, this utterance cannot be understood as anything other than the understanding of that spirit, by which he understands all things. For what is it for him to utter something, in this sense of "uttering," other than to understand it? For unlike a human being, he never fails to utter what he understands. Therefore, if that supremely simple* nature is nothing other than what his understanding is, just as he is the same as what his wisdom is, then it must be that in the same way he is nothing other than what his utterance is. But since it is already evident that the supreme spirit is only one, and in every way individual,[43] his utterance must be consubstantial* with him, so that they are not two spirits but one.

Chapter 30

*That this utterance does not consist of many words, but rather is one Word**

Why, then, should I hesitate over the question I left open earlier, namely, whether this utterance consists in several* words or in one?[44] For if this utterance is consubstantial with the supreme nature in such a way that they are not two, but one spirit, then of course that utterance is supremely simple,* just as the supreme nature is. Therefore, it does not consist of several words; rather, it is one Word, through whom all things were made.

Chapter 31

That this Word is not a likeness of created things but the truth of their essence, whereas created things are an imitation of that truth; and which natures are greater and more excellent than others

But behold! It seems to me that a question arises that is not easy and yet should in no way be left unresolved. For all words by which we say things in our mind (that is, think them) are likenesses and images of the things of which they are words. And every likeness or image is more or less true as it imitates more or less the thing of which it is a likeness. So what are we to hold about that Word by whom all things are uttered, and through whom all things were made? Is he or is he not a likeness of those things that were made through him? For if he is a true likeness of

---

43. Anselm argues for this claim in Chapter 37.
44. Anselm raised this question in passing in Chapter 12.

mutable things, he is not consubstantial* with the supreme immutability, which is false. On the other hand, if he is not an altogether true likeness of mutable things, but merely some sort of likeness, the Word of the supreme truth is not altogether true, which is absurd. But if he has no likeness to mutable things, how is it that they were patterned after him?

But perhaps none of this uncertainty will remain if we understand it in this way. The truth of a human being is said to exist in a living human being, whereas in a painted one there is the likeness or image of that truth. In the same way, the truth of existing is understood to be in the Word, whose essence exists so supremely that in a certain sense it alone exists, whereas in the things that by comparison with him in a certain sense do not exist, and yet have been made something through him and in accordance with him, there is judged to be an imitation of that supreme essence. Thus, the Word of the supreme truth, who himself is also the supreme truth, experiences no gain or loss depending on whether he is more or less like creatures; instead, it must be the case that every created thing is so much greater and more excellent the more it is like him who supremely exists and is supremely great.

For it is perhaps on this basis—no, not perhaps—it is *certainly* on this basis that every intellect judges that natures that are in some way living are more excellent than those that are not living, natures that perceive than those that do not perceive, and rational natures than those that lack reason. For since the supreme nature in his own unique way not merely exists but also lives and perceives and is rational, it is clear that of all existing things, what is in some way living is more like him than what is in no way living; and what in some way knows something, even through a bodily sense, is more like him than what perceives nothing at all; and what is rational is more like him than what is not capable of reason. And by a similar argument it is clear that certain natures exist more greatly or to a lesser degree than others. For just as something exists more excellently by nature if its natural essence is closer to the most excellent nature, so a nature exists more greatly if its essence is more like the supreme essence.

That this also is the case can, I think, be easily established. Suppose one first thinks of a substance that lives and is capable of perception and is rational. Then in thought one takes away its rationality, next its ability to perceive, then its life, and finally the bare existence that is all that remains. Who would not understand that the substance that is thus destroyed a little at a time is gradually brought to exist less and less, and finally not to exist at all? So if these things are taken away one at a time, they lead an essence down to a lesser and lesser existence; but if they are added in an orderly way, they lead it up to a greater and greater existence. So it is evident that a living substance exists more greatly than one that is not living, one that is capable of perception than one that is not capable of perception, and one that is rational than one that is not rational. And so there is no doubt that every essence exists more greatly and is more excellent to the extent that it is more like the essence that supremely exists and is supremely excellent.

And so it is sufficiently clear that in the Word, through whom all things were made, there is no likeness of those things but rather their true and unqualified* essence. By contrast, in the things that were made there is no unqualified and absolute essence; instead, there is barely an imitation of that true essence. Hence it must be that the Word is not more or less true depending on the likeness of created things; instead, every created nature stands at a higher level of essence and dignity the more it is seen to approach him.

Chapter 32

That the supreme spirit utters himself by his coeternal Word

But since this is so, how can he, who is the unqualified* truth, be the Word of those things of which he is not a likeness? For every word by which a thing is uttered by the mind is a likeness of that thing. And if he is not the Word of those things that were made through him, in what sense is he a Word? Surely every word is the word of some thing. Furthermore, if there were never any creature, there would be no word of a creature. What then? Are we to conclude that the Word, who is the supreme essence and lacks for nothing, would not exist at all if no creature ever existed? Or perhaps that the supreme essence, which the Word is, would indeed be eternal* through his essence, but he would not be a Word if nothing were ever made through him? For there can be no word of something that neither existed, nor exists, nor will exist.

But according to this argument, if no essence other than the supreme spirit ever existed, no word at all would exist in him. If no word ever existed in him, he would not utter anything within himself. Now for him, to utter something is the same as to understand it. So if he did not utter anything within himself, he would not understand anything. If he did not understand anything, it would follow that the supreme wisdom, which is nothing other than that same spirit, would not understand anything, which is utterly absurd. What then? If he did not understand anything, how would he be the supreme wisdom?

But then if nothing existed apart from him, what would he understand? Would he not understand *himself*? Indeed, how can it even be thought that the supreme wisdom at some time fails to understand himself, since the rational mind can remember not only itself but even the supreme wisdom and can understand both him and itself? For if the human mind were not capable of remembering or understanding either him or itself, it would in no way be able to distinguish itself from nonrational creatures or to distinguish him from all of creation by reasoning silently within itself, as my mind is doing now. Therefore, just as that supreme spirit is eternal, so too he eternally remembers and understands himself after the likeness of the rational mind—or rather, not after the likeness of anything; instead, he does so paradigmatically, and the rational mind does so after his likeness. Now if he understands himself eternally, he utters himself eternally. And if he utters himself eternally, his Word exists with him eternally. Therefore, whether he is thought to exist without any other essence existing, or along with other things that exist, his Word, coeternal with him, must exist with him.

Chapter 33

That by one Word he utters both himself and what he made

But behold! While I was asking about the Word by which the Creator utters all the things he made, it was the Word by which he utters himself, who made all things, that presented itself to me. Does he utter himself by one Word and the things he makes by some other Word? Or is the Word by which he utters whatever he makes the very same as the Word by which he utters himself? For the Word by which he utters himself must also be the very same thing that he is, just as was true of the Word by which he utters the things he made. For even if nothing other than the supreme spirit ever existed, reason nevertheless compels the conclusion that the Word by which he utters himself necessarily exists. And so what is truer than this: that his Word is nothing other than what he himself is? Therefore, if by a Word that is consubstantial* with himself he utters both himself and the things he makes, it is evident that the Word by which he utters himself and the Word by which he utters creation are one substance. So if there is one substance, how can there be two Words?

But perhaps the identity of the substance does not compel us to assert the unity of the word. For he who utters by means of these words has the same substance they have, and yet he is not a word. And of course the Word by which the supreme wisdom utters himself is most appropriately called his Word according to our earlier argument, since he bears a perfect likeness to him. For it cannot be denied by any argument that when the rational mind understands itself by thinking itself, an image of itself is born in its thought. Indeed, that very thinking of itself *is* its own image, formed to its own likeness as by its own impress. For whatever the mind desires to understand accurately, whether through corporeal imagination or through reason, it tries to impress a likeness of that thing in its thought, so far as it can. And the more truly it does this, the more truly it thinks of that thing. This fact is of course observed more clearly when the mind thinks of something other than itself, especially when it thinks of some body.* For when I think of someone I know who is absent, the gaze of my thought is formed into an image of him like the one that I committed to memory through the vision of my eyes. This image in thought is the word of the man whom I utter by thinking of him. Therefore, when the rational mind understands itself by thinking itself, it has within itself its own image, born from itself—in other words, its thought of itself, formed to its own likeness as by its own impress—although it is reason alone that can distinguish the mind from this image of itself.[45] This image of the mind is its word.

And so who could deny that in this way, when the supreme wisdom understands himself by uttering himself, he begets a likeness of himself that is consubstantial with himself: that is, his Word? Although nothing fully adequate can properly be said of such a uniquely excellent thing, he is not improperly called his likeness, and in the same way also his image[46] and figure and character.[47] By contrast, the Word by whom he utters creation is not the word of creation in a similar sense at all, since he is not a likeness of creation but rather its paradigmatic essence.[48] It follows, therefore, that he does not utter creation by a word of creation. So if he does not utter creation by a word of creation, by whose word *does* he utter creation? For what he utters, he utters by a word, and a word is the word (that is, the likeness) *of something*. Now if he utters nothing other than himself and creation, he cannot utter anything except by his own Word or by a word of creation. Therefore, if he utters nothing by a word of creation, whatever he utters, he utters by his own Word. Therefore, he utters both himself and whatever he made by one and the same Word.

Chapter 34

How he can be seen to utter creation by his own Word

But how can such different things—namely, the creating and the created essence—be uttered by one Word, especially since that Word is coeternal with him who utters it, whereas creation is not coeternal with him? Perhaps it is because he is himself the supreme wisdom and the supreme reason, in which all created things exist. For any work that is made according to a craft always—not only when it is made, but even before it is made and after it is destroyed—exists in that craft as nothing other than the craft itself. Therefore, when that supreme spirit utters himself, he utters all created things. For before they were made, and once they

---

45. That is, when the mind understands itself, there is no real distinction between the mind and its image of itself. The distinction is a purely conceptual one, one that is made by reason alone.

46. Cf. Colossians 1:15: "He is the image of the invisible God."

47. Cf. Hebrews 1:3: "He is the splendor of his glory and the figure of his substance." The Greek word translated as 'figure' is χαρακτήρ ('character').

48. See the argument of Chapter 31 for this distinction.

have already been made, and when they are destroyed or in any way changed, they always exist in him, not as what they are in themselves, but as what he himself is. For in themselves they are a changeable essence created according to an unchangeable reason; in him, however, they are that first essence and first truth of existing, and the more they are in any way like him, the more truly and excellently do they exist. And so in this way it can reasonably be asserted that when the supreme spirit utters himself, he also, by one and the same Word, utters whatever was made.

Chapter 35

That whatever was made is life and truth in his Word and knowledge

Now since it has been established that his Word is consubstantial with him and exactly like him, it follows necessarily that all the things that exist in him exist in his Word in just the same way. So whatever was made—whether it is living or non-living, or whatever it is in itself—is, in him, life and truth.[49] And since for the supreme spirit there is no difference between knowing and understanding or uttering, he must know all the things he knows in the same way that he utters or understands them. Therefore, just as all things are life and truth in his Word, so are they also in his knowledge.

Chapter 36

In what an incomprehensible way he utters or knows the things he made

From this it can be most clearly comprehended that no human knowledge can comprehend how that spirit utters or knows the things that were made. For no one doubts that created substances exist in themselves quite differently from how they exist in our knowledge. After all, in themselves they exist through their own essence, whereas in our knowledge it is not their essences but their likenesses that exist. So it follows that they exist more truly in themselves than in our knowledge to the extent that they exist more truly somewhere through their essence than through their likeness. And it is also clear that every created substance exists more truly in the Word, that is, in the understanding of the Creator, than in itself, to the extent that the creating essence exists more truly than a created essence. So if our knowledge is as much surpassed by created substances as their likeness falls

---

49. John 1:3–4, as Anselm read it (following Augustine), says, "All things were made through him [i.e., the Word], and without him was nothing made. That which was made is, in him, life."

short of their essence,[50] how will the human mind understand what that utterance and that knowledge are like, since they are far higher and truer than created substances?

Chapter 37

That whatever he is with respect to creation, his Word is also; nevertheless, the two of them together are not so in more than one way

Now since the arguments above clearly show that the supreme spirit made all things through his Word, did not the Word himself also make all things? For since he is consubstantial with him whose Word he is, he must be the supreme essence. But there is only one supreme essence, who is the only Creator and only origin of all created things. For he alone made all things from nothing, not through another, but through himself. So whatever the supreme spirit makes, his Word also makes, and in the same way.[51] Therefore, whatever the supreme spirit is with respect to creation, his Word is also, and in the same way. Nevertheless, the two of them together are not so in more than one way, for there is not more than one supreme creating essence. Therefore, just as he is the Creator and origin of things, so also is his Word; and yet they are not two, but one Creator and one origin.

Chapter 38

That one cannot say what they are two of, and yet they must be two

And so one must pay close attention to something that is quite unusual in the case of other things but seems to happen in the case of the supreme spirit and his Word. For it is certain that whatever they are in their essence, and whatever they are with respect to creation, is present in each of them individually, and in both of them together, in such a way as to be complete in both and yet not introduce any plurality into the two of them. For although the supreme spirit individually is completely the supreme truth and the Creator, and his Word individually is also the supreme truth and the Creator, nevertheless the two of them together are not two truths or two Creators.

---

50. Anselm explains in Chapter 62 that what is present in our minds when we think of some external object is not the thing itself (its essence) but merely an image of the thing (its likeness).

51. Cf. John 5:19: "For whatever [the Father] made, the Son also makes in the same way."

But although this is so, it is nevertheless in a strange way quite clear that the one whose Word exists cannot be his own Word, and the Word cannot be the one whose Word he is. Thus, in that which signifies either what they are substantially or what they are with respect to creation, they always keep an individual unity; but in virtue of the fact that the supreme spirit does not exist from the Word, whereas the Word exists from him, they admit an ineffable plurality.

Ineffable indeed—for although necessity compels that they be two, there is no way to express what they are two *of.* For even if they can be said to be two equals (or something else like that) in relation to each other, if it is asked what the thing is of which these relatives* are said, one will not be able to answer in the plural, as when two lines are said to be equal or two human beings to be similar. Certainly they are not two equal spirits, or two equal Creators, or two of anything that signifies either their essence or their relationship to creation. Nor are they two of anything that signifies the distinguishing relationship of one to the other; they are not two Words or two images. After all, the Word's being a Word or image implies a relationship to another: he must be the Word or image *of something.* These are the distinguishing characteristics of the Word, so much so that they cannot in any way be shared by the other. For he whose Word or image he is, is neither an image nor a Word.

So it is established that one cannot express what the supreme spirit and his Word are two *of,*[52] although they must be two because of their individual properties. For it is the distinguishing characteristic of the second that he exists from the first, and it is the distinguishing characteristic of the first that the second exists from him.

Chapter 39

That the Word exists from the supreme spirit by being born

This can, it seems, be expressed in no more familiar terms than by saying that it is the distinguishing characteristic of the second that he is born from the first, and it is the distinguishing characteristic of the first that the second is born from him. For it has certainly been established already[53] that the Word of the supreme spirit does not exist from him in the same way as the things that were made by him, but rather as Creator from Creator, supreme from supreme, and—to express their likeness in the briefest way possible—the very same from the very same, and in such a way that he in no way exists except from him. Therefore, since it is evident that the Word of the supreme spirit exists from him alone in such a way that he bears a perfect likeness to him as offspring to parent, and that he does not exist from him

---

52. In Chapter 79 Anselm takes up this question again.

53. In Chapter 29.

in the sense that he is made by him, he is indeed most appropriately thought of as existing from him by being born. Indeed, if we do not hesitate to say that countless things are born from the things from which they have their existence, even though they bear no likeness, as offspring to parent, to the things from which they are said to be born—for we say that hair is born from the head and fruit from a tree, although hair is not like the head and fruit is not like the tree—; if, I say, many such things are not absurdly said to be born, it is as much more fittingly said that the Word of the supreme spirit exists from him by being born, as he more perfectly bears a likeness to him, like that of offspring to parent, by existing from him.

Chapter 40

That most truly he is the parent and the Word his offspring

But if the Word is most appropriately said to be born and is so much like the one from whom he is born, why is he regarded as like him in the way that offspring is like a parent? Should it not rather be asserted that one is parent and the other is offspring the more truly, the more that the one by himself suffices completely for the birth of the other and he who is born expresses his likeness? For in other things that certainly have a relationship of parent to offspring, none of them begets in such a way that it needs no help and is by itself completely sufficient to beget its offspring, and none of them is begotten in such a way that it is exactly like its parent, with no admixture of unlikeness. Therefore, given that the Word of the supreme spirit exists so completely from his essence alone, and is like him in such a unique way, that no other offspring exists so completely from the essence of its parent alone or is so much like its parent, the relationship of parent to offspring certainly seems not to apply to anything so fittingly as it does to the supreme spirit and his Word. Therefore, the distinguishing characteristic of the supreme spirit is to be most truly parent, and the distinguishing characteristic of the Word is to be most truly offspring.

Chapter 41

That he most truly begets and the Word is begotten

Now this could not be the case unless it were equally true that he most truly begets and the Word is most truly begotten. Therefore, just as the earlier claim is clearly true, this claim must be absolutely certain. Therefore, the supreme spirit most truly begets and his Word is most truly begotten.

Chapter 42

That he is most truly begetter and Father, and the other is begotten and Son

At this point I should like to conclude (and perhaps I could) that he is most truly the Father, while the other is most truly the Son. But I think one should not overlook the question whether they are more properly called 'Father' and 'Son' or 'Mother' and 'Daughter,' since there is no distinction of sex in them. For if it is appropriate to call him 'Father' and his offspring 'Son' because they are both spirit, why would not a parallel argument show that it is appropriate for one to be Mother and the other Daughter, since they are both truth and wisdom?[54] Or is it because in those natures that do have a distinction of sexes, being a father or son is characteristic of the better sex, whereas being a mother or daughter is characteristic of the lesser sex? This is indeed naturally the case in most, but in some it is just the opposite, as in certain kinds of birds, in which the female sex is always larger and stronger, whereas the male is smaller and weaker. But surely the real reason why it is more appropriate for the supreme spirit to be called Father rather than Mother is that the first and principal cause of offspring is always in the father. For since the paternal cause always in some way precedes the maternal, it would be quite incongruous to apply the word 'mother' to that parent who begets his offspring without any other cause that either accompanies or precedes him. Therefore, it is most true that the supreme spirit is the Father of his offspring.

Now given that a son is always more like his father than a daughter is, and nothing is more like another than his offspring is like the supreme Father, it is most true that this offspring is not a daughter but a Son. Therefore, just as it is the distinguishing characteristic of the one that he most truly begets and of the other that he is most truly begotten, so it is the distinguishing characteristic of the one that he is most truly begetter and of the other that he is most truly begotten. And just as the one is most truly parent and the other most truly offspring, so the one is most truly Father and the other most truly Son.

---

54. This argument relies on the fact that in Latin the word for 'spirit' is masculine and the words for 'truth' and 'wisdom' are feminine.

Chapter 43

A reconsideration of what is common to both and the distinguishing characteristics of each

Having discovered so many and so great distinguishing characteristics of each, by which it is proved that there is a marvelous plurality—as ineffable as it is inevitable—in the supreme unity, it seems to me most delightful to reconsider so impenetrable a mystery again and again. For behold, it is impossible for him who begets to be the same as him who is begotten, and for the parent to be the same as the offspring—so much so that it is necessary that the begetter be one thing and the begotten something else, and that the Father be one thing and the Son something else. Nevertheless, it is necessary that he who begets be the same as him who is begotten, and that the parent be the same as the offspring—so much so that it is impossible for the begetter to be other than what the begotten is, and for the Father to be other than what the Son is.

Now the Father is one thing and the Son is another, so much so that it is altogether obvious that they are two; and yet that which they both are is so much one and the same thing that it is completely obscure what they are two *of*. For the Father is one thing and the Son another, so much so that when I speak of both, I see that I have spoken of two things; and yet that which is both Father and Son is so much one and the same thing that I do not understand *what* two things I have spoken of. For although the Father individually is completely the supreme spirit, and the Son individually is completely the supreme spirit, nevertheless, the Father-spirit and the Son-spirit are so much one and the same that the Father and the Son are not two spirits but one spirit.

Thus, just as the individual distinguishing characteristics of each do not admit of plurality, since they do not belong to both of them, so what is common to both keeps its individual unity, even though it belongs wholly to each. For just as there are not two fathers or two sons but one Father and one Son, since their individual distinguishing characteristics belong to them individually, so there are not two spirits but one, even though the Father is a complete spirit and the Son is also a complete spirit. In virtue of their relations they are opposed in such a way that neither takes on the distinguishing characteristic of the other; in virtue of their nature they are harmonious in such a way that each always has the essence of the other. For in virtue of the fact that one is the Father and the other is the Son, they are so different that the Father is never called the Son and the Son is never called the Father; and in virtue of their substance they are so much the same that the essence of the Son always exists in the Father and the essence of the Father always exists in the Son. For there are not different essences but the same essence, not several* essences, but one essence of both.

Chapter 44

How one is the essence of the other

Hence, if we say that one is the essence of the other, we are not straying from the truth but rather emphasizing the supreme unity and simplicity of their common nature. For if we say that the Father is the essence of the Son and the Son is the essence of the Father, we cannot understand this in the same way as when we talk about the wisdom of a man through which the man is wise. For a man cannot be wise through himself; but we do not mean that the Son exists through the Father and the Father through the Son, as if one could exist only through the other in the same way that a man can be wise only through wisdom. For just as the supreme wisdom is always wise through himself, so also the supreme essence always exists through himself. Now the Father is completely the supreme essence, and the Son is also completely the supreme essence. Therefore, the Father exists completely through himself, and the Son also exists completely through himself, just as each of them is wise through himself.

For that essence or wisdom which is the Son is no less perfect simply because he is an essence born of the Father's essence and a wisdom born of his wisdom. But he would indeed be a less perfect essence or wisdom if he did not exist through himself or were not wise through himself. For it is in no way contradictory that the Son both subsists* through himself and has being from the Father. For just as the Father has essence and wisdom and life in himself, so that it is not through someone else's but through his own essence that he exists, through his own wisdom that he is wise, and through his own life that he lives, so by begetting the Son he grants the Son to have essence and wisdom and life in himself,[55] so that it is not through someone else's essence, wisdom, and life but through his own that he subsists, is wise, and lives. Otherwise the being of the Father and the Son would not be the same, nor would the Son be equal to the Father. And we saw above[56] quite clearly how false that is.

Therefore, it is not contradictory that the Son both subsists through himself and exists from the Father, since this very power of subsisting through himself is necessarily something he has from the Father. For if some wise man teaches me his wisdom, which I formerly lacked, we would rightly say that he had taught me by means of that very wisdom of his. But although my wisdom would have its being and its wisdom from his wisdom, nonetheless, once it existed it would exist only through its own essence and be wise only through itself. So it is all the more true

---

55. Cf. John 5:26: "For just as the Father has life in himself, so he has granted the Son also to have life in himself."
56. In Chapters 29 and 43.

that the eternal Father's coeternal Son—who has being from the Father in such a way that they are not two essences—subsists, is wise, and lives through himself.

So if we say that the Father is the essence of the Son and the Son is the essence of the Father, this cannot be understood as meaning that either of them can subsist only through the other and not through himself. Rather, in order to indicate that they share the supremely simple and supremely unitary essence, it can be fittingly said and understood that each is the very same as the other in such a way that each has the essence of the other. Now for each of them there is no difference between having an essence and being an essence. And so by this argument, just as each has the essence of the other, each *is* the essence of the other; that is, one has the same being as the other.

Chapter 45

That the Son can more appropriately be called the essence of the Father than the Father can be called the essence of the Son; and that similarly the Son is the power and wisdom of the Father, and so on

But although this is true according to the argument we have examined, it is far more fitting to call the Son the essence of the Father than to call the Father the essence of the Son. For since the Father has his essence from no one but himself, it is not completely appropriate to say that he has anyone's essence but his own. By contrast, since the Son has his essence from the Father, and indeed the very same essence that the Father has, he can be most appropriately said to have the essence of the Father.

Now neither of them has his essence otherwise than by *being* that essence. Therefore, just as the Son is much more appropriately understood to have the essence of the Father than the Father to have the essence of the Son, so also the Son can be more fittingly called the essence of the Father than the Father can be called the essence of the Son. For this one expression indicates, with quite pointed brevity, not only that the Son has the same essence as the Father, but also that he has it from the Father. Thus, "the Son is the essence of the Father" means "the Son is an essence no different from the Father's essence; indeed, he is an essence from the Father." In the same way, therefore, the Son is the power, the wisdom or truth, and the justice of the Father, and whatever else belongs to the essence of the supreme spirit.

Chapter 46

*How some of the statements expressed in this way
can also be understood in another way*

Nevertheless, some of the statements that can be expressed and interpreted in this way seem to admit another interpretation—and not an inappropriate one—for the very same statement. For it is clear that the Son is the true Word, that is, the perfect understanding or perfect cognition, knowledge, and wisdom of the whole substance of the Father; in other words, he is that which understands and cognizes and knows and is wise concerning the very essence of the Father. Therefore, if one says that the Son is the understanding, wisdom, knowledge, and cognition or awareness of the Father, in the sense that he understands, is wise concerning, knows, and is aware of the Father, one in no way departs from the truth. Also, the Son can be most appropriately called the truth of the Father, not only in the sense that the truth of the Son is the very same truth as that of the Father, as we have already discussed, but also in the sense that in him is understood not an imperfect imitation but the unadulterated truth of the Father's substance, since he is nothing other than what the Father is.

Chapter 47

*That the Son is the understanding of understanding and
the truth of truth, and so on for similar attributes*

Now if the Father's substance is understanding, knowledge, wisdom, and truth, then, since the Son is the understanding, knowledge, wisdom, and truth of the Father's substance, it follows that he is the understanding of understanding, the knowledge of knowledge, the wisdom of wisdom, and the truth of truth.

Chapter 48

*That 'memory' signifies the Father just as 'understanding' signifies the
Son; and how the Son is the understanding or wisdom of memory,
as well as the memory of the Father and the memory of memory*

But what are we to hold about memory? Are we to judge that the Son is the understanding of memory, or the memory of the Father, or the memory of memory? Indeed, since it cannot be denied that the supreme spirit remembers himself, nothing could be more appropriate than to use 'memory' to signify the Father, just as we use 'Word' to signify the Son; for it seems that a word is born from the memory, as is more clearly seen in the case of our own mind. For since the human mind is not always thinking of itself, as it always remembers itself, it is clear that when it does think of itself, its word is born from its memory. Hence it is evident that if it were always thinking of itself, its word would always be born from its memory. For to think of a thing we remember is to utter it in our mind; the word of that thing, then, is that very thought, formed out of our memory after the likeness of the thing. And so from this we can quite clearly understand that his coeternal Word is born from the eternal memory of the supreme substance, who always utters himself, just as he always remembers himself. Therefore, just as the Word is fittingly understood to be an offspring, so the memory is quite appropriately called a parent.

Therefore, if the offspring that is born entirely from the supreme spirit alone is the offspring of his memory, nothing follows more logically than that he is his own memory. For it is not the case that by remembering himself he exists in his own memory as one thing exists in another, in the way that things in the memory of the human mind are not our memory itself. Rather, he remembers himself in such a way that he *is* his own memory.

And so it follows that just as the Son is the understanding or wisdom of the Father, so he is also the understanding or wisdom of the Father's memory. Now whatever the Son is wise about or understands, he likewise also remembers. So the Son is the memory of the Father and the memory of memory, that is, the memory that remembers the Father, who is memory; just as he is also the wisdom of the Father and the wisdom of wisdom, that is, the wisdom that is wise concerning the Father, who is wisdom. And the Son is indeed memory born from memory, just as he is wisdom born from wisdom; but the Father is memory or wisdom born from no one.

Chapter 49

That the supreme spirit loves himself

But behold! As I consider with delight the distinguishing characteristics and the common features of the Father and the Son, I find nothing that brings me greater delight to consider than their affection of mutual love. For how absurd it would be to deny that the supreme spirit loves himself, just as he remembers and understands himself, when even the rational mind can be shown to love itself and him in virtue of the fact that it can remember and understand itself and him! After all, the memory and understanding of a thing is idle and completely useless unless the thing itself is either loved or repudiated as reason requires. Therefore, the supreme spirit loves himself, just as he remembers and understands himself.

Chapter 50

That this love proceeds equally from the Father and the Son

Now to anyone who has reason it is perfectly clear that he does not remember or understand himself because he loves himself; rather, he loves himself because he remembers and understands himself. Furthermore, he cannot love himself unless he remembers and understands himself. For nothing is loved unless it is remembered and understood, and many things are remembered and understood that are not loved. It is therefore evident that the love of the supreme spirit proceeds from him in virtue of the fact that he remembers and understands himself. And since by "the memory of the supreme spirit" we mean the Father and by 'understanding' we mean the Son, it is clear that the love of the supreme spirit proceeds equally from the Father and the Son.

Chapter 51

That each loves himself and the other with an equal love

Now if the supreme spirit loves himself, undoubtedly the Father loves himself, the Son loves himself, and each loves the other, because the Father individually is the supreme spirit, and the Son individually is the supreme spirit, and both together are one spirit, and also because each equally remembers and understands himself and the other. And since what loves or is loved in the Father is exactly the same as what loves or is loved in the Son, it must be that each loves himself and the other with an equal love.

Chapter 52

That this love is as great as the supreme spirit

How great, then, is this love of the supreme spirit, which is thus common to the Father and the Son? If his love of himself is as great as his memory and understanding of himself, and his memory and understanding of himself is as great as his essence—and this cannot be otherwise—, then his love is indeed as great as he himself is.

Chapter 53

That this love is the very same thing that the supreme spirit is, and yet together with the Father and the Son he is one spirit

But what can be equal to the supreme spirit other than the supreme spirit? And so this love is the supreme spirit. Furthermore, even if no creature—that is, nothing other than the supreme spirit, who is the Father and the Son—ever existed, the Father and Son would nonetheless love both themselves and each other. And so it follows that this love is nothing other than what the Father and the Son are, namely, the supreme essence. Now since there cannot be more than one supreme essence, what is more necessary than that the Father and the Son and the love of each is one supreme essence? So this love is the supreme wisdom, the supreme truth, the supreme good, and whatever else can be said of the substance of the supreme spirit.

Chapter 54

That this love proceeds as a whole from the Father and as a whole from the Son, and yet he is only one love

We must carefully examine whether there are two loves, one proceeding from the Father and the other from the Son; whether there is one proceeding not as a whole from one but partly from the Father and partly from the Son; or whether there is neither more than one love, nor just one proceeding partly from each individually, but rather one and the same proceeding as a whole from each individually and from both at once. Now we can undoubtedly resolve this doubtful issue by noticing that he does not proceed from that in virtue of which the Father and the Son are more than one, but rather from that in virtue of which they are one. For the Father and the Son equally send forth so great a good, not from their relations, which are more than one (for the relation of Father is one thing and the relation of Son is another), but from their essence, which admits no plurality. Therefore, just as the Father individually is the supreme spirit and the Son individually is the supreme spirit, and the Father and the Son together are not two spirits but one, so also the whole love of the supreme spirit flows forth from the Father individually and from the Son individually, and what flows forth from the Father and the Son together is not two wholes, but one and the same whole.

Chapter 55

That this love is not their son

What then? Since this love has being equally from the Father and the Son, and since it is so much like them that it is in no way unlike them but is in every respect the same as they are, should it be considered their son or offspring? Now as soon as the Word is contemplated he gives most compelling proof that he is the offspring of him from whom he exists, for he bears the unmistakable image of his parent; whereas this love just as openly denies that he is an offspring, since when he is understood to proceed from the Father and the Son, he does not immediately exhibit to one who contemplates him his likeness to him from whom he exists, although the argument we have considered shows that he is indeed in every respect the same as the Father and the Son are.

Furthermore, if he is their offspring, either one of them is his father and the other is his mother, or they are both his father or mother. But all these possibilities seem inconsistent with the truth. For since he does not proceed from the Father any differently than from the Son, the truth will not permit dissimilar words to be used to express the Father's and the Son's relation to him. So it is not the case that one is his father and the other his mother. But no nature provides any example of two things, each of which equally has a complete and altogether identical relationship of father or mother to some one thing. Therefore, it is not the case that both the Father and the Son are the father or mother of the love that flows forth from them. And so the claim that this love is their son or offspring does not seem at all consistent with the truth.

Chapter 56

That only the Father is begetter and unbegotten, only the Son is begotten, and only the love is neither begotten nor unbegotten

Nevertheless, it seems that this love cannot absolutely be called 'unbegotten' in our common way of speaking, but neither can he be called 'begotten' as properly as the Son. For we are accustomed to say frequently that something is begotten from the thing from which it exists, as when we say that heat or light is begotten from fire, or an effect from its cause.[57] So in this sense the love that comes forth from the supreme spirit can in no way be called unbegotten. But on the other hand, he cannot be

---

57. Of course we do not say things like this in English. The verb *gigni*, which I have translated as "to be begotten" in view of its use in Trinitarian theology, is here being used in its wider sense to mean "to come to exist."

called 'begotten' as properly as the Word, since the Word is most truly offspring and Son, whereas it is clear that the love is in no way Son or offspring. And so it can be said—indeed, it ought to be said—that only he whose Word exists is begetter and unbegotten, since he alone is Father and parent and in no way exists from another; that only the Word is begotten, since he alone is Son and offspring; and that only the love of both is neither begotten nor unbegotten, since he is neither Son nor offspring, nor is it the case that he in no way exists from another.

Chapter 57

That this love is uncreated and Creator just as the Father and the Son are, and yet he and they together are not three, but one uncreated and one Creator; and that he can be called the Spirit of the Father and the Son

Now this love is individually the supreme essence, just as the Father and the Son are; and yet the Father, the Son, and the love of both are together not several* but one supreme essence, who alone having been made by no one made all things through nothing other than himself. Therefore, it must be that just as the Father individually and the Son individually are uncreated and Creator, so also this love individually is uncreated and Creator, and yet all three together are not several, but one uncreated and one Creator. And so nothing makes or creates or begets the Father; the Father alone does not make but rather begets the Son; and the Father and the Son equally neither make nor beget, but somehow (if one can put it this way) breathe out[58] their love. For although the supremely unchangeable essence does not breathe out in the way we do, nonetheless, it seems there may be no more appropriate expression for the way in which he sends forth his love—which proceeds from him ineffably, not by departing from him but by existing from him—than "breathing out."

Now if one can say this, then just as the Word of the supreme essence is his Son, so his love can be most fittingly called his Spirit.[59] Granted, he is essentially a spirit just as the Father and Son are. But they are not thought of as the spirit *of* something, since the Father does not exist from another, and the Son is not born from the Father by a breathing-out, as it were. This love, by contrast, is regarded as the Spirit of both, since he wondrously proceeds from both in his own inexpressible way by being breathed out. And because he is the communion of the Father

---

58. The Latin is *spirant*. In Trinitarian theology the Father is said to "beget" the Son; the Father and Son together are said to *spirate* the Holy Spirit.

59. That is, if one can say that he is "breathed out" (*spiratur*), he can appropriately be called the "Spirit" (*Spiritus*).

and Son, it seems not unreasonable for him to take as his own distinctive name one that is common to the Father and the Son, if the need for a distinctive name for him so requires. Indeed, if this is done—that is, if this love is distinctively designated by the word 'spirit,' which equally signifies the substance of the Father and the Son—it usefully serves to indicate that he is the very same thing that the Father and the Son are, although he has his being from them.

Chapter 58

That just as the Son is the essence or wisdom of the Father in the sense that he has the same essence or wisdom as the Father, so also the Spirit is the essence and wisdom (and similar things) of the Father and the Son

In the same way that the Son is the substance and wisdom and power of the Father in the sense that he has the same essence and wisdom and power as the Father, so also the Spirit of both can be understood to be the essence or wisdom or power of the Father and the Son, since he has exactly the same essence, wisdom, and power that they have.

Chapter 59

That the Father and the Son and their Spirit exist equally in one another

It is joyous to behold how the Father, the Son, and the Spirit of both exist in each other with such equality that none of them exceeds another. For aside from the fact that each of them is perfectly the supreme essence in such a way that all three together are nevertheless only one supreme essence, which cannot be apart from itself or outside itself or greater or less than itself, the same thing can be proved no less for each of them individually. For the Father exists as a whole in the Son and in their common Spirit, the Son exists in the Father and in that same Spirit, and that Spirit exists in the Father and in the Son, since the memory of the supreme essence exists as a whole in his understanding and in his love, his understanding exists in his memory and in his love, and his love exists in his memory and in his understanding. For indeed the supreme spirit understands and loves his whole memory, remembers and loves his whole understanding, and remembers and understands his whole love. Now by 'memory' we mean the Father, by 'understanding' the Son, and by 'love' the Spirit of both. Therefore, the Father, the Son, and the Spirit of both embrace one another and exist in one another with such equality that none of them is found to exceed another or exist apart from another.

Chapter 60

That none of them needs another in order to remember, understand, or love, since each individually is memory and understanding and love and whatever else is necessarily present in the supreme essence

But as I behold these things, something occurs to me that I think should be most carefully borne in mind. For we must understand the Father as memory, the Son as understanding, and the Spirit as love in such a way that the Father does not need the Son or their common Spirit, the Son does not need the Father or that same Spirit, and the Spirit does not need the Father or the Son. It is not as if the Father can remember through himself alone but can understand only through the Son and love only through the Spirit of himself and the Son; and the Son through himself can only understand, but remembers through the Father and loves through their Spirit; and that Spirit through himself can do nothing but love, but the Father remembers for him and the Son understands for him. For since each of these three is individually the supreme essence and supreme wisdom so completely that each remembers and understands and loves through himself, it must be that none of these three needs another in order to remember or understand or love. For each of them individually is essentially memory and understanding and love, and whatever else is necessarily present in the supreme essence.

Chapter 61

That nevertheless there are not three but one Father, one Son, and one Spirit of both

Here I see a question arise. If the Father is understanding and love just as he is memory, and the Son is memory and love in the same way that he is understanding, and the Spirit of both is no less memory and understanding than he is love, how is it that the Father is not a son and someone's spirit? And why is the Son not a father and someone's spirit? And why is that Spirit not someone's father and someone's son? After all, it was understood that the Father was memory, the Son understanding, and the Spirit of both love.

But this question is not difficult to answer if we consider the truths that reason has already discovered. For the Father is not the son or spirit of another simply because he is understanding and love, since he is not an understanding that is begotten or a love that proceeds from someone; rather, whatever he is, is only the begetter and the one from whom another proceeds. And the Son is not a father or someone's spirit simply because he remembers and loves by himself, since he is not a memory that begets or a love that proceeds from another in the way his own Spirit proceeds; rather, whatever existence he has is only begotten, and it is he from whom the Spirit proceeds. And the fact that he contains his own memory and understanding does not mean that the Spirit is a father or son, since he is not a memory that begets or an understanding that is begotten; rather, whatever he is only proceeds. So what prevents us from concluding that in the supreme essence there is only one Father, one Son, and one Spirit, not three fathers or three sons or three spirits?

Chapter 62

How it seems that many sons are born from them

But perhaps what I am now realizing contradicts this assertion. For there should be no doubt that the Father, the Son, and their Spirit each utters both himself and the other two, just as each understands both himself and the other two. Now if this is so, how is it that there are not as many words in the supreme essence as there are ones uttering and ones being uttered? For if several* human beings utter some one thing in their thought, there appear to be as many words of that thing as there are people thinking, since a word of that thing exists in the thoughts of each of them. Similarly, if one human being thinks of several things, there are as many words in the mind of the thinker as there are things being thought.

But in a human being's thought, when he thinks of something that exists outside his mind, the word of the thing that is thought is not born from the thing itself, since that thing is absent from the gaze of his thought; rather, the word is born from some likeness or image of the thing. That likeness or image exists in the memory of the one thinking; or else perhaps a bodily sense is conveying it into his mind from some present object right then as he is thinking. In the supreme essence, by contrast, the Father, the Son, and their Spirit are always present to one another—for, as we have already seen,[60] each exists in the others no less than in himself—in such a way that when they utter one another, each one who is uttered seems to beget his own word, just as when he is uttered by himself. How is it, then, that the Son, and the Spirit of him and the Father, beget nothing, if each of them begets his own word when he is uttered by himself or another? Now however many words we can prove are born from the supreme substance, by our earlier argument he must beget that many sons and send forth that many spirits. And so by this argument it seems that there are in him not only many fathers, sons, and [spirits] proceeding but also other relations.

---

60. In Chapter 59.

Chapter 63

How in him there is only one of one[61]

Now certainly the Father, the Son, and their Spirit—about whom it is already most certain that they truly exist—are not three who utter, even though each of them individually utters. Nor is there more than one thing uttered when each utters himself and the other two. For just as knowledge and understanding are present in the supreme wisdom, even so it is natural for that eternal and immutable knowledge and understanding always to behold as present that which it knows and understands. Now for the supreme spirit there is no difference between uttering something in this sense and beholding it in thought, as it were, just as the utterance of our mind is no different from the thinker's observation. Now the arguments we have already considered have made one thing quite certain: whatever is essentially present in the supreme nature belongs completely to the Father, the Son, and their Spirit individually; and yet if the same thing is said of the three of them together, it does not admit of plurality.[62]

Now it is established that just as knowledge and understanding belong to his essence, even so his knowing and understanding are nothing other than his uttering—that is, his always beholding as present—that which he knows and understands. Furthermore, the Father individually and the Son individually and their Spirit individually know and understand, and yet the three of them together are not several* who know and understand, but one who knows and one who understands. In the same way, therefore, it must be the case that each of them individually utters, and yet the three of them together are not three who utter but one who utters.

From this we can also clearly recognize that when the three of them are uttered, whether by themselves or by one another, it is not the case that more than one thing is uttered. After all, what is uttered there except their essence? So if that essence is only one, that which is uttered is only one. Therefore, if in them that which utters is one, and that which is uttered is one—for in them there is one wisdom that utters and one substance that is uttered—, it follows that there are not several words there but only one. So although each of them utters himself and all of them utter one another, it is impossible for there to be any Word in the supreme

---

61. That is, despite how things looked in the previous chapter, it is not the case that in God there are *many* sons born from *many* divine persons. Rather, in God there is only *one* Son born from *one* divine person (namely, the Father).

62. In other words, for any perfection you choose (call it *p*), if *p* belongs to God essentially, then the Father is fully *p*, the Son is fully *p*, and the Holy Spirit is fully *p*. And yet you cannot say that there are three things that are *p*; there is only one. See the argument in Chapter 38.

essence other than the one concerning whom it has been established[63] that he is born from him whose Word he is in such a way that he can be called his true image and is truly his Son.

I see in this something wonderful and inexplicable. For behold! Although it is evident that each of them—that is, the Father, the Son, and the Spirit of the Father and the Son—equally utters himself and the other two, and that there is only one Word there, nevertheless, it appears that the Word can in no way be called the Word of all three, but of only one of them. For it has been established that he is the image and Son of him whose Word he is, and obviously he cannot sensibly be called the image or Son of himself or of the Spirit who proceeds from him. For he is not born from himself or from the one who proceeds from him; nor does he by existing imitate himself or the one who proceeds from him. He certainly does not imitate himself, or bear to himself a likeness of existing, since imitation or likeness does not exist in just one thing; it requires more than one. And he does not imitate the Spirit or exist after his likeness, since he does not have his existence from the Spirit; rather, the Spirit has his existence from him. So the only remaining possibility is that he is the Word only of him from whom he is born and thereby has his existence, and after whose perfect likeness he exists.

Therefore, one Father, not several fathers; one Son, not several sons; and one proceeding Spirit, not several proceeding spirits, exist in the supreme essence. So although they are three in such a way that the Father is never the Son or the proceeding Spirit, the Son is never the Father or the proceeding Spirit, and the Spirit of the Father and the Son is never the Father or the Son; and although each individually is so complete that he needs no one, nonetheless, that which they are is so much one that, just as it cannot be said in the plural of each of them individually, so also it cannot be said in the plural of the three of them together. And although each equally utters himself, and all of them equally utter one another, nonetheless there are not several words there but only one; and that Word is not the Word of each individually or of all of them together but of only one.

Chapter 64

That although this cannot be explained, it must nevertheless be believed

The mystery of so sublime a thing seems to me to transcend every power of human understanding, and for that reason I think one should refrain from attempting to explain how this is true. After all, I think someone investigating an incomprehensible thing ought to be satisfied if his reasoning arrives at the knowledge that the thing most certainly exists, even if his understanding cannot fathom how it is so.

---

63. In Chapters 33 and 42.

Nor should we withhold any of the certainty of faith from beliefs that are asserted on the basis of necessary proofs and are contradicted by no other argument, simply because, owing to the incomprehensibility of their natural sublimity, they do not yield to explanation. Now what is as incomprehensible, as ineffable, as the one who is above all things? Therefore, if the conclusions we have reached thus far concerning the supreme essence have been asserted on the basis of necessary reasons, their solid certainty is in no way shaken even though the understanding cannot fathom them so as to be able to explain them in words. For if our earlier reflection[64] rationally comprehends that it is incomprehensible how that supreme wisdom knows the things he made, about which we ourselves must know so many things, who will explain how he knows or utters himself, about whom nothing, or scarcely anything, can be known by a human being? Therefore, if in uttering himself the Father generates and the Son is generated, "Who will tell of his generation?"[65]

Chapter 65

How a true conclusion has been reached regarding an ineffable thing

But once again, if the nature of his ineffability is like this—or rather, since it is indeed like this—how will any of our conclusions concerning the relation of the Father, the Son, and him who proceeds from them, remain intact? For if that has been explained by a sound argument, in what way is he ineffable? Or, if he is ineffable, how can our conclusions be correct? Is it that he could to some extent be explained, and therefore nothing prevents our conclusions from being true, but since he could not be thoroughly understood, he is therefore ineffable? But how could one reply to the point that was made earlier in this very discussion:[66] that the supreme essence is so much above and beyond every other nature that even if sometimes words are applied to him that are common to other natures, their meanings are in no way common? For what meaning did I understand in all the words I thought, if not the common and familiar one? So if the familiar meaning of words is foreign to him, none of my reasoning applies to him. How then is it true that something has been discovered about the supreme essence if what has been discovered is vastly different from him?

What then? Is it that in one way something has been discovered about an incomprehensible thing, and in another way nothing about it has been fully seen? After all, we often say many things that we do not properly express as they really

---

64. In Chapter 36.
65. Isaiah 53:8.
66. In Chapter 26.

are; rather, we signify through some other thing what we are either unwilling or unable to express properly, as when we speak in riddles. And we often do not see something properly as the thing itself actually is, but through some likeness or image, as when we look at someone's face in a mirror. In this way we do indeed both say and not say, or both see and not see, one and the same thing. We say and see through some other thing; we do not say or see through its own distinctive character.[67]

And so by this argument it is perfectly possible for our conclusions thus far about the supreme nature to be true and yet for that nature himself nevertheless to remain ineffable, if we suppose that he was in no way expressed through the distinctive character of his essence but somehow designated through some other thing. For all the words that seem applicable to that nature do not show him to me through his distinctive character so much as they hint at him through some likeness. For when I think of the significations of these words, I more readily conceive in my mind what I observe in created things than what I understand to transcend all human understanding. For by their signification they produce something in my mind that is much less than—that is in fact vastly different from—that which my mind is trying to come to understand through their tenuous signification. For the word 'wisdom' does not suffice to show me the one through whom all things were made from nothing and are preserved from nothingness. Nor can the word 'essence' express to me the one who through his unique exaltedness is far above all things and through his natural distinctive character is vastly beyond all things. So this is how it is the case *both* that his nature is ineffable, because words can in no way express him as he is, *and* that if reason can teach us to form any judgment about him through some other thing, as in a riddle, that judgment is not false.

Chapter 66

That through the rational mind one comes closest to knowing the supreme essence

Therefore, since it is evident that nothing about this nature can be perceived through his own distinctive character, but only through something else, it is certain that one comes closer to knowing him through that which is nearer to him because it is more like him. For whatever among created things is shown to be more like him must be more excellent by nature. Hence, because of its greater

---

67. "Distinctive character" represents the Latin *proprietas*. The *proprietas* of a thing is whatever it is *in itself*, by its very nature. Anselm is arguing that we do not know God by knowing his very nature. We do not have direct intellectual access to what he is in himself. Instead, whatever we know about God must be inferred indirectly through some likeness.

likeness such a thing gives more help to the investigating mind in coming closer to the supreme truth, and because of its more excellent created essence it more fully teaches what that mind ought to believe about the Creator. And so there is no doubt that the creating essence is known in a more profound way the more he is investigated through a creature that is closer to him. For the argument already considered above[68] leaves no room for doubt that every essence is like the supreme essence to the extent that it exists.

And so it is evident that just as the rational mind is the only thing among all creatures that can rise up to seek him, it is no less true that the rational mind is the only thing through which the mind itself can best make progress in finding him. For we have already realized that it comes especially close to him through the likeness of its natural essence. So what is more obvious than this: that the more diligently the rational mind tries to come to know itself, the more efficaciously it rises up to know him; and the more it neglects to look upon itself, the more it falls away from seeing him?

Chapter 67

That the mind itself is a mirror and image of him

The mind can therefore most fittingly be said to be like a mirror for itself, in which it might see (if I may put it that way) the image of him whom it cannot see face to face.[69] For if the mind alone among all created things can remember and understand and love itself, I do not see why one would deny that there is in it a true image of that essence who in virtue of remembering, understanding, and loving himself constitutes an ineffable Trinity. Or certainly it proves itself to be more truly his image by the fact that it can remember, understand, and love *him*. For that by which it is greater and more like him is that by which it is recognized as a truer image of him. Now it is altogether impossible to think that the rational creature was naturally given anything so preeminent and so much like the supreme wisdom as its ability to remember and understand and love that which is best and greatest of all things. Therefore, no creature was endowed with anything else that thus displays an image of the Creator.

---

68. In Chapter 31.

69. Cf. 1 Corinthians 13:12: "For now we see in a mirror, in a riddle, but then face to face."

Chapter 68

That the rational creature was made for loving him

And so it seems to follow that the rational creature should strive for nothing else so much as to express through voluntary action this image that has been stamped on it through its natural ability. For aside from the fact that it owes its very existence to the one who created it, if it recognizes that it can do nothing else so preeminent as to remember, understand, and love the supreme good, it will certainly be convinced that it ought to will nothing else so preeminently. For who would deny that whatever better things are in our power should be more in our will?

Furthermore, for the rational nature there is no difference between being rational and being able to discern the just from what is not just, the true from what is not true, the good from what is not good, and the greater good from the lesser good. But this ability is altogether useless for it, and utterly empty, unless it loves or repudiates what it discerns in accordance with the judgment of a true discernment. Hence, it is quite obvious that every rational thing exists in order that it might love something more or less, or reject it altogether, according as its rational discernment judges that the thing is more or less good, or not good at all. So nothing is more evident than that the rational creature was made in order that it might love the supreme essence above all other goods, since he is the supreme good—indeed, that it might love nothing but him or [what it loves] for his sake, since he is good through himself, and nothing else is good except through him.

Now it cannot love him unless it strives to remember and understand him. It is therefore clear that the rational creature ought to devote all its power and will to remembering and understanding and loving the supreme good, for which purpose it knows it has its very existence.

Chapter 69

That a soul that always loves him will at some time truly live happily

Now there is no doubt that the human soul is a rational creature. Therefore, it must have been made in order that it might love the supreme essence. So it must have been made either in order that it might love without end or in order that it might at some time lose this love, whether willingly or by force. But it is impious to suppose that the supreme wisdom made it in order that it might at some time either disdain so great a good or lose him by force even though it wills to hold on to him. So the only remaining possibility is that it was made in order that it might love the supreme essence without end.

Now it cannot do this unless it will always live. Therefore, it has been made in such a way that it will always live if it always wills to do what it was made for.

Furthermore, the supremely good and supremely wise and omnipotent Creator caused it to exist in order that it might love him, so it would be utterly absurd for him to cause it not to exist as long as it truly loved him; and he willingly gave life to something that did not love him in order that it might always love him, so it would be utterly absurd for him to take that life away, or to allow it to be taken away, from something that loves him in order that it will, necessarily, not love him—especially since there should be no doubt that he loves every nature that truly loves him. It is therefore evident that its life will never be taken away from a human soul if it always strives to love the supreme life.

So what sort of life will it have? After all, what good is a long life unless it is truly secure against the onslaught of troubles? For if someone as long as he lives is subject to troubles that he either fears or suffers, or else is deceived by a false security, is his life not miserable? By contrast, if someone's life is free from these things, he lives happily. But it is utterly absurd that any nature always leads a miserable life by always loving him who is supremely good and omnipotent. It is therefore clear that the human soul is such that if it preserves what it was made for, it will at some time live happily, truly secure from death itself and from all other troubles.

Chapter 70

That he gives himself as a reward to the one who loves him

Finally, it can in no way seem to be true that he who is most just and most powerful, who gave being to one that did not love him in order that it might be able to love him, would give no reward to one who loves him perseveringly. For if he gives no reward to one who loves him, he who is most just does not distinguish between one who loves what ought to be supremely loved and one who disdains it; nor does he love one who loves him—either that, or it does no good to be loved by him. But all those things are incompatible with his nature. Therefore, he rewards everyone who loves him perseveringly.

But what does he give as a reward? If he gave a rational essence to nothing in order that it might love him, what will he give to someone who loves him if he does not cease to love? If what serves love is so great, how great is that which repays love? And if such is the support of love, what will the benefit of love be like? For if the rational creature, which is useless to itself without this love, is so eminent among all creatures, surely nothing can be the reward of this love except that which is supereminent among all natures. For the very same good who thus demands to be loved compels the one who loves him no less to desire him. For who loves justice, truth, happiness, and incorruptibility in such a way that he does not also desire to enjoy them? So what will the supreme goodness give as a reward to one who loves and desires him, if not himself? For anything else he might give would not be a reward, since it would not recompense the love, or console the one who loves him, or satisfy the one who desires him. Either that, or if he wills to be loved and desired so that he might give something else as a reward, he does not will to be loved and desired for his own sake, but for the sake of something else. But in that case he does not will that he himself be loved, but rather that something else be loved—which it is impious to think.

Therefore, nothing is truer than this: that every rational soul, if it strives to love and desire the supreme happiness as it ought, at some time perceives him so as to enjoy him. Thus, what it now sees as if "in a mirror, in a riddle," it will then see "face to face."[70] Now it is utterly foolish to doubt whether one will enjoy him without end, since one who enjoys him cannot be tortured by fear or deceived by a false security; nor, having once experienced being without him, could one fail to love him; nor will he abandon one who loves him; nor will there be anything else more powerful than he that might separate them against their will. Therefore, any soul that has once begun to enjoy the supreme happiness will be happy eternally.

Chapter 71

That one who disdains him will be eternally miserable

From this of course it follows that a soul that disdains the love of the supreme good will incur eternal misery. One might say that for such disdain it would be more justly punished if it lost its very existence or life, since it did not use itself for what it was made for; but reason in no way allows that after so great a fault it should receive as its punishment the existence it had before any fault at all.[71] Certainly before it existed it could neither be at fault nor experience punishment. Therefore, if a soul that disdains what it was made for dies, so that it experiences nothing, or is nothing at all, it will be in the same state both when it is most greatly at fault and when it is without any fault; nor would the supremely wise justice distinguish between what is capable of no good and wills no evil, and what is capable of the greatest good and wills the greatest evil. Now it is quite obvious how absurd that is. So nothing could seem more logical, and nothing should be believed more certainly, than this: the human soul was made in such a way that if it disdains to love the supreme essence, it will suffer eternal misery. Thus, just as one who loves him will rejoice in an eternal reward, one who disdains him will suffer under an eternal punishment. And just as the former will experience immutable plenty, so the latter will experience inconsolable poverty.

---

70. 1 Corinthians 13:12.

71. In other words, nonexistence, which is the "existence" the soul had before it was guilty of any fault.

Chapter 72

That every human soul is immortal

But if the soul is mortal, it need not be the case that one who loves him is eternally happy or one who disdains him miserable. Therefore, whether it loves or disdains him whom it was created to love, it must be immortal. But if there are some rational souls that must be judged neither to love him nor to disdain him, as the souls of infants appear to be, what are we to hold about them? Are they mortal or immortal? Undoubtedly all human souls are of the same nature. Therefore, since it is established that some are immortal, it must be the case that every human soul is immortal.

Chapter 73

That it is either always miserable or at some time truly happy

Now since everything that lives is either never or at some time truly secure from all trouble, it must be no less true that every human soul is either always miserable or at some time truly happy.

Chapter 74

That no soul is unjustly deprived of the supreme good, and that it should strive after him with all its might

But I think it is undoubtedly most difficult, if not impossible, for any mortal to be able to comprehend through disputation which souls are to be unhesitatingly judged as so loving him whom they were made for loving that they deserve to enjoy him at some time, and which ones so disdain him that they deserve to be deprived of him forever, and how or by what merit those who apparently can be said neither to love nor to disdain him are assigned to eternal happiness or misery. Nevertheless, one should hold with absolute certainty that the supremely just and supremely good Creator of things does not unjustly deprive any soul of the good for which it was made, and that every human being ought to strive after that good by loving and desiring him with all his heart, and with all his soul, and with all his mind.[72]

---

72. Cf. Matthew 22:37: "You shall love the Lord your God with all your heart, and with all your soul, and with all your mind."

Chapter 75

That one ought to hope for the supreme essence

But the human soul could in no way exert itself in this effort if it despaired of being able to attain what it is striving for. Therefore, the hope of success is as necessary to it as persistence in struggling is useful.

Chapter 76

That one ought to believe in him[73]

But one cannot love or hope for what one does not believe. And so it is beneficial for the human soul to believe the supreme essence and those things without which he cannot be loved, so that by believing them it might strive for [*in*] him. I think the same thing can be signified fittingly and more briefly if one says "believe in [*in*] the supreme essence" instead of "by believing to strive for [*in*] the supreme essence." For if someone says that he believes in [*in*] him, he seems to make it quite clear both that he strives unto [*ad*] the supreme essence through the faith he professes, and that he believes those things that pertain to this striving. For someone who believes what does not pertain to striving for [*in*] him, or who does not strive unto [*ad*] him in virtue of what he believes, does not appear to believe in [*in*] him. And perhaps it would make no difference whether we say that someone believes "in [*in*] him" or "on [*ad*] him," just as "by believing to strive for [*in*] him" and "by believing to strive unto [*ad*] him" can be regarded as meaning the same thing, except for the fact that whoever comes to him by striving unto [*ad*] him will not remain outside him but will abide within him forever. This is more explicitly and readily signified by saying that one ought to strive "for [*in*] him" rather than "unto [*ad*] him."[74] And so by this argument I think it can be more fittingly said that one ought to believe "in [*in*] him" rather than "on [*ad*] him."

---

73. Much of the argument in this chapter turns on the question of which of two prepositions is most suitably used with the verbs *tendere* (to strive) and *credere* (to believe). Unfortunately, in English we have to use *four* different prepositions if we are not to outrage idiom, and the point is thus lost in translation. So in order to show what Anselm is doing, I have indicated the Latin preposition in brackets after each occurrence in the English.
74. Since the Latin *in* suggests the idea of motion *into* something, whereas *ad* merely suggests the idea of motion *toward* something.

Chapter 77

That one ought to believe equally in the Father, the Son, and their Spirit, both in each individually and in all three together

Therefore one ought to believe equally in the Father, the Son, and their Spirit, both in each individually and in all three together. For the Father, the Son, and their Spirit are each individually the supreme essence, and the Father and the Son along with their Spirit are together one and the same supreme essence, in whom alone every human being ought to believe, since he alone is the end at which they ought to aim through love in their every thought and action. From this it is evident that just as no one can strive for him unless he believes him, so also it does no one any good to believe him unless he strives for him.

Chapter 78

What is a living and what a dead faith

Therefore, with however great a certainty so great a thing is believed, that faith will be useless and like something dead unless through love it is strong and alive. For a faith that is accompanied and attended by love will by no means be idle when it has the opportunity to act; instead, it will exert itself to act quite frequently, which it could not do without love. That this is so can be proved by just this one fact: one who loves the supreme justice cannot disdain anything just or tolerate anything unjust. Therefore, since whatever acts, shows that it has life, without which it could not act, it is not absurd to say that an active faith is living, since it has the life of love without which it would not act, and that an idle faith is not living, since it lacks the life of love with which it would not be idle. Therefore, if not only one who has lost his sight is called blind, but also one who, though he ought to have it, does not, why cannot faith without love similarly be called dead,[75] not because it has lost its life (that is, its love), but because it does not have what it ought always to have? So, just as a faith that through love is active[76] is recognized as living, a faith that through disdain is idle is proved to be dead. And so it can quite appropriately be said that a living faith believes *in* what it ought to believe in,[77] whereas a dead faith merely believes what it ought to believe.

---

75. Cf. James 2:26: "Faith without action is dead."
76. Cf. Galatians 5:6: "Faith, which through charity is active."
77. Because, as was argued in Chapter 76, believing in [*in*] God implies striving for [*in*] God.

Chapter 79

What the supreme essence can in a certain sense be said to be three of

Behold! Clearly it is beneficial for every human being to believe in an ineffable threefold Unity and unified Trinity. They are indeed one and a Unity in virtue of one essence, but I do not know what it is in virtue of which they are three and a Trinity. For although I can say 'Trinity' because of the Father, the Son, and the Spirit of both, who are three, I cannot express by any one word what it is in virtue of which they are three, as if I were to say [they are a Trinity] in virtue of being three persons in the same way that I would say they are a Unity in virtue of being one substance. For they are not to be thought of as three persons, since whenever there are two or more persons, the persons subsist* separately from each other in such a way that there must be as many substances as there are persons. This is known to be true in the case of two or more human beings, who are as many individual substances as they are persons. Therefore, just as there is not more than one substance in the supreme essence, so also there is not more than one person.[78]

And so if anyone wishes to talk about this with someone, what will he say the Father, the Son, and the Spirit of both are three *of,* unless perhaps for lack of a strictly appropriate word he is forced to choose one of those words that cannot be said in the plural of the supreme essence in order to signify that which cannot be said by a suitable word? For example, he might say that this wondrous Trinity is one essence or nature and three persons or substances.[79] For these two words are more fittingly chosen to signify the plurality within the supreme essence, since 'person' is said only of an individual rational nature, and 'substance' is principally said of individuals, which especially constitute a plurality. For it is individuals that especially stand under (that is, underlie) accidents,* and therefore they more properly take the name of 'substance.'[80] Hence it had already become evident above[81] that the supreme essence, which does not underlie any accidents, cannot properly be called a substance unless 'substance' is being used instead of 'essence.'[82] Therefore, by this argument of necessity that supreme and unified Trinity or threefold Unity can be irreproachably called one essence and three persons or three substances.

---

78. The standard definition of 'person' was from Boethius, *Contra Eutychem* 4.4–5: "an individual substance of a rational nature." Anselm is arguing that in this sense of the word God cannot be three persons, since if he were, he would be three substances and therefore three gods.

79. See the Glossary entry for substance* (sense 3).

80. See the Glossary entry for substance* (sense 2).

81. In Chapter 36.

82. See the Glossary entry for substance* (senses 1 and 2).

Chapter 80

That he is Lord of all and rules all and is the only God

It therefore seems—indeed, it is unhesitatingly declared—that that which is called God is not nothing, and that the name 'God' is properly assigned only to this supreme essence. Surely everyone who says that God exists (whether one God or more than one) understands him to be nothing other than a substance that he thinks human beings ought to worship because of his preeminent dignity, and to entreat in any pressing need, beyond every nature that is not God. Now what is as deserving of worship because of his dignity, or as properly the object of prayer for anything at all, as the supremely good and supremely powerful spirit, who is Lord of all and rules all? For just as it has been established[83] that all things were made and are sustained through his supremely good and supremely wise omnipotence, so also it is altogether absurd to suppose that he is not the Lord of the things he made, or that they are ruled by something less powerful or less good or less wise, or even by no reason at all, but merely by the unstable disorder of chance. For it is he alone through whom it goes well for anything, without whom it goes well for nothing, and from whom and through whom and in whom all things exist.[84] Therefore, since he alone is not only the good Creator but also the most powerful Lord and most wise Ruler of all things, it is utterly clear that it is he alone whom all other natures should lovingly worship and worshipfully love with all their power, from whom alone they ought to hope for good things, to whom alone they ought to flee from troubles, to whom alone they ought to pray for anything at all. Truly, therefore, he is not merely God; he is the only God, ineffably three and one.

---

83. In Chapter 13.
84. Cf. Romans 11:36: "For from him and through him and in him all things exist."

Proslogion

Prologue

AFTER I HAD published, at the urging of some of my brethren, a short work as a pattern for meditation on the reason of faith, adopting the role of someone who, by reasoning silently within himself, investigates things he does not know, I began to wonder, when I considered that it is constructed out of a chaining together of many arguments, whether it might be possible to find a single argument that needed nothing but itself alone for proof, that would by itself be enough to show that God really exists; that he is the supreme good, who depends on nothing else, but on whom all things depend for their being and for their well-being; and whatever we believe about the divine nature. And so I often turned my thoughts to this with great diligence. Sometimes I thought I could already grasp what I was looking for, and sometimes it escaped my mind completely. Finally, I gave up hope. I decided to stop looking for something that was impossible to find. But when I tried to stifle that thought altogether, lest by occupying my mind with useless speculation it should keep me from things I could actually accomplish, it began to hound me more and more, although I resisted and fought against it. Then one day, when my violent struggle against its hounding had worn me down, the thing I had despaired of finding presented itself in the very clash of my thoughts, so that I eagerly embraced the thought I had been taking such pains to drive away.

Therefore, thinking that what I had rejoiced to discover would please a reader if it were written down, I wrote about it and about a number of other things in the work that follows, adopting the role of someone trying to raise his mind to the contemplation of God and seeking to understand what he believes. Since I had judged that neither this work nor the one I mentioned earlier deserved to be called a book, or to bear the name of an author, and yet I did not think they ought to be sent out without so much as a title by which they might induce someone who came across them to read them, I gave each a title. The first I called "A pattern for meditation on the reason of faith"; the second I called "Faith seeking understanding." But since both works had been transcribed under these titles by several readers, I was encouraged by a number of people (especially by Hugo, the Most Reverend Archbishop of Lyons, Apostolic Legate to France, who commanded me by his apostolic authority) to put my own name on these works. And so, in order to do so more suitably, I named the first *Monologion*, which means a speech made to oneself, and the second *Proslogion*, which means a speech made to another.

Chapters

Chapter 1

A rousing of the mind to the contemplation of God

Come now, insignificant mortal. Leave behind your concerns for a little while, and retreat for a short time from your restless thoughts. Cast off your burdens and cares; set aside your labor and toil. Just for a little while make room for God and rest a while in him. "Enter into the chamber" of your mind, shut out everything but God and whatever helps you to seek him, and seek him "behind closed doors."[1] Speak now, my whole heart: say to God, "I seek your face; your face, Lord, do I seek."[2]

Come now, O Lord my God. Teach my heart where and how to seek you, where and how to find you. Lord, if you are not here, where shall I seek you, since you are absent? But if you are everywhere, why do I not see you, since you are present? Truly "you dwell in unapproachable light."[3] And where is this "unapproachable light"? How am I to approach an unapproachable light? Who will lead me into it, so that I can see you in it? And by what signs am I to seek you? Under what aspect? I have never seen you, O Lord my God; I do not know your face. What shall he do, O Lord Most High? What shall he do, this distant exile from you? What shall your servant do, deeply troubled by his love for you and "banished far from your face"?[4] He longs to see you, but your face is too far away from him. He desires to approach your presence, but your dwelling is unapproachable. He wants to find you, but he does not know where you are. He aspires to seek you, but he does not know your face. Lord, you are my God, and you are my Lord, but I have never seen you. You have made me and remade me, you have given me every good thing that is mine, and still I do not know you. I was created so that I might see you, but I have not yet done what I was created to do.

How wretched human beings are! They have lost the very thing for which they were created. Hard and terrible was their fall! Alas! Think what they have lost and what they have found; think what they left behind and what they kept. They have lost the happiness for which they were created and found an unhappiness for which they were not created. They left behind the only source of happiness and kept what brings nothing but misery. Once "human beings ate the bread of angels,"[5] for which they now hunger; now they "eat the bread of sorrows,"[6] which once they did not know. Alas for the common lamentation of human beings, the

---

1. Matthew 6:6.
2. Psalm 27:8 (26:8).
3. 1 Timothy 6:16.
4. Psalm 51:11 (50:13).
5. Psalm 78:25 (77:25).
6. Psalm 127:2 (126:2).

universal outcry of the children of Adam! He was satisfied to the full; we sigh with hunger. He had everything he needed; we go begging. He happily possessed those things and abandoned them in misery; we unhappily do without them and miserably desire them, but alas, we remain empty-handed. Why did he not preserve for us, as he could easily have done, what we so woefully lack? Why did he thus shut us out from the light and cover us with darkness? Why did he take away our life and inflict death upon us? What wretches we are! Think whence we have been cast out, whither we have been driven; thrown down from so great a height, and buried so deep. From our homeland into exile; from the vision of God into our blindness; from the joy of immortality into the bitterness and terror of death. What a wretched change! From such great good into such great evil! O woeful loss, woeful sorrow, all is woeful!

Alas, wretched man that I am, one of the wretched children of Eve, far from the presence of God. What have I undertaken, and what have I accomplished? Where was I heading, and where have I come to? What was I reaching toward, and what do I long for? "I have sought the good,"[7] and "behold, confusion!"[8] I was heading for God but stumbled over myself. I sought rest in my solitude but "found trials and sorrows"[9] deep within. I wanted to laugh as my mind rejoiced, but I am forced to "cry out as my heart weeps."[10] Joy was hoped for, but look where the sighs are closing in.

"How long, O Lord?"[11] How long, O Lord, will you forget us? How long will you turn your face from us?[12] When will you look favorably upon us and hear us? When will you enlighten our eyes[13] and show us your face?[14] When will you give yourself to us again? Look favorably upon us, O Lord; hear us, enlighten us, show yourself to us. Give yourself to us again, that it might go well for us; for without you it goes so badly for us. Take pity upon our toils and strivings after you, for without you we can do nothing. You call us; come to our aid. I beseech you, Lord: let me not sigh in despair, but let me breathe hopefully again. I beseech you, Lord: my heart is made bitter with its desolation; sweeten it with your consolation. I beseech you, Lord: in my hunger I began to seek you; let me not depart from you empty. I have come to you starving; let me not leave unsatisfied. I have come as a beggar to one who is rich, as a pitiful wretch to one who has pity; let me not go back

---

7. Psalm 122:9 (121:9).

8. Jeremiah 14:19.

9. Psalm 116:3 (114:3).

10. Psalm 38:8 (37:9).

11. Psalm 6:3 (6:4).

12. Cf. Psalm 13:1 (12:1).

13. Cf. Psalm 13:3 (12:4).

14. Cf. Psalm 80:3, 7, 19 (79:4, 8, 20).

penniless and despised. If indeed "I sigh before I eat,"[15] grant that I might eat after I sigh. Lord, I am bent double; I can only look down. Raise me up so that I can turn my gaze upwards. "My sins are heaped up over my head" and entangle me; "like a heavy burden" they weigh me down.[16] Extricate me; lift my burdens, "lest like a pit they swallow me up."[17] Let me look up at your light, whether from afar or from the depths. Teach me how to seek you, and show yourself to me when I seek. For I cannot seek you unless you teach me how, and I cannot find you unless you show yourself to me. Let me seek you in desiring you; let me desire you in seeking you. Let me find you in loving you; let me love you in finding you.

I acknowledge, Lord, and I thank you, that you have created in me this image of you so that I may remember you, think of you, and love you. Yet this image is so eroded by my vices, so clouded by the smoke of my sins, that it cannot do what it was created to do unless you renew and refashion it. I am not trying to scale your heights, Lord; my understanding is in no way equal to that. But I do long to understand your truth in some way, your truth which my heart believes and loves. For I do not seek to understand in order to believe; I believe in order to understand. For I also believe that "unless I believe, I shall not understand."[18]

Chapter 2

That God truly exists

Therefore, Lord, you who grant understanding to faith, grant that, insofar as you know it is useful for me, I may understand that you exist as we believe you exist, and that you are what we believe you to be. Now we believe that you are something than which nothing greater can be thought. So can it be that no such nature* exists, since "the fool has said in his heart, 'There is no God'"?[19] But when this same fool hears me say "something than which nothing greater can be thought," he surely understands what he hears; and what he understands exists in his understanding,[20] even if he does not understand that it exists [in reality]. For it is one thing for an object to exist in the understanding and quite another to understand

---

15. Job 3:24.

16. Psalm 38:4 (37:5).

17. Psalm 69:15 (68:16).

18. Cf. Isaiah 7:9 in the Old Latin version: "Unless you believe, you will not understand." Anselm is here indebted to Augustine, who frequently appealed to this verse in explaining his views on the relationship between faith and reason.

19. Psalms 14:1 (13:1); 53:1 (52:1).

20. The word here translated 'understanding' is *intellectus*. The text would perhaps read better if I translated it as 'intellect,' but this would obscure the fact that it is from the same

that the object exists [in reality]. When a painter, for example, thinks out in advance what he is going to paint, he has it in his understanding, but he does not yet understand that it exists, since he has not yet painted it. But once he has painted it, he both has it in his understanding and understands that it exists because he has now painted it. So even the fool must admit that something than which nothing greater can be thought exists at least in his understanding, since he understands this when he hears it, and whatever is understood exists in the understanding. And surely that than which a greater cannot be thought cannot exist only in the understanding. For if it exists only in the understanding, it can be thought to exist in reality as well, which is greater. So if that than which a greater cannot be thought exists only in the understanding, then the very thing than which a greater *cannot* be thought is something than which a greater *can* be thought. But that is clearly impossible. Therefore, there is no doubt that something than which a greater cannot be thought exists both in the understanding and in reality.

Chapter 3

That he cannot be thought not to exist

This [being] exists so truly that it cannot even be thought not to exist. For it is possible to think that something exists that cannot be thought not to exist, and such a being is greater than one that can be thought not to exist. Therefore, if that than which a greater cannot be thought can be thought not to exist, then that than which a greater cannot be thought is *not* that than which a greater cannot be thought; and this is a contradiction. So that than which a greater cannot be thought exists so truly that it cannot even be thought not to exist.

And this is you, O Lord our God. You exist so truly, O Lord my God, that you cannot even be thought not to exist. And rightly so, for if some mind could think something better than you, a creature would rise above the Creator and sit in judgment upon him, which is completely absurd. Indeed, everything that exists, except for you alone, can be thought not to exist. So you alone among all things have existence most truly, and therefore most greatly; for whatever else exists has existence less truly, and therefore less greatly. So then why did "the fool say in his heart, 'There is no God,'" when it is so evident to the rational mind that you among all beings exist most greatly? Why indeed, except because he is stupid and a fool?

root as the verb *intelligere*, 'to understand.' Some of what Anselm says makes a bit more sense if this fact is constantly borne in mind.

Chapter 4

How the fool said in his heart what cannot be thought

But how has he said in his heart what he could not think? Or how could he not think what he said in his heart, since to say in one's heart is the same as to think? But if he really—or rather, *since* he really—thought this, because he said it in his heart, and did not say it in his heart, because he could not think it, there must be more than one way in which something is "said in one's heart" or "thought." In one way, to think a thing is to think the word that signifies that thing. But in another way, it is to understand what the thing is. God can be thought not to exist in the first way, but not at all in the second way. No one who understands what God is can think that God does not exist, although he may say these words in his heart with no signification at all, or with some peculiar signification. For God is that than which a greater cannot be thought. Whoever understands this properly, understands that this being exists in such a way that he cannot, even in thought, fail to exist. So whoever understands that God exists in this way cannot think that he does not exist.

Thanks be to you, my good Lord, thanks be to you. For what I once believed through your grace, I now understand through your illumination, so that even if I did not want to *believe* that you exist, I could not fail to *understand* that you exist.

Chapter 5

That God is whatever it is better to be than not to be; and that he alone exists through himself, and makes all other things from nothing

Then what are you, Lord God, than which nothing greater can be thought? What are you, if not the greatest of all beings, who alone exists through himself and made all other things from nothing? For whatever is not this is less than the greatest that can be thought, but this cannot be thought of you. What good is missing from the supreme good, through which every good thing exists? And so you are just, truthful, happy, and whatever it is better to be than not to be. For it is better to be just than unjust, and better to be happy than unhappy.

Chapter 6

*How God can perceive even though he is not a body**

Now it is better to be percipient, omnipotent, merciful, and impassible* than not. But how can you perceive if you are not a body? How can you be omnipotent if you cannot do everything? How can you be both merciful and impassible? If only corporeal things can perceive, because the senses exist in a body and are directed toward bodies, then how can you perceive? For you are not a body but the highest spirit, which is better than any body.

But if to perceive is just to know, or is aimed at knowledge—for whoever perceives knows according to the appropriate sense, as, for example, we know colors through sight and flavors through taste—then it is not inappropriate to say that whatever in some way knows also in some way perceives. Therefore, Lord, although you are not a body, you are indeed supremely percipient in the sense that you supremely know all things, not in the sense in which an animal knows things through its bodily senses.

Chapter 7

In what sense God is omnipotent even though there are many things he cannot do

But how are you omnipotent if you cannot do everything?[21] And how can you do everything if you cannot be corrupted, or lie, or cause what is true to be false (as, for example, to cause what has been done not to have been done), or many other such things?

Or is the ability to do these things not power but weakness? For someone who can do these things can do what is not beneficial to himself and what he ought not to do. And the more he can do these things, the more power misfortune and wickedness have over him, and the less he has over them. So whoever can do these things can do them, not in virtue of his power but in virtue of his weakness. So when we say that he "can" do these things, it is not because he has the power to do them, but because his weakness gives something else power over him. Or else it is some other manner of speaking, such as we often use in speaking loosely. For example, we sometimes say 'to be' instead of 'not to be,' or 'to do' instead of 'not to do' or 'to do nothing.' For often when someone denies that something exists, we say "It is as you say it is"; but it would seem more correct to say "It is not as you say it is not." Again, we say "This man is sitting just as that man is doing" or "This man is resting just as that man is doing"; but to sit is not to do anything, and to rest is to do nothing. In the same way, then, when someone is said to have the "power" to do or suffer something that is not beneficial to himself or that he ought not to do,

---

21. This chapter is full of word play in the Latin that does not all come across in English. The words for 'power' (*potentia*), 'weakness' (*impotentia*), and various forms of the verb 'can' (*posse*)—also translated here as 'have power'—all share a common stem. And the word for omnipotent (*omnipotens*) means literally "able to do everything" (*omnia potens*).

by 'power' we really mean 'weakness.' For the more he has this "power," the more power misfortune and wickedness have over him, and the less he has over them. Therefore, Lord God, you are all the more truly omnipotent because you can do nothing through weakness, and nothing has power over you.

Chapter 8

How God is both merciful and impassible*

But how are you both merciful and impassible? For if you are impassible, you do not feel compassion, and if you do not feel compassion, your heart is not sorrowful out of compassion for sorrow; and that is what being merciful is.[22] But if you are not merciful, how is it that you are such a comfort to the sorrowful?

So how, Lord, are you both merciful and not merciful? Is it not because you are merciful in relation to us but not in relation to yourself? You are indeed merciful according to what we feel, but not according to what you feel. For when you look with favor upon us in our sorrow, we feel the effect [*effectum*] of mercy, but you do not feel the emotion [*affectum*] of mercy. So you are merciful, because you save the sorrowful and spare those who sin against you; but you are also not merciful, because you are not afflicted with any feeling of compassion for sorrow.

Chapter 9

How the one who is completely and supremely just spares the wicked and justly has mercy on them

But how do you spare the wicked if you are completely and supremely just? For how does the one who is completely and supremely just do something that is not just? And what sort of justice is it to give everlasting life to someone who deserves eternal death? How then, O good God, good to the good and to the wicked, how do you save the wicked if this is not just and you do not do anything that is not just?

Or, since your goodness is incomprehensible, does this lie hidden in the unapproachable light in which you dwell?[23] It is indeed in the highest and most secret place of your goodness that the spring is hidden whence the river of your mercy flows. For although you are totally and supremely just, you are nonetheless kind even to the wicked, since you are totally and supremely good. After all, you would be less good if you were not kind to any wicked person. For one who is good both

---

22. In Latin, "sorrowful heart" is *miserum cor*; 'merciful' is *misericors*.
23. 1 Timothy 6:16.

to the good and to the wicked is better than one who is good only to the good, and one who is good to the wicked both in punishing and in sparing them is better than one who is good only in punishing them. So it follows that you are merciful precisely because you are totally and supremely good. And while it may be easy to see why you repay the good with good and the evil with evil, one must certainly wonder why you, who are totally just and lack for nothing, give good things to your evil and guilty creatures.

O God, how exalted is your goodness! We can see the source of your mercy, and yet we cannot discern it clearly. We know whence the river flows, but we do not see the spring from which it issues. For it is out of the fullness of goodness that you are kind to sinners, while the reason why you are lies hidden in the heights of goodness. True, out of goodness you repay the good with good and the evil with evil, but the very nature of justice seems to demand this. When you give good things to the wicked, however, one knows that he who is supremely good willed to do this, and yet one wonders why he who is supremely just could have willed such a thing.

O mercy, from what rich sweetness and sweet richness you flow forth for us! O immeasurable goodness of God, how intensely ought sinners to love you! You save the just whom justice commends and set free those whom justice condemns. The just are saved with the help of their merits, sinners despite their merits. The just are saved because you look upon the good things you have given them, sinners because you overlook the evil things you hate. O immeasurable goodness that thus "surpasses all understanding"![24] Let the mercy that proceeds from your great riches come upon me. Let that which flows forth from you flow over me. Spare me through your mercy, lest you exact retribution through your justice. For even if it is difficult to understand how your mercy coexists with your justice, one must nonetheless believe that it is in no way opposed to justice, because it flows out of your goodness, and there is no goodness apart from justice—indeed, goodness is actually in harmony with justice. In fact, if you are merciful because you are supremely good, and supremely good only because you are supremely just, then you are indeed merciful precisely because you are supremely just. Help me, O just and merciful God, whose light I seek, help me to understand what I am saying. You are indeed merciful because you are just.

So, then, is your mercy born of your justice? Do you spare the wicked because of your justice? If it is so, Lord, if it is so, teach me how it is so. Is it because it is just for you to be so good that you cannot be understood to be better, and to act so powerfully that you cannot be thought to act more powerfully? For what could be more just than this? And this would certainly not be the case if you were good only in punishing and not in sparing, and if you made only those not yet good to be good and did not do this also for the wicked. And so it is in this sense just that you

---

24. Philippians 4:7.

spare the wicked and make them good. And finally, what is not done justly should not be done, and what should not be done is done unjustly. So if it were not just for you to be merciful to the wicked, you should not be merciful; and if you should not be merciful, you would act unjustly in being merciful. But since it is wrong to say this, it is right to believe that you act justly in being merciful to the wicked.

Chapter 10

How God justly punishes and justly spares the wicked

But it is also just for you to punish the wicked. For what could be more just than for the good to receive good things and the wicked bad things? So how is it both just that you punish the wicked and just that you spare the wicked?

Or do you justly punish the wicked in one way and justly spare them in another? For when you punish the wicked, this is just because it accords with their merits; but when you spare the wicked, this is just, not because it is in keeping with their merits, but because it is in keeping with your goodness. In sparing the wicked you are just in relation to yourself but not in relation to us, in the same way that you are merciful in relation to us but not in relation to yourself. Thus, in saving us whom you might justly destroy, you are merciful, not because you experience any emotion, but because we experience the effect of your mercy; and in the same way, you are just, not because you give us our due, but because you do what is fitting for you who are supremely good. And so in this way you justly punish and justly pardon without any inconsistency.

Chapter 11

How "all the ways of the Lord are mercy and truth,"
and yet "the Lord is just in all his ways"

But is it not also just in relation to yourself, O Lord, for you to punish the wicked? It is certainly just for you to be so just that you cannot be thought to be more just. And you would by no means be so just if you only repaid the good with good and did not repay the wicked with evil. For one who treats both the good and the wicked as they deserve is more just than one who does so only for the good. Therefore, O just and benevolent God, it is just in relation to you both when you punish and when you pardon. Thus indeed "all the ways of the Lord are mercy and truth,"[25] and yet "the Lord is just in all his ways."[26] And there is no inconsistency

---

25. Psalm 25:10 (24:10).
26. Psalm 145:17 (144:17).

here, for it is not just for those to be saved whom you will to punish, and it is not just for those to be condemned whom you will to spare. For only what you will is just, and only what you do not will is not just. Thus your mercy is born of your justice, since it is just for you to be so good that you are good even in sparing the wicked. And perhaps this is why the one who is supremely just can will good things for the wicked. But even if one can somehow grasp why you can will to save the wicked, certainly no reasoning can comprehend why, from those who are alike in wickedness, you save some rather than others through your supreme goodness and condemn some rather than others through your supreme justice.

Thus you are indeed percipient, omnipotent, merciful, and impassible,* just as you are living, wise, good, happy, eternal,* and whatever it is better to be than not to be.

Chapter 12

That God is the very life by which he lives, and so on for similar attributes

But clearly, you are whatever you are, not through anything else, but through yourself. Therefore, you are the very life by which you live, the wisdom by which you are wise, and the very goodness by which you are good to the good and to the wicked, and so on for similar attributes.

Chapter 13

How he alone is unbounded and eternal, although other spirits are unbounded and eternal

Everything that is at all enclosed in a place or a time is less than that which is not restrained by any law of place or time. Therefore, since nothing is greater than you, you are not confined to any place or time; you exist everywhere and always. Since this can be said of you alone, you alone are unbounded and eternal.* So how can other spirits also be said to be unbounded and eternal?

And indeed you alone are eternal, because you alone of all beings do not cease to exist, just as you do not begin to exist. But how are you alone unbounded?

Is it that a created spirit is bounded compared to you but unbounded compared to a body*? Surely something is completely bounded if, when it is wholly in one place, it cannot at the same time be somewhere else. This is true only of bodies. On the other hand, something is unbounded if it is wholly everywhere at once, and this is true of you alone. But something is both bounded and unbounded if, when it is wholly in one place, it can at the same time be wholly in another place but not everywhere; and this is true of created spirits. For if the soul were not present as a whole in each part of its body, it would not as a whole sense each part. Therefore, Lord, you are uniquely unbounded and eternal, and yet other spirits are also unbounded and eternal.

Chapter 14

How and why God is both seen and not seen by those who seek him

Have you found what you were seeking, O my soul? You were seeking God, and you have found that he is the highest of all beings, than which nothing better can be thought; that he is life itself, light, wisdom, goodness, eternal happiness and happy eternity; and that he exists always and everywhere. If you have not found your God, how is he the one whom you have found, whom you have understood with such certain truth and true certainty? But if you have found him, why do you not perceive what you have found? Why does my soul not perceive you, O Lord God, if it has found you?

Or has it not found him whom it found to be light and truth? For how did it understand this, if not by seeing that light and truth? Could it have understood anything at all about you except by "your light and your truth"?[27] Therefore, if it has seen the light and the truth, it has seen you. If it has not seen you, it has not seen the light or the truth. Or perhaps it was indeed the light and the truth that it saw, but it has not yet seen you, because it saw you only in part and did not see you as you really are.[28]

O Lord my God, you who have fashioned and refashioned me, tell my longing soul what you are besides what it has seen, that it might see purely what it longs to see. It strives to see more, but beyond what it has already seen it sees nothing but darkness. Or rather, it does not see darkness, for in you there is no darkness;[29] it sees that it cannot see more because of its own darkness. Why is this, Lord, why is this? Is its eye darkened by its own infirmity, or is it dazzled by your splendor? Surely it is both darkened in itself and dazzled by you. Indeed it is both obscured by its own littleness and overwhelmed by your vastness. Truly it is both pinched by its own narrowness and vanquished by your fullness. How great is that light, for from it flashes every truth that enlightens the rational mind! How full is that truth, for in it is everything that is true, and outside it is only nothingness and falsehood! How vast it is, for in one glance it sees all created things, and it sees by whom and through whom and how they were created from nothing! What purity,

---

27. Psalm 43:3 (42:3).

28. Cf. 1 John 3:2.

29. Cf. 1 John 1:5.

what simplicity, what certainty and splendor are there! Truly it is more than any creature can understand.

Chapter 15

That God is greater than can be thought

Therefore, Lord, you are not merely that than which a greater cannot be thought; you are something greater than can be thought. For since it is possible to think that such a being exists, then if you are not that being, it is possible to think something greater than you. But that is impossible.

Chapter 16

That this is the unapproachable light in which he dwells

Truly, Lord, this is the unapproachable light in which you dwell.[30] For surely there is no other being that can penetrate this light so that it might see you there. Indeed, the reason that I do not see it is that it is too much for me. And yet whatever I do see, I see through it, just as a weak eye sees what it sees by the light of the sun, although it cannot look at that light directly in the sun itself. My understanding cannot see that light. It is too dazzling; my understanding does not grasp it, and the eye of my soul cannot bear to look into it for long. It is dazzled by its splendor, vanquished by its fullness, overwhelmed by its vastness, perplexed by its extent. O supreme and unapproachable light, O complete and blessed truth, how far you are from me while I am so close to you! How far you are from my sight while I am so present to yours! You are wholly present everywhere, and yet I do not see you. In you I move and in you I have my being,[31] and yet I cannot approach your presence. You are within me and all around me, and yet I do not perceive you.

Chapter 17

That in God there is harmony, fragrance, savor, softness, and beauty in his own ineffable way

Still, O Lord, you are hidden from my soul in your light and happiness, and so it still lives in its darkness and misery. It looks around, but it does not see your

---

30. Cf. 1 Timothy 6:16.
31. Cf. Acts 17:28.

beauty. It listens, but it does not hear your harmony. It smells, but it does not perceive your fragrance. It tastes, but it does not know your savor. It touches, but it does not sense your softness. For you have these qualities in you, O Lord God, in your own ineffable way; and you have given them in their own perceptible way to the things you created. But the senses of my soul have been stiffened, dulled, and obstructed by the long-standing weakness of sin.

Chapter 18

That there are no parts in God or in his eternity, which he himself is

Once again, "behold, confusion!"[32] Behold, once again mourning and sorrow stand in the way of one seeking joy and happiness. My soul hoped for satisfaction, and once again it is overwhelmed by need. I tried to eat my fill, but I hunger all the more. I strove to rise to the light of God, but I fell back down into my own darkness. Indeed, I did not merely fall into it; I find myself entangled in it. I fell before "my mother conceived me."[33] I was indeed conceived in darkness; I was born enshrouded in darkness. Truly, we all fell long ago in him "in whom we all sinned."[34] In him, who easily possessed it and wickedly lost it for himself and for us, we all lost what we desire to seek but do not know; what we seek but do not find; what we find but is not what we sought. Help me "because of your goodness, O Lord."[35] "I have sought your face; your face, Lord, will I seek. Turn not your face from me."[36] Lift me up from myself to you. Cleanse, heal, sharpen, "enlighten the eye"[37] of my soul so that I may look upon you. Let my soul gather its strength, and let it once more strive with all its understanding to reach you, O Lord.

What are you, Lord, what are you? What shall my heart understand you to be? Surely you are life, you are wisdom, you are truth, you are goodness, you are happiness, you are eternity, and you are every true good. These are many things; my narrow understanding cannot see so many things in one glance and delight in all of them at once. How then, Lord, are you all these things? Are they parts of you? Or rather, is not each of them all that you are? For whatever is composed of parts is not completely one. It is in some sense a plurality and not identical with itself, and it can be broken up either in fact or at least in the understanding. But such characteristics are foreign to you, than whom nothing better can be thought.

---

32. Jeremiah 14:19.

33. Psalm 51:5 (50:7).

34. Romans 5:12.

35. Psalm 25:7 (24:7).

36. Psalm 27:8–9 (26:8–9).

37. Psalm 13:3 (12:4).

Therefore, there are no parts in you, Lord, and you are not a plurality. Instead, you are so much a unity, so much identical with yourself, that you are in no respect dissimilar to yourself. You are in fact unity itself; you cannot be divided by any understanding. Therefore, life and wisdom and the rest are not parts of you; they are all one. Each of them is all of what you are, and each is what the rest are. And since you have no parts, and neither does your eternity, which you yourself are, it follows that no part of you or of your eternity exists at a certain place or time. Instead, you exist as a whole everywhere, and your eternity exists as a whole always.

Chapter 19

That God is not in a place or a time, but all things are in him

But if by your eternity you have been, and are, and will be, and if to have been is not the same as to be in the future, and to be is not the same as to have been or to be in the future, then how does your eternity exist as a whole always?

Is it that nothing of your eternity is in the past in such a way that it no longer exists, and nothing is in the future as if it did not exist already? So it is not the case that yesterday you were and tomorrow you will be; rather, yesterday, today, and tomorrow you *are*. In fact, it is not even the case that yesterday, today, and tomorrow you *are*; rather, you *are* in an unqualified* sense, outside time altogether. Yesterday, today, and tomorrow are merely in time. But you, although nothing exists without you, do not exist in a place or a time; rather, all things exist in you. For nothing contains you, but you contain all things.

Chapter 20

That he is before and beyond even all eternal things

Therefore you fill and embrace all things; you are before and beyond all things. And indeed you are before all things, since before they came into being, you already *are*.[38] But how are you beyond all things? In what way are you beyond those things that will have no end? Is it because they can in no way exist without you, whereas you do not exist any less even if they return to nothingness? For in this way you are in a certain sense beyond them. And is it also because they can be thought to have an end, whereas you cannot at all? Thus they do in one sense have an end, but you do not in any sense. And certainly what does not in any sense have an end is beyond what does in some sense come to an end. And do you not

---

38. Cf. Psalm 90:2 (89:2).

also surpass even all eternal things in that both your and their eternity is wholly present to you, whereas they do not yet possess the part of their eternity that is yet to come, just as they no longer possess the part that is past? In this way you are indeed always beyond them, because you are always present somewhere they have not yet arrived—or because it is always present to you.

Chapter 21

Whether this is "the age of the age" or "the ages of the ages"

So is this 'the age of the age' or 'the ages of the ages'?[39] For just as an age of time contains all temporal things, so your eternity contains even the very ages of time. This eternity is indeed 'an age' because of its indivisible unity, but it is 'ages' because of its boundless greatness. And although you are so great, Lord, that all things are full of you and are in you, nonetheless you have no spatial extension, so that there is no middle or half or any other part in you.

Chapter 22

That he alone is what he is and who he is

Therefore, you alone, Lord, are what you are; and you are who you are. For whatever is one thing as a whole and something else in its parts, and whatever has in it something changeable, is not entirely what it is. And whatever began to exist out of non-existence and can be thought not to exist, and returns to non-existence unless it subsists* through some other being; and whatever has a past that no longer exists and a future that does not yet exist: that thing does not exist in a strict and absolute sense. But you are what you are, since whatever you are in any way or at any time, you are wholly and always that.

And you are the one who exists in a strict and unqualified* sense, because you have no past and no future but only a present, and you cannot be thought not to exist at any time. And you are life and light and wisdom and happiness and eternity and many such good things; and yet you are nothing other than the one supreme good, utterly self-sufficient, needing nothing, whom all things need for their being and their well-being.

---

39. That is, is it more correct to identify God's eternity as *saeculum saeculi* or as *saecula saeculorum*? Both expressions (usually translated into English as "world without end" or "forever and ever") were found in Scripture and in the liturgy.

112

Chapter 23

That this good is equally Father, Son, and Holy Spirit; and that this is the "one necessary thing," which is the complete, total, and only good

This good is you, O God the Father; it is your Word, that is to say, your Son. For there cannot be anything other than what you are, or anything greater or less than you, in the Word by which you utter yourself. For your Word is as true as you are truthful, and therefore he is the same truth that you are and no other. And you are so simple* that nothing can be born of you that is other than what you are. And this good is the one love that is shared by you and your Son, that is, the Holy Spirit, who proceeds from you both. For this love is not unequal to you or to your Son, since you love yourself and him, and he loves himself and you, as much as you and he *are.* Moreover, the one who is equal to both you and him is not other than you and him; nothing can proceed from the supreme simplicity that is other than that from which it proceeds. Thus, whatever each of you is individually, that is what the whole Trinity is together, Father, Son, and Holy Spirit; for each of you individually is nothing other than the supremely simple unity and the supremely united simplicity, which cannot be multiplied or different from itself.

"Moreover, one thing is necessary."[40] And this is that one necessary thing, in which is all good—or rather, which is itself the complete, one, total, and unique good.

Chapter 24

A conjecture as to what sort of good this is, and how great it is

Bestir yourself, O my soul! Lift up your whole understanding, and consider as best you can what sort of good this is, and how great it is. For if particular goods are delightful, consider intently how delightful is that good which contains the joyfulness of all goods—and not such joyfulness as we have experienced in created things, but as different from that as the Creator differs from the creature. If created life is good, how good is the life that creates? If the salvation that has been brought about is joyful, how joyful is the salvation that brings about all salvation? If wisdom in the knowledge of created things is desirable, how desirable is the wisdom that created all things from nothing? In short, if there are many and great delights in delightful things, what kind and how great a delight is there in him who made those delightful things?

---

40. Luke 10:42.

Chapter 25

What great goods there are for those who enjoy this good

O those who enjoy this good: what will be theirs, and what will not be theirs! Truly they will have everything they want and nothing they do not want. There will be such goods of both body and soul that "neither eye has seen nor ear heard nor the human heart"[41] conceived. So why are you wandering through many things, you insignificant mortal, seeking the goods of your soul and of your body? Love the one good, in which are all good things, and that is enough. Desire the simple good, which is the complete good, and that is enough. What do you love, O my flesh? What do you long for, O my soul? It is there; whatever you love, whatever you long for, it is there.

If it is beauty that delights you, "the righteous will shine like the sun."[42] If it is swiftness, or strength, or the freedom of a body that nothing can withstand, "they will be like the angels of God";[43] for "it is sown an animal body, but it will rise a spiritual body,"[44] with a power that is not from nature. If it is a long and healthy life, there is a healthy eternity and eternal health, for "the righteous will live forever"[45] and "the salvation of the righteous is from the Lord."[46] If it is satisfaction, "they will be satisfied when the glory of God has appeared."[47] If it is drunkenness, "they will be drunk with the abundance of the house"[48] of God. If it is music, there the choirs of angels sing unceasingly to God. If it is some pleasure, not impure but pure, God "will give them to drink from the torrent of his pleasure."[49] If it is wisdom, the very wisdom of God will show itself to them. If it is friendship, they will love God more than themselves and one another as themselves, and God will love them more than they do themselves; for they will love God and themselves and one another through God, and God will love himself and them through himself. If it is concord, everyone will have but one will, for there will be no will among them but the will of God. If it is power, they will be omnipotent through their wills, just as God is through his. For just as God can do what he wills through himself, so they will be able to do what they will through God; for just as they will will only what God wills, so he will will whatever they will—and what he wills cannot fail

---

41. 1 Corinthians 2:9.

42. Matthew 13:43.

43. Matthew 22:30.

44. 1 Corinthians 15:44.

45. Wisdom 5:16.

46. Psalm 37:39 (36:39). The word for 'salvation' (*salus*) is the same as the word for 'health.'

47. Psalm 17:13 (16:15).

48. Psalm 36:8 (35:9).

49. Ibid.

to be. If it is wealth and honor, God will set his good and faithful servants over many things;[50] indeed, they will be called, and will truly be, "sons of God"[51] and "gods."[52] And where his Son is, there they too will be, "heirs of God and joint-heirs with Christ."[53] If it is true security, they will be certain that they will never in any way lose this security—or rather, this good: just as they will be certain that they will never give it up of their own accord, and that the loving God will never take it away against their will from those who love him, and that nothing more powerful than God will separate them from God against their will.

What great joy is there where so great a good is present! O human heart, O needy heart, heart that has known troubles, that is indeed overwhelmed by troubles: how greatly would you rejoice if you abounded in all these things! Ask your inmost self whether it can even comprehend its joy at such great happiness. And yet surely if someone else whom you loved in every respect as yourself had that same happiness, your joy would be doubled, for you would rejoice no less for him than for yourself. And if two or three or many more had that same happiness, you would rejoice as much for each of them as you would for yourself, if you loved each one as yourself. Therefore, in that perfect charity of countless happy angels and human beings, where no one will love anyone else less than he loves himself, each one will rejoice for each of the others just as he does for himself. If, then, the human heart will scarcely comprehend its own joy from so great a good, how will it be able to contain so many and such great joys? And indeed, since the more one loves someone, the more one rejoices in his good, it follows that, just as everyone in that perfect happiness will love God incomparably more than himself and all others with him, so everyone will rejoice inconceivably more in God's happiness than in his own, or in that of everyone else with him. But if they love God so much with "their whole heart, mind, and soul"[54] that their whole heart, mind, and soul are too small for the greatness of their love, they will truly rejoice so much with their whole heart, mind, and soul that their whole heart, mind, and soul will be too small for the fullness of their joy.

---

50. Cf. Matthew 25:21, 23.
51. Matthew 5:9.
52. Psalm 82:6 (81:6); John 10:34.
53. Romans 8:17.
54. Matthew 22:37.

Chapter 26

Whether this is the "fullness of joy" that the Lord promises

My God and my Lord, my hope and the joy of my heart, tell my soul whether this is that joy of which you tell us through your Son, "Ask and you shall receive, that your joy may be full."[55] For I have found a joy that is full and more than full. Indeed, when the heart, the mind, the soul, and the whole human being are filled with that joy, there will still remain joy beyond measure. The whole of that joy will therefore not enter into those who rejoice; instead, those who rejoice will enter wholly into that joy. Speak, Lord, tell your servant inwardly in his heart whether this is the joy into which your servants will enter who "enter into the joy of the Lord."[56] But surely the joy with which your chosen ones will rejoice is something "no eye has seen, nor ear heard, nor has it entered into the human heart."[57] Therefore, Lord, I have not yet expressed or conceived how greatly your blessed ones will rejoice. They will indeed rejoice as much as they love, and they will love as much as they know. How much will they know you then, Lord, and how much will they love you? Truly in this life "eye has not seen, nor has ear heard, nor has it entered into the human heart" how much they will love and know you in that life.

O God, I pray that I will know and love you that I might rejoice in you. And if I cannot do so fully in this life, I pray that I might grow day by day until my joy comes to fullness. Let the knowledge of you grow in me here, and there let it be full. Let your love grow in me here, and there let it be full, so that my joy here is great in hope, and my joy there is full in reality. O Lord, by your Son you command us—or rather, you counsel us—to ask, and you promise that we will receive,[58] that our joy may be full.[59] Lord, I ask what you counsel us through our "Wonderful Counselor."[60] Let me receive what you promise through your truth, that my joy may be full. O truthful God, I ask that I may receive, that my joy may be full. Until then, let my mind ponder on it, my tongue speak of it. Let my heart love it and my mouth proclaim it. Let my soul hunger for it, my flesh thirst for it, my whole being long for it, until I "enter into the joy of my Lord,"[61] who is God, Three in One, "blessed forever. Amen."[62]

---

55. John 16:24.

56. Matthew 25:21.

57. 1 Corinthians 2:9.

58. Matthew 7:7.

59. Cf. John 16:24.

60. Isaiah 9:6.

61. Matthew 25:21.

62. Romans 1:25.

Gaunilo's Reply on Behalf of the Fool

1   Someone who either doubts or denies that there is any such nature* as that than which nothing greater can be thought is told that its existence is proved in the following way. First, the very person who denies or entertains doubts about this being has it in his understanding, since when he hears it spoken of he understands what is said. Further, what he understands must exist in reality as well and not only in the understanding. The argument for this claim goes like this: to exist in reality is greater than to exist only in the understanding. Now if that being exists only in the understanding, then whatever also exists in reality is greater than it. Thus, that which is greater than everything else[1] will be less than something and not greater than everything else, which is of course a contradiction. And so that which is greater than everything else, which has already been proved to exist in the understanding, must exist not only in the understanding but also in reality, since otherwise it could not be greater than everything else.

He can perhaps reply:

2   "The only reason this is said to exist in my understanding is that I understand what is said. But in the same way, could I not also be said to have in my understanding any number of false things that have no real existence at all in themselves, since if someone were to speak of them I would understand whatever he said? Unless perhaps it is established that this being is such that it cannot be had in thought in the same way that any false or doubtful things can, and so I am not said to think of what I have heard or to have it in my thought, but to understand it and have it in my understanding, since I cannot think of it in any other way except by understanding it, that is, by comprehending in genuine knowledge the fact that it actually exists.

"But first of all, if this were true, there would be no difference in this case between having the thing in the understanding at one time and then later understanding that the thing exists, as there is in the case of a painting, which exists first in the mind of the painter and then in the finished work.

"Furthermore, it is nearly impossible to believe that this being, once someone had heard it spoken of, cannot be thought not to exist, in just the same way that even God can be thought not to exist. For if that were so, why bother with all this argument against someone who denies or doubts that such a nature exists?

---

1. Gaunilo regularly says "*maius omnibus*," which literally translated is "greater than everything." English idiom demands "greater than everything *else*," and I have translated it accordingly, but I thought it important to note the discrepancy.

"Finally, it must be proved to me by some unassailable argument that this being merely needs to be thought in order for the understanding to perceive with complete certainty that it undoubtedly exists. It is not enough to tell me that it exists in my understanding because I understand it when I hear about it. I still think I could likewise have any number of other doubtful or even false things in my understanding if I heard them spoken of by someone whose words I understand, and especially if I am so taken in by him that, as often happens, I believe him—as I still do not believe in that being.

3   "Accordingly, that example of the painter, who already has in his understanding the picture that he is going to paint, is not a close enough analogy to support this argument. For before that picture is painted, it is contained in the craft of the painter, and any such thing in the craft of a craftsman is nothing but a part of his intelligence. For, as Saint Augustine says, 'when a carpenter is about to make a chest in reality, he first has it in his craft. The chest that exists in reality is not a living thing, but the chest that exists in his craft is a living thing, since the soul of the craftsman, in which all those things exist before they are produced, is alive.'[2] Now how can they be living things in the living soul of the craftsman unless they are nothing other than the knowledge or intelligence of his soul itself? By contrast, except for things that are recognized as belonging to the nature of the mind itself, when the understanding upon hearing or thinking of something perceives that it is true, that truth is undoubtedly distinct from the understanding that grasps it. So even if it is true that there is something than which a greater cannot be thought, that thing, when it is heard and understood, is not the same sort of thing as a picture that exists in the understanding of the painter before it is painted.

4   "There is a further argument, which I mentioned earlier. When I hear someone speak of that which is greater than everything else that can be thought (which, it is alleged, can be nothing other than God himself), I can no more think of it or have it in my understanding in terms of anything whose genus or species I already know, than I can think of God himself—and indeed, for this very reason I can also think of God as not existing. For I do not know the thing itself, and I cannot form an idea of it on the basis of something like it, since you yourself claim that it is so great that nothing else could be like it. Now if I heard something said about a man I do not know at all, whose very existence is unknown to me, I could think of him in accordance with that very thing that a man is, on the basis of that knowledge of genus or species by which I know what a man is or what men are. Nonetheless, it could happen that the one who spoke of this man was lying, and so the man whom I thought of would not exist. But I would still be thinking of

---

2. *In Iohannem,* tractate 1, n. 17.

him on the basis of a real thing: not what that particular man would be, but what any given man is.

"But when I hear someone speak of 'God' or 'something greater than everything else,' I cannot have it in my thought or understanding in the same way as this false thing. I was able to think of the false thing on the basis of some real thing that I actually knew. But in the case of God, I can think of him only on the basis of the word; and one can seldom or never think of any true thing solely on the basis of a word. For in thinking of something solely on the basis of a word, one does not think so much of the word itself (which is at least a real thing: the sound of letters or syllables) as of the signification of the word that is heard. And in the present case, one does not do this as someone who knows what is customarily signified by the word and thinks of it on the basis of a thing that is real at least in thought. Instead, one thinks of it as someone who does not know the meaning of the word, who thinks only of the impression made on his mind by hearing the word and tries to imagine its signification. It would be surprising if one ever managed to reach the truth about something in this way. Therefore, when I hear and understand someone saying that there exists something greater than everything else that can be thought, it is in this way, and this way only, that it is present in my understanding. So much, then, for the claim that that supreme nature already exists in my understanding.

5   "Then I am offered the further argument that this thing necessarily exists in reality, since if it did not, everything that exists in reality would be greater than it. And so this thing, which of course has been proved to exist in the understanding, would not be greater than everything else. To that argument I reply that if we are to say that something exists in the understanding that cannot even be thought on the basis of the true nature of anything whatever, then I shall not deny that even this thing exists in my understanding. But since there is no way to derive from this the conclusion that this thing also exists in reality, there is simply no reason for me to concede to him that this thing exists in reality until it is proved to me by some unassailable argument.

"And when he says that this thing exists because otherwise that which is greater than everything else would not be greater than everything else, he does not fully realize whom he is addressing. For I do not yet admit—indeed, I actually deny, or at least doubt—that this being is greater than any real thing. Nor do I concede that it exists at all, except in the sense that something exists (if you want to call it 'existence') when my mind tries to imagine some completely unknown thing solely on the basis of a word that it has heard. How, then, is the fact that this greater being has been proved to be greater than everything else supposed to show me that it subsists* in actual fact? For I continue to deny, or at least doubt, that this has been proved, so that I do not admit that this greater being exists in my understanding or thought even in the way that many doubtful and uncertain things exist there.

First I must become certain that this greater being truly exists somewhere, and only then will the fact that it is greater than everything else show clearly that it also subsists in itself.

6 "For example, there are those who say that somewhere in the ocean is an island, which, because of the difficulty—or rather, impossibility—of finding what does not exist, some call 'the Lost Island.' This island (so the story goes) is more plentifully endowed than even the Isles of the Blessed with an indescribable abundance of all sorts of riches and delights. And because it has neither owner nor inhabitant, it is everywhere superior in its abundant riches to all the other lands that human beings inhabit.

"Suppose someone tells me all this. The story is easily told and involves no difficulty, and so I understand it. But if this person went on to draw a conclusion and say, 'You cannot any longer doubt that this island, more excellent than all others on earth, truly exists somewhere in reality. For you do not doubt that this island exists in your understanding, and since it is more excellent to exist not merely in the understanding, but also in reality, this island must also exist in reality. For if it did not, any land that exists in reality would be greater than it. And so this more excellent thing that you have understood would not in fact be more excellent.'—If, I say, he should try to convince me by this argument that I should no longer doubt whether the island truly exists, either I would think he was joking, or I would not know whom I ought to think more foolish: myself, if I grant him his conclusion, or him, if he thinks he has established the existence of that island with any degree of certainty, without first showing that its excellence exists in my understanding as a thing that truly and undoubtedly exists and not in any way like something false or uncertain."

7 In this way the fool might meet the objections brought against him up to this point. The next assertion is that this greater being is such that even in thought it cannot fail to exist, and that in turn rests entirely on the claim that otherwise this being would not be greater than everything else. To this argument he can make the very same response, and say, "When did I ever say that any such thing as that 'greater than everything else' exists in actual fact, so that on that basis I am supposed to accept the claim that it exists to such a degree that it cannot even be thought not to exist? Therefore, you must first prove by some absolutely incontestable argument that there exists some superior nature,* that is, one that is greater and better than all others that exist, so that from this we can also prove all of the qualities that that which is greater and better than all other things must necessarily possess." So instead of saying that this supreme thing cannot be *thought* not to exist, perhaps it would be better to say that it cannot be *understood* not to exist, or even to be capable of not existing. For in the strict sense of the word, false things cannot be understood, even though they can of course be thought in the same way that the fool thought that God does not exist.

Furthermore, I know with absolute certainty that I myself exist, but nonetheless I also know that I can fail to exist. But I understand beyond all doubt that the supreme being that exists, namely God, both exists and cannot fail to exist. Now I do not know whether I can think I do not exist even while I know with absolute certainty that I do exist. But if I can, why can I not do the same for anything else that I know with the same certainty? And if I cannot, it is not God alone who cannot be thought not to exist.

8 The rest of this book is argued so truly, so lucidly and magnificently, full of so much that is useful, and fragrant with the aroma of devout and holy feeling, that it should by no means be belittled on account of the claims made at the beginning, which are indeed accurately understood, but less compellingly argued. Rather, those claims should be demonstrated more solidly, and then the whole book can be accorded great honor and praise.

Anselm's Reply to Gaunilo

SINCE THE ONE who takes me to task is not that fool against whom I was speaking in my book, but a Christian who is no fool, arguing on behalf of the fool, it will be enough for me to reply to the Christian.

1 You say—whoever you are who say that the fool could say these things—that something than which a greater cannot be thought is in the understanding no differently from that which cannot even be thought according to the true nature of anything at all. You also say that it does not follow (as I say it does) that that than which a greater cannot be thought exists in reality as well simply because it exists in the understanding, any more than it follows that the Lost Island most certainly exists simply because someone who hears it described in words has no doubt that it exists in his understanding. I, however, say this: if that than which a greater cannot be thought is neither understood nor thought, and exists neither in the understanding nor in thought, then either God is not that than which a greater cannot be thought, or else he is neither understood nor thought, and exists neither in the understanding nor in thought. I appeal to your own faith and conscience as the most compelling argument that this is false. Therefore, that than which a greater cannot be thought is indeed understood and thought, and exists in the understanding and in thought. So either the premises by which you attempt to prove the contrary are false, or else what you think follows from them does not in fact follow.

You think that from the fact that something than which a greater cannot be thought is understood, it does not follow that it exists in the understanding; nor does it follow that if it exists in the understanding, it therefore exists in reality. But I say with certainty that if it can be so much as thought to exist, it must necessarily exist. For that than which a greater cannot be thought cannot be thought of as beginning to exist. By contrast, whatever can be thought to exist but does not in fact exist, can be thought of as beginning to exist. Therefore, it is not the case that that than which a greater cannot be thought can be thought to exist, but does not in fact exist. If, therefore, it can be thought to exist, it does necessarily exist.

Furthermore, if it can be thought *at all*, it necessarily exists. For no one who denies or doubts that something than which a greater cannot be thought exists, denies or doubts that if it did exist, it would be unable to fail to exist either in reality or in the understanding, since otherwise it would not be that than which a greater cannot be thought. But whatever can be thought, but does not in fact exist, could (if it did exist) fail to exist either in reality or in the understanding. So if that than which a greater cannot be thought can be thought at all, it cannot fail to exist.

But let us assume instead that it does not exist, although it can be thought. Now something that can be thought but does not exist, would not, if it existed, be that than which a greater cannot be thought. And so, if it existed, that than which a greater cannot be thought would not be that than which a greater cannot be thought, which is utterly absurd. Therefore, if that than which a greater cannot be thought can be thought at all, it is false that it does not exist—and much more so if it can be understood and can exist in the understanding.

I shall say something more. If something does not exist everywhere and always, even if perhaps it does exist somewhere and sometimes, it can undoubtedly be thought not to exist anywhere or at any time, just as it does not exist in this particular place or at this particular time. For something that did not exist yesterday but does exist today can be conceived of as never existing in just the same way that it is understood as not existing yesterday. And something that does not exist here but does exist elsewhere can be thought not to exist anywhere in just the same way that it does not exist here. Similarly, when some parts of a thing do not exist in the same place or at the same time as other parts of that thing, all its parts—and therefore the thing as a whole—can be thought not to exist anywhere or at any time. Even if we say that time always exists and that the universe is everywhere, nevertheless, the whole of time does not always exist, and the whole of the universe is not everywhere. And just as each individual part of time does not exist when the others do, so each can be thought never to exist. And just as each individual part of the universe does not exist where the others do, so each can be thought to exist nowhere. Moreover, whatever is composed of parts can, at least in thought, be divided and fail to exist. Therefore, whatever does not exist as a whole in all places and at all times, even if it does exist, can be thought not to exist. But that than which a greater cannot be thought, if it exists, cannot be thought not to exist. For otherwise, even if it exists, it is not that than which a greater cannot be thought— which is absurd. Therefore, there is no time and no place in which it does not exist as a whole; it exists as a whole always and everywhere.

Do you think the being about whom these things are understood can in any way be thought or understood, or can exist in thought or in the understanding? If it cannot, these claims about it cannot be understood either. Perhaps you will say that it is not understood and does not exist in the understanding because it is not *fully* understood. But then you would have to say that someone who cannot gaze directly upon the purest light of the sun does not see the light of day, which is nothing other than the light of the sun. Surely that than which a greater cannot be thought is understood, and exists in the understanding, at least to the extent that these things about it are understood.

2   And so I said in the argument that you criticize, that when the fool hears someone utter the words "that than which a greater cannot be thought," he understands

what he hears. Someone who does not understand it (if it is spoken in a language he knows) is rather feeble-minded, if indeed he has a mind at all.

Then I said that if it is understood, it exists in the understanding. Or does that which has been shown to exist necessarily in actual fact not exist in any understanding? But you will say that even if it exists in the understanding, it still does not follow that it is understood. Notice, however, that if it is understood, it does follow that it exists in the understanding. For when something is thought, it is thought by means of thinking; and what is thought by means of thinking exists in thinking just as it is thought. And in the same way, when something is understood, it is understood by means of the understanding; and what is understood by means of the understanding exists in the understanding, just as it is understood. What could be clearer than that?

After that I said that if it exists only in the understanding, it can be thought to exist in reality as well, which is greater. Therefore, if it exists only in the understanding, the very same thing is both that than which a greater *cannot* be thought and that than which a greater *can* be thought. Now I ask you, what could be more logical? For if it exists only in the understanding, can it not be thought to exist in reality as well? And if it can, does not the one who thinks it, think something greater than that thing is if it exists only in the understanding? So if that than which a greater *cannot* be thought exists only in the understanding, it is that than which a greater *can* be thought: What more logical conclusion could there be? But of course that than which a greater cannot be thought is not the same in anyone's understanding as that than which a greater can be thought. Does it not follow, therefore, that if that than which a greater cannot be thought exists in any understanding at all, it does not exist only in the understanding? For if it exists only in the understanding, it is that than which a greater can be thought, which is absurd.

3   But, you say, this is just the same as if someone were to claim that it cannot be doubted that a certain island in the ocean, surpassing all other lands in its fertility (which, from the difficulty—or rather, impossibility—of finding what does not exist, is called "the Lost Island"), truly exists in reality, because someone can easily understand it when it is described to him in words. I say quite confidently that if anyone can find for me something existing either in reality or only in thought to which he can apply this inference in my argument, besides that than which a greater cannot be thought, I will find and give to him that Lost Island, never to be lost again. In fact, however, it has already become quite clear that that than which a greater cannot be thought cannot be thought not to exist, since its existence is a matter of such certain truth. For otherwise it would not exist at all.

Finally, if someone says that he thinks it does not exist, I say that when he thinks this, either he is thinking something than which a greater cannot be thought, or he is not. If he is not, then he is not thinking that it does not exist, since he is not thinking it at all. But if he is, he is surely thinking something that cannot be thought not to exist. For if it could be thought not to exist, it could be thought to have a beginning and an end, which is impossible. Therefore, someone who is thinking it, is thinking something that cannot be thought not to exist. And of course someone who is thinking this does not think that that very thing does not exist. Otherwise he would be thinking something that cannot be thought. Therefore, that than which a greater cannot be thought cannot be thought not to exist.

4   When I say that this supreme being cannot be *thought* not to exist, you reply that it would perhaps be better to say that it cannot be *understood* not to exist, or even to be capable of not existing. But in fact it was more correct to say that it cannot be *thought* not to exist. For if I had said that this thing cannot be understood not to exist, you (who say that in the strict sense of the word false things cannot be understood) might well object that nothing that exists can be understood not to exist, since, after all, it is false that something that exists does not exist. Consequently, it is not God alone who cannot be understood not to exist. But if any of those things that most certainly exist can be understood not to exist, then other things that are certain can likewise be understood not to exist. If, however, we say 'thought' [rather than 'understood'] this objection will have no force if it is examined properly. For even if nothing that actually exists can be *understood* not to exist, everything can be *thought* not to exist, except for that which exists supremely. Indeed, all and only those things that have a beginning or end, or are made up of parts, as well as whatever does not exist always and everywhere as a whole (as I discussed earlier), can be thought not to exist. The only thing that cannot be thought not to exist is that which has neither beginning nor end, and is not made up of parts, and which no thought discerns except as wholly present always and everywhere.

So you should realize that you can indeed *think* of yourself as not existing even while you know with absolute certainty that you exist. I am amazed that you said you did not know this. For we think of many things as not existing that we know exist, and we think of many things as existing that we know do not exist—not judging, but imagining, that things are as we are thinking of them. And so we can in fact think of something as not existing even while we know that it exists, since we can think the one thing and know the other at the very same time. And yet we cannot think of something as not existing even while we know that it exists, since we cannot think of it as existing and not existing at the same time. So if someone distinguishes the two senses of this statement in this way, he will understand that in one sense nothing can be thought of as not existing when we know that it exists, and in another sense anything besides that than which a greater cannot be thought can be thought not to exist, even when we know that it exists. Thus God alone cannot be thought not to exist, but nonetheless it is also true that there are many things that cannot be thought not to exist while they actually exist. I think, however, that I adequately explained in my book the sense in which God is thought not to exist.[1]

5   Now as for the other objections you raise against me on behalf of the fool, anyone with much sense at all can easily see through them, so I had judged it best not to bother proving this. But since I hear that some readers think they have some force against me, I will deal with them briefly. First, you repeatedly say that I argue that that which is greater than everything else exists in the understanding; and that if it exists in the understanding, it also exists in reality, for otherwise that which is greater than everything else would not be greater than everything else. Nowhere in anything I said can such an argument be found. For "that which is greater than everything else" and "that than which a greater cannot be thought" do not have the same force in proving that the thing spoken of exists in reality. For if someone says that that than which a greater cannot be thought is not something existing in reality, or is capable of not existing, or can be thought not to exist, he is easily refuted. For whatever does not exist is capable of not existing, and whatever is capable of not existing can be thought not to exist. Now whatever can be thought not to exist, if it does exist, is not that than which a greater cannot be thought. And if it does not exist, it would not be that than which a greater cannot be thought *even if it were to exist*. But it makes no sense to say that that than which a greater cannot be thought, if it exists, is not that than which a greater cannot be thought, and that if it [does not exist but] were to exist, it would not be that than which a greater cannot be thought. It is therefore evident that it exists, that it is not capable of not existing, and that it cannot be thought not to exist. For otherwise, if it exists, it is not the thing spoken of; and if it [does not exist but] were to exist, it would not be the thing spoken of.

This does not seem to be so easily proved with regard to what is said to be greater than everything else. For it is not as evident that something that can be thought not to exist is not that which is greater than everything else that exists, as it is that such a thing is not that than which a greater cannot be thought. Nor is it indubitable that if there is something greater than everything else, it is the same as that than which a greater cannot be thought, or that if such a thing were to exist, there would not exist another thing just like it. But these things are certainly true of what is called "that than which a greater cannot be thought." For what if someone were to say that something exists that is greater than everything else that exists, and yet that this very thing can be thought not to exist, and that something greater than it can be thought, although that greater thing does not actually exist? Can it be just as easily inferred in this case that it is not greater than everything else that exists, as it was perfectly certain in the previous case that it was not that than which a greater cannot be thought? In the second case we would need another

---

1. See Chapter 4 of the *Proslogion*.

premise, besides the mere fact that this being is said to be "greater than everything else," whereas in the first case there was no need for anything more than the expression "that than which a greater cannot be thought." Therefore, since "that than which a greater cannot be thought" proves things about itself and through itself that cannot be proved in the same way about what is said to be "greater than everything else," you have unjustly criticized me for saying things I did not say, when they differ greatly from what I actually said.

If, however, this can be proved through some further argument, you should not have criticized me for saying something that can be proved. And that it can in fact be proved should be easily perceived by anyone who knows that it can be proved for that than which a greater cannot be thought. For that than which a greater cannot be thought cannot be understood as anything other than the one thing that is greater than everything else. Therefore, just as that than which a greater cannot be thought is understood and exists in the understanding, and therefore is affirmed to exist in actual fact, even so that which is said to be greater than everything else is with necessity inferred to be understood, to exist in the understanding, and consequently to exist in reality. So you see how right you were to compare me to that stupid man who was willing to affirm the existence of the Lost Island solely because the island would be understood if someone described it.

6   But you also raise the objection that all sorts of false or doubtful things can be understood, and exist in the understanding, in the very same way as the being I was talking about. I wonder what force you thought this objection could have against me. I was simply trying to prove something that was still in doubt, and for that it was enough for me to show that this being is understood, and exists in the understanding, *in some way or other*, since on that basis the argument would go on to determine whether it exists only in the understanding, like a false thing, or also in reality, like a real thing. For if false and doubtful things are understood, and exist in the understanding, in the sense that one who hears them spoken of understands what the speaker means, there is no reason that the being I was discussing could not be understood or exist in the understanding.

But how can these two claims of yours be consistent: first, that if someone spoke of false things, you would understand whatever he said; and second, that if what you heard is not had in thought in the same way that false things are, you would not say that you think it and have it in your thought, but rather that you understand it and have it in your understanding, since you cannot think this thing without understanding it, that is, comprehending in genuine knowledge that it exists in reality? How, I ask, can these be consistent: that false things are understood, and that to understand is to comprehend in genuine knowledge that something exists? You should realize that this objection has no force against me. If false things can indeed be understood in some sense, and your definition of understanding applies not to all but only to some cases of understanding, then I should not have been criticized for saying that that than which a greater cannot be thought is understood and exists in the understanding even before it was certain that it exists in reality.

7   Next, you say that it is nearly impossible to believe that when this thing has been spoken of and heard, it cannot be thought not to exist in the way that even God can be thought not to exist. Let those who have acquired even a meager knowledge of disputation and argument reply on my behalf. Is it rational for someone to deny [the existence of] what he understands, simply because it is said to be the same as something [whose existence] he denies because he does not understand it? Or if [its existence] is sometimes denied because it is only partly understood, and it is the same as something that is not understood at all, are not things in doubt more easily proved to be true of what exists in some understanding than of what exists in no understanding? Therefore, it is impossible to believe that someone would deny [the existence of] that than which a greater cannot be thought, which he understands to some extent when he hears of it, simply because he denies [the existence of] God, whose meaning he is not thinking of in any way. Or, if he also denies [the existence of] that than which a greater cannot be thought, because he does not fully understand it, is it not easier to prove [the existence of] what is understood to some extent than to prove what is not understood at all? So it was not irrational for me to prove against the fool that God exists by making use of the expression "that than which a greater cannot be thought," since he would understand that expression to some extent, whereas he might not understand 'God' at all.

8   You go to some trouble to show that that than which a greater cannot be thought is not the same sort of thing as a picture, not yet painted, in the understanding of the painter, but your argument is not to the point. I did not bring up the picture that is thought out beforehand in order to claim that it was the same sort of thing as the being I was discussing, but merely so I could show that something exists in the understanding that would not be understood to exist [in reality].

Again, you say that when you hear "that than which a greater cannot be thought," you cannot think it in accordance with some thing that you know by genus or species, or have it in your understanding, since you do not know the thing itself and cannot form an idea of it on the basis of something similar. But that is clearly wrong. For since every lesser good, insofar as it is good, is similar to a greater good, it is clear to every reasonable mind that by raising our thoughts from lesser goods to greater goods, we can certainly form an idea of that than which a greater cannot be thought on the basis of those things than which a greater can be thought. Who, for example, is unable to think (even if he does not believe that what he thinks exists in reality) that if something that has a beginning and end is good, then something that has a beginning but never ceases to exist is much better? And that just as the latter is better than the former, so something that has neither beginning nor end is better still, even if it is always moving from the past through the present into the future? And that something that in no way needs or is compelled to change or move is far better even than that, whether any such thing exists in reality or not? Can such a thing not be thought? Can anything greater than this be thought? Or rather, is not this an example of forming an idea of that than which a greater cannot be thought on the basis of those things than which a greater can be thought? So there is in fact a way to form an idea of that than which a greater cannot be thought. And so in this way it is easy to refute a fool who does not accept the sacred authority, if he denies that one can form an idea of that than which a greater cannot be thought on the basis of other things. But if an orthodox Christian were to deny this, he should recall that "since the creation of the world the invisible things of God—his everlasting power and divinity—have been clearly seen through the things that have been made."[2]

9   But even if it were true that that than which a greater cannot be thought cannot be thought or understood, it would not be false that [the expression] "that than which a greater cannot be thought" can be thought and understood. For just as one can use the word 'ineffable,' even though the thing that is said to be ineffable cannot be spoken of; and just as 'unthinkable' can be thought, even though the thing to which the word 'unthinkable' applies cannot be thought; in the same way, when someone says "that than which nothing greater can be thought," that which is heard can undoubtedly be thought and understood, even though the thing itself than which a greater cannot be thought cannot be thought or understood.

For even if someone is foolish enough to say that something than which a greater cannot be thought does not exist, he will surely not be shameless enough to say that he cannot understand or think what he is saying. Or, if such a person does turn up, not only should his words be repudiated, but he himself should be ridiculed. So anyone who denies the existence of something than which a greater cannot be thought surely understands and thinks the denial that he is making. Now he cannot understand or think this denial without its parts. And one part of it is "that than which a greater cannot be thought." Therefore, whoever denies this, understands and thinks that than which a greater cannot be thought. Now it is quite clear that something that cannot fail to exist can be thought and understood in the same way. And one who thinks this is thinking something greater than is one who thinks something that can fail to exist. Therefore, if, while he is thinking that than which a greater cannot be thought, he thinks that it can fail to exist, he is not thinking that than which a greater cannot be thought. But it is not possible for the same thing at the same time both to be thought and not to be thought. Therefore, someone who thinks that than which a greater cannot be thought does

---

2. Romans 1:20.

not think that it can, but rather that it cannot fail to exist. For this reason the thing that he is thinking exists necessarily, since whatever can fail to exist is not what he is thinking.

10   I believe I have now shown that my proof in the foregoing book that that than which a greater cannot be thought exists in reality was no weak argument, but a quite conclusive one, one that is not weakened by the force of any objection. For the signification of this expression has such great force that the thing it expresses is, from the mere fact that it is understood or thought, necessarily proved both to exist in reality and to be whatever we ought to believe about the divine nature. Now we believe about the divine nature everything that can be thought, absolutely speaking, better for something to be than not to be. For example, it is better to be eternal* than not eternal, good than not good, and indeed goodness itself rather than not goodness itself. That than which something greater cannot be thought cannot fail to be anything of this sort. So one must believe that that than which a greater cannot be thought is whatever we ought to believe about the divine nature.

I am grateful for your kindness both in your criticisms and in your praise of my book. For since you lavished such great praise on the things you found worthy of acceptance, it is quite clear that you criticized the things that seemed weak to you not from ill will but in a friendly spirit.

[Three Philosophical Dialogues]

Preface

AT VARIOUS TIMES I wrote three treatises pertaining to the study of Holy Scripture, all of them in question-and-answer form, with the person asking questions identified as 'Teacher' and the respondent as 'Student.' I did in fact write a fourth treatise in the same form—a very useful work, I believe, for those being introduced to dialectic—which begins with the words "*De grammatico.*" But since its subject matter is different from these three, I do not count it as belonging with them.

One of the three is *On Truth*: it considers what truth is, in what things truth is commonly said to be, and what justice is. The second is *On Freedom of Choice*: it considers what freedom of choice is, and whether human beings always have it, as well as how many distinctions there are in freedom of choice depending on whether someone has or lacks rectitude of will—freedom of choice having been given to rational creatures in order that they might preserve rectitude of will. In it I elucidated only the natural power of the will to preserve the rectitude that it received, not how necessary it is that the will be supported by grace. The third asks how the devil sinned by not remaining steadfast[1] in the truth, since God did not give him perseverance, which the devil could not have unless God gave it to him; for if God had given it, the devil would have had it, just as the good angels had it because God gave it to them. Although I did discuss the confirmation of the good angels in this treatise, I called it *On the Fall of the Devil* because what I wrote about the bad angels was the very heart of the question, whereas what I said about the good angels was a side issue.

Although I did not compose these treatises one right after the other, their subject matter and their similarity of form require that they be written together as a unit, and in the order in which I have listed them. So even if certain over-hasty persons have transcribed them in a different order before they were all finished, I want them to be arranged as I have instructed here.

---

1. Cf. John 8:44: the devil "did not remain steadfast in the truth." "Remained steadfast" (Latin: *stetit*) is literally "stood firm." The translation "remained steadfast" has certain advantages, not the least of which is that it allows the use of 'steadfastness' to translate the cognate noun *status* in *On the Fall of the Devil*, Chapter 6.

ON TRUTH

Chapters

Chapter 1

That truth has no beginning or end

STUDENT: Since we believe that God is truth,[2] and we say that truth is in many other things, I would like to know whether, wherever truth is said to be, we must acknowledge that God is that truth. For you yourself, in your *Monologion*, prove on the basis of the truth of speech that the supreme truth has no beginning or end: "Let anyone who can do so think of this: When did it begin to be true, or when was it not true, that something was going to exist? Or when will it cease to be true, and no longer be true, that something existed in the past? But given that neither of these is conceivable, and both statements cannot be true apart from truth, then it is impossible even to think that truth has a beginning or end. Finally, if truth had a beginning or will have an end, before it came into being it was then true that there was no truth, and after it has ceased to exist, it will then be true that there is no truth. Now nothing can be true apart from truth. So truth existed before truth existed, and truth will exist after truth has ceased to exist—which is an absolute absurdity. So, whether truth is said to have a beginning or end or is understood not to have a beginning or end, truth cannot be confined by any beginning or end."

---

2. Cf. John 14:6, where Christ says "I am the way, the truth, and the life."

So you say in your *Monologion*.[3] And for that reason I am eager for you to teach me a definition of truth.

TEACHER: I don't remember ever discovering a definition of truth; but if you like, let's inquire what truth is by examining the variety of things in which we say there is truth.

S: Even if I can't do anything else, I will at least help by listening.

Chapter 2

On the truth of signification, and on the two truths of a statement

T: Then let's inquire first what truth is in a statement, since we quite often call a statement true or false.

S: You inquire, and I will hold on to whatever you discover.

T: When is a statement true?

S: When what it states, whether by affirming or denying, is the case. For I say that it states something even when it denies that what-is-not is, since that is the way in which it states what is the case.

T: So do you think that the thing stated is the truth of the statement?

S: No.

T: Why not?

S: Because nothing is true except by participating in truth, and so the truth of what is true is in the true thing itself, whereas the thing stated is not in the true statement. Hence, we must say that the thing stated is not the truth of the statement, but the cause of its truth. For this reason it seems to me that the truth of a statement must be sought nowhere else but in the statement itself.

T: Then consider whether the statement itself, or its signification, or any of those things that are in the definition of 'statement,' is what you are looking for.

S: I don't think so.

T: Why not?

S: Because if that were so, the statement would always be true, since everything in the definition of 'statement' remains the same, both when what is stated is the

---

3. See Chapter 18 of the *Monologion*.

case and when it isn't. For the statement is the same, its signification is the same, and so forth.

T: Then what do you think truth is in a statement?

S: All I know is that when a statement signifies that what-is is, then there is truth in it, and it is true.

T: For what purpose is an affirmation made?

S: For signifying that what-is is.

T: So it ought to do that.

S: Certainly.

T: So when it signifies that what-is is, it signifies what it ought to.

S: Obviously.

T: And when it signifies what it ought to, it signifies correctly.

S: Yes.

T: Now when it signifies correctly, its signification is correct.

S: No doubt about it.

T: So when it signifies that what-is is, its signification is correct.

S: That follows.

T: Furthermore, when it signifies that what-is is, its signification is true.

S: Indeed it is both correct and true when it signifies that what-is is.

T: Then its being correct is the same thing as its being true: namely, its signifying that what-is is.

S: Indeed, they are the same.

T: So its truth is nothing other than its rectitude.[4]

S: Now I see clearly that this truth[5] is rectitude.

T: The case is similar when a statement signifies that what-is-not is not.

---

4. That is, its correctness. 'Rectitude' (*rectitudo*) is the abstract noun corresponding to 'correct' (*rectum*). I use 'rectitude' rather than 'correctness' for the sake of consistency: later in the dialogue there are passages where 'correctness' will not work as a translation for *rectitudo*, and since *rectitudo* is the most important technical term in the dialogue, it seemed important to signal its presence with a consistent translation.

5. "this truth": that is, the truth of statements.

S: I understand what you're saying. But teach me how I could respond if someone were to say that even when a statement signifies that what-is-not is, it signifies what it ought to. A statement, after all, has received the power to signify[6] both that what-is is, and that what-is-not is—for if it had not received the power to signify that even what-is-not is, it would not signify this.[7] So even when it signifies that what-is-not is, it signifies what it ought to. But if, as you have shown, it is correct and true by signifying what it ought to, then a statement is true even when it states that what-is-not is.

T: Certainly it is not customary to call a statement true when it signifies that what-is-not is; nonetheless, it has truth and rectitude, in that it is doing what it ought to. But when it signifies that what-is is, it is doing what it ought to in *two* ways, since it not only signifies what it received the power to signify but also signifies in keeping with the purpose for which it was made. We customarily call a statement correct and true according to the rectitude and truth by which it signifies that what-is is, not according to that by which it signifies that even what-is-not is. After all, what a statement ought to do depends more on the purpose for which it received its power of signification than on what was not the purpose for receiving signification; and the only reason it received the power to signify that a thing is when it is not, or that a thing is not when it is, was that it was not possible for it to be given only the power of signifying that a thing is when it is, or that it is not when it is not.

Therefore, the rectitude and truth that a statement has because it signifies in keeping with the purpose for which it was made is one thing; that which it has because it signifies what it received the power to signify is quite another. The latter is invariable for a given statement, whereas the former is variable, since a statement always has the latter but does not always have the former. For it has the latter naturally, while it has the former accidentally and according to its use. For example, when I say "It is day" in order to signify that what-is is, I am using the signification of this statement correctly, since this is the purpose for which it was made; consequently, in that case it is said to signify correctly. But when I use the same statement to signify that what-is-not is, I am not using it correctly, since it

---

6. "Has received the power to signify" is literally just "has received to signify" (*accepit significare*). Anselm uses this construction and others like it in the three dialogues to speak about the powers and capacities that things receive from whatever causes them to exist in the first place.

7. In other words, a false statement is still a meaningful statement: if I say "Abraham Lincoln served out his second term as president," I do manage to signify that Abraham Lincoln served out his second term, even though what I am signifying does not match the way things really are. The student therefore suggests that what statements were made for (what they "received the power to do") is signifying, period, and not necessarily signifying what is really the case.

was not made for that purpose; and so in that case its signification is said not to be correct. Now in some statements these two rectitudes or truths are inseparable: for example, when we say "Human beings are animals" or "A human being is not a stone." For this affirmation always signifies that what-is is, and this negation always signifies that what-is-not is not; nor can we use the former to signify that what-is-not is (since human beings are always animals) or the latter to signify that what-is is not (since a human being is never a stone).[8]

We began our inquiry with the truth that a statement has when someone uses it correctly, since it is according to this truth that common usage identifies a statement as true. As for the truth that it cannot fail to have, we will discuss that later.[9]

S: Then go back to what you began, since you have adequately distinguished for me between the two truths of statements—if, that is, you have shown that a statement has some truth even when it's a lie, as you say.

T: For the time being let these remarks suffice for our first topic, the truth of signification. After all, the same notion of truth that we examined in spoken statements will be found in all signs that are made for the purpose of signifying that something is or is not: for example, writing and sign language.

S: Then go on to the other things.

Chapter 3

On the truth of opinion

T: We also call a thought true when things are as we think they are (whether we think this through reason or in some other way) and false when they are not.

S: That's the custom.

T: So what do you think truth in thought is?

---

8. Anselm is noting that statements can be regarded as having two functions and therefore as being true in two different senses. Their real purpose is to signify what is the case, so they can be called true if they signify what is the case (that is the usual sense of 'true'); but they also have the power simply to signify, regardless of whether what they signify is the case, and so they can be called true if they simply signify. Any well-formed statement signifies (so Anselm says that this sort of truth is "invariable" and "natural"), but not every well-formed statement signifies what is the case (so Anselm says that this sort of truth is "variable"). The last two sentences note that there are certain statements in which the two truths cannot diverge: that is, if they signify anything at all, they signify what is the case. These are the affirmations of necessary truths and the negations of necessary falsehoods.

9. There is a brief discussion of this truth at the end of Chapter 5.

S: According to the reasoning we found persuasive in the case of statements, nothing can be more correctly called the truth of a thought than its rectitude. For the power of thinking that something is or is not was given to us in order that we might think that what-is is, and that what-is-not is not. Therefore, if someone thinks that what-is is, he is thinking what he ought to think, and so his thought is correct. If, then, a thought is true and correct for no other reason than that we are thinking that what-is is, or that what-is-not is not, its truth is nothing other than its rectitude.

T: Your reasoning is correct.

Chapter 4

On the truth of the will

Now Truth Itself says that there is also truth in the will when he says that the devil "did not remain steadfast in the truth."[10] For it was only in his will that he was in the truth and then abandoned the truth.

S: So I believe. For if he had always willed what he ought, he would never have sinned; and it was only by sinning that he abandoned the truth.

T: Then tell me what you understand truth to be in the will.

S: Nothing other than rectitude. For if he was in rectitude and in the truth so long as he willed what he ought—that is, that for the sake of which he had received a will—and if he abandoned rectitude and truth when he willed what he ought not, then we cannot understand truth in this case as anything other than rectitude, since both truth and rectitude in his will were nothing other than his willing what he ought.

T: You understand this well.

---

10. John 8:44.

Chapter 5

On the truth of natural and non-natural action

But we must equally believe that there is truth in action as well. As the Lord says, "One who does evil hates the light,"[11] and "One who does the truth comes to the light."[12]

S: I understand what you're saying.

T: Then consider, if you can, what truth is in action.

S: Unless I am mistaken, we must use the same reasoning about truth in action that we used earlier to identify truth in other things.

T: You're right. For if doing evil and doing the truth are opposites, as the Lord indicates by saying that "one who does evil hates the light" and "one who does the truth comes to the light," then doing the truth is the same as doing good, since doing good and doing evil are contraries. Therefore, if doing the truth and doing good are both opposed to the same thing, they have the same signification. Now everyone agrees that those who do what they ought, do good and act correctly.[13] From this it follows that to act correctly is to do the truth, since it is agreed that to do the truth is to do good, and to do good is to act correctly. So nothing is more obvious than that the truth of action is its rectitude.

S: I see no weakness in your reasoning.

T: Consider whether every action that does what it ought to is appropriately said to do the truth. You see, there is rational action, such as giving to charity, and nonrational action, such as the action of a fire that causes heat. So think about whether it would be appropriate for us to say that the fire is doing the truth.

S: If the fire received the power to heat from the one from whom it has being, then when it heats, it is doing what it ought to. So I don't see what is inappropriate about saying that the fire does the truth and acts correctly when it does what it ought to.

T: That's exactly how it seems to me. Hence we can note that there is one rectitude or truth in action that is necessary, and another that is not. When the fire heats, it does the truth and acts correctly out of necessity; but when human beings do good, it is not out of necessity that they do the truth and act correctly. Now when the Lord said that "one who does the truth comes to the light," he meant us to take 'do' not just to mean what is properly* called doing, but as substituting for any

---

11. John 3:20.
12. John 3:21.
13. "Act correctly" is literally "do rectitude."

verb. After all, he is not excluding from this truth or light someone who undergoes persecution "for righteousness' sake,"[14] or who is when and where he ought to be, or who stands or sits when he ought to, and so forth. No one says that such people are not doing good. And when the Apostle says that everyone will receive a recompense "according to his deeds,"[15] we should understand him to mean whatever we customarily identify as doing good or doing evil.

S: Ordinary language, too, uses 'to do' both of undergoing and of many other things that are not doings. Hence, if I am not mistaken, we can also include among right actions an upright will, whose truth we investigated earlier, before the truth of action.

T: You are not mistaken. For someone who wills what he ought to is said to act correctly and to do good; nor is he excluded from those who do the truth. But since we are discussing the upright will in the course of investigating the truth, and the Lord seems to speak specifically of the truth that is in the will when he says that the devil "did not remain steadfast in the truth," I wanted to give separate consideration to what truth is in the will.

S: I am glad you did it that way.

T: So since it is established that there is a natural truth in action as well as a non-natural truth, that truth in statements which we saw above cannot be separated from them should be classified as natural truth.[16] For just as fire, when it heats, does the truth, since it received the power to heat from the one who gave it being, so also the statement "It is day" does the truth when it signifies that it is day, whether it is actually day or not, since it received naturally the power to do this.

S: Now for the first time I see the truth in a false statement.

---

14. Matthew 5:10.

15. 2 Corinthians 5:10.

16. See Chapter 2. The truth that cannot be separated from a statement is its signifying whatever it "received the power to signify." This truth, Anselm says, is akin to the truth of natural action. Just as fire cannot help heating, "It is day" cannot help signifying that it is day. In this sense both the statement and the fire are doing what they received the power to do, and so they are both "doing the truth."

Chapter 6

On the truth of the senses

T: Do you think we have found every dwelling-place of truth apart from the supreme truth?

S: I now recall one truth that I don't find in the things you have discussed.

T: What is it?

S: There is truth in the bodily senses, although not always, since they sometimes deceive us. For sometimes when I see something through glass, my vision deceives me, since it sometimes reports to me that the body* I see beyond the glass is the same color as the glass, when in fact it is a different color; on the other hand, sometimes it makes me think that the glass has the color of the thing that I see beyond it, even though it doesn't. And there are many other cases in which vision and the other senses are deceptive.

T: I don't think this truth and falsehood is in the senses, but in opinion. For it is the interior sense that deceives itself; the exterior sense does not lie to it. Sometimes this is easy to recognize, but sometimes it is difficult. When a child fears the open maw of the sculpture of a dragon, it is easy to recognize that his vision is not responsible; his vision is reporting to the child exactly what it reports to adults. Rather, what is responsible is the child's interior sense, which is not yet adept at distinguishing between a thing and its likeness. This is the sort of thing that happens when we see someone who resembles someone else and we think he is the person he resembles, or when someone hears what is not a human voice and thinks it is a human voice. The interior sense is responsible for these as well.

Now what you say about glass is the case for the following reason. When vision passes through a body* that is of the same color as air—unless that body is denser or darker than the air—nothing prevents vision from taking on the likeness of the color that it sees beyond that body, any more than when it passes through air. This is what happens when, for example, vision passes through glass with its natural color (that is, in which there is no admixture of another color) or through perfectly pure water or crystal or something of a similar color. But when vision passes through another color—as, for example, through glass that is not its natural color, but to which some other color has been added—it receives the color that it encounters first. Hence, once it has received a color and been affected by it, any other color it encounters is received either less accurately or not at all; as a result, what it reports is the color it first received, either by itself or in conjunction with a color it encounters afterwards. For if vision is altered by a prior color to the full extent of its power to see color, it cannot perceive any other color at the same time; but if it is not altered to the full extent of its power to perceive color, it can perceive another color. For example, if it passes through some body, such as glass, that is so perfectly red that vision itself is completely altered by its redness, it cannot be altered by any other color at the same time. But if it does not find the redness it first encounters to exhaust its power to see color, it is (so to speak) not yet full; it can still take on another color, since its capacity was not satiated by the previous color. Someone who does not know this therefore thinks his vision is reporting that everything it perceives after taking on the first color is either partially or wholly of that same color. And so it happens that the interior sense blames its own shortcoming on the exterior sense.

Similarly, when a straight stick, part of which is in water and part of which is not, is thought to be broken; or when we think we see our own faces in a mirror; or when we think our vision or other senses are reporting that any number of things are otherwise than they really are, it is not the fault of the senses. They are reporting what they can, since that is what they received the power to do. Instead, the blame lies with the judgment of the soul, which does not discriminate well what the senses can or ought to do. To show that this is so would be more troublesome than fruitful for our present purposes, so I don't think we should take up this topic just now. Let it suffice to say that whatever the senses seem to report, whether they do so by their very nature or in virtue of some other cause, they are doing what they ought to. Hence they are acting correctly and doing the truth, and this truth is included in the truth of action.

S: I am happy with your reply, and I don't want you to spend any more time on this question about the senses.

Chapter 7

On the truth of the being[17] of things

T: Now consider whether, apart from the supreme truth, we should understand truth to exist in any thing besides those we examined above.

S: What could that be?

T: Do you think anything is,[18] in any time or place, that is not in the supreme truth and did not receive its being, insofar as it has being, from the supreme truth, or that can be anything other than what it is in the supreme truth?

S: That is unthinkable.

---

17. See the Glossary entry for essence* (sense 4).

18. As often in these dialogues, 'is' includes the meanings 'exists,' 'is a certain way,' and 'is the case.'

T: So whatever is, is truly, insofar as it is what it is in the supreme truth.

S: You can conclude without reservation that everything that is, is truly, since it is nothing other than what it is in the supreme truth.

T: So there is a truth in the being of all things that are, since they are what they are in the supreme truth.

S: I recognize that there is truth in their being in such a way that there can be no falsehood there, since whatever is falsely, is not.

T: Well said! But tell me whether anything ought to be different from what it is in the supreme truth.

S: No.

T: Therefore, if all things are what they are in the supreme truth, they are undoubtedly what they ought to be.

S: Indeed they are.

T: Now whatever is what it ought to be, is correct.[19]

S: It could not be otherwise.

T: So everything that is, is correct.

S: Nothing could be more logical.

T: So if both truth and rectitude are in the being of things because they are what they are in the supreme truth, it is clear that the truth of things is their rectitude.

S: Nothing could be plainer than the soundness of your argument.

Chapter 8

On the various meanings of 'ought' and 'ought not,' 'can' and 'cannot'

But how can we say, with respect to the truth of a thing, that whatever is ought to be, since there are many evil deeds that certainly ought not to be?

T: How is it surprising that the same thing both ought to be and ought not to be?

S: How can that be the case?

---

19. Literally, "is correctly." I could use "exists correctly," but the context makes clear that Anselm is not using the verb *esse* ('to be') solely to denote existence. Something can be what it ought to be, not merely by existing, but by being in the place it ought to be, having the characteristics it ought to have, and so on.

T: I know you do not doubt that nothing is at all, unless God either causes or permits it.

S: There is nothing I am more certain of.

T: Will you dare to say that God causes or permits anything unwisely or badly?

S: On the contrary, I contend that God always acts wisely and well.

T: Do you think that something caused or permitted by such great goodness and wisdom ought not to be?

S: What intelligent person would dare to think that?

T: Therefore, both what comes about because God causes it and what comes about because God permits it ought equally to be.

S: What you are saying is obviously true.

T: Then tell me whether you think the effect of an evil will ought to be.

S: That's the same as asking whether an evil deed ought to be, and no sensible person would concede that.

T: And yet God permits some people to perform the evil deeds that their evil wills choose.

S: If only he did not permit it so often!

T: Then the same thing both ought to be and ought not to be. It ought to be in that God, without whose permission it could not come about, acts wisely and well in permitting it; but if we consider the one whose evil will instigates the action, it ought not to be. In this way the Lord Jesus, who alone was innocent, ought not to have suffered death, and no one ought to have inflicted death on him; and yet he ought to have suffered death, in that he himself wisely and generously and usefully willed to suffer it. There are, after all, many ways in which one and the same thing takes on contrary attributes when considered in different ways. This often happens in the case of an action: for example, punishment.[20] Punishment involves both an agent and a patient, so it can be called both an action and a passion.[21] Even though

---

20. Anselm actually speaks of a blow (*percussio*). But the argument that follows, if it is to be rendered into English intelligibly, requires a noun with a cognate verb; that verb in turn must have a participle that is distinct in form from the noun. (The latter requirement rules out 'striking' and 'beating,' which appear in other translations.) 'Punishment,' with 'punish' and 'punishing' available, fits the bill, and is close enough in sense to *percussio* to allow me to keep intact the example Anselm uses in the last paragraph of this speech.

21. 'Patient' and 'passion' are technical terminology. A patient is someone who is on the receiving end of an action, as opposed to the agent, who performs the action. A passion is

'action' and 'punishment' and similar words that are derived from passive participles are used with an active signification, they seem to belong more to the patient than to the agent. In referring to that which acts, it would seem more appropriate to speak of 'acting' or 'punishing,' and to use 'action' and 'punishment' in speaking of that which undergoes the action. For 'acting' and 'punishing' get their name from the one who acts and punishes, as foresight gets its name from the one who foresees and restraint from the one who restrains—and those who act, punish, foresee, and restrain are active; by contrast, 'action' and 'punishment' are derived from those who are acted upon and punished, and they are passive.[22] But since—to give you one example from which you will understand the rest—just as there is not someone who punishes unless there is also someone who is punished, nor someone punished without someone who punishes, so punishing and punishment cannot exist without each other. Indeed, they are one and the same thing under different names, depending on the different roles being signified. That's why punishment is said to belong to both the one who punishes and the one who is punished.

Hence, one and the same action will be evaluated in the same or in opposite ways for the agent and the patient, according to whether the agent and patient themselves are evaluated in the same or in opposite ways. Therefore, when the one who punishes punishes correctly, and the one who is punished is punished correctly—as when a sinner is corrected by one with the authority to correct him—the action is correct on both sides, since on both sides there ought to be punishment. By contrast, when a just man is punished by a wicked man, since the just man ought not to be punished and the wicked man ought not to punish, the action is not correct on either side, since there ought not to be punishment on either side. But when a sinner is punished by someone who lacks the authority to punish him, it cannot be denied that the punishment is both correct and not correct, since it both ought to be and ought not to be: for the sinner ought to be punished, but this man ought not to punish him. But if you look to the judgment of the supreme Wisdom and Goodness and ask whether the punishment ought not to be (whether on one side only or on the part of both agent and patient), who would dare to deny that what is permitted by such great Wisdom and Goodness ought to be?

---

an undergoing as opposed to an action, which is a doing. If A punishes B, A is the agent and B the patient; A's punishing B is an action, and B's being punished by A is a passion.

22. Literally: "For [the nouns] 'acting' and 'striking' get their name from [the present participles] 'acting' and 'striking,' as [the noun] 'foresight' gets its name from [the present participle] 'foreseeing' and [the noun] 'restraint' from [the present participle] 'restraining'—and [the participles] 'acting,' 'striking,' 'foreseeing,' and 'restraining' are active; by contrast, [the nouns] 'action' (*actio*) and 'blow' (*percussio*) are derived from [the participles] *actum* and *percussum*, which are passive."

S: Let him deny it who dares; I certainly do not dare.

T: And what if you are thinking in terms of the nature of things: Would you say that when iron nails were driven into the Lord's body, his feeble flesh ought not to have been pierced, or that, once pierced by the sharp iron, he ought not to have suffered pain?

S: I would be speaking against nature.

T: So it can happen that according to nature an action or passion ought to be, while with respect to the agent or patient it ought not to be, since the agent ought not to do it and the patient ought not to undergo it.

S: I can't deny any of that.

T: Do you see, then, that it can happen quite often that the same action both ought to be and ought not to be, when considered in different ways?

S: You are showing this so clearly that I cannot fail to see it.

T: Now one thing I want you to know is that 'ought' and 'ought not' are sometimes used improperly*: for example, if I say that I ought to be loved by you. For if it's true that I ought to be loved by you, then I am under an obligation to do what I ought,[23] and I am at fault if I am not loved by you.

S: That follows.

T: But when I ought to be loved by you, the love is not to be demanded from me but from you.

S: I must admit that's true.

T: So when I say that I ought to be loved by you, it does not mean that there is something I ought to do, but that you ought to love me. Similarly, when I say that I ought not to be loved by you, this is understood to mean simply that you ought not to love me. We talk about abilities and inabilities in the same way: for example, if someone says that Hector was able to be defeated by Achilles, and Achilles was not able to be defeated by Hector. After all, the ability was not in the one who was able to be defeated, but in the one who was able to defeat him; nor was the inability in the one who could not be defeated, but in the one who could not defeat him.

S: I like what you're saying. In fact, I think it is useful to understand this.

T: You're right to think so.

---

23. Literally, "I am one who is indebted to pay back what I owe": the Latin plays on the fact that *debere* means both 'owe' and 'ought,' and that the noun *debitor* (debtor, one who is indebted) can mean 'one who has an obligation.'

Chapter 9

That every action signifies something true or false

But let's return to the truth of signification, which I began with in order to lead you from the better-known to the less well-known. For everyone talks about the truth of signification, but few consider the truth that is in the being of things.

S: Your leading me in that order has been a great help to me.

T: Then let us see how widespread the truth of signification is. For there is true and false signification not only in what we usually call signs, but also in all the other things we have discussed. After all, since no one should do anything but what he ought to do, by the very fact that someone does something, he says and signifies that he ought to do it. And if he ought to do what he does, he says something true; but if he ought not, he lies.

S: I think I understand, but since I have never heard this before, explain more clearly what you mean.

T: Suppose you were in a place where you knew there were both healthful and deadly herbs, but you didn't know how to tell them apart. And suppose someone were there who you did not doubt knew how to tell them apart, and when you asked him which were healthful and which deadly, he said that certain ones were healthful but then ate others. Which would you believe more: his words or his action?

S: I would believe his action more than his words.

T: Then he would have told you which were healthful by his action more than by his words.

S: That's true.

T: Similarly, if you didn't know that one ought not to lie, and someone lied in your presence, then even if he told you that he ought not to lie, he would tell you by his action that he ought to lie more than he would tell you by his words that he ought not. Likewise, when someone thinks or wills something, if you didn't know whether he ought to think or will it, then if you could see his will and thought, he would signify to you by that very action that he ought to think and will it. Now if he in fact ought to think or will it, he would be saying something true; but if not, he would be lying. And similarly, there is also true and false signification in the being of things, since by the very fact that something is, it says that it ought to be.

S: Now I see clearly what I had never realized before.

T: Let's go on to what remains.

S: You lead, and I'll follow.

Chapter 10

On the supreme truth

T: You will surely not deny that the supreme truth is rectitude.

S: Indeed, I cannot acknowledge it to be anything else.

T: Note that, while all the rectitudes discussed earlier are rectitudes because the things in which they exist either are or do what they ought, the supreme truth is not a rectitude because it ought to be or do anything. For all things are under obligations to it, but it is under no obligation to anything.[24] Nor is there any reason why it is what it is, except that it is.

S: I understand.

T: Do you also see that this rectitude is the cause of all other truths and rectitudes, and nothing is the cause of it?

S: I see that, and I notice that some of these other truths and rectitudes are merely effects, while others are both causes and effects. For example, the truth that is in the being of things is an effect of the supreme truth, and it is in turn a cause of the truth of thoughts and statements; and the latter two truths are not a cause of any other truth.

T: You have understood this well. Hence, you can now understand how I used the truth of statements in my *Monologion* to prove that the supreme truth has no beginning or end. For when I asked, "when was it not true that something was going to exist?"[25] I didn't mean that this statement, asserting that something was going to exist in the future, was itself without a beginning, or that this truth was God. Instead I meant that it is inconceivable that this statement could ever have been uttered without its also possessing truth. Therefore, since it is inconceivable that that truth could fail to exist if the statement existed in which that truth could exist, we understand that the truth which is the first cause of this truth existed without a beginning. After all, the truth of a statement could not always exist if

---

24. More literally: "the supreme truth is not a rectitude because it owes something. For all things owe [something] to it, but it owes nothing to anything." Recall that 'ought' and 'owe' are the same word in Latin.

25. Chapter 18 in the *Monologion*, as quoted at the beginning of the dialogue.

its cause did not always exist. For a statement that says something will exist in the future is not true unless in fact something will exist in the future; and nothing will exist in the future unless it exists in the supreme truth. The same reasoning applies to a statement that says something existed in the past. Since it is inconceivable that this statement, if uttered, could lack truth, it must be the case that the supreme cause of its truth cannot be understood to have an end. For what makes it true to say that something existed in the past is the fact that something really did exist in the past; and the reason something existed in the past is that this is how things are in the supreme truth. Therefore, if it was never possible for it not to be true that something was going to exist, and it will never be possible for it not to be true that something existed in the past, it is impossible for the supreme truth ever to have had a beginning or ever to have an end.

S: I see no way to object to your reasoning.

Chapter 11

On the definition of truth

T: Let's return to the investigation of truth that we have begun.

S: All of this is relevant to investigating truth, but return to what you wish.

T: Then tell me whether you think there is any other rectitude besides those we have discussed.

S: I don't think there is any, except that which is in corporeal things, which is very different from those we have discussed—for example, the rectitude[26] of a stick.

T: In what way do you think this differs from those?

S: In that this can be known through corporeal vision, whereas the others are perceived by reason.

T: Can't that rectitude of bodies* be understood and known through reason apart from the subject?[27] If, when a body is not present, you are in doubt whether its surface is straight, and it can be shown that it is not curved in any place, are you not grasping by reason that it must be straight?

---

26. That is, straightness.

27. "the subject": the physical object that has the property in question (in this case, straightness).

S: Certainly. But this same rectitude that is understood by reason in this way is also perceived by vision in the subject. The others, however, can be perceived only by the mind.

T: Then if I'm not mistaken, we can define truth as rectitude perceptible only by the mind.

S: I don't see any way someone saying that could be mistaken. For this definition of truth contains neither more nor less than it should, since the term 'rectitude' distinguishes truth from everything that is not called rectitude, and the phrase 'perceptible only by the mind' distinguishes it from visible rectitude.

Chapter 12

On the definition of justice

But since you have taught me that all truth is rectitude, and rectitude seems to me to be the same thing as justice, teach me also what I should understand justice to be. It seems, after all, that if it is right for something to be,[28] it is also just for it to be; and conversely, if it is just for something to be, it is also right for it to be. For it seems to be both just and right for fire to be hot and for all human beings to love those who love them. Indeed, if—as I believe—whatever ought to be is right and just, and nothing is right and just but what ought to be, then justice cannot be anything other than rectitude. Certainly justice and rectitude are the same in the supreme and simple* Nature, although he is not just and right because he is under any obligation.

T: So if justice is nothing other than rectitude, you have your definition of justice. And since we are speaking of the rectitude that is perceptible only by the mind, truth and rectitude and justice are all inter-defined, so that someone who knows one and not the others can attain knowledge of those he doesn't know through the one he does know. Or rather, someone who knows one cannot fail to know the others.

S: What then? Shall we say that a stone is just when it seeks to go from higher to lower, since it is doing what it ought to, in the same way that we say human beings are just when they do what they ought to?

T: We don't generally call something 'just' on the basis of that sort of justice.

S: Then why is a human being any more just than a stone is, if both act justly?

---

28. Here again, 'to be' includes the meanings 'to exist,' 'to be a certain way,' and 'to be the case.'

T: Don't you think what the human being does differs in some way from what the stone does?

S: I know that the human being acts spontaneously,[29] whereas the stone acts naturally* and not spontaneously.

T: That is why the stone is not called just: something that does what it ought to is not just unless it wills what it does.

S: Then shall we say that a horse is just when it wills to graze, since it willingly does what it ought to?

T: I did not say that something is just if it willingly does what it ought to, but that something is not just if it does not willingly do what it ought to.

S: Then tell me who is just.

T: I see that you are looking for a definition of the justice that deserves praise, just as its opposite, injustice, deserves reproach.

S: That's what I'm looking for.

T: Clearly that justice is not in any nature that is not aware of rectitude. For whatever does not will rectitude, even if it in fact retains rectitude, does not deserve praise for retaining it, and what does not know rectitude cannot will it.

S: That's true.

T: So the rectitude that wins praise for the one who retains it exists only in a rational nature, since only a rational nature perceives the rectitude of which we are speaking.

S: That follows.

T: Therefore, since all justice is rectitude, the justice that makes praiseworthy the one who preserves it does not exist anywhere at all except in rational natures.

S: That must be right.

T: Where, then, do you think this justice exists in human beings, who are rational?

S: Either in the will, or in knowledge, or in action.

T: If someone understands correctly or acts correctly, but does not will correctly, will anyone praise him for his justice?

S: No.

---

29. 'Spontaneously' is used as a technical term in this translation; the word does not have the connotations it has in ordinary usage. For a definition, see the Glossary.

T: Therefore, this justice is not rectitude of knowledge or rectitude of action, but rectitude of will.

S: It is either that or nothing.

T: Do you think we have reached an adequate definition of the justice we're investigating?

S: You had better say.

T: Do you think everyone who wills what he ought to wills correctly and has rectitude of will?

S: If someone unknowingly wills what he ought to—for example, if someone wills to lock the door against one who, unbeknownst to him, intends to kill someone in the house—then whether or not he has *some* rectitude of will, he doesn't have the rectitude of will we're asking about.

T: What do you say about someone who knows that he ought to will what he wills?

S: It can turn out that someone who knowingly wills what he ought to is also unwilling to be under that obligation. For example, if a robber is forced to give back the money he stole, he clearly does not will to be under that obligation, since he is forced to give it back because he ought to. But in no way does he deserve praise for this rectitude.

T: Someone who gives food to a starving pauper for the sake of an empty reputation[30] wills that he be under the obligation to will what he in fact wills. For he is praised because he wills to do what he ought to. What do you think about him?

S: His rectitude does not deserve praise, and so it is not sufficient for the justice we're asking about. But show me now what *is* sufficient.

T: Every will not only wills something but wills for the sake of something. Now just as we must examine what it wills, so also we must understand why it wills. In fact, a will should not be correct because it wills what it ought to will more so than because it wills it for the reason it ought to will. Hence, every will has a what and a why. For we do not will anything at all unless there is a reason why we will it.

S: We all recognize this in ourselves.

---

30. "for the sake of an empty reputation": *propter inanem gloriam.* Someone who gives food *propter inanem gloriam* does so in order to win praise for his generosity when in fact he is not generous but self-seeking. Anselm says that such a person "wills that he be under the obligation to will what he in fact wills" because if he were under no such obligation, he could not win praise for doing as he ought to do. Since he clearly wills the praise, he must also will the obligation.

T: But what do you think is the *why* on account of which everyone must will whatever he wills, if he is to have a praiseworthy will? *What* everyone must will is clear, after all, since someone who does not will what he ought to is not just.

S: It seems no less obvious to me that just as everyone must will *what* he ought, so also everyone must will it *because* he ought, in order for his will to be just.

T: You correctly grasp that these two things are necessary for the will to have justice: to will what it ought to, and because it ought to. But are they sufficient?

S: Why wouldn't they be?

T: Suppose someone wills what he ought because he is compelled, and he is compelled because he ought to will it. Doesn't he in a certain sense will what he ought to, because he ought to?

S: I cannot deny it. But he wills it in one way, and the just man in quite another.

T: Distinguish these two ways.

S: When the just man wills what he ought, he does not—insofar as he deserves to be called just—preserve rectitude for the sake of anything other than rectitude itself. But someone who wills what he ought only because he is compelled, or because he is bribed by some extraneous reward, preserves rectitude not for its own sake, but for the sake of something else—if he should be said to preserve rectitude at all.

T: Then a will is just when it preserves its rectitude for the sake of that rectitude itself.

S: Either such a will is just, or no will is.

T: Then justice is rectitude of will preserved for its own sake.

S: That is indeed the definition of justice for which I was looking.

T: Now consider whether perhaps something in it needs correcting.

S: I see nothing in it that needs to be corrected.

T: Neither do I, since there is no justice that is not rectitude, and no rectitude other than rectitude of will is called justice in its own right. For rectitude of action is called justice, but only when the action proceeds from a correct will. Rectitude of will, on the other hand, is always entitled to be called justice, even if it is impossible for what we correctly will to come about.

Now the use of the word 'preserved' might prompt someone to say that if rectitude of will is to be called justice only when it is preserved, then it is not justice as soon as we have it, and we do not receive justice when we receive rectitude of will; rather, we cause it to be justice by preserving it. After all, we receive and have rectitude of will before we preserve it. For we do not receive or initially have it because we preserve it; instead, we begin to preserve it because we have received it and have it.

But in response we can say that we simultaneously receive both the willing and the having of rectitude. For we have it only in virtue of willing it, and if we will it we thereby have it. Now just as we simultaneously have it and will it, so also we simultaneously will it and preserve it. For just as we do not preserve it except when we will it, so also there is no time at which we will it but do not preserve it; on the contrary, as long as we will it, we preserve it, and as long as we preserve it, we will it. Therefore, since we both will it and have it at the same time, we both will it and preserve it at the same time. Necessarily, we simultaneously receive both the having and the preserving of rectitude. And just as we have it as long as we preserve it, so also we preserve it as long as we have it. Nor does any absurdity follow from these statements. Indeed, just as the receiving of this rectitude is prior* in nature to having or willing it (since neither having nor willing it is the cause of receiving it, but receiving it is the cause of willing and having it) and yet receiving it is temporally simultaneous with having and willing it (since we simultaneously begin to receive it, to have it, and to will it, and no sooner do we receive it than we have it and will it), so also having or willing it, although prior in nature to preserving it, is nonetheless temporally simultaneous with preserving it. Hence, the one from whom we simultaneously receive the having, the willing, and the preserving of rectitude of will is also the one from whom we receive justice; and as soon as we have and will that rectitude of will, it is rightly called "justice."

Now the last phrase we added, "for its own sake," is so essential that rectitude is in no way justice unless it is preserved for its own sake.

S: I can't think of any objection.

T: Do you think this definition can be applied to the supreme Justice—insofar as we can talk about a thing about which nothing, or hardly anything, can be said properly*?

S: Although in him will and rectitude are not distinct, still, just as we speak of the power of divinity or the divine power or powerful divinity even though in the divinity power is nothing other than divinity, so also it is appropriate for us to speak of God's rectitude of will or voluntary rectitude or upright will. And we cannot so fittingly say of any other rectitude as we can of his that it is preserved for its own sake. For just as nothing else preserves that rectitude but itself, and it preserves itself *through* nothing else but itself, so also it preserves itself *for the sake of* nothing but itself.

T: Then we can unhesitatingly say that justice is rectitude of will that is preserved for its own sake. And since we have no present passive participle of the verb 'preserve,' we can use the perfect passive participle of the same verb in place of the present.[31]

S: It is extremely common for us to use perfect passive participles in place of the present passive participles that Latin doesn't have. Similarly, Latin has no perfect participles for active and neuter[32] verbs, so in place of the perfect participles that it doesn't have, it uses present participles. For example, I might say of someone, "that which he learned studying and reading, he doesn't teach unless forced." That is, "what he learned when he studied and read, he does not teach unless he is forced."[33]

T: Then we were right to say that justice is rectitude of will preserved for its own sake—that is, rectitude of will that is being preserved for its own sake. This is why the just are sometimes called "upright in heart," that is, upright in will, and sometimes simply "upright" without the addition of "in heart," since no one else is understood to be upright but those who have an upright will: for example, "Rejoice, all you upright in heart"[34] and "The upright will see and be glad."[35]

S: You have made the definition of justice clear enough even for children. Let's pass on to other things.

---

31. English, however, is better equipped with participles; the present passive participle is "being preserved." Anselm's point is best explained as follows: because of the lack of a present passive participle in Latin, the phrase "rectitude of will preserved for its own sake" is ambiguous. It can mean either "rectitude of will that is being preserved for its own sake" or "rectitude of will that has been (or was) preserved for its own sake." In his definition of justice, Anselm means us to understand the phrase in the first way.

32. By 'neuter' verbs Anselm seems to mean intransitive verbs that are active in form. 'Study' (*studere*) is an example of a neuter verb and 'read' (*legere*) of an active verb.

33. The differences between English and Latin grammar again make Anselm's point obscure. In his sample sentence, 'studying' and 'reading' are both present participles, while 'forced' is a past ("perfect") participle. His point is that, since the studying and the reading were in the past, whereas the being-forced is in the present, it would be more accurate to use the perfect participles of 'study' and 'read' and the present participle of 'force' rather than vice versa—the only problem being that Latin does not *have* those participles. Once again, English is better supplied: the relevant participles are 'having studied,' 'having read,' and 'being forced.'

34. Psalm 32:11 (31:11).

35. Psalm 107:42 (106:42).

Chapter 13

That there is one truth in all true things

T: Let's return to rectitude or, in other words, truth—since we are speaking of rectitude perceptible only by the mind, these two words, 'rectitude' and 'truth,' signify one thing, which is the genus* of justice—and ask whether there is only one truth in all the things in which we say there is truth, or whether there are several* truths, just as there are several things in which (as we have established) there is truth.

S: I very much want to know that.

T: It has been established that in whatever thing there is truth, that truth is nothing other than rectitude.

S: I don't doubt it.

T: So if there are several truths corresponding to the several things in which there is truth, there are also several rectitudes.

S: That is no less certain.

T: If there must be diverse rectitudes corresponding to the diversities of things, then these rectitudes have their being in virtue of the things themselves; and as the things in which they exist change, the rectitudes must also change.

S: Show me one example involving something in which we say there is rectitude, so that I can understand it in others as well.

T: I am saying that if the rectitude of signification differs from rectitude of will because the one is in the will and the other in signification, then rectitude of signification has its being because of signification and varies according to signification.

S: So it does. For when a statement signifies that what-is is, or that what-is-not is not, the signification is correct; and it has been established that this is the rectitude without which there is no correct signification. If, however, the statement signifies that what-is-not is, or that what-is is not, or if it signifies nothing at all, there will be no rectitude of signification, which exists only in signification. Hence, the rectitude of signification has its being through signification and changes along with it, just as color has its being and non-being through body.* For when a body exists, its color must exist; and if the body ceases to exist, its color cannot remain.

T: Color is not related to body in the same way that rectitude is related to signification.

S: Explain the difference.

T: If no one wills to signify by any sign what ought to be signified, will there be any signification by means of signs?

S: No.

T: And will it therefore not be right for what-ought-to-be-signified to be signified?

S: It will not be any less right, nor will rectitude demand it any less.

T: Therefore, even when signification doesn't exist, the rectitude in virtue of which it is right for what-ought-to-be-signified to be signified, and by which this is demanded, does not cease to exist.

S: If that rectitude ceased to exist, this would not be right, and rectitude would not demand it.

T: Do you think that when what-ought-to-be-signified is signified, the signification is correct on account of and in accordance with this very rectitude?

S: Indeed, I cannot think otherwise. For if the signification is correct through some other rectitude, there is nothing to keep it from being correct even if this rectitude ceases to exist. But in fact there is no correct signification that signifies what it is not right to signify, or what rectitude does not demand.

T: Then no signification is correct through any rectitude other than that which remains even when signification ceases.

S: That's clear.

T: So when rectitude is present in signification, it's not because rectitude begins to exist in signification when someone signifies that what-is is, or that what-is-not is not; instead, it's because at that time signification comes about in accordance with a rectitude that always exists. And when rectitude is absent from signification, it's not because rectitude ceases to exist when signification is not what it should be or there is no signification at all; instead, it's because at that time signification falls away from a rectitude that never fails. Don't you see that?

S: I see it so clearly that I cannot fail to see it.

T: Therefore, the rectitude by which signification is called correct does not have its being or any change because of signification, no matter how signification itself might change.

S: Nothing is clearer to me now.

T: Can you prove that color is related to body in the same way that rectitude is related to signification?

S: I am more apt now to prove that they are very dissimilar.

T: I think you now realize what the proper view is about the will and its rectitude, and about the other things that ought to have rectitude.

S: I fully understand that this very argument proves that however those other things may be, rectitude itself remains unchangeable.

T: Then what do you think follows concerning those rectitudes? Do they differ from one another, or is there one and the same rectitude for all things?

S: I admitted earlier that if there are several* rectitudes because there are several things in which they are observed, they must exist and change in accordance with those things; and it has been demonstrated that this does not happen at all. So it is not the case that there are several rectitudes because there are several things in which they exist.

T: Do you have any other reason for thinking that there are several rectitudes, other than the fact that there are several things in which they exist?

S: Not only do I realize that that's no reason, I also see that no other reason can be found.

T: Then there is one and the same rectitude for all things.

S: So I must acknowledge.

T: Furthermore, if there is rectitude in the things that ought to have it only because they are as they ought to be, and if this is precisely what it is for them to be correct, then it is evident that there is only this one rectitude for all of them.

S: Undeniably.

T: Therefore, there is one truth in all of them.

S: That, too, is undeniable. But explain this: Why do we speak of the truth *of* this or that particular thing as if we were distinguishing different truths, when in fact there aren't different truths for different things? Many people will hardly grant that there is no difference between the truth of the will and what is called the truth of action, or of one of the others.

T: Truth is said improperly* to be *of* this or that thing, since truth does not have its being in or from or through the things in which it is said to be. But when things themselves are[36] in accordance with truth, which is always present to those things that are as they ought to be, we speak of the truth of this or that thing—for example, the truth of the will or of action—in the same way in which we speak of the time of this or that thing despite the fact that there is one and the same time for all things that are temporally simultaneous, and that if this or that thing did

---

36. Again, 'are' includes the meanings 'exist,' 'are a certain way,' and 'are the case.'

not exist, there would still be time. For we do not speak of the time of this or that thing because time is in the things, but because they are in time. And just as time regarded in itself is not called the time of some particular thing, but we speak of the time of this or that thing when we consider the things that are in time, so also the supreme truth as it subsists in itself is not the truth of some particular thing, but when something is in accordance with it, then it is called the truth or rectitude of that thing.

ON FREEDOM OF CHOICE

Chapters

Chapter 1

That the power to sin does not belong to freedom of choice

STUDENT: Since free choice seems to be incompatible with the grace, predestination, and foreknowledge of God, I want to know what this freedom of choice is, and whether we always have it. For if freedom of choice is "the ability to sin and not to sin," as some are accustomed to say, and we always have that ability, then how is it that we ever need grace? On the other hand, if we do not always have it, why is sin imputed* to us when we sin without free choice?

TEACHER: I don't think freedom of choice is the power to sin and not to sin. After all, if this were its definition, then neither God nor the angels, who cannot sin, would have free choice—which it is impious to say.

S: Why not say that the free choice of God and the good angels is one thing, and our free choice is quite another?

T: Even though human free choice differs from that of God and the good angels, the definition of the word 'freedom' should still be the same for both. For example, even though one animal differs from another, whether substantially* or accidentally,* the definition of the word 'animal' is the same for all animals. Therefore, we ought to offer a definition of freedom of choice that contains neither more nor less than freedom; and since the free choice of God and the good angels cannot sin, "the ability to sin" does not belong in the definition of freedom of choice.

And finally, the power to sin is neither freedom nor a part of freedom—to understand this clearly, pay close attention to what I am about to say.

S: That's why I'm here.

T: Which will do you think is freer: one whose willing and ability not to sin are such that it cannot be turned away from the rectitude of not sinning, or one that in some way can be turned to sin?

S: I don't see why a will isn't freer when it is capable of both.

T: Do you not see that someone who has what is fitting and expedient in such a way that he cannot lose it is freer than someone who has it in such a way that he can lose it and be seduced into what is unfitting and inexpedient?

S: I don't think anyone would doubt that.

T: And you will say that it is no less indubitable that sinning is always unfitting and harmful.

S: No one in his right mind thinks otherwise.

T: Then a will that cannot fall away from the rectitude of not sinning is freer than a will that can abandon that rectitude.

S: I don't think anything could be more reasonably asserted.

T: Now if something diminishes freedom if it is added and increases freedom if taken away, do you think that it is either freedom or a part of freedom?

S: I cannot think so.

T: Then the power to sin, which if added to the will diminishes its freedom and if taken away increases it, is neither freedom nor a part of freedom.

S: Nothing could be more logical.

Chapter 2

That nonetheless, angels and human beings sinned through this power and through free choice; and although they were able to be slaves to sin, sin was not able to master them

T: So what is extraneous to freedom in this way does not belong to freedom of choice.

S: I cannot rebut your arguments at all, but it strikes me quite forcefully that in the beginning both the angelic nature and our own had the power to sin—if they had not had it, they would not have sinned. But if both human beings and angels sinned through this power, which is extraneous in this way to free choice, how can we say they sinned through free choice? And if they did not sin through free choice, it seems they sinned out of necessity. After all, they sinned either spontaneously* or out of necessity. And if they sinned spontaneously, how was it not through free choice? So if it was *not* through free choice, they apparently sinned out of necessity.

And there is something else that worries me about this power to sin. Someone who has the power to sin can be a slave to sin, since "one who commits sin is a slave to sin."[37] But someone who can be a slave to sin can be mastered by sin. In what way, then, was that nature created free, and what sort of free choice did it have, given that it could be mastered by sin?

T: It was through the power of sinning, and spontaneously, and through free choice, and not out of necessity that our nature,* and that of the angels, first sinned

---

37. John 8:34.

and were able to be slaves to sin; and yet sin was not able to master them in such a way that either they or their choice could be said not to be free.

S: I need you to explain that, because it's obscure to me.

T: The fallen angel and the first human being sinned through free choice, since they sinned through their own choice, which was so free that it could not be compelled to sin by any other thing. And so they are justly reproached, since, having this freedom of choice, they sinned: not because any other thing compelled them, and not out of any necessity, but spontaneously. They sinned through their choice, which was free; but they did not sin through that in virtue of which it was free, that is, through the power by which it was able not to sin and not to be a slave to sin. Instead, they sinned through that power they had for sinning; by that power they were neither helped into the freedom not to sin nor coerced into slavery to sin.

Now as for what you thought was the implication of their being able to be slaves to sin—namely, that sin was able to master them, and so neither they nor their choice was free—that doesn't follow. For if someone has the power not to be a slave, and no one else has the power to make him a slave, although he can be a slave through his own power, then as long as he exercises his power not to be a slave rather than his power to be a slave, nothing can master him and make him a slave. Suppose a free rich man can make himself the slave of a poor man. As long as he does not do so, he is still entitled to be called 'free,' and we don't say that the poor man is able to master him—or if we do say this, we say it improperly,* since it is not in the poor man's power to make him a slave, but in someone else's power.[38] Therefore, nothing prevents it from being the case that angels and human beings before their sin were free or had free choice.

Chapter 3

In what way they had free choice after they had made themselves slaves to sin, and what free choice is

S: You have convinced me that of course nothing prevents this before their sin, but how could they retain free choice after they had made themselves slaves to sin?

T: Even though they had subjected themselves to sin, they could not destroy the natural freedom of choice within themselves. What they could do, however, was to make themselves unable to exercise that freedom without some additional grace that they had not had before.

---

38. The "someone else" is of course the rich man himself.

S: I believe this, but I want to understand it.

T: Let's first examine what sort of freedom of choice they had before their sin, since it is quite certain that they did in fact have free choice.

S: I'm eager to do so.

T: For what purpose do you think they had this freedom of choice: in order to attain what they willed, or in order to will what they ought to and what was expedient for them to will?

S: In order to will what they ought to and what was expedient to will.

T: So they had freedom of choice for the sake of rectitude of will—since as long as they willed what they ought to, they had rectitude of will.

S: Yes.

T: When we say that they had freedom for the sake of rectitude of will, some ambiguity remains unless we add something. So I ask you this: In what way did they have that freedom for the sake of rectitude of will? Was it in order to attain rectitude without a giver when they did not yet have it; or to receive a rectitude they did not yet have, if it were given to them later so that they might have it; or to abandon the rectitude they had received and then, by their own power, to reclaim what they had abandoned; or to preserve always the rectitude they had received?

S: I do not think they had freedom in order to attain rectitude without a giver, since they were not able to have anything that they did not receive.[39] And we must not say that they had freedom in order to receive from a giver a rectitude they did not yet have, so that they *would* then have it, since we must not believe that they were created without an upright will. Still, we should not deny that they had the freedom to receive that same rectitude if they abandoned it and then were given it back by the one who first gave it to them. We often see this in human beings who by heavenly grace are brought back to righteousness from unrighteousness.

T: You're right that they were able to receive that lost rectitude if they were given it back; but we are asking about the freedom they had before they sinned—since undoubtedly they had free choice—not about a freedom that none of them would need if they never abandoned the truth.

S: Then I'll go on and reply to the other possibilities you asked about. It's not true that they had freedom in order to abandon rectitude, since to abandon rectitude of will is to sin, and you showed earlier[40] that the power to sin is neither freedom nor a

---

39. Cf. 1 Corinthians 4:7: "What do you have that you did not receive?" See also *On the Fall of the Devil*, Chapter 1.

40. In Chapter 1.

part of freedom. And they didn't receive freedom in order to reclaim, by their own power, the rectitude they had abandoned, since this rectitude was given to them in order that they might never abandon it—for indeed, this very power to reclaim the rectitude they had abandoned would engender carelessness about preserving the rectitude they had. The only remaining possibility, then, is that freedom of choice was given to the rational nature in order that it might preserve the rectitude of will it had received.

T: You have replied ably to the questions I asked. But we still need to investigate the purpose for which the rational nature ought to have preserved rectitude. Was it for the sake of rectitude itself, or for the sake of something else?

S: If freedom had not been given to that nature so that it might preserve rectitude of will for the sake of rectitude itself, freedom would not have been the capacity for justice, since it has been established[41] that justice is rectitude of will preserved for its own sake. But we believe that freedom of choice contributes to justice. Therefore, we must unhesitatingly assert that the rational nature received freedom for no other purpose than preserving rectitude of will for the sake of rectitude itself.

T: Therefore, since every freedom is a power, freedom of choice is the power to preserve rectitude of will for the sake of rectitude itself.

S: It can't be anything else.

T: So it is now clear that a free choice is nothing other than a choice that is able to preserve rectitude of will for the sake of rectitude itself.

S: It is indeed clear. Now as long as the rational nature had rectitude, it could preserve what it had. After it has abandoned rectitude, however, how can it preserve what it does not have? Therefore, if there is no rectitude that can be preserved, there is no free choice that can preserve it. For one cannot preserve what one does not have.

T: Even if it lacks rectitude of will, the rational nature nonetheless has what is properly its own. For I believe we have no power that by itself suffices for action. And yet even in the absence of those things without which we can't exercise our powers at all, we are nonetheless said to have those powers within ourselves. In the same way, no instrument is sufficient by itself for any action or task;[42] and

---

41. In *On Truth*, Chapter 12.

42. "Action or task" renders a form of the Latin *operati* (and later, *opus*). These are broad terms that can refer to everything from painting a picture to entertaining an idea. Basically, to exercise any power one has is to *operati*; and the exercise of that power, or the product of that exercise of power, is an *opus*. Anselm makes no clear distinction here between a power and an instrument, and he will soon speak of the power of vision as the "instrument or

yet even in the absence of those things without which we cannot make use of the instrument, we are nonetheless correct to affirm that we have the instrument for some particular action or task. And so that you can understand this in many cases, I will show it to you in one: no one who has vision is said to be entirely unable to see a mountain.

S: Someone who is unable to see a mountain certainly does not have vision.

T: Then someone who has vision has the power and the instrument for seeing a mountain. And yet if there is no mountain there and you say to him, "see the mountain," he will answer you, "I can't, because there's no mountain there. If there were a mountain, I could see it." Similarly, if there were a mountain but no light, and someone instructed him to look at the mountain, he would reply that he couldn't, because there's no light; but if there were light, then he could. Again, if both a mountain and light were present to the person who has vision, but something were interfering with his vision (say, if someone were keeping his eyes shut), he would say that he could not see the mountain; but if nothing were interfering with his vision, then undoubtedly he would have the power to see the mountain.

S: Everyone knows all that.

T: So do you see that the power of seeing some body* is one power in the one who sees, another power in the object to be seen, and another in the medium (that is, neither in the one seeing nor in the thing to be seen); and in the medium there is one power in something that gives aid to vision and another in something that does not impede vision (that is, when nothing that could impede vision actually does so)?

S: I see it clearly.

T: There are, then, these four powers. If any one of them is lacking, the other three cannot accomplish anything, either individually or all together. And yet when the other three are missing, we do not deny that a person who has vision has vision, or the instrument or power for seeing, or that the visible thing can be seen, or that light can aid vision.

---

power for seeing." Elsewhere he speaks of the power of will as the "instrument for willing": see Chapter 7 and *De concordia* 3.11.

Chapter 4

In what way those who do not have rectitude have the power to preserve rectitude

The fourth of these, however, is improperly* called a power. For the only reason we say that something that typically impedes vision gives the power of seeing when it does not impede vision is that it does not take away vision. But the power to see light consists in only three things, since in that case what is seen and what aids vision are the same. Doesn't everyone know this?

S: Certainly.

T: So when there's nothing there for us to see, we're in total darkness, and our eyes are closed or blindfolded, we still have the power to see any visible thing—so far as it pertains to us. What, therefore, is to prevent us from having the power to preserve rectitude of will for the sake of rectitude itself, even in the absence of rectitude, as long as we have reason, by which we can know rectitude, and will, by which we can retain it? For freedom of choice consists of reason and will.

S: You have convinced me that this power of preserving rectitude of will is always present in rational nature, and that this power was free in the choice of the first human being and the angels, from whom rectitude of will could not be taken away against their will.

Chapter 5

That no temptation compels anyone to sin against his will

But how is the choice of the human will *now* free in virtue of this power, given that quite often a person whose will is right abandons that rectitude against his will because he is compelled by temptation?

T: No one abandons rectitude except by willing to do so. Therefore, if 'against one's will' means 'unwillingly,'[43] no one abandons rectitude against his will. For someone can be tied up against his will, since he is unwilling to be tied up; he can be tortured against his will, since he is unwilling to be tortured; he can be killed against his will, since he is unwilling to be killed; but he cannot will against his

---

43. *nolens*: the word most naturally describes someone who performs an action grudgingly or prefers to act otherwise, but Anselm takes it here in the more precise sense of "not willing the action in question."

will, since he cannot will if he is unwilling to will. For everyone who wills, wills his own willing.

S: Then how is it that someone is said to lie against his will when he lies in order to avoid being killed, since he does not lie without willing to lie? For just as it is against his will that he lies, so also it is against his will that he wills to lie. And if it is against his will that he wills to lie, he is unwilling to will to lie.

T: Perhaps he is said to lie against his will because, when he so wills the truth that he lies only for the sake of his life, he both wills the lie for the sake of his life and does *not* will the lie for its own sake, since he wills the truth. And so he lies both willingly and unwillingly. For a will by which we will a thing for its own sake, as when we will health for its own sake, is different from a will by which we will a thing for the sake of something else, as when we will to drink wormwood for the sake of health. Hence, on the basis of these two wills, it could perhaps be said that his lying is both against his will and not against his will. So when he is said to lie against his will because insofar as he wills the truth he does not will to lie, this is not inconsistent with my saying that no one abandons rectitude of will against his will; for in lying, he wills to abandon rectitude of will for the sake of his life. And in virtue of that will he does not abandon rectitude against his will; rather, he abandons it willingly—and that is the will of which we are speaking now. We are, after all, speaking of the will by which he wills to lie for the sake of his life, not of that by which he does not will the lie for its own sake.

Or in any event he certainly lies against his will because it is against his will that he must either lie or be killed—that is, it is against his will that he is in this difficulty, so that of necessity one of these two possibilities must come about. For although it is necessary that he either lie or be killed, it is not necessary that he be killed, since he can avoid being killed if he lies; and it is not necessary that he lie, since he can avoid lying if he is killed. Neither of these is determinately a matter of necessity, since both are in his power. And so although it is against his will that he must either lie or be killed, it does not follow either that he lies against his will or that he is killed against his will.

There is another argument as well that is often used to explain why someone is said to do against his will, unwillingly, and from necessity what he nonetheless does willingly. If it would be difficult to do something, and so we don't do it, we say that we can't do it, and that we abandon it from necessity or against our will. And if it would be difficult to refrain from doing something, and so we do it, we claim to do it against our will, unwillingly, and from necessity. So in this sense someone who lies to avoid death is said to lie against his will, unwillingly, and from necessity, since he cannot avoid the lie without risking death. Therefore, just as someone who lies for the sake of his life is improperly* said to lie against his will, since he is willing to lie, so also it is not properly said that his *willing* to lie is against his will, since he does not will to lie otherwise than willingly. For just as when he lies, he wills that lying, so also when he wills to lie, he wills that willing.

S: I can't deny what you're saying.

T: Then in what way is that will not free, given that no external power[44] can bring it into subjection without its consent?

S: Can't we, by a similar argument, say that the will of a horse is free, since it willingly serves the bodily appetite?

T: The two cases are not similar. In the horse, the will does not subject itself; instead, being subjected naturally,* it always of necessity* serves the bodily appetite. In a human being, by contrast, as long as the will itself is right, it does not serve what it ought not to serve, and is not subjected to what it ought not to be subjected to, and it is not turned aside from rectitude by any external power, unless it willingly consents to what it ought not. And it has this consent, as is clearly seen, not naturally or of necessity, like the horse, but through itself.

S: You have met my objection about the will of the horse. Go back to where we were.

T: Will you deny that something is free from another thing if it cannot be compelled or prevented by that other thing unless it is willing to be?

S: I don't see how I could deny it.

T: Then also explain in what way an upright will is victorious and in what way it is vanquished.

S: To persevere in willing rectitude itself is for it to overcome; to will what it ought not is for it to be overcome.

T: I believe that unless the will itself is willing, temptation cannot keep an upright will from rectitude or compel it to do what it ought not, so that it wills against rectitude and wills what it ought not.

S: Nor can I see any reason to think that's false.

T: Then who can say that a will is not free for preserving rectitude, and free from temptation and sin, if no temptation can turn it aside from rectitude to sin (that is, to willing what it ought not) unless it is willing? Therefore, when it is overcome, it is not overcome by something else's power, but by its own.

S: What has been said shows that.

---

44. "external power": *aliena potestas* (and later, *aliena vis*). Literally, "power belonging to something else."

T: Don't you see that it follows from this that no temptation can overcome an upright will? For if it can, it has a power of overcoming and overcomes by its own power. But that can't be, since the will is overcome solely by its own power. Therefore, temptation cannot in any way overcome an upright will; and when we say that temptation can do this, we are speaking improperly.* For this expression simply means that the will can submit itself to temptation—just as when we say that a weak man can be overcome by a strong man, we are not speaking of his own power but of someone else's, since this simply means that the strong man has the power to overcome the weak.

Chapter 6

In what way our will is powerful against temptations, even though it seems weak

S: Even though I cannot find anything wrong with the arguments by which you make every assault subject to our will and do not permit any temptation to master it, I cannot pretend that there is no weakness in the will, which almost all of us experience when we are overcome by the vehemence of temptation. So unless you show how the power for which you've argued is consistent with the weakness that we feel, my mind can't be at ease with this question.

T: This weakness in the will of which you speak: In what do you think it consists?

S: In the fact that one cannot persevere in clinging to rectitude.

T: If it is because of its weakness that the will does not cling to rectitude, it is turned away from rectitude by some external power.

S: I grant that.

T: And what power is that?

S: The power of temptation.

T: That power does not turn the will away from rectitude unless the will itself wills what temptation has suggested.

S: That's true. But that temptation itself by its power compels the will to will what it has suggested.

T: How does it compel the will to will: in such a way that the will could in fact not will, but only with great difficulty; or in such a way that it is completely unable not to will?

168

S: Although I must admit that we are sometimes so beleaguered by temptations that it would be difficult for us not to will what they suggest, I can't say that they ever overwhelm us to such an extent that we are completely unable not to will what they tell us to will.

T: I don't know how one could say that. For if a human being wills to lie in order to avoid death and preserve his life for a time, who will say that it is impossible for him to will not to lie in order to avoid eternal death and live forever? Hence, you should no longer doubt that this powerlessness[45] to preserve rectitude, which you say we experience in our wills when we consent to temptations, is not a matter of impossibility but of difficulty. For we commonly say that we can't do something, not because it is impossible for us to do it, but because we can do it only with difficulty. But this difficulty does not destroy the will's freedom; it can assail but it cannot defeat an unwilling will. In this way, then, I think you can see how the power of the will, which is vindicated by truthful reasoning, is consistent with the weakness that our humanity experiences. For just as difficulty in no way destroys the will's freedom, so also that weakness—which we say is in the will precisely because it cannot retain its rectitude without difficulty—does not take away the will's power to persevere in rectitude.

Chapter 7

How the will is more powerful[46] than temptation, even when it is overcome by temptation

S: I can't at all deny what you have proved, but I also can't by any means affirm that the will is more powerful than temptation when it is overcome by temptation. After all, if the will to preserve rectitude were more powerful than the onslaught of temptation, the will, in willing what it retains, would resist temptation more powerfully than temptation would assail the will. For the only way I know my will is more or less powerful is that I will more or less powerfully. So when I will what

---

45. "powerlessness": *impotentia*, the same word that is generally translated 'weakness' in this chapter.

46. "more powerful": *fortior*. Anselm relies heavily in this chapter on the adjective *fortis* ('strong,' 'powerful') and various cognates, and ideally an English translation would stick with one word and its cognates. Unfortunately, considerations of English idiom make this impossible. So the reader should bear in mind that *fortis* is translated variously as 'strong,' 'powerful,' and 'forceful'; *fortius* as 'more powerfully' and 'more forcefully'; and *fortitudo* as 'strength' and 'force.'

I ought less powerfully than temptation urges me to do what I ought not, I don't see how temptation is not more powerful than my will.

T: I see that you've been misled by an equivocation on the word 'will.'

S: I would like to understand that equivocation.

T: 'Will' is said equivocally in much the same way as 'sight.' We use the word 'sight' to refer to the instrument for seeing, that is, the ray proceeding through the eyes by which we see light and things that are in light; we also use it to refer to the activity[47] of that instrument when we make use of it, that is, vision. Similarly, we use the word 'will' to refer to the instrument for willing, which is in the soul, and which we direct to willing this or that, just as we direct sight to seeing various things; and we also use it to refer to the exercise of the will that is the instrument for willing, just as we use the word 'sight' to refer to the exercise of the sight that is the instrument for seeing.[48] Now we have the sight that is the instrument for seeing even when we are not seeing anything, whereas the sight that is its activity is in us only when we are seeing something. Similarly, the will that is the instrument for willing is always in the soul, even when it is not willing anything—for example, when one is asleep—but we have the will that I am calling the exercise or activity of that instrument only when we are willing something. So the will that I am calling the instrument for willing is always one and the same, no matter what we will; but the will that is its activity is as multifarious as the many objects and occasions of our willing—just as the sight that we have even in darkness or with our eyes closed is always the same, no matter what we see, whereas the sight that is its activity, which is also called vision, is as various as the varied objects and occasions of our seeing.

S: I clearly understand and admire this distinction between two senses of 'will,' and I think I now realize the error I fell into because I didn't know it. Still, go on with what you've begun.

T: Then since you understand that there are two wills, the instrument for willing and its activity, in which of these two do you think the strength of willing resides?

S: In the will that is the instrument for willing.

T: Suppose you know a man who is so strong that if he restrains a wild bull, the bull can't move, and you see him restraining a ram in such a way that the ram breaks free from his grasp. Will you think that he is less strong in restraining the ram than in restraining the bull?

---

47. "activity": *opus*. See note 42.

48. Cf. *De concordia* 3.11, in which Anselm distinguishes three different senses of 'will.'

S: I will judge that he is equally strong in either action, but I will acknowledge that he is not using his strength equally, since he acts more forcefully on the bull than on the ram. The man is strong because he has strength, whereas his action is called strong because it is done forcefully.

T: In the same way you must understand that the will I am calling the instrument for willing has an inseparable strength, insuperable by any external power, which it sometimes uses more and sometimes less in willing. Hence, it by no means abandons what it wills more forcefully when it is offered what it wills less forcefully; and when it is offered what it wills more forcefully, it immediately lets go of what it does not will with equal force. And then the will—which we can call the activity of this instrument, since it is actively at work when it wills something—this will as activity, I say, is called more or less strong as the action is done more or less forcefully.

S: I must admit that what you have explained is quite clear to me now.

T: Then you see that when a human being assailed by temptation abandons his rectitude of will, he is not torn away from rectitude by any external power; rather, his will turns itself to that which he wills more forcefully.

Chapter 8

That not even God can take away rectitude of will

S: Can God, at any rate, take away rectitude from the will?

T: You must understand in what sense he can't. He can indeed reduce to nothing the whole substance that he has made from nothing, but he cannot take away rectitude from a will that has it.

S: I am very eager for you to offer an argument for this claim of yours, which I have never heard before.

T: We are speaking of the rectitude of will in virtue of which a will is called just: that is, rectitude that is preserved for its own sake. Now no will is just unless it wills what God wills it to will.

S: One that does not will this is clearly unjust.

T: Then for any will that preserves rectitude, its preserving rectitude of will for the sake of rectitude itself is the same as its willing what God wills it to will.

S: So one must acknowledge.

T: If God takes away this rectitude from someone's will, he does so either willingly or unwillingly.

S: He cannot do so unwillingly.

T: So if he takes away rectitude from someone's will, he wills what he does.

S: Undoubtedly.

T: So if he takes away rectitude from someone's will, he does not will that that person should preserve rectitude of will for the sake of rectitude itself.

S: That follows.

T: But it has already been settled that for everyone who preserves rectitude, preserving rectitude of will in this way is the same as willing what God wills him to will.

S: Even if that hadn't been settled, it would still be true.

T: Therefore, if God takes this much-discussed rectitude away from someone, he does not will that person to will what he wills him to will.

S: Nothing could be more logical, but nothing could be more impossible.

T: Therefore, nothing is more impossible than for God to take away rectitude of will. Nonetheless, he is said to do this when he does not prevent someone from abandoning rectitude. Moreover, the devil or temptation is said to take away rectitude, or to overcome the will and tear it away from the rectitude it possesses, because unless he promised[49] something or threatened to take away something that the will wills more than rectitude, the will would by no means turn itself away from the rectitude that it does in fact will to some extent.

S: What you say appears so evident to me that I don't think anything could be said against it.

Chapter 9

That nothing is freer than an upright will

T: And so you see that nothing is freer than an upright will, since no external power can take away its rectitude. If, when it wills to lie in order not to lose life or well-being, we say that it is compelled by fear of death or torture to abandon the truth, that is certainly not true. For it is not compelled to will life more than truth;

---

49. Reading *promitteret* for *permitteret*.

but since an external power prevents it from preserving both, it chooses what it wills more. And certainly the will does so spontaneously* and not against its will, although its being in a position where it must abandon one or the other is not spontaneous but against its will. For it has no less strength for willing truth than for willing well-being, but it wills well-being more forcefully. For if it saw right before its eyes the eternal glory that it would immediately attain if it preserved the truth, and the torments of hell to which it would be given over without delay if it lied, there's no question that it would quickly be found to have strength enough to preserve the truth.

S: That's clearly true, since it would show greater strength for willing eternal well-being for its own sake, and truth for the sake of the reward, than for preserving temporal well-being.

Chapter 10

How someone who sins is a slave to sin, and that it is a greater miracle when God restores rectitude to someone who abandons it than when he restores life to a dead person

T: So rational nature always has free choice, since it always has the power to preserve rectitude of will for the sake of rectitude itself, although sometimes with difficulty. But once a free will abandons rectitude because of the difficulty of preserving it, the will is thereafter a slave to sin because of the impossibility of recovering rectitude through its own power. Thus it becomes "a spirit going on its way and not returning,"[50] since "one who commits sin is a slave to sin."[51] Indeed, just as no will before it had rectitude could acquire it unless God gave it, so also, once it has abandoned the rectitude it received, it cannot regain it unless God restores it. And I think it is a greater miracle when God restores to a will the rectitude it has abandoned than when he restores to a dead man the life he has lost. For a body, in dying out of necessity, does not sin so as never to regain life; but a will, by abandoning rectitude through its own power, deserves always to lack rectitude. And if someone spontaneously* inflicts death upon himself, he does not take away from himself what he was never going to lose; but someone who abandons rectitude of will throws away what he ought always to have preserved.

S: I see that what you are saying about the slavery by which "one who commits sin is a slave to sin," and about the impossibility of recovering rectitude once it

---

50. Psalm 78:39 (77:39).
51. John 8:34.

is abandoned unless it is restored by him who first gave it, is entirely true; and it should be ceaselessly contemplated by all to whom rectitude is given, in order that they might always retain it.

Chapter 11

That this slavery does not take away freedom of choice

But with this claim you have quite dampened my excitement, since I was thinking it was already firmly established that human beings always have freedom of choice. So I insist that you explain this slavery to me, lest it might perhaps seem incompatible with freedom. For both this freedom and this slavery are in the will, and it is in virtue of the will that human beings are free or slaves. So if they are slaves, how are they free? Or if they are free, how are they slaves?

T: If you distinguish carefully, they are, without any inconsistency, both free and slaves when they do not have rectitude. After all, it is *never* in their power to acquire rectitude when they don't have it; but it is always in their power to preserve it when they do have it. Because they cannot return to rectitude from sin, they are slaves; because they cannot be torn away from rectitude, they are free. But they can be turned back from sin, and from slavery to sin, only by someone else, whereas they can be turned away from rectitude only by themselves; and they cannot be deprived of their freedom either by themselves or by someone else. For they are always by nature free to preserve rectitude if they have it, even when they do not have the rectitude that they might preserve.

S: I am satisfied with the compatibility you have shown between freedom and slavery, so that they can both exist in the same person at the same time.

Chapter 12

Why, when human beings do not have rectitude, we say that they are free, since rectitude cannot be taken away from them when they have it, rather than saying that those who have rectitude are slaves, since they cannot recover it by their own power when they do not have it

But I very much want to know why, when human beings do not have rectitude, we say that they are free, since no one else can take it from them when they have it, rather than saying that when they do have it, they are slaves, since they cannot recover rectitude by their own power when they do not have it. For because they cannot return from sin, they are slaves; because they cannot be torn away from rectitude, they are free; and just as they can never be torn away from it if they have it, so also they can never return to it if they do not have it. Hence, just as they are always free, so also, it seems, they are always slaves.

T: This slavery is nothing other than the inability not to sin. For whether we call it the inability to return to rectitude or the inability to recover rectitude or have it again, human beings are slaves to sin only because, since they cannot return to rectitude or recover it or have it again, they are unable not to sin. By contrast, when they have rectitude, they do not have the inability not to sin. Therefore, when they have rectitude, they are not slaves of sin. But they always have the power to preserve rectitude, both when they have rectitude and when they do not; and so they are always free.

As for your asking why, when human beings do not have rectitude, we say that they are free, since no one else can take it from them when they have it, rather than saying that when they do have rectitude, they are slaves, since they cannot recover it by their own power when they do not have it: that's like asking why, when the sun is not present, we say that people have the power to see it, since they can see it when it *is* present, rather than saying that when the sun is present they are unable to see it, since when it is not present they cannot themselves cause it to be present. For even when the sun is not present, we have within ourselves the power of vision by which we see it when it is present; and in the same way, when rectitude of will is lacking in us, we nonetheless have within ourselves the aptitude for understanding and willing by which we can preserve it for its own sake when we have it. And when we have everything we need in order to see the sun except its presence, the only power we lack is the one that its presence confers upon us; and in the same way, when we lack rectitude, the only inability we have is the one that its absence causes in us. Therefore, human beings always have freedom of choice, but they are not always slaves of sin. They are slaves of sin only when they do not have upright wills.

S: If I had reflected carefully on what you said earlier when you divided the power of seeing into four powers,[52] I would not have been uncertain about this; so I acknowledge that I'm to blame for my uncertainty.

T: I will forgive you now if from here on out you will keep what we say in the forefront of your mind as much as will be necessary, so that we won't have to repeat it.

S: I appreciate your kindness. But don't be surprised if just one hearing should not be enough to keep these things, which I have not been used to thinking about, always clearly before my mind's eye.

T: Tell me whether you are still in doubt about anything in the definition of freedom of choice that we have offered.

---

52. In Chapter 3.

Chapter 13

That "the power to preserve rectitude of will for the sake of rectitude itself" is a perfect definition of freedom of choice

S: There is one thing that still worries me a bit about the definition. We often have a power to preserve something, but the power is not free in such a way that it cannot be impeded by any external force. So when you say that freedom of choice is the power to preserve rectitude of will for the sake of rectitude itself, consider whether perhaps we ought to add something to indicate that this power is so free that it cannot be overcome by any force.

T: If the power to preserve rectitude of will for the sake of rectitude itself could sometimes be found apart from the freedom that we have come to understand, it would be a good idea to add what you say. But since the stated definition is perfect in terms of genus* and differences,* so that it includes neither more nor less than the freedom we are investigating, it cannot be understood to need any addition or deletion. For 'power' is the genus of freedom. By adding 'to preserve' we distinguish it from every power that is not a power to preserve, for example, a power to laugh or to walk. By adding 'rectitude' we distinguish it from the power to preserve gold or whatever else is not rectitude. By adding 'of will' we distinguish it from the power to preserve the rectitude of other things, such as a stick or an opinion. By the phrase 'for the sake of rectitude itself' we distinguish it from the power to preserve rectitude of will for the sake of something else, as when rectitude is preserved for the sake of money, or naturally.* For a dog preserves rectitude of will naturally when it loves its puppies or its kindly master.

Therefore, since there is nothing in this definition but what is necessary to include the freedom of choice of a rational will and to exclude everything else, and freedom is sufficiently included and everything else sufficiently excluded, our definition is surely neither overly broad nor overly narrow. Do you think so?

S: It certainly seems perfect to me.

T: Then tell me whether you have any further questions about this freedom, on the basis of which an action, be it good or bad, is imputed* to someone—for that is the only freedom we are discussing now.

Chapter 14

How this freedom is divided

S: You still need to set out how this freedom is divided. For although freedom as defined in this way is common to every rational nature, God's freedom is very different from that of rational creatures, and theirs in turn differs from one creature to another.

T: There is a freedom of choice that is from itself, neither made by nor received from anyone else; it belongs to God alone. There is another freedom of choice that is made by and received from God; it belongs to angels and human beings. The freedom that is made or received either has rectitude that it preserves, or lacks rectitude. That which has rectitude has it either separably or inseparably. That which has rectitude separably belonged to all the angels before the good were confirmed and the bad fell, and it belongs now to all human beings before death who have rectitude. That which has rectitude inseparably belongs to elect angels and human beings—but to angels after the fall of the reprobate and to human beings after their death. Now that which lacks rectitude lacks it either recoverably or irrecoverably. That which lacks it recoverably belongs only to human beings in this present life who lack it, although many do not recover it. That which lacks it irrecoverably belongs to reprobate angels and human beings—but to angels after their fall, to human beings after this life.

S: With God's assent you have so completely explained the definition and division of freedom that I can't find anything else I need to ask about them.

ON THE FALL OF THE DEVIL

Chapters

28: That the power to will what he ought not was always good, and that willing
itself is good with respect to its essence

Chapter 1

That "What do you have that you did not receive?" is said even to the angels; and that nothing is from God but good and being; and that every good has being and every being is good

STUDENT: When the Apostle says "What do you have that you did not receive?"[53] is he saying this only to human beings, or to angels as well?

TEACHER: No creature has anything from itself. For if a thing does not have itself from itself, how can it have *anything* from itself? In short, since there are only two sorts of things—the Creator and what he created—whatever being anything has must be either God's own being or created being.[54]

S: That is indeed clear.

T: But neither the Creator nor what he created can have their being from any source other than God himself.[55]

S: That is no less clear.

T: So he alone has from himself whatever he has, and all other things have nothing but what they have from him. And just as what they have from themselves is nothing, so also what they have from him is something.

S: I don't think it's obviously true that what other things have from God is something. After all, who else brings it about that the many things we see passing from being to non-being are not what they used to be, even if they do not pass completely into nothingness? And who causes what-is-not not to be, unless it is he who causes everything that is to be? Similarly, if something is only because God makes

---

53. 1 Corinthians 4:7.

54. More literally: "In short, since nothing exists but the one being who created and the things created by that one being, it is clear that nothing at all can be had but the one who created and what he created." It sounds odd to say that God and his creation "can be had," but Anselm adopts this formulation because the argument takes off from a question about what creatures *have*. Since (as he will go on to argue) God has his own being from himself, it is proper to say that God "is had" by himself; since creatures have whatever they are from God, it is proper to say that what God creates "is had" by creatures.

55. More literally: "But neither the Creator nor what is created can be had except from the Creator."

it, it must be the case that what-is-not is not only because God doesn't make it. Therefore, just as those things that are have from him their being something, so also those that are not, or that pass from being to non-being, seem to have from him their being nothing.

T: It is not only someone who causes what-is-not to be, or causes what-is not to be, who is said to cause something to be or not to be. Rather, someone who can cause something not to be but refrains from doing so is also said to cause something to be; and someone who can cause something to be but refrains from doing so is also said to cause something not to be. For example, it is not only someone who robs another who is said to cause him to be naked or not to be clothed, but also someone who can prevent the robber but fails to do so. But this is said properly* of the former, whereas it is said improperly of the latter. For when it is said of the latter that he caused someone to be naked or not to be clothed, this simply means that although he could have caused the man to remain clothed or not to be naked, he didn't do so.

It is in this way that God is said to do many things that he does not do, as when he is said to lead us into temptation[56] because he does not spare us from temptation even though he could, or to cause what-is-not not to be, since he does not cause it to be even though he could. But if you would consider the things that are when they pass into non-being, it is not God who causes them not to be. After all, not only does no other essence* exist unless God makes it, but what God has made cannot persist even for a moment unless God preserves it; therefore, when he stops preserving what he made, that which used to be does not return to non-being because God causes it not to be, but because he stops causing it to be. For when God, as if in anger,[57] destroys something and thereby takes away its being, its non-being is not from God. Rather, when God takes away its being, like something of his own that he has lent—something he made and preserved in order that the thing might be—it returns to the non-being that it had from itself and not from God before it was made. After all, if you ask for your cloak back from someone to whom you willingly lent it temporarily when he was naked, he does not have his nakedness from you; instead, when you take away what was yours he returns to what he was before you clothed him.

So surely, just as whatever is from the supreme Good is good, and every good is from the supreme Good, so also whatever is from the supreme Being has being, and every being is from the supreme Being.[58] Therefore, since the supreme Good

---

56. Cf. Matthew 6:13, Luke 11:4: "Lead us not into temptation."

57. "As if in anger," because Anselm does not wish to imply that God actually experiences the emotion of anger. Cf. *Proslogion*, Chapter 8.

58. The word translated 'being' in this paragraph is *essentia*. See the Glossary entry for essence* (sense 4).

is the supreme Being, it follows that everything good has being and every being is good. So since nothing and non-being do not have being, they are not good. And so nothing and non-being are not from him from whom only good and being come.

S: I now see clearly that just as good and being come only from God, so also whatever comes from God is good and has being.

T: Now when we read in the Holy Scriptures, or when we say in conformity with them, that God causes evil or causes something not to be,[59] you must not in the least suppose that I deny the point being made in those words or find fault with its being said in that way. But we should not so much cling to the improper words that conceal the truth as diligently seek the proper truth that lies hidden in many forms of expression.

S: That would go without saying for anyone who isn't either stupid or dishonest.

T: Go back to what you started with, and consider whether it can be said not only to human beings but also to angels that they have nothing they did not receive.

S: It's quite clear that this is true of angels no less than of human beings.

Chapter 2

Why it seems that the devil did not receive perseverance because God did not give it

So it is clear that the angel who remained steadfast in the truth persevered because he had perseverance, that he had perseverance because he received it, and that he received it because God gave it. It follows, then, that the one who "did not remain steadfast in the truth"[60] did not persevere because he did not have perseverance, that he did not have perseverance because he did not receive it, and that he did not receive it because God did not give it. So then I want you to explain to me, if you can, what the angel's fault was. After all, he did not persevere because God did not give him perseverance, and he could have nothing but what God gave him. For I am certain—even though I don't see how it could be true—that his damnation by the supremely Just was just, and he could not have been damned justly apart from some fault.

---

59. As we read in Isaiah 45:7, for example: "I form the light, and create darkness: I make peace, and create evil: I the LORD do all these things."
60. John 8:44.

T: Why do you think it follows that if the good angel received perseverance because God gave it, then the evil angel did not receive it because God did not give it?

S: Because if its being given to the good angel was the cause of its being received, I think its not being given to the evil angel must have been the cause of its not being received. Now if we posit that it was not given, I see that this necessarily entails that it was not received; and we all know that when we don't receive something we want, it's not the case that it isn't given because we don't receive it, but rather we don't receive it because it isn't given. Finally, everyone I've heard or read asking this question always (as far as I can remember) brings it to a point with the following argument: if the good angel received perseverance because God gave it, the evil angel did not receive it because God did not give it. And I don't recall ever seeing a rejoinder to that reasoning.

Chapter 3

That God did not give perseverance because the evil angel did not receive it

T: That reasoning has no force at all, since it's possible for not-giving not to be the cause of not-receiving, even if giving were always the cause of receiving.

S: So if we posit the not-giving, the not-receiving doesn't necessarily follow. Therefore, there can be receiving even if there is no giving.

T: That's not so.

S: I'd like you to show me an example that illustrates what you're saying.

T: If I offer you something and you receive it, I do not give it because you receive it, but rather you receive it because I give it, and the giving is the cause of the receiving.

S: Right.

T: What if I offer that very same thing to someone else and he doesn't receive it?[61] Is it the case that he doesn't receive it because I don't give it?

S: No, it seems that you don't give it because he doesn't receive it.

T: So in this case not-giving is not the cause of not-receiving, and yet if I posit that I didn't give it, that causes it to follow that he didn't receive it. You see, for one thing to cause another is not the same as for the *positing* of a thing to cause

---

61. That is, does not accept it, refuses it.

something else to follow. For example, burning is not the cause of fire, but fire is the cause of burning; and yet if we posit that there is burning, this always causes it to follow that there is fire. For if there is burning, there must be fire.

S: I have to admit you're right.

T: Then I think you understand that even though you received because I gave, it does not therefore follow that the one who did not receive did not receive because I didn't give; and yet it does follow that if I didn't give, he didn't receive.

S: I do understand, and I am pleased that I understand.

T: Do you still doubt that just as the reason the angel who remained steadfast received perseverance is that God gave it, so also the reason God did not give perseverance to the angel who did not remain steadfast is that the angel did not receive it?

S: You haven't shown me that yet. All you have succeeded in proving is that just because the reason the good angel received perseverance is that God gave it, it doesn't *follow* that the reason the bad angel didn't receive it is that God didn't give it. If you intend to claim that in fact the reason God didn't give it to the bad angel is that the angel didn't receive it, I want to know why he didn't receive it. It was either because he wasn't able to or because he didn't will to. Now if he lacked either the power or the will to receive it, God did not give them to him, since if God had given them, the angel certainly would have had them. Therefore, since he could not have either the power or the will to receive perseverance unless God gave them to him, in what way did he sin by not receiving what God gave him neither the power nor the will to receive?

T: God did give him the will and the power to receive perseverance.

S: Then he received what God gave, and he had what he received.

T: He did indeed receive it and have it.

S: Then he received and had perseverance.

T: He didn't receive it, and therefore he didn't have it.

S: Didn't you say that God gave him, and that he received, the will and the power to receive perseverance?

T: I did. But I didn't say that God gave him the receiving of perseverance, only that God gave him the will and the power to receive perseverance.

S: Then if he had the will and the power, he received perseverance.

T: That doesn't follow necessarily.

S: I don't see why not, unless you'll explain it to me.

T: Have you ever begun something with the will and the power to complete it, but then you failed to complete it because your will had changed before you finished?

S: Often.

T: Then you had the will and the power to persevere in something in which you did not in fact persevere.

S: I did indeed have the will, but I didn't persevere in that will, and therefore I didn't persevere in the action.

T: Why didn't you persevere in that will?

S: Because I didn't will to persevere.

T: As long as you willed to persevere in the action, didn't you will to persevere in that will itself?

S: I can't deny it.

T: Then why do you say you didn't will to persevere in it?

S: I would reply again that I willed to persevere but didn't persevere in that will, except that I see this would go on forever, with you always asking the same question and me always giving the same reply.

T: That's why you shouldn't say, "I didn't will to persevere in that will because I didn't will to persevere in willing that will." Instead, when asked why you did not persevere in that action in which you had the will and the power to persevere, you can reply that it was because you didn't persevere in that will. If you are then asked why you didn't persevere in that will, you should adduce a different cause, namely the reason why this deficiency in your will came about, rather than saying that it was because you didn't persevere in willing that will. For the latter reply merely restates the very thing that is being asked about, that is, the fact that you didn't persevere in the will to persevere in that action.

S: I realize that I didn't see what I should say.

T: So tell me in one word what it is to persevere in doing something as far as the thing requires.

S: To *finish* doing it. For when someone perseveres in writing, we say that he finishes writing; and when someone perseveres in leading, we say that he finishes leading.

T: Then let's likewise say, even though the expression is not in common use, that to persevere in willing is to finish willing.[62]

S: Very well.

T: So when you did not finish doing what you had the will and the power to finish, why didn't you finish doing it?

S: Because I didn't finish willing it.

T: Then in the same way you must say that the devil, who received the will and the power to receive perseverance and the will and power to persevere, did not receive perseverance and did not persevere because he did not finish willing.

S: But then again I want to know why he didn't finish willing. After all, when you say he did not finish willing what he willed, that just amounts to saying that he no longer willed what he had once willed. So when he no longer willed what he had once willed, why did he not will it, unless it was because he did not have the will? I don't mean the will he had had before, when he willed it, but the will he didn't have when he didn't will it. Why, then, did he not have this will, unless it was because he didn't receive it? And why didn't he receive it, unless it was because God didn't give it?

T: Again I say that it's not the case that he didn't receive it because God didn't give it; instead, God didn't give it because he didn't receive it.

S: Explain that.

T: He spontaneously* forsook the will he had. Now as long as he possessed what he later abandoned, he received his possessing it; and in the same way he could have received his always retaining what he abandoned. But since he abandoned it, he did not receive his always retaining it. Therefore, it was because he abandoned it that he did not receive his retaining it—and it's not the case that he didn't receive it because God didn't give it, but instead God didn't give it because he didn't receive it.

S: Who would not understand that it's not because he abandoned it that he didn't will to retain it, but rather it's because he didn't will to retain it that he abandoned

---

62. Anselm's procedure is much clearer in the Latin. In the first three instances Anselm took the verb and added the prefix *per*. Thus *facere* (to do) became *perficere* (to bring to completion), *scribere* (to write) became *perscribere* (to write in full), and *ducere* (to lead) became *perducere* (to lead to the destination). Anselm now proposes to do the same with the word *velle* (to will), thereby coining a new word, *pervelle*, which will mean 'to will to the end, to will with complete perseverance.' In the translation I have represented *per* by the verb 'to finish': thus, *perficere* is 'to finish doing,' *pervelle* 'to finish willing,' and so on.

it? For not willing to retain something one has is always prior to willing to abandon it; after all, someone wills to abandon something he has because he does not will to retain it. So I am asking if there was a reason why he did not will to retain what he had, other than God's not giving him the will to retain it.

T: Not willing to retain something is not always prior to willing to abandon it.

S: Explain to me when it isn't.

T: When you do not will to retain a thing, but rather to abandon it, for its own sake: for example, if a live coal is placed in your bare hand. In such a case, perhaps, your not willing to retain the thing is prior to your willing to abandon it, and you will to abandon it because you do not will to retain it. After all, before you have it you do not will to retain it, and yet you cannot will to abandon it except when you have it.

By contrast, when you have something that you do not will to retain, but only for the sake of something else, and that you will to abandon only for the sake of something else, and you more strongly will something else that you cannot have unless you abandon what you have: in that case your willing to abandon something is prior to your not willing to retain it. For example, when a miser wills to retain a coin, but he more strongly wills bread, which he cannot have unless he spends his coin, his willing to spend—that is, to abandon—the coin is prior to his not willing to retain it. He does not, after all, will to spend the coin because he does not will to retain it; rather, he does not will to retain it because in order to have bread he must spend it. Moreover, before he has it, he wills to have it and to retain it; and while he has it, he in no way lacks the will to retain it, so long as he need not abandon it.

S: That's true.

T: Therefore, not willing to retain something is not always prior to willing to abandon it; instead, willing to abandon something is sometimes prior.

S: I can't deny it.

T: I therefore say that it was not because his will was faulty—God having failed to give him the will—that he did not will what and when he ought to have willed; but instead, by willing what he ought not, he cast out his good will when an evil will came to exist within him. Hence, it is not the case that he did not have or receive a persevering good will because God did not give it to him; but rather, God did not give it to him because he deserted that will by willing what he ought not, and by deserting it did not retain it.

S: I understand what you're saying.

Chapter 4

In what way he sinned and willed to be like God

T: Do you still doubt that it was not because he did not will to retain what he had that the devil abandoned it, but rather it was because he willed to abandon it that he did not will to retain it?

S: I don't doubt that that *could* be true, but you haven't yet convinced me that it really *is* true. So show me first what he willed to have that he did not have, so that he willed to abandon what he did have, as you illustrated in the case of the miser. Then, if there's no possible objection, I will acknowledge that I don't doubt it really is true.

T: You don't doubt that he did in fact sin, since a just God could not condemn him unjustly, but you are asking in what way he sinned.

S: Exactly.

T: If he had persevered in preserving justice, he would never have sinned or been wretched.

S: That is what we believe.

T: And no one preserves justice except by willing what he ought or abandons justice except by willing what he ought not.

S: No one would doubt that.

T: So he abandoned justice, and thus sinned, by willing something that he ought not to have willed at that time.

S: That follows, but I'm asking what it was he willed.

T: Whatever he had, he ought to have willed.

S: Certainly he ought to have willed what he had received from God, and he did not sin by willing it.

T: Then he willed something that he did not have and that he ought not to have willed at that time, just as Eve willed to be "like the gods"[63] before God willed that.

S: I cannot deny that that follows too.

T: Now he could not will anything but justice or something advantageous. For happiness, which every rational nature wills, consists in advantageous things.

---

63. Cf. Genesis 3:5, where the serpent tells Eve, "You will be like the gods, knowing good and evil."

S: We can see this to be true in ourselves, since we will nothing but what we think is either just or advantageous.

T: But he could not sin by willing justice.

S: That's true.

T: Therefore, he sinned by willing something advantageous that he did not have and ought not to have willed at that time, but that could have served to increase his happiness.

S: Clearly that is the only way in which he could have sinned.

T: I believe you understand that by inordinately willing something in addition to what he had received, he stretched out his will beyond the bounds of justice.

S: I now see clearly that he sinned both by willing what he ought not and by not willing what he ought. It is also evident that it was not the case that he willed more than he ought because he did not will to retain justice. On the contrary, he did not retain justice because he willed something else; and by willing that, he abandoned justice—as you showed in the case of the miser, the coin, and the bread.

T: Now when he willed this thing that God did not want him to will, he willed inordinately to be like God.

S: If God must be thought of as so unique that nothing else like him can be thought,[64] how could the devil will what he could not think? After all, he was not so dense that he didn't know that nothing else can be thought to be like God.

T: Even if he didn't will to be completely equal to God, but instead willed something less than equality with God that was contrary to God's will: by that very fact he willed inordinately to be like God, since he willed something by his own will, which was not subjected to anyone else. For it is the prerogative of God alone to will anything by his own will in such a way that he does not follow any higher will.

S: That's true.

T: Now he did not merely will to be equal to God by presuming to have a will of his own; he willed to be even *greater* than God, in that he placed his own will above God's will by willing what God didn't want him to will.

S: That's quite clear.

T: I believe it's obvious to you now from the arguments offered above that the devil spontaneously* stopped willing what he ought and justly lost what he had, since

---

64. This expression recalls Anselm's description of God as "something than which nothing greater can be thought" in the *Proslogion*, beginning with Chapter 2.

he spontaneously and unjustly willed what he didn't have and what he ought not to have willed.

S: I think nothing could be more obvious.

T: So although the good angel received perseverance because God gave it, it's not the case that the evil angel did not receive it because God didn't give it; rather, God didn't give it because he didn't receive it, and he didn't receive it because he didn't will to receive it.

S: You have given such satisfactory answers to my questions that both the truth of your premises and the validity of your arguments are firmly fixed in my understanding.

Chapter 5

That before the fall of the evil angels, the good angels were able to sin

T: Do you think the good angels were likewise able to sin before the evil angels fell?

S: I think so, but I would like to understand this through reason.

T: You know for certain that if they were not able to sin, they preserved justice out of necessity* and not in virtue of their power. Therefore, they did not merit grace from God for remaining steadfast when others fell any more than they did for preserving their rationality, which they could not lose. Nor, if you consider the matter rightly, could they properly be called just.

S: That's what reason shows.

T: So suppose that those who fell had not sinned, even though they were able to. They would have been greater than the angels who were not able to sin, insofar as they would have been genuinely just and would have merited grace from God. Hence, it follows either that elect human beings will turn out to be better and greater than the good angels, or that the reprobate angels will not be adequately replaced, since the human beings who are received in their place will not be such as they themselves were going to be.[65]

---

65. This cryptic argument depends in part on Anselm's views in *Cur Deus Homo*, Book 1, Chapters 16–18, where he argues that some human beings will fill up the places in heaven that should have been occupied by the angels who fell. If those views are borne in mind, Anselm's argument here can be understood in the following reformulation. The bad angels were (obviously) able to sin. But what about the good angels? Either they too were

S: I think both these conclusions must be utterly rejected.

T: Therefore, the good angels were able to sin before the fall of the evil angels, just as has been shown in the case of those who fell.

S: I don't see how else things could be.

Chapter 6

How the good angels have been confirmed in their steadfastness and the evil angels in their fall

T: And so the good angels willed the justice that they had, rather than that additional something which they didn't have. As far as their own will was concerned, they lost that good (as it were) for the sake of justice; but they received it as a reward for justice, and they remained forever in secure possession of what they had. Hence, they have progressed so far that they have attained everything they could will, and they no longer see what more they could will; and because of this they are unable to sin. By contrast, the evil angels willed that additional something which God did not yet will to give them, rather than willing to remain steadfast in the justice in which they were created. By the judgment of that very justice, they not only failed utterly to obtain that on account of which they scorned justice but also lost the good they had. Therefore, the angels are distinguished in the following way: those who cleave to justice can will no good that they do not enjoy, and those who abandon justice can will no good that they do not lack.

S: Nothing could be more just or more beautiful than this distinction. But if you can tell me, I would like to hear what sort of advantageous thing this was that

---

able to sin or they weren't. Suppose they weren't. Then their actions were neither just nor meritorious. But in that case, saved human beings would actually be *better* than the good angels, since human beings are able to sin and therefore can act justly and meritoriously. And we can't say that human beings are better than angels. So suppose instead we cling to the view that saved human beings are *not* better than the good angels. It would follow that human beings, like the good angels, act neither justly nor meritoriously. But that can't be true either, since saved human beings are supposed to fill up the gap left by the desertion of the evil angels. Now those evil angels were able to sin, which means that if they *hadn't* sinned, they would have acted justly and meritoriously. If saved human beings do not act justly and meritoriously, they are not fitting replacements for the rebel angels ("they will not be such as [the reprobate angels] were going to be"). Therefore, since the assumption that the good angels were unable to sin leads to all sorts of dead ends and absurdities, we must conclude that they were able to sin.

the good angels justly spurned and thereby advanced, and the evil angels unjustly desired and thereby fell away.

T: I don't know what it was. But whatever it might have been, all we need to know is that it was something they were able to attain, which they did not receive when they were created, in order that they might advance to it by their own merit.

S: And let this be enough for our discussion of this point.

Chapter 7

Questions: Is the will, and its turning to what it ought not, the very evil that makes them evil? And why can't the rational creature turn from evil to good on its own, as it can turn from good to evil on its own?

But I don't know what it is—as soon as I hope I've finally answered one question, I see more questions sprouting up from the roots of those I've already mowed down. Now that I quite clearly see that unrestrained concupiscence was the only reason the rebel angel could have fallen into this extreme lack of anything good, I am very troubled about the source of this inordinate will. For if that will was good, then it was on account of a good will that he fell from such great good into such great evil. Moreover, if it was good, then God gave it to him, since he had nothing from himself. So if he willed what God gave him to will, what was his sin? On the other hand, if he had this will from himself, he had something good that he did not receive.

Now if that will is evil and is also something, the problem arises again: his evil will must have been from God, who is the source of whatever is something. And once again one can ask what his sin was in having the will God gave him, or how God could give an evil will. If, however, this evil will was from the devil himself and is also something, then the devil had something from himself, and not every essence* is good; nor will evil be nothing, as we are accustomed to say, since an evil will is an essence. On the other hand, if an evil will is nothing, it was on account of nothing, and therefore without cause, that he was so harshly condemned. And what I'm saying about will can equally well be said about concupiscence or desire, since both concupiscence and desire are will; and just as there is good and evil will, so also there is good and evil concupiscence and good and evil desire.

Now suppose someone said that a will is an essence* and is therefore something good, but that it becomes a good will by turning to what it ought but is called a bad will when it turns to what it ought not. Then I notice that whatever I said about the will can be said about this turning of the will. For I am very troubled about the source of the perverse turning of the devil's will, and about the other things I said just now about the will. And there is still something else that bewilders me whenever I think about this turning of the will, namely, why God made that excellent and sublime nature such that it could turn its will from what it ought to will to what it ought not to will but could not turn from what it ought not to will to what it ought. For it seems that such a creature ought to have received from such a Creator the power to do the good for which it was created, rather than the evil it was created to avoid. The same question can be asked about our own nature, since we believe that no human being can have a good will unless God gives it, whereas we can have an evil will at any time if God merely permits it.

Chapter 8

That neither the will nor its turning is the very evil that makes them evil

T: I don't think we can deny that both the will and its turning are something. For even if they are not substances,* it still cannot be proved that they are not essences,* since there are many essences besides those that are properly* called substances. Moreover, a good will is no more a something than is a bad will, nor is a bad will more an evil than a good will is a good. For a merciful, generous will is no more a something than a merciless, rapacious will; nor is the latter more an evil than the former is a good. Therefore, if an evil will is the very evil because of which someone is called evil, it would follow that a good will is the very good by which someone is made good. But then it would turn out that an evil will is nothing at all, if it is that very evil that we believe to be nothing; and then a good will would also be nothing, since it is no more a something than an evil will is. So we would be forced to hold that the very good that makes beings good is nothing, since it is the good will, which would be nothing. But no one for a moment supposes that a good will, or good itself, is nothing. Therefore, an evil will is not the very evil that makes beings evil, just as a good will is not the very good that makes them good.

Now what I said about the will can also be applied to the will's turning: the turning by which a will turns from stealing to bestowing is no more a something than that by which the very same will turns from generosity to greed. And so on, for all the things I said about the will a moment ago.

S: What you say seems right to me too.

T: Therefore, neither the evil will nor the wicked turning of the will is the very evil that makes an angel or human being evil—that is, the very evil that we claim is nothing—nor is the good will or the good turning of the will the good that makes them good.

Chapter 9

That injustice is that very evil and is nothing

S: Then what are we to say is the very evil that makes them evil, and what is the very good that makes them good?

T: We ought to believe that justice is the very good in virtue of which both angels and human beings are good, that is, just, and in virtue of which the will itself is said to be good or just; whereas injustice is the very evil that we claim is nothing other than a privation of good, which makes them and their will evil. And consequently, we hold that injustice is nothing other than the privation of justice. For when a will was initially given to the rational nature, it was, simultaneously with that giving, turned by the Giver himself to what it ought it to will—or rather, it was not turned but *created* upright. Now as long as that will remained steadfast in the rectitude in which it was created, which we call truth or justice, it was just. But when it turned itself away from what it ought to will and toward what it ought not, it did not remain steadfast in the original rectitude (if I may so call it) in which it was created. When it abandoned that rectitude, it lost something great and received in its place nothing but its privation, which has no essence,* and which we call 'injustice.'

Chapter 10

How evil seems to be something

S: I grant what you say about evil's being a privation of good, but I equally see that good is a privation of evil. And just as I perceive that in the privation of evil something else comes about that we call 'good,' so also I notice that in the privation of good something else comes about that we call 'evil.' Now there are certain arguments proving that evil is nothing. For example, it has been argued that evil is nothing but a flaw or corruption, which exists only in some essence,* and the more flaws and corruptions there are in an essence, the more they reduce it to nothingness; and if that essence falls completely into nothingness, the flaws and corruptions will also be found to be nothing. But even if this or some other argument is offered to show that evil is nothing, my mind cannot endorse that view, except by faith alone, unless someone refutes my contrary argument proving that evil is something. For when we hear the name[66] 'evil' there would be no reason for

---

66. *nomen*: I have chosen to translate *nomen* consistently as 'name,' since that makes the best sense of Anselm's arguments on the whole; but readers should bear in mind that *nomen* can also have the more general meaning 'word' and the narrower meaning 'noun.'

our hearts to fear what they understand to be signified by that name if in fact it signified nothing. Moreover, if the word 'evil' is a name, it surely has a signification; and if it has a signification, it signifies. But then it signifies *something*. How, then, is evil nothing, if what the name 'evil' signifies is something? Finally, consider what peace there is, what rest, while justice endures: so that in many cases it seems that justice, like chastity and forbearance, is nothing but restraint from evil. But when justice is gone, what varied, troublesome, and multifarious feelings take possession of the soul; like a cruel master they force their wretched slave to be anxious about so many depraved and wearisome deeds and to labor so painfully in doing them. It would be astonishing if you could show that *nothing* accomplishes all this.

Chapter 11

That one cannot prove on the basis of the names that evil and nothing are something, but rather that they are quasi-something

T: I imagine you're not crazy enough to say that *nothing* is something, even though you cannot deny that 'nothing' is a name. So, if you cannot prove that nothing is something based on the name 'nothing,' how do you think you're going to prove that evil is something based on the name 'evil'?

S: An example that resolves one controversial issue by bringing in another is useless. For I don't know what nothing is either. So, since the question at hand concerns the evil that you say is nothing, if you want to teach me what I should understand evil to be, first teach me what I should understand nothing to be; and then you will respond to the other considerations, besides the name 'evil,' that I said induced me to think evil is something.

T: Now given that there is no difference at all between being nothing and not being something, how can one say what that which is not something *is*?

S: If there isn't something that is signified by the name 'nothing,' then that name doesn't signify anything; and if it doesn't signify anything, it's not a name. But surely it *is* a name. Therefore, although no one would say that nothing is something, but instead we must always say that nothing is nothing, still, no one can deny that the name 'nothing' has a signification. But if this name does not signify nothing, but instead signifies something, then it seems that what it signifies cannot be nothing but instead is something. Therefore, if what it signifies is not nothing but instead is something, how will it be true that this word signifies that which is nothing? After all, if 'nothing' is said truly, then what is signified by the name is truly nothing, and therefore it isn't something. Hence, if what is signified by this name is not nothing but instead is something—as the argument seems to show—then it is falsely and inappropriately called by that name. But on the other hand, if (as everyone agrees) that which is named 'nothing' truly is nothing and in no way is something, could anything at all follow more logically than this: that this word signifies nothing, that is, doesn't signify anything? And so why is it that the name 'nothing' does not signify nothing but instead something, and also does not signify something but instead nothing?

T: Perhaps signifying nothing is not inconsistent with signifying something.

S: Suppose they're not inconsistent. Then either this word signifies nothing when taken in one way and something when taken in another way, or else we will have to find a thing that is both something and nothing.

T: What if both turn out to be true? That is, what if we can find two ways of understanding this name and also find one and the same thing to be both something and nothing?

S: I would like to know both.

T: It is agreed that as far as its signification goes, the word 'nothing' is in no way different from 'not-something.' And nothing is more obvious than this: 'not-something' by its signification requires that every thing whatsoever, and anything that is something, is to be excluded from the understanding, and that no thing at all or what is in any way something is to be included in the understanding. But since there is no way to signify the exclusion of something except by signifying the very thing whose exclusion is signified—for no one understands what 'not-human' signifies except by understanding what a human is—the expression 'not-something' must signify something precisely by eliminating that which is something. On the other hand, by excluding everything that is something, it signifies no essence* that it requires to be included in the hearer's understanding. Therefore, the expression 'not-something' does not signify any thing or that which is something.

Therefore, the expression 'not-something' under different aspects both in some way signifies a thing and something and in no way signifies a thing or something. For it signifies by excluding; it does not signify by including. The same argument applies to the name 'nothing,' which excludes everything that is something: by what it eliminates, it signifies something rather than nothing, and by what it includes, it signifies nothing rather than something. Therefore, it is not necessary that nothing be something just because its name signifies something in a certain way; but rather, it is necessary that nothing be nothing, because its name signifies something in that particular way. And so in this way it is not inconsistent for evil to be nothing and yet for the name 'evil' to have a signification, given that it signifies something by excluding it and does not include any thing.

S: I can't deny that the name 'nothing' in some way signifies something, as you've just argued; but it is quite well-known that the something that is signified in that way by this name is not named 'nothing.' Nor when we hear this name do we take it as standing for the thing that it signifies in that way. So I am asking about the item[67] that we use this name to stand for and that we understand when we hear this name—I mean, I'm asking what that item is. After all, it is what this name properly* signifies; this name is a name because it signifies that item, not because it signifies something by denying, in the way you explained earlier. That name is reckoned among names precisely because it signifies that item, and that item is called 'nothing.' I am asking how that item is something if it is properly called 'nothing,' or how it is nothing if the name that signifies it signifies something, or how one and the same item is both something and nothing. I ask the same questions about the name 'evil,' both about what it signifies and about what is named 'evil.'

T: You are right to ask these questions, since even though the argument given above shows that 'evil' and 'nothing' signify something, what they signify is not evil or nothing. But there is another argument showing that they signify something and that what they signify is something—yet not really something, but quasi-something.

You see, the form of an expression often doesn't match the way things are in reality.[68] For example, 'to fear' is active according to the form of the word even though fearing is passive in reality. And in the same way 'blindness' is something according to the form of the expression, even though it is not something in reality. For we say that someone has blindness and that there is blindness in him in just the same way that we say someone has vision and that there is vision in him, even though blindness is not something, but instead not-something, and to have blindness is not to have something but rather to lack that which is something. After all, blindness is nothing other than non-vision or the absence of vision where there ought to be vision; and non-vision or the absence of vision is not something in cases where there ought to be vision any more than it is in cases where there ought not to be vision. Therefore, blindness is not something in the eye, just because there ought to be vision in the eye, any more than non-vision or the absence of vision is something in a stone, where there ought not to be vision. And there are many other similar cases in which things that are not something are called

---

67. There is no word in the Latin corresponding to 'item.' I use it to avoid a confusing string of neuter pronouns with different referents in the sentences that follow. 'Thing' would not work, because the Student is not committed to the notion that whatever is referred to by 'nothing' qualifies as a thing; indeed, he is committed to just the opposite, which is why he avoids words like 'something' and 'thing' and formulates his question using only neuter demonstrative pronouns.

68. Literally: "many things are said according to form that are not so in reality."

something according to the form of the expression, in that we speak of them as we speak of things that really exist.

It is in this way, then, that 'evil' and 'nothing' signify something; and what they signify is something, not in reality, but according to the form of the expression. For 'nothing' does not signify anything other than not-something, or the absence of those items that are something. And evil is not anything other than not-good, or the absence of good where it is required or fitting that good should be. Now that which is not anything other than the absence of what is something is certainly not itself something. Therefore, evil is truly nothing, and nothing is not something; and yet in a certain way evil and nothing *are* something, because we speak of them as if[69] they were something when we say, "He did nothing" or "He did evil," or "What he did is nothing" or "What he did is evil," in the same way in which we say "He did something" or "He did what is good," or "What he did is something" or "What he did is good." That's why, when we utterly deny that what someone says is something, we say "That which you say is nothing." For 'that' and 'which' are properly* said only of that which is something; and when they are used in the expression I just mentioned, they are not said of that[70] which is something, but of that which is spoken of as if it were something.

S: You have succeeded in meeting the argument based on the name 'evil' by which I thought I could prove that evil is something.

Chapter 12

That the angel could not have his first will from himself; and that 'can' is applied to many things because of something else's power and 'cannot' because of something else's lack of power

You still need to show me how I can reply to the other considerations that strive to persuade me that evil is something.[71]

T: In order for us to be able to elucidate the truth of the matter, we will have to begin a little further back. But it's important for you not to be content merely to

---

69. "as if": Latin, *quasi*; hence the expression "quasi-something" above.

70. Reading *dicuntur de eo* for *dicuntur eo*.

71. The "other considerations" raised in Chapter 10 are finally answered in Chapter 26. As the Teacher indicates in his next speech, Chapters 12–25 set up the philosophical account needed to make the claims of Chapter 26 compelling, and those chapters should be read with the considerations of Chapter 10 in mind. This is not to say, of course, that Chapters 12–25 are interesting *only* for the light they shed on the problem raised in Chapter 10; on the contrary, they are arguably the philosophical centerpiece of *On the Fall of the Devil*.

understand each of the things I say individually, but to gather them all up in your memory at the same time and see them in one glance, as it were.

S: I will be as attentive as I can. But if I prove to be somewhat slower than you might wish, don't become annoyed at having to wait for me as you see that my slowness requires it.

T: Well, let's suppose that right now God is making an angel that he wills to make happy, and he's not making the angel all at once but rather part by part. Up to this point the angel has been made apt to have a will, but he does not yet will anything.

S: Suppose whatever you like, and explain what I am asking about.

T: Do you think this angel can will anything on his own?

S: I don't really understand what you mean by "on his own." For as you said earlier,[72] no creature has anything that it did not receive, and no creature can do anything on its own.

T: By "on his own" I mean in virtue of what he already has. For example, someone who has feet and whatever else suffices for the ability to walk can walk on his own, whereas someone whose feet are injured cannot walk on his own. This is the sense in which I am asking whether the angel who is already apt to will but does not yet will anything can will something on his own.

S: I think he can, if at some point he wills.

T: You're not answering my question.

S: How so?

T: My question is about someone who is willing nothing, and about the possibility[73] that precedes the fact; but your answer is about someone who wills, and about the possibility that comes about with the fact. For whatever is, by the very fact that it is, can be. But not everything that is could be before it was. So when I ask whether this angel who wills nothing can will, I am asking about the possibility before he wills, by which he can move himself to will; but when you reply that if he wills, he can will, you are talking about the possibility that comes about with that will itself. For necessarily, if he wills, he can will.

S: I know that there are two possibilities, one that is not yet realized in fact, and one that is already realized in fact. But I also can't help but know this: if anything can be in the sense that it now actually exists, then if at any time it did not exist,

---

72. In Chapter 1.

73. possibility: *potestas*, the abstract noun corresponding to the verb *posse*, which I have been translating 'can.'

it previously could exist. After all, if it could not have existed, it would never have existed. So I think my reply was perfectly adequate: since, given that he wills, he can will, it must be the case that before he willed, he could will.

T: Do you think that what is nothing has nothing at all and therefore has no power,[74] and that without power there is absolutely nothing it can do or be?

S: I can't deny that.

T: I believe that before the world was made, it was nothing.

S: You're right.

T: Therefore, before it existed, there was nothing it could do or be.

S: That follows.

T: Therefore, before it existed, it could not exist.

S: And I say that if it could not exist, it was impossible for it ever to exist.

T: That was both possible and impossible before it existed. It was impossible for the world, since the world did not have the power to exist; but it was possible for God, who had the power to make the world. Therefore, the world exists because before it was made, God could make it, not because before it existed the world itself could exist.

S: I can't rebut your argument, but our normal way of speaking is against you.

T: That's not surprising. Many things are said improperly* in ordinary speech; but when it is incumbent upon us to search out the heart of the truth, we must remove the misleading impropriety to the greatest extent possible and as much as the subject matter demands. Because of such impropriety in speaking we quite

---

74. "power": again, *potestas*. Part of Anselm's point in this chapter is to distinguish two senses of *potestas*: to say that *x* has the *potestas* to be *y* might just mean that it is possible for *x* to be *y*, but it might mean something more, namely that *x* can bring it about that *x* is *y*. (Consider two examples: a banana has the *potestas* to be digested in the first sense but not in the second, since it cannot throw itself into your intestines and bombard itself with digestive enzymes and so forth. By contrast, I have the *potestas* to be in Chicago in both senses: it is possible for me to be in Chicago, and I myself have the power to bring it about that I am in Chicago.) The problem is that in English we have a ready-made distinction between these two senses. For the first we use 'possibility' and for the second we use 'power.' Anselm must therefore labor to make clear a distinction we already have firmly entrenched in ordinary language. The analogue in English would be to distinguish between two uses of 'can': when I say that the banana can be digested I am using a sense of 'can' that implies mere possibility, but when I say that I can be in Chicago I am using a sense of 'can' that implies a power.

often apply the word 'can' to a thing, not because it can do anything, but because something else can; and we apply the word 'cannot' to a thing that can do something, simply because some other thing cannot. For example, if I say "a book can be written by me," the book certainly can't do anything, but I can write the book. And when we say "this man cannot be defeated by that man," we understand this to mean simply, "that man cannot defeat this man."[75] This is why we say that God cannot undergo anything harmful to himself or do anything wicked, since he is so powerful in his blessedness and justice—or rather, since in him blessedness and justice are not distinct things but a single good, he is so all-powerful in his unitary good—that no thing can do what would harm the supreme Good. Hence, he can neither be corrupted nor lie.[76]

Therefore, whatever does not exist cannot, before it exists, exist through its own power; but if some other thing can cause it to exist, then it can exist through something else's power. Now although there are many ways to draw distinctions involving power or lack of power, let this be enough for now: 'can' is applied to many things not because of their own power, but because of something else's power; and 'cannot' is applied to many things not because of their own lack of power, but because of something else's lack of power. So I am speaking of his own power when I ask about the newly created angel whom we are imagining, who up to this point has been made apt to have a will but does not yet will anything. Can he will anything on his own? Answer in terms of his own power.

S: If he is already apt to will and lacks nothing but the willing itself, I don't see why he can't will on his own. After all, someone who is apt to see, but doesn't see anything, who is placed in the light but with his eyes closed, can see on his own. Why, then, couldn't someone who is not willing will on his own in the same way that someone who is not seeing can see on his own?

T: Because the one who is not seeing has vision and a will by which he can move vision. We, however, are speaking of an angel who has no will. So answer this question: If a thing moves itself from not willing to willing, does it will to move itself?

S: If I say that it is moved without willing, what will follow is that it is moved by something else rather than by itself—except perhaps if someone suddenly closes his eyes in anticipation of a blow or is compelled by something disadvantageous to will what he did not will before. For in those cases I'm not sure whether he first moves himself to this will.

---

75. Cf. *On Truth*, Chapter 8.

76. Cf. *Proslogion*, Chapter 7.

T: No one is compelled by fear or the expectation of something disadvantageous, or incited by love of something advantageous, to will something, unless he first has a natural* will to avoid what is disadvantageous or have what is advantageous. By that will he moves himself to other wills.

S: I can't deny that.

T: You must acknowledge, therefore, that whatever moves itself to will, first wills to move itself.

S: Yes.

T: Therefore, that which wills nothing can in no way move itself to will.

S: I can't object.

T: So it must be the case that the angel who has already been made apt to have a will but nonetheless does not will anything cannot have his first will from himself.

S: I have to grant you that, since that which wills nothing can will nothing on its own.

T: Now he cannot be happy unless he wills happiness. By 'happiness' I don't mean happiness in accordance with justice, but the happiness that everyone wills, even the unjust. After all, everyone wills his own well-being. For leaving aside the fact that every nature* is said to be good, we commonly speak of two goods and of two evils that are contrary to them. One good is that which is called "justice," whose contrary evil is injustice. The other good is what I think can be called "the advantageous"; its opposite evil is the disadvantageous. Now not everyone wills justice, and not everyone avoids injustice, whereas not merely every rational nature, but indeed everything that can be aware of it wills the advantageous and avoids the disadvantageous. For no one wills anything unless he thinks it is in some way advantageous for himself. So in this way everyone wills his own well-being and wills against his own unhappiness. It is of happiness in this sense that I said just now that no one can be happy unless he wills happiness. For no one can be happy either in having what he does not will or in not having what he does will.

S: There's no denying that.

T: And someone who does not will justice *ought* not be happy.

S: That's equally true.

Chapter 13

That, having received only the will for happiness, he would not be able to will anything else or to refrain from willing happiness; and that no matter what he might will, his will would be neither just nor unjust

T: Then let's say that God first gives him only the will for happiness and see whether, in virtue of having received a will, he is now able to move himself to will something other than happiness.[77]

S: Continue what you have begun. I'm ready to understand.

T: It is agreed that he does not yet will anything besides happiness, since he has not received the will for anything else.

S: That's true.

T: So I'm asking you whether he can move himself to will something else.

S: I can't see how someone who wills nothing besides happiness would move himself to will anything other than happiness. After all, if he wills to move himself to will something else, he wills something else.

T: Therefore, just as he could not will anything at all on his own when no will had yet been given him, so also he cannot have any other will from himself if he has received only the will for happiness.

S: Yes.

T: What if he thought something would contribute to his attaining happiness? Couldn't he move himself to will that?

S: I'm not sure how to reply. If he can't, I don't see how he's willing happiness, since he can't will that through which he thinks he can attain happiness. On the other hand, if he can, I don't understand in what sense he can't will anything other than happiness.

T: If someone wills something, not for the sake of the thing he appears to will but for the sake of something else, which should one properly judge him to be willing: that which he is said to will, or that for the sake of which he wills?

S: Surely that for the sake of which he seems to will.

---

77. "other than happiness": literally, "other than what he received to will."

T: So someone who wills something for the sake of happiness is not willing anything other than happiness. Therefore, it can be true both that he wills what he thinks will contribute to his happiness and that he wills only happiness.

S: That's quite clear.

T: I still want to know whether, having received only this will, he can refrain from willing happiness.

S: He cannot simultaneously both will it and refrain from willing it.

T: That's true, but it's not what I'm asking. I'm asking whether he can abandon that will and move himself from willing happiness to refraining from willing it.

S: If he does that unwillingly, it is not he who is doing it. On the other hand, if he does it willingly, he is willing something other than happiness. But he *doesn't* will anything other than happiness. So I think it's obvious that there's no way he can, on his own, will anything other than the one thing he received the power to will.[78]

T: You have understood this well. But now tell me whether someone who wills nothing other than happiness, and who cannot refrain from willing happiness, can keep from willing happiness more and more, the greater he understands it to be.

S: If he didn't will happiness more and more, the greater and better he understood it to be, then either he wouldn't be willing happiness at all, or else he would will something else on account of which he would not will the better thing.[79] But we are supposing that he wills happiness and nothing else.

T: Then the higher he realizes happiness can be, the more he wills to be happy.

S: Undoubtedly he does.

T: Therefore, he wills to be like God.

S: Nothing could be more obvious.

T: What do you think: would his will be unjust if he willed in this way to be like God?

S: I don't want to call him just, since he would be willing what is not fitting; nor do I want to call him unjust, since he would be willing out of necessity.

T: Now we said that someone who wills only happiness wills only advantageous things.

S: Yes.

---

78. "received the power to will": literally, "received to will."
79. That is, happiness.

T: Then suppose someone who willed nothing but advantageous things could not have those that are greater and truer. Would he will lesser things—whichever ones he could make use of?

S: Indeed, he could not refrain from willing any of the very lowest, if he couldn't have greater ones.

T: Since he would will the lowest advantageous things, the impure things in which irrational animals take pleasure, wouldn't his will be unjust and blameworthy?

S: How would his will be unjust or deserve reproach, given that it would be willing what it did not receive the power not to will?

T: And yet it is well-established that his will, whether it wills the highest advantageous things or the lowest, is the work and gift of God, just as his life and his power of sensation are, and that there is neither justice nor injustice in it.

S: Undoubtedly.

T: Therefore, insofar as it is an essence,* it is something good; but as far as justice and injustice are concerned, it is neither good nor bad.

S: Nothing could be clearer.

T: But he ought not to be happy if he does not have a just will. Indeed, someone who wills what neither can nor ought to be the case cannot be either completely or commendably happy.

S: That is quite evident.

Chapter 14

That the case would be similar if he had received only the will for rectitude, and that he received both wills simultaneously in order that he might be both just and happy

T: Then let's consider the will for justice. If this same angel were given only the will for what it is fitting that he will, could he will anything else? And could he refrain on his own from willing justice?[80]

S: What we found regarding the will for happiness must also turn out to be completely true of this will too.

---

80. "willing justice": literally, "willing what he had received to will."

T: Therefore, he would not have either a just or an unjust will. For just as if he were given only the will for happiness, his will would not be unjust even if he willed unfitting things, since he would not be able to refrain from willing them, so also if he were given only the will for justice, his will would not be just simply because he willed what is fitting, since he would have received that willing in such a way that he would not be able to will otherwise.

S: That's right.

T: Therefore, since he cannot be called just or unjust for willing only happiness or for willing only what is fitting when he wills in that way out of necessity, and since he neither can nor ought to be happy unless he wills to be happy and wills it justly, God must create both wills in him in such a way that he both wills to be happy and wills it justly. This added justice governs his will for happiness so as to curtail its excess without eliminating its power to exceed. Thus, since he does will to be happy, he can exceed the limits of justice; but since he wills it justly, he does not will to exceed them. And thus, having a just will for happiness, he both can and ought to be happy. By refraining from willing what he ought not to will, even though he could will it, he deserves to be unable ever to will what he ought not, and by always retaining justice through a disciplined will he deserves not to lack happiness in any way. On the other hand, if he abandons justice through an undisciplined will, he deserves to be deprived of happiness altogether.

S: I cannot imagine anything more fitting.

T: Remember that earlier, when we were examining the will for happiness by itself, without the restraint we added so that it might subject itself to God, we said there would be no justice or injustice in it no matter what it willed.

S: I remember that well.

Chapter 15

That justice is something

T: Now do you think that this item which, when added to the will, governs the will so that it does not will more than what it is fitting and expedient for it to will, is something?

S: No sensible person will think that it is nothing.

T: This, as I believe you fully realize, is nothing other than justice.

S: It cannot be thought to be anything else.

T: So it is certain that justice is something.

S: Indeed, it is something outstandingly good.

Chapter 16

That injustice is nothing other than the absence of the justice there ought to be

T: Before it received this justice, was the will obligated to will and to refrain from willing in accordance with justice?

S: The will did not owe[81] what it did not have because it had not received it.

T: But once it had received justice, you have no doubt that it was obligated, unless it were to lose justice by coercion.

S: I think it is always bound by this obligation, whether it retains what it received or spontaneously* abandons it.

T: You're right. But what if the will abandons the justice that was so usefully and so wisely added to it—abandons it without being compelled by any lack or any coercion, but by spontaneously exercising its own power, that is, by willing more than it ought to? Will anything remain in that will besides what we imagined it to have before justice was added to it?

S: Since nothing was added but justice, once justice is lost it is certain that nothing will remain besides what was there before, except that the justice it received made the will a debtor to justice and left behind, as it were, certain beautiful traces of itself when justice was abandoned. For the very fact that it remains a debtor to justice shows that it had been adorned with the nobility of justice. And it is quite just that what has once received justice should always be a debtor to justice, unless it lost justice by coercion. Certainly, if a nature is shown to have once had justice, and to be always obligated to have so noble a good, it is thereby proved to be of far greater dignity than a nature that is known never to have had this good or to have been obligated to have it.

---

81. Bear in mind that 'ought,' 'owe,' and 'is obligated' all translate the same Latin word: *debet*. The cognate noun, *debitrix*, is translated 'debtor.'

T: You have thought this through very well. But add this to your view: the more praiseworthy a nature that had and ought to have this good is shown to be, the more blameworthy a person who does not have what he ought is proved to be.[82]

S: I heartily agree.

T: Pinpoint for me what it is in this nature that shows it to be praiseworthy and what makes the person blameworthy.

S: Its having had or being obligated to have justice is what shows the nature's dignity; not having justice is what makes the person corrupt. For his being obligated was brought about by the one who gave him justice, whereas his not having justice was brought about by the one who abandoned justice. After all, he is obligated because he had received it, whereas he does not have it because he forsook it.

T: So what you condemn in the will that did not remain steadfast in justice is not its being a debtor to justice, but its not having justice.

S: What I condemn in it is precisely the absence of justice, or in other words, its not having justice. For as I have already said, its being a debtor to justice confers honor, whereas its not having justice brings disgrace; and the more honorable it is to have justice, the more dishonorable it is to lack justice. Indeed, the only reason that the will is dishonored by not having justice through its own fault is that it is honored by being obligated to have justice by the goodness of its Giver.

T: Don't you judge that a will that does not have the justice it ought to have is unjust, and that there is injustice in it?

S: Who would judge otherwise?

T: I believe you would find nothing in it to condemn if it weren't unjust and there weren't injustice in it.

S: Nothing at all.

T: Therefore, what you condemn in it is nothing other than injustice and its being unjust.

S: I cannot condemn anything else in it.

T: So if, as you just said, you do not condemn anything in it other than the absence of justice and its not having justice, and if it is also true that you do not condemn anything in it other than there being injustice in it, in other words, its being unjust, then clearly its injustice or its being unjust is nothing other than the absence of justice or its not having justice.

---

82. For a precise statement of the distinction between nature and person that is implicit here, see *On the Virginal Conception*, Chapter 1.

S: There's no way there can be any difference between them.

T: Therefore, just as the absence of justice and not having justice have no essence,* so also injustice and being-unjust have no being, and therefore they are not something but rather nothing.

S: Nothing could be more logical.

T: Remember also that we've already agreed that once justice has been lost, nothing but the obligation to justice remains in him beyond what he had before he received justice.

S: Right.

T: But before he had justice he was not unjust and did not have injustice.

S: No.

T: Therefore, either there is no injustice in him and he is not unjust once justice has been lost, or else injustice and being-unjust are nothing.

S: No conclusion could be more inevitable.

T: And you conceded that once he has abandoned justice he has injustice and is unjust.

S: I could hardly fail to realize that!

T: Therefore, his injustice or being-unjust is nothing.

S: You have caused me to know what I used to believe without knowing it.

T: I suppose you also already know why, even though injustice is nothing but the absence of justice and being-unjust is nothing but not having justice, it is only after he has abandoned justice and not before he was given it that this absence of justice is called injustice, and not having justice is being unjust, and both are worthy of reproach. The reason is simply this: the absence of justice is dishonorable only where there ought to be justice. For example, not having a beard is not dishonorable for a man who is not yet supposed to have a beard, but once he ought to have a beard it is unbecoming for him not to have one. In the same way, not having justice is not a defect in a nature that is not obligated to have justice, but it is disgraceful for a nature that ought to have it. And to whatever degree his being supposed to have a beard shows his manly nature, to that degree his not having it disfigures his manly appearance.

S: I now understand quite well that injustice is nothing other than the absence of justice where there ought to be justice.

Chapter 17

Why an angel who abandoned justice cannot return to it

T: When we stipulated that only the will for happiness had been given to the angel we discussed earlier, we saw that he could not will anything else.

S: We saw that clearly.

T: Now that he has forsaken justice and retains only the will for happiness that he had before, can the angel who abandoned justice return by his own power to the will for justice, which he could not obtain before it was given to him?

S: Far less so can he return to it now. After all, he could not have justice then because of the way his nature had been created, whereas now he ought not to have it because of his desert and his fault.

T: Then there is no way he can have justice from himself when he doesn't have it, since he cannot have it from himself either before he receives it or after he has abandoned it.

S: He shouldn't have anything from himself.

Chapter 18

In what sense the evil angel made himself unjust and the good made himself just; and that the evil angel owes thanks to God for the goods he received and abandoned, just as the good owes thanks for the goods he received and preserved

T: Isn't there a sense in which, when he had justice, he was able to give himself justice?

S: How could he do that?

T: We use the word 'make' in many ways. For example, we say that we "make" something when we make a thing exist, and also when we can make it not exist but we refrain from doing so. And in this latter way he was able to give himself justice, since he was able to take it away from himself and also able not to take it away. In the same way, the one who remained steadfast in the truth in which he was made did not make himself not have it, although he could have; and thus he both gave himself justice and received all this from God. For both angels received from God the having of justice, the ability to retain justice, and the ability to abandon it. God gave them this last ability so that they could, in a certain sense, give justice to themselves. For if there was no sense in which they were able to take away justice from themselves, there was also no sense in which they were able to give it to themselves. Therefore, the one who in this sense gave himself justice received from God the very fact that he gave himself justice.

S: I see that they were able to give themselves justice by not taking it away from themselves; but one angel gave it to himself, while another took it away from himself.

T: Then do you see that each ought to give God equal thanks for his goodness, and that the devil is no less obligated to render God his due simply because he took away from himself what God gave him and was unwilling to receive what God offered?

S: I see that.

T: So an evil angel always owes thanks to God for the happiness that he took away from himself, just as a good angel always owes thanks for the happiness that he gave himself.

S: That's quite true.

T: I believe you realize that the only way God can make something unjust is by not making an unjust thing just even though he can. For until someone has received justice, he is neither just nor unjust; and once someone has received justice, he does not become unjust unless he spontaneously* abandons justice. Therefore, just as a good angel made himself just by not taking justice away from himself even though he could, so also God makes an evil angel unjust by not giving justice back to him even though he can.

S: That's easy to see.

Chapter 19

That the will, insofar as it has being, is a good; and that no thing is an evil

T: Let's return to our discussion of the will and recall what we discussed earlier, namely, that before the will receives justice, the will for happiness is not an evil but something good, no matter what it wills. It follows that when it abandons the justice it received, if it is the same essence* it was before, it is something good insofar as it has being; but insofar as the justice that was once in it is no longer there, it is called evil and unjust. For if willing to be like God were evil, the Son of God would not will to be like the Father; and if willing the lowest pleasures were evil, the will of brute animals would be called evil. But the will of the Son of God is not evil, since it is just; and the will of a nonrational animal is not called evil, since it is not unjust.

Hence, it follows that no will is an evil;[83] on the contrary, every will is a good insofar as it has being, since it is the work of God, and it is evil only insofar as it is unjust. Now only two sorts of things are called evil: an evil will, and whatever is called evil on account of an evil will (for example, an evil human being or an evil action); therefore, nothing is more evident than that no thing is an evil. Evil is nothing other than the absence of justice that has been forsaken, either in a will or in some other thing on account of an evil will.

Chapter 20

In what sense God makes both evil wills and evil actions;
and in what sense they are received from him

S: Your disputation is constructed out of such true, necessary, and evident arguments that I would see no argument that could undermine it, except that I find it entails something I think should not be said, and I cannot see how that conclusion could fail to be true if what you say is also true. For if willing to be like God is not nothing or evil, but something good, it could be had only from him from whom comes everything that is. Therefore, if an angel did not have anything he did not receive, then whatever he had, he received from the one from whom he had it. But what did he receive from God that God did not give? Therefore, if he had the will to be like God, he had it because God gave it to him.

T: How would it be surprising if we acknowledge that God gives an evil will by not preventing it even though he can—especially since the power to will anything at all is from him alone—in the same way in which God is said to lead us into temptation when he does not free us from it?

S: Looked at in that way, it doesn't seem absurd.

T: Now it is not unusual for us to speak of giving not only when someone willingly hands something over but also when someone grudgingly lets it go. So, since there is no giving without receiving, it is also not incongruous for us to speak of receiving not only when someone accepts what has been handed over but also when someone presumes to take what is unlawful.

---

83. Notice, Anselm does not say that no will is evil (*nullam voluntatem esse malam*), since obviously the devil's will is evil. He says that no will is *an* evil (*nullam voluntatem esse malum*): that is, every will, insofar as it has being, is a good.

S: What you say strikes me as neither incongruous nor unusual.

T: Then suppose we say that when the devil willed what he ought not, he both received this from God, since God permitted it, and did not receive it from God, since God did not consent. How would this be contrary to the truth?

S: Nothing in that statement seems incompatible with the truth.

T: So when the devil turned his will to what he ought not, both that willing and that turning were something, and nonetheless he had this something from no source other than God, since he could neither will anything nor move his will unless permitted by God, who makes all natures, substantial* and accidental,* universal and individual. For insofar as the will and the turning or movement of the will is something, it is good and is from God. But insofar as the will lacks justice, which it ought not to be without, it is not an unqualified* evil, but something evil; and its being evil is not from God, but from the one who wills or moves his will. Injustice, after all, is an unqualified evil, since it is nothing other than evil, which is nothing. By contrast, the nature in which there is injustice is something evil, since it is something, and something distinct from injustice, which is evil and nothing. Therefore, that which is something is brought about by God and is from God, but that which is nothing, that is, evil, is brought about by the unjust person and is from him.

S: Certainly we have to acknowledge that God brings about the natures of all things. But who would grant that he brings about the individual actions of perverse wills or the depraved movement of the will by which an evil will moves itself?

T: What's so surprising about our saying that God brings about the individual actions that are brought about by an evil will, since we acknowledge that he brings about the individual substances that are brought about by an unjust will and a dishonorable action?

S: I have no objection to make. I can't deny that any given action is genuinely something, and I refuse to say that anything that genuinely has some essence* is not brought about by God. And this argument of yours in no way accuses God or excuses the devil; in fact, it completely excuses God and accuses the devil.

Chapter 21

That the evil angel could not foreknow that he was going to fall

But I would like to know whether the rebel angel foreknew that he was going to abandon justice.

T: When you ask whether the angel who did not remain steadfast in the truth foreknew that he was going to fall, it's important to distinguish what sort of knowledge you mean. If you're asking about the knowledge that exists only when something is understood through a conclusive argument, then I reply emphatically that what can fail to be the case cannot be known, since what can fail to be the case cannot be shown by any conclusive argument to be the case. So it is clear that there was no way he could foreknow his own fall, which was not necessarily going to happen. After all, suppose this fall was not going to happen. Do you think he could have foreknown it if it was not going to happen?

S: It seems that what can fail to happen in the future cannot be foreknown, and that what is foreknown cannot fail to happen in the future. But I now recall that most celebrated question about divine foreknowledge and free choice. For although it is so authoritatively asserted and so usefully held—so much so that we should in no way doubt it because of any human reasoning—that divine foreknowledge and free choice are compatible with each other, they nonetheless seem to be irreconcilably opposed as far as the reasoning goes by which we examine them. Hence, we see that many people who consider this question are so inclined to one alternative that they entirely abandon the other, dying as they sink beneath the waves of unbelief; many, however, are tossed to and fro as if by opposing winds and are in danger of maintaining contradictory opinions. Therefore, since it is agreed that there is divine foreknowledge of all actions done by free choice and that none of them is a matter of necessity, it still seems that what is foreknown can fail to happen in the future.

T: For the time being I will reply briefly. God's foreknowledge is not properly* called foreknowledge. To him, everything is always present, so he does not have foreknowledge of what is future but simply knowledge of what is present. So since the argument regarding foreknowledge of a future thing differs from that regarding knowledge of a present thing, divine foreknowledge need not have the same implications as the foreknowledge we are asking about now.

S: I agree.

T: Let's return to the question at hand.

S: I'm happy to do as you say, but on the understanding that when I ask again about the issue I just mentioned, you will not refuse to give me the answer that God will deign to show you. For the resolution of that problem is absolutely crucial, whether someone has already come up with it or will come up with it in the future. I must admit that I have not yet read an argument anywhere that was sufficient for me to understand how the problem is resolved—except in that divine authority that I believe without hesitation.

T: When we come to that question, if we do, we will have whatever success God gives us.[84] For now, however, since the argument given above shows that the fallen angel could not foreknow his fall with the sort of foreknowledge that depends upon a thing's being necessary, listen to another argument that rules out any prior expectation of his fall not only through foreknowledge but even through rational calculation or any suspicion.

S: I am eager to hear it.

T: If, while he was remaining steadfast in his good will, he foreknew that he was going to fall, he either willed that this should happen, or he didn't.

S: One of these must be true.

T: But if, along with his foreknowledge, he at some time had the will to fall, he had already fallen in virtue of that evil will.

S: What you say is evident.

T: So it's not the case that before his fall he knew he was going to fall and also willed to fall.

S: No objection can be raised against your conclusion.

T: But if he foreknew he was going to fall and did *not* will it, then the more he willed to remain steadfast, the more his distress made him wretched.

S: That can't be denied.

T: And the more he willed to remain steadfast, the more just he was; and the more just he was, the happier he deserved to be.

S: Undeniably so.

T: Therefore, if he knew he was going to fall but did not will his fall, then the happier he deserved to be, the more wretched he actually was—and that's absurd.

S: I can't deny that that follows, but we often recognize that this happens not only without any absurdity but even in a praiseworthy way and through heavenly grace. For often—if I may mention a few things about the sufferings of the just—the more just someone is, the more he is moved by compassion for the plight of another. And we often see that someone who is more steadfast in justice is more brutally persecuted by the unjust.

T: The case is not the same for human beings as it is for that angel. The nature of human beings has now been made capable of suffering countless misfortunes because of the sin of our first parent, and out of this capacity for suffering, grace

---

84. Anselm takes up the issue at length in *De concordia*.

works incorruptibility for us in many ways. The angel, by contrast, had not yet deserved to suffer any evil because of some previous sin.

S: You have met my objection. It is obvious that this argument not only denies the evil angel foreknowledge of his fall but also eliminates any opinion that he was going to fall.

T: And there is something else that I think shows convincingly that he did not in any way conceive his future sin beforehand. Certainly he would have conceived it as either coerced or spontaneous.* Now he would not have supposed there was anything that might ever coerce him, and as long as he willed to persevere in the truth he could in no way think he was going to abandon it by his will alone. For it has already been shown that as long as he had an upright will, he willed to persevere in that will. Therefore, as long as he willed to persevere in retaining what he had, I can't see any way he could have so much as suspected that he was going to abandon it by his will alone, without any additional cause playing a role. I don't deny that he knew he could change the will that he was retaining. I just mean that he could not have thought that with no other cause acting upon him, he would ever spontaneously change the will that he willed to persevere in retaining.

S: Anyone who attentively understands what you are saying will see clearly that the evil angel could in no way know or think that he was going to do the evil act that he did.

Chapter 22

That he knew he ought not to will that which he sinned by willing, and that he knew he deserved punishment if he sinned

But I also want you to show whether he knew he ought not to will that which he willed when he sinned.

T: You shouldn't be in doubt about that if you think through what was said earlier. For if he hadn't known that he ought not to will that which he unjustly willed, he wouldn't have been aware that he ought to retain the will that he abandoned. And so he would not have been just by retaining, or unjust by abandoning, the justice that he would not have known. In fact, if he didn't know that he ought to be content with what he had received, he also could not have refrained from willing to have more than he had. And finally, since he was so rational that nothing prevented him from making use of reason, he was not ignorant of what he ought to will and what he ought not to will.

S: I don't see how your argument can be refuted, but even so, it seems to me that it prompts a certain question: if he knew that he ought not to abandon what he had received, surely he knew equally well that he would deserve punishment if he abandoned it. How, then, could someone who had received an ineliminable will for happiness spontaneously* will that which would bring him wretchedness?

Chapter 23

That he should not have known that he would be punished if he sinned

T: Just as it is certain that he must have known he would deserve punishment if he sinned, so also he should not have known that he would be punished if he sinned.

S: How did he not know that, if he was so rational that his rationality was not prevented from knowing the truth, as ours is often prevented by the burden of this corruptible body?

T: Because he was rational, he was able to understand that it would be just for him to be punished if he sinned. But since God's "judgments are a great abyss"[85] and "his ways are unsearchable,"[86] the angel could not have known for certain whether God would in fact do what he could justly do. Suppose someone were to say this: "There is no way the angel could have believed that God would damn his own creature, which he had made out of his great goodness, because of the creature's fault—especially since there had been no example of avenging justice prior to the angel's injustice. And he would have been certain that God had so wisely established the number of those who were meant to enjoy him that, just as it contained nothing superfluous, so also it would have been incomplete if it had been reduced. He would have been certain, too, that so outstanding a work of God would not remain incomplete in any part. If human beings had already been created, he could not have known by any reasoning that God was going to substitute human nature for the angelic or angelic nature for the human if either fell, instead of each nature's being restored to the state in which it was created, to fill its own proper place and not that of another. Or, if human beings had not yet been created, far less could he have thought they were going to be created as a substitute for another nature." If someone were to say all this, is there anything unreasonable in it?

S: To me it seems reasonable rather than unreasonable.

T: Let's return to what I had said, namely, that he should not have had this knowledge, since if he had known this, he, as one who both willed and had happiness, could not have spontaneously willed that which would make him wretched.

---

85. Psalm 36:6 (35:7).
86. Romans 11:33.

Therefore, he would not have been just for not willing what he ought not, since he would not have been able to will it.

Now consider another argument about whether he should have had the knowledge you're asking about. If he had known he would be punished, either he would have sinned or he wouldn't.

S: One of those would have been the case.

T: If he sinned even though he had foreseen such punishment, and even though he lacked nothing and there was nothing compelling him, he would be that much more deserving of punishment.

S: Yes.

T: So this foreknowledge was not beneficial for him.

S: Indeed, foreknowing his punishment was not beneficial for one who was going to sin.

T: Now if he hadn't sinned, he would have refrained from sinning either by his good will alone, or out of fear of punishment.

S: There's no other possibility.

T: But he showed by his action that he would not have refrained from sinning solely out of love for justice.

S: Undoubtedly.

T: But if he had refrained from sinning out of fear, he would not be just.

S: It is clear that he should not have known at all that the punishment now inflicted upon him was going to follow his sin.

Chapter 24

That even the good angel should not have known this

Now we believe that both the angel who remained steadfast in the truth and the angel who did not were endowed with equal knowledge when first created. But I don't see why this knowledge was denied to the angel whose good will was so tenacious that it was sufficient for him to refrain from sinning.

T: Still, if he had foreknown this punishment, he neither could have nor should have disregarded it.

S: So it seems.

T: Therefore, just as the love of justice was sufficient by itself for him not to sin, so also his hatred of that punishment would have been sufficient by itself for him not to sin.

S: Nothing could be clearer.

T: So there would have been two causes of his not sinning: one honorable and useful, the other not honorable and useless: that is, the love of justice and the hatred of punishment. For it is not honorable not to sin solely out of hatred of punishment, and hatred of punishment is useless for not sinning in a case where the love of justice is sufficient by itself.

S: There's no objection I could raise.

T: Then isn't his perseverance more resplendently satisfactory when only one cause of that perseverance is seen in him, a cause that is both useful and honorable because it is spontaneous,* than if at the same time another cause were to present itself, one that is useless and dishonorable because it is understood to be necessary*?

S: What you are saying is so evident that I am now glad he didn't know what a little while ago I wanted him to have known—except that we can't deny he has that knowledge now, since thanks to the example of the angel who sinned he can't help having it.

Chapter 25

That even if the good angel is said to be no longer able to sin solely because he now has this knowledge because of the fall of the devil, this is to his glory

T: Although both the good and the evil angel are now certain that such a fault will be followed by such punishment, this knowledge is different in each, the cause of the knowledge is not the same, and its result is different. For what the evil angel knows by his own experience, the good angel learned solely by someone else's example. The evil angel knows it by one means, because he did not persevere; the good angel knows it by another means, because he did persevere. Hence, just as the evil angel's knowledge is to his discredit, since his not persevering was blameworthy, so also the good angel's knowledge is to his glory, since his persevering was praiseworthy. So if the good angel is said to be no longer able to sin solely because he has this knowledge, it is perfectly clear that just as the knowledge itself, which was acquired by his praiseworthy perseverance, is glorious, so also the inability to sin that arises out of that glorious knowledge is to his glory. Therefore, just as the evil angel deserves reproach for being unable to return to justice, so also the good angel deserves praise for being unable to desert justice. For just as the evil angel cannot now return to justice because he deserted it by his evil will alone, so also the good angel is no longer able to desert justice because he remained in it by his good will alone. So it is clear that just as the evil angel's punishment for sin is his inability to recover what he abandoned, so also the good angel's reward for justice is his inability to abandon what he retained.

S: Your discussion of the good angel's knowledge and his inability to sin would be very appealing—if, as you say, it is because he persevered that the good angel comes to have this knowledge and the inability to sin. But in fact it seems that he acquired them, not because he persevered, but because the rebel angel did not persevere.

T: If you're right, the good angel can rejoice over the fall of the rebel angel inasmuch as it was beneficial for him that the evil angel fell, since he acquired this knowledge—in virtue of which he can no longer sin or be wretched—not because of his own good deserts, but because of someone else's evil deserts. And all of that is wildly absurd.

S: The more absurd it seems—as you point out—that the fall of the sinful angel was advantageous for the angel who remained steadfast, the more necessary it is for you to show that the good angel did not receive the knowledge in question because the evil angel sinned.

T: You must not say that the good angel attained this knowledge because the evil one sinned, but rather that he attained this knowledge *through the example of the fallen angel* because the evil angel sinned. For if neither had sinned, God would have given both the same knowledge by some other means because of the merit of their perseverance, without the example of anyone's fall. After all, no one will say that God could not have given his angels this knowledge by some other means. Therefore, since the evil angel sinned, God used his example to teach the good angel what he was going to teach anyway: not on account of some lack of power, because he could not teach it in any other way, but through that greater power of his through which he was able to bring good out of evil, so that no evil would remain disordered in the realm of all-powerful wisdom.

S: What you say is very appealing.

T: And so it is evident that even if the good angel were no longer able to sin solely because he knows that the sin of the evil angel was met with punishment, even so, this inability would not diminish his praiseworthiness but would be the reward for his having preserved justice. But you know, because it became clear earlier,[87] that

---

87. In Chapter 6.

the reason he cannot sin is that by the merit of his perseverance he has come to the point where he no longer sees what more he could will.

S: I haven't forgotten any of what we found out earlier through the investigations of reason.

Chapter 26

What it is we fear when we hear the word 'evil,' and what causes the deeds that injustice is said to cause, given that injustice and evil are nothing

But even though you have answered all my questions, there is something else I'm eager for you to explain. Since evil is nothing, what is it we fear when we hear the word 'evil'? And what causes the deeds that injustice, which is an evil, seems to cause, for example, in a robber or a lustful person?

T: I will answer you briefly. The evil that is injustice is always nothing; but the evil that is misfortune is undoubtedly sometimes nothing, as in the case of blindness, and sometimes something, as in the case of sadness and pain. And we always hate the misfortune that is something. So when we hear the word 'evil,' we do not fear the evil that is nothing, but the evil that is something, which follows from the absence of good. For many misfortunes that are evil and are something follow from injustice and blindness, which are evil and are nothing; and it is the former that we fear when we hear the word 'evil.'

Now when we say that injustice causes robbery, or that blindness causes someone to fall into a ditch, we must in no way understand this to mean that injustice or blindness causes something; rather, it means that if there had been justice in the will and sight in the eyes, neither the robbery nor the fall into the ditch would have happened. It's like when we say that the absence of the rudder drives the ship into the rocks or that the absence of the reins causes the horse to run wild; that simply means that if there had been a rudder on the ship and reins for the horse, the winds would not have driven the ship and the horse would not have run wild. For in the same way that a ship is controlled by the rudder and a horse by the reins, the human will is governed by justice and the feet by vision.

S: You have so thoroughly put my mind at rest concerning the evil that is injustice that every difficulty about it that used to trouble me has been cleared up. For this evil seems to generate a difficulty: if it were an essence,* it would be from God, since it is necessary that whatever is something is from him, and it is impossible that sin or injustice be from him. But I see that there is nothing threatening to a correct faith if the evil that is misfortune should sometimes be something.

220

Chapter 27

From what source evil entered the angel who used to be good

But don't grow weary of giving brief answers to my foolish questions, so that I might know how to answer those who ask the same thing. After all, it's not always easy to respond wisely to someone who asks a foolish question. So I ask this: From what source did the evil that is called injustice or sin first enter the angel who had been created just?

T: You tell me: From what source does nothing enter something?

S: Nothing neither enters nor goes away.

T: Then why do you ask from what source injustice entered, given that injustice is nothing?

S: Because when justice departs from where it was, we say that injustice comes in.

T: Then use the clearer and more proper* expression, and ask about the departure of justice. For often an apt question makes for an easier answer, while an inept question make the answer more difficult.

S: Then why did justice depart from the just angel?

T: If you want to speak properly, justice did not depart from the angel; rather, the angel abandoned justice by willing what he ought not to will.

S: Why did he abandon justice?

T: In saying that he abandoned it by willing what he ought not, I indicate clearly both why and how he abandoned it. He abandoned justice *because* he willed what he ought not to will, and he abandoned it *by* willing what he ought not to will.

S: Why did he will what he ought not?

T: No cause preceded this will, except that he was able to will.

S: Did he will it because he was able to will it?

T: No, because the good angel was likewise able to will it, but he didn't. No one wills what he can will simply because he can, with no other cause, although no one ever wills anything unless he can will it.

S: Then why did he will it?

T: Simply because he willed it. For there was no other cause by which his will was in any way incited or attracted. Instead, his will was its own efficient cause, if I may put the matter that way, and its own effect.

Chapter 28

That the power to will what he ought not was always good, and that willing itself is good with respect to its essence

S: If that power to will, and the willing itself, were something, they were good and were from God.

T: Both were something. The power indeed was something good, a spontaneous* gift of God, whereas the willing was good according to its essence* but bad in that it was done unjustly—and yet it was from God, since whatever is something comes from God. Indeed, any given person has from God not only what God spontaneously gives him, but also what he steals unjustly with God's permission. And just as God is said to do what he permits to be done, so also he is said to give what he permits to be stolen. Therefore, since it was with God's permission that the angel stole his exercise of the power God had spontaneously given him, he had this exercise of power—which is nothing other than the willing itself—from God. For willing is nothing other than exercising the power to will, just as speaking is nothing other than exercising the power to speak.[88]

---

88. See *De concordia* 3.11.

On the Incarnation of the Word

To THE LORD and father of the whole church in pilgrimage on earth, the Supreme Pontiff Urban:[1] brother Anselm, in his life a sinner, by his habit a monk, by the command or permission of God called bishop of the see of Canterbury, offers due submission with humble service and fervent prayers.

1   Because divine providence chose Your Holiness, to whom God entrusted the guardianship of Christian faith and life and the governance of his church, there is no one to whom one might more properly appeal if anything contrary to Catholic faith arises in the church, so that it might be corrected by your authority; nor is there anyone to whom one might more properly show a response to such error, so that it might be examined by your sound judgment. Therefore, just as there is no one to whom I can more fittingly address this letter, so too there is no one to whom I would more gladly send it than Your Wisdom, so that if anything in it requires amendment, it will be corrected by your censure, and if anything in it hews to the rule of truth, it will be reinforced by your authority.

When I was still abbot in the monastery at Bec, a certain clergyman[2] in France ventured this assertion: "If in God the three persons are just one thing and not three things (each person a thing in himself taken separately, like three angels or three souls, but such that they are altogether the same in will and power), then the Father and the Holy Spirit were incarnate along with the Son." When this claim had made its way to me, I began a letter in opposition to this error; but when it was only partly written I decided it was not worth finishing, thinking there was no need, since the one against whom it was written had himself abjured his error at the council convened by Rainaldus, the venerable Archbishop of Rheims—and also because I could not imagine that anyone would not realize he was in error. But unbeknownst to me, some of my brothers transcribed the part of the letter that I had written and gave it to others to read. I point this out so that if anyone comes across that part, he will leave it aside as incomplete and not fully worked out (although there is nothing false in it), and instead seek out this letter, where I have more diligently undertaken and completed what I undertook there. For after I had been seized and held for the episcopate in England by I know not what arrangement of God, I heard that the originator of the aforementioned novelty was persisting in his error, saying that he had abjured his statement only because he was afraid of being killed by the people.

For this reason, therefore, certain brothers compelled me by their requests to answer the question by which this fellow had been so exercised that he thought

---

1. Urban II, pope from 1088 to 1099.
2. Roscelin of Compiègne (roughly 1050 to 1125).

there was no way he could escape from it without becoming entangled with either an incarnation of God the Father and the Holy Spirit or a multiplication of gods. I plead this as my excuse, lest anyone should think I was so arrogant as to suppose that the Christian faith in all its strength required the help of my defense. Indeed, if I, a trivial and inconsiderable fellow, should try to write something to add strength and support to the Christian faith, when there are so many holy and wise people all over the world, I would indeed be judged arrogant and could appear worthy of ridicule. For if other people were to see me well-supplied with stakes and ropes, and the other usual equipment for trying to secure and steady things that are wavering, working to strengthen Mount Olympus so that no force would shake it or cause it to fall, it would be amazing if they could contain their laughter and derision. How much more so, then, with that "stone" that was "cut out of the mountain without hands and struck and crushed the statue" that Nebuchadnezzar saw in his dream, which has now become "a great mountain that filled the whole earth."[3] If I should try to support it with my arguments and steady it, as if it were wavering, so many holy and wise people who rejoice that they are secure upon its eternal steadfastness could grow angry with me and attribute my efforts not to sober-minded diligence but to frivolous self-aggrandizement. So if in this letter I have engaged in disputation concerning the steadfastness of our faith, it is not in order to strengthen that faith, but to satisfy the requests of the brethren who required this of me.

But if that man who put forward the aforementioned view has, by God's correction, returned to the truth, let him by no means suppose that I am saying anything against him in this letter, since he is no longer what he once was. For if he was "once darkness, but is now light in the Lord,"[4] the darkness that no longer exists does not require rebuke, but rather the light that now is shining deserves approval. Nevertheless, whether he has yet returned to the light or not, since I understand that many are troubled by this same question, even if their faith conquers the reasoning that they think contradicts the faith, I do not think it is wasted effort to dissolve the contradiction.

But before I speak to this question, I shall preface a few words in order to curb the presumption of those who with abominable insolence dare to raise as an objection to one of the articles of the Christian faith the fact that they cannot grasp it by their own intellect. With witless arrogance they judge that what they cannot understand is in no way possible, rather than acknowledging in humble wisdom that many things are possible that they are unable to comprehend. Indeed, no Christian ought to argue that something the Catholic Church believes with her

---

3. Daniel 2:34–35.
4. Ephesians 5:8.

heart and confesses with her lips[5] is not true. Instead, always holding that same faith unswervingly, loving it, and living in accordance with it, a Christian ought to seek the reason of its truth as humbly as he can. If he is capable of understanding, let him give thanks to God. If he is not, let him not brandish his horns to scatter,[6] but instead let him bow his head in reverent submission.

For human wisdom trusting in itself can more quickly tear out its own horns by brandishing them than it can roll this stone by pushing. For as soon as some people have begun to produce, as it were, horns of self-confident knowledge—not realizing that "if someone thinks he knows something, he does not yet know it as he ought to know it"[7]—they often presume to rise to the very loftiest questions of the faith before they have developed spiritual wings through the firmness of their faith. This is how it comes about that they absurdly attempt to climb up through their understanding to those things that first require the ladder of faith: as Scripture says, "Unless you believe, you will not understand."[8] And when they do this, they are compelled to fall into manifold errors because their intellect fails them. For it is obvious that they do not have the firmness of faith, given that they raise objections against the truth of that faith, which has been made firm by the holy fathers, simply because they cannot themselves understand what they believe. It is as if bats and owls, which see the sky only at night, should dispute about the midday sun with eagles, who behold the sun itself with unflinching eyes.

So first our heart must be cleansed by faith; Scripture describes God as "cleansing their hearts by faith."[9] And first our eyes must be enlightened by our keeping the Lord's commandments, since "the command of the Lord is bright, enlightening the eyes."[10] And first we ought to become little children through our humble obedience to the testimonies of God, in order that we might learn the wisdom that the testimony of the Lord gives, for "the testimony of the Lord is sure, giving wisdom to little children."[11] This is why the Lord says, "I thank you, Father, Lord of heaven and earth, that you have hidden these things from the learned and wise,

---

5. Cf. Romans 8:8.

6. In the Old Testament the horn is regularly a symbol of power and aggression. The nearest parallels to Anselm's usage in the Latin Vulgate are in Psalm 43:6 (44:5), "In you we will scatter our enemies with the horn"; Ezekiel 34:21, "And with your horns you scattered all the weak sheep"; and Zechariah 1:19, "These are the horns that have scattered Judah and Israel and Jerusalem." The close parallel with Ezekiel suggests that by "scattering" Anselm is talking about the disturbing effect that undisciplined skepticism has on those whose faith is weak.

7. 1 Corinthians 8:2.

8. Isaiah 7:9 in the Old Latin text.

9. Acts 15:9.

10. Psalm 19:8 (18:9).

11. Psalm 19:7 (18:8).

and have revealed them to little children."[12] First, I say, we must set aside the things of the flesh and live according to the spirit. Only then can we investigate perceptively the deep things of faith. For someone who lives according to the flesh is carnal or sensual. Of such a person Scripture says that "the sensual man does not perceive the things that are of the Spirit of God";[13] but one who "by the Spirit puts to death the deeds of the flesh"[14] is made spiritual, and of him we read that "the spiritual man judges all things, and he himself is judged by no one."[15] For it is true that the more abundantly we take nourishment in Holy Scripture from those things that feed us through obedience, the more acutely we are brought to those things that satisfy us through understanding. Indeed, someone who ventures to say, "I have more understanding than all my teachers," is speaking in vain unless he is bold to add, "because your testimonies are my meditation."[16] And someone who proclaims, "I have more understanding than my elders," is lying unless he is well-acquainted with what follows: "because I have sought out your commandments."[17] There is no room for doubt about what I say: one who has not believed will not understand. For one who has not believed will not experience, and one who has not experienced will not know. For as much as experiencing a thing is superior to hearing about it, so much does the knowledge of someone who has experience surpass that of someone who merely hears.

And not only is the mind forbidden to rise to understanding higher things apart from faith and obedience to God's commandments, but understanding once granted is taken away and faith itself is destroyed if one does not take care to preserve a good conscience. For the Apostle says of certain people, "Although they had known God, they did not glorify him as God or give thanks; but their thoughts became empty, and their foolish hearts were darkened."[18] And when he commanded Timothy to "fight the good fight," he spoke of "preserving faith and a good conscience, which some have rejected and suffered shipwreck regarding the faith."[19] Let no one, therefore, be in a hurry to plunge into the thicket of divine questions unless he has first sought in firmness of faith the weight of good character and wisdom, lest he should run carelessly and frivolously along the many side-roads of sophistries and be snared by some obstinate falsehood.

---

12. Matthew 11:25.
13. 1 Corinthians 2:14.
14. Romans 8:13.
15. 1 Corinthians 2:15.
16. Psalm 119:99 (118:99).
17. Psalm 119:100 (118:100).
18. Romans 1:21.
19. 1 Timothy 1:18–19.

And since everyone ought to be admonished to approach questions concerning Holy Scripture as cautiously as possible, those dialecticians—or rather, heretics of dialectic—in our own day who suppose that universal substances are nothing but empty air,[20] who cannot understand color to be anything but body or human wisdom to be anything but the soul, ought to be blown far away from any engagement with spiritual questions. Indeed, in their souls, reason—which ought to be the ruler and judge of everything in a human being—is so wrapped up in bodily imaginations that it cannot extricate itself from them; their reason cannot discriminate between those bodily imaginations and the things that ought to be contemplated by reason itself, alone and unmixed. For they do not yet even understand how the plurality of human beings in the species are one human being. How, then, will they comprehend how the plurality of persons in that most hidden and most exalted nature—each of whom individually is perfect God—are one God? Their minds are too dark to distinguish between a horse and its color. How, then, will they distinguish between the one God and his several relations? And finally, they cannot understand how something can be human without being an individual; there is no way they will understand anything to be human unless it is a human person, since every individual human being is a person. How, then, will they understand that the Word assumed human being but did not assume a person: that is, that the Word assumed another nature, not another person? I have said these things so that no one will venture to investigate the most exalted questions concerning the faith before he is ready—or so that if he does venture to do so, the difficulty or impossibility of understanding them will not dislodge him from the truth to which he has held fast by faith. Now we must come to the matter on account of which I have undertaken to write this.

2   This fellow who is said to claim that the three persons are like three angels or three souls says this (so I hear): "The pagans defend their law, the Jews defend their law, so we Christians ought also to defend our faith." Let us hear how this Christian defends his faith. He says, "If the three persons are just one thing and not three things (each person a thing in himself taken separately, like three angels or three souls, but such that they are altogether the same in will and power), then the Father and the Holy Spirit were incarnate along with the Son."

Look at what this fellow says, at how this Christian defends his faith. Surely he either intends to acknowledge three gods or else does not understand what he is saying. Now if he acknowledges three gods, he is not a Christian. And if he affirms what he does not understand, no one should believe him. The reply to this man should not be made using the authority of Holy Scripture, since either he does not believe Scripture or he interprets it in some perverse sense: For what does Holy

---

20. "empty air": *flatus vocis*, literally, "the breathing of a voice." The expression is associated in particular with Roscelin.

Scripture say any more clearly than that there is one and only one God? Instead, his error should be exposed on the basis of reason, which he tries to use to defend himself. Now in order to do this more easily and concisely, I will speak only of the Father and the Son, since these two persons are clearly distinguished from one another by their own proper designations. The name 'Holy Spirit,' after all, is not foreign to the Father and the Son, since both of them are spirit and both are holy. But what we will find in the case of the Father and the Son regarding the unity of substance and plurality of persons, we will recognize in the case of all three persons, without any room for doubt.

So let him say, "If the two persons, the Father and the Son, are not two things." Let us ask first what he means by 'two things.' We do after all believe that each person is that which is common to both and is also that which is proper to himself. The person of the Father is God, which is common to him and the Son, and is also Father, which is proper to him. Similarly, the person of the Son is God, which is common to him and the Father, and is also Son, which is said only of this person. So in these two persons one feature is common, namely God, and two features are proper, namely Father and Son. All those features that are common to them—for example, omnipotent, eternal*—are understood in the meaning of the one common term 'God.' And the features that are proper to the individual persons—as begetter or begetting is proper to the Father, and Word or begotten to the Son—are signified by these two names, 'Father' and 'Son.' So when he says that these two persons are two things, I want to know what he is calling two things: what is common to them, or the individual characteristics that are proper to the individual persons. Now if he is saying that the two proper characteristics (namely, Father and Son) are two things, but in such a way that what is common is just one thing and not more than one, there was no point in saying that, since no Christian professes that the Father and the Son are just one thing in terms of these proper characteristics, but two things. After all, we typically apply the word 'thing' to whatever we say is something in any way, and when we say 'Father' or 'Son' of God, we are saying something of God. And everyone knows that in God the Father is not the Son and the Son is not the Father, even though in one human being a father is a son and a son is a father, if one and the same human being is both a father and a son. The reason for this is that in God 'Father' and 'Son' are said as opposites, whereas in one human being they are not said in opposition to each other—rather, he is said to be a father with respect to a different son and a son with respect to a different father.

So in this way there is nothing to prevent our saying that the two persons, the Father and the Son, are two things, provided that we understand what sort of things they are. The Father and the Son are two things in such a way that what we understand in these two things is not their substance but their relations. But this fellow makes it clear by what he says next that this is not the way in which he understands the two persons to be two things. For when he says, "If the three persons are just one thing and not three things" he adds, "each person a thing in himself taken separately." He seems to mean 'separately' in a way that makes it impossible for the Father and the Son both to be present at the same time in the same human being. This, he thinks, is the only way to keep the Father from sharing the Son's Incarnation. For he does not see how, if one believes that there is one and only one God who is Father and Son, the Father and the Son can be separated in such a way that they are not both in the same human being at the same time, in virtue of the separateness by which being the Father and being the Son are distinct, given that fatherhood and sonship are distinct from one another. Therefore, either he is speaking of some other way in which the Father is separate from the Son, other than the separateness in terms of their being Father and Son to each other through their proper characteristics—since he does not understand that their being separate in this way is enough to make Incarnation foreign to the Father; indeed, he thinks that if the Father and the Son exist at the same time, it follows that the Father shares the Son's Incarnation—or else he is talking about that very separateness, in which case he is wasting his efforts, since as I have already said, the Christian faith does understand the Father and the Son to be two things in precisely this sense.

Now when he says, "like three angels or three souls," he shows quite clearly that he is *not* talking in terms of the separation or plurality that exists in them on account of their proper characteristics. Clearly we do not say of numerically one thing that it is two angels or two souls, nor do we say of two angels or two souls that they are numerically one anything, in the way that we do say of numerically one God that he is both Father and Son and of the Father and Son that they are numerically one God. For we believe and say that God is Father and God is Son, and conversely, that the Father is God and the Son is God. And yet we do not believe or say that there is more than one God, but rather that there is numerically one God as a nature, even though the Father and the Son are not one, but two. For we call something an angel or a soul according to substance, not according to relation. For although the name 'angel' is taken from the angels' function ('angel' means 'messenger'), we use it to indicate the substance, just as we use 'soul' for a species of substance. He shows that he understands this by saying, "like three angels or three souls," without differentiating the two cases. And so what he means is the sort of plurality or separateness that a plurality of angels or souls have, that is, the sort that a plurality of substances have. He seems to indicate this meaning quite clearly when he adds, "but such that they are altogether the same in will and power," since he is understanding will and power in this plurality of things in the same way as in a plurality of angels or souls. And that makes no sense if one is thinking of the divine persons as a plurality of things in accordance with the proper characteristics of the persons, not in accordance with what is said of them in common. After all, there is no will or power belonging to the Father or to the Son according to their proper characteristics—that is, according to fatherhood or sonship—but only according to the substance of the Godhead that is common to them both. Therefore, if he means that the three persons are three things in accordance with those proper characteristics, it is clear how unnecessary it was for him to say this; when he goes on to add, "like three angels or three souls," it is also clear how absurd his words are.

3   But if he is saying that the persons are two things according to that which is common to them—that is, as each of them individually and the two of them at once are one perfect God—then I must first ask whether he is a Christian. I believe he will reply that he is. So then he believes that there is one God, and that this one God is three persons, that is, Father, Son, and Holy Spirit, and that only the person of the Son was incarnate, although with the cooperation of the other two persons. But someone who believes these things also affirms that someone who sets out to make any claims that contradict them is not a Christian. So if this fellow believes these things, he also denies that someone who argues against them is a Christian. Now let us see whether this fellow is trying to undermine this faith. When he says (I will continue to speak just of two persons, meaning what I say to be understood as applying to all three), "If the two persons are one thing and not two, like two angels or two souls, it follows that the Father too was incarnate if the Son was incarnate," I take it that his reasoning goes like this:

> If God is numerically one and the same thing, and that very thing is the Father and is also the Son, how can it be that the Father is not incarnate as well, given that the Son is incarnate? Clearly an affirmation and its negation are not both true of one and the same thing at one and the same time. But it is perfectly fine to affirm something of one thing and deny it of another thing at one and the same time. For it is not the case that one and the same Peter both is an apostle and is not an apostle. Even if we speak of that one person by two different names, and say of him under one name that he is an apostle and under another name that he is not—for example, "Peter is an apostle" and "Simon is not an apostle"—it is not the case that both statements are true; one of them is false. By contrast, it is possible for "Peter is an apostle" and "Stephen is not an apostle" both to be true, since Peter and Stephen are two different people. So if the Father and the Son are numerically one thing and not two distinct things, it is not true that something ought to be affirmed of the Son and denied of the Father or affirmed of the Father and denied of the Son. Therefore, whatever the Father is, the Son is too; and what is said of the Son should not be denied of the Father. But the Son was incarnate, so the Father too was incarnate.

But if this reasoning is sound, the heresy of Sabellius[21] is true. For if whatever is said of one person is also said of another, on the grounds that the two persons are one thing, it follows that because 'Son' and 'Word' and 'begotten' are said of the Son, they must also be said of the Father. And just as the Father is Father and Begetter and Unbegotten, these things must also be said of the Son. And if that is the case, the Father is not distinct from the Son nor the Son from the Father. Therefore, they are not two persons, but one. After all, the reason they are said to be two persons is that the Father and the Son are believed to be distinct from one another, assuming that God is both Father and Son. For a father is always the father *of* someone, and a son is always the son *of* someone; but a father is never his own father, and a son is never his own son. Rather, a father is distinct from the one whose father he is, and similarly a son is distinct from the one whose son he is. Hence, if, in God, the Father and the one whose Father he is are not distinct, and the Son and the one whose Son he is are not distinct, it is false to say of God that he is Father or Son. For if there is not in God someone distinct from the Father whose Father he is, God cannot be a Father. And similarly, if there is not in God someone distinct from the Son whose Son he is, God cannot be a Son. And from that it will follow that there is no basis for speaking of two persons in God: for we speak of two persons on the grounds that God is a Father and God is a Son, and a father is always distinct from a son.

So do you see how our faith is destroyed by the opinion of this fellow who supposes that if the plurality of persons in God are one thing and not a plurality of things, it follows that the Father was incarnate along with the Son? If this inference of his is correct, then what follows is not only what I have already said about the Father and the Son, but such extensive confounding of all three persons that whatever is said properly of any one of them must be said of all three in common. Consequently there will be no basis for distinguishing from one another the Father, the Son, and the Holy Spirit who proceeds from the Father and the Son, as I have shown in the case of the Father and the Son. Nor will there be any relation in God, since there is no relation in God other than that in accordance with which the persons are distinguished one from another. Therefore, there will not be a plurality of persons. For on the supposition that one thing is three persons, either what he says does not follow, or else all the conclusions I have drawn follow at once—for the strength of the inference is similar in each case. Why, then, does he proceed to the Incarnation, as if that alone raised a difficulty, and not say instead, "If the three persons are one thing, they are not three persons"? For he

---

21. Sabellius taught that Father, Son, and Holy Spirit are not distinct persons in God but merely different ways in which an utterly unitary God relates to his creation. He was excommunicated by Pope Calixtus I in 220.

can raise this question both independently of the Incarnation and on the basis of the Incarnation.

4   On the other hand, if he means to assert outright that the three persons, insofar as each is God, are not one thing, but three things, each person in himself a thing as three angels are, then it is unmistakably clear that he is setting up three gods. Perhaps, though, he was not the one who said, "like three angels or three souls," but merely affirmed that the three persons are three things, without adding any comparison, and the man who sent me his question offered this comparison on his own. Why, then, is he fooled—or why does he fool others—by this word 'thing,' given that the word 'God' signifies this very thing? Surely he will either deny that God is that thing in which we profess that there are three persons—indeed, that thing that we profess to be three persons—or else, if he does not deny this, it follows that he must affirm that the persons are not one God but three gods, just as he claims that they are not one thing but three things. I leave it to Christians to judge how impious these claims are.

But he will reply, "My saying 'three things' does not compel me to acknowledge three gods, since these three things together are one God." To this we say: Therefore, each of these three things—that is, each person—is not God; instead, God is composed of three things. Therefore, the Father is not God, the Son is not God, and the Holy Spirit is not God, since 'God' must not be said of any one person or of two, but only of all three persons named together. And that likewise is impious. For if that is the case, God is not a simple nature but is composed of parts. Yet anyone who has a simple understanding, one that is not overloaded by a surfeit of phantasms, understands that simple things as such are superior to composites as such, since necessarily every composite can be divided either in reality or in the understanding. Such division is unintelligible in the case of simple things, since no intellect can divide up into parts something that cannot be conceived to have parts. Therefore, if God is composed of three things, either no nature is simple, or there is some nature that is in one respect superior to God's nature—and it is no great mystery just how false both of these alternatives are. Even if this fellow belongs to those modern dialecticians who believe that nothing exists apart from what they can grasp through their imaginations, and he does not think there is anything that has no parts, he will at least not deny that he understands that if there *were* something that could not be dissolved either in reality or in the understanding, it would be greater than what can be dissolved, even if only in the understanding. And so if every composite can be dissolved, at least in thought, when he says that God is composite, he is saying that he can understand something greater than God. So his understanding passes beyond God, which no understanding can do.

5   But let us see what he adds as if to drive away the absurdity that seems to result if these three persons are three things: "but such that there is one will and power of these three things." Here we must ask whether these three things are of divine

nature insofar as they are understood separately from each other, or in accordance with their common will and power, or neither only in accordance with what they possess individually nor only in accordance with what is common to them, but in accordance with both at once. Clearly if they possess deity in accordance with what they are separately, they are three gods. In that case, they can be understood to be the same without reference to their will and power, since proper characteristics are always understood separately from common characteristics and vice versa. But in fact the divine nature can in no way be understood apart from will and power.

Now if the persons taken singly or two at a time or all three at once are God in accordance with their one will and power, what are these three separate things doing there? For some other thing would have to bring them together into the unity of the Godhead, and they would not be sufficient for perfection or for any contribution to God's existence. After all, if one will and power is sufficient for God's perfection, what are these three things that God needs, and for what purpose does he need them? For we believe that God needs nothing. So it is pointless to conceive of these three things in God.

And if it is not just these three things, and not just the one will and power, but all these taken together that compose God, I will note again that God is a composite, and that things that are not in themselves God or gods make up God. Or if he says that these three things bear the name 'God' in virtue of their power or will, as a human being is called 'king' in virtue of his royal power, then 'God' is not the name of a substance; rather, those three whatever-they-ares are called three 'gods' accidentally,* in the way that three human beings who have the same royal power are called three 'kings.' Three human beings, after all, cannot be one king. And there is no need to point out how blasphemous all this is.

I would need to fill a sizeable volume if I undertook to write out all the absurdities and impieties that result if indeed it follows that if one divine person is incarnate, the other two must also be incarnate, on the grounds that those three persons are one thing in accordance with what we say in common of all three; or if, because only the Son was incarnate, it follows that the three persons are three separate things, as this fellow against whom I am writing supposes. Therefore, it is clear that he ought not to be eager to engage in disputes about profound matters, and especially about those in which error is dangerous.

6   But perhaps he will say to me: "You think the conclusions you draw follow necessarily if I am right about the inferences I make. But the inferences I make seem just as necessary to me as yours do to you. So show that my conclusions do not in fact follow, and then I will acknowledge with you that nothing absurd follows if the Son alone was incarnate or if the three persons are one thing. If you fail to show this, you do not solve the problem but merely compound it by joining me in proving that many absurdities follow from these assumptions. And if those absurd conclusions must be rejected, both of us equally ought to conclude that if only the

Son was incarnate, the three persons are not one thing, and that if they are one thing, all three were equally incarnate."

It is therefore incumbent upon me to show in what respect he is mistaken, and how it does not follow that if the Son alone was incarnate, the three persons are three separate things, or that if the three persons are one thing, all three were incarnate. Now the fact that God is both one, single, individual, and simple* nature* and also three persons has been set forth by the unassailable arguments of the holy fathers, and especially of blessed Augustine, following the apostles and evangelists. And if anyone will think it worth his while to read my two little works, the *Monologion* and *Proslogion*, which I wrote mainly so that what we hold by faith concerning the divine nature and persons, leaving aside the Incarnation, could be proved by necessary reasons, independently of the authority of Scripture—if, I say, anyone should be willing to read these works, I think he will find in them discussions of this matter that he will not be able to refute and will not wish to belittle. If in those books I have said anything that I did not read elsewhere (or do not remember having read elsewhere) as a reply on behalf of our faith to those who refuse to believe what they do not understand, and ridicule those who do believe, or to assist the devout inquiry of those who humbly seek to understand what they most steadfastly believe, I do not think I should be reproached in any way. For I have not said it as if I were teaching something that our teachers did not know or correcting something they did not say well, but as saying something that they were silent about—something that nevertheless does not contradict what they said, but harmonizes with it. But to save those who read this letter the trouble of looking into those other writings in order to know, not just by faith but by evident argument, that the three persons are not three gods but only one, and yet that God's being incarnate according to one person does not necessitate his being incarnate according to the others, I will say something here that I think will be sufficient to refute the opinion of this self-styled defender of our faith.

He says explicitly that either the Father and the Holy Spirit were incarnate along with the Son, or else the three persons are three separate things—separate to so great a degree, in his estimation, that neither the Father nor the Holy Spirit is in the Son. After all, if the other two persons are in the Son and the Son is in a human being, they too are in that human being. Hence, since the three persons are all in one and the same human being, he thinks it follows that if they are one thing, there is no way for the person of the Son to be incarnate in that human being apart from the other two persons. He does not, however, deny that there are three persons or that the Son was incarnate. Now as was shown above, if the three persons are three separate things, either it follows that there are three gods, or else the other absurdities I have already discussed are true. Therefore, with the help of the one and only God, I will now show briefly, first, that even if there are three gods, that will not help avert an incarnation of the Father and the Holy Spirit (which he thinks we can avoid only by positing a multitude of gods), and second, that there is only one God, not more than one. Then I will make it clear that although the one God is three persons, the incarnation of one person not only does not necessitate the incarnation of the others but in fact makes their incarnation impossible.

7   It belongs to the divine nature to be always and everywhere in such a way that nothing is ever or anywhere without its presence. If this were not so, it would by no means have power everywhere and always, and what does not have power everywhere and always is in no way God. For even if he says that it is not the divine substance, but its power, that is everywhere and always, he will still not deny that power is either accidental* or substantial* with respect to the divine nature. Power is certainly not accidental with respect to God, since every substance can either exist or be understood without its accident, whereas God can neither exist nor be understood without power. Yet if power is substantial with respect to God, it is either a part of his essence* or the very same thing that is his whole essence. Now it is not a part, since, as was said above, that which has parts can be dissolved either in reality or in the understanding, and that is altogether alien to God. Therefore, the being of God and of his power are one and the same. And so, just as God's power is always and everywhere, so too whatever God is is everywhere and always. Therefore, when the aforesaid self-styled defender of our faith says that there are three gods, he cannot show how they are separate in the way that he thinks is necessary in order to save the Father and the Holy Spirit from being incarnate. So this multiplicity of gods cannot help him defend the Father and the Holy Spirit from being incarnate, since in his multiplying of gods we cannot find the distinction without which, on his own view, such a defense cannot succeed at all.

8   Here is a straightforward argument for the conclusion that there is only one God, and not more than one: either God is not the supreme Good, or there are many supreme Goods, or there is only one God and not more than one. Now no one denies that God is the supreme Good, since whatever is less than something else is in no way God, and whatever is not the supreme Good is less than something else, since it is less than the supreme Good. And clearly the supreme Good does not admit plurality within itself in such a way that there are several* supreme Goods. For if there are several supreme Goods, they are equal; but the supreme Good is the one that so surpasses other goods that it has neither superior nor peer. Therefore, there is one and only one supreme Good. So there are not several gods, but one and only one God, just as there is one and only one supreme Good. And the same reasoning that applies to the supreme Good proves also that one cannot in any way speak of more than one supreme substance or essence or nature.

9   Though this one and only God is three persons—Father, Son, and Holy Spirit—it is not necessary, as my opponent thinks, that if the Son is incarnate, the other persons are incarnate as well; rather, this is impossible. For he does not deny

that there is a plurality of persons, precisely because the persons are distinct from one another—after all, if they were not distinct from one another, they would not be a plurality. But in order to lay out more concisely and easily what I want to say, I shall speak only of the Father and the Son, as I did above; it will be clear from what is said about them how we ought to understand what is true of the Holy Spirit.

Now *qua* substance the Father and the Son are not a plurality or distinct from each other, since they are not two substances; the Father is not one substance and the Son a distinct substance, but rather the Father and the Son are one and the same substance. Yet *qua* person they are a plurality and distinct from each other, since the Father and the Son are not one and the same person, but two persons distinct from each other. So he says, "If the Son is incarnate, and the Son is not a different thing from the Father, but numerically one and the same thing as the Father, then it is necessary that the Father too is incarnate. For it is impossible that numerically one and the same thing at a given time both is and is not incarnate in one and the same human being." But I say that if the Son is incarnate, and the Son is not numerically one and the same person that the Father is, but a distinct person, then it is not necessary that the Father is incarnate as well. For it is possible for one person to be incarnate in one human being and at the same time for a distinct person not to be incarnate in that same human being. He replies: "If God the Son is incarnate, and the God who is the Son is not distinct from, but is numerically one and the same as, the God who is the Father, then although the Father and the Son are indeed distinct persons, it seems more necessary that the Father be incarnate along with the Son on account of their oneness in deity than it seems possible for him not to be incarnate too on account of their distinctness as persons."

Notice how the one who says this is limping with both feet when it comes to the Incarnation of the Son of God. Someone who understands his Incarnation properly believes that the Son assumed human being not into a unity of nature but into a unity of person, whereas this fellow dreams that human being was assumed by the Son of God into a unity of nature rather than into a unity of person. For if that were not his view, he would not say that it is more necessary for the Father to be incarnate along with the Son because the Father and the Son are one God than it is possible for the Father not to be incarnate as well because they are a plurality of persons. So anyone who thinks that this Incarnation is according to the unity of nature in such a way that the Son cannot be incarnate without the Father, and who does not understand that it is in accordance with the unity of person in such a way that the Father cannot be incarnate along with the Son, is limping with both feet (that is, in both respects) when it comes to the Incarnation of the Son of God, who is one nature with the Father and a distinct person from the Father. Certainly God did not assume human being in such a way that the nature of God and of human being are one and the same, but in such a way that the person of God and of the human being are one and the same. This can only be the case in one divine person, since it is unintelligible for distinct divine persons to be one and the same person as one and the same human being. For if one human being is one person with each of a plurality of persons, it is necessary that a plurality of persons that are distinct from one another are one and the same person, which is impossible. For this reason, once God is incarnate according to any one person, it is impossible for him to be incarnate also according to another person.

10   Now although it was not our aim in this letter to show why God assumed human being into a unity of person with the Son rather than into a unity with either of the other persons, I think some reason for this ought to be given, since the topic has come up. Certainly if the Holy Spirit had become incarnate, as the Son did, the Holy Spirit would have been the son of a human being, and so there would have been two sons in the divine Trinity: the Son of God and the son of a human being. The result would have been a confusing uncertainty whenever we talked about "God the Son," since each would be both God and a son, although one would be the Son of God and the other the son of a human being. There would also have come to be an inequality of sorts between the divine persons—who ought to be equal in every respect—*qua* sons; the one who was son of the greater parent would be superior in dignity, whereas the one who was the son of the lesser parent would be subordinate in his lowliness. For the dignity of being Son of God exceeds the dignity of being the son of a human being as much as the greatness of divine nature exceeds the greatness of human nature. So if the Holy Spirit had been born of a virgin, then given that the Son of God would have only the more exalted birth that is from God, whereas the Holy Spirit would have only the lesser birth that is from a human being, one divine person would be greater than another according to the dignity of his birth, which is absurd.

Now if the Father had assumed human being into a unity of person with himself, the plurality of sons in God would have caused the same absurdities, plus an additional one. For if he had been the Son of a virgin, two persons in the Trinity would have taken the name of 'grandson,' since the Father would be the grandson of the virgin's parents, and the Son would also be the grandson of that same virgin,[22] even though he would not derive in any way from her.

Therefore, since it is impossible for there to be any absurdity, however trivial, in God, it was not appropriate for any divine person to be incarnate other than the Son. For nothing absurd follows from his becoming incarnate. That the Son is said to be less than the Father and the Holy Spirit according to his humanity does not mean that those two persons are superior to the Son, since the Son possesses the very same majesty by which they are greater than the Son's humanity; and by virtue of that majesty the Son is, like them, greater than his own humanity.

---

22. Because he would be the Son of the Father, who would in turn be the son of the virgin. See the parallel arguments given in *Cur Deus Homo*, Book 2, Chapter 9.

And there is another reason why incarnation is more suitable to the Son than to another person. The person who was to become incarnate was going to pray for the human race, and the human mind understands well enough that it is more fitting for the Son to pray to the Father than for any other person to pray to any other person—although it is not divinity that makes this prayer, but humanity that prays to divinity. The Son of God makes such prayer because a human being is the Son of God by unity of person.

Moreover, the person who was to assume human being was going to come in order to fight against the devil and in order to intercede for human beings, as I have said. Both the devil and human beings willed to make themselves like God through an act of robbery when they exercised their own wills. And since this was an act of robbery, it was an act of falsehood, since they were not able to will this otherwise than unjustly. For the will of an angel or of a human being is his own when it is contrary to the will of God; someone who wills what God forbids has no author of his will but himself, and so his will is his own. Even if a human being at some time subjects his will to that of another human being, his will is still his own if it is contrary to God; for he subjects it to someone else only in order to achieve something that he himself wills, and so he is the author of his own subjection of his will to another. Hence, his will is his own; it is not subjected to another. Now it is the prerogative of God alone to have his own will, a will that is not subjected to another. So those who exercise their own will are trying by an act of robbery to be like God and are guilty of depriving God (as far as they are able) of the dignity that rightly belongs to him and the superiority that is his alone. For if there is any other will that is not subjected to another, God's will will not be superior to all others, and it will not be the only will to which no other will is superior. Therefore, none of the three divine persons could more fittingly "empty himself, receiving the form of a slave"[23] in order to wage war against the devil and intercede on behalf of human beings, who by an act of robbery arrogated to themselves a false likeness of God, than the Son who, being "the splendor of eternal light"[24] and the true image of the Father,[25] "did not regard his being equal with God as an act of robbery."[26] Rather, in virtue of his true equality and likeness, he said, "I and the Father are

---

23. Philippians 2:7.

24. These words are taken from a liturgical text sung in the week before Christmas. Cf. Wisdom 7:26, "He is the brightness of eternal light"; Hebrews 1:3: "He is the splendor of glory."

25. Cf. 2 Corinthians 4:4: "He is the image of God"; Colossians 1:15: "He is the image of the invisible God."

26. Philippians 2:6.

one"[27] and "Whoever sees me also sees the Father."[28] For no one acts more justly in vanquishing or punishing the guilty, or acts more mercifully in sparing them or interceding for them, than the one whom they are proved to have particularly wronged. Nor is anything more fittingly put in opposition to falsehood in order to vanquish it, or applied to falsehood in order to heal it, than is truth. For those who arrogated to themselves a false likeness to God appear to have sinned in particular against the one who is believed to be the true likeness of God the Father. But as has been said, he took human being into a unity of person, so that the two natures, human and divine, would be one person.

11   I think it would be useful to say something about this unity of person, which we most steadfastly believe is not from two persons in Christ; for some things that are said about it could cause those who do not understand clearly to think that Christ exists from two persons and in two persons. For some people say, "How do we say that in Christ there are not two persons as there are two natures? After all, before assuming human being, God was a person; and he did not cease to be a person after he had assumed human being. And the assumed human being is a person, since we know that every individual human being is a person. So the divine person who existed before the Incarnation is distinct from the human person who was assumed. Therefore, since Christ is both God and a human being, there seem to be two persons in him." This reasoning appears to show that there are two persons in Christ on the grounds that God is a person and the assumed human being is a person.

But that is not the case. For as in God one nature is a plurality of persons and a plurality of persons are one nature, so too in Christ one person is a plurality of natures and a plurality of natures are one person. For as the Father is God, the Son is God, and the Holy Spirit is God, and yet they are not three gods, but one God, so too in Christ God is a person and the human being is a person, and yet there are not two persons, but one person. It is not the case that God is one thing and the human being another *in Christ*, even though God is one thing and human being another. Rather, he is himself God who is also a human being. For "the Word made flesh"[29] assumed another nature, not another person. The expression 'human being' signifies only the nature that is common to all human beings. By contrast, when we use a demonstrative and say 'this human being' or 'that human being,' or when we use the proper name 'Jesus,' we designate a person. A person has a collection of distinguishing characteristics along with the nature; it is by those characteristics that human being in general is made an individual and is distinguished from other individuals. When Christ is designated in this way, the

27. John 10:30.
28. John 14:9.
29. John 1:14.

expression signifies not just any human being, but the one who was announced by an angel, is both God and a human being, is Son of God and son of the Virgin, and is whatever else it is true to say of him either as God or as human. For the Son of God cannot be designated or named personally apart from the Son of Man, nor can the Son of Man be designated or named personally apart from the Son of God, since he who is the Son of God is the very same as the one who is the Son of Man, and the same collection of distinguishing characteristics belongs both to the Word and to the assumed human being. But it is impossible for one and the same collection of distinguishing characteristics to belong to distinct persons or for two persons to be predicated of each other. After all, the same collection of distinguishing characteristics does not belong to both Peter and Paul, and Peter is not called 'Paul' or Paul 'Peter.'

So when "the Word was made flesh," he assumed the nature that is all that is signified by the word 'human being' and is always distinct from divine nature. He did not assume another person, since he has one and the same collection of distinguishing characteristics as the assumed human being. For human being is not one and the same thing as the human being assumed by the Word—that is, Jesus. As has been said, by the expression 'human being' we mean only the nature, whereas by the expression 'assumed human being' or the name 'Jesus' we mean, in addition to the nature (that is, in addition to human being) the collection of distinguishing characteristics, which is one and the same for both the assumed human being and the Word. For this reason we do not say that the Word and human being, without qualification, are one and the same person—which would imply that that human being is no more one and the same person as the Word than any given human being is—but instead that the Word and that assumed human being, who is Jesus, are one and the same person. Similarly, we do not believe that that human being is one and the same person as God, without qualification, but that he is one and the same person as that divine person who is the Word and the Son—otherwise we would seem to be professing that this human being is the same person as the Father or the Holy Spirit. But since the Word is God and that assumed human being is a human being, it is true to say that God and a human being are one and the same person, so long as we understand 'God' to designate the Word and 'human being' to designate the son of the Virgin.

I have not been able to look at any of the writings of the man to whom I am responding in this letter, apart from what I set forth above. But I think the truth of the matter is so evident from what I have said that anyone with understanding will see that nothing that is said against it has any power of truth.

12   But if this man has been called back from positing a multiplicity of gods and now denies a plurality of persons in God, he is doing this because he does not know what he is talking about. He is not conceiving God or his persons, but something along the lines of a plurality of human persons; and since he sees that

one human being cannot be a plurality of persons, he says that God too cannot be a plurality of persons. For they are not called three persons because they are three separate things, as three human beings are, but because they bear a certain likeness to three separate persons. Let us examine this in the case of the Father and the Son; the same reasoning should be understood to hold for the Holy Spirit as well.

So let us posit a human being who is only a father and not a son, and his son, who is only a son and not his father: Adam and Abel. And we say of Adam the father and Abel the son that the father is not a son and the son is not a father, since Adam and Abel are two human beings and two separate persons, and there is no one whose son Adam is and no one whose father Abel is. It is in this way that we profess that in God, the Father is not the Son and the Son is not the Father, even though they are not two gods, since the Father does not have a father and the Son does not have a son. Similarly, the Holy Spirit is not a father or a son, because there is no one whose father he is or whose son he is. So the Father and the Son and the Holy Spirit are called three persons, not because they are three separate things, but because they are three and are distinct from one another, and cannot be said of one another (as we showed for 'father' and 'son' in the case of distinct human persons).

13   But if he denies that 'three' can be said of one and 'one' of three in such a way that the three are not said of each other, as we do in the case of the three persons and one God, on the grounds that he does not see an instance of this in other things and cannot comprehend it in God, let him put up with the fact that there is something in God that his understanding cannot penetrate. That nature is above all other things and free from every law of place and time and composition of parts: let him not compare it to things that are hemmed in by place or time or are composed of parts. Rather, let him believe that something exists in that nature that cannot exist in those other things; let him accede to Christian authority and not dispute against it.

Nevertheless, let us see whether we can in some respect find in created things that are subject to the law of place and time and composition of parts an example of what he denies in God. Let us imagine a spring from which there rises and flows a river that later opens out into a lake. Call it "the Nile." We speak of the spring, the river, and the lake so separately that we do not call the spring 'river' or 'lake' or the river 'spring' or 'lake' or the lake 'spring' or 'river.' And yet the spring is called 'the Nile,' the river is called 'the Nile,' and the lake is called 'the Nile.' The spring and the river are both the Nile; the spring and the lake are both the Nile; the river and the lake are both the Nile. Moreover, all three together—the spring, the river, and the lake—are the Nile. Nonetheless, whether we call one or two or all three of them 'the Nile,' they are not distinct Niles, but one and the same Nile. So the spring, the river, and the lake are three, and yet they are one Nile, one stream, one nature, one body of water; and we cannot say what they are three *of*, since they are not three Niles or three streams or three bodies of water or three natures, nor are they three springs or three rivers or three lakes. So in this example 'one' is said of the three and 'three' of the one, and yet the three are not said of each other.

Suppose he objects that neither the spring nor the river nor the lake individually, nor any two of them together, are the complete Nile; rather, they are parts of the Nile. In that case, let him conceive the whole Nile as existing for its entire lifetime, so to speak, from the time it begins to exist until it ceases to exist. After all, that whole does not exist all at once in either a place or a time, but only part by part; and it will not be complete until it ceases to exist. In this respect it is like an utterance, which is incomplete as long as it is still springing forth from the mouth, and no longer exists once it has been completed. Anyone who entertains this analogy and attentively understands it will recognize that the whole Nile is the spring, the whole Nile is the river, and the whole Nile is the lake, but the spring is not the river or the lake, the river is not the lake or the spring, and the lake is not the spring or the river. For the spring is not the same as the river or the lake, even though the river and the lake are the very same thing that the spring is, that is, the same Nile, the same stream, the same body of water, the same nature. So these three are said of one complete whole and the one complete whole of the three, and yet the three are not said of each other. Of course, this holds in a quite different and more perfect way in that supremely simple nature, which is supremely free from every law of place or time. Yet if this is evident in any way at all in a thing that is composed of parts and exists in place and time, it is not impossible to believe that it exists perfectly in that supremely free nature.

And one must also bear in mind that the spring is not from the river or from the lake, the river is from the spring alone and not from the lake, and the lake is from the spring and from the river—and in such a way that the whole river is from the whole spring and the whole lake is from the whole spring and from the whole river. This is how we speak of the Father, the Son, and the Holy Spirit. And one must also bear in mind that the river is from the spring in a different way from that in which the lake is from both the spring and the river, so that the lake is not called a river. Similarly, the Word is from the Father in a different way from that in which the Holy Spirit is from both the Father and the Word, so that the Holy Spirit is not a Word or a Son, but proceeds [from the Father and the Son].

14   I want to add a further comparison, since although there is a great disanalogy in this case, it nonetheless has some similarity to the Incarnation of the Word. Perhaps someone who reads this will make light of it, but I will mention it anyway, since I would not reject it if someone else said it. If the river ran through a pipe from the spring to the lake, would it not be the river alone that is "piped," so to speak, even though the river is not a different Nile from the spring and the lake— just as only the Son was incarnate, even though he is not a different God from the Father and the Holy Spirit?

15 But since these earthly things are very far removed from the supreme nature, let us with his help raise our minds to that nature and contemplate in it, though briefly and partially, the things we have been saying. God is nothing other than simple eternity itself. Now it is inconceivable that there should be a plurality of eternities. For if there is more than one eternity, they are either outside each other or within each other. But nothing is outside eternity, so an eternity is not outside eternity. Moreover, if eternities are outside each other, they exist in different places or times, which is incompatible with eternity. And so there are not several eternities existing outside each other. But if instead it is said that there are several eternities within each other, one must recognize that however many times an eternity is repeated within an eternity, there is only one and the same eternity. For a nature that when repeated within itself always comes together into a perfect unity is more exalted than one that admits plurality within itself. For where there is plurality, there is also diversity; and where there is diversity, there is not perfect harmony. For a perfect harmony is one that comes together into a single identity and one and the same unity. Therefore, if a perfect harmony is better than an imperfect one, and it is impossible for there to be anything imperfect in the supreme Good—which is eternity itself—it is not possible for the nature of eternity to admit plurality. Hence, however many times eternity is repeated within eternity, it is always only one and the same eternity.

Similar remarks apply to many other things. For example, omnipotence within omnipotence is only one omnipotence. And (to offer an analogy from characteristics that the divine nature does not have) a point within a point is only one point. For a point, such as the midpoint of the earth or a point of time (that is, the present time) has a certain resemblance to eternity, a resemblance that is quite helpful in contemplating eternity. I will examine this matter in greater detail elsewhere;[30] for now it will be enough to note that a simple point (that is, one that has no parts) is indivisible, as eternity is. For this reason a point together with a point without any interval is only one point, and in the same way an eternity together with an eternity is only one eternity.

Therefore, since God is eternity, there is not a plurality of gods; for God is not outside God, and God within God does not add numerically to God. Therefore, there is always only one and the same God. And so when God is born of God, given that what is born is not outside that from which it is born, the offspring is in the parent and the parent is in the offspring: that is, the Father and the Son are one God. And when God proceeds from God the Father and God the Son, he does not depart and go outside God; God—that is, God the Holy Spirit—remains in the God from whom he proceeds, and the Father and Son and Holy Spirit are one God. And since this birth and this procession have no beginning—for otherwise

---

30. *On the Procession of the Holy Spirit* 9.

the eternity born and the eternity proceeding would have a beginning, which is false—we neither should nor can in any way think that God began to be Father or Son or Holy Spirit.

16 Yet even as the divine substance preserves an eternal* and singular unity, the nature of these relative qualities—Father and Son, proceeding and proceeded-from—retains an inseparable plurality. For just as it is necessary that God is always one and the same, not many, so too in accordance with these relations the Father is never the same as his Son and the one who proceeds is never the same as the one from whom he proceeds. Rather, the Father is always distinct from the Son, the one who proceeds is always distinct from the one from whom he proceeds, and the Persons can never be said of each other. Therefore, when God is born of God or God proceeds from God, the substance cannot lose its singularity and the relations cannot lose their plurality. For this reason, in God something one is three and what are three is one, and yet the three are not said of each other. And even though no perfect analogy for this can be found in other things, we should not find it incredible that this is true of the nature that is above all things and is unlike all other things. Now the Latins call these three 'persons,' whereas the Greeks call them 'substances.' Thus, just as we say that in God one substance is three persons, they say that one person is three substances, signifying by 'substance' exactly what we signify by 'person,' so that they do not differ from us in the faith in the slightest respect.

Now we cannot in this life see God "as he is,"[31] and so blessed Augustine in his book *On the Trinity* has carefully examined, as though "through a mirror and in a riddle,"[32] how the Son is born of the Father and the Holy Spirit proceeds from the Father and the Son, and yet is not himself a Son; and I have investigated these things myself to the best of my ability in the *Monologion*,[33] which I mentioned above. If anyone is interested in knowing why, given that there is no sex in the supreme being, the parent is called Father rather than Mother and the offspring is called Son rather than Daughter, or why the Father alone is unbegotten, the Son alone begotten, and the Holy Spirit neither begotten nor unbegotten, he will find these matters treated explicitly in that book.[34]

---

31. 1 John 3:2.

32. 1 Corinthians 13:12.

33. See the *Monologion*, Chapter 29 and following.

34. See the *Monologion*, Chapters 42 and 56.

Cur Deus Homo
Commendation of the Work to Pope Urban II

EVER SINCE THE days of the apostles, many of our holy fathers and teachers have spoken of the reason of our faith,[1] in order to refute the foolishness of unbelievers and break down their obstinacy, and also in order to nourish those who, because their hearts have already been purified by faith, have come to take delight in the reason of that faith—reason for which we too should hunger, once we have attained the certainty of faith. Indeed, they have spoken so often and so well that we cannot hope for anyone in our day or in the years to come who will be their equal in the contemplation of the truth. Nevertheless, I do not think we should find fault with anyone who is firmly established in faith and desires to expend his labor in investigating its reason. For "brief are the days of man,"[2] so even our holy fathers and teachers were not able to say everything they could have said had they lived longer; and the reason of truth is so abundant and so deep that mortals cannot come to the end of it. Moreover, the Lord never ceases to bestow gifts of grace upon his Church, for he has promised to be with her "even to the end of the age."[3] And—leaving aside all the other places in which Holy Scripture urges us to search for reason—when it says, "Unless you believe, you will not understand,"[4] it is clearly admonishing us to direct our energies toward understanding, since it is teaching us the right way to make progress toward understanding. Finally, since I take the understanding that we achieve in this life to be intermediate between faith and vision, I think that the more progress someone makes toward understanding, the closer he comes to that vision for which we all long.

Although I am a man of very little knowledge, these considerations give me such great strength that I will endeavor to raise myself up just a little to gaze upon the reason of the things we believe, so far as heavenly grace sees fit to grant it to me. And when I discover something that I had not previously seen, I will gladly reveal it to others, so that I may learn from others' judgment what I ought to maintain with confidence.

For this reason, my lord and father, Pope Urban, whom all Christians should love with reverence and revere with love, whom the providence of God has appointed Supreme Pontiff in his Church, I submit the enclosed work for Your Holiness to examine—for there is no one to whom I could more properly address

---

1. For an explanation of what Anselm means by "the reason of faith," see the Introduction, pp. vii–viii.

2. Job 14:5.

3. Matthew 28:20.

4. Isaiah 7:9 in the Old Latin text.

it—so that your authority may give approval to those things in it that are worthy of acceptance and may correct those things that require amendment.

Preface

Thanks to certain people who made copies for themselves of the first parts of the enclosed work without my knowledge, before it was completed and fully thought through, I have been forced to complete it (as well as I could) more hastily than I cared to, and therefore more briefly than I had intended. If I had been allowed freedom from distractions and enough time to work on it, I would have included and added quite a few things that I have left unsaid.[5] For it was in the midst of great turmoil in my heart—God knows the source of this trouble and why I have suffered from it—that I undertook this work in England in response to a request and finished it as an exile in the province of Capua.[6]

Because of the subject matter of this work I have named it *Cur Deus Homo*,[7] and I have divided it into two short books. The first presents the objections of unbelievers who reject the Christian faith because they think it is contrary to reason, and the answers given by believers. It goes so far as to prove by necessary reasons—leaving Christ out of the picture, as if nothing concerning him had ever taken place—that it is impossible for any human being to be saved apart from Christ. But the second book—which again proceeds as though nothing were known of Christ—demonstrates, by means of argument and truth that is no less evident, that human nature was established in order that the whole human being, both body and soul, should at some time enjoy blessed immortality, and that it was necessary that the purpose for which human beings were made should in fact be achieved, but only through the agency of a God-man, and that it was necessary that everything we believe about Christ should take place.

I ask everyone who might want to copy this book to put this short preface before the beginning, along with the chapter titles of the whole work, so that anyone into whose hands it falls will be able to see from its face, so to speak, whether there is anything in the whole body that might merit his attention.

---

5. See the Introduction (pp. x–xi) for an account of what Anselm would have "included and added."

6. Anselm began *Cur Deus Homo* in 1095. As a result of a quarrel with King William II in which many of his own bishops sided against him, Anselm went into exile in November 1097. He spent part of his exile in the Lombard duchy of Capua as a guest of his former pupil, the abbot of San Salvatore at Telese. He finished *Cur Deus Homo* there in 1098.

7. That is, *Why God [Became] a Human Being* or *Why a God-Man?* As is usual, I have left the title of the work in Latin.

Chapters

Book One

BOOK ONE

Chapter 1

The question on which the whole work hangs

I have received frequent and quite eager requests from many people, both by word of mouth and in letters, that I make a written record of the reasoning that I am accustomed to offer in answer to those who ask about the reason of a certain question of our faith. They say that my reasoning is pleasing to them, and they think it fully answers their questions. They do not seek such an explanation in order to achieve faith through reason, but rather so that they can delight in the understanding and contemplation of things they already believe, and so that they may be "always ready," to the best of their ability, "to give an answer to all who demand" from them "the reason of the hope that is in" us.[8] This is the question that unbelievers commonly raise as an objection against us, deriding Christian simplicity as foolishness, and that many believers often ponder in their own hearts: By what reason or necessity did God become a human being and, as we believe and profess, restore life to the world by his own death, when he could have accomplished this through some other person, whether angelic or human, or even by his own will alone? Not only the learned but even many who are unlettered ask this question and look for a rational answer. So there are many people who are asking for a discussion of this question, and although the investigation seems extremely difficult, the solution can be understood by anyone and is appealing to everyone because of its usefulness and the beauty of its reasoning. For this reason I will attempt to present to those who make this request what God sees fit to reveal to me, even though the holy fathers have said what ought to be sufficient on this subject. Now because an inquiry that takes the form of questions and answers is more accessible, and consequently more pleasing, to many people, especially to those whose intellects are sluggish, I will take as my partner in dialogue one of those who have been pressing me on this matter, the one whose urging has been most insistent. Thus, Boso[9] will ask the questions and Anselm will reply, as follows:

---

8. 1 Peter 3:15.

9. Boso was a monk of Bec for whose intellectual abilities Anselm had particularly high regard. When Anselm went to Canterbury as archbishop he summoned Boso there to serve as a philosophical companion; and Anselm's treatise *On the Virginal Conception, and On Original Sin,* a companion piece to *Cur Deus Homo,* is addressed to Boso. Boso eventually became the fourth abbot of Bec, 1124–1136.

BOSO: Just as right order requires that we believe the deep matters of Christian faith before we undertake to examine them by reason, so too I think we would be derelict if we did not strive to understand what we believe, once we have been made steadfast in faith. For this reason, since I think I have such faith in our redemption—thanks to God's prevenient grace—that there is nothing that could uproot me from the steadfastness of that faith even if I could not get any rational grasp on what we believe, I am asking you to explain something to me that, as you know, many others are asking along with me: Given that God is omnipotent, by what necessity and reason did he assume the lowliness and weakness of human nature in order to restore human nature?

ANSELM: What you are asking of me is too high for me. And I am afraid to deal with loftier matters,[10] lest someone should suppose or even see that I have failed to give a satisfactory answer and think that I have fallen away from the truth in this matter, rather than that my understanding is not equal to the task of grasping it.

B: You should not be afraid of that so much as you should remember that it often happens in discussing some question that God reveals what was previously hidden; and you should place your hope in God's grace, that if you freely share what you have received by grace, you will become worthy to receive the loftier things that you have not yet attained.

A: I see another reason that it is hardly possible, or even not possible at all, for us to examine this question to the fullest extent on this occasion. A full treatment requires knowledge of power, of necessity, of will, and of certain other things; and these are interrelated in such a way that none of them can be considered fully apart from the others. And for that reason an investigation of these things requires a work of its own,[11] a work that would not, I think, be terribly easy but would also not be altogether without its usefulness—for ignorance of those things makes certain matters difficult that become easy once one knows them.

B: You can speak briefly to these issues at the appropriate points, so that we may have enough for the work at hand and may postpone to another occasion whatever else needs to be said.

A: I also shrink from your request because the subject matter is not merely precious but, just as it concerns one who is "beautiful in his appearance beyond the children of men,"[12] so too is it beautiful in its reasoning beyond the understanding of men. Hence, just as I am accustomed to grow indignant at incompetent painters when I see that the Lord himself is portrayed as ugly in his appearance, so too I am afraid

---

10. Cf. Psalm 131:2 (130:1); Ecclesiasticus 3:22.

11. The Lambeth Fragments appear to be Anselm's drafts of a work along these lines.

12. Psalm 45:2 (44:3).

that the same thing will happen to me if I presume to discuss such a beautiful subject in unworthy and inelegant language.

B: Nor should that deter you. For if anyone can speak better, you will allow him to do so; and if your language does not please someone, you will not prevent him from writing more beautifully. But so that I may rule out all your excuses: you will be doing what I ask, not for the learned but for me and those who join me in making this request.

Chapter 2

In what way the things to be said are to be accepted

A: Since I see your earnest appeal and that of the ones who join you in making this request out of charity and pious zeal, I will try to the best of my ability, with God's help and your prayers (which you who make this request have often promised me when I asked for them for this very purpose), not so much to reveal the answer you are seeking as to seek it in company with you. But I want everything I say to be accepted on the following terms: If I say something that is not confirmed by a greater authority, even if I appear to prove it by reason, it should be accepted with confidence only as what seems true to me for the time being, until God in some way reveals something better to me. If I prove to be able to give a satisfactory answer to your question to any extent at all, it ought to be quite clear that someone wiser than I am could do this much more completely. Indeed, it is important to recognize that no matter what someone might be able to say on this topic, there are still loftier reasons for so great a matter that remain hidden.

Chapter 3

The objections of unbelievers and the replies of believers

B: Allow me, then, to use the words of unbelievers. For since we are seeking to investigate the reason of our faith, it is appropriate for me to set forth the objections of those who are completely unwilling to accede to that faith without reason. They seek reason because they do not believe, whereas we seek it because we believe. Nonetheless, it is one and the same thing that we all seek. And if you offer any response that appears to contradict sacred authority, allow me to bring it to your attention so that you can explain how there is no contradiction.

A: Go right ahead.

B: Unbelievers who deride our simplicity object that we injure and insult God when we say that he descended into a woman's womb, was born of a woman, grew by being nourished by milk and human foods, and (not to mention many other things that do not appear to be suitable for God) suffered fatigue, hunger, thirst, beatings, and crucifixion and death between thieves.

A: We do not injure or insult God at all. On the contrary, we praise and proclaim the ineffable depth of his mercy, giving thanks with our whole hearts. For the more wondrously and unexpectedly he has rescued us from the great and well-deserved evils in which we once were, and restored us to the great and undeserved goods that we had lost, the greater is the love and generosity that he has shown toward us. If they attentively considered how fitting a way this was to accomplish the restoration of humankind, they would not deride our simplicity but join with us in praising God's wise benevolence. For it was fitting that just as death entered the human race through the disobedience of a human being, so too life should be restored by the obedience of a human being.[13] It was fitting that just as the sin that was the cause of our damnation had its origin from a woman, so too the author of our justice and salvation should be born of a woman. And it was fitting that the devil, who through the tasting of a tree defeated the human being whom he persuaded, should be defeated by a human being through the suffering on a tree that he inflicted. And there are many other things that, if carefully considered, demonstrate the indescribable beauty that belongs to our redemption, accomplished in this way.

Chapter 4

That unbelievers think these responses lack necessity and are merely pictures, as it were

B: All these things are beautiful, and they have to be treated like pictures. But if there is nothing sturdy underneath them, unbelievers do not think they provide a sufficient explanation for why we ought to believe that God willed to undergo the things we say he underwent. When someone wants to produce a picture, he chooses something sturdy on which to paint, so that his painting will last. No one paints on water or in the air, since no traces of the picture would remain there. So when we offer unbelievers these instances of what you say is fitting as pictures of an actual fact, they think it is as though we are painting on a cloud, since they hold that what we believe is not an actual fact at all, but a fiction. Therefore, one must first demonstrate the rational solidity of the truth: that is, the necessity that

---

13. Cf. Romans 5:19.

proves that God should or could have humbled himself to the things that we proclaim about him. Only then should one expound on considerations of fittingness as pictures of this truth, so that the body of truth, so to speak, might shine all the more brightly.

A: Does not this seem to be a sufficiently necessary reason that God ought to have done the things we say: that the human race—such a precious work of God—had utterly perished, and that it was not fitting that God's purpose for human beings should be completely annihilated, and that his purpose could not be brought to fulfillment unless the human race were liberated by its Creator himself?

Chapter 5

That human redemption could not have been brought about by anyone but a divine person

B: If this liberation were said to have been brought about somehow by someone other than a divine person, by either an angel or a human being, the human mind would accept this much more readily. For God could have made a sinless human being—not from the sinful mass[14] and not from another human being, but as he made Adam—and it seems that he could have accomplished this same work by means of this man.

A: Do you not understand that human beings would be rightly judged to be subservient to any other person whatsoever who redeemed them from eternal death? And if that were the case, they would by no means be restored to that dignity that they were going to have if they had not sinned, since they who were not going to be subservient to anyone but God and were going to be in every respect equal to the good angels would instead be subservient to someone who was not God, someone to whom the angels would not be subservient.

---

14. The expression 'sinful mass' (*massa peccatrix*) derives from Augustine, who referred to the human race variously as a 'mass of sin(s),' a 'mass of wrath,' and a 'mass of perdition.'

Chapter 6

In what way unbelievers cast aspersions on our claim that God redeemed us by means of his own death, and that in this way he demonstrated his love toward us, and that he came in order to subdue the devil on our behalf

B: That is what they find particularly baffling—I mean that we call this liberation "redemption." They say to us, "In what captivity were you being held, in what prison, under whose control, from which God could not liberate you except by redeeming you at the cost of so many labors and, in the end, of his own blood?" When we say to them:

> He redeemed us from our sins and from his own wrath and from hell and from the power of the devil, whom he himself came to subdue on our behalf, because we could not do so ourselves; and he redeemed for us the kingdom of heaven. And by doing all these things in this way, he showed us how much he loved us.

They reply:

> If you say that God—who you say created all things by his command—could not have accomplished all these things simply by commanding them, you are contradicting yourselves, since you are making him out to be powerless. On the other hand, if you acknowledge that he *could* have done all this simply by commanding it, but that he did not *will* to do it except in the way you describe, how will you be able to show that he is wise, when you claim that he willed to suffer such indignities for no reason at all? For all the things you mention reside in God's will. God's wrath is just his will to punish. So if he does not will to punish human sin, human beings are free from their sins and from God's wrath and from hell and from the power of the devil, since they suffer all these things on account of their sins; and they receive all the things of which they are deprived on account of their sins. For who holds power over hell and the devil, and to whom does the kingdom of heaven belong, if not God, who made all things? And so whatever you fear, whatever you desire, it is all subject to God's will, which nothing can oppose. So if indeed God was unwilling to save the human race except in the way you describe, when he could have done so through his will alone, face up to how you are impugning his wisdom—to put it mildly. After all, no one would judge a man to be wise if, without reason, he expended great effort to do something he could have done quite easily. Moreover, if you offer no proof

at all that God could not have saved humanity in some other way, you have no argument to defend your claim that by doing it in the way you describe, God showed how much he loves you. After all, if he could not have done it in any other way, then presumably it was necessary that he show his love in this way. But if he could have saved humanity in some other way, what reason is there for him to do and to undergo the things you describe in order to show his love? He does not undergo such things for the good angels: Does he not show them how much he loves them? And as for your claim that he came in order to subdue the devil on our behalf: What are you thinking, that you should dare to say this? Doesn't God's omnipotence rule everywhere? So how did God need to come down from heaven in order to overcome the devil?

It seems that unbelievers can raise these objections against us.

Chapter 7

That the devil had no just claim on humanity; and why it seems that he had such a claim, thus requiring God to liberate humanity in this way

Now we are also accustomed to say that in order to liberate humanity God was obligated to act against the devil through justice before he acted through force, so that when the devil killed him who did not deserve death and who was God, he would justly lose the power that he held over sinners. Otherwise, God would have inflicted unjust force on the devil, since the devil justly had possession of human beings, whom he had not captured by force, but who had delivered themselves up to him of their own accord.

But I do not see how this has any cogency. If either the devil or human beings were their own, or belonged to anyone other than God, or remained in the power of anyone other than God, then maybe this would be the right thing to say. But since in fact neither the devil nor human beings belong to anyone other than God or stand outside God's power, on what grounds was God obligated to do anything with his own, about his own, or in his own, other than to punish his own slave who had persuaded a fellow slave to abandon their common master and transfer allegiance to him, a traitor harboring a fugitive, a thief who received a thief along with what he had stolen from his master? For both of them were thieves, since at one thief's persuasion the other thief stole himself from his master. If God were to do this, what could be done more justly? What injustice would there be if God, the judge of all, were to remove human beings from the control of one who had them unjustly in his possession, in order to punish them by some means other than the devil, or in order to spare them? For although human beings were justly tormented by the devil, he was tormenting them unjustly. Human beings deserved to be punished, and there was no one by whom they might be more appropriately punished than the one to whom they gave their consent for sinning. But there was no merit on the devil's part that entitled him to punish them; in fact, the more he was spurred on to doing this by an impulse for wickedness rather than drawn to it by a love of justice, the more he acted unjustly in doing it. For he was not doing this at God's command, but by the permission of God's incomprehensible wisdom, which orders even evils in a good way.

I also think that those who hold that the devil had some just claim to possess humanity are brought to this view because they see that humanity was justly subject to the devil's persecution and that God justly permitted it; and on those grounds they suppose that the devil justly inflicted it. But it can happen that one and the same thing is both just and unjust according to different ways of looking at it, and accordingly it is judged to be wholly just or wholly unjust by people who do not examine it attentively. For example, suppose someone unjustly strikes an innocent man and as a result deserves, as a matter of justice, to be struck himself. Yet if the victim ought not to avenge himself but goes ahead and strikes the one who struck him, he is acting unjustly. So this second blow is unjust on the part of the one who strikes the blow, because he ought not to have avenged himself; but it is just on the part of the one who is struck, because by unjustly striking someone else he deserved, as a matter of justice, to be struck himself. Thus, one and the same action is both just and unjust according to different ways of examining it, and it can happen that one person judges it to be simply* just and another to be simply unjust. And so it is in this way that the devil is said to persecute human beings justly, since God justly permits this and human beings justly suffer it. But even when we say that human beings justly suffer it, they are not said to suffer it justly with respect to their own justice, but because they are punished in accordance with God's just judgment.

Now someone might bring up the "handwriting of the decree" that the Apostle says was "against us"[15] and was erased by the death of Christ, thinking that it signifies that before the passion of Christ the devil justly—as though under the handwritten terms of an agreement—demanded sin from human beings as interest on the first sin that he had persuaded them to commit, and also as punishment for sin; and he might seem to prove by this that the devil did have some just claim on humanity. I do not think the passage should be understood in that way at all. That handwriting is clearly not the devil's, since it is called the handwriting "of the decree," and the decree was not the devil's, but God's. For it was decreed by the just judgment of God and confirmed, as it were, in writing that human beings who had sinned of their own accord would not be able on their own to avoid either sin or the punishment for sin. For they are "a spirit that goes forth and does not

---

15. Colossians 2:14.

return,"[16] and "one who commits sin is a slave to sin,"[17] and one who sins should not be left unpunished unless mercy spares the sinner and frees him and leads him back. Hence, we should not think that this handwriting provides any justification for the devil's persecution of human beings. Finally, just as there is no injustice at all in a good angel, so too there is no justice whatsoever in an evil angel. Therefore, there was nothing in the devil because of which God was obligated not to use force against him in order to liberate humanity.

Chapter 8

How even though the lowly things we say of Christ do not pertain to his divinity, it seems absurd to unbelievers that they are said of him even as a human being; and why they think this human being did not die of his own accord

A: When God does something, his will ought to be reason enough for us, even if we do not see why he willed it, since God's will is never irrational.

B: That is true, provided that we already agree that God in fact did whatever we are talking about. After all, many people will not in any way concede that God wills something if it seems contrary to reason.

A: What seems to you to be contrary to reason when we confess that God willed the things that we believe concerning his Incarnation?

B: To put it in a few words: that the Most High should stoop to such lowly things, and that the Almighty should expend such effort to do something.

A: Those who say this do not understand what we believe. For we claim that the divine nature is undoubtedly impassible,* that it cannot in any way be brought down from its lofty heights, and that it expends no effort in anything it wills to do. But we say that the Lord Jesus Christ is true God and true man, one person in two natures and two natures in one person. So when we say that God was subject to lowliness or weakness, we do not understand this according to the sublimity of his impassible nature but according to the weakness of the human substance that he bore. In this way it is evident that no reason opposes our faith, since we are not indicating any lowliness in the divine substance but instead pointing out that there is one person of both God and man. So we do not mean that there was

---

16. Psalm 78:39 (77:39). The word for 'spirit' is often translated 'breath.'
17. John 8:34.

any degradation of God in his Incarnation; rather, we believe that human nature was exalted.

B: Suppose you're right, and nothing that is said of Christ with respect to human weakness is attributed to the divine nature. Even so, this human being was the one whom the Father called his beloved Son, in whom he was well-pleased,[18] whom the Son made to be one with himself. So how can it be shown to be just or reasonable for God to treat him, or allow him to be treated, in this way? What sort of justice is it for the most just human being of all to be handed over to death for the sake of a sinner? If any human being condemned an innocent man in order to set a guilty man free, would he not be judged worthy of condemnation himself? In fact, the matter seems to return to the same absurdity that I explained earlier. For if God could not save sinners in any other way than by condemning a just man, where is his omnipotence? On the other hand, if he could but he did not will to do so, how will we defend his wisdom and justice?

A: God the Father did not, as you seem to think, treat him in that way or hand over an innocent man to death for the sake of a guilty man. For God the Father did not compel him to die, or allow him to be killed, against his will. Rather, he endured death of his own accord in order to save human beings.

B: Even if it was not against his will, since he consented to the Father's will, it still seems that in a way the Father compelled him by commanding him. Scripture says, after all, that Christ "humbled himself, being made obedient" to the Father "to the point of death, even death on the Cross; for this reason God has also exalted him."[19] It also says, "He learned obedience from the things he suffered,"[20] and that the Father "did not spare his own Son, but handed him over on behalf of us all."[21] And the Son says, "I did not come to do my own will, but the will of him who sent me."[22] And on the way to his passion, he says, "I am doing exactly as the Father has commanded me."[23] And again, "The cup that the Father has given me: will I not drink it?"[24] And elsewhere, "Father, if it is possible, let this cup pass from me. Yet not as I will, but as you will."[25] And "Father, if it is not possible for this cup to pass from me unless I drink it, your will be done."[26] In all these passages it

---

18. Cf. Matthew 3:17, 17:5; Mark 1:11; Luke 3:22.

19. Philippians 2:8–9.

20. Hebrews 5:8.

21. Romans 8:31.

22. John 6:38.

23. John 14:31.

24. John 18:11.

25. Matthew 26:39.

26. Matthew 26:42.

appears that Christ endured death because obedience compelled him, rather than because his own spontaneous will determined it.

Chapter 9

That he died of his own accord; and what is meant by "He was made obedient to the point of death," and by "for this reason God has also exalted him," and by "I have not come to do my own will," and by "God did not spare his own Son," and by "Not as I will, but as you will"

A: It seems to me that you are not distinguishing properly between (1) what he did because obedience demanded it and (2) what was done to him because he preserved obedience, and which he endured, but not because obedience demanded it.

B: I need you to explain this more clearly.

A: Why did the Jews persecute him to the point of death?

B: For no other reason than this: in the way he lived and in what he said, he held unswervingly to truth and justice.

A: I believe that God demands this of every rational creature, and the rational creature owes this to God by way of obedience.

B: It is right and proper for us to acknowledge this.

A: So that man owed this obedience to God the Father, and his humanity owed it to his divinity; and the Father demanded this of him.

B: No one could doubt that.

A: So now you see what he did because obedience demanded it.

B: That's true; and now I see what he endured that was inflicted on him because he persevered in obedience, since death was inflicted upon him because he remained steadfast in obedience, and he endured death. But I do not understand how obedience did not demand this.

A: If human beings had never sinned, would they deserve to suffer death, or would it be right for God to demand this of them?

B: What we believe is that if human beings had never sinned, they would not die, and God would not demand death of them. But I want to hear from you the reason for this.

A: You do not deny that the rational creature was created just, and that it was created in order to be happy in enjoying God.

B: No.

A: But you would not at all suppose it is fitting for God to compel what he created just, and for the sake of happiness, to be wretched, and not on account of any guilt. And it is wretched for a human being to die against his will.

B: It is evident that if human beings had not sinned, it would not be right for God to demand death from them.

A: It follows that God did not compel Christ, in whom there was no sin, to die. On the contrary, Christ endured death of his own accord. His obedience consisted not in abandoning his life, but in preserving justice; and he persevered in justice with such fortitude that he incurred death.

It can also be said that the Father commanded that he die, since he commanded that on account of which he incurred death. So it was in that way that he "did as the Father commanded" him, and drank "the cup that he gave," and was "made obedient" to the Father "to the point of death," and "learned obedience from the things he suffered"—learned, that is, how far one ought to maintain obedience. Now the expression "he learned," which is used in this passage, can be understood in two ways. Either it is used for "he made others learn,"[27] or else it means that he learned by experience what he already knew intellectually. As for the Apostle's statement that "He humbled himself and was made obedient to the point of death, even death on the cross," to which he adds, "for this reason God has also exalted him and given him a name that is above every name": this is like David's words, "He drank from the brook along the road; for that reason he has exalted his head."[28] It doesn't mean that he could in no way have come to this exaltation except through the obedience of death, and that this exaltation was granted to him only as a reward for this obedience. For even before he suffered, he himself said that all things were entrusted to him by the Father,[29] and that everything the Father had was his.[30] Rather, what it means is that he himself, together with the Father and the Holy Spirit, had ordained that he would reveal to the world the loftiness of his omnipotence in no other way than through death. And since it had been ordained that this would come about only through that death, it is surely appropriate to say that it came about because of that death, since it came about through that death.

After all, if we aim at doing something, but we decide that we will first do some other thing through which our ultimate aim will be achieved, then once the preliminary thing has been done, if what we aim at comes about, it is correctly

---

27. That is, to mean "he taught."
28. Psalm 110:7 (109:7).
29. Luke 10:22.
30. John 16:15.

said to come about *because* the preliminary thing has been done, since it had been ordained that the ultimate aim would be achieved only through the preliminary thing. For example, suppose there is a river I can cross either on horseback or by boat, but I decide I am not going to cross it except by boat. Since there is no boat available, I put off crossing the river. Now when a boat becomes available, if I cross the river, it is rightly said of me that I crossed the river *because* the boat became available. And we speak this way not only when we have resolved to attain our ultimate aim only *through* some preliminary step, but even when we have merely decided to attain our ultimate aim only *after* some preliminary step, not through it. For example, suppose someone puts off eating because he has not yet attended a celebration of mass that day. Once he has done what he willed to do first, it would be appropriate to say to him, "Have something to eat now, *because* you have now done the thing on account of which you were putting off eating." So it is not at all an unusual way of speaking when Christ is said to have been exalted *because* he endured the death through which, and after which, he decreed that he would bring about that exaltation. This expression can also be understood in the same way as the passage in which we read that the Lord grew in wisdom and in grace before God:[31] not that this was actually the case, but that he conducted himself as though this were the case. For he was exalted after his death as though he were being exalted because of his death.

Now his statement that "I have not come to do my own will, but the will of him who sent me" is the same sort of thing as "My teaching is not my own."[32] If someone has something from God and not from himself, he ought to say it is not his own so much as it is God's. Now no human being has the truth that he teaches, or a just will, from himself, but from God. Therefore, Christ did not come to do his own will but the Father's will because the just will that he had was not from humanity but from divinity. But God "did not spare his only Son, but handed him over for our sake" simply means that God did not set him free. We find many expressions like this in Holy Scripture. Now where he says, "Father, if it is possible, let this cup pass from me; yet not as I will, but as you will," and "If this cup cannot pass unless I drink it, let your will be done," by his own will he means the natural desire for well-being by which human flesh shrank from the pain of death. He speaks of the Father's will, not in the sense that the Father wanted the Son's death rather than his life, but because the Father was unwilling that the human race should be restored unless a human being accomplished something as great as that death was. The demands of reason were such[33] that no one else was able to accomplish this, and that is why the Son said the Father willed his death, which

---

31. Luke 5:22.

32. John 7:16.

33. Reading *quia poscebat ratio* for *quia non poscebat ratio*.

the Son himself willed to suffer rather than that the human race should not be saved. It was as though he said, "Because you do not will that the reconciliation of the world should come about in any other way, I say that you will my death in this way. Therefore, let this will of yours be done—that is, let my death take place—so that the world may be reconciled to you." After all, we often say that someone wills *a* because he doesn't will *b*, and if he willed *b*, *a* would not come about. For example, we say that someone wants to put out a light because he is unwilling to close the window through which a wind comes in that blows out the light. It is in this sense, then, that the Father willed the death of the Son: he was unwilling for the world to be saved unless a human being accomplished something so great, as I have said. Given that no one else could do this, and that the Son so fervently desired the salvation of human beings, the Father's will had the same effect as if he had commanded the Son to die. Hence, he did "as the Father commanded" him, and he drank "the cup that the Father gave" him, "obedient to the point of death."

Chapter 10

Another way in which the same passages can be understood correctly

It can also be rightly understood that the Father "commanded him"—but did not compel him—through that generous will by which the Son was willing to die for the salvation of the world; it was in that way that the Father gave him the "cup" of his passion and "did not spare" him "but handed him over for us" and willed his death, and that the Son himself was "obedient to the point of death" and "learned obedience from the things he suffered." For according to his humanity he did not have from himself his will to live justly, but from the Father; and in the same way, it could only be from "the Father of lights," from whom comes "every best gift and every perfect gift,"[34] that he had that will by which he was willing to die in order to accomplish so great a good. And just as the Father is said to "draw" someone by giving him a will, so too it is not inappropriate to say that the Father "impels" someone. For just as the Son says of the Father, "No one comes to me unless the Father has drawn him,"[35] so too he could have said, "unless the Father has impelled him." And in a similar way he could have said, "No one risks death for my name's sake unless the Father has impelled or drawn him." After all, given that someone is drawn or impelled by his will to that which he wills unswervingly, it is fitting to affirm that God, who gives him such a will, is drawing or impelling him. In this drawing or impelling we do not find any necessity resulting from violence, but only the spontaneous and loving clinging to the good will that one has received. So

---

34. James 1:17.
35. John 6:44.

since it is undeniable that the Father drew or impelled the Son to his death in this way, by giving the Son that will, who will not understand that according to the same reasoning, the Father commanded him to endure death of his own accord and gave him the cup that he willingly drank? And if it is correct to say that the Son did not spare himself, but handed himself over for us of his own spontaneous will, who will deny that it is also correct to say that the Father, from whom he had such a will, "did not spare" him, "but handed him over for us" and willed his death? In this way too, by unswervingly and of his own accord preserving the will he had received from the Father, the Son "was made obedient" to the Father "to the point of death" and "learned obedience from the things he suffered"—that is, he learned how great a deed was to be done out of obedience. For there is true and unalloyed obedience when a rational nature, not from necessity but spontaneously,* preserves the will it has received from God.

And there are other ways in which we can correctly understand the claim that the Father willed the Son's death, although the ones already given can suffice. Just as we say that someone wills when he causes another person to will, so too we say that someone wills when he does not cause the other person to will but approves of his willing. For example, when we see someone bravely willing to suffer some hardship in order to bring to completion what he rightly wills, we acknowledge that we will that he endure such suffering; yet we do not will or love his suffering but rather his will. We are also accustomed to say of someone who can prevent something but does not prevent it that he wills the thing he does not prevent. So, since the Son's will was pleasing to the Father, and since the Father did not prevent him from willing or from carrying out what he willed, it is correct to affirm that the Father willed that the Son endure death so generously and for so great a benefit, even though he did not love the Son's suffering. Now he said that the cup could not pass unless he drank it, not because he could not have avoided death if he had wanted to, but because (as I have said) it was impossible for the world to be saved in any other way; and he unswervingly willed to suffer death rather than that the world should not be saved. He spoke those words in order to make it clear that the human race could not be saved except through his own death, not to indicate that there was no way he could have avoided dying. And all the other passages that say similar things about him should be expounded in such a way that we believe he did not die out of any necessity but of his own free will. He was, after all, omnipotent; and we read of him that "he was offered because he himself willed it."[36] And he says himself, "I am laying down my life in order that I might take it up again. No one is taking it from me, but I am laying it down of my own accord. I have the power to lay it down, and I have the power to take it up again."[37]

---

36. Isaiah 53:7.
37. John 10:17–18.

Therefore, it cannot be at all correct to say that he was compelled to do something that he does by his own power and of his own will.

B: But the mere fact that God allows him to be treated in that way, even though he was willing, does not seem suitable for such a Father with respect to such a Son.

A: On the contrary: it is especially appropriate for such a Father to consent to such a Son if what the Son wills is praiseworthy because it honors God and useful because it procures the salvation of human beings, which could not be accomplished in any other way.

B: We are still trying to figure out how that death can be shown to be reasonable and necessary. Otherwise, it seems that the Son should not have willed it and the Father should not have compelled or permitted it. What we're asking about, after all, is why God could not have saved humanity in some other way, or, if he could have, why he willed to do it in this way. For it seems unfitting for God that humanity should be saved in this way, and it is also not obvious what efficacy that death had for saving humanity. It would be quite astonishing if God were so pleased by the blood of an innocent man, or so much in need of his blood, that he would not or could not spare the guilty unless the innocent man were killed.

A: Since in this debate you are playing the role of those who are unwilling to believe anything unless it has first been demonstrated by reason, I want to strike a deal with you: we will not accept anything unsuitable, however slight, concerning God; and we will not throw out any argument, however modest, that is not defeated by some weightier argument. For just as an impossibility follows from anything unsuitable in God, however slight, so too necessity accompanies every argument, however modest, that is not defeated by some weightier argument.

B: Nothing in this discussion would please me more than for us to keep this agreement.

A: The question concerns only God's Incarnation and the things that we believe about the human being assumed in the Incarnation.

B: That's right.

A: So let's suppose that God's Incarnation and the things we say about that human being had never happened, and let's agree that human beings were made for a happiness that cannot be possessed in this life, that no one can attain such happiness unless his sins are forgiven, and that no human being passes through this life without sin. And let's assume the other things in which we must have faith in order to attain eternal salvation.

B: Agreed, since there does not seem to be anything impossible or anything unsuitable for God in these claims.

A: It follows that remission of sins is necessary for human beings if they are to attain happiness.

B: So we all believe.

Chapter 11

What it is to sin and to make recompense for sin

A: We must therefore investigate this question: "What is the rational basis on which God forgives the sins of human beings?" In order to do this more clearly, we should first see what it is to sin and what it is to make recompense for sin.

B: It is your job to explain and my job to listen.

A: If angels and human beings were always to pay back to God what they owe, they would never sin.

B: I cannot deny it.

A: And so sinning is nothing other than failing to pay back what one owes to God.

B: What is the debt that we owe to God?

A: Every will of a rational creature ought[38] to be subject to God's will.

B: Nothing could be truer.

A: This is the debt that angels and human beings owe to God. No one who discharges this debt sins, and everyone who fails to discharge it sins. This is the justice or rectitude of will that makes people just or upright in heart, that is, in will. This is the only and the complete honor that we owe to God and that God requires of us. For only such a will does works that are pleasing to God when it has the power to do them; and when it does not have the power, it is by itself pleasing to God, since no deed is pleasing without it. Someone who does not pay back to God the honor that is owed him takes from God what is rightly his and dishonors God; and this is what sinning is.

Now as long as someone fails to return what he has stolen, he remains in a state of guilt. And it is not enough for him just to restore what he has taken. Rather, because of the affront that he has perpetrated, he ought to pay back more than he took. For example, if someone injures another's health, it is not enough for him to restore the other person's health unless he also makes recompense for the damage

---

38. The words 'ought' and 'owes' both translate *debet*; the noun form *debitum* is translated as 'debt' or 'what one owes.'

he inflicted by causing pain. In the same way, if someone violates another's honor, it is not enough for him to pay back that honor if he does not also offer something satisfactory to the one he has dishonored, as compensation for the harm he caused by dishonoring him. It is important to notice this as well: when someone repays what he took unjustly, he owes something that could not have been demanded from him if he had not stolen what belonged to another. It is in this way, therefore, that all those who sin ought to repay God the honor they have stolen from him; and this is the recompense that every sinner ought to make to God.

B: Since we have undertaken to follow reason, I have nothing I could raise as an objection to anything you have said. But you are scaring me just a little.

Chapter 12

Whether it is fitting for God to forgive sin by mercy alone, without any repayment of the debt

A: Let's go back and see whether it is fitting for God to forgive sin by mercy alone, without any repayment of the honor that has been taken from him.

B: I don't see why it isn't fitting.

A: Forgiving sin in this way is the same as not punishing it. But to order sin in the right way when no recompense is made *just is* to punish sin. So if sin is not punished, it is left unordered.

B: What you say is reasonable.

A: But it is not fitting for God to leave anything unordered in his kingdom.

B: I fear I would be sinning if I wanted to say anything else.

A: So it is not fitting for God to leave sin unpunished in this way.

B: That follows.

A: And there is something else that follows if sin is left unpunished in this way: someone who sins will have the same standing before God as someone who does not sin. And that does not befit God.

B: I cannot deny it.

A: Pay attention to this as well. Everyone knows that the justice of human beings is subject to this law: what God gives as a reward is proportionate to the greatness of a person's justice.

B: That's what we believe.

A: But if sin is neither discharged nor punished, it is subject to no law.

B: I cannot see it any other way.

A: Then if injustice is forgiven by mercy alone, it is freer than justice, which is utterly absurd. Indeed, the absurdity goes so far as to make injustice like God, since injustice is subject to no law just as God is subject to no law.

B: I cannot escape your reasoning. But since God commands us to forgive unreservedly those who sin against us,[39] he seems to be caught in a contradiction, by commanding us to do what it is unfitting for him to do.

A: There is no contradiction here. God commands us to do this so that we will not arrogate to ourselves what belongs to God alone. For the right to exact vengeance belongs only to the one who is Lord of all. When earthly powers act correctly in doing this, it is really God himself, by whom they were ordained for this very purpose, who does it.

B: You have taken away the contradiction I thought was involved. But there is another point on which I would like to have your response. God is so free that he is subject to no law and to no one's judgment; he is so kind that nothing kinder can be conceived. Moreover, nothing is right or fitting except what he wills. Given all that, it seems surprising for us to say that he in no way wills to forgive harm done to himself, or that it is not fitting for him to do so, considering that we often ask his mercy even for harm we have done to *others*.

A: What you say about God's freedom and will and kindness is true. But we need to understand these things reasonably, so that we do not appear to contradict God's dignity. Freedom, after all, is only for what is expedient or fitting; and what acts in a way that is unfitting for God should not be called kindness. Now as for the claim that what God wills is just and what he does not will is not just, we should not take this to mean that if God wills something unsuitable, it is just, simply because God wills it. If God wills to lie, it does not follow that it is just to lie. What follows is that he isn't God. For there is no way that a will can will to lie unless truth has been corrupted in it—or rather, unless it has become corrupted by abandoning truth. So saying "If God wills to lie" is equivalent to saying "If God's nature is such that he wills to lie"; it therefore does not follow that lying is just. Or else we can understand this as we would understand the statement, "If this is true, then that is true," when made about two impossibilities; for neither is actually true. Thus, if someone were to say, "If water is dry, then fire is wet," neither of these is true. And so it is true to say "If God wills this, it is just" only of things that it is not unsuitable for God to will. After all, if God wills that it rain, it is just for it to

---

39. Matthew 6:12.

rain; and if God wills that a certain person be killed, it is just for that person to be killed. Hence, given that it is not fitting for God to do anything unjustly or inordinately, it does not pertain to his freedom, kindness, or will that he should leave unpunished a sinner who does not repay God what he took from him.

B: You have taken away any ground for objection I thought I had.

A: Now notice a further reason that it is not fitting for God to do this.

B: I will gladly pay attention to whatever you say.

Chapter 13

That there is nothing less tolerable in the order of things than for a creature to take away the honor that is owed to the Creator and not restore what he has taken

A: Nothing is less tolerable in the order of things than for a creature to take away the honor that is owed to the Creator and not restore what he has taken.

B: Nothing could be clearer than that.

A: And nothing is more unjustly tolerated than something than which nothing is less tolerable.

B: That is fairly obvious.

A: So I think you will not say that God ought to tolerate that than which nothing is more unjustly tolerated, namely, a creature's not paying back to God what he has taken from him.

B: On the contrary, I see that this must be emphatically denied.

A: Furthermore, there is nothing that supreme Justice—which is simply God himself—preserves more justly in his governance of things than his own honor, since nothing is greater or better than God.

B: Here again, nothing could be clearer than that.

A: There is therefore nothing that God preserves more justly than the honor of his own dignity.

B: I have to concede that.

A: Do you think he keeps his honor unimpaired if he allows it to be taken from him and not paid back, and does not punish the one who took it?

B: I wouldn't dare say that.

A: Necessarily, then, when God's honor is taken away, either it is paid back or else punishment follows. Otherwise, either God would not be just toward himself, or he would lack the power to enforce either repayment or punishment. And it is impious even to think such a thing.

Chapter 14

In what way the punishment of a sinner is an honoring of God

B: I recognize that nothing more reasonable could be said. But I would like to hear from you whether the punishment of a sinner is itself an honoring of God, or in what way it honors God. After all, if the punishment of a sinner does not bring honor to God, then when a sinner does not repay what he has taken but instead is punished, God loses his honor in such a way as not to recover it. And that appears to contradict the things you have said.

A: It is impossible for God to lose his honor. Either a sinner spontaneously repays what he owes or else God exacts it from the sinner against his will. For either someone offers to God by his own spontaneous* will the subjection that he owes, whether by not sinning or by making restitution for sin, or else God brings him into subjection against his will by tormenting him—thus showing that he is his Lord, which the sinner refused to acknowledge voluntarily. It is important to recognize here that just as a human being in sinning steals what belongs to God, so too God in punishing takes away what belongs to the human being. You see, it is not only what someone already possesses that can be said to belong to him, but also what is in his power to have. Human beings were made in such a way that they have the power to be happy if they do not sin. So when, because of their sin, they are deprived of happiness and of every good thing, they are spending what is their own—unwillingly, of course—to pay back what they have taken. For although God does not use what he takes in order to benefit himself, in the way that a human being takes money from someone else and uses it for his own purposes, he does use what he takes for his own honor, just in virtue of the fact that he takes it. For by taking control of the sinner and what belongs to him, God demonstrates that all these things are subject to himself.

Chapter 15

Whether God allows his honor to be violated even to a limited extent

B: I like what you're saying. But there is another matter on which I would like to have your response. If God ought to preserve his honor in the way you have proved, why does he allow it to be violated even to a limited extent? For if something is allowed to be harmed in any way, it is not being guarded completely and perfectly.

A: Nothing can be added to God's honor or taken away from it, as far as God is concerned. For God himself is his own incorruptible and utterly immutable honor. But when a creature preserves the ordering that belongs to it and has been, as it were, commanded for it—whether the creature preserves that ordering naturally* or rationally—it is said to obey God and honor him. This is especially true of a rational nature, which has been given the power to understand what it owes. When a rational nature wills what it owes, it honors God, not because it bestows anything on God, but because it spontaneously* subjects itself to God's will and governance, and it preserves both its own ordering within the whole universe and, so far as it can, the beauty of the universe itself. But when it does not will what it owes, it dishonors God as far as it itself is concerned, because it does not spontaneously subject itself to God's governance, and it disrupts the order and beauty of the universe as much as it can, although it in no way harms or tarnishes God's power or dignity.

For if the things encompassed by the revolution of the heavens were to will not to be beneath the heavens or to be removed from the heavens, it would not be at all possible for them not to be beneath the heavens or for them to flee from the heavens without approaching the heavens. From wherever they might start, wherever they might go, and by whatever path they might take, they would still be beneath the heavens; and the farther away they drew from one part of the heavens, the closer they would come to the part that lies opposite. In the same way, although a human being or an evil angel may be unwilling to be subject to God's will and ordering, he has no power to escape it. If he flees from God's commanding will, he runs into God's punishing will. And if you ask by what path he runs from one to the other, the answer is just this: by God's permitting will. And supreme wisdom transforms the sinner's perverse will or action into order and beauty for the universe. Thus, leaving aside the fact that God brings good out of evil in many ways, both a spontaneous recompense for perversity and the infliction of punishment on one who does not make recompense have their proper place and a beautiful ordering in the same universe. If divine wisdom did not add these wherever perversity tries to disturb correct order, a certain ugliness would arise from the violation of the beauty of order in the very universe that God ought to make orderly, and God would seem to fall short in his governance. Since these two conclusions are as impossible as they are absurd, it is necessary that every sin is followed by either recompense or punishment.

B: You have completely met my objection.

A: It is therefore clear that no one can honor or dishonor God as far as what is in God himself is concerned; but as far as what is in the creature is concerned, someone appears to honor or dishonor God when he either subjects his own will to God's will or withdraws his will from subjection to God's.

B: I don't know what I could say to the contrary.

Chapter 16

The reason that human beings are to make up for the number of angels who fell

A: I shall add something further.

B: Keep talking until I get tired of listening.

A: It is agreed that God set out to restore the number of angels who fell by replacing them with human nature, which he created without sin.

B: We believe this, but I would like to have some rational explanation for it.

A: You have misled me. We set out to discuss nothing but God's Incarnation,[40] and now you're throwing in extra questions for me.

B: Don't be angry: "God loves a cheerful giver."[41] And the best way for anyone to show that he is cheerful in giving what he has promised is to give more than he promised. So answer my question willingly.

A: We must not doubt that God foreknew the number of rational natures who either are or will be happy in the contemplation of God, a number so reasonable and complete that it is not fitting for it to be greater or smaller. After all, either God does not know the number of such natures that it is most fitting for him to establish, which is false; or else, if he does know, he will establish those natures in the number that he understands to be most fitting for this purpose. Therefore, either the angels who fell were created in order to be within that number, or else they fell of necessity because they were superfluous and therefore could not persevere, which is an absurd thing to think.

---

40. See Chapter 10.

41. 1 Corinthians 9:7.

B: What you say is an obvious truth.

A: Therefore, since they were supposed to belong to that number, either their number must be restored, or else the number of rational natures, which God foreknew as complete, will remain incomplete.

B: Undoubtedly they must be replaced.

A: Then they must be replaced with human nature, since there is no other nature by which they can be replaced.

Chapter 17

That they cannot be replaced by other angels

B: Why can't either those angels themselves, or else additional angels, take the place of the angels who fell?

A: When you come to see the difficulty of our own restoration, you will understand the impossibility of their reconciliation.[42] And additional angels cannot take their place because (not to mention how that seems to impugn the perfection of the original creation)[43] it would not be right for them to do so unless they could be such as the other angels would have been if they had not sinned. Now those original angels would have persevered without having seen God's vengeance upon sin; but once the original angels fell, that would be impossible for the additional angels who would be meant to take their place. For these two are not equally praiseworthy if they remain steadfast in the truth: one who has known no punishment for sin, and one who is always face to face with an eternal punishment. Certainly we must by no means suppose that the good angels were confirmed because of the fall of the evil angels; rather, they were confirmed as a result of their own merit. If the good angels had sinned when the evil angels did, they would have been damned along with them; and in the same way, if the unjust angels had remained steadfast along with the just angels, they too would have been confirmed. In fact, if some angels had to fall in order for any angels to be confirmed, then either no angel would ever have been confirmed, or else it was necessary that some angel fall and be punished in order for the other angels to be confirmed. And both of those possibilities are absurd. And so those who remained steadfast were confirmed in exactly the same way as all the angels would have been confirmed if they had remained

---

42. See Book 2, Chapter 21.

43. Presumably because it would suggest that God had not created the right number of angels to begin with.

steadfast. I explained the way in which the good angels were confirmed, so far as I was able, where I discussed why God did not give the devil perseverance.[44]

B: You have proved that the evil angels must be replaced by human nature, and it is apparent from this reasoning that the number of elect human beings will be no less than the number of reprobate angels. But if you can, show whether there will be more elect human beings than there are reprobate angels.

Chapter 18

Whether there will be more holy human beings than there are evil angels

A: If the angels, before some of them fell, existed in that perfect number of which we have spoken,[45] then human beings were created for no other purpose than to take the place of the lost angels. In that case it is clear that there will be no more elect human beings than evil angels. On the other hand, if all the angels together did not make up that perfect number, then human beings must make up for both what was lost and what was originally lacking. In that case, there will be more elect human beings than reprobate angels, and we will say that human beings were not created solely to replenish that diminished number, but also to complete what was not yet completed.

B: Which of these views should we prefer: that the angels were originally created in that perfect number, or that they were not?

A: I will tell you what seems true to me.

B: That's all I can ask of you.

A: If human beings were created after the fall of the evil angels, as some people read Genesis, I do not see how I can give a definite proof of either alternative on that basis. I think it's possible that the angels were originally created in that perfect number and that human beings were created afterwards in order to replenish that diminished company. But it's also possible that the angels did not exist in that perfect number because God was delaying (as he is still delaying) the fulfillment of that number because he was going to create human nature at the proper time, thereby either simply completing the number that was not yet complete or else also restoring it, if it had been diminished.

---

44. See *On the Fall of the Devil*, Chapters 2–6.

45. That is, the perfect number of all rational natures who are or will be happy. See Chapter 16.

On the other hand, if the entire creation was made all at once, and the "days" by which Moses seems to indicate that the world was not made all at once must be understood as something other than the days that we experience in our own lives, I cannot see how the angels were created in that complete number. Indeed, it seems to me that if they were, then either some angels or human beings had to fall, or else there would be more of them in the heavenly city than the fitting nature of that perfect number demanded. Therefore, it seems that if all things were created at once, the angels and the first two human beings were incomplete in number in such a way that if no angel fell, human beings would simply make up for what was lacking; but if some angel were lost, human beings would also replace what fell. And human nature, which was weaker, would vindicate God and confound the devil if the devil blamed his fall on his own weakness, since human nature remained steadfast despite being weaker. And even if human nature fell, it would defend God all the more against the devil and against itself, since although it was created very weak and subject to death, in the elect it would rise from such weakness to even greater heights than those from which the devil had fallen; for human nature would be owed equality with the good angels, who, because they persevered, were exalted after the fall of the evil angels.

On the basis of these arguments it seems more likely to me that the angels did not originally exist in that complete number in which the heavenly city will be made perfect. For if human beings were not created simultaneously with the angels, it is possible that this is true; and if they were created simultaneously (which is the prevailing opinion, since Scripture says, "He who lives forever created all things simultaneously"),[46] this appears to be necessary. Even if we understand the perfection of the creation of the world to be more a matter of the number of natures than of the number of individuals, it is still necessary that human nature was created in order to complete its perfection; otherwise, human nature would be superfluous, which we would not dare to say even of the nature of the smallest worm. So human nature was made to take its own place in creation, and not merely to supply the place of individuals of another nature. Hence, it is clear that even if no angel had been lost, human beings would still have their own place in the heavenly city. And so it follows that the angels did not exist in that perfect number before some of them fell; for if they did, it was necessary for some angels or human beings to fall, since no one could remain in the heavenly city outside that perfect number.

B: You have really accomplished something.

A: And there is another argument, it seems to me, that lends considerable support to the view that the angels were not created in that perfect number.

B: Tell me.

---

46. Ecclesiasticus 18:1.

A: If the angels were created in that perfect number, and human beings were created exclusively to replace the lost angels, it is clear that unless the angels had fallen from happiness, human beings would never have risen to happiness.

B: That is evident.

A: Now suppose someone were to say that elect human beings will exult as much over the loss of the angels as they will rejoice in their own exaltation, because undoubtedly their exaltation would not take place unless the angels' fall had taken place. How can the elect be spared this perverse rejoicing? Or how will we say that human beings are taking the place of the angels who fell, given that if the angels had not fallen, they would have remained free from this sin—the sin of rejoicing over others' fall—whereas human beings will not be able to avoid this sin? Indeed, how will they deserve to be happy when they are guilty of this sin? And finally, how could we dare to say that God is unwilling or unable to bring about this replacement without this sin?

B: Isn't this just like the case of the Gentiles, who were called to faith because the Jews rejected it?

A: No. If all the Jews had believed, the Gentiles would have been called anyway, because "in every race"[47] one who fears God and does justice is acceptable to God."[48] But because the Jews did not heed the apostles, there was an opportunity at that time for the apostles to turn to the Gentiles.

B: I don't see any way I could object to what you are saying.

A: How would it come about, do you think, that individual people would rejoice over another's fall?

B: Only if each person will be certain that he would not be where he is unless someone else had fallen from that very place.

A: So if no one had that certainty, there would be no basis for anyone's rejoicing over another's downfall.

B: So it seems.

A: Do you think any of them will have such certainty if they greatly outnumber the angels who fell?

B: There is no way I can think any of them will or ought to have such certainty. How, after all, could anyone know whether he was created to make up for what had been lost from, or instead to fill up what had been left incomplete in, the full

---

47. *gens*: the singular form of *gentes*, 'Gentiles' or 'the nations.'
48. Acts 10:35.

complement of the city that is to be established? Yet all of them will be certain that they were created in order to make that city perfect.

A: So if there will be more elect human beings than reprobate angels, it will be neither possible nor reasonable for any human being to know that he was exalted to heaven only because of another's fall.

B: That's true.

A: So no one will have any reason to rejoice over another's downfall.

B: That follows.

A: And so since we see that the unseemly conclusion that necessarily follows if elect human beings will not outnumber reprobate angels does not follow if they will, and since it is impossible that there will be anything unseemly in that city, it appears to be necessary that the angels were not originally created in that perfect number, and that there will be more blessed human beings than there are wretched angels.

B: I do not see any rational basis to deny this.

A: I think another argument can be given for this same view.

B: You ought to expound that argument as well.

A: We believe that this bodily mass of the world will be transformed into something better,[49] and that this will not take place until the number of elect human beings is brought to completion and that blessed city is made perfect; but once the city is made perfect, the transformation of the bodily mass of the world will no longer be delayed. From this it can be concluded that God has intended from the beginning to bring both to perfection at the same time, for two reasons: because the lesser nature that would not be aware of God would by no means be perfected before the greater nature that would enjoy God, and because that lesser nature, transformed into something better, would in its own way rejoice, as it were, in the perfection of the greater nature. Indeed, every creature would exult in its own glorious and wondrous consummation, eternally sharing its joy, each in its own way, with the Creator, with itself, and with every other creature. For a creature that is not aware of God would exhibit naturally,* through God's governance, what the will does spontaneously* in a rational nature. And we are accustomed to join in rejoicing over the exaltation of those who are greater than we are, as when

---

49. 2 Peter 3:13.

we rejoice with exultation on the festival of the birthdays of the saints,[50] rejoicing over their glory.

This view seems to be supported by the fact that if Adam had not sinned, God would nevertheless have delayed perfecting that city until the number that he was awaiting had been completed from human beings and they had been transformed into the immortal immortality of bodies (if I may so express it). You see, they had a sort of immortality in paradise: the power not to die. But that power was not itself immortal, since it could die, in such a way that human beings would no longer be able not to die.

If it is in fact true that God intended from the beginning to bring that rational and blessed city to completion at the same time as this earthly and nonrational nature, it seems that either (1) that city was not complete in the number of angels before the fall of the evil angels, but God was waiting to complete it with human beings when he would transform the corporeal nature of the world into something better; or else (2) if it was perfect in number, it was not perfect in confirmation, and its confirmation was to be delayed—even if no one in it sinned—until the transformation of the world that we await; or (3) if that confirmation was not to be delayed, then the transformation of the world was to be moved forward so that it would take place along with the confirmation.

(Not 3) But it is completely irrational that God should, from the very beginning, intend to transform the newly created world as soon as he created it, and to destroy those things that would not exist after the transformation, even before the reason they were created in the first place became evident. It therefore follows that the angels did not exist in that perfect number in such a way that their confirmation would not be long delayed; for if that had been the case, the transformation of the world would have had to take place immediately, which is not fitting.

(Not 2) Now it seems unfitting for God to will to delay that confirmation until the future transformation of the world, especially since he completed the confirmation so quickly for some beings, and also since it can be understood that at the time when human beings sinned, he would have performed this confirmation for them if they had not sinned, just as he did for the angels who persevered. For although they would not yet have been promoted to that equality with the angels that human beings would ultimately attain when they formed part of that perfect number, it does seem that if they had been victorious—so that, though tempted, they did not sin—they and all their progeny would have been confirmed in the justice they possessed, so that they would no longer be able to sin; just as, because they were defeated and sinned, they were so weakened that they could not by their own efforts be free from sin. For who would dare to say that injustice had more

---

50. The feast days of the saints are celebrated on the day of their birth into the heavenly kingdom, that is, on the day of their earthly death.

power to bind the human being in slavery when he consented to its first persuasion than justice would have had power to confirm him in freedom when he cleaved to it in the face of the first temptation? For since the whole of human nature was in our first parents, the whole of human nature in them was overcome in such a way that it sinned, with the exception of that one man whom God knew how to keep free from Adam's sin, even as he knew how to make him from a virgin without a man's seed; and in the same way, the whole of human nature would have been victorious in them if they had not sinned.

(1) So the only thing left to say is that the original number of angels was not enough to complete the heavenly city, but it was to be completed with human beings. And if all these things are true, there will be more elect human beings than there are reprobate angels.

B: The things you say seem extremely reasonable to me. But what shall we say about the Scripture that says God "established the limits of the peoples according to the number of the sons of Israel"?[51] Because the words 'angels of God' are found in place of 'sons of Israel,'[52] some people expound this passage as meaning that the number of elect human beings is to be set according to the number of good angels.

A: This is not inconsistent with the view I have set forth, so long as it is not certain that the number of angels who fell is exactly the same as the number who remained. For if there are more elect angels than reprobate angels, it is both necessary that elect human beings replace the reprobate angels and possible that the number of blessed human beings is equal to the number of blessed angels. And thus there will be more just human beings than unjust angels. But keep in mind the agreement we made before I began to answer your questions: "If I say something that is not confirmed by a greater authority, even if I appear to prove it by reason, it should be accepted with confidence only as what seems true to me for the time being, until God in some way reveals something better to me."[53] For I am certain that if I say anything that undoubtedly contradicts Scripture, it is false; and I do not wish to maintain it once I have recognized the contradiction. But there are matters in which it is possible to hold any of a number of views without danger, and the issue we are now discussing is one of those, since I do not think there is any danger to the soul if we do not know whether there will be more elect human beings than lost angels, and we favor one of these possibilities over the other. If in such matters we expound the divine writings in such a way that they seem to support different

---

51. Deuteronomy 32:8.

52. The Greek translation of the Old Testament, the Septuagint, had the words 'angels of God' instead of 'sons of Israel,' as did Latin versions that were translated from the Septuagint rather than directly from the Hebrew.

53. Quoted verbatim from Chapter 2.

views, and we find no passage that settles what we must unhesitatingly hold, I do not think anyone ought to find fault with us.

Now as for the passage you brought up—"he established the limits of the peoples," that is, of the nations, "according to the number of the angels of God," which in another translation reads, "according to the number of the sons of Israel"—since both translations either signify the same thing or signify different things but without any contradiction, we should understand that both 'the angels of God' and 'the sons of Israel' signify only the good angels, or only elect human beings, or both the angels and elect human beings together (that is, the whole heavenly city); or that 'the angels of God' signifies only the holy angels and 'the sons of Israel' only the just human beings; or that 'the sons of Israel' signifies only the angels and 'the angels of God' just human beings. If both expressions signify only the good angels, then that is the same as if only 'the angels of God' had been used. But if they signify the whole heavenly city, the verse means that the peoples (that is, the multitudes of elect human beings) will continue to be exalted, or there will continue to be peoples in this present age, so long as the predestined number of that city has not yet been made complete by human beings.

But I do not now see how 'the sons of Israel' can mean only the angels, or both angels and holy human beings. By contrast, it is not strange for holy human beings to be called 'sons of Israel,' just as they are called 'sons of Abraham.'[54] They can also rightly be called 'angels of God' in virtue of the fact that they imitate angelic life and are promised likeness and equality with the angels in heaven, and also because all who live justly are angels of God for the same reason that they are called 'confessors' or 'martyrs.' For one who confesses and bears witness to God's truth is a messenger—that is, an angel—of God.[55] And if an evil human being is called a devil, as the Lord called Judas a devil,[56] because they are alike in evil, then why shouldn't a good human being be called an angel because he imitates an angel's justice? Therefore, we can (or so I think) say that God established "the limits of the peoples according to the number" of elect human beings because there will be peoples and the procreation of human beings in this world until the number of the elect is made complete; and once it is complete, the begetting of human beings that takes place in this life will come to an end.

On the other hand, if we take 'the angels of God' to mean the holy angels alone and 'the sons of Israel' to mean only just human beings, there are two ways in which we can understand the claim that "God established the limits of the peoples according to the number of the angels of God": either that as many people

---

54. Galatians 3:7.

55. As Anselm knows, *martyr* is the Greek word for one who bears witness, and *angelos* for a messenger.

56. John 6:70–71.

(that is, as many human beings) will be exalted as there are holy angels of God, or that there will be peoples until the number of the angels of God is filled up from human beings. And I can see only one way in which we can expound the claim that he "established the limits of the people according to the number of the sons of Israel," namely, that as was said above, there will be peoples in this present age until the number of holy human beings is completed. Either translation implies that the number of human beings who will be exalted is the same as the number of angels who remained; but even though the lost angels will be replaced by human beings, it does not follow from this that the number of angels who fell is the same as the number who persevered. But if that claim is made, one will have to find some mistake in the arguments given above, which seem to establish that the angels did not exist in that perfect number I have talked about before some of them fell, and that there will be more elect human beings than evil angels.

B: I do not regret compelling you to say these things about the angels, for it was not done in vain. Now return to the point from which we digressed.

Chapter 19

That human beings cannot be saved without recompense for sin

A: It has been established that God intended for human beings to replace the angels who fell.

B: Certainly.

A: So in the heavenly city the human beings who are taken up into that place as replacements for the angels ought to be such as the angels whom they are replacing were going to be in that city: in other words, they should be such as the good angels are now. Otherwise, those who fell would not in fact be replaced, and it would follow either that God cannot complete the good thing that he has undertaken, or else that he regrets having undertaken so great a good—both of which are absurd.

B: Indeed, it is right that human beings should be equal to the good angels.

A: Did the good angels ever sin?

B: No.

A: Can you think that a human being who sinned at one time and never made recompense to God for his sin, but is simply let off without punishment, is equal to an angel who never sinned?

B: I can think such words and say them, but I cannot conceive their meaning, in the same way that I cannot understand that falsity is truth.

A: Therefore, it is not fitting for God to exalt sinful human beings to replace fallen angels without recompense for sin, since truth does not allow them to be raised to equality with the blessed.

B: That is what reason shows.

A: Now leave aside the fact that human beings ought to be made equal to the angels, and just consider human beings themselves. Should God promote them in this way to any happiness, even the happiness they had before they sinned?

B: Tell me what you think, and I will examine it as well as I can.

A: Let's suppose some rich man holds in his hand a precious pearl that has never been touched by any impurity. Suppose no one else can take it out of his hand unless he himself permits it, and that he plans to put it away in his treasury, where all his costliest and most precious possessions are found.

B: I conceive this as clearly as if it were right in front of us.

A: Suppose he permits some envious person to grab that pearl out of his hand and cast it into the mud, even though he could prevent this; and afterwards he takes it out of the mud and puts it away, still muddy and unwashed, in some clean and costly place, to be stored in that condition from then on. Would you think him wise?

B: How could I? Would it not be far better for him to keep and store his pearl clean rather than dirty?

A: Wouldn't God be acting in a similar way? He held human beings in his hand, so to speak, in paradise; they were sinless, destined to be companions for the angels. If he had willed to prevent the devil, the devil would not have been able to tempt human beings; so he allowed the devil, enraged with envy, to cast them down into the mire of sin—with their consent, admittedly. So wouldn't God be acting in a similar way if he led human beings, stained with the grime of sin and without any washing (that is, without any recompense), even back into the paradise from which they had been cast out, to remain in that condition forever?

B: I do not dare deny that if God did this, the analogy would hold; and for that reason I do not grant that he can do it. For in that case it would appear that either he could not accomplish what he had set out to do or else that he had come to regret the good thing he had set out to do; and neither of those can be true of God.

A: Therefore, you must hold with the utmost certainty that without recompense—that is, without a spontaneous payment of the debt—God cannot leave sin unpunished and a sinner cannot attain happiness, even such happiness as he had before he sinned. For without recompense human beings would not be restored, even to the state they were in before they sinned.

B: I cannot in any way contradict your arguments. But then why do we say to God, "forgive us our debts"?[57] Why does every nation pray to the god in which it believes that he will forgive their sins? If we pay what we owe, why do we pray for God to forgive it? Is God unjust, so that he demands again what has already been paid? On the other hand, if we do not pay our debt, why do we pray in vain for God to do something that he cannot do, because it would be unfitting for him to do it?

A: Someone who does not pay it says "forgive" in vain. But someone who does pay it asks for forgiveness, because his asking forgiveness is part of his payment. God, after all, owes nothing to anyone, but every creature is in debt to him. For that reason it is not appropriate for a human being to deal with God as though they were on an equal footing. But there is no need for me to answer your questions about this matter right now. Once you come to see why Christ died, perhaps you will see on your own the answer to your question.

B: Then the answer you have already given is enough for me for the time being. But you have shown that human beings cannot attain happiness in a state of sin or be released from sin unless they repay what they took by sinning—shown it so clearly, in fact, that I could not doubt it even if I wanted to.

Chapter 20

That recompense ought to be proportionate to sin, and that human beings cannot make recompense on their own

A: I think you will also not doubt that recompense ought to be proportionate to sin.

B: Otherwise sin would remain disordered to some extent, and that cannot be the case if God leaves nothing disordered in his kingdom. And it was settled in advance that any unseemliness, however small, is impossible in God.[58]

A: Then tell me: What will you give God in payment for your sin?

B: Repentance, a contrite and humble heart, acts of self-denial and a great variety of bodily labors, mercy in giving and forgiving, and obedience.

---

57. Matthew 6:12.

58. See Chapter 10.

A: What are you giving to God in all these things?

B: Do I not honor God when out of fear and love for him I cast down temporal happiness in heartfelt contrition, when I trample underfoot the pleasures and repose of this life in acts of self-denial and labor, when I bestow my own possessions in giving and forgiving, when I submit my very self to God in obedience?

A: When you repay God what you already owe him even if you have not sinned, you should not count this as payment for the debt you owe for sinning. And you owe God all the things you have mentioned. In this mortal life your love and (this is where prayer comes in) your desire to reach the state for which you were created, and your sorrow that you are not yet there, and your fear of not reaching it, ought to be so great that you should not experience any happiness except in things that give you help or hope in reaching that state. For if you do not love and desire it in accordance with its nature, and feel sorrow that you do not yet have it and that there remains such great uncertainty whether you will ever have it, then you do not deserve to have it. This involves fleeing the repose and worldly pleasures that call the soul away from that true repose and pleasure, except insofar as you know they support your effort to reach that state. As for giving, you ought to regard yourself as doing that because you owe it, as you understand that what you give, you do not have from yourself, but from the one of whom both you and the one to whom you give are servants. And nature teaches you that you should do to your fellow servant, that is, to your fellow human being, what you want him to do to you,[59] and that someone who is not willing to give what he has ought not to receive what he does not have. As for forgiving, I will say briefly that vengeance does not belong to you in any way, as we said above.[60] For you do not belong to yourself, and the one who has wronged you does not belong to you or to himself. Rather, both of you are servants of the one Lord who created you from nothing; and if you take revenge on your fellow servant, you arrogantly presume to exercise on him the judgment that rightly belongs to the Lord and Judge of all. And as for obedience, what are you giving to God that you do not already owe? For you owe everything you are, everything you have, and everything you can do to his command.

B: I no longer dare to say that in any of these things I am giving something to God that I do not already owe.

A: Then what will you give to God in payment for your sin?

B: If even when I do not sin I owe God my very self and everything I can do, lest I sin, then I have nothing that I can give in payment for my sin.

---

59. Matthew 7:12.
60. See Chapter 12.

A: Then what will become of you? How will you be able to be saved?

B: If I think about your arguments, I don't see how I can be saved. But if I turn to my faith, I have hope in the Christian faith, "which is active through love,"[61] that I can be saved. I also have hope because we read that "if an unjust man turns from injustice and does justice,"[62] all his injustices are forgotten.

A: But that is addressed only to those who either looked for Christ before he came or believe in him now that he has come. But when we set out to investigate by reason alone whether it was necessary for Christ to come in order to save humanity, we agreed to treat Christ and the Christian faith as though they had never existed.

B: Indeed we did.

A: Then let us proceed by reason alone.

B: Although you are leading me into difficulties, I still very much want you to proceed in the way you set out.

Chapter 21

How serious sin is

A: Let's suppose you do not owe all the things you just suggested you could offer in payment for your sin, and let's examine whether they could be sufficient recompense for a single sin as small as, say, one glance contrary to God's will.

B: If it weren't for the fact that I hear you raising this question, I should have thought I could wipe out this sin with just one act of remorse.

A: You have not yet come to grips with how serious sin is.

B: Show me now.

A: Imagine that you found yourself under God's watchful eye and someone said to you, "Look over there," but God said, "I do not in any way want you to look." Now ask yourself in your own heart what there is, among all the things that are, for the sake of which you ought to take that look, contrary to the will of God.

B: I find nothing on account of which I ought to do so, unless perhaps I were in such a bind that it would be necessary for me to do it in order to avoid committing some greater sin.

---

61. Galatians 5:6.
62. Ezekiel 18:27.

A: Set that case of necessity aside and just think about whether you can commit that sin in order to save your own life.

B: I see quite clearly that I can't.

A: Not to drag this out any longer: What if it were necessary that either the whole world and whatever is not God perish and return to nothing, or else you do such a small thing contrary to God's will?

B: When I think about the action itself, I see that it is something exceptionally insignificant. But when I recognize that it is contrary to God's will, I understand that it is something exceptionally serious and not commensurable with any loss. Yet we often justifiably act contrary to someone's will in order to keep his possessions safe, and afterwards he approves what we did contrary to his will.

A: This is true in the case of a person who sometimes does not understand what is useful for himself or who cannot replace what he loses. But God needs nothing; and if all things perished, he could replace them, just as he made them in the first place.

B: I must admit that I ought not to do anything contrary to God's will, even to preserve the whole of creation.

A: What if there were many worlds, as full of creatures as this one is?

B: Even if there were infinitely many worlds spread out before me, I would give the same answer.

A: Nothing you can do would be more correct. But now suppose you did in fact take that look contrary to God's will. Consider what you might be able to give in payment for that sin.

B: I have nothing greater to give than what I said earlier.

A: That is how seriously we sin every time we knowingly do something, however small, contrary to the will of God; for we are always under his watchful eye, and he always commands us not to sin.

B: As I hear it, we are living very dangerously.

A: It is evident that God demands recompense according to the size of the sin.

B: I cannot deny it.

A: So you do not make recompense unless what you pay back is greater than the thing for the sake of which you ought not to have committed the sin.

B: I see that reason requires this, and I also see that this is completely impossible.

A: And God cannot, because he ought not, exalt to happiness anyone who is in any way liable for the debt of sin.

B: This conclusion is serious indeed.

Chapter 22

What injury human beings did to God when they allowed themselves to be overcome by the devil, for which they cannot make recompense

A: Hear yet another reason that it is no less difficult for human beings to be reconciled to God.

B: If faith did not give me comfort, the first reason alone would compel me to give up hope.

A: Listen anyway.

B: Go ahead.

A: Human beings in paradise, created without sin, were (so to speak) put in God's place between God and the devil so that they would overcome the devil by not consenting to his temptation to sin, thus vindicating and honoring God and confounding the devil—for then the weaker ones on earth would not have sinned though the devil tempted them, whereas the stronger one in heaven had sinned though no one tempted him. And although human beings could have accomplished this easily, they allowed themselves—not coerced by any power, but simply giving in to temptation of their own accord—to be overcome in accordance with the devil's will and contrary to the will and honor of God.

B: What are you getting at?

A: Judge for yourself whether it is not contrary to God's honor for human beings to be reconciled to him when they are still guilty of the insult and wrong they have done to God, unless they have first honored God by overcoming the devil, just as they dishonored God by being overcome by the devil. Now that victory ought to be like this: just as human beings were strong and immortal in power when they gave their consent for sin to the devil, thereby justly incurring the punishment of mortality, so too, weak and mortal as they have made themselves, they will overcome the devil through the pain of death in such a way as not to sin at all. But they cannot do this as long as they are conceived with the wounds of the first sin and born in sin.

B: I say again that reason proves what you are saying, and yet what you are saying is impossible.

Chapter 23

What human beings took away from God when they sinned, which they cannot repay

A: Note one further condition that must be met if human beings are to be justly reconciled but that is no less impossible.

B: You have already put forward so many things we ought to do that nothing you add can make me any more afraid.

A: But listen.

B: I'm listening.

A: What did human beings take from God when they allowed themselves to be overcome by the devil?

B: You should say, as you started to, because I don't know what else they could add to the evils you have already set forth.

A: Did they not take from God whatever he intended to make out of human nature?

B: Undeniably.

A: Think in terms of uncompromising justice and judge on that basis whether human beings make recompense to God that is equal to their sin unless, by overcoming the devil, they restore the very thing they took from God by allowing themselves to be overcome by the devil: so that, as the devil took what was God's and God lost it through humanity's defeat, so too the devil will lose it and God recover it through humanity's victory.

B: Nothing more uncompromising or more just can be conceived.

A: Do you think supreme justice can transgress this justice?

B: I don't dare think so.

A: Therefore, there is no way human beings either should or can receive from God what God intended to give them, unless they pay back to God everything they took from him, so that God will recover this through human beings just as he lost it through human beings. There is only one way that this can be accomplished: just as, through one who was defeated the whole of human nature was corrupted and, as it were, leavened with sin—and God does not exalt any sinner to perfect that heavenly city—so too, through one who is victorious, as many human beings will be justified from sin as were going to complete that number, which human beings were created in order to complete. But there is no way for a sinful human being to do this, since a sinner cannot justify a sinner.

B: Nothing is more just, and nothing is more impossible. But these considerations seem to spell the end of divine mercy and human hope when it comes to the happiness for which human beings were created.

Chapter 24

That as long as they do not repay God what they owe, they cannot be happy; and that they are not excused because of their inability

A: Be patient just a little while longer.

B: What more do you have to say?

A: If a human being is called unjust because he does not repay what he owes to another human being, one who does not repay what he owes to God is all the more unjust.

B: If he is able to repay it and does not do so, he is truly unjust. But if he is not able to repay it, how is he unjust?

A: Perhaps if he is not responsible for that inability, he can be excused to some extent. But if the inability is his fault, it does not excuse him from repaying what he owes, just as it does not mitigate his sin. Suppose someone orders his servant to perform some task. Suppose he shows the servant a pit from which there is no way to get out, and he warns the servant not to fall into it. But the servant ignores his master's command and warning; of his own accord he throws himself into the ditch he was shown, so that there is no way he can perform the task he was assigned. Do you think his inability to perform the task he was assigned can in any way serve to excuse him for not performing it?

B: Not at all. Instead it serves to magnify his fault, since he brought that inability on himself. He has sinned in two ways: he did not do what he was commanded to do, and he did what he was warned not to do.

A: Human beings are without excuse in just the same way. For of their own accord they bound themselves to a debt they are unable to pay, and it is by their own fault that they made themselves unable to repay not only what they already owed before they sinned (namely, not to sin), but also what they owe because they sinned. Their inability is itself a fault, since it is not something they ought to have—in fact, they ought not to have it. For just as it is a fault not to have what one ought to have, so too it is a fault to have what one ought not to have. Therefore, just as it is a fault in human beings that they do not have the ability they received in order to be able to avoid sin, so too it is a fault in them that they have the inability in virtue of which they cannot hang on to justice or avoid sin or give anything in repayment for what they owe on account of sin. After all, they spontaneously did what caused them to lose that ability and fall into that inability. (For not having the ability they ought to have is the same thing as having the inability they ought not to have.) For that reason their inability to repay God what they owe, which brings it about that they do not repay, does not excuse human beings for not repaying it, since an effect of sin does not excuse the sin that it in turn brings about.

B: This is very dire, but it must be the way things are.

A: Therefore, a human being who does not repay God what he owes is unjust.

B: That is all too true. For he is unjust because he does not repay, and he is unjust because he cannot repay.

A: Now no unjust person will be admitted to happiness. Happiness is a state of fullness in which nothing is lacking, and so it is suitable only for those in whom justice is so pure that there is no injustice in them.

B: I do not dare believe otherwise.

A: So someone who does not repay God what he owes cannot be happy.

B: I can't deny that that follows.

A: Now you might want to say that God, who is merciful, forgives the debt of those who call upon him—precisely *because* they cannot repay it. But there are only two things God can be said to forgive: either that which human beings ought to repay of their own accord but cannot—that is, that which could make recompense for sin, which ought not to be committed even to preserve everything that is not God; or that which he was going to take away from them against their will as punishment, as I explained above—that is, happiness. Now if God forgives what human beings ought to repay of their own accord, precisely because they cannot repay it, isn't that the same as God's forgiving what he cannot have? But it is a travesty to attribute that sort of mercy to God. And if, on account of their inability to repay what they ought to repay of their own accord, God forgives what he was going to take away against their will, he is lightening the punishment of human beings and making them happy on account of sin, because they have what they ought not to have. For they ought not to have this inability, and for that very reason, as long as they have it without recompense, it is sin for them. But mercy of this sort is altogether contrary to God's justice, which does not permit anything other than punishment to be repayment for sin. Hence, it is impossible for God to be merciful in this way, just as it is impossible for God to be contrary to himself.

B: I see that we need to look for some other mercy in God besides this.

A: Assume that God does forgive someone who does not repay what he owes, precisely because he cannot repay it.

B: I wish that were really true.

A: As long as he does not repay it, either he wills to repay it or he does not. But if he wills what he cannot do, he is lacking something. On the other hand, if he does not will it, he is unjust.

B: Nothing could be clearer.

A: But whether he is lacking or unjust, he is not happy.

B: That too is obvious.

A: Therefore, as long as he does not repay it, he cannot be happy.

B: If God follows the rational demands of justice, wretched mortals cannot escape it, and God's mercy seems to perish.

A: You asked for reason; you must accept reason. I do not deny the mercy of God, who saves men and beasts, as he has multiplied his mercy.[63] But we are speaking now about that final mercy by which he makes human beings happy after this present life. And I take it that by the arguments given above, I have shown compellingly that this happiness ought not to be given to any but those whose sins are completely forgiven, and that this forgiveness ought not to take place unless the debt that is owed on account of sin is repaid, according to the magnitude of the sin. If you think any objection can be raised to those arguments, you ought to say so.

B: In fact I see that none of your arguments can be weakened in the slightest respect.

A: I don't think so either, provided that they are examined well. Besides, if even one of all the arguments I have put forward has the strength of invincible truth, that ought to be enough. For the truth is secured against all doubt equally well, whether it is demonstrated invincibly by just one argument or by several.

B: That is certainly true.

---

63. Cf. Psalm 36:7 (35:7–8).

Chapter 25

That of necessity human beings are saved through Christ

How then will human beings be saved, given that they cannot themselves pay what they owe and ought not to be saved unless they pay it? Or how will we have the effrontery to say that God, "who is rich in mercy"[64] beyond human understanding, cannot bestow this mercy?

A: At this point you ought to ask those who do not believe that Christ is necessary for human salvation—those on whose behalf you are speaking—to say how human beings can be saved apart from Christ. If they cannot do so in some way, they should stop mocking us and instead draw near and join us who do not doubt that human beings can be saved through Christ; or else they should give up hope that we can be saved in any way at all. If they recoil from this, let them believe in Christ along with us, so that they can be saved.

B: As I have from the beginning, I will ask you to show me the reason according to which human beings are saved through Christ.

A: Since even unbelievers don't deny that human beings can somehow be made happy, and since it has been fully demonstrated that if we assume Christ does not exist, we cannot find any way human beings can be saved, isn't that sufficient proof that human beings can be saved through Christ? After all, human beings can be saved either through Christ, or by some other means, or by no means. So if it is false that they can be saved by no means or by some other means, it is necessary that they can be saved through Christ.

B: Suppose someone who grasped the reason that it cannot be by any other means, but didn't understand how it can be through Christ, should wish to claim that this cannot be the case either through Christ or in any other way. How will we respond to him?

A: How should one respond to someone who insists that what must be the case is impossible, simply because he does not know how it is the case?

B: That he is a fool.

A: Then one should pay no attention to what he says.

B: True, but one still ought to show him the reason of what he thinks is impossible.

A: Do you not understand, on the basis of what we said above, that it is necessary that some human beings will attain happiness? For if it is unfitting for God to

---

64. Ephesians 2:4.

bring human beings who are in any way blemished to that state for which he created them unblemished, lest he seem to regret the good he had undertaken or to be unable to achieve his purpose, much more so is it impossible, on account of that same unfittingness, that no human being is advanced to the state for which he was created. So either some recompense for sin, of the sort we showed earlier ought to exist, must be found outside the Christian faith—and no reasoning can reveal any such thing—or else one must believe in that faith without doubting. For if one has concluded by means of a necessary argument that something is really and truly the case, one ought not to fall into any doubt about it, even if one does not grasp the reason for how it is the case.

B: What you say is true.

A: So what more is there for you to ask?

B: I did not get involved in this discussion so that you would take away my doubts about the faith, but so that you would show me a reason for my certainty. You have already led me by reason to see that sinful human beings owe God, on account of their sin, something that they cannot repay but that they must repay if they are to be saved. Now I want you to lead me further, so that I understand on the basis of rational necessity that all the things the Catholic faith requires us to believe about Christ if we want to be saved must be true, and how they are efficacious for human salvation, and in what way God saves human beings through his mercy, given that he does not forgive their sin unless they repay him what they owe on account of sin. And to make your arguments more solidly grounded, start from a long way back so that you build them on a firm foundation.

A: May God help me now, since you are not making any allowances for me or taking into account the weakness of my knowledge in imposing so great a task on me. But I will try, since I have already begun, trusting not in myself but in God; and I will do whatever I can, with his help. But to keep from wearing out someone who wants to read this by going on too long without a break, let's separate the earlier discussion from what is still to be said by making a fresh start.

BOOK TWO

Chapter 1

Human beings were created just, in order that they might be happy

A: It should not be doubted that God made rational nature just, in order that it might be happy in enjoying him. For it is rational in order that it might distinguish between the just and the unjust, between the good and the bad, and between the greater good and the lesser good. Otherwise, it would have been made rational in vain, and God did not make it rational in vain. Therefore, there is no doubt that it was made rational for this purpose.

A similar argument proves that it received this power of discernment so that it might hate and avoid evil, so that it might love and choose good, and so that it might love and choose the greater good to a greater degree. Otherwise God would have given it this power of discernment in vain, since its discernment would be in vain if it did not love and avoid things in accordance with its discernment; and it is not fitting that God should bestow so great a power in vain. And so it is certain that rational nature was made for the purpose of loving and choosing the supreme Good above all other things, not for the sake of something else, but for his own sake. After all, if rational nature loves the supreme Good for the sake of something else, it loves something else and not the supreme Good. Now it cannot love the supreme Good for its own sake unless it is just. Therefore, it was made rational and just at the same time so that it would not be rational in vain.

Now given that it was made just so that it might choose and love the supreme Good, it was made to be just either so that it would at some time attain what it loves and chooses, or not. But if was not made just so that it would attain what it loves and chooses in this way, its being made just, so that it loves and chooses this, would be in vain, and there would be no reason why it ever ought to attain what it loves. Therefore, as long as it continues to act justly by loving and choosing the supreme Good, which is the purpose for which it was made, it will be unhappy, because it will lack something against its will, by not having what it desires—which is altogether absurd. Consequently, rational nature was made just in order that it might be happy in enjoying the supreme Good, that is, God. Therefore, human beings, who are rational in nature, were made just in order that they might be happy in enjoying God.

Chapter 2

That they would not die if they had not sinned

It is easy to prove that human beings were made such that they would not die of necessity, because, as we have already said,[65] it is incompatible with God's wisdom and justice that he should compel those whom he made just for the sake of eternal happiness to suffer death apart from any guilt. So it follows that if they had never sinned, they would never die.

Chapter 3

That they will rise again with the body in which they live in this life

This affords a clear proof of the future resurrection of the dead. If human beings are to be perfectly restored, they certainly ought to be reestablished as what they were going to be if they had not sinned.

B: It cannot be otherwise.

A: If human beings had not sinned, they were going to be transformed into incorruptibility along with the bodies that they bore. Accordingly, therefore, it must be the case that when they are restored, they will be restored along with the bodies in which they lived in this life.

B: What answer will we give if someone says that this ought to be done for those in whom the human race will be restored, but it need not be done for the reprobate?

A: Nothing is understood to be more just or more fitting than this: just as, if human beings had persevered in justice, their whole being—that is, soul and body—would be eternally happy, so too, if they persevere in injustice, their whole being will likewise be eternally wretched.

B: Though you have spoken concisely, you have offered me an adequate account of these matters.

---

65. In Book 1, Chapter 9.

Chapter 4

That God will complete what he began in human nature

A: On the basis of these considerations it is easy to recognize that either God will complete what he began in human nature or else he made so sublime a nature for so great a good in vain. And since we know that God made nothing more precious than rational nature, which he created so that it might rejoice in him, it is utterly foreign to him that he should allow any rational nature to perish entirely.

B: A rational heart cannot think otherwise.

A: It is therefore necessary that he complete what he began in human nature. And as we have said, this can take place only through a perfect recompense for sin, which no sinner can make.

B: I now understand that it is necessary for God to complete what he has begun, lest he seem to fall short in his undertaking in a way that is not fitting.

Chapter 5

That although it is necessary that this be done, God is not compelled by necessity to do it; and that there is a necessity that eliminates or diminishes gratitude, and a necessity that increases gratitude

But if this is so, it seems that God is, as it were, compelled to secure human salvation by the necessity of avoiding what is unfitting. So how can it be denied that he does this more for his own sake than for ours? Or if this is so, what gratitude do we owe him for what he does for his own sake? And how will we ascribe our salvation to his grace if he saves us out of necessity?

A: There is a necessity that eliminates or diminishes gratitude to a benefactor, and there is a necessity that increases the gratitude one owes for a benefit. When someone confers a benefit unwillingly because of the necessity to which he is subject, he is owed little or no gratitude. But when he spontaneously* subjects himself to the necessity of conferring a benefit, and he does not remain subject to the necessity against his will, then he surely deserves greater gratitude for his benefit. In fact, this should not be called necessity, but grace (*gratia*), since he undertook it or remains subject to it freely (*gratis*), with nothing compelling him. For example, suppose today you spontaneously promise you will give something tomorrow, and by that same will you do give it tomorrow. It is necessary that you fulfill your promise tomorrow if you can, or else be a liar; but the one to whom you give it owes you no less gratitude for the benefit you have conferred than he would have if you had not made the promise, since you did not hesitate to put yourself under an obligation to him before the time of the giving. This is how things are when someone spontaneously vows to pursue a holy way of life. After he has made the vow, he is obligated by necessity to carry it out, lest he incur the damnation of an apostate; and in fact he can be compelled to carry out the vow if he is unwilling. Yet if he willingly carries out his vow, he is more pleasing to God, not less, than if he had not made the vow, since for God's sake he has renounced not only the common way of life but even his own self-determination. And we should say that he leads a holy life not out of necessity, but by the same freedom by which he made his vow.

Much more, then, should we offer all our gratitude to God if he does the good for human beings that he set out to do, even though it would not be fitting for him to fall short in the good he has undertaken; for he undertook it for our sake, not for his own sake, since he lacks nothing. After all, when God made human beings, he knew what they were going to do. And yet because, in his goodness, he created them, he spontaneously obligated himself (as it were) to bring to completion the good thing that he had undertaken.

Finally, God does nothing out of necessity, since he is in no way compelled to do or prevented from doing anything. And when we say that God does something as though out of the necessity of avoiding dishonorableness (which God certainly does not fear), we should understand this more properly as meaning that he does it out of the necessity of preserving honorableness. This necessity is nothing other than the immutability of his honorableness, which he has from himself and not from another, and for that reason it is improperly* called necessity. Nevertheless, let us say that it is necessary that the goodness of God, because of its immutability, complete what it has begun in human beings, even though the whole of this good work is a matter of grace.

B: Agreed.

Chapter 6

That only a God-man can make the recompense through which human beings are saved

A: But this can be accomplished only if there is someone who in payment for human sin gives God something greater than everything other than God.

B: So we have agreed.[66]

---

66. See Book 1, Chapter 21.

A: And someone who can give God something of his own that surpasses everything that is less than God must himself be greater than everything that is not God.

B: I can't deny it.

A: But nothing other than God surpasses everything that is not God.

B: That's true.

A: Therefore, no one other than God can make this recompense.

B: That follows.

A: But no one other than a human being ought to make it, since otherwise human beings would not make recompense.

B: Nothing seems more just.

A: So if, as we have agreed, it is necessary that the heavenly city be made complete by human beings, and that cannot be the case unless this recompense is made—a recompense that only God can make and only human beings owe—then it is necessary that a God-man make this recompense.

B: Blessed be God! We have now discovered something great concerning the subject of our investigation. So continue as you have begun. For I have hope that God will help us.

Chapter 7

That it is necessary that one and the same being be perfect God and perfect man

A: We must now investigate how a God-man can exist. After all, divine nature and human nature cannot be transformed into each other, so that a divine nature becomes a human nature or a human nature divine; nor can they be combined in such a way that a third nature, neither altogether divine nor altogether human, emerges from the two of them. Anyway, if it were possible for one nature to be turned into the other, either it would be only God and not a human being, or only a human being and not God. Or if they were combined in such a way that from the two corrupted natures a third nature came to exist—in the way that from two individual animals, a male and a female, of different species, a third animal is born that does not preserve either the father's or the mother's nature intact, but instead possesses a third, mixed nature derived from both—that third nature would be neither a human being nor God. So the God-man for whom we are looking cannot come to be from divine and human nature either by the transformation of one into the other or by a corruptive mixing of the two into a third nature: for these things cannot happen, or if they could happen, they would be unavailing for what we are seeking.

If, on the other hand, these two intact natures are said to be conjoined in such a way that the human being is distinct from God, and it is not one and the same being that is both God and human, it is impossible for the two of them to do what needs to be done. God will not do it, because he will not owe the debt; the human being will not do it, because he will not be able to. Therefore, in order for the God-man to do this, it is necessary that the one who is going to make this recompense be both perfect God and perfect man, since only one who is truly God can make it, but only one who is truly human owes it. Therefore, since it is necessary that a God-man be found, one who preserves both natures intact, it is no less necessary that these intact natures come together into one person, just as a body and a rational soul come together into one human being. There is no other way for one and the same being to be perfect God and perfect man.

B: I like everything you say.

Chapter 8

That it is fitting for God to assume a human being from Adam's race and from a woman who is a virgin

A: It now remains for us to ask from where and in what way God will assume a human nature. Either he will assume it from Adam or he will make a new human being in the same way that he made Adam, from no other human being. But if he makes a new human being not of Adam's race, this new man will not belong to the human race that is born of Adam. And for that reason he will not owe a recompense for the human race, since he will not belong to the human race. For just as it is right that a human being should make recompense for human guilt, so too it is necessary that the one who makes recompense be either the sinner himself or someone of the same race. Otherwise neither Adam nor his race will make recompense for itself. Therefore, just as sin was transmitted to all human beings from Adam and Eve, so too only they or someone born from them ought to make recompense for human sin. Since Adam and Eve cannot do it, the one who will do it must be descended from them.

Furthermore, if Adam and his whole race had not sinned, they would have remained steadfast through themselves, without the aid of any other creature. Analogously, it is fitting that if that same race rises again after its fall, it should arise and be rescued through itself. For no matter who restores it to its original state, it will certainly stand through the one through whom it will recover its state. And God showed clearly that whatever he was going to make of human nature, his will was to make it from Adam. He showed this by originally making human nature in Adam alone and then, when he created the woman so that human beings would be propagated from both sexes, willing to make her from Adam and from no other. Hence, if Adam's race is rescued by some human being who does not belong to that same race, it will not be restored to the same dignity that it would have had if Adam had not sinned. Consequently, its restoration will not be complete, and God's purpose will seem to fail—and both of these are unfitting. Therefore, the human being through whom Adam's race is to be restored must be assumed from Adam.

B: If we follow reason, as we set out to do, there is no escaping this conclusion.

A: Now let's ask whether God ought to assume a human nature from a father and mother, like other human beings, or from a man without a woman, or from a woman without a man. For in whichever of these three ways the assumed nature comes to be, it will be from Adam and from Eve, from whom every human being of either sex is. And none of these three ways is any easier for God than another, so that it would be more appropriate for the nature to be assumed in that way.

B: You are proceeding well.

A: But there's no need for much effort to show that this human being will be pro-created in a purer and more honorable way from a man alone or from a woman alone than from the commingling of the two, as are all other human offspring.

B: That is enough.

A: So he ought to be assumed either from a man alone or from a woman alone.

B: There is no other possibility.

A: There are four ways in which God can make a human being: from a man and a woman, as everyday experience shows; or from neither a man nor a woman, as he created Adam; or from a man without a woman, as he made Eve; or from a woman without a man, which he had never done. So in order to prove that this last way was within his power and had been held in reserve for this very deed, nothing was more fitting than for him to assume the human being whom we are seeking from a woman without a man. And there is no need for debate about whether this would be done more worthily from a virgin or a non-virgin. Rather, one should assert without hesitation that it was right for the God-man to be born from a virgin.

B: You are speaking in accordance with my heart's desire.

A: Is what we have said solid? Or is it something insubstantial, like clouds, as you said unbelievers claim in their objections against us?[67]

B: Nothing could be more solid.

A: Then paint, not on an insubstantial fiction, but on the solid truth, and say that it is altogether fitting that just as human sin and the cause of our damnation had its beginning from a woman, so too the cure for sin and the cause of our salvation should be born from a woman. And so that women will not despair of membership in the company of the blessed because so great an evil proceeded from a woman, it is fitting that so great a good should proceed from a woman so that their hope might be restored. Paint this too: given that it was a virgin who was the cause of all evil for the human race, it is all the more fitting that it should be a virgin who will be the cause of all good. And paint this as well: given that the woman whom God made from a man without a woman was made from a virgin, it is altogether fitting that the man who will come to be from a woman without a man should likewise be made from a virgin. But let these be enough for now of the pictures that can be painted on the fact that the God-man ought to be born of a virgin woman.

B: These pictures are exceedingly beautiful and reasonable.

Chapter 9

That it is necessary that the Word alone and a human being come together in one person

A: Now we must also investigate in which person God, who is three persons, assumes a human being. After all, it is not possible for more than one person to assume one and the same human being into unity of person, so it is necessary that this be done in one person only. But I think I said enough, for the purposes of this present inquiry, concerning this unity of person between God and a human being, and in which divine person it is most appropriate for this to be done, in the letter *On the Incarnation of the Word* addressed to Lord Pope Urban.[68]

B: Nonetheless, touch briefly here on the reason the person of the Son ought to be incarnate rather than that of the Father or the Holy Spirit.

A: If any other person becomes incarnate, there will be two sons in the Trinity: the Son of God, who is a son before the Incarnation, and the person who will be son of the virgin through the Incarnation. And then there will be an inequality among

---

67. See Book 1, Chapter 4.

68. See *On the Incarnation of the Word*, Chapter 10.

the persons, who ought always to be equal, with respect to the nobility of their births. For the person who is born from God will have a nobler birth than the one who is born of the virgin. Moreover, if the Father is incarnate, there will be two grandsons in the Trinity, since the Father will be the grandson of the virgin's parents through the assumed human being; and the Word, even though he will not derive in any way from a human being, will nonetheless be the virgin's grandson, because he will be the Son of the virgin's son. All these results are unfitting, and they do not arise in the Incarnation of the Word. And there is another reason that it is more fitting for the Son to be incarnate than the other persons: it sounds more fitting for the Son to pray to the Father than for any other person to pray to any other person. Moreover, both human beings, for whom he was going to intercede, and the devil, whom he was going to defeat, had arrogated to themselves a false likeness to God through a will of their own. Thereby they sinned more particularly, as it were, against the person of the Son, who is believed to be a true likeness to the Father. And so the one to whom more particular injury was done is the one to whom the punishment or pardon for that fault is more fittingly entrusted. Therefore, since inescapable reason has led us to the conclusion that divine and human nature must come together into one person, and that this cannot be done in more than one divine person, and that it is evident that it is done more fittingly in the person of the Word than in the other persons, it is necessary that God the Word and a human being come together into one person.

B: The path along which you are leading me is so well-fortified by reason in every direction that I see I cannot turn aside from it to the right or to the left.

A: It is not I who lead you; rather, the one of whom we are speaking, without whom we can do nothing,[69] leads us wherever we keep to the path of truth.

Chapter 10

That this human being does not die out of obligation; and in what way he can or cannot sin; and why he or an angel deserves praise for justice, even though they cannot sin

Now at this point we ought to investigate whether this human being will die out of obligation, in the way that all other human beings die out of obligation. But given that Adam would not have died if he had not sinned, all the more will this man not be obligated to die; for in him there can be no sin, since he will be God.

---

69. Cf. John 15:5.

B: I want you to linger on this point for just a bit, for it seems to me that whether we say that he is or that he is not able to sin, a serious difficulty arises either way. If we say that he cannot sin, it seems we should find that difficult to believe. If I might speak of him for a moment not as though he had never existed (as we have done up to this point) but as one whom we know and whose deeds we know: Who would deny that he was able to do many things that we call sins? To take just one example, how can we say that he was not able to lie, which is always a sin? When he spoke to the Jews about the Father and told them, "If I say that I do not know him, I will be a liar, like you,"[70] he uttered the words "I do not know him." Who would say that he was incapable of uttering those same five[71] words without the others, so as to say just "I do not know him"? And if he had done so, he would have been a liar, as he says himself; and to be a liar is to be a sinner. Therefore, since he was able to do that, he was able to sin.

A: He was both able to say that and not able to say that.

B: Explain that.

A: All power follows will. When I say that I can speak or walk, the stipulation "if I will" is understood. If there is no implicit reference to willing, it is not power but necessity. After all, when I say that I can be dragged off or overcome unwillingly, this is not my power; it is necessity and someone else's power. In fact, "I can be dragged off or overcome" is equivalent to "Someone else can drag me off or overcome me." And so we can say of Christ that he was able to lie if we implicitly add, "If he willed." And since he could not lie unwillingly, and he could not will to lie, it can equally well be said that he was not able to lie. And so in this way he was both able and not able to lie.

B: Let us now return to inquiring about him as though he did not yet exist, in the way we began. So I say: If he will not be able to sin because, as you say, he will not be able to will to sin, then he will preserve justice out of necessity, and so he will not be just in virtue of his freedom of choice. So what thanks will he be owed for his justice? After all, we are accustomed to say that God made angels and human beings capable of sin so that they would merit thanks and praise for preserving justice through freedom of choice when they could have abandoned it, whereas they would not be owed thanks and praise if they were just of necessity.

A: Shouldn't the angels who are now unable to sin be praised?

---

70. John 8:55.

71. Actually, Anselm says 'three,' since the expression translated "I do not know him" is *non scio eum.*

B: Certainly they should, because they earned their present inability to sin by not willing to sin when they were able to sin.

A: What do you say about God? He cannot sin, and he did not earn his inability to sin by not sinning when he had the power to sin. Shouldn't he be praised for his justice?

B: On this point I want you to give an answer on my behalf. For if I say he should not be praised, I know I'm lying; yet if I say he should be praised, I fear I will undermine the argument I gave concerning the angels.

A: It is not because they were able to sin that the angels should be praised for their justice; it is because, as a result of that fact, they in a certain sense have *from themselves* their inability to sin. In this respect they are a little like God, who has from himself whatever he has. For we say that a person gives something when he can take it away but does not; and we say that someone causes something to be when he can cause it not to be but does not. And so, since in this way the angels had the power to take justice away from themselves but did not, and since they had the power to cause themselves not to be just but did not, it is correct to assert that the angels gave themselves justice and caused themselves to be just. In this way, then, they have justice from themselves—since a creature cannot have justice from itself in any other way. And for this reason they should be praised for their justice, and they are just freely and not of necessity, since it is improper to speak of necessity where there is neither compulsion nor constraint. Hence, because God has from himself in a perfect way whatever he has, he is supremely worthy of praise for the good things that he has and preserves not by any necessity but, as I said above,[72] by the eternal* immutability that belongs to him alone. So it is in this way that the human being who will himself be God will be just from himself and will therefore be worthy of praise: because every good thing that he will have, he will have from himself, not of necessity but freely. For although the human nature will have from the divine nature whatever it will have, it will be one and the same person who will have it from himself, since the two natures will be one person.

B: You have convinced me by these arguments: I see clearly both that he will not be able to sin and that, nevertheless, he will be worthy of praise for his justice. But I think we should now investigate why—given that God can make a human being like this—he did not make the angels and the two first human beings in such a way that they likewise would not be able to sin but would deserve praise for their justice.

A: Do you understand what you are saying?

---

72. Near the end of Book 2, Chapter 5.

B: I *think* I understand. That's why I'm asking why God didn't make them that way.

A: Because it neither should nor could come about that each of them would be the very same person as God, as we say this man is. And if you ask why God did not do this for as many of them as there are divine persons, or at least for one of them, my answer is that reason in no way required that it be done at that time; instead, reason forbade it altogether, since God does nothing without reason.

B: I am embarrassed that I asked the question. Say what you were going to say.

A: Let us say, therefore, that he will not be obligated to die, since he will not be a sinner.

B: I have to concede that.

Chapter 11

That he dies of his own power; and that mortality does not belong to pure human nature

A: But it remains now to investigate whether he is able to die according to human nature, for according to divine nature he will always be incorruptible.

B: Why should we have any doubt about this, since he will be a true human being, and every human being is naturally mortal?

A: I think mortality belongs not to pure human nature but rather to corrupted human nature. Indeed, if human beings had never sinned and their immortality had been immutably confirmed, they would still be true human beings, no less than now; and when mortals rise again into incorruptibility,[73] they will still be true human beings, no less than now. After all, if mortality belonged to true human nature, there is no way there could be an immortal human being. So neither corruptibility nor incorruptibility belongs to bare human nature, since neither of them makes or destroys a human being; rather, one has the power to make a human being wretched, the other to make him blessed. But since there is no human being who does not die, 'mortal' is included in the definition of 'human being' by the philosophers, who did not believe that a whole human being ever could or ever can be immortal.[74] So the fact that he will be a true human being is not sufficient to show that this human being ought to be mortal.

---

73. 1 Corinthians 15:42.

74. Anselm specifies 'a whole human being' because some philosophers did believe in the immortality of the *soul*.

B: Then it is up to you to look for another argument to prove that he can die, since if you don't know one, I certainly don't.

A: There is no doubt that just as he will be God, so too will he be omnipotent.

B: That's true.

A: So if he wills to do so, he will be able to lay down his life and take it up again.[75]

B: If he cannot do this, it doesn't seem that he is omnipotent.

A: Therefore, he will be able never to die, if he so wills, and he will be able to die and rise again. Now it makes no difference to his power whether he lays down his life with no one else causing him to do so or he permits someone else to cause him to lay down his life.

B: Undoubtedly.

A: So if he wills to permit it, he can be killed; and if he does not will to permit it, he cannot.

B: Reason leads us unswervingly to this conclusion.

A: Reason has also taught us that he must have something greater than everything that is less than God, and that he gives this to God of his own accord and not out of obligation.

B: That's right.

A: But no such thing can be found either below him or outside him.

B: That's true.

A: So it must be found *in* him.

B: That follows.

A: So he will give either himself or something of his own.

B: I cannot understand it any other way.

A: We must now ask what sort of thing this giving ought to be. After all, he will not be able to give God himself or something of his own as though God did not already possess it, since every creature belongs to God.

B: That's right.

A: So we must understand his giving as follows: he will lay down himself or something of his own for the honor of God in a way that he is not obligated to do.

---

75. Cf. John 10:17–18.

B: That follows from what was said earlier.

A: If we say that he will give himself to obey God, so that by persevering in pre-serving justice he subordinates himself to God's will, that will not be a case of giving something that God does not demand of him as a debt; for every rational creature owes such obedience to God.

B: That cannot be denied.

A: And so it is in some other way that he must give God himself or something of his own.

B: Reason drives us to that conclusion.

A: Let's see whether that means giving his life: in other words, laying down his life or delivering himself over to death for the honor of God. For God will not demand this from him as a debt, since because there will be no sin in him, he will not be obligated to die, as we have said.

B: I cannot understand it any other way.

A: Let's consider further whether this is fitting according to reason.

B: Speak, and I will gladly listen.

A: Since humanity sinned through pleasure, is it not fitting for humanity to make recompense through pain? And since humanity was overcome by the devil so eas-ily that it could not have been any easier, and thereby dishonored God by sinning, is it not just for the human being who makes recompense for sin to overcome the devil with such great difficulty that it could not be any greater, and thereby honor God? And is it not appropriate that humanity, which in sinning took itself away from God as much as possible, should in making recompense give itself to God as much as possible?

B: Nothing could be more reasonable.

A: Now there is nothing more painful or more difficult a human being can do for the honor of God than to suffer death of his own accord and not out of obligation; and there is no greater way for a human being to give himself to God than to deliver himself up to death for the honor of God.

B: All these things are true.

A: So the one who is going to will to make recompense for human sin ought to be such that he can die if he so wills.

B: I see clearly that the human being about whom we are inquiring ought to be such that he will not die of necessity, since he will be omnipotent, or out of obligation, since he will never be a sinner, and also such that he can die of his own free will, since this will be necessary.[76]

A: And there are many other reasons why it is extremely fitting for him to be like human beings and to have dealings with them, without sin: reasons that are apparent through themselves in his life and deeds more straightforwardly and more clearly than they can be proved by reason alone, apart from experience. For who will set forth how necessarily and how wisely this was brought to pass: that the one who was going to redeem human beings from the way of death and destruction and, by teaching, lead them back to the way of life and eternal blessedness, should himself have dealings with human beings and in those dealings, when he taught them by his words how they ought to live, should offer himself as an example? Now how would he give himself as an example to those who are weak and mortal that they should not depart from justice on account of injuries, insults, pain, or death, unless they knew that he himself had experienced all these things?

Chapter 12

That although he shares our misfortunes, he is not unhappy

B: All these considerations show clearly that he ought to be mortal and to share our misfortunes. But all these misfortunes make us unhappy, so won't he be unhappy?

A: Not in the least. For just as having something advantageous against one's will does not make one happy, so too experiencing some misfortune wisely, willingly, and not under necessity, does not make one unhappy.

B: I have to grant that.

Chapter 13

That he does not possess ignorance along with our other infirmities

But tell me whether he will possess ignorance, along with our other infirmities, as part of the likeness to human beings that he ought to have.

A: Why do you doubt that God knows everything?

---

76. "this will be necessary": this phrase does not mean that his death will take place as a result of necessity, but that his ability to die of his own free will is a necessary condition for his making recompense for human sin.

B: Because even though he will be immortal in virtue of his divine nature, he will nonetheless be mortal in virtue of his human nature. So, in the same way, why can't this human being be genuinely ignorant, just as he will also be genuinely mortal?

A: Supreme Wisdom will of course act wisely in assuming the human being into unity of person with God, and so he will not assume in that human being what is in no way useful but instead quite harmful, to the work that this human being is going to carry out. Ignorance would not be useful to him in any way; on the contrary, it would be harmful in many respects. How, after all, will he carry out the many great works he is going to do unless he possesses enormous wisdom? How will human beings believe him if they know that he is ignorant? Even supposing they don't know he is ignorant, what purpose would such ignorance serve for him? Finally, given that only what is known is loved, just as there will be no good thing that he does not love, so too there will be no good thing that he does not know. Now no one has perfect knowledge of the good unless he knows how to distinguish it from evil, and no one knows how to distinguish good from evil if he is ignorant of evil. So just as the one of whom we are speaking will have complete knowledge of every good, so too he will not be ignorant of any evil. Therefore, he will possess all knowledge, though he may not show it openly in his dealings with human beings.

B: What you say seems right for when he is an adult; but infancy is not a suitable time for wisdom to appear in him, and so there will be no need for him to possess wisdom in his infancy and, therefore, it will not be fitting for him.

A: Have I not said that this Incarnation will be done wisely? God will assume mortality wisely; for he will use it wisely, in that he will put it to a very beneficial use. But he cannot assume ignorance wisely, since ignorance is never beneficial but always harmful, except perhaps when an evil will is thwarted by ignorance—but there will never be an evil will in him. For even if sometimes ignorance is not harmful in any other way, it is harmful simply by taking away the good of knowledge. And (to answer your question briefly) from the moment he begins to exist, this man will always be filled with God, just as he will be filled with himself.[77] Hence, he will never be without God's power, strength, and wisdom.

B: Although I never doubted that this was always the case in Christ, I have asked about it so that I might hear the reason for it. For we are often certain of something but do not know how to prove it rationally.

---

77. This may mean either "He will have all the attributes of God because he will himself be God" or "He will have all the attributes of God just as he will have all the attributes of a human being."

Chapter 14

How his death outweighs the number and magnitude of all sins

I now ask you to teach me how his death outweighs the number and magnitude of all sins, since you have shown[78] that a single sin that we regard as extremely insignificant is so infinite that even if one were shown an infinite number of worlds, as full of creatures as this one, and they could not be kept from falling into nothingness unless someone took a single glance contrary to the will of God, it should still not be done.

A: Suppose that man were present and you knew who he was. And suppose someone said to you, "Unless you kill this man, this whole world and everything that is not God will perish." Would you do it in order to save every other creature?

B: I wouldn't do it even if I were shown an infinite number of worlds.

A: What if someone then said to you, "Either you kill him, or all the sins of the world will come upon you"?

B: I would reply that I would rather take up all other sins—not only all the sins of this world that have been or will be, but also, in addition to these, every sin that can even be conceived—than this one sin. I think I ought to give this reply not only about killing him but even about any minor injury that might be done to him.

A: You are right to think that. But tell me: Why does your heart judge in such a way that it fears one sin in injuring this man more than all other sins that can be conceived, given that all sins whatsoever are against him?

B: It's because a sin that is committed against his person is incomparably more serious than all conceivable sins that are not against his person.

A: What will you say about the fact that often someone willingly endures damage to his person in order to keep from suffering greater damage to his possessions?

B: God has no need for this sort of endurance, because all things are subject to his power, as you said earlier[79] in reply to a question of mine.

A: Good answer. We therefore see that sins not committed against the person of God, no matter how great or how numerous they are, cannot be compared to the destruction of this man's bodily life.

B: That is quite clear.

---

78. In Book 1, Chapter 21.
79. In Book 1, Chapter 21.

A: How great a good do you think his life is, given that its destruction is so evil?

B: If every good thing is as good as its destruction is evil, his life is an incomparably greater good than those sins are evils, since its destruction is unfathomably greater than those sins.

A: You're right. Consider also that sins are as worthy of hatred as they are bad, and that his life is as worthy of love as it is good. From this it follows that his life is more worthy of love than those sins are worthy of hate.

B: I cannot fail to understand this.

A: Do you think that so great and so lovable a good can be sufficient to discharge the debt that is owed for the sins of the whole world?

B: Indeed, it can do infinitely more.

A: Then do you see how, if his life is given for sins, it overcomes them all?

B: Clearly.

A: So if giving one's life is accepting death, then just as the giving of his life outweighs all the sins of human beings, so too does his accepting death.

B: It is firmly established that this is true of all the sins that do not impinge upon the person of God.

Chapter 15

How his death wipes out the sins even of those who put him to death

But now I see another question that needs to be asked. If killing him is as great an evil as his life is a good, how can his death overcome and wipe out the sins of those who killed him? Or, if it does wipe out the sin of one of them, how can it also wipe out the sin of other human beings? For we believe that many human beings have already been saved and that countless others are being saved.

A: The Apostle has given the answer to this question. He wrote, "If they had known, they would never have crucified the Lord of Glory."[80] A sin committed knowingly is so different from a sin done through ignorance that this evil, which is so extremely serious that they could never have committed it if they had known what they were doing, is venial because it was done in ignorance. No human being could ever knowingly will to kill God. And so those who killed God in ignorance did not fall into that infinite sin to which no other sins can be compared. For in

---

80. 1 Corinthians 2:8.

our effort to discern how great a good his life is, we did not examine how grave the destruction of his life would be if done in ignorance, but as though it were done knowingly—though in fact no one ever did or could do it knowingly.

B: You have rationally demonstrated that the killers of Christ could attain forgiveness of their sin.

A: What more is left for you to ask? At this point you see how the necessity of reason shows that the heavenly city is to be completed by human beings, and that this can be done only through forgiveness of sins, which no human being can have except through a human being who is himself God and reconciles sinners to God by his own death. Therefore, we have clearly discovered Christ, whom we confess to be both God and man and to have died for our sake. And now that we know this without any doubt, we must not hesitate to believe that everything Christ says is assuredly true, since God cannot lie, and that all the things he did were done wisely, even if we do not grasp the reason for them.

B: What you say is true, and I do not doubt in the least that what he said is true or that what he did was done in accordance with reason. But I do make this request. There are things in the Christian faith that unbelievers think either should not be done or cannot be done. Explain to me the reason according to which they should or can be done—not in order to confirm me in faith, but in order to cause one who is already confirmed to have the joy of understanding the truth of that faith.

Chapter 16

How God assumed a sinless human being from the sinful mass; and concerning the salvation of Adam and Eve

That is why I am asking that you will disclose the reason of the things that I have yet to investigate, in the same way that you have already revealed the reason of the things discussed above. The first is how God assumed a sinless human being from the "sinful mass"[81]—that is, from the human race, the whole of which had been infected with sin—as though drawing out something unleavened from what is leavened. For although the conception of this human being is pure, and free from the sin of carnal pleasure, the Virgin from whom he was assumed was "conceived in iniquities, and in sins did" her "mother conceive" her;[82] and she was born with original sin, since she too sinned in Adam, "in whom all have sinned."[83]

---

81. For an explanation of the expression 'sinful mass,' see note 14 in Book 1, Chapter 5.
82. Psalm 51:6 (50:7).
83. Romans 5:12.

A: Once it has been established that this human being is God and the one who reconciles sinners, there is no doubt that he is completely without sin. But that cannot be the case unless he is assumed without sin from the sinful mass. If we cannot grasp the reason by which God's wisdom accomplished this, we should not be astonished; instead we should reverently tolerate the fact that in the hidden depths of so great a matter there is something we do not know. Indeed, God restored human nature more wonderfully than he first established it.[84] Of course the two things are equally easy for God, but before they existed human beings had not sinned so as to deserve never to be brought into being, whereas by sinning after they had been made, they deserved to lose both what they had been made to be and the purpose for which they had been made—although they did not completely lose what they had been made to be, so that there would be something for God to punish or to have mercy on, neither of which would have been possible if they had been reduced to nothing. So God restored human beings more wonderfully than he first established them insofar as he restored them from a sinful state, contrary to what they deserved, whereas he did not establish them from a sinful state or contrary to what they deserved. And how great a thing it is for God and a human being to come together into one in such a way that one and the same person is both God and man, each nature being preserved intact! So who would presume even to think that the human mind can penetrate how wisely and how wonderfully so inscrutable a work was accomplished?

B: I agree that no human being in this life can completely reveal so great a mystery, and I am not asking you to do what no human being can do, but just to do as much as you can. For your claim that more exalted reasons lie hidden in this matter will be more persuasive if I have seen you point out one reason than if, by saying nothing, you show that you do not understand any reason for it.

A: I see I can't escape your demands. But if I can show what you are asking for, even in a small way, let us give thanks to God. If I can't, let the things proved above be sufficient. After all, since it has been established that God ought to become a human being, there is no doubt that he has the wisdom and the power to accomplish this without sin.

B: I am happy to agree to that.

A: It was of course necessary that the redemption Christ brought about should benefit not only those who were alive in his day but others as well. Imagine, then, that there is a king, and the entire populace of one of his cities, with the exception of one man (who is nonetheless of their race), has sinned against him in such a

---

84. Cf. the offertory prayer said quietly by the priest in the Roman rite: "O God, who wonderfully created, and yet more wonderfully restored, the dignity of human nature."

way that none of them can do what is necessary to escape the death penalty. But the one innocent man has such favor with the king that he can reconcile them by means of some service that will greatly please the king, and he has such love for the guilty that he is willing to do this for all who put their trust in his help. He will do this service on a day that has been fixed according to the king's will. And since not all of those who are to be reconciled can come together on that day, the king, in view of the magnitude of this service, makes a concession: he will release from all past guilt all those who profess, either before or after that day, that they want to attain pardon through the deed that will be done on that day and to become parties to the agreement made there. And if they should happen to sin again after this pardon, they will again receive pardon through the efficacy of that same agreement, provided that they are willing to make appropriate recompense and then to amend their lives. But none of them will be allowed to enter the king's palace until the deed is done by which they are absolved of guilt.

In keeping with this analogy, since not all those who were to be saved could be present when Christ accomplished this redemption, there was such power in his death that its effect extends even to those who are absent in time or place. That his death ought to benefit not only those who are present is easy to recognize in virtue of the fact that not enough people could be present at his death as are necessary to build up the heavenly city—not even if everyone who was alive anywhere in the world at the time of his death were admitted to that redemption. For there are more demons than there were human beings alive on that day, from whom the number of fallen angels would have to be replaced.

Nor should it be believed that there was ever a time, from the moment human beings were created, that this world—together with its creatures, which were created for the use of human beings—was so bereft that it did not contain a single person from the human race who attained the purpose for which human beings were created. After all, it seems unfitting that God should allow the human race, and the things he created for the use of those who would make the heavenly city complete, to be pointless, as it were, even for a moment. For they would appear to exist in vain in some measure so long as they are seen to stop short of the purpose for which they were principally created.

B: By a fitting argument, and one that seems subject to no objection, you show that from the moment human beings began to exist, there was never a time without someone who belonged to the reconciliation without which every human being would have been made in vain. We can conclude that this is not merely fitting but indeed necessary. For if this is more fitting and more reasonable than the opposite (namely, that at some time there was no one in whom God's purpose in making human beings was realized), and if there is nothing that undermines this argument, it is necessary that at every time there has been someone who belonged to the aforesaid reconciliation. Hence, it should not be doubted that Adam and

Eve belonged to that redemption, even though divine authority does not teach this explicitly.

A: And it seems incredible that God should exclude the two of them from his purpose at the very time that he made them and immutably purposed that from them he would make all the human beings whom he was going to exalt to that heavenly city.

B: On the contrary, we ought to believe that they were created above all so that they might be in the company of those for whose sake they were created.

A: You have examined this well. Yet before the death of Christ no soul could gain entrance to heaven, as I said earlier about the king's palace.

B: So we believe.

A: Now the Virgin from whom the man we are discussing was assumed was among those who were cleansed from their sins by him before his birth; and he was assumed from her in her cleansed state.

B: I very much like what you say, except for one thing. He ought to have his cleanness from sin from himself, but he would appear to derive this condition from his mother and to be clean through her rather than through himself.

A: That's not so. His mother's cleanness, through which he is clean, was itself from him; therefore, he was clean through himself and from himself.[85]

B: That sounds good. But I think there's something else we need to investigate. Earlier we said that he was not going to die of necessity, and now we see that his mother was clean through his future death; and if she had not been clean, he could not have come to exist from her. So how is it that he did not die of necessity, given that he could not even exist unless he was going to die? After all, if he had not been going to die, the Virgin from whom he was assumed would not have been clean, since there was no way for her to be clean except by believing in the fact of his death; and he could not be assumed from her unless she was clean. So if he did not die of necessity after he had been assumed from the Virgin, it was possible for him not to have been assumed from the Virgin after he had already been assumed, which is impossible.

---

85. The nuances of the Latin can be made clearer if we use the name 'Christ' to designate "the man whom we are discussing": his mother's cleanness, through which Christ is clean, was itself from Christ; therefore, Christ too (i.e., as well as his mother) was clean through Christ and from Christ.

A: If you had reflected properly on what was said earlier,[86] you would, I think, understand that this question has already been answered.

B: I don't see how.

A: When we investigated whether he was able to lie, did we not show that there are two powers involved in lying: the power to will to lie, and the power to lie? And that although he had the power to lie, he had from himself the lack of any power to will to lie? And that for that very reason he deserves praise for the justice by which he preserved truth?

B: Yes.

A: Similarly, when it comes to preserving his life, there is the power to will to preserve it and the power to preserve it. So if someone asks whether the God-man was able to preserve his life so that he would never die, it should not be doubted that he always had the power to preserve it, although he was not able to will to preserve it so that he would never die; and since it was from himself that he had this inability to will, he laid down his life not of necessity but by a free power.

B: These two powers of his—the power to lie and the power to preserve life—are not exactly alike. In the case of the power to lie, it follows that if he willed to lie, he was able to lie. But in the case of the power to preserve his life, it seems that if he had willed not to die, he was no more able not to die than he was able not to be what he was. For he was a human being precisely in order that he might die, and he was able to be assumed from the Virgin because of her faith in his future death, as you said earlier.

A: You think that he was unable not to die, or that he died of necessity, because he was unable not to be what he was; but you might just as well claim that he was unable to will not to die, or that he willed of necessity to die, because he was unable not to be what he was. For it is every bit as true that he became a human being in order that he might *will* to die as it is that he became a human being in order that he might die. Hence, just as you ought not to say that he was unable to will not to die or that he willed of necessity to die, so too one ought not to say that he was unable not to die or that he died of necessity.

B: On the contrary: since the same reasoning applies to both dying and willing to die, it seems that both of them were necessary in his case.

A: Who was this who spontaneously* willed to make himself a human being, so that by this same immutable will he might die, and so that the Virgin from whom

---

86. In Book 2, Chapters 10 and 11.

this human being would be assumed would be made clean through faith in this certainty?

B: It was God, the Son of God.

A: Was it not shown earlier[87] that God's will is not compelled by any necessity, but rather that when it is said to do something of necessity, it is preserving itself by its own spontaneous immutability?

B: Yes, that was shown; but conversely, we see that what God immutably wills cannot not be, but necessarily is. Hence, if God willed that this human being should die, he was unable not to die.

A: By virtue of the fact that the Son of God assumed a human being with the will that he should die, you prove that this human being was unable not to die.

B: That's how I understand it.

A: From what has been said, is it not likewise clear that the Son of God and the assumed human being are a single person, so that one and the same being is both God and man, the Son of God and the son of the Virgin?

B: Yes.

A: So it was by his own will that this human being was unable not to die and did die.

B: I cannot deny it.

A: Therefore, since God's will does nothing by any necessity, but only by its own power, and since his will was God's will,[88] he did not die of any necessity, but solely by his own power.

B: I cannot quarrel with your arguments, since I cannot in any way undermine either your premises or the conclusions you draw. Still, what I said earlier continues to strike me: if he had willed not to die, he could not have avoided dying, any more than he could have not been what he was. For he was truly going to die, since

---

87. See Book 2, Chapters 5 and 10.

88. Taken strictly, Anselm's words seem to commit him to a heretical view called "monothelitism," according to which there is only one will in Christ, the divine will. But by Anselm's day it had long been settled that there are two wills in Christ: both a divine will and a human will. (For according to orthodoxy, there are two complete and intact natures in Christ: the divine nature and a human nature. And will is an essential feature of each, so that any being with both natures would have to have two wills.) Moreover, the arguments of Book 1, Chapters 8 and 9, clearly involve attributing a human will to Christ. Presumably, then, what Anselm means here is that Christ's human will always freely accorded with his divine will.

if he had not been truly going to die, the faith in his future death through which both the Virgin from whom he was born and many others had been cleansed from sin would not have been true. And if that faith had not been true, it could not have been of any benefit. Therefore, if he was able not to die, he was able to make untrue what was already true.

A: Why was it true, before he died, that he was going to die?

B: Because he himself willed it spontaneously and with an immutable will.

A: So if, as you say, he was unable not to die because he was truly going to die, and he was truly going to die because he himself spontaneously and immutably willed this, it follows that he was unable not to die because, and only because, he willed to die with an immutable will.

B: Right. But whatever the reason may have been, it is still true that he was unable not to die and that it was necessary that he die.

A: You are hung up on nothing. As the saying goes, you're looking for knots in a bulrush.[89]

B: Have you forgotten what I said to counter your excuses at the beginning of our discussion—namely, that you should do what I was asking, not for the learned but for me and for those who joined me in making this request?[90] So bear with me as I ask questions that reflect the slowness and dullness of our minds, and satisfy me and them with your answers even to childish questions, just as you set out to do.

Chapter 17

That there is no necessity or impossibility in God; and that there is compelling necessity and non-compelling necessity

A: We have already said that it is improper to say that God cannot do something or that God does something of necessity. In fact, all necessity and impossibility are subject to God's will; his will is not subjected to any necessity or impossibility. For nothing is necessary or impossible except because God himself wills it to be so, whereas it is far from the truth to say that God wills or does not will anything on account of necessity or impossibility. Hence, because God does all and only those things that he wills, just as no necessity or impossibility precedes his willing or not-willing, so too neither does any necessity or impossibility precede his doing

---

89. Bulrushes are smooth; they have no knots or nodes. The proverb refers to finding difficulties where in fact there are none.

90. At the end of Book 1, Chapter 1.

or not-doing, even though he wills and does many things immutably. Now when God does something, after it has been done it can no longer not have been done, but rather it is always true that it has been done; and yet it is not rightly said that it is impossible for God to bring it about that what is past is not past—for in this case there is no necessity of not bringing it about, or impossibility of bringing it about, at work, but only the will of God, who, because he is himself the truth, wills that the truth be always immutable, just as he is. In the same way, if he immutably resolves to do something, then although what he resolves to do, before it is done, cannot fail to come about in the future, nonetheless there is not in God any necessity of doing it or impossibility of not doing it, since only God's will is at work in him. For to say that God "cannot" do something is not to deny any power in God, but rather to signify his invincible power and strength. For all it means is that nothing can make God do the thing that we say is impossible.[91]

For this sort of expression is quite common, in which a thing is said "to be able," not because there is a power in it, but because there is a power in another thing; and in which a thing is said "not to be able," not because there is a lack of power in it, but because there is a lack of power in some other thing. For example, we say "This man can be overcome" for "Someone can overcome him," and "He cannot be overcome" for "No one can overcome him." After all, to be able to be overcome is not a power, but a lack of power; and not to be able to be overcome is not a lack of power but a power. Nor do we say that God does something of necessity on the grounds that there is any necessity in him, but because there is some necessity in something else, just as I said was true of lack of power, when he is said not to be able. For all necessity is either compulsion or constraint; these two necessities are related to each other as contraries, just like necessary and impossible. For whatever is compelled to exist is constrained from not existing, and what is compelled not to exist is constrained from existing, just as what is necessary to exist is impossible not to exist, and what is necessary not to exist is impossible to exist, and vice versa. But when we say that something is necessarily the case or necessarily not the case in God, we do not mean that there is any compelling or constraining necessity in him; rather, we signify that in all other things there is a necessity constraining them from acting, and compelling them not to act, contrary to what is said of God. For when we say that it is necessary that God always speaks the truth, and that it is necessary that he never lies, this simply means that there is in God such steadfastness in preserving the truth that it is necessary that no thing can make it the case that he does not speak the truth or that he lies.

---

91. More literally: For nothing else is understood [by such statements] than that no thing can bring it about that God does the thing that is denied to be possible.

For this reason, when we say that this human being, who through unity of person (as was said above)[92] is himself the very same as God, the Son of God, was unable not to die or to will not to die after he was born of the Virgin, this does not signify any lack of power in him to preserve, or to will to preserve, his own immortal life; rather it signifies (1) the immutability of his will, by which he spontaneously made himself a human being so that, persevering in that same will, he might die, and (2) the fact that no thing was able to change that will. For it would not be power, but a lack of power, if he were able to will to lie or to deceive or to change his will, which he previously willed to be immutable. And if, as I said above,[93] when someone spontaneously resolves to do something good and by that same will afterwards accomplishes what he resolved to do, then even though he can be compelled to do it if he is unwilling to make good on his promise, he should still not be said to do of necessity what he does, but rather to do it by the free will by which he originally resolved to do it—for we should not say that something is done or not done out of necessity or out of a lack of power when what is actually active is neither necessity nor lack of power but will—if, I say, this is true in the case of human beings, much more so should we refrain from speaking of any necessity or lack of power at all in the case of God, who does nothing but what he wills, and whose will cannot be compelled or constrained by any power. For in Christ the diversity of natures and unity of person worked in such a way that if the human nature could not do what needed to be done for the restoration of human beings, the divine nature did it; and if it was not at all fitting for the divine nature, the human nature exhibited it. And it was not two distinct persons, but he himself who, existing perfectly as both divine and human, through his human nature paid what human nature owed and through his divine nature was able to do what was beneficial. Finally, the Virgin, who through faith was made clean so that he could be assumed from her, in no way believed that he was going to die except because he willed, as she had learned from the prophet who said of him, "he was offered because he himself willed it."[94] Hence, because her faith was true, it was necessary for things to be in the future as she believed they were going to be. Now if again it bothers you that I say "it was necessary," remember that the truth of the Virgin's faith was not the cause of his dying spontaneously; rather, because this was going to be in the future, her faith was true. Hence, if it is said that "It was necessary that he die by his will alone, because her faith, or the prophecy, which came beforehand, was true," this is equivalent to saying, "It was necessary that this was going to be the case in the future, because this was going to be the case in the

---

92. Book 2, Chapters 7 and 9.
93. Book 2, Chapter 5.
94. Isaiah 53:7.

future." But that sort of necessity does not compel a thing to be; rather, the thing's being is what brings about the necessity of its being.

You see, there is antecedent necessity, which is the cause of something's being; and there is subsequent necessity, which the thing itself brings about. It is a case of antecedent and[95] efficient necessity when it is said that the heavens revolve because it is necessary that they revolve, whereas it is a case of subsequent necessity—and necessity that brings nothing about but rather is brought about—when I say that you are speaking of necessity because you are speaking. For when I say this, I signify that nothing can make it the case that while you are speaking you are not speaking, not that anything is compelling you to speak. For the violence of their natural condition compels the heavens to revolve, whereas no necessity brings it about that you speak. Now wherever there is antecedent necessity there is also subsequent necessity; but it is not the case that where there is subsequent necessity there is automatically also antecedent necessity. For we can say, "It is necessary that the heavens revolve, because they revolve"; but it is not similarly true that you are speaking because it is necessary that you speak. This subsequent necessity runs through all times[96] in the following way. Whatever was, necessarily was. Whatever is, necessarily is and necessarily was going to be. Whatever will be, necessarily will be. This is the necessity that, where Aristotle discusses singular and future propositions, seems to destroy contingency and show that all things are of necessity.[97] Because that faith in or prophecy about Christ, namely, that he was going to die willingly and not of necessity, was true, it was necessary—in terms of this subsequent necessity, which does not bring anything about—that the actual event should be this way. It was by this necessity that he became a human being, by this necessity that he did and suffered whatever he did and suffered, by this necessity that he willed whatever he willed. For because these things were going to take place in the future, they took place of necessity; and because they in fact took place, they were going to take place of necessity; and because these things took place, they took place of necessity. And if you want to know the true necessity of all the things that he did and suffered, know that all these things were of necessity because he himself willed them. But no necessity preceded his will. Therefore, given that the only reason they took place is that he willed them, it follows that if he had not willed them, they would not have taken place. And so in this way no one took his life from him; instead, he laid it down and took it up again, since he had the power to lay down his life and take it up again, as he himself says.[98]

---

95. This 'and' as well as the next one should be treated as epexegetic: that is, they function like 'that is' or 'in other words.'

96. or 'tenses': the word is the same in Latin (*tempora*).

97. Aristotle, *De interpretatione* 9.

98. John 10:18.

B: You have satisfied me that it cannot be proved that he was subject to death by any necessity, and I do not regret having pressed you to do this.

A: I take it that we have presented a solid explanation of how God assumed a sinless human being from the sinful mass, but I do not at all think one should deny that there is any other reason besides the one we have given—not to mention the fact that God can do what human reason cannot comprehend. Yet because this reason seems sufficient to me, and also because if I decided to look into the other reason now, it would be necessary to investigate what original sin is and how it is transmitted from our first parents to the whole human race (apart from the man whom we are discussing), and to look into certain other questions that require a treatise to themselves, let us be content with what we have already said in accordance with reason, and go forward with what remains of the task we have undertaken.

B: As you wish—but on one condition: that you treat this other reason, which for now you evade discussing, as a debt that at some point you will repay, with God's help.

A: Since I know that I want to do just that, I will not deny your request. But because I am uncertain of the future, I will not be so bold as to make a promise, but I will entrust this to God's providence.[99]

Chapter 18

How by Christ's life restitution is made to God for human sins; and how Christ both owed and did not owe suffering

But now say something about what you think remains to be resolved concerning the question you raised at the outset, on account of which many other questions have arisen.

B: The kernel of the question was this: Why did God become a human being in order to save human beings through his death, given that it seems he could have accomplished this in some other way? In reply you showed by many necessary reasons that the restoration of human nature ought not to have been left undone, and that it could not be brought about unless humanity paid what it owed to God on account of sin. Only humanity owed this debt, but it was so great that only

---

99. Anselm's uncertainty is not just the usual acknowledgment that we cannot be sure of what will happen in the future, but a recognition that both the pressure of his administrative duties and his own failing health might well keep him from writing further on these topics. Nonetheless, he did in fact repay his "debt" by writing *On the Virginal Conception, and On Original Sin*, which he dedicated to Boso.

God could pay it; thus, there had to be one and the same being who was both God and human. For this reason it was necessary for God to assume a human being into unity of person, so that one who in his nature owed the debt and could not repay it would be the same person as one who could repay it. Then you showed that the human being who would be God ought to be assumed from a virgin and by the person of the Son of God, and you showed how it was possible for him to be assumed without sin from the sinful mass. And you proved quite compellingly that this man's life was so sublime and so precious that it could suffice to pay what was owed for the sins of the whole world, and infinitely more besides. So what is left now is to explain how his life repays God for the sins of human beings.

A: Since he allowed himself to be killed for the sake of justice, did he not give his life for the honor of God?

B: If I can understand what I do not hesitate to believe—even if I do not see how it was reasonable for him to do this, given that he had the power both to preserve justice unswervingly and to preserve his own life eternally—I will acknowledge that what he spontaneously gave to God for God's honor is something that cannot even be compared to anything that is not God and something that can make restitution for all the debts of every human being.

A: Do you not understand that when (as we discussed earlier)[100] he bore with generous patience the things that were inflicted on him because he obediently preserved justice—injuries and slanders and death on the cross between thieves—he gave an example to human beings that they ought not to turn aside from the justice that they owe to God, because of any suffering they might experience? And he would not have given this example if he had exercised his power and turned aside from the death that was inflicted upon him for the sake of justice.

B: It seems there was no need for him to give this example. After all, we know that even before Christ came, many people had given a sufficient example by courageously enduring death for the sake of truth, and John the Baptist did so after Christ came but before he died.

A: No human being other than Christ ever gave God, in dying, something that he was not at some point going to lose of necessity anyway, and none ever repaid God what he did not owe. Christ, by contrast, spontaneously offered the Father what he was never going to lose of necessity, and he repaid on behalf of sinners what he did not owe for himself. He gave his most precious life—indeed, he gave his very self, so great a person, with such great willingness—for the sake of those whom he owed nothing but punishment, even though he in no way lacked for anything for his own sake or was compelled for anyone else's sake. Much more so, then, did he

---

100. Book 1, Chapter 9.

give an example, so that every person will, when reason demands it, unhesitatingly render to God on his own behalf what he will at some point lose without delay.

B: You are getting very close to what I am longing for. But bear with me as I ask a question that perhaps you will think it is foolish for me to ask, but that I would not be able to answer readily if someone asked it of me. You say that when he died, he gave what he did not owe. But no one will deny that when he gave this example in such a way, he did something better and pleased God more than he would have if he had not done this. And no one will say that he did not owe what he understood to be better and more pleasing to God. How, then, will we claim that he did not owe God what he did, namely, what he knew to be better and more pleasing to God, especially given that a creature owes God everything it is and everything that it knows [is good] and has the power to do?

A: Granted, a creature has nothing from itself. But when God leaves it up to a creature either to do something or not to do it, he gives each alternative to the creature as something of its own, so that even if one alternative is better, neither is determinately required; rather, whether the creature does the better alternative or the other, we say that it ought to do what it does. And if it does what is better, it has a reward, because it spontaneously gives something of its own. For example, although virginity is better than marriage, neither is determinately required of human beings; rather, both someone who makes use of marriage and someone who prefers to remain a virgin are said to do what they ought to do. No one, after all, says that either virginity or marriage ought not to be chosen. Instead, we say that someone ought to act according to what he prefers before he has settled on one or the other; and if someone remains a virgin, he looks forward to a reward for the spontaneous gift that he is offering to God. Therefore, when you say that a creature owes God what it knows is better and has the power to do, that is not always true if you mean the creature owes it as a matter of obligation, and you do not add the qualification, "If God commands it." For, as I have said, human beings do not owe virginity as a matter of obligation; instead, they ought to make use of marriage if that is what they prefer.

Perhaps the word 'ought'[101] is bothering you, and you cannot understand how there can be owing without any obligation. In that case, you should know that 'ought'—like 'can,' 'cannot,' and 'necessity'—is sometimes said, not because it is in the things of which it is said, but because it is in something else. For example, when we say that the poor ought to receive alms from the rich, this is equivalent

---

101. 'Owe' and 'ought' are the same word in Latin. English idiom makes it impossible to stick consistently with one translation. Up to this point in the chapter 'owe' has been the prevailing (but not invariable) translation, but from here to the end of the chapter 'ought' will be more common.

to saying that the rich ought to give alms to the poor. After all, one should exact this obligation from a rich person, not from a poor one. We say too that God ought to rule over all things, not because he is under an obligation in this respect, but because all things ought to be subject to him; and we say that God ought to do what he wills, because what he wills ought to be the case. Thus, when some creature wills to do what it has the prerogative either to do or not to do, it is said to do what it ought to do, because what it wills ought to be the case. And so when (as we have said) the Lord Jesus willingly underwent death, which it was his prerogative either to suffer or not to suffer, it was true that he ought to do what he did, because what he willed ought to come about; but it was also not the case that he ought to do it, because he was not under an obligation to do it. For he himself is both God and a human being. Therefore, in terms of his human nature, from the time he was a human being his divine nature (which is distinct from his human nature) conferred on him this prerogative: that whatever he possessed was his own, so that there was nothing he ought to give, other than what he willed to give. But in terms of his person, whatever he possessed, he had it from himself in such a way, and was so perfectly self-sufficient, that he did not owe any repayment to anyone and did not need to give anything in order to be repaid.

B: I now see clearly that there is no sense in which he was under an obligation to give himself over to death for God's honor, as my argument seemed to show, and that nevertheless he did what he ought to do.

A: That honor in fact belongs to the whole Trinity. For because he is himself God, the Son of God, he offered himself to himself, as to the Father and to the Holy Spirit, for his own honor. That is, he offered his humanity to his divinity, which is one and the same as the divinity of the three persons. But in order to say more clearly what we mean, while abiding in this same truth, let us adopt the usual way of speaking and say that the Son freely offered himself to the Father. For this is the most suitable way to express it, since in [the name of] one Person we understand God as a whole, to whom as a human being he offered himself; and the names of Father and Son kindle intense devotion in the hearts of those who hear that the Son is said to intercede with the Father in this way on our behalf.

B: I accept this most willingly.

Chapter 19

How very reasonable it is that his death brings about human salvation

A: Let us now examine, as well as we can, how very reasonable it is that his death brings about human salvation.

B: That is what my heart is longing for. For although I think I understand this, I want you to show how the rational account holds together.

A: Now there is no need to set forth how great a thing it is that the Son freely gave.

B: That is already sufficiently clear.

A: And you will not judge that the one who freely gave so great a gift to God should go unrewarded.

B: On the contrary, I see that it is necessary that the Father reward the Son. Otherwise, he would appear to be either unjust, if he were unwilling to reward him, or powerless, if he were unable to reward him; and neither of these is true of God.

A: Someone who gives a reward either gives the other person what he does not have or cancels a debt that can be demanded from him. But before the Son did such a great thing, everything that was the Father's was also his; and he never owed any debt that could be canceled. So what reward will be given to one who lacks for nothing, one to whom nothing can be given and for whom no debt can be canceled?

B: I see on the one hand that a reward is necessary, and on the other that it is impossible. For it is necessary that God pay what he owes, yet there is also nothing for him to pay.

A: If such a great and well-deserved reward is not given either to the Son or to anyone else, it will seem that the Son did so great a deed in vain.

B: It is impious to suppose such a thing.

A: Then it is necessary that the reward be given to someone else, since it cannot be given to him.

B: That conclusion is inescapable.

A: If the Son should will to give someone else what was owed to himself, could the Father rightfully prevent him or deny the reward to the one to whom the Son gives it?

B: On the contrary, I understand that it is just and necessary that the Father pay the reward to the one to whom the Son wills to give it, since it is proper for the Son to give what belongs to him, and the Father cannot pay what he owes except to someone other than the Son.

A: To whom will he more fittingly give the fruit and reward of his death than to those for whose salvation he made himself a human being, as truthful reasoning has taught us, and to whom, as we have said, he gave an example by dying for the sake of justice? For their imitation of him will be unavailing if they do not share in what he has earned. And whom will he more justly make heirs of the reward he does not need, and of the abundance of his own riches, than his own kindred and brothers, whom he sees languishing in poverty and deep misery, bound by their many and great debts, so that what they owe for their sins is forgiven and they are given what they lack on account of their sins?

B: The world can hear nothing more reasonable, nothing sweeter, nothing more desirable. For my part, this gives birth to such assurance in me that I can no longer express the great joy with which my heart exults. For it seems to me that God rejects no one who approaches him under this name.

A: That is so, provided that one approaches him as one ought. And Holy Scripture—which is established on the firm foundation of the solid truth that we have in some measure glimpsed, with God's help—teaches us in every place how we ought to approach participation in such great grace and how we ought to live under it.

B: Truly, whatever is built on this foundation is established on solid rock.[102]

A: I think I have now to some extent given a satisfactory answer to your question, although someone better than I am could do so more fully, and there are more and greater reasons for this matter than my mind, or any mortal mind, can grasp. It is also clear that God had no need at all to do the thing we have been discussing; rather, unchangeable truth demanded it. Now because of the unity of person, God is said to do what this man did; nonetheless, God had no need to come down from heaven in order to overcome the devil or in order to act justly against the devil in order to set human beings free. Instead, God demanded that humanity overcome the devil and that humanity, which had offended against God through sin, make recompense through justice. For God owed the devil nothing but punishment, and humanity owed him nothing but defeat, so that those whom he had defeated would in turn vanquish him. Whatever else was demanded of humanity was owed to God, not to the devil.

Chapter 20

How great and how just is God's mercy

As for God's mercy, which seemed to you to vanish when we were considering God's justice and human sin,[103] we have found it to be so great and so consonant with justice that it cannot be thought to be greater or more just. What, indeed,

---

102. Cf. Luke 6:47–48.
103. Book 1, Chapter 24.

can be understood to be more merciful than for God the Father to say to a sinner condemned to eternal torments, with no way to redeem himself, "Take my only-begotten Son, and offer him on your behalf," and for the Son himself to say, "Take me and redeem yourself"? For when they call us and draw us to the Christian faith, it is as though they were saying those things. And what is more just than for one who is paid a price greater than every debt to cancel every debt, if the price is paid with the proper affection?

Chapter 21

That it is impossible for the devil to be reconciled

As for the devil's reconciliation, which you asked about,[104] you will understand that it is impossible if you attentively consider the reconciliation of humanity. For just as humanity could be reconciled only through a God-man who would be able to die, through whose justice God would be repaid what he lost through human sin, so too the damned angels can be saved only through a God-angel who can die and through his justice restores to God what the sins of the other angels have taken away. And just as it was not right for human beings to be rescued by another human being who was not of the same race, even if he were of the same nature, so too no angel ought to be saved by another angel, even though they are all of one nature, since unlike human beings they are not of the same race. For it is not the case that all angels are from one angel, as all human beings are from one human being.

Another thing that prevents their restoration is the fact that just as they fell without anyone else harming them, so too they ought to get back up without anyone else helping them, which is impossible for them. For there is no other way for them to be restored to the dignity that they were originally going to have, since if they had not sinned, they would have remained steadfast in the truth through their own power that they had received, without help from anyone else. Hence, if anyone thinks that our Savior's redemption ought to be extended to them, he will be convinced rationally that he has irrationally fallen into error. I do not mean that the price of his death does not outweigh in its magnitude all the sins of human beings and angels, but that immutable reason forbids the restoration of the lost angels.

---

104. Book 1, Chapter 17.

Chapter 22

That the truth of the Old and New Testaments has been proved in what has been said

B: I think everything you say is reasonable and cannot be contradicted, and I understand that through this answer to the one question we have put forward, everything that is contained in the Old and New Testaments has been proved. For your proof that God had to become a human being is such that, even if one were to eliminate the few things you introduced from our books in order to say something about the three divine persons and about Adam, you would satisfy not only Jews but also pagans by reason alone; and the God-man himself establishes the New Testament and confirms the Old. Therefore, just as one must confess that the God-man himself is truthful, so too no one can doubt that everything contained in the Old and New Testaments is true.

A: If we have said anything that requires correction, I will not spurn correction if it is made reasonably. But if what we take ourselves to have discovered by reason is strengthened by the testimony of truth, we should ascribe it not to ourselves but to God, "who is blessed forever. Amen."[105]

---

105. Romans 1:25; cf. Romans 9:5, 2 Corinthians 11:31.

On the Virginal Conception, and On Original Sin

Chapters

Though I should wish in all things to honor, if I can, your pious will, my brother and dearest son, Boso, I regard myself as most greatly in your debt when I understand that I am the one who instilled such a will in you. Now I am certain that when you read in *Cur Deus Homo*—a book that you in particular, among others, encouraged me to write, in which I took you as my partner in dialogue—that it seems there can be another explanation, besides the one I offered there, for how God took a sinless human being out of the sinful mass of the human race,[1] your eager mind is strongly aroused to investigate what that reason might be. So I fear you would think me unjust if I should conceal from your zealous interest what I believe about that topic. I will therefore speak briefly about my view of this matter, in such a way that I do not repudiate anyone's faithful opinion about it or stubbornly defend my own opinion if it can be shown by reason to conflict with the truth. Nonetheless, I do regard the reason I offered in *Cur Deus Homo* to be utterly firm and sufficient if one examines it carefully. After all, nothing prohibits there being a plurality of reasons for one and the same thing, any one of which can be sufficient by itself.

Chapter 1

What original and personal justice and injustice are

So in order to see in what way God assumed a sinless human being from the sinful mass of the human race, we must first investigate original sin, since that alone gives rise to this question. For if it becomes evident how Christ could not be subject to original sin, it will be clear how the assumption or conception of that human being was free from all sin.

---

1. See *Cur Deus Homo*, Book 2, Chapter 17.

There is no doubt that 'original' is denominated* from 'origin.' So if original sin exists only in human beings, it appears to be called 'original' either from the origin of human nature, because it exists from the original beginning of human nature in virtue of being transmitted from the very origin of human nature, or from the origin or beginning of each particular person, because it was transmitted in his origin. But it does not appear that original sin derives from the beginning of human nature, since the origin of human nature was just; for our first parents were created just, without any sin. And so it seems that original sin is so called from the origin of each particular human person. Now if someone were to say that sin is called 'original' because individual human beings derive it from those from whom their nature has its origin, I will not contradict him, provided that he does not deny that original sin is transmitted in conjunction with the origin of each person. For although in every human being there is both the nature by which he is a human being, just as all other human beings are, and the person by which he is distinguished from others (as when someone is called 'this fellow' or 'that man,' or is called by his own name, such as 'Adam' or 'Abel'), and although each one's sin is in both the nature and the person—for Adam's sin was in both the human being, that is, in the nature, and in the particular man named 'Adam,' that is, in the person—nonetheless, there is both the sin that everyone receives along with his nature in his own origin and the sin that someone does not receive with his nature but commits himself once he is a person distinct from other persons. That which is received in one's origin is called 'original'; it could also be called 'natural,' not because it derives from the essence of the nature, but because it is received along with the nature on account of the nature's corruption. By contrast, the sin that all human beings commit once they are persons can be called 'personal,' since it is done by the vice of a person. Justice can be called 'original' and 'personal' on the same grounds. Thus, Adam and Eve were 'originally' (that is, at their very beginning, as soon as they were human beings) and without delay just together. Justice, however, can be called 'personal' when someone unjust receives a justice that he did not have from his origin.

Chapter 2

How human nature was corrupted

So if Adam and Eve had preserved their original justice, those who would be born from them would have been originally just, in the same way that Adam and Eve were just. But since they sinned personally, even though they were originally strong and uncorrupted and had the power always to preserve justice without difficulty, everything they were became weakened and corrupted: after their sin, their bodies were like those of brute animals, subject to corruption and carnal appetites, while their souls were infected with carnal affections from the corruption of the body and its appetites, as well as from the lack of the goods that it lost. And because the whole of human nature was in them, and nothing of human nature was outside them, the whole of human nature was weakened and corrupted.

What was left in human nature, therefore, was the debt of the justice, whole and sound and without any injustice, that human nature had received, and the debt of making recompense for having abandoned justice, along with the corruption that it had incurred on account of sin. If it had not sinned, it would have produced offspring that were such as God had made human nature to be; but since it did sin, it produces offspring that are such as it has made itself by sinning. Therefore, since by itself it can neither make recompense for sin nor recover the justice it has abandoned, and since "the body, which is corrupted, weighs down the soul"[2]—especially when, as in infancy and in the mother's womb, the body is so weak that one cannot even understand justice—it appears to be necessary that in infants human nature is born with the debt of making recompense for the first sin, which it had the power to avoid always, and with the debt of having original justice, which it had the power to preserve always. Nor does its powerlessness in those infants excuse human nature for not paying back in them what it owes, since it brought that powerlessness upon itself by abandoning justice in its first parents, in whom the whole of human nature existed; and it is always indebted to have the power that it received for the sake of always preserving justice. This condition can be regarded as original sin in infants.

Let us also add the sins of the more immediate ancestors, which are repaid "unto the third and fourth generation."[3] For one might wonder whether all these are to be reckoned as original sin or not. Yet because I do not wish to be seen as trivializing original sin by raising this question, I will stipulate that original sin is such that no one could show it to be any more serious.

Chapter 3

That sin exists only in a rational will

But whether original sin is this whole thing[4] or something less, I think it cannot in any way be said to exist in an infant before the infant has a rational soul, just as there was no justice in Adam before he was made a rational human being. For even if Adam and Eve had produced offspring without having sinned in the meantime,

---

2. Wisdom 9:15.

3. Cf. Exodus 20:5 ff.

4. By 'this whole thing' (*hoc totum*) Anselm appears to mean the combination of the effects of the sin of Adam and Eve with the effects of the sins of our more immediate ancestors.

justice would not and could not have been in their seed before it was formed into a living human being. So if the seed of a human being is not capable of acquiring justice before it becomes a human being, it also cannot acquire original sin before it is a human being.

Indeed, there is no doubt that original sin is an instance of injustice. After all, given that every sin is an instance of injustice and original sin is sin, original sin is clearly an instance of injustice. If someone were to say that not every sin is an instance of injustice, he would be saying that it is possible for there to be some sin in a person and yet, at the same time, for there to be no injustice in that person—and that seems unintelligible. Now if someone were to say instead that original sin should not be called sin in an unqualified sense, but only with the qualification 'original' (in the same way that a stuffed animal is not truly an animal, but a stuffed animal),[5] it would of course follow that an infant that has no sin but original sin is free of sin, and that the Virgin's Son was not the only one among human beings to be sinless in his mother's womb and at his birth, and that either an unbaptized infant that dies without any sin other than original sin is not damned or else it is damned without sin. But we do not accept any of these claims. Therefore, every sin is a case of injustice, and original sin is sin without qualification. Hence, it follows that original sin is a case of injustice. Furthermore, if God damns a human being only on account of injustice, and he damns someone on account of original sin, it follows that original sin is nothing other than injustice. And if this is so, and injustice is nothing other than the absence of the justice that is owed—for it is evident that there is injustice only in a nature that ought to have justice but lacks it—original sin is clearly included in that definition of injustice.

Now given that justice is rectitude of will preserved for its own sake, and that such rectitude cannot exist except in a rational nature, it follows that only a rational nature owes justice, just as only a rational nature is capable of having justice. So since injustice can exist only where justice ought to be, original sin, which is a case of injustice, exists only in a rational nature. Now the only rational natures are God, angels, and the human soul, in virtue of which a human being is called rational and without which one is not a human being. Therefore, since original sin does not exist in God or angels, it exists only in the rational soul of the human being.

One must also realize that justice can exist only in the will, given that justice is rectitude of will preserved for its own sake. Therefore, injustice too can exist only in the will. After all, the absence of justice is called 'injustice' only where justice ought to be. And so, apart from justice and injustice themselves, nothing is called

---

5. Anselm actually uses the example of a person in a painting (*pictus homo*), but that example does not work unambiguously in English if one preserves the Latin construction, so I have substituted an example that does the same work but allows for more grammatical flexibility.

'just' or 'unjust' except a will and whatever else is so called on account of a just or unjust will. We call a human being, an angel, a soul, or an action just or unjust on the basis of the will.

Chapter 4

That nothing is just or unjust in itself except for justice and injustice; and that nothing is punished other than the will

For nothing—no substance, no action, nor anything else—considered in itself is just except for justice, or unjust or a sin except for injustice: not even the will itself in which justice or injustice exists. For the power of the soul by which the soul wills something, which can be called the "instrument" for willing (as sight is the instrument for seeing), which we name "the will," is one thing; the justice by which the will is called "just" when it has it, and "unjust" when it lacks it, is another thing. The affections and exercises of this instrument are also called "wills," but that is too involved a matter to pursue here.[6]

Not even the appetites that the Apostle calls "the flesh," which "lusts against the spirit,"[7] and "the law of sin,"[8] which is "in the members, opposing the law of the mind,"[9] are just or unjust considered in themselves. For they do not make a person who experiences them just or unjust; they make someone unjust only when he consents to them by his will when he should not. For that same Apostle says that there is "no condemnation for those who are in Christ Jesus, who walk not according to the flesh,"[10] that is, who do not consent to the flesh with their wills. After all, if they made someone unjust who merely experienced them without consenting to them, condemnation would follow. Hence, merely experiencing them is not a sin; consenting to them is a sin. And in fact, if they were unjust in themselves, then whenever consent is given to them, they would make someone or something unjust. Yet when brute animals consent to them, the animals are not called unjust. Furthermore, if these appetites were sins, they would be taken away in baptism, when every sin is washed away; but it is quite clear that this does not happen. So it is not in their being that there is any injustice, but only in a rational will that follows them in an inordinate way. When a will resists them by delighting in the law of God according to the inner person,[11] that will is just. For he calls the

---

6. See *De concordia* 1.11.

7. Galatians 5:17.

8. Romans 7:25.

9. Romans 7:23.

10. Romans 8:1.

11. Cf. Romans 7:22, 25.

justice that the law enjoins both "the law of God," because it is from God, and "the law of the mind," because it is understood through the mind, just as the Old Law is called "the law of God," because it is from God, and "the law of Moses," because it was handed down through Moses.

My claim that no action is called unjust in itself, but only on account of an unjust will, is clear in the case of actions that can sometimes be performed without injustice: for example, killing a human being, as Phineas did,[12] and sexual intercourse, as in marital relations or among brute animals. This is not as easy to understand when it comes to actions that can never be performed without injustice, such as perjury and certain other actions that ought not even to be mentioned. Yet consider both an action by which something comes into being—an action that exists only so long as something is coming into being and passes out of existence once that thing has been brought about—and the product that comes into being and remains in existence. For example, when someone writes what ought not to be written, the action of writing passes out of existence, but it brings into being certain marks that remain in existence. If the action were a sin, then once the action passed out of existence, the sin likewise would pass out of existence and would no longer exist. And if the product were a sin, then as long as the product remained in existence, the sin would never be wiped away. Yet in fact we observe that very often sins are not destroyed when the action is destroyed, and that they are destroyed even though the product is not destroyed. Hence, neither the action that passes out of existence nor the product that remains in existence is ever a sin.

Finally, if the bodily members and senses by means of which voluntary actions are done unjustly are blamed for those actions, they can respond, "God subjected us, and the power that is in us, to the will, so that when the will commands us, we cannot fail to move ourselves and to do what it wills. Indeed, the will moves us as its instruments; it is the will that performs the deeds we appear to do. And we cannot resist the will on our own; the deeds it performs cannot fail to be done. We ought not, and we cannot, fail to obey the master whom God has set over us. When we obey the will, we are obeying God, who gave us this law." What sin, therefore, is committed by the bodily members or the senses or their deeds, which God has made subject to the will in this way, when they preserve the order that God has made for them? So the entirety of whatever they do is to be attributed to the will.

Since this is the case, someone might wonder why the bodily members and the senses are punished for the will's fault. But that is not in fact what happens. Only the will is punished. For only what is contrary to someone's will is a punishment for that person, and only what has a will experiences punishment. Now the bodily members and the senses do not will anything through themselves. So just as the

---

12. Numbers 25:7 ff.

will is operative in the members and the senses, it is tormented or pleased through them. Anyone who resists this claim should realize that what experiences and acts in the senses and the bodily members is nothing other than the soul, in which the will exists; and so it is nothing other than the soul that is tormented or pleased through them. Nevertheless, in our ordinary way of speaking we call the actions done by an unjust will "sins," on the grounds that there is sin in the will by which they are done; and some are given names that signify that they are done unjustly, such as "fornication" and "lie." But what we understand when we consider the action or utterance as such is different from what we understand when we consider whether it was done justly or unjustly.

Finally, all being is from God, from whom nothing unjust comes. Hence, no being is unjust in itself.

Chapter 5

That the evil that is sin or injustice is nothing

Now injustice, like blindness, is absolutely nothing at all. For blindness is nothing other than the absence of sight where sight ought to be; and that absence is no more something in an eye, where sight ought to be, than it is in a log, where sight ought not to be. Nor is injustice some sort of thing that infects and corrupts the soul, as a poison does to the body, or that does something, as it seems to be when a vicious person does evil deeds. When a wild animal breaks its chains and goes on a rampage, or when a helmsman abandons the rudder and leaves his ship at the mercy of winds and waves, so that it wanders aimlessly and drifts into danger, we say that the absence of the chains or of the rudder did this—not meaning that their absence is something or that it did anything, but rather that if they had been present, they would have kept the wild animal from going on a rampage and the ship from running into disaster. In the same way, when a wicked human being goes on a rampage and is driven into those dangers of the soul that are evil deeds, we cry out that injustice does these things. But this does not mean that injustice is a being or that it does anything. It means rather that when justice is absent, the will, to which all voluntary movements of the whole human being are subject, is inconstant, unrestrained, and ungoverned; driven by various appetites, it throws itself and everything subject to it into all manner of evil—and that if justice were present, it would keep all this from happening.

From these considerations it is easy to recognize that injustice has no being, even though ordinary usage calls the affections and acts of an unjust will, which are something considered in themselves, "injustice." By this very same reasoning we understand that evil is nothing. For just as injustice is not anything other than the absence of justice that there ought to be, so too evil is not anything other than the absence of goodness that there ought to be. Now no being, however evil we might say it is, is nothing; and for a thing to be evil is not for it to be something. For *any* being to be evil is nothing other than for it to lack some good that it ought to have; and for a being to lack a good that ought to be present is not for it to be anything. Hence, for any being, for it to be evil is not for it to be anything.

I have made these brief remarks concerning the evil that is injustice, an evil that is always unquestionably nothing. There is also the evil that is disadvantage, on the basis of which disadvantages are called evils. Disadvantage is sometimes nothing, as in the case of blindness and deafness, but sometimes it seems to be something, as in the case of pain and sorrow.[13] In any event, I think I have shown adequately in *On the Fall of the Devil*[14] that justice is rectitude of will preserved for its own sake, that injustice is nothing other than the absence of justice that ought to be present and that injustice has no being, that all being is from God, and that nothing is from God but what is good. But I dealt more fully with justice in *On Truth*.[15]

Chapter 6

That nonetheless, when God punishes on account of sin, he does not punish on account of nothing

Certain people, when they hear that sin is nothing, are accustomed to say, "If sin is nothing, why does God punish human beings on account of sin, since no one ought to be punished on account of nothing?" This is a trivial question, but since they do not understand what they are asking, I should offer them a brief reply.

Even though the absence of justice is equally nothing both where justice ought to be and where it ought not to be, it is still right for God to punish sinners, not on account of nothing but on account of something. For, as I said in the aforementioned book,[16] God requires of them, against their wills, the honor that is due to himself, which they refused to offer him spontaneously; and he deals with them separately from the just, according to a fitting order, so that there will be nothing out of order in his kingdom. But he does not punish creatures in which justice ought not to be on account of their lacking justice, that is, on account of nothing, because he does not require justice of them, and the fitting order of the whole universe does not demand it. And so when God punishes on account of sin, which is the absence of the justice that is owed—an absence that is nothing—it is not the case that he is punishing on account of nothing at all; and it is true that God does

---

13. See *On the Fall of the Devil*, Chapter 26.
14. Chapters 9–11, 15, 16, 19, and 26.
15. Chapters 12 and following.
16. See *Cur Deus Homo*, Book 1, Chapters 12 and 14.

not punish on account of nothing unless there is something on account of which he ought to punish.

Chapter 7

In what way the seed of a human being is said to be unclean and to be conceived in sins, even though there is no sin in it

I think by now it has become quite evident from what I have said that sin and injustice are nothing, that they exist only in a rational will, and that no being is properly called "unjust" other than a will. And so it appears to follow that either an infant has a rational soul (without which it cannot have a rational will) from the very moment of conception, or else original sin is not present in it as soon as it is conceived. Now no one thinks it has a rational soul from the very moment of conception. For it would follow that every time a human seed[17] perishes, even from the very moment of its reception, before it attains human form, the human soul in it is damned because it is not reconciled through Christ, which is completely absurd. So we must emphatically reject this horn of the dilemma.

Yet if an infant does not have sin from the very moment of conception, why does Job say to God, "Who can make clean one who was conceived from unclean seed? Who but you, who alone have being?"[18] And how is there truth in what David says: "In iniquities was I conceived, and in sins my mother conceived me"?[19] I will therefore investigate, if I can, in what sense infants are said to be conceived from unclean seed, in iniquities, and in sins, even though sin does not exist in infants from the very moment of their conception.

Certainly Scripture often asserts that something is the case when it is not, on the grounds that it is certain that such a thing will be the case. It is in this sense that God says to Adam regarding the forbidden tree, "On the very day you eat from it, you will die":[20] not that on that day he underwent bodily death, but that on that day he received the necessity of dying some day. And Paul speaks in a similar way about the necessity of dying some day: "But if Christ is in you, the body

---

17. The Latin for 'seed' is *semen*, but Anselm clearly does not have in mind what we call 'semen,' since he will talk about the *semen* that Christ received from his mother. Rather, by *semen* he means whatever it is that grows in a mother's womb and is eventually born. Keep in mind that Anselm does not know enough about embryology to give any precise characterization of the *semen*, which is why translating *semen* as 'fetus' (as is sometimes done) or 'embryo' seems wrong.

18. Job 14:4.

19. Psalm 51:5 (50:7).

20. Genesis 2:17.

is dead on account of sin, but the spirit is alive on account of justification."[21] After all, the bodies of those to whom he was writing were not already dead, but they were going to die on account of sin, since "through one human being sin entered into this world, and through sin, death."[22] Thus, when Adam sinned, we all sinned in him: not because we, who did not even exist yet, sinned, but because we were going to come from him in the future, and at that time the necessity came about that when we did exist, we would sin, since "by the disobedience of one, many were made sinners."[23]

We can understand in a similar way the claim that a human being is conceived from unclean seed, in iniquities, and in sins: not that there is the uncleanness of sin, or sin or iniquity, in the seed, but because from the seed and from the moment of conception from which a human being begins to exist, he receives the necessity that once he has a rational soul, he will have the uncleanness of sin, which is nothing other than sin and iniquity. For even if a child is conceived as a result of vicious concupiscence, there is no more fault in the seed than there would be fault in spit or blood simply because someone spat or bled as a result of an evil will. It is not, after all, the spit or the blood that is blamed, but the evil will. So it is clear how sin does not exist in infants from the moment of their conception and yet, at the same time, how the texts I quoted from Scripture are true. There is no sin in infants because they do not have a will, without which sin is not present; and yet sin is said to be present, because they carry in their seed the necessity of sinning once they are human beings.

Chapter 8

That there was neither sin nor the necessity of future sin in the seed received from the Virgin

If, as I believe, these things are true, there is no sin in that which is received into the offspring from the parent, since it has no will. And so it is clear that there could not be any stain of sin in that which the Son of God assumed into his person from the Virgin. I have said, however, that the seed is transmitted from the parents with a necessity of future sin, once it is animated by a rational soul. This is indeed the case for only one reason, namely, that (as I have said) human nature is born in infants with a debt of making recompense for the sin of Adam and, as I have

---

21. Romans 8:10.
22. Romans 5:12.
23. Romans 5:19.

proposed,[24] the sin of their immediate parents. Human nature is in no way capable of making such recompense; and so long as it fails to make this recompense, it is sinning. Left to itself, it does not have the power on its own to possess the justice that it abandoned. Indeed, a soul that is weighed down by a corrupted body[25] cannot even understand justice, and what does not understand justice cannot preserve or possess justice. Now if it can be shown that the seed received from the Virgin is free from these necessities, it will be clear that it did not contract any necessity of sin.

It can be easily demonstrated that that seed does not suffer from the necessity according to which human nature on its own cannot recover justice by its own power, and by which the body that is corrupted weighs down the soul, so that in its fully developed state it requires the help of grace to preserve the justice it has received, and in infancy it cannot even understand justice. We can show this on the basis of the personal unity of the assuming nature and the assumed nature, provided that we first exempt that seed from the necessity of making recompense for the sins of our first parents as well as those of its more immediate ancestors. Now if it can be understood to be free from the debt of our first parents, there will be no question that no debt accrues to it from its more immediate ancestors either. Therefore, with God's help I will try first to look for a way to make this evident, so that once I have demonstrated it, there will be no need to devote much effort to other matters.

Chapter 9

Why the sin by which the human race is damned is ascribed to Adam more than to Eve, even though he sinned after her and because of her

I think the first question that needs to be asked in this regard is why the sin by which the human race is damned is more often and more particularly ascribed to Adam than to Eve, even though she sinned first, and Adam sinned after her and because of her. For the Apostle says, "Death reigned from Adam to Moses, even over those who did not sin in the likeness of the transgression of Adam."[26] And many other passages seem to incriminate Adam rather than Eve.

This is done, I think, because the two of them are understood together in the name of the chief member of the couple, in the way that a whole is often signified by the part; or because Adam, together with his rib, could still be called 'Adam,'

---

24. proposed, but not affirmed: Anselm will in fact argue in Chapter 24 that the sins of one's immediate parents are not included in original sin.

25. Wisdom 9:15.

26. Romans 5:14.

even though his rib was fashioned into a woman—for we read that God "made them male and female and blessed them, and he called their name 'Adam' on the day in which they were created";[27] or else because if only Eve had sinned and not Adam, it would not have been necessary for the whole human race to perish but only for Eve. For God could have made another woman from Adam, in whom he had created the seed of all human beings; and by that other woman made from Adam, God's purpose would have been fulfilled. For these same reasons, I will signify them both by the name 'Adam,' except when it is necessary to distinguish the two of them.

Chapter 10

Why those who were not Adam's accomplices are burdened by his sin

It is through creation that all the offspring of Adam are human beings, through propagation that they are Adam, and through the individuation by which they are distinguished from others that they are persons. For it is not *from* Adam, but *through* Adam, that they possess their being human. Just as Adam did not make himself a human being, he also did not make the reproductive nature that he possessed; rather God, who created Adam a human being, made this nature in him so that human beings would be propagated from him. Now there is no doubt about the basis on which all his offspring incur the debt about which we are speaking. It is not because they are human beings or because they are persons. After all, if it is because they are human beings or persons that they are all liable for this debt, then Adam would necessarily have been constrained by this debt before he sinned, since he too was a human being and a person—and that is altogether ridiculous. The only remaining possibility, then, is that all his offspring are debtors for no other reason than that they are Adam: not, however, because they are Adam without qualification, but because they are Adam the sinner. Otherwise it would follow that even if Adam had never sinned, those who were propagated from him would nevertheless have been born owing this debt—an impious conclusion.

It is appropriate to repeat here what I said earlier[28] about why they are all burdened by the sin or debt of Adam because they are propagated from him, even though they were not accomplices in his sin. When God made Adam, he made a reproductive nature in him, and God placed this nature under his control so that he would use it in accordance with his own will, so long as he should will to be subject to God. For Adam would not use this nature in accordance with bestial and irrational passion, but in accordance with a human and rational will. After

---

27. Genesis 5:2.
28. See Chapter 2.

all, it is proper to beasts to will nothing in conjunction with reason, whereas it is proper to human beings to will nothing apart from reason. They are always under the obligation to do this, since Adam received this power and was able to preserve it always. God also gave him this gift of grace: so long as he did not sin, those whom he generated by the workings of nature and will would be just, as soon as they came to possess a rational soul—in the same way that God, apart from the workings of natural propagation or any created will, had created Adam both rational and just all at once.

In fact, the same argument that shows that rational nature was created just (an argument I laid out in the aforementioned work)[29] also proves that if there had been no preceding sin, those who were propagated from human nature necessarily would have been just as soon as they were rational. For the one who created the first human being without generation from parents also creates those who come into being from him through the created reproductive nature. Therefore, if there had been no preceding sin, every human being, just like Adam, would be both just and rational. But since Adam refused to be subject to God's will, that reproductive nature—though it remained intact—was not subject to his will, as it would have been if he had not sinned. He also lost the grace that he had the power to retain for all those who would be propagated from him, and all who are propagated by the workings of the nature that he had received are bound by his debt. Therefore, because human nature, which existed wholly in Adam in such a way that there was nothing of it outside him, dishonored God by sinning without any necessity, and could not by itself make recompense for its sin, it lost the grace that it had received and could have retained always for those who would be propagated from it; and every time it is propagated by the reproductive nature that it was given, it contracts sin and, with it, the punishment for sin.

Chapter 11

That propagation from the Virgin is not subject to the law and merits of natural propagation; and that there are three courses of events

We must now carefully investigate whether this inheritance (so to speak) of sin and of the penalty of sin is justly transmitted to the human being who was propagated from Adam through the Virgin. It is of course clear that Adam received a nature for propagating only through both a man and a woman together. Human nature does not have the power—and we recognize that it is impossible—for a man alone or a woman alone to generate a human being solely by the workings of his or her own nature and will. For just as the dust of the earth had not received a nature

---

29. See *Cur Deus Homo*, Book 2, Chapter 1.

or will that could act so as to bring about the first man from it, even though God could make a man from it, so too, it was not the nature or will of a human being that acted so as to make a woman from a man's rib or a man from a woman alone. Rather, God by his own power and will made one man from the dust and another man from a woman alone, and a woman from a man alone. For although nothing comes about unless God's will either brings it about or permits it, some things are brought about by God's will and power alone, others by a created nature, and others by a creature's will. But just as a created nature can bring about nothing by itself except what it has received from God's will, so too a creature's will can do nothing at all by itself except what the creature's nature supports or allows. It was God's will alone that made the natures of things in the beginning, giving to some natures a will suited to them, so that natures and wills would fulfill their functions in the course of events in accordance with the order that God laid down for them. And God's will continues to do many things by using those natures and wills to accomplish what they would never do according to their characteristic role and purpose.

It is the work of God's will alone when the sea offers a dry path through itself to God's people, when the dead arise, when water is suddenly turned to wine, when human hearts are taught by the Holy Spirit things that they do not know either through themselves or through another creature, when unwholesome wills are turned by the governance of grace alone from their own impulses to what is beneficial, and when many other things come about that neither a creature nor its will would do in its ordinary course of activity.

Nature moves light things upward and heavy things downward. Nature makes the earth produce countless plants and trees and makes them bear fruit, sometimes when a will has previously cultivated and sown seed, but sometimes without any prior activity on the part of a will. And nature does many other things that we know more easily from what we see than from what we are taught.

Things like the following are attributed to will: taking a trip, building, writing, speaking, and similar things that only a will does.

Therefore, since, if we examine them carefully, all things that come about come about either by God's will alone or by nature in accordance with the power granted it by God or by a creature's will, and since those things that neither a created nature nor a creature's will but God alone brings about are always miraculous, it is evident that there are three courses of events: miraculous, natural, and voluntary. The miraculous is in no way subservient to the others or to their law; rather, it freely controls them. Nor does it do them any injury when it appears to supersede them, since they have nothing but what they have received from it, and whatever it has given them is subordinate to it. Therefore, since the propagation of a man from the Virgin alone is not natural or voluntary but miraculous (just like the propagation that produced a woman from a man alone and the creation of a man from the dust), it is clear that it is in no way subject to the laws and merits of the propagation that both nature and will accomplish, though separately (for in such a case what will does is distinct from what nature does). Nevertheless, Adam, who is from something that was not a human being, and Jesus, who is from a woman alone, and Eve, who is from a man alone, are all just as much genuine human beings as is any man or woman who is from both a man and a woman. Now every human being is either Adam or from Adam, but Eve is from Adam alone, and all others are from Adam and Eve. For since Mary, from whom alone Jesus came, is from Adam and Eve, Jesus cannot but be from both Adam and Eve. And it was fitting that in this way the one who was to redeem the human race should be, and be born from, the father and mother of all.

Chapter 12

That it would not be right for Adam's evils to be transmitted to that man

And the following considerations likewise make it easy to understand how the son of the Virgin was not subject to the sin or debt of Adam. Adam was created just, free from sin and its much-discussed debt and from punishment for sin, happy, and capable of always preserving the justice that he had received and thereby also preserving the freedom and happiness of which I have spoken. Therefore, since he did not preserve for himself these good things, even though he could have preserved them forever without any difficulty, he robbed himself of them and subjected himself to their opposites. And so he was made a slave to sin or injustice, and to a debt that he could not repay, and to that unhappiness that consists in his powerlessness to recover the good things that he had lost. It was only by failing to preserve those good things, even though he had the power to preserve them for himself, that he was able to rob himself of the good things he had possessed and attract evils that he had not possessed; accordingly, he was not able to rob others of those good things or inflict evil things upon them unless he had the power to preserve those things for them but failed to do so. Now it was only for those whose propagation had been made subject to his will that he was able to preserve these good things; therefore, he was not able to transmit the aforementioned evils to any person whose generation was not, and could not be, in any way accomplished either by the reproductive nature bestowed on him or by his will—even if that person were propagated from him. Therefore, there was no basis, and it would not have been right, for Adam's evils to be transmitted to the man who was conceived by the Virgin.

Chapter 13

That even if he were not God, but merely a human being, it would still have been necessary for him to be such as the first human being was created

Furthermore, if by the pure sight of reason we gaze attentively upon God's wise justice, we will understand that it would be altogether absurd for any necessity deriving from someone else's sin or debt or punishment to be transmitted to that human being through a seed that was produced and brought into being not by any created nature, or by any creature's will, or by any power bestowed on a nature, but solely by God's own will, which set apart from the Virgin this seed so that by a new power a human being would be begotten who would be free from sin. This would be true even if that seed came to be a mere human being and were not assumed into a divine person. After all, the rational mind clearly recognizes that God ought not to have made this man, whom he propagated solely by his own will and power, subject to any evil, for the same reason that he ought to have made Adam just, and not burdened by any debt or disadvantage: namely, that it would be altogether unfitting for God's wise and all-powerful goodness to make a rational nature subject to any evil by his own will alone, out of matter in which there was no sin. Anyone who does not understand this does not recognize what is unfitting for God. Therefore, even if God had made a mere human being in this way I have described, it would have been necessary for him to be endowed with no less justice and happiness than Adam was when he was first made.

Chapter 14

That the passages saying human beings are conceived from unclean seed and in iniquities do not contradict the argument I have offered, even if they do apply properly to certain cases

Now suppose someone's mind does not grasp what I have said concerning the seed of a human being, namely, that there is no sin in it before there is a rational soul, but that it is said to be unclean with sin and iniquity on account of its future uncleanness, once it is a human being. Suppose such a person thinks that the human seed is unclean from its very conception on the grounds that (to quote the passages I myself raised as objections) Scripture says, "Who can make clean what was conceived from unclean seed?" and "In iniquities was I conceived, and in sins did my mother conceive me." I will not devote much effort here to make him understand what he is incapable of understanding, for I have no need to do so. But I do ask that he pay attention to the brief reply I am about to make.

Those who wrote these words meant them to be understood either as applying to every human seed or as applying only to that which is produced in conjunction with the experience of the sensuality that would have belonged exclusively to brute animals had human beings not sinned. If they meant them to apply to every human seed, it follows that such great men asserted that the seed received from the Virgin alone was unclean—and it is impious to believe such a thing. So they did not write these things about that seed. Rather, if they were speaking of any human seed according to the second sense, they meant their words to apply only to seed that is conceived in sensuality. But this in no way contradicts our argument, which claims that the seed received from the Virgin is clean, even though it is from the sinful mass.

Chapter 15

How the sinful mass is not wholly sinful

Just as blindness is not in every part of a human being, even though the human being is called blind, but is only in the eye, where sight ought to be—for blindness is not in a hand or foot—and deafness is only in the ear, even though the human being is called deaf, so too, even though the mass of the human race is called sinful, there is not sin in every part of it, but only (as I have said)[30] in the will; and as we know, no seed has a will at the moment of its conception. Therefore, if the things I have said are examined carefully, we can now freely conclude—with no sound or plausible argument to contradict us—that no reasoning, no truth, no understanding allows that any share of the sin of the sinful mass either could have or should have affected the human being who was conceived by the Virgin alone, even though he was taken out of that sinful mass; and this would have been the case even if he were not God.

Chapter 16

Why John, and others who likewise were miraculously conceived, are not of themselves free from sin

Someone might bring up the cases of John the Baptist and others who were propagated from those who were sterile and in those whose reproductive nature was dead because of old age, objecting that by a similar argument they too should have been born without sin and the punishment for sin, since they were miraculously

---

30. See Chapter 3.

conceived. But it must be understood that such cases are far removed from the argument that shows that the virginal conception was free from all necessity of sin. For it is one thing for God to do something unheard-of, unexpected, and unknown to nature, and quite another for him to heal a nature that has been weakened by age or infirmity and call it back to its proper work. After all, if Adam had not sinned, he would not have grown weak from age, or indeed from any cause; thus, no fall would have impeded the working of the reproductive nature created in him, the exercise of which was subjected to his power (as has been said)[31]. So what we find with John and similar cases is not something new given to Adam's nature, as was granted in the son of the Virgin, but the restoration of what had been enfeebled by its own causes. Therefore, since these people were generated by means of the natural propagation granted to Adam, they neither can nor should at all be assimilated to the one whose miraculous conception we are now discussing, in such a way that it could be shown that they are free from the bondage of original sin.

Chapter 17

Why God was incarnate, given that he could have made from Adam a sufficient number of non-divine human beings without sin

Perhaps someone will say, "If a mere human being who was not God could have been made from Adam without any contagion of sin, as you claim, why was it necessary for God to be incarnate? God could have redeemed sinners through one such sinless man, or else, by a similar miracle, he could have created as many as were necessary to complete the heavenly city."

I shall respond to this briefly. God became a human being because a human being who was not God would not have been sufficient to redeem others, as I showed in the work I have mentioned so often.[32] And he did not create as many human beings as were necessary because if no one who came about through natural propagation were saved, the nature that God had created in Adam would have been in vain; it would have seemed as if God were correcting a mistake that he had made. And it is not fitting for the highest wisdom to do this for any nature.

A little earlier[33] I set out to investigate how we can understand that the seed received from the Virgin, in which (as has been shown) there was no sin, was free from all the necessities in which all other human beings are conceived. I was confident that if I could first establish by reason that it was exempt from the necessity of

---

31. See Chapter 11.

32. See *Cur Deus Homo*, Book 2, Chapter 6.

33. See Chapter 8.

the sin and debt of Adam and of its more immediate ancestors, I would be able to show that it was free from all the other necessities—the inability to recover by one's own effort the justice that human nature abandoned, and the soul's being weighed down by the body that is corrupted, especially in infants—on the grounds that this human being was God. And so I began by asking how we could understand this to be true regarding the necessity of Adam's sin and debt, so that afterwards I might more easily discover what I was looking for in those other cases. And by the abundant grace of him whose sinless conception is our theme, not only have we come to know that he was free from all sin and debt and the necessities I have described, but in addition we have proved by intelligible reasoning that the human being conceived in this way ought to have been endowed with no less justice or happiness than that with which Adam was created—even if he were not God, but merely a human being. For both these things seemed equally unreasonable: that sin or the punishment for sin should fall on him from any ancestors through such propagation, and that God should spontaneously make a rational nature unjust, or should make a rational nature unhappy who did not deserve it on account of injustice.

Chapter 18

It was not necessary that God be conceived from a just virgin, as if he could not have been conceived from a sinful woman; but it was fitting that he should be conceived in this way

Therefore, although the Son of God was most truly conceived from a most pure virgin, this did not happen by necessity, as if a just offspring could not reasonably be generated from a sinful parent through this sort of propagation. Rather, this happened because it was fitting for the conception of this human being to come about from a most pure mother. Indeed it was fitting that the Virgin should be radiant with a purity than which no greater can be thought, except for that of God himself. For to her God the Father entrusted the gift of his only Son, whom he loved as himself, as one begotten from his own heart and equal to himself, so that there should be by nature one and the same Son of both God the Father and the Virgin; and the Son himself chose to make her substantially his mother; and the Holy Spirit willed and worked so that the one from whom he himself proceeded would be conceived and born from her. Now in the book in which I offered my other explanation for what is under discussion here, I also explained how the Virgin herself was purified by faith before that conception.[34]

---

34. See *Cur Deus Homo*, Book 2, Chapter 16.

Chapter 19

How the explanation offered here both harmonizes with and differs from the one I offered elsewhere

To my intellect it seems that each of these two explanations is, by itself, a sufficient answer to the question at hand; but the two of them taken together abundantly satisfy a mind that is seeking both force in reasoning and suitability in action. And although both explanations are aiming at the same conclusion, they do differ in this respect: the one I have offered here shows, with no argument to contradict it, that God ought to have produced a just offspring, and nothing other than a just offspring, through such propagation even from the substance of a sinful virgin, since sin exists nowhere in human nature except in the will; by contrast, my previous argument proves that even if there were sin in the entire being of the Virgin, she could nonetheless have been purified through faith for the sake of this pure conception. Moreover, my argument here explicitly exempts this human being from every necessity of death or of any corruption or effort, whereas the other argument seems to leave that issue open, although it is resolved by a sufficient argument if one looks into the matter carefully. Hence, it is evident on the basis of either argument that our Lord and Redeemer endured all his sufferings solely by his most gracious will.

Chapter 20

That he who was born of the Virgin had original justice in place of original sin

It seems to me that I have adequately shown what I set out to show: that there was no rational basis on which original sin could be transmitted from his ancestors to the human being who was conceived by the Virgin, but rather that he should have been made just and happy, as reason demands. Therefore, since from his very origin (in the sense I have explained)[35] from a just Father according to his divine nature and from a just mother according to his human nature he was born just, it is quite appropriate to say that he had original justice in place of the original injustice that all other children of Adam have from their origin.

---

35. See Chapter 1 for different senses of 'origin.'

Chapter 21

Why he could not possess personal injustice

But it would be superfluous to argue the point that personal injustice did not touch him, since the human nature in him was never without the divine, and his soul was never weighed down against his will or in any way hindered by the corruptible body. Because his soul—or rather the whole human being—together with the Word of God, who is God, always existed as one person, he was never without the perfect justice, wisdom, and power that, in terms of his person, he always possessed from himself as God, although in terms of his natures, the human nature received from the divine nature whatever it possessed.

I do not deny that there may be some other reason, besides the one I have given here and the one I offered elsewhere,[36] why God assumed a sinless human being from the sinful mass, as something unleavened from what is leavened. If someone shows it to me, I will accept it gladly; and I will not hold on to my own reasons if they can be shown to contradict the truth—though I do not think they can.

Chapter 22

On the magnitude of original sin

Moreover, original sin can be neither greater nor less than I have said, since once an infant becomes rational, human nature in him does not have the justice that it received in Adam and that it ought always to have; and as I explained earlier,[37] the fact that it lacks the power to have justice does not excuse it for not having justice. Yet I do not think that original sin is in every respect as grave as I made it out to be earlier. For, since my aim was to show that original sin did not belong to the human being who was conceived by the Virgin, I stipulated that original sin was such that no one could add to it, so that (as I remarked) I would not appear to be making light of it for the sake of my inquiry. But now I will say explicitly what I think about this topic.

I do not think Adam's sin passes to infants in such a way that they ought to be punished for it in just the same way as if they themselves as individuals had personally committed it, like Adam himself. But on account of that sin it has come to pass that no infant can be born without sin, from which damnation follows. For when the Apostle says that "death reigned from Adam to Moses, even over those

---

36. See *Cur Deus Homo*, particularly Book 2, Chapter 16.
37. In Chapter 2.

who did not sin in the likeness of Adam's transgression,"[38] he seems to signify expressly that neither Adam's transgression itself nor anything as great is imputed to them personally, even though in his writings he describes all the children of Adam, except for the Virgin's son, as "sinners"[39] and "children of wrath."[40] For when he says, "even over those who did not sin in the likeness of Adam's transgression," this can be understood as if he said, "even over those who did not sin as much as Adam sinned by transgressing." And when he says, "the law came in so that sin might be abundant,"[41] we should understand either that before the law the sin of "those who did not sin in the likeness of Adam's transgression" was less than the sin of Adam, or else, if it was not less than Adam's, that after the law sin was abundant in them over and above the sin of Adam—though when I consider this latter alternative, I cannot make sense of it. In *Cur Deus Homo* I laid out my views on the gravity of this sin and its recompense, as you have already read. Nevertheless, it is true that no one is restored to the state for which human beings were created and a reproductive nature was given to them, and no one is rescued from the evils into which human nature has fallen, except through recompense for that sin by which human nature threw itself into those evils.

Someone might say, "If these individuals do not have Adam's sin, how can you claim that none of them is saved except through recompense for Adam's sin? How does a just God demand from them recompense for a sin that is not theirs?" But in fact God does not demand from any sinner more than he owes; yet since no sinner can pay back as much as he owes, Christ alone, on behalf of all who are saved, pays back more than they owe, as I have already explained in that oft-cited work.

Still, we need to examine yet another explanation for the fact that sin is less in infants than it was in Adam, even though it passes to all of them from him. For "through one human being"—that is, through Adam—"sin entered into this world, and through sin, death."[42]

Chapter 23

Why and how it passes to infants

Yet one will not understand why it is less in them unless one understands why and how it is present in them in the first place. Although I just explained this above, to the extent that it was needed in order to answer my question, it will not be

---

38. Romans 5:14.
39. Romans 5:8.
40. Ephesians 2:3.
41. Romans 5:20.
42. Romans 5:12.

pointless to repeat it here briefly. Certainly it cannot be denied that infants were in Adam when he sinned. But they were in him causally, or materially, as in his seed; they are in themselves personally. For in him they were the seed itself, whereas in themselves each of them is individually a distinct person. In him they were not distinct from him, but in themselves they are distinct from him. In him they were Adam; in themselves they are themselves. Therefore, they were in him, but they were not themselves, since they did not yet exist.

Perhaps someone will say, "When you say that other human beings 'were' in Adam, this 'being' is like nothing. It's inconsequential. It should not even be called 'being.'" Well, then, let him say that the being by which Christ was in Abraham according to his seed, and in David, and in the other fathers, was nothing or empty or false. Let him say this of the being by which all things that are from seed were in their seeds. Let him say that God made nothing when he first made in their seeds all the things that are reproduced from seed. If truly this did not exist, the things we see existing would not exist; let him then say that this is nothing, that it is something empty. For if it is not true that the things nature reproduces from seeds first exist in those seeds, those things would not in any way be from those seeds. Now it is the height of foolishness to say these things, and so the being by which all other human beings were in Adam was not false or empty but true and solid; and when God made them to be in Adam, what he made was not something inconsequential. Nonetheless, as I have said, in Adam they were not distinct from Adam, and therefore they existed in quite a different way from how they exist in themselves.

Now although it is incontestable that they all existed in Adam, only the Virgin's son was in Adam in a very different way from the others. All the others were in Adam in such a way that they would be from him by means of the reproductive nature that had been subjected to his power and will, whereas Christ alone was not in Adam in such a way that he would come to be from Adam by means of his nature or will. For in the case of all the others, it had been given to Adam at the time of his sin to be both the one from whom they were to come and the one from whom they would exist; but in the case of Christ it had been given to Adam to be the one from whom he was to come but not to be the one from whom he would exist—for it was not in Adam's power that Christ should be propagated from him. Nor was it in Adam's power that he should come to exist from some other being, or from nothing. It was not, therefore, up to Adam that Christ should exist in any way, since it was not in the power of Adam's nature or of his will that Christ should exist in any way. Nonetheless, there was in Adam the nature from which Christ would be propagated—though by God's power, not Adam's. For although will had sown the seed and nature had given it growth in our ancestors up to the Virgin Mother, so that the Virgin herself was brought into being from Adam by an order partly natural and partly voluntary, just as everyone else was, in her no creaturely will sowed her offspring, and no nature gave it growth. Rather, "the

Holy Spirit" and "the power of the Most High"[43] miraculously propagated a man from a virgin woman. Therefore, in the case of all others, it was in Adam—that is, in his power—that they should exist from him; but in the case of Christ, it was not in Adam that he should exist in any way, just as it was not in the dust from which the first man was made that he should exist miraculously from the dust, and just as it was not in the man that Eve should exist from him in the way in which she was made. But neither was it in any of those from Adam to Mary in whom he existed that he should exist. And yet he did exist in them, because that from which he was going to be assumed existed in them—in the same way that Adam existed in the dust from which the first human being was made, and Eve existed in the man from whom she was made: not by any creature's will or power, but by divine power alone. Yet his coming into being sprang from a greater and more miraculous grace, since they were mere human beings, but he was the God-man. And so he was in Adam at the time of Adam's sin in a very different way from those who were procreated according to the voluntary and natural order. Therefore, in a certain way Adam makes those who are procreated when human will sows the seed and nature gives them growth, through the power that will and nature have received; but it is God alone who made this man, even though he is from Adam, because he did not come to be through Adam but through himself, as though from himself.

What, therefore, would be more fitting for displaying the great goodness of God and the fullness of the grace that he granted to Adam, than that those whose being was in Adam's power, so that through him they would be what he was naturally, should likewise be under the sway of his free choice, so that he would propagate them to be such as he was himself in his justice and happiness? Therefore, this was granted to him. Yet although he had been placed on such a pinnacle of grace, he spontaneously abandoned the goods that he had received for the purpose of preserving them both for himself and for them; and for that reason his children lost what their father took away from them by not preserving it, although he could have given it to them simply by preserving it himself. This seems to me to be a sufficient reason—provided that we pay heed to pure justice itself, leaving aside our own wills, which so often seriously hinder the mind from understanding rectitude—why the sin and evils of Adam pass to infants. But I shall say a few words about how, in my view, that sin passes to them.

As I have said, there is sin from the nature and sin from the person. That which is from the person can be called 'personal,' whereas that which is from the nature can be called 'natural' but is usually called 'original.' And just as personal sin is transmitted to the nature, so too natural sin is transmitted to the person, in the following way. Adam's nature required him to eat; it was created to require this. But his eating from the forbidden tree came not from his natural will but from

---

43. Luke 1:35.

his personal will—that is, from his own will. Yet what the person did, he did not do without the nature. For the person was what was called 'Adam'; the nature was what was called 'human being.' Therefore, the person made the nature sinful, since when Adam sinned, human being sinned. It was not because he was a human being that he was driven to the presumption of eating the forbidden fruit; rather, he was drawn to it by his own will—a will that the nature did not require, but to which the person gave birth.

What takes place in infants is like this, only in the other direction. Indeed, what caused them to lack the justice they ought to have was not their personal will, as was the case with Adam, but the natural deficiency that the nature itself has received from Adam. For there was nothing of human nature that was outside Adam; in him human nature was stripped of the justice that it had possessed, and it always lacks justice unless it receives help. It is for this reason—because the nature subsists in persons and persons do not exist without the nature—that the nature makes the persons of infants sinful. In this way, a person deprived the nature of the good of justice that it had possessed in Adam, and the nature, having become deficient, makes all the persons whom it procreates from itself to be sinful and unjust in virtue of that same deficiency. In this way the personal sin of Adam is transmitted to all those who are propagated naturally from him, and in them it is original or natural sin.

But clearly there is a great distance between Adam's sin and theirs, since he sinned by his own will, whereas they sin by the natural necessity that Adam's own and personal will earned for them. Yet although no one will doubt that unequal sins are not punished equally, the condemnation for original sin is like that for personal sin in this respect: no one is admitted into the kingdom of God, for which human beings were made, except through the death of Christ, for only the death of Christ pays back what is owed on account of Adam's sin. Nevertheless, not everyone earns equal torment in hell. For after the day of judgment every angel and every human being will be either in the kingdom of God or in hell. So in this way it is true both that the sin of infants is less than Adam's sin, and yet that no one is saved apart from that universal recompense by which sin both great and small is forgiven. Now why there is no recompense apart from that death, and how through that death there is salvation for human beings, I have investigated and explained in the aforementioned book, so far as God granted it to me.

Chapter 24

That the sins of ancestors after Adam are not counted in the original sin of their descendants

Now I do not hold that the sins of one's more immediate ancestors belong to original sin. Certainly if Adam had not had the power to pass along his own justice to those whom he was going to generate, there is no way he could have transmitted his own injustice to them. So, given that no one after Adam has had the power to preserve his own justice for his children, I see no reason why the sins of more immediate ancestors should be imputed to the souls of their descendants. Furthermore, no one doubts that infants do not preserve rectitude of will for the sake of rectitude itself. In this respect, therefore, they are all equally unjust, since they have none of the justice that every human being ought to have. This absence of justice passes to all of them from Adam, in whom human nature deprived itself of this justice. For even if in Adam some justice remained in human nature, so that it was able to preserve an upright will in some matters, it was at any rate deprived of the gift by which it could conserve justice for itself for the benefit of its posterity; thus it cannot reproduce itself in any of them with any justice at all. Indeed, human nature could not take away from itself in infants anything more than all justice and the happiness that is not given to anyone who lacks any of the justice that is owed.

And it does not seem possible that the injustice of one's more immediate ancestors can increase this absence of justice, than which no greater deprivation can pass to infants from Adam's sin. For where there is no justice, no justice can be taken away. But where justice cannot be taken away, no injustice can be added. Therefore, unjust parents cannot add any injustice to their infants beyond the absence of justice I have already described. On the other hand, where there is no justice, nothing prevents justice from being added. Therefore, if unjust parents are said to add some injustice to their infants, it seems more probable and more possible that just parents can give some justice to their infants. If that happens, the children of the just possess some justice. But if that is the case, they suffer less severe condemnation than the children of the unjust if they die unbaptized; or if they are saved, they are among the elect because of some antecedent merit of their own. But the Apostle Paul denies this in the passage where he uses the example of Jacob and Esau to prove that no one is saved except by grace that precedes any merits.[44] And so since just parents do not bestow justice on their children before baptism, neither do unjust parents add injustice to their children.

But someone might say, "Unjust parents do not add any injustice to their children, from whom they cannot take away any justice. But they do make more

---

44. Romans 10:9–13.

serious the original injustice that their children possess from Adam. Therefore, the just also make original injustice less severe in their children. Hence, given that the children of the just are less unjust than the children of the unjust, they deserve less condemnation." If someone has the nerve to say this and can show that it is true, let him say it. I am not so daring, since I see the children of both the just and the unjust being chosen for the grace of baptism and being rejected from it. And if someone does say this, he will not be able to prove it. In fact, someone is more just than another just person only if by his will he either pursues or avoids more strongly what he ought to; similarly, someone is more unjust than another unjust person only if he either loves or spurns more strongly what he ought not. Therefore, if it cannot be shown that as soon as infants have souls, one wills more or less strongly what he ought or ought not than does some other, no one can prove that one infant is born more or less just than any other. Therefore, it does not seem that the just by means of their own justice make original injustice less serious in their children; and equally, it does not seem that the unjust by means of their own injustice make original injustice more serious in their children. Therefore, if unjust parents cannot by their own sin increase original sin in their children, either in number or in severity, it seems to me that the sins of parents after Adam are not counted in the original sin of infants.

I do not deny that many great benefits of both body and soul are imparted to children on account of the good deserts of their parents, and that because of the sins of their parents, children and grandchildren are tormented in this life by various trials "unto the third and fourth generation,"[45] and perhaps further, and that they lose goods even in their souls that might have come to them from their parents if they had been just. (It would require too much space to offer examples here.) But I say that original sin is equal in all naturally conceived infants, just as Adam's sin, which is the cause of their being born in original sin, belongs to all of them equally.

Chapter 25

How the parents' sins harm their children's souls

Yet if in fact the parents' sins sometimes harm their children's souls, I think this happens, not because God imputes those sins to the children, or because he leads them into[46] certain misdeeds on account of their parents, but rather because he sometimes leaves the children of the unjust in their sins because of their parents'

---

45. Exodus 20:5.

46. "Lead into" is *inducere*, the same word used in the petition of the Lord's Prayer, "Lead us not into temptation." See Matthew 6:13 and Luke 11:4.

merits, just as he often rescues the children of the just from their sins because of their parents' merits. No one, after all, is free from sin unless God sets him free. For that reason, when God does not set someone free, he is said to "lead him into" sin, and when he does not soften someone, he is said to "harden"[47] him. It does in fact seem rather more reasonable that on account of the parents God should leave a sinful soul, to which he owes nothing but punishment, in its sins so that it should be punished for them, than that he should burden such a soul with someone else's sins and torment him for those. Therefore, there is no contradiction in saying, on the one hand, that original sin is the same in all, that "the son will not bear the iniquity of the father"[48] and "everyone will bear his own burden,"[49] that each will receive "according to his deeds" in the body, "whether good or evil,"[50] and also, on the other hand, that God visits the sins of the parents on the children "unto the third and fourth generation" (even if this happens in the soul) and whatever else we read that seems to indicate that the sins of the parents harm the souls of their children. Indeed, the soul of the child does not die for its father's sin, but for its own; nor does anyone bear "the iniquity of his father," but his own iniquity, when he is left in his own sins; no one bears anyone's burden but his own, and no one receives according to his father's deeds, but according to his own deeds in the body. Yet, since it is because of his parents' sins that he is not set free from his own evils, the evils that he bears are imputed to his parents' sins.

Chapter 26

How, nevertheless, no one bears the sin of his father, but his own sin

Now if someone objects that all who are not saved by faith, which is in Christ, bear the iniquity and burden of Adam—meaning by this to prove that either infants should likewise bear the iniquities of their other ancestors or else they should not bear Adam's—let him pay close attention to the fact that infants do not in fact bear Adam's sin, but their own. Adam's sin was one thing and the sin of infants is another, since they differ in the way I have explained. Adam's sin was the cause; the sin of infants is the effect. Adam lacked the required justice not because anyone else abandoned it but because he abandoned it; infants lack it, not because they themselves left it behind, but because someone else left it behind. So Adam's sin is not the same as the sin of infants. And when the Apostle says, in the passage I

---

47. Exodus 4, 7–11, and 14, *passim*; Deuteronomy 2:30; Joshua 11:20; John 12:40; Romans 9:18. See also *De concordia* 2.2.

48. Ezekiel 18:20.

49. Galatians 6:5.

50. 2 Corinthians 5:10.

quoted above, that "death reigned from Adam to Moses even over those who did not sin in the likeness of the transgression of Adam," he makes it quite clear that the sin of infants is something other than the sin of Adam, just as he indicates that their sin is less than his.

It follows, then, that when an infant is damned on account of original sin, he is damned on account of his own sin and not Adam's. For if he did not have sin of his own, he would not be damned. In this way, therefore, he bears his own iniquity and not Adam's, even though he is said to bear Adam's iniquity on the grounds that the iniquity of Adam's sin was the cause of the infant's. Now this cause of infants' being born in sin was in Adam; it is not in their other ancestors, for in them (as I have explained) human nature does not have the power to reproduce just children. Hence it does not follow that there is sin in infants because of the sin of their other ancestors, as it does follow that there is sin in infants because of Adam's sin.

Chapter 27

What original sin is, and that it is equal in all

I therefore understand original sin to be nothing other than the sin that is in an infant as soon as it has a rational soul, no matter what might have taken place in the body before it was ensouled (some corruption of its members, for example) or what might happen in the future in either the soul or the body. For the reasons given above, I think this original sin is the same in all naturally propagated infants, and that all who die in it alone are equally damned. Any sin that is added to original sin in a human being is personal sin; and just as a person is born sinful because of the nature, so too the nature is made more sinful by a person, since when any person sins, human being sins.

I cannot understand this sin that I call 'original' to be anything else in infants but the deprivation of required justice that I discussed above, which was brought about by Adam's disobedience. As a result of his disobedience, all are children of wrath;[51] for the spontaneous* abandonment of justice that human nature committed in Adam accuses the nature, and the inability to recover justice does not (as I have explained) excuse persons. This deprivation of justice is accompanied by deprivation of happiness, so that just as they are without any justice, so too are they without any happiness. Because of these two deprivations they are banished into exile in this life, and unless they are protected by divine governance, they are constantly exposed to sins and miseries that befall them at every point and attack them from every direction.

---

51. Cf. Ephesians 2:3.

Chapter 28

Against those who do not think infants should be damned

There are some whose minds are unwilling to accept that infants who die unbaptized ought to be damned solely on account of this injustice of which I have spoken, since no human being judges that they deserve to be blamed for some other person's sin, and because infants are not yet just and capable of understanding at that age; and they do not think that God should judge innocent children more strictly than human beings would judge them. What needs to be said to them is that the way God ought to treat infants is different from the way human beings ought to treat them. A human being ought not to demand from a nature what he himself did not give and what is not owed to him; nor does one human being justly accuse another for being born with a fault with which he was born himself, and from which he is cleansed only through someone else. God, by contrast, rightly demands from a nature what he gave that nature, and what is justly owed to him.

But even this judgment by which infants are damned is not, if one thinks it over, very far removed from the judgment of human beings. Suppose a man and his wife who have been promoted to some great dignity and possession, not by their own merit but by grace alone, together commit some serious crime for which there is no excuse, and because of this crime they are justly dispossessed and reduced to servitude. Who would say that the children they have after their condemnation do not deserve to be subjected to servitude as well, but rather should by grace be restored to those good things that their parents justly lost? This is how things stand with our first parents and the children whom they had in that exile from happiness and into misery to which they had been justly condemned on account of their own fault. And so similar judgments should be made about these similar cases, except that the judgment about the latter case should be stricter to the extent that their wrongdoing can be shown to be more indefensible.

Finally, every human being is either saved or damned. Everyone who is saved is admitted into the kingdom of heaven, and everyone who is damned is shut out. Whoever is admitted is made like the angels, in whom there never was and never will be any sin; and that cannot take place as long as there is any stain of sin in him. And so it is impossible for any human being to be saved with any sin, however small. Hence, if what I have called original sin is any sort of sin, it is necessary that every human being born in original sin is damned unless that sin is forgiven.

Chapter 29

In what way their inability to have justice excuses them after baptism

I have said that the inability to have justice does not excuse the injustice of infants. So perhaps someone will ask, "If there is sin—that is, injustice—in an infant before baptism, and it is not excused because of the infant's inability to have justice, as you claim, and if the only sin forgiven in baptism is the sin that was present before baptism, then, given that after baptism the infant is still without justice for as long as it remains an infant, and is not capable of understanding the justice it ought to preserve (assuming that justice is indeed rectitude of will preserved for its own sake), how is the infant not unjust even after it has been baptized? Therefore, if a baptized infant dies in infancy but not immediately after baptism, when it does not yet know how to repent, it departs from this life unjust, even as it would have done before baptism, because it does not have the required justice and its inability to have justice does not excuse it; nor is it admitted to the kingdom of God, into which no unjust person is welcomed. The Catholic Church does not accept this. But if an infant is forgiven in baptism for a sin that will be committed later in infancy, why not also for those sins that it will commit in later life?"

My answer is that in baptism the sins that existed before baptism are completely wiped out. For this reason, the original inability to possess justice is not imputed as sin to those who have already been baptized, as it was before. Therefore, just as before baptism this inability could not excuse the absence of justice because that inability was culpable, so also after baptism that inability completely excuses the absence of justice, since the inability remains but is no longer culpable. This is how it happens that the justice that infants owed before baptism, without anything to excuse them, is not demanded from them as something required once they have been baptized. So as long as it is solely because of that original inability that they do not possess justice, they are not unjust, since there is no absence of required justice in them. For something is not required if it is impossible and not at all culpable. So if they die in this state, they are not damned, because they are not unjust. Instead, through the justice of Christ, who gave himself on their behalf, and through the justice of the faith of their mother the Church, which believes on their behalf, they are saved as though they were just.

I have offered this brief account of original sin so far as my own understanding permits, more by way of exploration than assertion, until God reveals a better account to me in some way. But if anyone has come to a different view, I will reject no one's opinion if it can be proved true.

On the Procession of the Holy Spirit

1　We Latins profess that the Holy Spirit proceeds from the Son; the Greeks deny this, and they do not accept the authority of the Latin teachers whom we follow on this point. Since they, like us, have great reverence for the Gospels, and since in every other respect they believe exactly what we believe concerning the Triune God—for we are firm in our belief in this same doctrine—I hope that by the help of that same Holy Spirit they can be led by reason from what they unequivocally profess to what they do not accept: provided that they would rather yield to unshakeable truth than struggle for empty victory.

There are, to be sure, many who could accomplish this better than I can; but many people have laid this burden upon me, and because of what I owe to the love of truth, and for the sake of their charity and devout will, I dare not refuse their request. I therefore call upon the Holy Spirit himself to be gracious in directing me to this end. And so, having this hope, on account of the lowliness of my knowledge I leave higher things to those who know more than I do, and I shall attempt what they are asking me to do: employing the faith of the Greeks, and the things they unwaveringly believe and profess, to prove by utterly solid arguments what they do not believe.

They of course believe that there is one and only one God, that God is perfect, and that God has no parts but is as a whole whatever he is. They also profess that this God is Father and Son and Holy Spirit, in such a way that if we say "Father" or "Son" or "Spirit" alone, or both "Father and Son" or "Father and Holy Spirit" or "Son and Holy Spirit," or all three together—"Father and Son and Holy Spirit"— it is one and the same whole and perfect God who is referred to, even though the name* 'Father' and the name 'Son' do not signify the same as the name 'God.' For *being God* is not the same as *being the Father* or *being the Son*. Now the name 'Holy Spirit' is taken as a relative* name: 'Holy Spirit' is understood as the spirit *of someone*. For although the Father is holy and a spirit, and the Son is holy and a spirit, the Father is not the spirit *of someone*, and the Son is not the spirit *of someone*, in the way that the Holy Spirit is the spirit *of someone*. For the Holy Spirit is the Spirit *of God* and the Spirit *of the Father* and *of the Son*. Granted, the Greeks deny that the Holy Spirit proceeds from the Son, but they do not deny that he is the Spirit of the Son.

They also believe and profess that God exists from God by being born and that God exists from God by proceeding: for God the Son exists from God the Father by being born, and God the Holy Spirit exists from God the Father by proceeding. And they do not think that the God who is born is a God other than the one from whom he is born or the one who proceeds, although God admits of plurality according to the names signifying that there is one from whom someone is born, and there is one who is born from someone, and there is one who proceeds. In accordance with this plurality the Father and the Son and the Holy Spirit are more than one, and distinct from each other. For when God is said to be Father, what is signified is that he is one from whom someone is born; and when God is named "Son," what is understood is that he is one who is born from someone; and when God is called "Holy Spirit," he is pointed out as one who proceeds from someone (for we do not understand 'Spirit' absolutely, but as meaning "Spirit of God"). But when it is said that the Son is from the Father and the Holy Spirit is from the Father, what is understood is that what the Son is, he has from the Father, and what the Holy Spirit is, he has from the Father. But the Son and the Holy Spirit are understood as being from the Father in different ways: the Son is from his Father, that is, he is from God, who is his Father; but the Holy Spirit is not from God his Father, but just from God, who is the Father. Therefore, the Son, insofar as he is from God, is said to be God's Son; and the one from whom the Son is, is his Father. By contrast, the Holy Spirit is not God's Son insofar as he is from God; and the one from whom the Holy Spirit exists is not his Father.

It is also certain that God is not the Father or Son or Spirit of anyone other than God, and that God is not some thing other than the Father and the Son and the Holy Spirit. And just as there is one God, so too there is only one Father, one Son, and one Holy Spirit. Hence, in that Trinity there is no Father other than the Father of that very Son, no Son other than the Son of that very Father, and no Holy Spirit of any spirit other than the Spirit of that very Father and Son. And so this is the only cause of plurality in God, so that Father and Son and Holy Spirit cannot be said of each other;[1] instead, they are distinct from each other, for God exists from God in the two ways I have explained.

This whole business can be called a relation. After all, because the Son exists from God by being born and the Holy Spirit by proceeding, they are related to each other in virtue of this distinction of birth and procession in such a way that they are distinct and different from each other. And when a substance has its being from a substance, two unshareable relations come about if names are imposed on the substance on the basis of those relations. For when a human being exists by being begotten of a human being, the human being from whom he exists is called a father, and the human being who exists from that human being is called a son. Accordingly, it is impossible for a father to be the son whose father he is, and it is impossible for a son to be the father whose son he is. But there is nothing to prevent a father from being a son or a son from being a father: one human being is both a father and a son because he is a father with respect to one man and a son with respect to another. Obviously, since Isaac is the father of Jacob and the son of Abraham, a father is a son and a son is a father, without any contradiction, because

---

1. That is, the name 'Father' cannot be predicated of the Son or Holy Spirit, and so on.

he is called "father" with respect to someone other than his father and "son" with respect to someone other than his son. But it is not possible for one and the same Isaac to be the father of the son whose father he is or to be the son of the father whose son he is.

So it is in the case of God. God is Father and Son and Holy Spirit, and God is Father only of that very Son, and Son only of that very Father, and Spirit only of that very same Father and Son. Therefore, the Father is not the Son or the Holy Spirit, the Son is not the Father, and the Holy Spirit is not the Father. Indeed, since the Son exists from the Father and the Holy Spirit exists from the Father, and the one from whom someone exists cannot himself be the one who exists from him, and the one who exists from someone cannot himself be the one from whom he exists, as I have already explained, it follows that the Father is not the Son or the Holy Spirit and that neither the Son nor the Holy Spirit is the Father. Now, since it has not yet been established that the Holy Spirit exists from the Son and proceeds from the Son, I need (for the time being) to state another explanation for the fact that the Son is not the Holy Spirit and the Holy Spirit is not the Son. It is this: the Son has existence from the Father by being born, whereas the Spirit has existence from the Father not by being born, but by proceeding. Moreover, the Son cannot be his own Spirit, and the Spirit cannot be the one whose Spirit he is.

Having set forth these preliminaries, let us investigate how indivisible unity and unshareable plurality are related to each other in God. We who say that the Holy Spirit proceeds from the Son, and the Greeks who disagree with us on that point, are united in our unwavering belief in and profession of these things. We should therefore agree unequivocally on whatever follows from them necessarily. Now from the distinctive character of the unity of God, which has no parts, it follows that whatever is said of the one God, who is as a whole whatever he is, is said of the whole God the Father and of the Son and of the Holy Spirit, for each is the only and whole and perfect God. But the opposing relations I discussed earlier, which arise from the fact that God exists from God in the two ways I explained, prevent the Father and the Son and the Holy Spirit from being said of each other and prevent what is proper to one from being attributed to the others. So the consequences of this unity and this relation blend together in such a way that the plurality that follows from the relation does not pass over into statements that express the simplicity of that unity, and the unity does not prevent plurality in statements where the relation is signified: so much so that the only limit to what the unity entails is what is incompatible with some opposition of relation, and the relation has its full scope up to the point where the inseparable unity sets a boundary.

This will become clearer if we make use of some examples. It is of course easy to recognize how the simplicity of unity excludes the plurality that there is in the signification of relative names. After all, we profess that the Father is not the Son or the Holy Spirit, and the Son is not the Father or the Holy Spirit, and the Holy

Spirit is not the Father or the Son. It follows, therefore, that the Father, the Son, and the Holy Spirit are distinct from each other and a plurality. But the Father is God, and the Son is God, and the Holy Spirit is God. And so what could be more logical, if the plurality of persons maintains its distinctive character, than to conclude that the Father, the Son, and the Holy Spirit are a plurality of gods, each distinct from the others? But the inviolable simplicity of the Godhead, which we believe to be the one and only God, in no way allows this conclusion. In this way the unity of God's essence* forestalls a consequence of the relative names.

In considering how the plurality of relations precludes a consequence of the unity, it is helpful first to set forth some of the consequences of that plurality that are not opposed to the unity. We say that the one God is Father and is Son and is Holy Spirit, and that there is one and the same God whether we speak of one or two or all three together. Therefore, if God is eternal,* it follows necessarily in virtue of the unity of the Godhead that the Father is eternal, the Son is eternal, and the Holy Spirit is eternal. And because they—whether each individually or more than one at a time—are one God, there is only one eternal. The inference is similar if God is said to be creator, or just, or any of the other things in which no relation (as set forth earlier) is understood.

Now let us examine how a relation constrains this consequence of the unity of God. We say that God is the Father. So, since the Father and the Son and the Holy Spirit are one God, the unity of God demands that the Son be the Father and the Holy Spirit be the Father; but the relation, which prevents the Son and the Holy Spirit from being the Father, precludes this. Indeed, nature does not allow, and understanding does not grasp, that one who exists from someone is the one from whom he exists, or that one from whom another exists is the one who exists from him. Now the Son and the Holy Spirit exist from the Father. Hence, neither the Son nor the Holy Spirit can be the Father, even though God is the Father, and the Father and Son and Holy Spirit are one and the same God.

We find exactly the same thing if we say that God is the Son. The unity of God would support the inference that the Father and the Holy Spirit are the Son. But the Father from whom the Son exists cannot be the one who exists from him; and the Holy Spirit, who exists from the Father by proceeding, is not the one who exists from the Father by being born. Likewise, if we say that God is the Holy Spirit, the unity I have described requires that the Father and the Son are also the Holy Spirit. But the Father, from whom the Holy Spirit exists, cannot be the one who exists from him; and the Son, who exists from the Father by being born, is not the one who exists from that same Father by proceeding, that is, the Holy Spirit. (Later, when it becomes evident that the Holy Spirit exists from the Son, it will also be clear that for that reason as well the Son cannot be the Holy Spirit and the Holy Spirit cannot be the Son.)

Let us examine further how the oppositions set forth above forestall the consequences of the unity we have described. God exists from God. Once this claim has been accepted, it follows that because one and the same God is Father and Son and Holy Spirit, in virtue of this identity God the Father is both God from God[2] and God from whom God exists, and likewise the Son is both God from God and God from whom God exists, and so also for the Holy Spirit. But to ask whether any one of them is God from whom God exists is simply to examine whether any of them is God who exists from God. For God cannot exist from God unless both (1) the Father or Son or Holy Spirit exists from God and (2) God exists from the Father or Son or Holy Spirit. So let us look closely at whether any one of them is God who exists from God, and it will be clear whether any of them is God from whom God exists.

The Father cannot exist from God, because of the opposition already stated. For since there is no God other than Father or Son or Holy Spirit, or two of them, or the three together, God the Father cannot exist from God unless he exists from the Father, that is, from himself, or from the Son, or from the Holy Spirit, or from two or three of them. He cannot exist from himself, because what exists from something and that from which it exists cannot be one and the same. He does not exist from the Son, because the Son exists from him, and therefore he cannot exist from the Son. He does not exist from the Holy Spirit, because the Holy Spirit exists from him, and he cannot be the one who exists from him. The same argument based on opposition shows that the Father cannot exist from two or three of them at once. But it must be the case that God the Son exists from God the Father, because the Father does not exist from the Son. The Son of course cannot exist from the Son, that is, from himself, because what exists from something and that from which it exists are not one and the same. But whether the Son exists from the Holy Spirit or the Holy Spirit exists from the Son will be shown later. But first let us say whether, given the inference stated earlier, the Holy Spirit exists from the Father or from himself. Obviously he must exist from the Father, because no opposition precludes this. For the Father does not exist from him, and it is impossible for him to exist from himself, since what exists from something cannot be one and the same as that from which it exists. In all these conclusions nothing inhibits the consequence of the one identity other than an opposition that I have set forth earlier. Now what we find in these conclusions must take place immutably in everything that we say about God.

---

2. "God from God": creedal language. God the Son (and only God the Son) is described in the Nicene Creed as "God from God, Light from Light, true God from true God"; that Anselm is here inquiring whether the Father and the Holy Spirit are also God from God shows a decided boldness, and perhaps also a desire to shock so that he can later soothe.

Now we must investigate, on the basis of these incontestable arguments, whether the Son exists from the Holy Spirit or the Holy Spirit from the Son. According to the argument given earlier, either the Father exists from the Son or the Son exists from the Father; and likewise either the Father exists from the Holy Spirit or the Holy Spirit exists from the Father. I say that, in the same way, either the Son exists from the Holy Spirit or the Holy Spirit exists from the Son. One who denies this must also deny that there is one and only one God, or that the Son is God, or that the Holy Spirit is God, or that God exists from God: for what I say follows from these claims.

Moreover, neither the Son nor the Holy Spirit exists from the Father otherwise than by existing from the *essence** of the Father, which is one in him with the Son and the Holy Spirit. Therefore, when it is said that the Son exists from God the Father, if the Father and the Holy Spirit are one and the same God, it follows from the unity of the Godhead that the Son also exists from the Holy Spirit. In the same way, when we profess that the Holy Spirit exists from God the Father, if the Father and the Son are one and the same God, it follows from that same unity of the Godhead that the Holy Spirit also exists from the Son. From these observations it is clearly seen that either the Son exists from the Holy Spirit or the Holy Spirit exists from the Son—since it cannot be the case that both those claims are true or that both are false.

Therefore, if it can be shown that the Son does not exist from the Holy Spirit, it must be the case that the Holy Spirit exists from the Son. For suppose someone says that, from the fact that the Father and the Holy Spirit are one God, it does not follow that the Son exists from the Father and the Holy Spirit (even if no other fact stands in the way of this conclusion), or that, from the fact that the Father and the Son are one God, it does not follow that the Holy Spirit exists from the Father and the Son (even though the Son does not exist from the Holy Spirit). Let him consider this: given that God exists from God, either the whole exists from the whole, or a part from a part, or the whole from a part, or a part from the whole. But God has no part, so it is impossible for God to exist from God as a whole from a part, or as a part from a whole, or as a part from a part. Necessarily, therefore, if God exists from God, the whole exists from the whole. Therefore, when the Son is said to exist from God, who is Father and Holy Spirit, either the Father is one whole and the Holy Spirit is another whole, so that the Son exists from the Father-whole and not from the Holy Spirit-whole, or else, if the Father and the Holy Spirit are the same whole God, then, given that the Son exists from the whole God, and that one whole God is Father and Holy Spirit, it follows necessarily that the Son exists equally from the Father and from the Holy Spirit, provided that no other fact is inconsistent with that conclusion. In the same way, when it is said that the Holy Spirit exists from the whole God, who is Father and Son, either the Father is one whole and the Son another whole, in such a way that the Holy Spirit exists from the Father-whole and not from the Son-whole, or else, since the Holy Spirit exists from the Father, he cannot fail to exist from the Son—unless the Son exists from the Holy Spirit. For there is no other basis for denying that the Holy Spirit exists from the Son.

Someone might object: "You say that because the Father and the Holy Spirit are one God, it follows that because the Son exists from the Father, he exists from the Holy Spirit; or else because the Holy Spirit exists from the Father, he also exists from the Son, because the Father and the Holy Spirit are the same God. But if that is true, then because the Father begets the Son, the Father must also beget the Holy Spirit, because the Son and the Holy Spirit are one and the same God. And because the Holy Spirit proceeds from the Father, then from the fact that the Son and the Holy Spirit are one God it follows that the Son also proceeds from the Father, just as the Holy Spirit does. But if the fact that the Son and the Holy Spirit are one God does not entail that both are begotten and both proceed, the fact that the Father and the Holy Spirit are one God evidently does not entail that the Son exists from the Holy Spirit, and the fact that the Father and the Son are the same God does not entail that the Holy Spirit exists from the Son, as you say."

I reply: The Son and the Holy Spirit do indeed have being from the Father, but in different ways, since one has being from the Father by being born and the other by proceeding. Consequently, they are distinct from each other in the way I have discussed. For that reason, when one is born, the other—who is distinct from him precisely because he is not also born, but proceeds—cannot be born along with him; and when one proceeds, the other—who is distinct from him precisely because he does not also proceed, but is born—cannot proceed along with him. And that is why in this case the unity does not have that implication: the plurality that arises from the birth and procession precludes it. For even if there were no other basis for the Son and Holy Spirit to be more than one, this basis alone would suffice for their being distinct. But when I say that from the fact that the Father is one God with the Son or with the Holy Spirit, it follows that either the Father exists from the Holy Spirit or else the Holy Spirit exists from the Son, no plurality arises in that case that would preclude what the unity implies, because I am not saying that both are true, but only that one or the other is true.

Therefore, if the claims that I identified earlier—the claims that I said we and the Greeks equally believe—are true, it follows by an unequivocal and insuperable necessity that either the Son exists from the Holy Spirit or the Holy Spirit exists from the Son. Now it is clear from the Catholic Faith that the Son does not exist from the Holy Spirit. For God exists from God in only two ways: by being born, as the Son, or by proceeding, as the Holy Spirit. Now the Son is not born from the Holy Spirit. For if the Son is born from the Holy Spirit, he is the Son of the Holy Spirit, and the Holy Spirit is his Father. But neither the Son nor the Holy Spirit is the Father or the Son of the other. Therefore, the Son is not born from the Holy Spirit. And it is no less clear that the Son does not proceed from the Holy Spirit, for if he did, he would be the Spirit of the Holy Spirit. That, clearly, we deny when we say and believe that the Holy Spirit is the Spirit of the Son. For he cannot be the Spirit of his own Spirit. Therefore, the Son does not proceed from the Holy Spirit; consequently, the Son does not exist from the Holy Spirit in any way. And so it follows by an insuperable argument that the Holy Spirit exists from the Son, just as he exists from the Father.

2   Perhaps the Greeks will deny that the Holy Spirit is God from God, as the Son is God from God, because it is on this basis that we prove that the Holy Spirit exists and proceeds from the Son; and [the claim that the Holy Spirit is God from God] does not appear in the Creed, about which they find fault with us for having added the procession of the Holy Spirit from the Son. But one who thinks this way must deny either that the Father is God from whom the Holy Spirit exists, or that the Holy Spirit is God who exists from the Father, or that what the Holy Spirit is exists from the Father. And no Christian entertains the idea that the Father or the Holy Spirit is not God. So let us examine whether the Holy Spirit is, from the Father, the very thing that he essentially is—as I discovered that a certain bishop in the city of Bari,[3] favorably disposed, perhaps, to the Greeks, was unwilling to profess. For if the Holy Spirit is not, from the Father, the very thing that he is, then, given that he is one and the same God as the Father, it will be impossible to find any basis for his being distinct from the Father. After all, it is not because the Father has a Son and the Holy Spirit does not have a Son that the Holy Spirit is distinct from the Father. Yes, one can *prove* on that basis that the Father and the Holy Spirit are distinct from each other, but that is not the *cause* of their being distinct persons. For instance, if there are two human beings, one of whom has a son and the other of whom does not, although we can *show* on that basis that they are distinct, that is not *why* they are distinct from each other: whether either of them has a son or not, they do not lose their distinctness. So it is in the case of the Father and the Holy Spirit. It is not because one has a Son and the other does not that they are distinct; rather, it is because they are distinct that there is nothing to prevent their being dissimilar with respect to having or not having a Son.

A similar response can be given if someone says that the Son is distinct because the Holy Spirit does not proceed from him, as he proceeds from the Father. Indeed, if I may speak with those who deny that the Holy Spirit proceeds from the Son, just as the fact that the Son does not have the Holy Spirit proceeding from him, as the Father does, is not the cause of his being distinct from the Father—for then it would follow that if the Holy Spirit did proceed from the Son, the Son would not be distinct from the Father—so too it is not because the Holy Spirit does not have a Son or Spirit proceeding from him, as the Father does, that the Holy Spirit is

---

3. At the Council of Bari in 1098, convened by Pope Urban II. Anselm appeared before the council at the pope's request in order to defend the Latin doctrine of the procession of the Holy Spirit from the Father and the Son.

distinct from the Father. And just as it is not because the Son has a Father, and the Father does not have a Father, that the Son is distinct from the Father—for if the Father did have a Father, he would still be distinct from the Son—so too it is not because the Holy Spirit proceeds from someone and the Father does not proceed from anyone that the Holy Spirit is distinct from the Father—for if the Father did proceed from someone, the Holy Spirit would still be no less distinct from the Father from whom he proceeds. So it is quite clear that the reason the Holy Spirit is distinct from the Father is not that the Holy Spirit does not have a Son or a Spirit proceeding from him, as the Father does, or that the Holy Spirit proceeds from someone and the Father does not proceed from anyone.

Nor does the fact that the Holy Spirit is the Spirit *of* the Father provide a basis for understanding that the Holy Spirit is distinct from the Father unless the Holy Spirit has his existence from the Father. For the fact that someone is distinct from another can be understood prior to someone's being *of* another, although someone cannot be *of* another unless he is distinct from that other. For example, when we say that a human being is someone's lord or someone else's vassal,[4] we understand that he is distinct from the one whose lord or vassal he is *before* he is that person's lord or vassal. And so in the same way, if the Holy Spirit does not exist from the Father, there is nothing to prevent us from understanding that the Holy Spirit is distinct from the Father before we understand that he is of the Father. So the fact that the Holy Spirit is the Spirit of the Father does not make him distinct from the Father unless he is distinct from the Father precisely because he is the Spirit of the Father, just as the Son is distinct from the Father precisely because he is the Son of the Father, which is nothing other than his existing from the Father by being born.

And so it appears that the Holy Spirit is distinct from the Father precisely because he has from the Father the being that he is—although in his own way, differently from the Son. But let us look into this more carefully. Surely either the Holy Spirit came to be distinct from the Father after he came to be what he is, or he has the basis for being distinct from the Father in his very existing. For it does happen that someone is what he is before he is distinct, and it also happens that someone comes to be distinct in his very existing; but it is not possible for someone to be distinct before he is what he is. For before any human being came to exist from the first human being, he was a human being, but he wasn't a distinct human being [from some other human being]. But as soon as someone came to exist from him, the one from whom she[5] came to exist became a distinct human being after

---

4. The word translated "vassal" is *homo*, human being, but Anselm has in mind here the feudal relationship of lord and vassal.

5. Anselm continues with masculine pronouns because *homo* ("human being") is masculine, but I have used feminine pronouns in referring to the second human being because it makes the sentence much easier to read.

he already existed, and she who came to exist from him had both her being, and her being distinct, simultaneously. So, as I have said, either the Holy Spirit became distinct from the Father after he already existed, or else he has, by the very fact of existing, the basis for our saying that he is distinct. But if he came to be distinct from the Father after he already existed, then—given that he is a distinct person only because he is distinct from the Father—there have not always been three persons, because this person has not always existed, as the Holy Spirit has not always been distinct from the Father. And so, since these conclusions are false, it is clear that the Holy Spirit has the basis for being distinct in his very existing.

Now he can exist in only one of two ways: from someone, as the Son exists, or from no one, as the Father exists. If he exists from no one, as the Father does, then either they both exist through themselves so that neither has anything from the other, and the Father and the Holy Spirit are two gods; or, because they are one God, if both exist from no one, there is absolutely nothing that can be found in the Christian faith to distinguish one from the other, and instead the Father and the Holy Spirit are one and the same, and one person—conclusions that are abhorrent to the true faith. So it is not true that the Holy Spirit exists from no one. Now if he exists from someone, he cannot exist from anyone other than God, who is Father and Son and Holy Spirit. Now he cannot exist from himself, since no person can exist from himself. So if someone denies that he exists from the Son, he cannot deny that he exists from the Father.

Now suppose someone says that although the Holy Spirit does not have being from the Father, he can still be understood to be distinct from the Father in virtue of the fact that he proceeds from the Father. I judge that this, too, requires a response, so that no objection can be made against our discussion of this matter that our response does not forestall. And no one should be surprised that I devote so much attention to this, since the one who, as I discovered, did not hold that the Holy Spirit has what he is from the Father is of considerable authority among his own people, and at that time I did not have an opportunity to respond to him.

Someone who claims that the Holy Spirit is distinct from the Father solely in virtue of the fact that he proceeds from the Father, even if he does not exist from the Father, understands "proceeding from the Father" in one of two ways: either as just being sent or given by the Father, so that the Holy Spirit proceeds from the Father only when the Father sends or gives him, or as being from the Father. But if proceeding from the Father is the same as being given or sent, the Holy Spirit proceeds equally from the Son and from the Father, since the Holy Spirit is likewise sent and given by the Son. Moreover, if the Holy Spirit's proceeding is the same as his being sent or given, he is not distinct from the Father and he does not proceed from the Father except when he is given or sent, which I think no one holds. For the Holy Spirit is always distinct from the Father, even before there is any creature; but he is only given or sent to a creature. Yet it should not be said that it is accidental* to him to be given or sent. Receiving the Holy Spirit is accidental for someone, because something comes to be the case for him that was not the case before, something that can fail to be the case; but the Holy Spirit is everywhere and cannot undergo change, so nothing comes to be the case for the Holy Spirit that was not the case before. For when a blind man is in the light but does not perceive the light, the light is neither increased nor diminished. And if his blindness is dispelled, and the blind man perceives the light, the change is in him, not in the light. And so it is clear that the Holy Spirit is not distinct from the Father in virtue of procession understood in this sense, as being nothing other than his being sent or given. It is therefore obvious that he has being from the Father by proceeding from the Father, and that he is distinct from the Father in virtue of this, just as the Son is distinct from the Father precisely because he exists from the Father. Therefore, the Holy Spirit is God from God and proceeds from God, because the Holy Spirit is God and the Father is God, and the Holy Spirit exists and proceeds from the Father.

And if we say that two processions of the Holy Spirit can be identified—one when he exists from the Father, another when he is given or sent—I do not think there is any need to deny this, so long as both processions are understood in their proper sense. We understand that the Lord spoke fittingly of the procession by which the Spirit is given or sent when he said, "The Spirit blows (*spirat*) where he wills, and you hear his voice, and you do not know where he comes from or where he is going."[6] For clearly he could have put it in this way: you do not know from where he proceeds or to where he departs. For when the Spirit is given, he comes and proceeds as if from a secret place; and when the Spirit is taken away, he goes and departs as if to a secret place. Concerning this procession it can be said that the Spirit's proceeding is the same thing as his being sent.

Therefore, whether the Holy Spirit proceeds from the Father only by existing from the Father, or only when he is given or sent and proceeds for the purpose of sanctifying a creature, or in both ways, it follows that he proceeds from the Son. For if he exists from the Father, he is God from God; and from this it follows, as I have explained, that he also exists and proceeds from the Son. For he proceeds from the one from whom he exists, and he exists from the one from whom he proceeds. Now if he proceeds only when he is sent or given, he proceeds from the Son, by whom he is sent and given. If he proceeds in both ways, he is recognized as proceeding equally from the Son in both ways. So notice: we see that the Holy Spirit is God from God, and proceeds from God, which is not stated in the aforementioned Creed. So if the reason they deny that the Holy Spirit exists and proceeds from the Son is that the Creed says nothing about this, they will likewise deny that he exists and proceeds from God, because that same Creed says nothing about that either. Or, if they cannot deny this, let them not be afraid to join us in

---

6. John 3:8.

professing that the Holy Spirit exists and proceeds from the Son, just because they find nothing to that effect in the Creed.

But they will say, "The statement that the Holy Spirit proceeds from the Father is a sufficient expression in the Creed of the fact that he proceeds from God, since the Father is God." And we likewise say that when the Holy Spirit is said to proceed from God, it is plainly indicated that he proceeds from the Son, since the Son is God. Here is my question: Are we to understand that the Holy Spirit exists from the Father because he exists from God, or rather that he exists from God because he exists from the Father? Granted, either claim can be proved from the other claim: if the Holy Spirit exists from the Father, he exists from God, and if he exists from God, he exists from the Father, because no relation (as discussed before) stands in the way. But it is not likewise the case that each is the *cause* of the other. For if the Holy Spirit's existing from the Father is the cause of his existing from God, when we say that he exists from the Father, we are not to understand that he exists from the Father's being God: that is, from the divine essence. Instead, we are to understand that he exists from God's being Father: from that in virtue of which he is related to the Son. And then it will turn out that the divine essence in the Holy Spirit is not from the Godhead of the Father, but from a relation, which is an extraordinarily stupid thing to say.

Yet even if someone is willing to accept this, it still follows that the Holy Spirit proceeds from the Son as well as from the Father. For there is no relation of father without a relation of son, just as there is no relation of son without a relation of father. Therefore, if neither relation exists without the other, nothing can exist from the relation of father without existing from the relation of son. It will follow, therefore, that the Holy Spirit exists from both relations if he exists from either. And so if the Holy Spirit exists from the Father in virtue of the relation, he will likewise exist from the Son in exactly the same respect. But since no one is foolish enough to say this, it must be believed and professed that the reason the Holy Spirit exists from the Father is that he exists from God. Now the Son is every bit as much God as the Father is: the Father and the Son are the one and only true God. Therefore, if the Holy Spirit exists from the Father because he exists from God, who is Father, it cannot be denied that he also exists from the Son, because he exists from God, who is Son.

3   Let us also consider what the Lord says in the Gospel. He says, "And this is eternal life, that they may know you, the only true God, and Jesus Christ, whom you have sent."[7] Now either we should understand "the only true God" in such a way that the only true God is not signified when we name only the Father or when we name only the Son, but instead the only true God is understood only when we speak of both Father and Son together, or else the only true God is understood

---

7. John 17:3.

when we name only the Father or only the Son. But if the only true God is not understood when only the Father or only the Son is named, without adding the other as well, then the Father is not perfect God and the Son is not perfect God; instead, God is composed of Father and Son. But we believe that the Father is the perfect and only true God, and the Son likewise is the perfect and only true God. Therefore, when we name the Father alone or the Son alone, what we understand—leaving aside the relation by which each is related to the other—is precisely the only true God, one and the same God whom we recognize in speaking of either of them.

And so when the Lord said, "And this is eternal life, that they may know you, the only true God, and Jesus Christ, whom you have sent," if he had added, "and the Holy Spirit proceeds from this only true God," who would have the temerity to exclude the Son from that procession, given that the Father is neither more nor less the only true God than the Son is? Accordingly, given that one and the same only true God is understood when the Father alone or the Son alone is spoken of, and when both are named together, what could be clearer than this: When the Holy Spirit is said to proceed from the Father, he proceeds from the only true God, who is Father and Son? So if, when the Son said that he and the Father are the only true God, he had said that the Holy Spirit proceeds from the only true God, it would be understood that the Holy Spirit proceeds from the Son. Undoubtedly, then, when the Son says that the Holy Spirit proceeds from the Father,[8] he signifies that the Holy Spirit proceeds from himself.

4   The Lord also speaks of "the Holy Spirit, the Paraclete, whom the Father will send in my name."[9] And he says, "When the Paraclete has come, whom I will send to you from the Father."[10] How are we to understand "whom the Father will send in my name"? Is it that the Holy Spirit will have his name, so that when the Father sends the Holy Spirit, that is the same thing as sending the Son? But "whom I will send to you from the Father" cannot have that meaning, since the Son sends the same Spirit whom the Father sends, and the Son does not send the Son. Finally, we do not read anywhere, and we altogether deny, that the Holy Spirit is the Son. And so what else does "whom the Father will send in my name" mean, if not that the Son also sends the one whom the Father sends—just as when he says, "whom I will send from the Father," this means the same as "I and the Father will send him"? For the Son is the name of the one who said "My Father will send him in my name." Therefore, saying "The Father will send him in my name" is the same as saying that the Father will send him in the name of the Son. And what does it mean to say that the Father will send him in the name of the Son but that the

---

8. John 15:26.
9. John 14:26.
10. John 15:26.

Father will send him as the Son sends him, so that in the Father's sending we understand the Son's sending? But how are we to understand "Whom I will send from the Father"? Surely he is sent by the one from whom the Son sends him. Now he sends him from the Father. Therefore, he is sent by the Father. But the one by whom he is sent is the one who sends him. And so when the Son says, "I will send him from the Father," it is understood that the Father sends him. What, then, does "I will send him from the Father" mean? Exactly this: I will send him as the Father sends him, so that my sending and the Father's sending are one and the same.

And so, since the Son so carefully shows that the Father's sending and his own sending are one and the same, so that the Father sends only when the Son sends, and the Son sends only when the Father sends, what does he intend to signify or to be understood, but that the Holy Spirit is related to the Father no differently from how he is related to the Son, and that he is no more of one than of the other? For that reason it is quite difficult—no, it is impossible—to show how he does not proceed from both. How can it be, after all, that the Holy Spirit is given by both the Father and the Son at once, and that he is of both, if he does not exist from both at once? How can it be, after all, that the Son gives the Holy Spirit, rather than that the Holy Spirit gives the Son, or that the Holy Spirit is of the Son, rather than that the Son is of the Holy Spirit, if not because the Son does not exist from the Father and the Holy Spirit together, as the Holy Spirit exists from the Father and the Son together? Therefore, if the Holy Spirit does not exist from the Son, he is not given by the Son and he is not said to be of the Son, just as the Son is not given by the Holy Spirit and is not said to be of the Holy Spirit, because he does not exist from the Holy Spirit. If, however, they say that the Holy Spirit, too, sends the Son, as the Son himself says through the prophet—"And now the Lord God has sent me, and his Spirit [has sent me]"[11]—this must be understood as applying to the human being whom he assumed, who appeared in the world by the one will and plan of the Father and the Holy Spirit in order to redeem the world.

Yet I ask those who deny that the Holy Spirit exists and proceeds from the Son how they understand that he is the Spirit of the Son in such a way that the Son sends him as his own Spirit. Do they think the Father gave the Holy Spirit to the Son as though the Son did not have the Spirit from himself? For the Son has the Spirit either from himself or from another. But he cannot have the Spirit from another unless he has the Spirit from the Father. So he received the Spirit from the Father, from whom he has the Spirit; and the Father gave the Holy Spirit to the Son as to one who did not have the Spirit from himself. If that is so, then—given that the Father and the Son and the Holy Spirit are equals, and each is sufficient unto himself—they need to explain what the reason was, or what deficiency there was on the part of the Son, so that the Father gave his Spirit to the Son, rather

---

11. Isaiah 48:16.

than giving his Son to the Holy Spirit. We do not deny that the Son has the Holy Spirit from the Father *in that* the Son has being from the Father, and so it is from the Father that he has the Spirit existing from himself, just as the Father has, since the being of the Father and of the Son is the same. For the Son's receiving from the Father the essence from which the Holy Spirit proceeds is not the same as his receiving the Holy Spirit from the Father. When it is said that the Son has from the Father the essence from which the Holy Spirit proceeds, no deficiency on the part of the Son is implied. But when it is said that the Son receives the Holy Spirit, whom he does not have from himself as the Father does, from the Father, this seems to mean that the Son has something less than the Father has, and that the Holy Spirit is given to him to supply this lack. But there does not appear to be any reason why the Son needs the Holy Spirit more than the Holy Spirit needs the Son. For if someone replies that the Holy Spirit is given to the Son so that when the Son, too, along with the Father, gave the Holy Spirit, grace would be attributed to him equally along with the Father, this is an earthbound opinion, far removed from an understanding of the Godhead, as if God needs help from God as one human being needs help from another. For if the Father gives the Holy Spirit to the Son, God gives God to God. After all, the Father is God, and the Son is God, and the Holy Spirit is God—and one and the same God. But we do not understand that God receives God from God, unless by this we mean that God exists from God, as the Son and the Holy Spirit do. Therefore, the Holy Spirit is said to be the Spirit of the Son for this reason, and this reason alone: he exists from the Son.

5   We read that after the resurrection the Lord breathed on his disciples and said to them, "Receive the Holy Spirit."[12] What does this breathing mean? We know, after all, that the breath that proceeded from his mouth at that time was not the Holy Spirit; therefore, we believe that this breathing was done with some deeper meaning. And what more correct or more suitable understanding can there be of this action than that he did it in order for us to understand that the Holy Spirit proceeds from him? It is as though he said, "Just as you see that this breath, by which I signify to you the Holy Spirit in the way that what is not sensible can be signified by sensible things, proceeds from the depth of my body and from my person, know also that the Holy Spirit, whom I signify to you by this breath, proceeds from the mystery of my Godhead and from my person." For we believe and profess one person of the Word and of a human being, and in that person two natures, divine and human.

But perhaps they will say, "Of course that breath did not have human substance,[13] and yet he sent it forth as his own. So we are taught by this sort of giving

---

12. John 20:22.

13. "did not have human substance": literally, "was not of human substance" (that is, Christ's breath, though human, neither contained nor exemplified the essence *human being*).

of the Holy Spirit that when the Son gives the Holy Spirit, he sends and gives his own Spirit, but not from the essence of his divinity." Well, then, let those who take this view (if there are any) say that, just as breath is not human nature when it is sent forth by a human being, so too the Holy Spirit is not a divine substance when he is given or sent by God the Son—something no Christian professes. And if they do not deny that when we hear "by the Word of the Lord were the heavens set in place, and by the Spirit[14] of his mouth all the heavenly hosts,"[15] we are to understand "the Spirit of the Lord's mouth" in this passage as the Holy Spirit, let them say that he is not of the essence of the Lord, though he is called the Spirit of the Lord's mouth, on the grounds that the spirit that generally proceeds from a human mouth is not of the substance of the one from whose mouth it proceeds. If they are not so bold as to say that the Spirit of God is not of the essence of God, and they understand these words drawn from sensible things—"the Spirit of his mouth"—to mean that the Holy Spirit proceeds from the mystery of the essence of the one of whom he is said to be "the Spirit of his mouth," let them also admit that the same Holy Spirit proceeds from the essence of the one of whom he is said to be "the Spirit of his lips." For in the prophet we read concerning Christ that "by the Spirit[16] of his lips he will slay the wicked man."[17] So either let them point out the difference between "the Spirit of his mouth" and "the Spirit of his lips"—which cannot be done—or else let them grant that the Holy Spirit proceeds equally from the one of whom he is described as the Spirit of his mouth and the one of whom he is described as the Spirit of his lips. Or suppose they say that we should by no means understand "the Spirit of his lips" in that passage as the Holy Spirit, but rather as the words of his preaching, which he formed in the typical human way out of this airy breath (*spiritus*): for it is by his words that he slays the wicked, since by teaching he repels wickedness from human beings. In fact sensible words, and this sensible breath, do not accomplish this; rather, it is the Holy Spirit, of whom God says through the prophet, "I will take away the heart of stone from your flesh, and I will give you a heart of flesh, and I will place my Spirit in the midst of you."[18] So it is the Holy Spirit who slays the wicked when he turns their hearts from wickedness to righteousness. And if we understand "the wicked man" as the antichrist, "whom the Lord Jesus will slay by the Spirit of his mouth,"[19] I do not

---

14. "Spirit" here is *spiritus*, usually translated "breath" in this passage from the Psalms. Up to this point the word for breath had been *flatus*, but the appearance of *spiritus* in this Scripture inevitably suggests the Holy Spirit (*spiritus sanctus*) to Anselm.

15. Psalm 33:6 (32:6).

16. Here again the word is *spiritus* and is usually translated "breath."

17. Isaiah 11:4.

18. Ezekiel 36:26.

19. 2 Thessalonians 2:8.

think anyone ascribes such great power as much to the breath of a human voice as to the divine Spirit.

So if the Holy Spirit is signified by all these expressions—as the Spirit of the mouth of the Lord by whose word the heavens were set in place, that is, the Spirit of the mouth of the Father; as the Spirit of the mouth of the Lord Jesus; and as the Spirit of his lips—there is no apparent reason why we ought to understand the Spirit as proceeding more from the mouth of the Father than from the mouth of the Son. And if by the "mouth" of the Father we understand the essence of the Father—for his mouth is nothing other than his essence, so that just as the Word of the Lord is from his essence, so too the Spirit of the Lord is from his essence— what is more obvious than this: just as the Spirit of the mouth of the Father exists and proceeds from the essence of the Father, so too the Spirit of the mouth and of the lips of the Son exists and proceeds from the essence of the Son? For I do not suppose anyone understands "By the Word of the Lord were the heavens set in place, and by the Spirit of his mouth all the heavenly hosts" to refer to transitory words and to a breath that is formed from air and sent forth by the mouth of a speaker.

But however someone might try to expound these passages, it is enough that the Lord's breathing upon the disciples, which I have noted, was done in order to signify that the Spirit whom he gave proceeded from the mystery of the same person from whose inmost being the Spirit whom he breathed on them proceeded. Finally, when Holy Scripture signifies some mystery through likenesses drawn from sensible things, the things that signify and the things signified cannot be alike in every respect: that would not be likeness, but identity.

Perhaps someone might venture to say that this breathing was simply done by the wisdom of God without any spiritual signification. But I think no one would be irrational enough to think that.

6   Moreover, the Son says of the Holy Spirit, "He will not speak from himself, but whatever he hears, he will speak."[20] What does "He will not speak from himself" mean, if not "What he speaks, he will have from another"? And what does "What he speaks, he will have from another" mean, if not "He will have from another the knowledge of the things of which he speaks"? That is why, after he says, "He will not speak from himself," he adds, "but whatever he hears, he will speak." What is it for the Holy Spirit to hear, if not to learn (as it were), and what is it for him to learn, if not to receive knowledge? Therefore, given that his knowledge is nothing other than his essence, he has his essence from the one from whom he hears the things that he speaks and that he teaches, since for him speaking is the same thing as teaching. Now he does not hear or have his essence from another except from either the Father or the Son. But if he has his essence from the Father, by

---

20. John 16:13.

the argument given earlier he also has it from the Son. This is why that same Son says, "He will glorify me, because he will receive what is mine and declare it to you."[21] This is surely the same thing as "He will hear from me—that is, he will know from me—what he will declare to you." When he said, "Whatever he hears, he will speak," he did not specify from whom he will hear; but when he says, "he will receive what is mine," he clearly shows that he, along with the Father, is the one from whom the Holy Spirit will receive knowledge or essence, so that no one will attribute to the Father alone what the Holy Spirit hears from another. For when the Son says, "He will not speak from himself, but whatever he hears, he will speak," and "he will declare it to you," this signifies that the Holy Spirit exists and proceeds from the one from whom he hears. Thus, when the Son says, "he will receive what is mine and declare it to you," he clearly shows that the Holy Spirit has his essence and proceeds from what is his, that is, from his essence. For whatever is not the divine essence is inferior to the Holy Spirit, and he does not receive anything from what is inferior to him. Hence, when the Son says, "he will receive what is mine," what he signifies by "what is mine" is precisely his essence.

7   Perhaps they could try to interpret the Son's words, "He will receive what is mine and declare it to you," differently from how I have explained them. But what will they say about this: "No one knows the Father except the Son, nor does anyone know the Son except the Father and those to whom the Son has chosen to reveal him"?[22] We hear that no one knows the Father or the Son except the Father or the Son, and those to whom the Son reveals him. Now he is not saying "No one" in the sense of "No human being," but rather as if he said "No one at all." Obviously if he had meant "No human being," he would not have added "except the Father," since the Father is not a human being. And when he says "nor does anyone know the Father," human persons are no more included than any other persons in this three-syllable word, 'anyone.'[23] So no one *at all* has this knowledge except the Father and the Son, and those to whom the Son himself reveals it. And so either the Holy Spirit does not know the Father and the Son—a wicked view to hold— or the Son reveals to the Holy Spirit the knowledge of himself and of the Father: knowledge that is nothing other than the essence of the Holy Spirit himself.

They might reply, "Sure, according to the strict implications of the words he uses, the Son does not ascribe this knowledge to anyone but himself and the Father, and those to whom he himself reveals it; but we should not grant that the Holy Spirit is excluded from it, or that he receives it from the Son. For the Father

---

21. John 16:14.

22. Matthew 11:27.

23. "in this three-syllable word, 'anyone'": *in hac monosyllaba dictione, videlicet «quis»*, literally, in this one-syllable word, *quis*.

and the Son know each other precisely through that in virtue of which they are one with the Holy Spirit, and so when he says that the Father and the Son know each other, the Holy Spirit must be understood along with them. And when the Son reveals this knowledge, he does not reveal it to the Holy Spirit, but to a creature." If that is what they say, then we immediately and resolutely draw this conclusion: "Here is a place where, as far as the words that he utters go, the Truth[24] clearly denies that the Holy Spirit knows the Father and the Son unless the Son reveals this knowledge; but they say we should not so much pay attention to the words as to the unity of the essence, which is one and inseparable in the three persons. Much more, then, should we insist on a consequence of that unity, of which I spoke earlier, when no authority contradicts it—not in words, not in meaning—or states anything that is contrary to it or in any way incompatible with it."

And so let the Greeks choose one of these two, if they do not wish to be in open warfare against the truth: either the Holy Spirit does not know the Father and the Son unless the Son reveals this knowledge, or else, because the Father and the Son are one with the Holy Spirit in that by which they know each other, it follows necessarily that the Holy Spirit is included in that same knowledge. There is simply no middle ground if they do not want to deny altogether that the Holy Spirit has this knowledge or that the words of the Truth are true: two conclusions that any genuine faith must abhor. For here is how the Truth speaks: "No one knows the Son except the Father, nor does anyone know the Father except the Son, and those to whom the Son has chosen to reveal him." If they choose to affirm that the Holy Spirit knows the Father and the Son through the Son's revelation, the Holy Spirit has knowledge from the Son, and his knowledge is nothing other than his essence. Therefore, he exists and proceeds from the Son, since he proceeds from the one from whom he exists. Suppose they say instead that when the Father and the Son are said to know each other, it follows that their Holy Spirit shares in this knowledge, because the essence through which they know each other is the same for the Holy Spirit. Then when they read that the Holy Spirit proceeds from the Father,[25] of whom the Son says "I and the Father are one,"[26] let them join with us in professing that he undoubtedly proceeds from the Son as well, because the Father and the Son have the same essence.

8   Now someone might object that when we say the Son is born from the Father, and the Holy Spirit proceeds from the Father and the Son, we are setting up hier-archies and relations of before-and-after. We are in effect saying that the Holy Spirit cannot exist until the Son is born from the Father, so that the Holy Spirit comes after the Son. So it would be more correct to say that the Son and the Holy

---

24. "the Truth": that is, God the Son (John 14:6).

25. John 15:26.

26. John 10:30.

Spirit are equally from the Father—the Son by being born, the Holy Spirit by proceeding—in such a way that the Son is not from the Holy Spirit and the Holy Spirit is not from the Son, just as light and heat are equally from one sun, and the light is not from the heat or the heat from the light.

If someone raises this objection to what we have said, we reply that we are not setting up hierarchies of dignity in God, who is one, nor are we setting up relations of before-and-after in eternity, which is outside all time, in the existence of the Son from the Father and the existence of the Holy Spirit from the Father and the Son. For all of us who hold the Christian faith are alike in professing that the Son is not less than the Father and does not come after the Father, even though he exists from the Father. In the same way, we who say that the Holy Spirit exists or proceeds from the Son profess that he is not less than the Son and does not come after the Son. Indeed, although light and heat proceed from the sun and cannot exist unless the sun from which they proceed exists, we understand that none of these three—the sun, the light, and the heat—comes before or after the others. If this is the case even in these temporal things, it makes far less sense to think that in eternity, which is not enclosed in time, the aforementioned three persons can be understood as taking on relations of before-and-after in their existing.

As for the claim that the Son and the Holy Spirit can both be from the Father alone in such a way that the Son is not from the Holy Spirit and the Holy Spirit is not from the Son, just as light and heat proceed at the same time from the one sun in such a way that neither exists from the other, this is not a successful objection to our view. For when we say that the Son exists from the Father and the Holy Spirit exists from the Father, we profess that God the Son and God the Holy Spirit exist from God the Father, and that these three persons are only one God, and that the very same exists from the very same. But in the case of the sun, we do not say that the sun exists from the sun, although light or heat exists from the sun; nor do we say that the sun and what exists from the sun are the very same, or that the three are one sun. For if the sun and the light were one sun, or if the sun and the heat were likewise one sun, it would have to be the case either that the light exists from the heat, because it would exist from the whole sun, which would be the very same thing as the heat, or else that the heat would exist from the light, because it would have its existence from the sun, which would not differ in essence from the light.

Nevertheless, let us suppose that the Son and the Holy Spirit exist equally from the Father alone, in the way that heat and light exist from the one sun. If that is the case, on what basis can those who say this profess that the Holy Spirit is of the Son but deny that the Son is of the Holy Spirit? Just as no reasoning allows for heat to be of the light or light to be of the heat, truth does not make room for the Holy Spirit to be of the Son more than the Son is of the Holy Spirit. For that reason, if they do not dare to deny that the Holy Spirit is of the Son, let them deny that the Son and the Holy Spirit exist equally from the Father alone in the way that light and heat exist from one sun. So if they raise this objection I have spelled out, concerning the sun's light and heat, it neither supports their view nor undermines ours.

9   So as not to exclude the Son altogether from sharing with the Father in this procession of the Holy Spirit, they claim (so we have been told) that the Holy Spirit proceeds *from* the Father *through* the Son. But it is not clear how this can be understood, especially since they nowhere provide any text on the basis of which they can prove this explicitly. Perhaps they think they have support in the passage where we read of God that "from him and through him and in him are all things,"[27] so that all things are from the Father and through the Son and in the Holy Spirit, and the Holy Spirit is included in the meaning of "all things" that are through the Son. Of course we have no hesitation in agreeing that all things exist from the Father and through the Son and in the Holy Spirit; but saying that the Holy Spirit is among all the things that the Apostle says exist in this way makes us very uneasy indeed. For it is impossible to include just one of these three persons among "all things" and exclude the other two. And if the Father and the Son and the Holy Spirit are among "all things" that are from the Father and through the Son and in the Holy Spirit, let any reasonable mind perceive what great confusion results. Therefore, when the Apostle says "from him and through him and in him are all things," we are undoubtedly supposed to understand "all things" as "all things created by God," which exist "from him and through him and in him" as one thing exists from another and through another and in another. For whatever was made is not the same as God, but other than God. But the Holy Spirit is not other than God, but the very same as what the Father is and what the Son is.

Indeed there is no other conceivable ground on which they can show that the Holy Spirit proceeds from the Father through the Son, as they say. For since the Father and the Son do not differ in the unity of Godhead, and the Holy Spirit proceeds from the Father precisely from his Godhead, it follows, given that the same Godhead belongs to the Son, that there is no way to make sense of the idea that the Holy Spirit proceeds *from* the Godhead of the Father *through* the Godhead of the Son and not *from* the Godhead of that same Son. Perhaps someone might say that the Holy Spirit does not proceed from the Godhead of the Father, but from his Fatherhood, and does not proceed from the Godhead of the Son, but from his Sonship—a view that chokes on its own evident stupidity.

Suppose someone says that when I claim that the Holy Spirit proceeds from the Godhead of the Father and of the Son, I cannot separate the Godhead of the Holy Spirit from that of the Father and of the Son, since there is one and the same Godhead of the three; and so it follows that if he proceeds from the Godhead of the Father and of the Son, he proceeds from his own Godhead as well, and

---

27. Romans 11:36.

consequently that the Holy Spirit proceeds from himself. I note that I have already given a sufficient response to this earlier: no person can exist from himself. For although the Son exists from the essence of the Father, and the Son's essence is not other than the Father's, but one and the same as the Father's, the Son does not exist from himself, but from the Father alone. And in the same way, although the Holy Spirit exists from the essence of the Father and of the Son, which is one and the same as his own essence, he does not exist from himself, but only from the Father and the Son.

They will say, "Why can we not likewise say that the Holy Spirit proceeds from the Father through the Son, just as we say that all things were made by the Father through the Word, who is the Son? When the Father makes things through his Word, he does not make them through anything other than what he himself is, that is, through the essential power that is the same as the Word's; nevertheless, he is said to make them through the Word. Why, then, should we not likewise say that the Holy Spirit proceeds from the Father through the Word, even though he proceeds from the Father only from that and through that which is the same in him as in the Son, although he proceeds from him not as a creature but as the very same that he is?"

Let us see what follows if we say this, and let us be at peace with one another. Certainly the things that were made by the Father through the Word were made by that very Word. For the Word himself says, "Whatsoever things" the Father "has made, the Son likewise makes."[28] So let us say that when the Holy Spirit proceeds from the Father through the Son, he likewise proceeds from the Son, just as whatever was made by the Father through the Word was likewise made by that very Word.

But perhaps they mean that the Holy Spirit proceeds from the Father through the Son in the way that when a spring flows into a river and the river feeds into a lake, the lake is said to be from the spring through the river. But in that case the river is not in the spring, but outside the spring, whereas the Son is in the Father, not outside the Father. So the Holy Spirit does not exist from the Father through the Son in the way that the lake exists from the spring through the river. But even if that were the case, it could not be denied that the Holy Spirit exists from the Son, even though he exists from the Father through the Son, just as we must profess that the lake exists from the river, even though it exists from the spring through the river. Suppose someone denies that the lake exists from the river, on the grounds that the river first exists from the spring. Then let him also say that he does not exist from his father, but from Adam, because he exists from Adam

---

28. John 5:19. More usually, in English translations, "Whatever the Father does, the Son does likewise." The Latin verb *facere* does duty for both "make" and "do," but Anselm of course has God's creative activity in mind here, so "do" is the better translation in context.

through his father. Let him also say that the Son of the Virgin does not exist from Mary, or from David, or from Abraham, because they existed first from Adam. Let him also say that what was said to Abraham is false: "In your seed will all the peoples be blessed";[29] as is what was said to David, "From the fruit of your body I will set one on your throne";[30] as is what was said to Mary, "Blessed is the fruit of your womb."[31] Let him also say that Christ was not the seed or fruit of them, but of Adam, because they descend from Adam. But on this reading the Son of the Virgin does not exist even from Adam; he exists from the dust from which Adam was made.

But they will carry the argument further: "We are right to say that the Holy Spirit does not proceed from the Son, but from the Father through the Son, even though he exists from the Father and from the Son, just as you say the lake exists from the spring and from the river. The dispute between us, after all, is about the word 'procession': you[32] say that there is a procession from the Son, and we deny that. Look: you clearly see that the river proceeds from the spring as its original source, whereas the lake does not proceed from the river but is fed by the river, although it has being from the river. In the same way, therefore, even though the Holy Spirit has being from the Son, he nonetheless is not properly said to proceed from the Son; rather, he is said to proceed from the Father as his source."

Perhaps this would be the right thing to say if the Son, in being born from the Father, proceeded outside the Father, and the Holy Spirit were understood to be from the Father first, and then from the Son only after some interval had elapsed, in the way that the river, in flowing from the spring, proceeds outside the spring and feeds into the lake after some lapse of time, and the lake exists from the spring first, and then from the river. That is why the lake exists from the spring through the river, not from the river through the spring. But the Son, in being born from the Father, does not go outside the Father; he remains in the Father, and does not differ from the Father in place or time or essence. And that from which the Holy Spirit proceeds is one and the same in the Father and the Son. For these reasons, it cannot be understood, and should not be said, that the Holy Spirit proceeds from the Father and not from the Son. Therefore, there does not seem to be any basis for saying that the Holy Spirit does not proceed from the Son, but from the Father through the Son, since even if he does proceed through the Son, he must also proceed from the Son.

---

29. Genesis 22:18.

30. Psalm 132:11 (131:11).

31. Luke 1:42.

32. "You" is plural here and in the next sentence, so the sense is "You Latins" rather than "You, Anselm."

Nonetheless, suppose someone wants to say that the Son proceeds from the Father more properly than the Holy Spirit proceeds from the Son, even though the Holy Spirit does exist from the Son (just as someone might think the river proceeds from the spring more than the lake proceeds from the river), so as to avoid conceding that the Holy Spirit proceeds from the Son, from whom he has being, as the lake has being from the river. If so, we do not deny that one being born proceeds in some way from the one from whom he is born, and we assert that the Holy Spirit proceeds in his own way, not as if from two springs, but from one spring—yet in such a way that the procession of the Son does not lose the designation "nativity" and the procession of the Holy Spirit does not acquire it. So there is no reason that the Son should be said to proceed from the Father more than the Holy Spirit from the Son.

Let us investigate more carefully how the lake exists equally from the spring and from the river, so that something that is eternal* can be understood through something that is in time and place, and we can thereby recognize that the Holy Spirit exists from the Father and the Son. For as I wrote in my letter *On the Incarnation of the Word* to Pope Urban of blessed memory,[33] there are many points found in this examination that apply, by a certain analogy, to the one God and the three persons. It is clear that it is one and the same body of water that is called "spring" and "river" and "lake," not three bodies of water, even though the spring, the river, and the lake are three. And so let us distinguish between the spring and the river and the lake, and let us see what each of them, although they are three, is understood to be in a single body of water.

Water bubbles up from the depths in the spring; it flows down from the spring in the river; it feeds the lake and remains there. So by "spring" we understand the water bubbling up from the depths, by "river" that the water flows from the spring, and by "lake" that the water is gathered there into one. But we see that the river does not exist from that by which the water is called a spring, but rather from that which the water is: that is, from water. Nor does the lake exist from that by which the water is called a spring or a river, but rather from the water itself, which is one and the same in the spring and in the river. So the lake does not exist from that by which the spring and the river differ but from that in which they are one. Therefore, given that the spring is not that from which the lake exists more than the river is, it makes no sense to say that the lake exists more from the spring than from the river. And so in the same way, when God is said to be Father or Son or Holy Spirit, what is understood in these three is one essence and one God—the name 'God' signifies that essence—but by 'Father' we understand God begetting,

---

33. See *On the Incarnation of the Word* in this volume, pp. 223–44. An earlier draft of the letter, found on pp. 456–65, is addressed "To all lords and fathers and brothers who are devoted to the catholic and apostolic faith who will see fit to read this letter."

by 'Son' God begotten, and by 'Holy Spirit' God in some unique and mysterious way proceeding. Therefore, just as the lake does not exist from that by which the spring and the river are distinct from each other, but from the water in which they are one, so too the Holy Spirit does not exist from that by which the Father and the Son are distinct from each other, but from the divine essence in which they are one. Therefore, given that the Father is not that from which the Holy Spirit exists more than the Son is, there is no way to make sense of the claim that the Holy Spirit exists more from the Father than from the Son.

10   And if they say that he cannot exist from two causes or (in other words) from two sources, we reply that we do not believe that the Holy Spirit exists from that in virtue of which the Father and the Son are two, but from that in which they are one; and in the same way we do not say that they are two sources of the Holy Spirit, but one source. Clearly, when we say that God is the source of creation, we understand the Father and the Son and the Holy Spirit to be one source, not three sources, as they are one creator, not three creators, even though the Father and the Son and the Holy Spirit are three: for it is through that in which they are one, not through that by which they are three, that the Father or the Son or the Holy Spirit is source or (in other words) creator. Therefore, just as the Father is source and the Son is source and the Holy Spirit is source, and yet they are not three sources, but one, so also when the Holy Spirit is said to be from the Father and from the Son, he is not from two sources, but from one, which is the Father and the Son, just as he is from the one God, who is Father and Son—if, that is, God should be said to have a source or cause.

For it seems that only something that begins to exist has a source, and only an effect has a cause; and the Holy Spirit never began to exist and is not the effect of anything. After all, what begins to exist advances from non-existence to existence, and the name 'effect' seems to be properly applied to a thing that is brought about. Nonetheless, because it is true that the Son exists from the Father and the Holy Spirit exists from the Father and the Son, it can be said without incongruity that the Father is in a certain way the source of the Son, and the Father and the Son are the source of the Holy Spirit, provided that this is understood in its own ineffable way (since there is no other way to express it). And yet we do not profess two sources—one, the Father, source of the Son; the other, the Father and the Son, source of the Holy Spirit—just as we do not believe that the Father, from whom the Son exists, is a different God from the Father and the Son, from whom the Holy Spirit exists, although each is from the same God or (in other words) from the same source in his own way, one by being born, the other by proceeding— provided that this procession is understood in a unique and ineffable way. For 'procession' is said in many ways, among which this way is understood to be the only one of its kind, just as the nativity of the Son is recognized as the only one its kind. This is also exactly how we understand the claim that the Father is the cause of the Son and the Father and the Son are the cause of the Holy Spirit. For we cannot say that there are two causes—one cause of the Son and another cause of the Holy Spirit—but one cause, since there are not two gods, but one God, from whom the Son and the Holy Spirit exist.

11   Someone might ask why, when the Lord said, "When the Paraclete comes, the Spirit of truth, who proceeds from the Father,"[34] he did not add "and from the Son" or "and from me," if that is how he wanted to be understood. But it is not unusual in what he says for him to attribute something as if to the Father alone or to himself or to the Holy Spirit when he means what he says about one to be understood as applying to the others. For when he says, "Blessed are you, Simon Bar-Jonah, because flesh and blood has not revealed this to you, but my Father, who is in heaven"[35] are we not to understand that the Son and the Holy Spirit revealed this along with the Father? For since the Father does not reveal in virtue of being Father but in virtue of being God, and the Son and the Holy Spirit are that same God, it follows that what the Father reveals, the Son and the Holy Spirit reveal. Likewise, when he says, "No one knows the Son except the Father, nor does anyone know the Father except the Son, and those to whom the Son chooses to reveal him,"[36] as if the Son alone knows and reveals the Father and himself, and the Father alone knows the Son, we should understand revealing and knowing in this passage as common to the three persons, since the Father and the Son and the Holy Spirit know and reveal, not through that by which they are distinct from each other, but through that by which they are one. And when he says that the Father knows the Son and the Son knows the Father and reveals himself and the Father, he clearly wants it to be understood that the Father knows the Holy Spirit, and the Son knows and reveals the Holy Spirit, since the Holy Spirit is the very same as what the Father and the Son are. Likewise, when he says, "One who sees me, also sees the Father,"[37] we are not to exclude the Holy Spirit, since one who sees that in which the Father and the Son and the Holy Spirit are one cannot see one of these three without the other two. Concerning the Holy Spirit he also says to the apostles, "But when the Spirit of truth comes, he will teach you all truth,"[38] as if only the Holy Spirit teaches all truth, when in fact he does not teach all truth without the Father or without the Son. For he does not teach all truth in virtue of being the Spirit of someone (namely, the Spirit of the Father and the Son), but in virtue of being one with the Father and the Son, that is, in virtue of being God.

---

34. John 15:26.
35. Matthew 16:17.
36. Matthew 11:27.
37. John 14:9.
38. John 16:13.

Do you see, therefore, how in the passages I have put forward, what he attributes to only one person cannot be denied of the other two? We read many such things in Holy Scripture, so that what is said of one person alone is understood to apply equally to all three. For whatever is affirmed of one person ought to be understood equally of the others, except (as I have said) when we see that the respect in which they differ from each other stands in the way. Accordingly, when we believe that the Holy Spirit proceeds from the Father, given that God proceeds from God—that is, the essence of the Holy Spirit proceeds from the essence of the Father, which is understood to be one in the three persons—we must profess that he likewise exists from the Son, if the Son does not exist from him. For the Holy Spirit exists from what the Son is and what the Father is.

But one of you will say: "We understand that the Son and the Holy Spirit reveal what the Father alone is said to reveal, and that the Father and the Holy Spirit reveal and know what only the Son is said to do, and that the Father and the Son teach what only the Holy Spirit is promised to teach, because what we read of only one in one passage is explicitly signified of the others in some other passage. But although this passage says that the Holy Spirit proceeds from the Father, we do not read anywhere else that he proceeds from the Son, and that fact warns us not to assert, on the basis of our own reasoning, something that is not said anywhere."

To this we reply that, on the contrary, we are taught by the things said in this way that we should understand similar passages, in which such things are not said, in the same way, especially when we see perfectly clearly that what is not said follows by rational necessity, and with no argument to contradict it, from the things that *are* said. After all, when the Lord says to the Father, "And this is eternal life, that they know you, the only true God, and Jesus Christ, whom you have sent,"[39] are we therefore to exclude the Holy Spirit from this saving and life-giving knowledge, just because we nowhere read, "And this is eternal life, that they know the Father, the only true God, and the Holy Spirit" or "This is eternal life, that they know the Son, the only true God, and the Holy Spirit"? Or when we read that "As the Father has life in himself, so also he has granted the Son to have life in himself,"[40] will we say that the Holy Spirit has not been granted by the Father, from whom he exists, to have life in himself, as the Father and the Son have life in themselves, just because the Son never says this of the Holy Spirit as he says it of himself? Likewise, when he says, "The Father is in me, and I in the Father,"[41] and "One who sees me, also sees the Father,"[42] will we deny that the Holy Spirit is in the Father and the Son, and the Father and the Son are in

---

39. John 17:3.
40. John 5:26.
41. John 14:10.
42. John 14:9.

the Holy Spirit, or that one who sees the Son sees the Holy Spirit just as he sees the Father, if we do not find a passage in which these things are said explicitly of the Holy Spirit as they are stated about the Father and the Son?

No, indeed. Because the Father and the Son and the Holy Spirit are one and the same God, when it is said that knowing the "only true God," the Father and the Son, is eternal life, the Holy Spirit must be included inextricably in that knowledge. And when we read that "As the Father has life in himself, so also he has granted the Son to have life in himself," we should not suppose that this life does not belong to the Holy Spirit or that he does not have it in himself. And when we hear, "The Father is in me, and I in the Father," and "One who sees me, also sees the Father," we ought to recognize through what is said in these passages that the Holy Spirit is not outside the Father and the Son, and the Father and the Son are not outside the Holy Spirit, and that when the Son is seen, the Holy Spirit also is seen, just as the Father is. For just as the Father, the Son, and the Holy Spirit are not distinct gods, so too God does not have anything in himself other than God, and God is not outside God, and God is not unlike God.

Finally, where in any prophet or evangelist or apostle do we read *in those words* that the one God is three persons, or that the one God is a Trinity, or that God exists from God? Not even in that Creed, in which the procession of the Holy Spirit from the Son is not stated, do we find the name 'person' or 'Trinity.' But these quite evidently follow from what we do read there, and for that reason we unwaveringly believe them with our heart and profess them with our mouth.[43] Therefore, we ought to accept with certainty not only the things we read in Holy Scripture but also the things that follow from them by rational necessity, with no other argument to contradict them.

12   Although what has already been said could suffice, I will nonetheless say something further by which it can be known that the Holy Spirit exists from the Son. The Greeks profess along with us that the Holy Spirit is the Spirit of God and the Spirit of the Father and the Spirit of the Son. And so I ask whether they understand him to be God's Spirit and the Father's Spirit and the Son's Spirit in the same way, or in different ways. Now it is certain that he is not said to be God's Spirit as a possession, as we speak of someone's horse or someone's house. For the one who possesses is greater than what is possessed, but God is not greater than the Holy Spirit, since the Holy Spirit is God, and God is not greater than God. Nor is he called God's Spirit as a limb of God, like a human being's hand or foot, for God has no limb or other part. How, then, are we to understand that he is God's Spirit, if not precisely in the sense that what he is, he is from God? But the name 'Father' does not signify anything other than the God who is Father, or his relation

---

43. Cf. Romans 10:10: "For one believes with the heart and so is justified, and one professes with the mouth and so is saved."

to the Son, by which he has the name 'Father.' And one should say the same sort of thing about the Son. After all, what is understood by the name 'Son' other than the God who is Son, or the relation by which he is related to the Father, by which he is called 'Son'? But there is no sense to be made of the idea that the Holy Spirit is the Spirit of the Father or of the Son in virtue of the Father and the Son's being distinct, rather than in virtue of the fact that the two are one and the same God. Hence, the meaning is the same when he is said to be the Spirit of God and the Spirit of the Father and the Spirit of the Son.

But he is called the Spirit of God and the Spirit of the Father because he exists and proceeds from God and from the Father, and so he also exists and proceeds from the Son, because he is called the Spirit of the Son in the same sense. For when the Holy Spirit is called the Spirit of God and the Spirit of the Lord, if we do not understand "the Spirit of the Son" in the same sense as we understand "the Spirit of the Father," we will either exclude the Son from the name 'God' or the name 'Lord,' or else "the Spirit of God" and "the Spirit of the Lord" will be understood in two different ways. But where do they get this view? Where do we find in Holy Scripture that when we read of "the Spirit of God" or "the Spirit of the Lord," we are not to understand this in the same way of the Father and of the Son? Or where do we find something from which this claim follows? Suppose they say, "When he is called the Spirit of the Father, this is understood in two ways: he is the Spirit of the Father because he exists from the Father and because he is given by the Father. By contrast, he is the Spirit of the Son only because he is given by the Son." Where are they getting this from? That is what I would like to know. And if they say that it is not stated in any authoritative writing, and it does not follow from anything written there, why do they find fault with us for saying that the Holy Spirit proceeds from the Son on the grounds that they do not read those words anywhere, even though we understand that it follows by necessity from things that we do read and believe?

Therefore, let them judge for themselves which view they ought to accept, even though Holy Scripture is silent on both of them: our view, that the Holy Spirit proceeds from the Son, which we prove follows from things we truthfully believe, or their view, that the Holy Spirit is the Spirit of the Father and the Spirit of the Son in two different senses, which they cannot prove from authority or by reason or on the basis of any other claims that are certain. Surely either they should desist from this view of theirs—if, that is, they really do say, as I have heard, that the Holy Spirit is the Spirit of the Father and the Spirit of the Son in two different senses—because they cannot find anywhere a text that says it or any basis on which to prove it, or they should at least not find fault with us, who say that the Holy Spirit proceeds from the Son, even though we do not find that stated in those exact words, because we show that it follows from things that they and we equally believe. But if they desist from their assertion, let them believe along with us that the Holy Spirit is the Spirit of the Father and the Spirit of the Son in the same way, and let them understand that he proceeds from the Son as he proceeds from the Father. And if they stop finding fault with us, let them join us in professing the truth by which they recognize that they should not find fault.

13   They also find fault with us for having added to that Creed, which we and they equally accept and uphold, the claim that the Holy Spirit proceeds from the Son; and they ask why this was done, and why it was not first shown to their church, so that the proposed addition could be considered together and added by common consent. To this, I say, we have a sufficient response.

If the question is why it was done, we say that it was necessary so that certain less intelligent people, who did not realize that the Holy Spirit's proceeding from the Son is encompassed by claims that the whole church believes, and follows from them, would not perhaps hesitate to believe it. Just how necessary this was, we recognize through those who do deny it because it was not included in the Creed. So, because necessity compelled it, no argument prevented it, and true faith embraced it, the Latin church faithfully asserted what it recognized should be believed and professed. For we know that not everything we ought to believe and profess is stated in that Creed, and those who set it forth did not intend that the Christian faith should be restricted to believing and professing only what they stated in the Creed. To give just one example, that Creed does not say that the Lord descended into hell, and yet we and the Greeks equally believe that he did.

If, however, they say that the Creed, which is reckoned to be of such great authority, should not have been corrupted in any way, we do not regard it as corruption where we add nothing that is opposed to what is said there. And even though we can defend the claim that this addition was not a corruption, if someone insists on making a stink about this, we reply that we did not corrupt the Creed; we published another, new Creed. For like the Greeks we revere and keep intact the old Creed, translated according to the distinctive features of the Greek language; but we published this new Creed, which we use more frequently in the hearing of the people, expressed in idiomatic Latin, with the addition discussed above.

Now as for the question why this was not done with the consent of the Greek church, we reply that it was too difficult for the Latins to gather the Greek bishops to consult with us on this matter; and there was no need to call into question something about which they had no doubt. After all, what church is there, even one spread throughout just one kingdom, that is not permitted to establish something that is in keeping with a correct faith and is profitably read or sung in the people's assembly? How much more, then, was it permitted for the Latins to state unwaveringly something about which all peoples and all kingdoms that use Latin equally agree?

14   Let us briefly summarize what was accomplished above through many arguments. It is established by incontestable argument that the Holy Spirit exists from

the Son, as he exists from the Father, and yet he does not exist from them as from two distinct [sources], but as from one. For the Holy Spirit exists from that in virtue of which the Father and the Son are one, that is, he exists from God; he does not exist from that in virtue of which they are distinct from each other. But because the God from whom the Holy Spirit exists is Father and Son, for that reason it is said truly that he exists from the Father and from the Son, who are two. And because the Father is not prior or posterior to the Son, or greater or less than the Son, and neither is more or less God than the other, the Holy Spirit does not exist from the Father before he exists from the Son, or from the Son before he exists from the Father, nor is one existing from the Father either greater or less than one existing from the Son, nor does he exist from one any more or less than he exists from the other. For if there were before and after, or greater or less, or if he existed from one more or less than from the other, it would follow by necessity that either the Holy Spirit would not exist from that in which the Father and the Son are one, or else that this one [God] would not be perfectly and unqualifiedly* one; instead, there would be some distinction there, on the basis of which there would be the discrepancy I have described in the Holy Spirit's existing from one and the same [God]. But it cannot be said that the Holy Spirit does not exist from that in which the Father and the Son are one—otherwise he would not exist from God—and it should not be believed that there is anything in that very one on the basis of which there is some distinction. Therefore, there is no before or after, no greater or less, and the Holy Spirit does not exist from the Father any more or less than he exists from the Son, or from the Son any more or less than he exists from the Father. For one and the same Holy Spirit, who exists as a whole all at once from the whole God, cannot exist more or less from the one and supremely simple God.

And if it is said that the Holy Spirit exists principally from the Father, as if he exists more from the Father than from the Son, this should not be understood to mean that any of the aforementioned differences apply. It can, however, be appropriately asserted on the grounds that the Son has from the Father what he is, and therefore the Son has from the Father, from whom he exists, the very fact that the Holy Spirit exists from him. Since, however, the Son has being from the Father in such a way that he is altogether the very same as what the Father is, and one and the same God, just as the only and simple God cannot be greater or less than himself, or prior or posterior to himself, or have any diversity within himself, so too the Son is not prior or posterior to the Father, or greater or less than the Father, and he does not have within himself any diversity from the Father. Instead, just as he has perfect being from the Father, so too he has from the Father his being equal to the Father and like him in every respect, indeed, his being the very same as the Father. Hence, just as the Father is not more God than the Son is, even though the Son has being from the Father, so too the Holy Spirit does not exist more from the Father than from the Son, even though the Son has from the Father the fact that the Holy Spirit exists from the Son. For insofar as the Son is one and the same as the Father—that is, insofar as he is God—he and the Father are not distinct, and they are not dissimilar in any respect; for the Father and the Son are not distinct gods, and they are not dissimilar in the way they are what they are. Rather, they are distinct in virtue of the fact that one is Father and the other is Son. And just as the Son is not a God distinct from the Father, so too as God he does not have anything from another rather than from himself. For when we speak of "God from God," the Son from the Father, we do not interpret this to mean one God from another God, but one and the same God from one and the same God, even though we do say that one exists from another, namely, the Son from the Father. For as was stated above, although God does not receive any multiplicity in terms of the name that signifies the unity, he necessarily allows for plurality in terms of the names that signify that God exists from God. Therefore, if it is said that the Holy Spirit exists principally from the Father, this means precisely that the Son himself, from whom the Holy Spirit exists, has from the Father the very fact that the Holy Spirit exists from him. For what he is, he has from the Father. This is not like the way we say of created things that something is "principally" such-and-such; there we intend to signify that what is said to be "principally" such-and-such is more so than that to which it is compared. For example, when some master's steward feeds the family of the household at his master's command, it is rightly said that the master feeds them principally, and more so than the steward. For not everything that belongs to the master belongs equally to the steward, as whatever belongs to the Father belongs equally to the Son.

Perhaps someone will pose a question and say, with amazement, "How can it be understood that something has being from something, and the thing from which it exists is not in some way more principal and of greater stature, and the thing that is from it is not less and, as it were, secondary—especially when what is from something seems to need what it is from in order to exist, whereas the thing from which it exists in no way needs the thing that exists from it?" The right response to give here is that just as God's essence is very different from and unlike a creature's essence, so also when we say that God exists from God by being born or proceeding, this birth or procession must be understood in a very different way from the way in which we speak of something's being born or proceeding in other things. For in God there is nothing prior or posterior—not in nature, not in time, not in any power; there is no more or less; there is nothing deficient in any respect. Rather, the whole that he is, is not so much equal or similar to or coeternal with itself as it is the very same as itself; and he is utterly sufficient by himself for himself, and nothing is born or proceeds in him as if it were advancing from non-being to being. Therefore, just as our intellect cannot pass beyond eternity so as to make a judgment about its beginning (so to speak), so too it cannot, and should not, think or make a judgment about this birth or procession through some likeness to a creature. But because both what is born and what proceeds is not other than that from which it is born or proceeds, which is the one and only God, just as one and the same God is not greater or less than himself, so too in the three—that is, in the Father and the Son and the Holy Spirit—there is not something greater or less, nor is one any more or less what he is than another, even though it is true that God exists from God by being born and proceeding.

Take note: we have seen with what great truth, and by how great a necessity, it follows that the Holy Spirit proceeds from the Son. Now if this is not true, either one of the claims from which we have said this follows is false, which is contrary to the Christian faith that we uphold along with the Greeks, or else we have not drawn our conclusions logically, which cannot be shown. Therefore, if it is not true, the Christian faith is destroyed. And it is clear to anyone who understands, that if it is held to be false, no truth can arise from it. And let us consider what happens if it is asserted as true. Surely, if it is true that the Holy Spirit proceeds from the Son as from the Father, it follows that he is the Spirit of the Son as of the Father, and he is sent and given by the Son as by the Father—claims that divine authority teaches—and no falsehood follows at all. But since the denial that the Holy Spirit proceeds from the Son leads to such great falsity that the claims that, as we have shown, follow from it are destructive to the Christian faith and generate no truth, whereas the assertion of that procession confirms the truth, as we showed, and brings no falsehood of any kind along with it, let a rational heart reflect on what reason there could be to exclude it from the Christian faith. Finally, if it is an error to believe in the procession of the Holy Spirit from the Son, divine authority itself is leading us into this error, since it teaches us both the claims from which that procession follows and the claims that follow from it, nor does it deny that procession anywhere or affirm anything that is in any way inconsistent with it. So if someone objects that we must not affirm that procession because divine authority nowhere expressly states it, let him also say that we must not deny it because divine authority nowhere denies it or affirms anything inconsistent with it. And we say that divine authority does sufficiently affirm that procession, because it asserts claims from which it is proved and in no way expresses any claim on the basis of which we would have to deny it.

15   It is therefore evident, as I promised earlier, that beyond the fact that the Son exists by being born and the Holy Spirit by proceeding, there is this additional reason—namely, that the Holy Spirit exists from the Son—why they cannot be said of each other; and for this reason alone the Son cannot exist from the Holy Spirit. For because, as I have said, either the Son exists from the Holy Spirit or the Holy Spirit exists from the Son, if the Holy Spirit did not exist from the Son, it would follow that the Son exists from the Holy Spirit. And so it is clear through the arguments offered above that the Father is God from whom God exists, and is not God from God; and the Son is God from God, and God from whom God exists; and the Holy Spirit is God from God, but is not God from whom God exists. And although there are two who exist from the Father—namely, the Son and the Holy Spirit—there are not two gods from the Father, but one God, who is

Son and Holy Spirit. And although the one from whom the Son exists and the one who exists from the Son are two—namely, the Father and the Holy Spirit—they are not two gods, but one God, who is Father and Holy Spirit. And although the Holy Spirit exists from two—namely, from the Father and from the Son—he does not exist from two gods, but from one God, who is Father and Son.

But if the Father and Son and Holy Spirit are considered two at a time, it is clear from what has been said that either (1) one exists from the other because the other does not exist from him or (2) one does not exist from the other because the other exists from him. For if we examine the Father and the Son, we see that the Son exists from the Father because the Father does not exist from him, and that the Father does not exist from the Son because the Son exists from the Father. Similarly, if we consider the Father and the Holy Spirit, we find that the Holy Spirit exists from the Father because the Father does not exist from him, and that the Father does not exist from the Holy Spirit because the Holy Spirit exists from him. So also if we look carefully at how the Son and the Holy Spirit are related to each other, we will understand that the Holy Spirit exists from the Son because the Son does not exist from him, and the Son does not exist from the Holy Spirit because the Holy Spirit exists from the Son. And so what I said earlier becomes clear: although the aforementioned relations exist in the one, they cannot impose their plurality on the unity, and the unity cannot impose its singularity on the relations.

16   Moreover, there are six differences between the Father and the Son and the Holy Spirit that arise from these names: having a Father, not having a Father; having a Son, not having a Son; having a Spirit proceeding from himself, and not having a Spirit proceeding from himself. Each of the three has one of these differences proper to himself, by which he differs from the other two, and two that are both common and proper in that what he has in common with one is that by which he differs from the other. For the Father alone has a Son; by that he differs from the other two. He has the Holy Spirit proceeding from himself, which is common to him and the Son, by which he differs from the Holy Spirit. Like the Holy Spirit, he does not have a Father, but in that he differs from the Son. The Son alone has a Father; by this he differs from the Father and the Holy Spirit. As has been said, he has in common with the Father that the Holy Spirit proceeds from him, which distinguishes him from that same Holy Spirit. He lacks a Son, however, as does the Holy Spirit, and by that he is distinguished from the Father. It is only the Holy Spirit from whom no other proceeds. As I have said, he has in common with the Father that he does not have a Father, in which he is unlike the Son. And, as has already been shown, he has in common with the Son that he does not have a Son, by which he is unlike the Father. And so it is the Father alone who exists from no one and from whom the other two exist; by contrast, it is only the Holy Spirit who exists from the other two and from whom no one exists; it is only the Son who exists from one and from whom one exists. But all three have in common the fact

that they have relations to the other two. For the Father is related to the Son and Holy Spirit as to those who exist from him; the Son is related to the Father and to the Holy Spirit in that he exists from the Father and the Holy Spirit exists from him; and the Holy Spirit is related to the Father and the Son in that he exists from both.

Therefore, each possesses his own distinctive characteristics, and no other has the same combination of those characteristics, in something like the way human persons differ. For what makes human persons distinct from one another is that no person has the same combination of characteristics that belong to any other. There is, however, a difference between these two cases. In the case of human persons, if there is one person, there is one human being; and if there is one human being, there is one person. Moreover, if there are several* persons, there are also several human beings; and if there are several human beings, there cannot fail to be several persons as well. In the case of God, however, although there are three persons, there is nevertheless one God; and although there is one God, the persons nevertheless by no means lose their plurality. And so what is said about God in relation to God allows for a plurality of persons, just as in the case of several human beings; but in that which God is in himself—that is, in God—he preserves an indivisible singularity, like that of one human being. For there is a plurality of human persons only in a plurality of human beings, and one human being does not receive a plurality of persons; but the one God is three persons, and the three persons are one God. And so in this way God does not wholly preserve the distinctive characteristics of other persons, whether of one or of many.

As for why this is so, although I have said a fair bit about this in the letter *On the Incarnation of the Word* I mentioned earlier, I will nevertheless repeat it briefly here. It often happens that a plurality of things come together as one under the same name and the same quantity that each had before they became one. Indeed, if we add a point to a point without any distance between them, or an equal line to an equal line, or place an equal surface on an equal surface, what comes about is just one point, one line, one surface. Anyone who cares to investigate this will find similar examples in many cases. And so in this way, although there are not many eternities, if we nonetheless speak of an eternity in an eternity, there is only one eternity; and light in light is only one light. In the same way, if whatever is said of God's essence is folded back on itself, it neither grows in quantity nor admits plurality. But since God is eternity, just as nothing at all is outside eternity, so too nothing at all is outside God; and just as eternity in eternity is only one eternity, so too God in God is only one God.

Now we hold on the basis of the true faith that God exists from God by being born and God exists from God by proceeding. But because there is nothing outside God, when God is born from God or when God proceeds from God, the one being born or the one proceeding does not depart outside God; rather, he remains in God. Since, therefore, God in God is only one God, when God is born from

God, the one begetting and the one begotten are only one God; and when God proceeds from God, the one proceeding and the one from whom he proceeds are just one God. From this it follows inevitably that because God has no parts, but is as a whole whatever he is, the whole Father, the whole Son, and the whole Holy Spirit are one and the same God, and not distinct gods. Hence, because the Father and the Son and the Holy Spirit are only one God, even though they are God from God and God in God, they preserve in their Godhead a likeness to the unity of a single human being; but because God exists from God either by being born or by proceeding, and what exists from something cannot be one and the same as that from which it exists, they are a plurality of persons in accordance with the names that signify these relations, like a plurality of distinct human beings.

One should note, however, that God does not exist without a person, and a person does not exist without God, and that sometimes we attribute the distinctive characteristic of each person to each person, but sometimes we attribute to one person, as if it were his own distinctive characteristic, something he has in common with the others. For example, when we say, "The Father is the only one of the three persons who exists from no one, the Son is the only one who exists from one and from whom one exists, and the Holy Spirit is the only one from whom no one exists," in naming the persons we attribute to each his own distinctive characteristic. By contrast, when we read, "No one knows the Son except the Father, nor does anyone know the Father except the Son,"[44] and "No one knows the things of God except the Spirit of God,"[45] although it looks as if Scripture denies of the other persons what it says of one, in fact what it attributes to one as if it were his own characteristic is common to them all. For neither the Father nor the Son lacks knowledge of himself or of the things of God, and the Holy Spirit does not lack knowledge of the Son. But enough was said earlier about why and when what is said as if it were true of only one is understood as applying to the others.

I have ventured to write these things about the procession of the Holy Spirit on behalf of the Latins, against the Greeks, at the urging of others, trusting not in myself but in that same Holy Spirit, and I have taken the opportunity to add something about the unity of the Godhead and the Trinity of persons, although there are countless people among those who use Latin who can do this better than I can. Therefore, let whatever I have said that is worthy of acceptance be attributed not to me, but to the Spirit of truth; but if I have stated something that is in any way in need of correction, let that be ascribed to me, not to the judgment of the Latin world.

---

44. Matthew 11:27.

45. 1 Corinthians 2:11.

On the Harmony of God's Foreknowledge, Predestination, and Grace with Free Choice (*De concordia*)

I SHALL TRY, with God's help, to set forth in writing what God sees fit to show me concerning those three questions about the apparent incompatibility between free choice and God's foreknowledge, predestination, and grace.

Question 1: On foreknowledge and free choice

1.1   Certainly God's foreknowledge seems to be incompatible with free choice, since it is necessary that the things God foreknows are going to be, whereas things done by free choice do not result from any necessity. And if they are in fact incompatible, it is impossible that God's foreknowledge, which foresees all things, coexists[1] with something's happening through free choice. If that impossibility can be shown not to exist, however, the apparent incompatibility is completely eliminated. Let us therefore suppose that both divine foreknowledge (which seems to imply that all future things are necessary) and free choice (by which, supposedly, many things come about without any necessity) exist, and see whether it is impossible that they coexist. If it is impossible, something else that is impossible will result from it. (For what is impossible is something such that, if one assumes it, something else impossible follows.) Now if some future thing is going to be without necessity, God foreknows it, since he foreknows all future things. But what God foreknows is, necessarily, going to be just as he foreknows it. Therefore, it is necessary that some future thing is going to be without necessity. So to anyone who understands this correctly, the foreknowledge that entails necessity does not in any way appear to be incompatible with the freedom of choice that eliminates necessity: for it is necessary that what God foreknows is going to be, and God foreknows that something is going to be without any necessity.

But you will reply: "You are still not eliminating the necessity either that I sin or that I do not sin. After all, God foreknows that I will sin, or else that I will not sin, and so it is necessary that I sin, if in fact I do sin, or else it is necessary that I do not sin, if in fact I do not sin." To this I reply that you should not say, "God foreknows that I will sin or not sin, period," but rather, "God foreknows that I will sin or not sin without necessity." That way it follows that whether you

---

1. "coexists": *simul esse*. Ordinarily one would translate the Latin as "exists at the same time," but Anselm will argue that strictly speaking God's foreknowledge does not exist at any time: it is timelessly eternal.

sin or do not sin, either outcome will happen without necessity, since God foreknows that what will happen is going to come about without necessity. So do you see that it is not impossible for God's foreknowledge, which is the basis for our saying that the future things God foreknows are necessary, to coexist with free choice, through which many things come about without necessity? For if it is impossible, something impossible follows from it. But nothing impossible follows from this.

Perhaps you will say, "Your claim that it is necessary that I will sin or not sin without necessity, because God foreknows this, does not assuage my worries about this necessity. Necessity seems to imply compulsion or constraint. So if it is necessary that I sin through my will, I understand this as meaning that I am compelled by some hidden power to will to sin; and if I do not sin, that I am constrained from willing to sin. For that reason it seems to me that if I sin, I sin by necessity, and if I do not sin, it is by necessity that I do not sin."

1.2   I say that it is important to realize that we often say something is necessary that is not compelled by any power, and that something is necessarily not the case that is not eliminated by any constraint. For example, we say that it is necessary for God to be immortal and that it is necessary for God not to be unjust. This is not because there is some power that compels God to be immortal or prevents him from being unjust, but because nothing can bring it about that he is not immortal or that he is unjust. And so, when I say, "It is necessary that you will sin or not sin by your will alone, just as God foreknows," this should not be taken to mean that something is preventing your will from being what it will not be or compelling your will to be what it will be. For indeed God, who foresees that something is going to be from the will alone, foreknows the very fact that the will is not compelled or constrained by any other thing, and thus that what is done by the will is done freely. Therefore, I think that if these matters are considered attentively, there is no inconsistency that would prevent God's foreknowledge from coexisting with freedom of choice.

Moreover, if one carefully considers the meaning of the word, merely by saying that something is foreknown, one is stating that it is going to be. For only what is going to be is foreknown, since only what is true can be known. So when I say that if God foreknows something, it is necessary that it is going to be, that is the same as saying that if it will be, it will be by necessity. But that necessity does not compel or constrain anything to be or not to be. It is because something is posited as existing that its existence is said to be necessary, and because something is posited as not existing that its non-existence is said to be necessary: not because necessity compels or constrains it to be or not to be. For when I say, "If it will be, it will be by necessity," the necessity here does not precede the positing of the thing, but follows from it. The same is true of "What will be, will be by necessity." For this necessity simply means that what will be cannot at the same time not be.

But it is equally true that something was and is and will be not from necessity, and that it is necessary that everything that was was, that everything that is is, and that everything that will be will be. For a thing's being past is not the same as a past thing's being past, and a thing's being present is not the same as a present thing's being present, and a thing's being future is not the same as a future thing's being future—just as a thing's being white is not the same as a white thing's being white. After all, a board is not always necessarily white, since before it was made white, it was able not to be made white; and once it is white, it can be made not-white. And yet it is always necessary that a white board be white, since neither before it is white nor after it is white can it be made to be both white and not-white at the same time. Similarly, a thing is not by necessity present, since before it was present, it was possible that it not become present; and once it is present, it can become not-present. Yet it is necessary that a present thing always be present, since neither before it is present nor after it is present can it be both present and not-present at the same time. In the same way, a given thing (say, an action) is not by necessity something future, since before it is, things can turn out in such a way that it is not going to be in the future. Yet it is necessary that what will be in the future will be in the future, since what is future cannot at the same time not be future. And similar things are true about what is past. A given thing is not by necessity past, since before it was, it was possible for it not to be; but it is necessary that what is past is always past, since what is past cannot at the same time not be past. But a past thing is different in one respect from a present or future thing: it can never come about that something that is past becomes not-past, in the way that something that is present can become not-present, and something that is not by necessity future can become not-future.

And so when a future thing is said to be future, what is said is necessary, since a future thing is never not-future—as happens whenever we say of any x that it is x.[2] For when we say "Every human being is a human being" or "If he is a human being, he is a human being" or "Every white thing is white" or "If it is white, it is white," what is said is necessary, since something cannot be and not be at the same time. In fact, if it is not necessary that every future thing be future, some future thing is not future, which is impossible. Therefore, by necessity every future thing is future, and by necessity if something is future, it is future; for 'future' is being said of something future. But this is by subsequent necessity, which does not compel anything to be.

1.3   But when it is said that some thing is going to be in the future, the thing is not always by necessity, even though it is going to be in the future. For if I say "Tomorrow there will be a rebellion among the people," the rebellion will

---

2. Literally, "as often as we say the same of the same."

nevertheless not be by necessity. For before the rebellion takes place, it is possible for things to turn out such that it does not take place, even though it will in fact take place. Yet it is sometimes the case that a thing that is said to be future is by necessity: for example, if I say "Tomorrow there will be a sunrise." Therefore, if I say with necessity that some future thing is future, this is either in the way in which tomorrow's future rebellion is by necessity future or else in the way in which tomorrow's future sunrise is by necessity future. But the rebellion, which will not be by necessity, is said to be future only by subsequent necessity, because this is a case of saying of a *future* thing that it is future. For if tomorrow's rebellion is future, it is by necessity future. Tomorrow's sunrise, by contrast, is understood to be future in accordance with *two* necessities: both antecedent necessity, which brings it about that a thing exists (for the fact that its future existence is necessary accounts for why it will exist), and subsequent necessity, which does not compel anything to be (for the fact that it is future is what accounts for its being future by necessity). Hence, when we say that it is necessary that what God foreknows to be future is future, we are not always claiming that the thing is by necessity future, but that a future thing is by necessity future. After all, it cannot be future and not future at the same time. If we say simply "If God foreknows something," without adding 'future,' the meaning is the same, since 'foreknow' implies 'future.' To foreknow is simply to know something future, and so if God foreknows something, it must be future. Therefore, it does not always follow from God's foreknowledge that a thing is by necessity future, since although God does foreknow all future things, he does not foreknow all future things by necessity; instead, he foreknows some future things on the basis of the free will of a rational creature.

Moreover, it is important to note that, just as it is not necessary for God to will what he wills, so too it is not necessary in many instances for human beings to will what they will. And just as it is necessary that whatever God wills is the case, so too it is necessary that whatever human beings will is the case—in those matters that God has made subject to human will, so that if they will something, it comes about, and if they do not will it, it does not come about. For since what God wills cannot not be, it follows that when God wills that a human will not be compelled or constrained by any necessity to will or not to will, and that its effect follow the will, it is necessary that the human will is free and that what it wills is the case. In such a case, therefore, it is true that a sinful deed that a human being wills to perform comes about by necessity, even though he does not will by necessity. Now if you ask whether the sin of the will itself, when it sins by willing, is by necessity, the right response is that just as the will does not will by necessity, so also there is not a sin on the part of the will by necessity. Nor does that will act by necessity— for if it did not will spontaneously,* it would not be acting—even though, as I just said above, it is necessary that what it does comes about. For given that in this case its sinning is nothing other than its willing what it ought not, the will's sin is not necessary in just the same way that its willing is not necessary. Nonetheless, it is true that if a human being wills to sin, it is necessary that he sins—but in accordance with the necessity that I said above neither compels nor constrains.

And so a free will (1) is able not to will what it wills but also (2) is unable not to will what it wills and (3) necessarily wills what it wills. For, given that it is free, (1) before it wills, it is able not to will. But (2) once it is willing, it is unable not to will; rather, (3) its willing is necessary, since it is impossible for it both to will and not to will the same thing at the same time. By contrast, since it has been granted to the will that what it wills is the case and what it does not will is not the case, the will's deed is voluntary or spontaneous, since it is brought about by a spontaneous will, and yet it is necessary in two ways: both because it is compelled by the will to come about, and because what comes about cannot at the same time not come about. But the freedom of the will is what brings about these two necessities, since before they exist, the will can avoid them. God, who knows all and only truth, sees all these things as either spontaneous or necessary; and as he sees them, so they are.

On this basis it is clear that there is no incompatibility at all between God's foreknowing all things and there being many things that are done by free will. Things that are done by free will are such that before they are, it can turn out that they never are; and yet they are in a certain sense by necessity—a necessity that, as I have said, derives from free will.

1.4   There is another way to see that not everything God foreknows is by necessity, but rather that some things come about through the freedom of the will. For when God wills or does something—whether we say this according to the unchangeable present of eternity in which nothing is past or future, but all things are at once without any motion (as when we say, not that he has willed or is going to will, or has done or is going to do, but simply that he wills or does), or according to time (as when we say that he is going to will or is going to do what we know he has not yet done)—it cannot be denied that he knows what he wills and does, or that he foreknows what he is going to will and is going to do. So if God's knowing or foreknowing imposes necessity on all the things he knows or foreknows, it follows that there is nothing he does or wills freely, whether according to eternity or according to some time, but that he wills and does all things by necessity. Given that it is absurd even to entertain such a thought, it is not true that whatever God knows or foreknows to be is necessarily the case, or that whatever God knows or foreknows not to be is necessarily not the case. So there is nothing to prevent his knowing or foreknowing that something in our wills and actions is done or will exist through free choice, so that even though it is necessary for what he knows or foreknows to exist, there are many things that exist not by any necessity, but instead by free will, as I showed above.

Indeed, why would it be surprising that in this way something is a result of freedom and is also by necessity, given that there are many things that take on opposite descriptions when considered in different ways? After all, what could be more opposite than going toward and going away from? And yet we see that when someone goes from one place to another, the very same going is both a going toward and a going away from; he goes away from one place and goes toward another place. Similarly, suppose we observe the sun beneath a certain point of the heavens, as it hastens toward this same point while always illuminating the heavens. We see that the place from which it is drawing away is the same place to which it is approaching, and it unceasingly draws near the very place from which it is at the same time departing. It is also evident to those who understand the sun's course that if we observe the heavens, the sun always moves from west to east; but if we instead pay attention to the earth, the sun always moves from east to west. And thus the sun always moves opposite to the firmament, though it also moves with the firmament, though more slowly; and the same movement is observed in the case of all the planets. In this way, then, no inconsistency arises if (in keeping with the arguments given above) we say that something is future by necessity, given that it is future, and also that the very same thing is not compelled by any necessity to be future—except by that necessity that is brought about by free will, as I said above.

1.5   Now someone might try to use what Job says to God about human beings— "You have fixed their limits, which cannot be transgressed"[3]—to argue that no one has ever been able to hasten or delay the day of his death, even though we might think that someone acts by free will in a way that brings about his own death. But that is no objection to what we said above. For because God does not err and sees nothing but truth, whether that truth comes about by freedom or by necessity, something is said to be immutably fixed with regard to him that, with regard to human beings, is subject to change up until it happens. This is also the sort of thing the Apostle Paul says concerning those who "according to God's purpose"[4] are "called to be saints":[5] "Those whom he foreknew, he also predestined to be conformed to the image of his Son, that he might be the firstborn among many brothers. Now those whom he predestined, he also called. And those whom he called, he also justified. Now those whom he justified, he also glorified."[6] Indeed, this purpose according to which they are called to be saints is immutable in eternity, in which there is neither past nor future but only present. But in the human beings themselves it is sometimes mutable because of freedom of choice. For in eternity it is not the case that something was or will be, but only that it is; nonetheless—and without any inconsistency—in time something was or will be. And in just the

---

3. Job 14:5.

4. Romans 8:28.

5. Romans 1:7.

6. Romans 8:29–30.

same way, something that in eternity cannot be changed is proved, without any inconsistency, to be changeable in time until it exists, thanks to free will. Now although in eternity there is only a present, it is not a temporal present like ours, but an eternal* present that encompasses all times. Just as every place, and those things that are in any place, are contained in the present time, so too every time, and those things that are at any time, are enclosed all at once in the eternal present. So even though the Apostle says that God "foreknew," "predestined," "called," "justified," and "glorified" his saints, none of these is earlier or later in God; rather, they are to be understood as existing all at once in the eternal present. For his eternity does have its "all at once," which contains all those things that exist together in one place or one time, as well as all those that exist in diverse places or times.

And in order to make it clear that he was not using those verbs with a temporal signification, the Apostle used past-tense verbs to describe things that are still in the future. For God has not yet in time "called," "justified," or "glorified" those whom he foreknew who have yet to be born. Thus we can see that the Apostle used past-tense verbs for lack of a verb tense that signifies the eternal present, because things that are temporally past are completely immutable, much as the eternal present is. In fact, in this respect temporally past things are more like things in the eternal present than temporally present things are, since things in the eternal present can never not be present, just as temporally past things can never not be past, whereas all temporally present things that pass away come to be not present.

It is in this way, therefore, that Holy Scripture speaks of things that come about by free choice as necessary. It is speaking in terms of eternity, in which everything that is true, and only what is true, is unchangeably present. It is not speaking in terms of time, in which our wills and our actions do not always exist—and just as, so long as they do not exist, it is not necessary that they exist, so too it is often not necessary that they ever exist. For example, I am not always writing or willing to write; and just as, while I am not writing or willing to write, it is not necessary that I write or will to write, so too it is in no way necessary that I ever write or will to write.

Now since we have discerned that a thing exists differently in time from how it exists in eternity, so that it is sometimes true that something does not exist in time that does exist in eternity, and that its existence is past in time but not past in eternity or future in time but not future in eternity, there does not seem to be any reason to deny that in the same way something can be mutable in time that is immutable in eternity. Indeed, there is no more opposition between being mutable in time and being immutable in eternity than there is between not existing at a given time and always existing in eternity, or between having existed or being yet to exist in time and not having existed or not being yet to exist in eternity. For I am not saying that something never exists in time that always exists in eternity, but merely that it does not exist at some time. For example, I am not saying that what I will do tomorrow—which always exists in eternity—does not exist at any time; I am merely denying that it exists today. And when we deny that something was or will be in eternity that was or will be in time, we are not claiming that what was or will be in time does not exist in any way in eternity. We are simply saying that it does not exist in eternity in a past or future way; rather, it exists there unceasingly in its own present way. And there does not appear to be any danger of inconsistency in these statements. In this way, then, there is no contradiction involved in saying that something is mutable in time until it exists but abides immutably in eternity—not before it exists or after it exists, but unceasingly, because nothing exists in eternity according to time. For the very fact that something exists temporally, and that before it exists it is able not to exist, exists there eternally, as I have already said. I think it is sufficiently clear from what I have said that God's foreknowledge is in no way incompatible with free choice. The power of eternity, which encloses every time and everything that exists at any time, accomplishes this.

1.6   But since we do not have free choice in all matters, it is important to investigate the extent and the nature of that freedom of choice that we believe human beings always possess, and what choice itself is. For choice is not the same thing as the freedom by which choice is called free. We talk about freedom and choice in many contexts. For example, we say that someone has the freedom either to speak or to keep silent, and that it is up to his choice which of the two he wills. And we often speak in similar ways of freedom and choice that are not always present or are not necessary for the salvation of our souls. The only question at issue now, however, concerns that choice and that freedom without which human beings cannot be saved, once they are able to make use of them. For many people complain bitterly because they think free choice has no influence on salvation or damnation and that the only thing that matters is the necessity arising from God's foreknowledge. Therefore, since human beings, once they have reached the age of reason, are not saved apart from their own justice, we need to examine the choice and the freedom that are under discussion here, because they are the seat of justice. We must first explain justice, and then freedom and choice.

Now any justice, be it great or small, is rectitude of will preserved for its own sake. And the freedom at issue here is the power to preserve rectitude of will for the sake of that rectitude itself. I take myself to have established these definitions by evident arguments, the former in the treatise I composed *On Truth* and the latter in the one I published *On Freedom [of Choice]*. In the latter I also showed how this freedom exists naturally and inseparably in human beings, even though they do not always employ it, and that it is so powerful that nothing can take the aforesaid rectitude, that is, justice, away from a human being who has it, so long as he wills to employ it. Now justice is not natural. Rather, in the beginning it was separable both from the angels in heaven and from human beings in paradise; and it remains separable in this life from those who have it—not, however, by necessity, but by their own wills. But since it has been established that the justice by which someone is just is the rectitude of will of which I have spoken, and that rectitude is in someone only when he wills what God wills him to will, it is evident that God cannot take that rectitude away from someone against that person's will, since God cannot will this. But neither can he will for someone who has it to abandon it unwillingly, because of some necessity, for that would mean God was willing for someone not to will what God wills for him to will, which is impossible. It follows, therefore, that God wills that an upright will be free for the purpose of willing rightly and preserving that very rectitude; and when a will has the power to do what it wills, it acts freely in doing what it does. And from this we can see quite clearly that it is possible for a will and its action to be free, consistently with God's foreknowledge, as was shown above.

Let us now offer an example of an upright (that is, a just) will, freedom of choice, and choice itself, and how an upright will is tempted to abandon rectitude, and how it preserves rectitude by free choice. Suppose someone has a settled intention to preserve truth, since he understands that it is right to love the truth. Such a person already has an upright will and rectitude of will. But the will is one thing, and the rectitude by which it is upright is another. Now suppose someone else comes up to him and threatens him with death unless he tells a lie. We see now that it is up to his choice whether he will abandon life for the sake of rectitude of will or abandon rectitude of will for the sake of life. This choice, which can also be called a judgment, is free, because the reason by which he understands rectitude teaches that this rectitude ought always to be preserved out of love for that rectitude itself, and that whatever might be offered as an inducement to abandon rectitude should be held in contempt, and because it is up to his will either to reject or to choose something in accordance with his reason's understanding. For will and reason were given to rational creatures principally for this purpose. So this person's voluntary choice to abandon rectitude is not compelled by any necessity, even though he is assaulted by the anguish of death. For although it is necessary that he give up either life or rectitude, there is no necessity that determines which he will preserve and which he will abandon. His will alone determines what he will hold on to in this case; and where only the will's selection holds sway, the power of necessity does nothing. And since there is no necessity for him to abandon the rectitude of will that he possesses, it is clear that he does not lack freedom, the power to preserve rectitude. For this power is always free. For this is the freedom that I have said is the power to preserve rectitude of will for the sake of that rectitude itself. It is in virtue of this freedom that both the choice and the will of a rational nature are said to be free.

1.7 Given that we believe that God foreknows or knows all things, it remains for us to consider whether God's knowledge is from things or things have their being from his knowledge. For if God has his knowledge from things, it follows that things are prior to God's knowledge and thus are not from God, since they cannot be from God unless they are from his knowledge. On the other hand, if everything that exists has its being from God's knowledge, God is the culprit and instigator in all evil deeds, and therefore he does not act justly in punishing the wicked—a conclusion we cannot support.

But in fact this question can be readily answered once we realize that the good that is justice is genuinely something, whereas the evil that is injustice lacks existence altogether. I showed this quite clearly in my treatise *On the Fall of the Devil* and in the short work that I entitled *On the Virginal Conception, and On Original Sin*. For injustice is not a quality or an action or any being; it is merely the lack of the justice that ought to be present, and its only place is in the will where justice ought to be. It is in virtue of this just or unjust will that all rational natures and all their actions are called either just or unjust. Indeed, every quality and every action and whatever has any being is from God, from whom all justice and no injustice comes. So God brings about all things, whether they are brought about by a just or an unjust will—that is, both good and evil deeds. In the case of good deeds, he brings about both what they are and their being good, whereas in evil deeds he brings about what they are, but not their being evil. In every case, for a thing to be just or good is for that thing to be something; but in no case does a thing's being unjust or bad consist in its being something. After all, to be good or just is to have justice, and having justice is something, whereas to be bad or unjust is to lack the justice that something ought to have, and lacking justice is not something. So justice is something and injustice is nothing, as I have said.

But there is another good, which is called 'advantage,' the opposite of which is the evil that we call 'affliction.' This evil is in some cases nothing, as is true of blindness; but in some cases it is something, as is true of pain. When this evil is something, we do not deny that God brings it about, since he "brings about peace and creates evil,"[7] as we read. For God himself creates afflictions by which he disciplines and purifies the just and punishes the unjust. So it is only with respect to the evil that is injustice, by which something is called unjust, that we are certain that evil is never something, and that in no case is a thing's being unjust its being something. And just as God does not bring about injustice, so too he does not bring it about that something is unjust. Nonetheless, he brings about all actions and all motions, since he brings about the things by which and from which and through which and in which they come about, and no thing has any power for willing or acting unless God gives it. Moreover, willing itself, which is sometimes just and sometimes unjust, is nothing other than employing the will and the power of willing that God gives. Insofar as it has being, it is good and is from God. When it exists rightly, it is good and just; when it does not exist rightly, it is bad and unjust solely in virtue of not existing rightly. Now existing rightly is

---

7. Isaiah 45:7.

something, and it is from God; not existing rightly is not something, and it is not from God. For when someone uses a sword or his tongue or the power of speaking, the sword or tongue or power of speaking is not one thing when it is used rightly but another when it is used wrongly; and in the same way, the will that we use for willing (just as we use reason for reasoning) is not one thing when someone uses it rightly and another when he uses it wrongly. When the will is just, it is neither more nor less what it essentially is than when it is unjust; and it is by the will that either a substance or an action is called just or unjust. And so in all good wills and good actions God brings about both what they essentially are and their being good, whereas in evil wills and evil actions God does not bring about their being evil, but only what they essentially are. For just as things have their essence from God alone, so too they have rectitude from God alone.

Now the absence of this rectitude of which I am speaking—the absence that is injustice—is found only in the will of a rational creature, which ought always to possess justice. Why, then, does a creature not always have the justice that it ought always to have? And how does God bring about good things entirely by his goodness but evil things entirely through the fault of human beings or the devil? And how does a human being do good things through his free choice with the help of grace but evil through the operation of his own will alone? And what part does God play in evil things, without being to blame for them, and what part do human beings play in good things, so that they deserve praise for them, in such a way that nevertheless the good things a human being does ought clearly to be imputed to God and the bad things to the human being? God will, I trust, grant that the answers will become clearer when we discuss grace and free choice. For the moment I will simply say that the evil angel lacks justice because he abandoned it and then was never given it back, whereas a human being lacks it because he cast it away in his first parents and then either was never given it back or received it and then rejected it.

I believe that, with the help of God's grace, we have shown that it is not impossible for God's foreknowledge to coexist with free choice, if one carefully examines what we have said, and that no insuperable objection can be raised.

Question 2: On predestination and free choice

2.1   So, placing our hope in the one who has guided us this far, let us now undertake to resolve the disharmony that appears to exist between predestination and free choice. As will become evident in what follows, we made a good deal of progress on this score in our earlier discussion.

Predestination seems to be the same thing as preordination or predetermination. So when God is said to predestine something, we understand this to mean that he preordains it: that is, he determines that it will happen in the future. But what God determines will happen in the future seems to happen by necessity; hence, it is necessary that whatever God predestines will happen. Therefore, if God predestines the good and bad actions that are done, nothing is done by free choice, but everything is a result of necessity. On the other hand, if he predestines only good actions, only good actions come about by necessity, and there is free choice only with respect to bad actions—which is completely absurd. So it is not only good actions that God predestines. Now if free choice does certain good deeds by which people become just apart from predestination, God does not predestine all the good deeds that make people just; hence, neither does God predestine the just themselves, who are just through the deeds of free choice. Therefore, God did not foreknow them, since "those whom he foreknew, he also predestined."[8] But it is false that God did not foreknow some good deeds or some just people. It is not therefore just any good deeds done by free choice alone that make people just, but only those that God predestines. Therefore, if God predestines all things, and whatever is predestined is by necessity, then given that nothing done by free choice comes about by necessity, it appears to follow that wherever predestination holds sway, free choice is nothing; or if we stipulate that there is free choice in some cases, predestination will disappear in those cases.

2.2   Before I answer the question, it is first important to see that predestination is not only of good things. We can also speak of predestination of bad things, in the same way that God is said to bring about the bad things that he does not in fact bring about, on the grounds that he permits them. For God is said to "harden"[9] someone when he does not soften him, and to "lead him into temptation"[10] when he does not set him free from temptation. So it is not inappropriate if we say in this sense that God predestines the wicked and their evil deeds when he does not rectify them and their evil deeds. But he is said to foreknow and predestine the good in a stricter sense, because in them he brings about both what they are and the fact that they are good, whereas in the evil he brings about only what they are essentially, not the fact that they are evil, as was said above.[11] One should also be aware that just as foreknowledge is not said properly* to be in God, neither is predestination, since for him nothing is either before or after, but all things are present to him at once.

2.3   Let us now investigate whether certain things that will happen through free choice can be predestined. Now to be sure, there is no room to doubt whether

---

8. Romans 8:29.

9. Exodus 4, 7–11, and 14, *passim*; Deuteronomy 2:30; Joshua 11:20; John 12:40; Romans 9:18.

10. Matthew 6:13; Luke 11:4.

11. In 1.7.

there is some discrepancy between God's foreknowledge and his predestination. On the contrary, as God foreknows, so too does he predestine. In the question on foreknowledge, we came to recognize quite clearly that certain future things that will be done through free choice are foreknown, without any contradiction. Hence, evident truth and reason teach that certain future things that will be done through free choice are likewise predestined, without any inconsistency. For God neither foreknows nor predestines any future just person by necessity. After all, someone who does not preserve justice by free will does not have justice. So although things that are foreknown and things that are predestined necessarily take place, nonetheless some things that are predestined and foreknown do not come about by that necessity that precedes a thing and brings it about, but by the necessity that follows a thing, as we said above. Although God predestines these things, he does not bring them about by compelling or restraining the will, but by leaving the will in its own power. But although the will does employ its own power, it does not bring about anything that God does not bring about: in the case of good things, by his grace; in the case of bad things, not by his own fault but by the fault of the will. This will become clearer when we discuss grace, as we have promised to do. Now there is no mistake in foreknowledge; God foreknows what is true in just the way in which it will be, whether necessary or spontaneous. In the same way, there is no change in predestination; God predestines in just the way something is in his foreknowledge. And just as what is foreknown is immutable in eternity even though in time it is subject to change before it exists, this is true too of everything included in God's predestination.

So if one attends carefully to what we have said, it is clear that predestination does not rule out free choice and free choice is not opposed to predestination, since all the considerations by which we showed that free choice is not incompatible with foreknowledge equally show that free choice is compatible with predestination. Therefore, whenever something occurs through the action of a spontaneous will, as when someone wrongs another and then is killed by him in retaliation, those who complain, "This was foreknown and predestined by God and so it was done by necessity and could not have turned out otherwise," are without justification. Indeed, neither the one who angered the other by wronging him, nor the one who took revenge, acted by necessity. Each acted by his will alone. For neither of them would have done what he in fact did if he had not willed spontaneously.

Question 3: On grace and free choice

3.1 It now remains to investigate grace and free choice, with the help of that same grace. This question arises because in some places Holy Scripture speaks in such a way that it seems free choice is unavailing for salvation and grace does everything, whereas in other places it speaks as if the whole of our salvation rests on our own free will. Concerning grace the Lord says, "Without me you can do nothing"[12] and "No one comes to me unless my Father draws him."[13] And the Apostle Paul says, "What do you have that you have not received?"[14] And he says of God, "He has mercy on whom he wills, and he hardens whom he wills."[15] And "It is not of the one who wills or of the one who runs, but of God who has mercy."[16] And we find many other passages that seem to attribute our good works and our salvation to grace alone, apart from free choice. Also, many claim to prove by experience that human beings are never empowered with free choice of any kind. They observe that too many people to count put forth an enormous effort of body and mind but make no progress at all because they are weighed down by some difficulty, or indeed impossibility—or else they do make great progress but then suddenly fall away with no hope of recovery.

On the other hand, that very same Scripture shows in the following way that we do have free choice. God says through Isaiah, "If you are willing and listen to me, you will eat the good things of the land."[17] And David says, "Who is the one who wills life, who loves to see good days? Restrain your tongue from evil, and let not your lips speak deceit. Turn away from evil and do good."[18] And the Lord says in the Gospel, "Come to me, all you who labor and are burdened, and I will refresh you. Take my yoke upon you and learn from me, for I am gentle and lowly of heart, and you will find rest for your souls."[19] And there are many, indeed countless, other passages that seem to stimulate free choice to act rightly and reproach it for failing to heed admonitions. Divine authority would by no means do this if it did not recognize some freedom of will in human beings. And there would be no basis on which God could justly repay both the good and the wicked according to their deserts if no one did anything good or wicked through free choice.

Therefore, since we find some statements in Holy Scripture that appear to speak in favor of grace alone, and others that are thought to uphold free choice alone apart from grace, there have been certain arrogant people who have thought the whole efficacy of the virtues rests in freedom of choice alone, and there are many in our own day who have given up all hope that free choice is anything at all. And so our aim in this question is to show that free choice coexists with grace and works

---

12. John 15:5.

13. John 6:44.

14. 1 Corinthians 4:7. Much of *On the Fall of the Devil* is devoted to understanding the implications of Paul's question.

15. Romans 9:18.

16. Romans 9:16.

17. Isaiah 1:19.

18. Psalm 34:12–14 (33:13–15).

19. Matthew 11:28–29.

together with it in many cases, just as we have already found that free choice is compatible with foreknowledge and predestination.

3.2   It is important to keep in mind that, as I said above, this question concerns only the free choice without which no one merits salvation once he has attained the age of reason; and similarly, it concerns only the grace without which no human being is saved.[20] For every creature exists by grace, since every creature was created by grace; and by his grace God gives many good things in this life without which a human being can be saved. To be sure, in infants who die baptized before they can make use of their free choice, the compatibility that we are looking for does not appear, since in them grace alone brings about their salvation without their free choice. It is, after all, by grace that others are granted the will to come to the assistance of these children by their own faith. So the compatibility of grace and free choice that we are exploring needs to be shown only in the case of those who have attained the age of reason, since our present question is applicable only to them.

Now there is no doubt that whoever among them is saved is saved on account of justice. For it is to the just that the promise of eternal life is made, since "the just will live forever, and their reward is with the Lord."[21] And sacred authority shows in many places that justice is rectitude of will. One example will suffice. When David said, "The Lord will not desert his people, and he will not abandon his heritage, until justice is transformed into judgment,"[22] in order to teach us what justice is, he added this question: "And who are in accord with justice?" He replies, "All those who are upright in heart":[23] that is, those who are upright in will. For although we believe and understand with our heart just as we will with our heart, the Holy Spirit does not judge someone to have an upright heart if he believes or understands rightly but does not will rightly; for such a person is not using his rectitude of faith and understanding for the purpose for which believing rightly and understanding rightly were given to the rational creature, namely, for willing rightly. For that matter, we should not even say that someone has an upright understanding if he does not will rightly in accordance with it; and we should not say that someone has anything other than a dead faith if he does not will to act rightly in accordance with his faith, since faith is given for this purpose.[24] We are therefore correct to understand David as meaning "upright in will" when he says "upright in heart." But to make sure that no one thinks the divine authority calls someone just or upright when he upholds rectitude of will only for the sake of something else, we say that justice is rectitude of will preserved for its own

---

20. Reading *salvatur* for *salvator*.

21. Wisdom 5:16.

22. Psalm 94:14–15 (93:14–15).

23. Psalm 94:15 (93:15).

24. Cf. *Monologion,* Chapter 78.

sake. For someone who preserves rectitude of will only for the sake of something else does not love rectitude of will, but instead loves that for the sake of which he preserves rectitude of will. And for that reason he does not deserve to be called just, and such rectitude does not deserve the name of justice.

When we were discussing foreknowledge and free choice, we gave an example that showed that the rectitude I call justice can coexist with free choice. That example allows us to understand quite readily that the same holds true in many other cases. Therefore, if we can show that no creature can attain this rectitude except through grace, the harmony between grace and free choice in human salvation that we are seeking will be evident.

3.3   Now there is no doubt that a will wills rightly only because it is upright. Vision is not acute because it sees acutely; rather, it sees acutely because it is acute. And in the same way, a will is not upright because it wills rightly; rather, it wills rightly because it is upright. And when it wills this rectitude, it undoubtedly is willing rightly. Therefore, it wills rectitude only because it is upright. But a will's being upright is the same thing as its having rectitude. So it is clear that it wills rectitude only because it has rectitude. I do not deny that an upright will wills rectitude that it does not yet have, when it wills greater rectitude than it has. But I do say that it cannot will any rectitude at all if it does not have rectitude in virtue of which it wills rectitude.

Let us now examine whether anyone who does not have this rectitude can in some way acquire it from himself. Certainly he cannot acquire it from himself except by either willing or not willing. Now no one can acquire rectitude from himself by willing, since he cannot will it if he does not have it. And no one with any sense is going to suppose that someone who does not have rectitude of will can attain it on his own by not willing. So there is no way a creature can have it from himself. But neither can a creature have it from another creature. For a creature cannot save another creature; and in the same way, a creature cannot give another creature something on the basis of which it deserves to be saved. And so it follows that no creature has this rectitude of will I have been talking about except through God's grace. We have, however, shown that this rectitude can be preserved through free choice, as I said above. Therefore, thanks to God's generosity, we have found that his grace for saving human beings is compatible with free choice. Thus, his grace alone can save a person whose free choice does nothing, as happens with infants; and in those who have reached understanding his grace always assists their natural free choice, which without grace is powerless to attain salvation, by giving their wills the rectitude that they preserve through free choice.

And even if God does not give grace to everyone (for "He has mercy on whom he wills and hardens whom he wills"[25]), he nonetheless does not give it to anyone

---

25. Romans 9:18.

on the basis of some preceding merit, since "Who has given first to God, so that God will repay him?"[26] If, however, the will, by preserving through free choice what it has received, merits an increase of the justice it has received or power for a good will or some reward, these are all fruits of the first grace and "grace for grace."[27] So it should all be attributed to grace, since "it is not of the one who wills" that he wills "or of the one who runs" that he runs, "but of God who has mercy."[28] For these words are addressed to all but God alone: "What do you have that you have not received? And if you have received, why do you boast as if you had not received?"[29]

3.4   I take myself to have shown in my treatise *On Freedom of Choice* how the freedom of a will that holds on to the rectitude it has received is not overwhelmed by some necessity that causes it to abandon rectitude; rather, it is assailed by some difficulty to which it yields willingly, not unwillingly. But it will be useful to say something about the ways in which grace assists free choice in preserving rectitude once it has been received, although I will not be able to list all of them, since grace helps in so many ways.

Certainly no one preserves this rectitude that has been received otherwise than by willing it. And no one can will it unless he has it. But it is quite impossible for anyone to have it otherwise than by grace. Therefore, just as no one receives rectitude unless grace comes first, no one preserves rectitude unless that same grace continues. So even though rectitude is preserved through free choice, the preserving of rectitude should not be attributed to free choice so much as it should be attributed to grace, since free choice has and preserves rectitude only through prevenient and subsequent grace. Now grace follows upon its previous gift in such a way that, whether the grace be great or small, it never ceases to give that gift unless free choice wills something else and thereby abandons the rectitude it has received. For this rectitude never ceases to be present in the will unless the will wills something else that is incompatible with rectitude. For example, someone receives the rectitude of willing sobriety and then throws it away by willing immoderate pleasure from drinking. When he does this, it is by his own will, and therefore by his own fault, that he loses the grace he had received. Grace also helps free choice when it is under pressure to abandon the rectitude it has received. Grace helps by mitigating or altogether removing the power of the temptation that assails free choice, or by increasing the felt strength of rectitude[30] itself. And finally, since

26. Romans 11:35.

27. John 1:16.

28. Romans 9:16.

29. 1 Corinthians 4:7.

30. "by increasing the felt strength of rectitude": *augendo affectum eiusdem rectitudinis*. This could mean either increasing the feeling of rectitude or increasing the love of rectitude, but

all things are at God's disposal, whatever happens to a human being that helps free choice receive or preserve this rectitude of which I am speaking should be attributed entirely to grace.

I have said that every instance of justice is rectitude of will preserved for its own sake. From this it follows that everyone who has this rectitude has justice and is just (since everyone who has justice is just). But I do not hold that eternal life is promised to all the just; it is promised only to those who are just without any injustice. For they are the ones who are properly and without qualification called "just" and "upright in heart." Some people, after all, are just in one respect and unjust in another: for example, someone who is chaste but envious. The blessedness of the just is not promised to such people, for just as true blessedness is without any shortcoming, so too it is granted only to those who are just without any injustice. For since the blessedness that is promised to the just will be a likeness to the angels of God,[31] it follows that just as there is no injustice in the good angels, so too no one with any injustice will have fellowship with them. Now it is not part of our aim here to show how a human being comes to be free from all injustice, but we do know that this is possible for a Christian through holy efforts and through God's grace.

3.5   If one gives careful consideration to what I have said, it becomes quite clear that when Holy Scripture says something in favor of grace, it is not completely setting aside free choice; nor, when it speaks in favor of free choice, is it excluding grace—as if grace alone or free choice alone were sufficient for human salvation, as those who raise this question suppose. And in fact we should understand these divine words as meaning that neither grace alone nor free choice alone accomplishes human salvation, except in the case of infants, as I have explained.

Indeed, when the Lord says, "Without me you can do nothing,"[32] he does not mean "Your free choice is powerless" but "Your free choice can accomplish nothing without my grace." And the verse, "It is not of the one who wills or of the one who runs, but of God who has mercy,"[33] does not say that free choice accomplishes nothing at all in the one who wills or runs; what it means is that the fact that the person wills or runs should be attributed to grace and not to free choice. (For we should understand this verse to be saying that it is not of the one who wills *that he wills* or of the one who runs *that he runs*.) Suppose someone gives clothing to a person who is naked, to whom he does not owe anything and who cannot provide himself with any garment. Even though the person who was naked has the power

---

the former seems to give a better parallel to "mitigating or altogether removing the power of the temptation."

31. Cf. Matthew 22:3, Luke 20:36.

32. John 15:5.

33. Romans 9:16.

to use or not use the clothing he has been given, still, if he does use it, the fact that he is clothed should not be attributed to him but to the one who gave him the clothing. So we could say something like this: "It is not of the one who is clothed that he is clothed, but of the one who has mercy," that is, of the one who gave him the clothing. And this would be even more appropriate to say if the one who gave the clothing had also given the power to preserve and use the clothing—as God, when he gives a human being this much-discussed rectitude, also gives him the power to preserve and use it, since he has already given free choice for preserving and using rectitude. On the other hand, if the person who was naked, and to whom nothing was owed, were not given clothing or threw away the clothing that he had been given, his nakedness would be attributed to him alone. Thus, when God grants willing and running to someone who was conceived and born in sin,[34] to whom he owes nothing but punishment, "it is not of the one who wills or of the one who runs, but of God who has mercy"; and it is not of God, but of the one who does not receive this grace, or who receives it but then spurns it, that he persists in his hardness and sinfulness.

We should adopt the same interpretation of other passages in which Scripture speaks in favor of grace: that is, that they do not eliminate free choice. Similarly, when God's word speaks in such a way that it appears to ascribe human salvation to free choice alone, we are not to understand that as separate from grace in any way. By way of analogy, natural intercourse does not produce offspring without a father, nor does it do so except through a mother; yet we do not understand this to deny a role to either the father or the mother in the generation of offspring. In the same way, grace and free choice are not in conflict; they come together to justify and save human beings.

3.6   Still, in relation to the passages in which Scripture seems to urge free choice to will and act rightly, one might ask why it urges human beings to act rightly— and why it blames them when they do not obey—given that no one can possess or receive such rectitude unless grace gives it. Consider how the earth, without any effort on our part, brings forth countless plants and trees that do nothing to nourish human nature, or even kill us, whereas those that are most necessary to sustain our lives require tremendous effort and someone to cultivate them, and they do not grow without seeds. In the same way, human hearts require no teaching or effort in order to sprout, effortlessly, thoughts and wills that are in no way useful for salvation or are actually harmful; but it is only through seeds of the proper sort and with diligent cultivation that they conceive and produce the thoughts and wills without which we do not make progress toward the soul's salvation. This is why the Apostle calls those who benefit from this work of cultivation "God's husbandry."[35]

---

34. Psalm 51:5 (50:7).
35. 1 Corinthians 3:9.

The seed of this husbandry is the word of God—not, indeed, the word, but the meaning that is perceived through the word. For a mere sound, without meaning, establishes nothing in the heart.

And it is not only the meaning of the word of God that is a seed of right willing; so too is every meaning or understanding of rectitude that the human mind conceives through hearing or reading or through reason or in whatever other way. For no one can will anything but what he has first conceived in his heart. And willing to believe what ought to be believed is willing rightly. Therefore, no one can will this unless he knows what ought to be believed. That is why when the Apostle said, "Everyone who calls upon the name of the Lord will be saved," he added, "But how will they call upon him in whom they have not believed? And how will they believe in him of whom they have not heard? And how will they hear without a preacher? And how will there be preachers unless they are sent?"[36] And shortly afterwards, "Therefore, faith is from hearing, but hearing is through the word of Christ."[37] Now we should understand "faith is from hearing" to mean that faith is from what the mind conceives as a result of hearing: not that the mind's conception by itself brings about faith, but that faith cannot exist apart from that conception. Faith—one's believing what one hears—comes about when, through grace, rectitude of will is added to the conception. "Hearing is through the word of Christ," that is, through the word of those who preach Christ. Now there are no preachers unless they are sent, and their being sent is a matter of grace. So the preaching itself is a grace, since what proceeds from grace is itself a grace. And the hearing is a grace, and the understanding that comes from hearing is a grace, and rectitude of will is a grace. But the sending, the preaching, the hearing, the understanding: these are all nothing unless the will wills what the mind understands. And the will cannot do this unless it has received rectitude; for it wills rightly when it wills what it ought to. Thus, what the mind conceives as a result of hearing the word is the seed sown by the preacher, and rectitude is the "growth" given by God, without whom "neither the one who plants nor the one who waters is anything, but God who gives the growth."[38]

So just as God in the beginning miraculously made grain and other things that sprang forth from the earth to nourish human beings, without a cultivator or seeds, so too did he wondrously make the hearts of the prophets and apostles, and indeed the Gospels, fertile with the seeds of salvation, without any human teaching. From those seeds we take whatever we sow wholesomely in "God's husbandry" for the nourishment of our souls, just as what we grow for the nourishment of our bodies comes from the first seeds of the earth. For there is nothing we preach

---

36. Romans 10:13–15.

37. Romans 10:17.

38. 1 Corinthians 3:7.

that is useful for spiritual salvation but what the Holy Scriptures, miraculously made fertile by the Holy Spirit, have revealed or contain within themselves. Even if by reason we say something that we cannot point to explicitly in Scripture, or prove from what Scripture says, it is by Scripture that we know whether we should accept or reject it. For if it is a conclusion of straightforward reasoning and does not contradict anything in Scripture (since just as Scripture opposes no truth, so too it gives aid to no falsehood), we accept that conclusion on the authority of Scripture precisely because Scripture does not deny what is being said according to reason. But if Scripture is unmistakably opposed to our opinion, then even if our reasoning seems unassailable to us, we must not think it is supported by the truth in any way. And so it is in this way that Holy Scripture contains the authority of every conclusion of reason: by either explicitly affirming it or in no way denying it.

Let us now look at some examples of how the word is a seed. When those to whom it is said, "If you are willing and listen to me,"[39] hear those words, they understand and conceive what is meant by willing and listening: namely, obeying. For someone who listens but does not obey is said not to listen. But they cannot obey unless they are willing. Now to will to obey is to will rightly. And no one can will rightly unless he has rectitude of will, which no human being has except through grace. But rectitude in willing something is given only to one who has the understanding to will and understands what he ought to will. And so we see that the words "If you are willing and listen to me" are a seed that in no way bears fruit through itself, apart from the addition of rectitude, but that rectitude itself is not given except by means of seeds.

Similarly, when God says, "Turn to me,"[40] this is a seed that does not bear fruit as long as God does not turn a person's will so that it wills the turning that one thinks of when one hears the word "turn"; but without this seed no one can will to turn to God. It is also to those who have already turned that he says, "Turn to me": either so that they will turn to him all the more, or so that they will preserve their turning. But those who say, "Turn us, O God,"[41] have already turned to some extent, since they have an upright will when they will to be turned. They pray in virtue of what they have already received, in order that their turning might be increased, like those who were already believers and said, "Increase our faith."[42] It is as if both were saying, "Increase in us what you have already given us; bring

---

39. Isaiah 1:19, quoted above in 3.1.

40. Isaiah 45:22: "Turn to me and you will be saved, all the ends of the earth. For I am God and there is no other."

41. Psalm 85:4 (84:5): "Turn us, O God of our salvation, and cause your indignation against us to cease."

42. Luke 17:5. Luke records that it was the apostles who said this.

to completion what you have already begun." And what I have shown in these examples should be taken to apply in similar cases.

So just as the earth does not naturally produce without seeds those things that are especially necessary for the health of our body, so too the soil of the human heart does not bring forth the fruit of faith and justice without appropriate seeds. Yet just as our farmers continue to sow their fields in hope of an appreciable harvest even though God does not grant growth to every seed, so too God commands those who toil in his fields to sow his word in hope and with great earnestness, even though God does not cause all those seeds to bear fruit. We have shown, I think, that it is not pointless to urge people toward faith in Christ and toward those things that faith demands, even though they do not all respond to this encouragement.

3.7   I noted that one might also ask why those who do not accept God's word are blamed, given that they cannot accept it unless grace directs their wills. For the Lord says of the Holy Spirit, "He will convict[43] the world of sin . . . because they do not believe in me."[44] Although it is perhaps difficult to answer this question, I should not withhold the response that, by God's gift, I am able to make. It is important to keep in mind that an inability that derives from guilt does not excuse the one who has the inability, so long as the guilt remains. Hence, in the case of infants, in whom God requires of human nature the justice that it received in our first parents, together with the power to preserve it for all its descendants, their inability to have justice does not excuse them, since human nature fell into this inability through its own fault. Indeed, the very fact that it does not have what it cannot get back through its own power just is the inability to have justice into which human nature fell because it spontaneously abandoned what it had the power to preserve. Therefore, because human nature abandoned justice by sinning, the inability that human nature inflicted on itself by sinning is imputed to it as sin. And it is not only the inability to have justice that is imputed as sin to the unbaptized; so too is the inability to understand justice, for this too derives from sin. It is also reasonable for us to assert that the wasting away and corruption of the dignity, strength, and beauty with which human beings were first created is to be imputed to human nature as a fault. For it has thereby diminished the honor and praise of God as far as it was able, since the wisdom of an artisan is praised and proclaimed in accordance with the dignity of his work. Therefore, as much as human nature diminished or spoiled in itself the precious work of God, for which God himself was to be glorified, so much did it dishonor God by its own fault. And this is accounted so great a sin that it is wiped out only by the death of God.

Indeed, the sacred authority bears ample witness to the fact that the very motions or appetites to which we are subject (like brute animals) on account of the

---

43. This is the same word translated 'blame' in the preceding sentence.

44. John 16:8–9.

sin of Adam are themselves imputed to us as sin. These are the motions that the Apostle calls "flesh" and "concupiscence,"[45] and he makes it clear that he endures them against his will by saying, "What I hate, that I do"[46]—that is, I desire it unwillingly. In fact, when the Lord says of the bare motion of anger, without any overt deed or word, "He who is angry with his brother will be liable to judgment,"[47] he shows very clearly that it is no trivial fault from which so grave a condemnation, a sentence of death, follows. It is as if he were to say, "Someone who does what human beings ought not to do, and what they would not do unless they sinned, should be cut off from human beings." And when Paul says of those who unwillingly experience the flesh, that is, concupiscences, "There is no condemnation for those who are in Christ Jesus, who do not walk according to the flesh"[48]—that is, who do not consent to the flesh with their will—he is undoubtedly indicating that condemnation does follow for those who are not in Christ as often as they experience the flesh, even if they do not walk according to it. For human beings were made in such a way that they ought not to experience the flesh, just as we said of anger. So if anyone pays careful attention to what I have said, he will have no doubt that those who because of their own fault cannot accept the word of God are rightly to be blamed.

3.8   But for those to whom the grace of Christian faith has been given, just as the original injustice with which they are born is forgiven in baptism, so too all guilt for the inability and for all the corruption they have incurred on account of the sin of our first parents, by which God is dishonored, is excused. After baptism they are not blamed for any guilt that was in them before baptism, even though the corruption and appetites that are a punishment for sin are not instantaneously removed in baptism; and no transgression is imputed to them after baptism except what they have done by their own will. From this it is evident that the corruption and evils that were a punishment for sin and remain after baptism are not sins in themselves. For indeed only injustice is a sin in itself; those things that follow from injustice are regarded as sins on account of their cause, until the injustice is forgiven. After all, if they were sins in themselves, they would be destroyed in baptism, in which all sins are washed away by the blood of Christ. Moreover, if they were properly called sins, they would be sins even in brute animals; it is a consequence of sin that our nature bears these ills and is in that way like the brute animals.

There is something else, greatly to be feared, that can be discerned in the first sin of human nature. Because a human being is a "spirit that goes forth and does

---

45. Romans 7:7–8.
46. Romans 7:15.
47. Matthew 5:22.
48. Romans 8:1.

not return,"[49] once someone falls spontaneously (I am speaking now only of voluntary sins), he can in no way get back up unless he is lifted up by grace. Rather, unless he is restrained by God's mercy, by his own deserts he goes from sin to sin until he sinks into a bottomless pit of sins, an unimaginable depth, to the point that even what is good comes to be hateful and deadly to him. This is why the Lord says to the apostles, "If the world hates you, know that it hated me before you."[50] And the Apostle says, "We are a lovely fragrance before God . . . to some an odor of death unto death, but to others a fragrance of life unto life."[51] This is why it is said of God that "he has mercy on whom he wills and hardens whom he wills."[52] But he does not have mercy equally on all those on whom he has mercy, and he does not harden equally all those whom he hardens.

3.9 But why does the punishment for sin continue for us in this life after sin itself has been wiped out? That is another question, one that does not belong to our discussion here. Yet I will say briefly that if the faithful were immediately changed into a state of incorruption upon their baptism or martyrdom, merit would be done away with, and human beings would not be saved by any merit, except for those who were first to believe and had no one to serve as an example for them. Indeed, both faith and hope would be lacking, and without them no one who has understanding can merit the kingdom of God. For faith and hope have to do with things that are not seen. And since people would see that those who turned to Christ immediately passed over into incorruptibility, there would be no one who could so much as will to withdraw from such great happiness as he beheld. Therefore, in order that we might with greater glory attain through the merit of faith and hope the happiness that we desire, we remain, so long as we are in this life, in this state that is no longer imputed to us as sin, even though it came about as a result of sin.

Furthermore, we are not promised through baptism and Christian faith the happiness that Adam had in paradise before he sinned, but the happiness that he was going to have once the number of human beings had been brought to fullness: the number, that is, of those who were to be taken up in order to complete the heavenly city, which was to comprise angels and human beings, where human beings will not bear offspring, as they would have done in paradise. If those who turn to Christ passed immediately into that state of incorruption, there would be no human beings from whom that number could be filled up, since no one who saw such happiness could fail to hasten toward it. I think this is what the Apostle

---

49. Psalm 78:39 (77:39).

50. John 15:18.

51. 2 Corinthians 2:15–16.

52. Romans 9:18.

is saying of those "who by faith . . . did the works of justice."[53] "All of them," he writes, "having gained approval through the witness of faith, did not receive what was promised, because God had provided something better for us, so that apart from us they would not attain fulfillment."[54] For if one were to ask what better thing God had provided for us, on account of which "they did not receive what was promised," I see no more fitting answer than what I said earlier: if, when they had gained approval, the happiness promised to the just had not been postponed, merit would be destroyed for those who knew this by experience and not by faith. Furthermore, the procreation of human beings by which we ourselves came to be born would have stopped, since all people would have run toward the incorruptibility they saw to be present. And so it was a great good that God provided for us when he put off the receiving of the promise by the saints who had "gained approval through the witness of faith," both so that we might be brought into being and so that faith would remain, by which we like them merit what has been promised and together with them are brought to fulfillment.

And there is another reason why the baptized and martyrs do not immediately become incorruptible. Suppose someone had planned to give great honors to his slave at some future time, but because of some fault for which the slave can in no way make recompense on his own, he gives the slave a severe beating. After the beating, at a time he has determined, he is going to throw the slave into a terrible prison where he will be subjected to intense and painful torture. If someone who has great influence in the eyes of the master makes recompense on behalf of the slave and reconciles him to the master, the blows that the guilty slave deservedly endured before recompense was made, while he was still at fault, are not wiped out. But the greater torments to which he had not yet been subjected are averted, because of the reconciliation that has been interposed. And the honors that (had he not sinned) he was going to receive at the proper time, and that (had he not been reconciled) he was going to lack once he sinned, will now be given to him without any change, just as had been decreed from the beginning, because a complete recompense has been made. Indeed, if before the reconciliation he had been deprived of those honors in the same way that he would have been deprived of them irrecoverably after his fault if he had not been reconciled, there would have been no room for reconciliation to help him recover them. But since he could not be deprived of an honor that he did not yet have and was not yet supposed to have, a reconciliation could intervene and prevent the deprivation—but only if the slave, while he is still recovering from the beating, vows in heart and word to be faithful to his master and to amend his own behavior, and only if he fulfills his vow.

---

53. Hebrews 11:33.
54. Hebrews 11:39–40.

This is how things stand between God and human beings. When human nature first sinned, the punishment inflicted on it was that it would always produce offspring of the sort we see infants are, and that after this life it would be forever banished to hell and exiled from the kingdom of God for which it was created, unless someone were to accomplish on behalf of human nature the reconciliation that it could not make for itself. Now there was no one by whom human nature could be reconciled, except for Christ. So in all infants begotten naturally, human nature is born with sin and is under punishment for sin. When this nature accepts reconciliation, the punishment inflicted upon it before the reconciliation deservedly remains. But the torments that it was going to suffer in hell are forgiven in those whom Christ has redeemed, and they are given the kingdom of God that they were going to receive at the proper time after their sojourn in the earthly paradise—but only if they persevere to the end in the faith that they promise in their baptism.

3.10   Now some people claim that experience proves that free choice has no power, since many people put forth an enormous effort to live well but (so they say) make no progress at all because some impossibility stands in their way, or else they do make progress but then fall away with no hope of recovery. But this claim does not undermine the conclusion that we have demonstrated by reason: free choice does have power in conjunction with grace. That those who make an effort make no progress or fall away after they do make progress results, I hold, not from any impossibility but from a difficulty—sometimes a severe difficulty, but sometimes one that could be easily overcome. It is, after all, extremely common for us to say that something is impossible for us when we cannot accomplish it without difficulty. And if each of us will attentively examine the motions of our own wills, we will recognize that we never abandon the rectitude of will received through grace except by willing something else that we cannot will at the same time as we will rectitude. Clearly, we do not do this because our power to preserve rectitude—the power that is itself freedom of choice—has failed; what fails is our will to preserve rectitude. And that will fails, not of itself, but because another will drives it out, as I have explained.

3.11   Now since this discussion particularly involves the will, I think I should say something in greater depth about the will that I believe will be helpful. Just as our bodies have limbs and the five senses, each apt for its respective uses, which we employ as instruments—for example, the hands are apt for grasping, the feet for walking, the tongue for speaking, and sight for seeing—so too our souls have within themselves certain powers that they employ as instruments for fitting uses. There is reason in the soul, which the soul employs as its instrument for reasoning, and the will, which it employs for willing. After all, neither reason nor will is the whole soul; each is something in the soul. Therefore, since each of these instruments has its nature, its dispositions, and its uses, let us distinguish in the will, which is our present concern, the instrument, its dispositions, and its uses. We can call these dispositions in the will its 'affections,' since the instrument for willing is affected by its dispositions. That is why when a human soul wills something very intensely, we say that it is goaded [*affecta*] into willing something, or that it wills it passionately [*affectuose*].

'Will,' in fact, appears to be said equivocally. It has three senses: the instrument for willing, the affection of the instrument, and the uses of that instrument. The instrument for willing is the power of the soul that we employ for willing, just as reason is the instrument for reasoning that we employ when we reason and sight is the instrument for seeing that we employ when we see. The affection of this instrument is that by which the instrument itself is disposed in such a way to will something (even when one is not thinking of what it wills) that if that thing comes to mind, the instrument wills it, either immediately or at the appropriate time. The instrument for willing is disposed in this way to will health, even when one is not thinking of health, so that as soon as health comes to mind, it wills health. It is also disposed in this way to will sleep, even when one is not thinking of sleep, so that when sleep comes to mind, it wills sleep at the appropriate time. After all, it is never disposed in such a way that it at some time wills illness or wills never to sleep. And in a just person, that same instrument is disposed in a similar way to will justice, even when the person is asleep, so that he wills justice as soon as he thinks of it. By contrast, the use of that instrument is what we have only when we think of the thing we will.

Now the instrument for willing, its affection, and its use are all called 'will.' We call the instrument 'will' when we say that we turn our will toward various things: now to willing to walk, now to willing to sit, now to willing this or that. Human beings always have this instrument, although we do not always employ it. In the same way, we always have sight, which is the instrument for seeing, even when we do not employ it, as when we are sleeping. And when we do employ it, we turn it now to seeing the sky, now to seeing the earth, now to something else. And similarly, we always have the instrument for reasoning, which is reason, which we do not always employ, and which we turn to various things when we engage in reasoning. By contrast, the affection of the instrument for willing is called 'will' when we say that someone always has the will that things be well with him. For in this case what we are calling 'will' is the affection of that instrument by which this person wills that things be well with him. We use 'will' in the same way when we say of a holy person that even when he is asleep and is not thinking about it, he unceasingly has the will to live justly. And when we say that one person has this will to a greater degree than another person, what we mean by 'will' is nothing other than the affection of the instrument for willing by which each wills to live justly. It is not, after all, the instrument itself that one person has to a greater degree and another person to a lesser degree. Now the use of this instrument is called will when someone says, "Right now I have the will to read" (that is, right now I will to read), or "Right now I have the will to write" (that is, right now I will to write). For just as to see is to use sight, which is the instrument for seeing, and its use is vision or sight (where 'sight' signifies the same as 'vision'—for 'sight' also signifies the instrument of sight), so too, to will is to use the will that is the instrument for willing, and its use is the will that exists only when we are thinking about what we will.

So the will that is the instrument is a single, unitary thing. That is, there is only one instrument for willing in a human being, just as there is only one reason, that is, only one instrument for reasoning. But the will by which this instrument is affected is twofold. For just as sight has multiple dispositions (a disposition to see light, a disposition to see figures by means of light, [and] a disposition to see colors [by means of figures][55]), so too the instrument for willing has two dispositions that we call "affections." One of these is a disposition to will advantage; the other is a disposition to will rectitude. Indeed, the will that is the instrument wills nothing but either advantage or rectitude. Whatever else it wills, it wills either for the sake of advantage or for the sake of rectitude; even if it is mistaken, it takes itself to be relating everything it wills to them. In virtue of the affection for willing advantage, a person always wills happiness and being happy, whereas in virtue of the affection for willing rectitude, he wills rectitude and being upright, that is, just. Now someone wills something for the sake of advantage when, for example, he wills to cultivate land or to work so that he will have that by which he can safeguard his life and health, which he judges to be advantageous. But he wills something for the sake of rectitude when, for example, he wills to work at learning so that he might know how to live rightly, that is, justly. By contrast, the will that is the use of this much-discussed instrument exists only when someone thinks of what he wills, as has been said. The divisions of this will are manifold, but I will not talk about them now, though perhaps I will elsewhere.[56]

Now 'to will' is equivocal, just like 'to see.' For we say that someone sees not only if he is employing his sight but also if he is not, but has the disposition to see; and in the same way, we say that someone wills not only if he employs the instrument for willing when thinking of what he wills but also if he is not employing it, because he has the affection, that is, the disposition, for willing.

And here is another way we can see that the will that is the instrument for willing is one thing, the will that is its affection is another, and the will that is the use of that instrument is still another. Even when a just person is asleep and not thinking of anything, he is said to have the will to live justly; when an unjust person is asleep, he is said not to have a will to live justly. The will that we say the

---

55. The bracketed words translate a conjectural emendation by the editor of the critical edition.

56. See the Lambeth Fragments, section 8, for more on this topic.

unjust person does not have is the very same will that we say the just person has. But obviously, when we say that the unjust person who is asleep does not have the will to live justly, we are not saying that he lacks the will that I have called the instrument for willing, since all human beings always have that will, whether they are asleep or awake. Hence, since the will that is said to be in a good person is none other than that which is said not to be in a wicked one, the will that we indicate is in the good person is not the instrument, but that by which the instrument is disposed. Now there is no doubt that the will that is use is not in someone who is asleep (unless he is dreaming), so when we say that the will to live rightly is in a just person who is asleep, that does not mean the will that is use. So the will as affection is not the same as either the will as instrument or the will as use. And everyone knows that the will as instrument is not the same as the will as use, since when I say that I do not have the will to write, no one takes this to mean that I do not have the instrument for willing. Therefore, the will as instrument is one thing, the will as affection is another, and the will as use is yet another.

Now the will as instrument moves all the other instruments that we employ spontaneously,* both those that are in us (such as hands, the tongue, and sight) and those that are outside us (such as a pen and an ax), and it brings about all voluntary motions. In fact, it moves itself by means of its own affections. Hence, it can be described as an instrument that moves itself. I say that the will as instrument brings about all voluntary motions, but if we consider this attentively, it is truer to say that God brings about everything that is done by either nature or will, since God creates nature and the instrument for willing together with its affections, without which that instrument brings about nothing.

3.12   From these two affections, which we also call wills, derives all human merit, whether good or bad. These two wills also differ in that the one that is for willing advantage is inseparable, whereas the one that is for willing rectitude was originally, as I said above,[57] separable from the angels and our first parents, and is still separable from those who remain in this present life. They also differ in that the one that is for willing advantage is not itself the thing that it wills, whereas the one that is for willing rectitude is rectitude. In fact, only someone who has rectitude wills rectitude; it is only in virtue of rectitude that anyone can will rectitude. But it is obvious that this rectitude belongs to the will that is the instrument. We indicate this when we call justice "rectitude of will preserved for its own sake." This is also the truth of the will in which, as the Lord charges, the devil did not remain steadfast, as I explained in my treatise *On Truth*.[58]

We must now investigate the way in which, as I have said, human merits— whether for salvation or for damnation—proceed from these two wills that I call

---

57. In 1.6.

58. See *On Truth*, Chapter 4.

"dispositions" or "affections." Rectitude as such is not a cause of any evil, and it is the mother of all good merit. It gives aid to the spirit as it lusts against the flesh,[59] and it shares in the spirit's delight in the law according to the inner human being,[60] that is, according to that same spirit. Now if anything evil ever seems to proceed from rectitude, it does not in fact come from rectitude, but from something else. It is through rectitude that the apostles were "a lovely fragrance before God." That they were "an odor of death unto death" before some did not proceed from the apostles' justice, but from the wickedness of those who wished them evil.[61] But the will that is for willing advantage is not always evil; it is evil only when it consents to the flesh that lusts against the spirit.[62]

3.13   But in order that this might be understood more clearly, we need to look into how the will came to be so vicious and so prone to evil—for we must not believe that God made the will that way in our first parents. Now although I have explained that it was on account of sin that human nature incurred corruption and appetites like those of brute animals, I have not said how such a will arose in human beings in the first place. Indeed, vicious appetites are not the same as a vicious will that consents to such appetites. Therefore, I think it is worth asking how such a will came to be present in human beings. But if we pay attention to the original creation of rational nature, we will easily detect the cause of such a will. God's aim was to make rational nature both just and happy for the purpose of enjoying God himself. Now rational nature could not be either just or happy without the will for justice and happiness. Indeed, the will for justice is itself justice. The will for happiness, by contrast, is not happiness, since not everyone who has the will for happiness has happiness. Now as everyone agrees, happiness includes a sufficient amount of appropriate advantages without any deficiency, whether we mean angelic happiness or the happiness that Adam had in paradise. For although the happiness of the angels is greater than the happiness that belonged to human beings in paradise, it cannot on that account be denied that Adam possessed happiness. A heat can be great and without any coldness, and yet there can be a greater heat; and a coldness can be great and without any heat, and yet there can be a greater coldness. In the same way, there is no reason to deny that Adam was happy in paradise and was without any deficiency, even though angelic happiness was greater. Indeed, to have something in a lesser degree than another is not always to be deficient. To be deficient is to lack something when one ought to have it, and that was not the case with Adam. For where there is deficiency, there is unhappiness. But God did not make rational nature unhappy without some antecedent

---

59. Cf. Galatians 5:17.

60. Cf. Romans 7:22.

61. Cf. 2 Corinthians 2:15–16, and see above at 3.8.

62. Cf. Galatians 5:17.

fault, given that he created rational nature in order to understand and love himself. Therefore, God made human beings happy, without any deficiency. Therefore, rational nature received, at one and the same moment, the will for happiness and happiness itself, the will for justice (that is, rectitude, which is justice itself), and free choice, without which it could not preserve justice.

Now God ordered these two wills or affections in such a way that the will that is the instrument would use the will that is justice to command and govern under the instruction of the spirit, which is also called mind and reason; and it would use the other disposition for obedience without any disadvantage. Indeed, he gave happiness to human beings (to say nothing of angels) for their advantage, whereas he gave them justice for his own honor. But he gave justice to them in such a way that they were able to abandon it, so that if they did not abandon it, but instead preserved it with perseverance, they would merit exaltation to fellowship with the angels. But if they did abandon it, they would in no way be able to recover it thereafter on their own. Not only would they not attain the happiness of the angels, but they would be deprived of the happiness they did have; and declining into the likeness of brute beasts, they would be subject like them to corruption and to the appetites that we have so often mentioned. Yet their will for happiness would remain, so that they would be justly punished with deep unhappiness by being deprived of the goods that they had lost. Therefore, they lost happiness because they abandoned justice. Though they had received a good will, and had received it for their good, their wills now burn with the desire for advantages that they cannot fail to will. And since they cannot take possession of those true advantages they have lost, which were fitting for rational nature, their wills turn to false advantages, suited to brute animals, at the prompting of their animal appetites. And in this way, when they will such things inordinately, they either refuse rectitude when it is offered to them or they spurn it once they have received it; but when they will such things licitly, they do not do this.

So in this way the will as instrument, which was created good insofar as it has being, and just, and capable of preserving the justice it had received, became evil through free choice: not evil insofar as it has being, but insofar as it has become unjust through the absence of that justice that it spontaneously abandoned and that it ought always to have. It has also become incapable of willing the justice it abandoned. For when it does not have justice, it cannot will justice through free choice, in the way that when it does have justice, it can preserve justice through free choice. The will for advantage was also created good insofar as it is something; but it became evil, that is, unjust, because it was not subordinated to justice, apart from which it ought not to will anything. Therefore, since the will as instrument became unjust spontaneously, once it has abandoned justice it remains unjust and a servant of injustice by necessity, so far as its own power is concerned, because it cannot by itself return to justice, apart from which it is never free, since its natural freedom of choice is otiose without justice. The will has also become a servant of its own affection for the advantageous, since in the absence of justice it cannot will anything except what the affection for the advantageous wills. (I speak of both the instrument and the affection as "willing," since both the instrument and the affection are will, and both wills are appropriately described as willing. For the instrument wills in virtue of its affection, and the affection through which the instrument wills also wills. Similarly, we say both that a person sees and that sight sees: the person sees in virtue of sight, and the sight through which he sees also sees.) Hence, we can say without any absurdity that the affections of that will that I have called an instrument of the soul are, as it were, instruments of that instrument, since the will as instrument does nothing apart from its affections. Therefore, once the will as instrument loses its instrument for willing justice (in other words, once it loses rectitude), there is no way it can will justice, unless its rectitude is restored through grace. Therefore, since no one ought to will otherwise than justly, whatever the will wills apart from rectitude, it wills unjustly. By contrast, all those appetites that the Apostle calls "flesh" and "concupiscence" are not evil or unjust insofar as they have being; they are called unjust because they are present in a rational nature where they ought not to be. In brute animals, of course, they are not evil or unjust, because they ought to be there.

3.14   From what was said above we can now discern that the reason human beings do not always possess justice—which they ought to possess without interruption—is that they can in no way attain or recover it by their own power. It is also clear that God brings about good deeds solely through his own goodness, since he creates the will with free choice and gives the will the justice by which it acts, whereas he brings about evil acts solely through the fault of human beings, since he would not bring them about if human beings did not will to do them. Nonetheless, he does bring it about that evil deeds exist, since he is the creator of the will in human beings, which they employ apart from justice; and therefore it is solely the fault of human beings that their acts are evil. It is not the fault of God, who created the human will with freedom of choice and granted it justice so that it might never will otherwise than justly; it is the fault of human beings, who abandoned the justice that they had the power to preserve. So in good deeds God is responsible both for their being good through their essence and for their being good through justice, whereas in evil deeds God is responsible only for their being good through their essence, not for their being evil through the absence of the justice that ought to be in them (since that absence is not anything). Human beings, however, are responsible in good deeds for their not being evil, since they did not abandon justice and do evil even though they could have, but instead preserved justice through free choice in cooperation with prevenient and subsequent grace.[63]

---

63. "In cooperation with prevenient and subsequent grace" translates *dante et subsequente gratia*. The difference among various translations testifies to the obscurity of the expression,

But in evil deeds they alone are responsible for their being evil, because they do them solely by their own unjust will.

I think I can now fittingly conclude my discussion of these three difficult questions, which I undertook in hope of God's help. If I have said in it what[64] ought to satisfy any inquirer, I give no credit to myself, since it was not I but God's grace with me. I will say this, however: when my mind was uneasily searching for an account of these matters as I asked these questions, if someone had given me the answers that I have written here, I would have been grateful, because he would have satisfied me. Therefore, since what I came to understand about this topic by God's revelation greatly pleased me, and I realized that it would likewise be pleasing to others if I wrote it down, I decided to give freely to those who ask for it what I have myself freely received.[65]

---

but I am convinced that Anselm means to refer to the dynamic of prevenient and subsequent grace described above in 3.4.

64. Reading *quid* for *qui*.

65. Cf. Matthew 10:8: "You have received freely; give freely."

The Lambeth Fragments[1]

[1. On possibility and impossibility]

STUDENT: There are several matters on which I have long wanted your response. Among them are power and inability, possibility and impossibility, necessity and freedom. I am listing them all together as subjects for investigation, because it seems to me that knowledge of each of them is connected with knowledge of the others. I will explain to you in part what motivates me to ask about them, so that once you have answered my questions about them, I will be able to make progress more easily on the other matters that I am concerned about.

You see, we sometimes say that there is power in something in which there is no power. For no one denies that whatever can [do something], can do [it] in virtue of its power. So when we say that what does not exist can exist, we are saying that there is power in that which does not exist, as when we say that a house that does not yet exist can exist—and I just cannot understand that. After all, there is no power in that which does not exist.

I will say again: that which in no way exists has no power. Accordingly, it does not have a power for being or for not being. And so it follows that what does not exist both cannot exist and cannot not exist. And what goes along with the negative statement, "what does not exist cannot exist," is that what does not exist is such that (a) it is not possible for it to exist, (b) it is impossible for it to exist, and (c) it is necessary that it does not exist. Or, if we take the other negation, "what does not exist cannot not exist," we find that what does not exist is such that (a) it is not possible for it not to exist, (b) it is impossible for it not to exist, and (c) it is necessary that it exists. Therefore, because that which in no way exists cannot exist, it is impossible for it to exist and necessary that it does not exist; but from the fact that it cannot not exist, it follows that it is impossible for it not to exist and necessary that it exists.

Furthermore, what cannot exist is not able to exist. And what is not able to exist is unable to exist. Similarly, what cannot not exist is not able not to exist, and what is not able not to exist is unable not to exist. Therefore, what does not exist cannot exist, cannot not exist, is unable to exist, and is unable not to exist. But equally,

---

1. I have followed the order of the fragments as they appear in the edition of F. S. Schmitt, "Ein neues unvollendetes Werk des hl. Anselm von Canterbury," *Beiträge zur Geschichte der Philosophie und Theologie des Mittelalters* Band 33, Heft 3 (1936), 22–43. I have, however, added headings of my own and made somewhat different divisions in the text.

what is unable to exist is able not to exist, and what is unable not to exist is able to exist. Therefore, what does not exist is both able and unable to exist, and similarly able [and unable] not to exist. Therefore, it equally has power and inability with respect to both existing and not existing.

But all these conclusions are perfectly ridiculous. For the following never hold [of the same thing] at the same time: (1) "it is impossible for this to exist" and "it is impossible for this not to exist"; (2) "it is necessary for this to exist" and "it is necessary for this not to exist"; (3) "this has the power to exist" and "this has an inability to exist"; (4) "this has the power not to exist" and "this has an inability not to exist." So, given that these things are impossible, that from which they follow is also impossible: namely, that "what in no way exists both cannot exist and cannot not exist, since it has no power." But I cannot at all figure out how this is false.

Another thing that motivates me to ask about impossibility and necessity is that we say that something is impossible for God, such as lying, or that God is something out of necessity, such as being just. For impossibility suggests inability, and necessity suggests violence. But there is neither inability nor violence in God. After all, if God preserves the truth because of an inability to lie or is just as a result of violence, he is not truthful or just freely. Now you might reply that this impossibility and this necessity signify an unconquerable strength in God. But in that case I will ask why this strength is designated by words that signify weakness.

These and perhaps other questions force me into a certain puzzlement about power and possibility and their contraries, and about necessity and freedom. My perplexities may be childish, but I ask you nonetheless to teach me how I might respond to someone who posed the same questions to me. For I must admit, I don't know how to.

[2. On the verb 'to do']

TEACHER: Even if your questions seem childish to you, their answers are not so easy for me that your questions strike me as contemptible. For I can see from a mile away that once I begin to reply to you, you will call me to greater things. Still, I should not restrain myself from matters in which God grants me the ability to answer you, just because I cannot solve all the problems you end up raising. Now in order to investigate the matters you have asked about, I understand that it is necessary first to set down something about the verb 'to do' and about what is properly attributable to something as 'its own,' so that I will not be compelled to insert a digression on those matters when the need arises. You just be sure to hold your questions in memory.

431

S: Whatever you set down beforehand will not displease me, as long as you get back to what I asked about.

T: The verb 'to do' [*facere*] is commonly used for any verb, of whatever signification, whether finite or infinite, even for 'not to do.' For if one asks concerning someone, "What is he doing?" if we pay careful attention, we see that 'do' is being used for any verb that might be used in reply, and that whatever verb is used in reply is used for 'do.' After all, no verb is correctly used in the reply to someone who asks, "What is he doing?" unless that verb is understood in the "doing" about which that person is asking. When the answer is given that "He is reading" or "He is writing," this has the same force as "This is what he is doing: he is reading" or "This is what he is doing: he is writing."

Now any verb can be used in reply to someone who asks this question. This is quite clear in many cases, as in "He is singing" or "He is dictating." In some cases, however, one might have doubts: for example, "He is," "He is living," "He can," "He owes," "He is named," "He is called." But no one will complain if the answer to "What is he doing?" is "He is in church" or "He is living like a good man" or "He has power[2] over the whole city in which he lives" or "He owes a great deal of money" or "He is named [i.e., renowned] above all his neighbors" or "He is called before all others, wherever he may be."

So any verb can on some occasion be used in response to someone who asks, "What is he doing?" provided that there is someone who knows how to do this properly. And so any verbs whatsoever that are used in response to someone who asks "What is he doing?" are used, as I have said, in place of 'to do' in the response, and 'to do' is used for them in the question, since what is said in response is what is being asked about, and what is asked in the question is what is being addressed in response.

Moreover, everything of which some verb is said is a cause that what is signified by the verb is the case; and in our common way of speaking, every cause is said to 'bring about' [*facere*][3] that of which it is the cause. Hence, everything of which any verb is predicated brings about what is signified by that verb. I will pass right

---

2. "Has power" translates *potest*, which was translated 'can' in the previous sentence. Some of these examples obviously work better in Latin than they do in English. Keep in mind, too, that the question translated "What is he doing?" can also be translated "What does he do?" or even, loosely, "What's the deal with him?" Some of Anselm's proposed answers work a bit better as responses to the latter questions.

3. Anselm's point in this section and the next is about the variety of uses of the Latin verb *facere*, not of course about the variety of uses of the English verb 'to do,' so it seems silly to me to make up awkward and unidiomatic uses of the verb 'to do' so that we can keep a consistent English translation of *facere*. Indeed, there is some advantage for readers in seeing which English expressions are used throughout these translations to correspond to *facere*.

over those verbs that according to their signification are properly cases of bringing about, such as 'to run' and similar verbs; what I am saying can be recognized even in other verbs that seem foreign to this property of bringing about. For in this way someone who sits brings about sitting, and one who undergoes brings about an undergoing, since if there were not someone who underwent there would be no undergoing, nor would anything be named unless there were something that is named, and nothing would in any way be said to exist unless that which is said to exist were first thought. According to the foregoing argument, then, whenever a verb is predicated of any thing at all, what is signified is that the thing brings about [*facit*] what is expressed by that verb. For that reason, it is not altogether ground-less that in our common way of speaking, 'to do' [*facere*] is used for any verb.

S: What you say is clear to someone who desires to understand, although I do not yet understand your aim in saying it.

T: You will come to understand it in what follows.

[3. On the senses of 'to do']

The verb 'to do' [*facere*] is commonly used for any verb, of whatever signification, whether finite or infinite, even for 'not to do.' For if one asks concerning someone, "What is he doing?", if we pay careful attention, we see that 'do' is being used for any verb that might be used in reply, and that whatever verb is used in reply is used for 'do.' After all, no verb is correctly used in the reply to someone who asks, "What is he doing?" unless that verb is understood in the "doing" about which that person is asking. When the answer is given that "He is reading" or "He is writ-ing," this has the same force as "This is what he is doing: he is reading" or "This is what he is doing: he is writing."

Now any verb can be used in reply to someone who asks this question. This is quite clear in many cases, as in "He is singing" or "He is dictating." In some cases, however, one might have doubts: for example, "He is," "He is living," "He can," "He owes," "He is named," "He is called." But no one will complain if the answer to "What is he doing?" is "He is in church" or "He is living like a good man" or "He has power over the whole city in which he lives" or "He owes a great deal of money" or "He is named [i.e., renowned] above all his neighbors" or "He is called before all others, wherever he may be."

So any verb can on some occasion be used in response to someone who asks "What is he doing?", provided that there is someone who knows how to do this properly. And so any verbs whatsoever that are used in response to someone who asks "What is he doing?" are used, as I have said, in place of 'to do' in the response, and 'to do' is used for them in the question, since what is said in response is what is being asked about, and what is asked in the question is what is being addressed in the response.

'To do' is often used for negative verbs, even for 'not to do.' For example, someone who does not love virtues and does not hate vices *does* ill, and someone who does not do what he ought not to do *does* well. In this way 'to do' is used for any verb, whether positive or negative, and every verb is 'to do.'

Moreover, everything of which some verb is said is a cause that what is signified by the verb is the case; and in our common way of speaking, every cause is said to 'bring about' [*facere*] that of which it is the cause. Hence, everything of which any verb is predicated brings about what is signified by that verb. I will pass right over those verbs that according to their signification are properly cases of bringing about, such as 'to run' and similar verbs; what I am saying can be recognized even in other verbs that seem foreign to this property of bringing about. For in this way someone who sits brings about sitting, and one who undergoes brings about an undergoing, since if there were not someone who underwent there would be no undergoing, nor would anything be named unless there were something that is named; and nothing would in any way be said to exist unless that which is said to exist were first thought. For when it is said that "A human being exists" or "A human being does not exist," the significate of this name is conceived in the mind before it is said to exist or not to exist; and for that reason what is conceived is a cause that 'exists' is said of a human being. Also, if we say, "A human being is an animal," the human being is a cause of his being an animal and being called an animal. I do not mean that the human being is a cause that an animal exists, but that the human being is a cause that he himself is an animal and is called an animal. For by means of the name 'human being' the whole human being is signified and conceived, and animal is a part of that whole. And so in this case the part follows from the whole in this way, because where the whole is, the part must also be. So because the whole human being is conceived in the name 'human being,' the whole human being is himself a cause that he is an animal and is called an animal, since the conception of the whole is a cause that the part is conceived in it and is said of it. In this way, then, whenever 'is' is said of anything at all—whether without qualification, as in "A human being exists,"[4] or with some qualification, as in "A human being is an animal" or "A human being is healthy"—the prior conception of a human being is a cause of his being said to be or not to be; it is also a cause that what is said is understood. According to the foregoing argument, then, whenever a verb is predicated of any thing at all, what is signified is that the thing brings about [*facit*] what is expressed by that verb. For that reason, it is not altogether groundless that in our common way of speaking, 'to do' [*facere*] is used for any verb, and every verb is said to involve doing. Indeed, in the Gospel the Lord uses 'do' (or 'act,' which is the same thing) for any verb when he says, "Everyone who acts badly hates the light" and "One who does the truth comes to

---

4. The word for "exists" is the same as the word for "is."

the light."[5] Someone acts badly who does what he ought not to do, or does not do what he ought to do—where 'do' again is understood as standing in for any verb. For someone who is where or when he ought not to be, or who sits or stands where or when he ought not to, and someone who is not or does not sit or does not stand where or when he ought to, acts badly. By contrast, someone does the truth who does what he ought to do and does not do what he ought not to do. Similarly, someone who is or sits or stands where or when he ought to, and someone who is not or does not sit or does not stand where or when he ought not to, does the truth. In this way the Lord includes every positive or negative verb in 'to do.'

[4. On the modes of bringing about]

There is another point to consider about that same verb, namely, in how many different ways we say 'to do' in our regular usage. Although this division has many parts and is rather involved, I shall nonetheless say something about it—as much as I think will be of use for what we are going to say and can give some help to someone who might wish to carry out a more thorough investigation.

Some causes are called 'efficient'—for example, someone who does some writing; others by contrast with them are not called efficient—for example, the material out of which something is made. Nonetheless, *every* cause (as I have said) is said to 'bring about' [*facere*], and everything that is said to bring about is named a cause. Now anything that is said to bring about either brings it about that something is or brings it about that something is not. So every bringing-about can be said to be either a 'bringing about being' or a 'bringing about non-being.' These two affirmations are contraries. Their negations are 'not bringing about being' and 'not bringing about non-being,' respectively. But the affirmative 'bringing about being' is sometimes put in place of the negative 'not bringing about non-being'; conversely, 'not bringing about non-being' is sometimes put in place of 'bringing about being.' Similarly, 'bringing about non-being' and 'not bringing about being' are put in place of each other. For sometimes someone is said to bring it about that evil things are, because he does not bring it about that they are not; and not to bring it about that evil things are not, because he brings it about that they are; and to bring it about that good things are not, because he does not bring it about that they are; and not to bring about good things, because he brings it about that they are not.

Let us now provide a classification of 'bringing about.' Now since, as has been explained, bringing about is always of either being or non-being, it will be incumbent upon us to add 'being' and 'non-being' to the individual modes of bringing about, so that they are explicitly distinguished. Accordingly, we predicate 'bring

---

5. John 3:20–21.

about' in six modes: two modes in which the cause (1) brings about the being, or (2) does not bring about the non-being, of the very thing that it is said to bring about; and four modes (3–6) in which the cause either brings about or does not bring about the being or non-being of something else. For we say that a given thing brings it about that something is, either (1) because it brings about the being of the very thing it is said to bring about, or (2) because it does not bring about the non-being of that very thing, or (3) because it brings about the being of some other thing, or (4) because it does not bring about the being of some other thing, or (5) because it brings about the non-being of some other thing, or (6) because it does not bring about the non-being of some other thing.

(1) In the first mode, when someone fatally stabs a person, he is said to bring it about that that person is dead. For in this case he brings about through himself the very thing he is said to bring about.

(2) I do not have an example of the second mode in the case of bringing it about that someone is dead, unless I imagine someone who could revive a dead person but does not will to do so. If this were the case, he would be said to bring it about that the person is dead according to the second mode, because he would not bring it about that the person is not dead. Examples are plentiful in other sorts of cases. For example, we say that someone brings it about that bad things exist, because he does not bring it about that they do not exist, although he has the power to do that.

(3) It is according to the third mode that someone is said to have killed another, that is, to have brought it about that he is dead, because he commanded that he be killed, or because he brought it about that the killer had a sword, or because he provoked the killing; also, if someone is said to have killed himself because he did something on account of which he was killed. For the people in these cases did not bring about through themselves what they are said to have brought about. That is, they did not kill or bring it about that someone was dead or was killed; rather, they brought this about by bringing something else about. They accomplished through an intermediary what they are said to have brought about.

(4) It is in the fourth mode when we say that someone killed another person because he did not offer weapons to the victim before he was killed, or because he did not forestall the killer, or because he did not do something such that, if he had done it, the victim would not have been killed. In these cases too the people did not kill through themselves; rather, it was by *not* bringing about something else that they brought about what they are said to have brought about.

(5) The fifth mode is when someone is said to have killed another because he brought it about that the victim was unarmed by taking away his weapons, or because by opening a door he brought it about that the killer was not locked in where he was being detained. Here again the one who is said to have killed did not kill through himself, but through something else, by bringing it about that something else did not exist.

(6) It is according to the sixth mode when someone is charged with killing because he did not, by taking away the killer's weapons, bring it about that the killer was not armed, or because he did not whisk away the victim so that he would not be accessible to the killer. In these cases too he did not kill through himself, but through something else, that is, by not bringing it about that something else did not exist.

The same classification applies to bringing about non-being. For whatever is said to bring about the non-being of something is said to do so either (1) because it brings about the non-being of that very thing, or (2) because it does not bring about the being of that thing, or (3) because it brings about the being of some other thing, or (4) because it does not bring about the being of some other thing, or (5) because it brings about the non-being of some other thing, or (6) because it does not bring about the non-being of some other thing. We can find examples of these in the killing of a human being, just as I did for bringing about being.

(1) Just as someone who kills brings it about that someone is dead, in the first mode of bringing about being, so too he brings it about that someone is not alive, in the first mode of bringing about non-being.

(2) I do not have an example in the second mode of bringing it about that someone is not living, unless, as I did above, I imagine someone who can revive a dead person. For if he is unwilling to do so, he will be said in the second mode to bring it about that the person is not living, because he does not bring it about that he is living. For although being dead and not being alive are not the same thing—after all, something is not dead unless it is deprived of life, whereas many things are not alive but are not deprived of life: for example, a stone—nonetheless, just as killing someone is nothing other than bringing it about that someone is dead and not alive, so too reviving someone is the same thing as bringing it about that someone is living and not dead. Of course there are many examples of this second mode in other cases. For example, someone is said to bring it about that good things do not exist because he does not bring it about that they exist even though he has the power to do so.

The examples that were given for bringing about being will suffice for the other four modes, in which someone brings about or does not bring about the being or non-being of something else.

[5. On the modes of bringing about non-being]

Let's now talk about 'bringing about non-being,' which I have said can also be classified in six modes. These modes are in every respect the same as the modes of 'bringing about being' except that in this case they are modes of 'bringing about non-being' rather than 'bringing about being.'

(1) The first mode of 'bringing about non-being' is when something is said to bring about non-being because it brings about the non-being of the very thing whose non-being it is said to bring about. For example, someone who kills a human being is said to bring it about that he is not alive, because he brings about the very thing he is said to bring about.

(2) The second mode is when something is said to bring about non-being because it does not bring about the being of the very thing whose non-being it is said to bring about. The only way I can offer an example of this mode in bringing it about that a human being is or is not alive is to imagine someone who can bring it about that a dead person is alive. If he did not do so, he would be said to bring it about that the dead person is not alive because he did not bring it about that the dead person is alive. In any event, there are plenty of examples in other cases. For example, suppose it is someone's job to bring it about that a house is illuminated at night. If he does not do what he is supposed to, he is said to bring it about that the house is not illuminated, because he does not bring it about that the house is illuminated.

(3) The third mode is when something is said to bring about non-being because it brings about the being of something other than the thing whose non-being it is said to bring about, as when we say that A brought it about that B is not alive because A brought it about that B's killer was in possession of a sword.

(4) The fourth mode is when something is said to bring about non-being because it does not bring about the being of something else, as when A is said to have brought it about that B is not alive, because before B died A did not bring it about that B was armed.

(5) The fifth mode is when something is said to bring about the non-being of something because it brings about the non-being of something else, as when A is said to bring it about that B is not alive because before B was killed A brought it about that B was not armed.

(6) The sixth mode is when something brings about the non-being of something because it does not bring about the non-being of something else, as when [A is said to bring it about that B is not alive because] A does not bring it about that B's killer is not armed by taking away his arms, even though he can take them away.

And note that although 'bringing about being' and 'not bringing about non-being' are put in place of each other, they do in fact differ. Properly speaking, someone brings about being who brings it about that something exists that did not exist, whereas 'not bringing about non-being' does not apply any more to someone who brings it about that something exists than it does to someone who does not bring about either being or non-being. 'Bringing about non-being' and 'not bringing about being' differ in the same way. Properly speaking, someone brings about non-being who brings it about that what used to exist no longer exists, whereas 'not bringing about being' is said equally of one who brings it about that what used to exist no longer exists and of one who does not bring about either being or non-being.

Now I offered these examples of 'bringing about being' and 'bringing about non-being' using efficient causes, because these provide clearer cases of what I wanted to show. But just as the aforesaid six modes are discerned in efficient causes, so too they are also found in non-efficient causes, if anyone should care to examine them attentively.

[6. More on the modes of 'bringing about']

S: I see it clearly.

T: I have taken these examples from efficient causes, because what I want to show is clearer in efficient causes. But just as efficient causes in the five modes following the first do not bring about what they are said to bring about, but, as I have repeatedly shown through examples, are said to bring about what the first brings about—the second mode by not bringing about the non-being of what the first mode brings about, the third by bringing about the being of something else, the fourth by bringing about the non-being of something else, the fifth by not bringing about the being of something else,[6] and the sixth by not bringing about the non-being of something else—so too non-efficient causes are also said to bring about, in accordance with the same modes. For some of them are proximate, though not efficient, causes that what they are said to bring about is the case; and others are remote causes, not that it is the case but that something else is the case. For example, a window brings it about that the house is bright. It is not an efficient cause, but it is a proximate cause through which the light brings it about that what the window is said to bring about is the case. It is a proximate [rather than a remote] cause because it causes this to be the case through itself and not through another. This is in the first mode of bringing about, since in its own way [i.e., non-efficiently] it brings about the very thing that it is said to bring about. But if, when there is no window or the window is closed, the window is said to bring it about that the house is dark according to the second mode, it is said to bring it about that the house is dark on the grounds that it does not bring it about that the house is not dark. On the other hand, suppose we say that the one who made the window brings it about that the house is bright, or that someone who did not make a window brings it about that the house is dark; or suppose someone says that his land feeds him. These are all remote causes because they do not bring about through themselves [what they are said to bring about]. Rather, someone

---

6. The Teacher here reverses the order of the fourth and fifth modes as described in sections 4 and 5.

brings it about through the window that he made, or that he didn't make when he should have; and the land brings it about through the produce that it yields. And so, whether they are efficient or non-efficient, causes in the first or second mode can be called proximate, whereas others are remote.

The negations—'not bringing about being' and 'not bringing about non-being'—are divided into the same number of modes. One can recognize this by using the examples I gave above for 'bringing about being' and 'bringing about non-being' if one converts the affirmations into negations and the negations into affirmations. If in doing this someone wishes to preserve the order I followed above, in the four modes after the second, let him state affirmatively in the third mode what I said negatively in the fourth, and let him put negatively in the fourth mode what was expressed affirmatively in the third. Similarly, let him make the fifth mode the sixth and the sixth mode the fifth. And it should be noted that in the negative modes, the first mode is purely a negation and does not imply anything else, whereas the other five present a negation that is equivalent to the contrary of the corresponding affirmation. For someone who revives someone else is said in the second mode 'not to bring it about that he is dead' as equivalent to 'bringing it about that he is not dead,' and 'not to bring it about that he is not alive' as equivalent to 'bringing it about that he is alive.' Now if we say of any of the following that he does not bring it about that someone is dead, or that he does not bring it about that someone is not alive, this is understood as meaning that the one of whom we are speaking brings it about (so far as this is in his power) that someone is not dead or that someone is alive:

> (3) in the third mode, one who brings it about that the intended victim is armed by providing him with a weapon; or
>
> (6) in the sixth mode, one who does not bring it about that the intended victim is unarmed, even though he has the power to take away his weapons; or
>
> (5) in the fifth mode, one who brings it about that the person bent on killing is unarmed by taking away his weapons; or
>
> (4) in the fourth mode, one who, by refusing him a weapon, does not bring it about that the person bent on killing is armed.[7]

---

7. Reading *non facit illum esse armatum* for *non facit illum non esse armatum*. Anselm says earlier in this section that the fourth mode of the negation 'not bringing about being,' which (4) is intended to exemplify, "put[s] negatively . . . what was expressed affirmatively in the third" mode of 'bringing about being.' The third mode of bringing about being is exemplified above (section 4) as follows: "someone is said to have . . . brought it about that [someone else] is dead . . . because he brought it about that the killer had a sword." Consequently, the fourth mode of not bringing about being has to be that someone is said not to have brought it about that someone else is dead because he did not bring it about that the killer was armed. Accordingly, we can see that the second *non* is in error.

The same basis for the division that I laid out in the case of 'bringing about being' or 'bringing about non-being' applies to any verb that is conjoined with 'bring about' in a similar way, as for example if I say "I bring it about that you bring something about" or "I bring it about that you write something," or "I bring it about that something is brought about" or "I bring it about that something is written."

[7. On the modes of other verbs]

These modes that I have laid out in the case of 'bring about' are also found in other verbs in a somewhat similar way. Although not all the modes apply to all verbs, one or more of them will apply in particular cases, and especially in verbs that take other verbs as their complements, such as 'ought' and 'can.' These take verbs as their complements when we say "I can read" or "I can be read" or "I ought to love" or "I ought to be loved." There are also verbs that do not take a verb as a complement, but rather some thing, as in "to eat bread" and "to burn wood." And there are some verbs that have no complement at all, for example, "to lie down" or "to sleep"—although some such verbs do appear to take a verb as their complement, as in "The people sat down to eat and drink and rose up to play."[8] But that is not actually the case. "The people sat down to eat and drink and rose up to play" is not said in the same way as "He wills to eat and drink and play." For the former expression is resolved as follows: "The people sat down in order to eat and drink and rose up in order to play."

Some of the modes described above are also found in the verb 'to be.' Certainly the first two modes are easy to recognize. The other four, which involve bringing it about or not bringing it about that something else exists or does not exist, are more difficult to grasp, since there are many ways in which things bring it about or do not bring it about that something else exists or does not exist. But I shall say a few words on this subject, and you will be able to observe in Scripture or in common speech similar points that I will not discuss explicitly.[9]

The verb 'to be' also resembles the verb 'to do.' For something is said to be what it is not, not because it is what it is said to be, but because there is some other cause that this is said. For example, someone is said to be a foot for the lame and an eye for the blind,[10] not because he is what he is said to be, but because he serves as a foot or as an eye. And the lives of the just who confront many struggles because of their desire for eternal life are said to be blessed, not because they in fact are, but because their lives are a cause of their being blessed at some future time.

---

8. Exodus 32:6.
9. Nothing more is said on this subject.
10. Job 29:15.

We also note a similarity between the verb 'to have' and the verb 'to do.' Someone who has no eyes is said to have eyes, not because he in fact has eyes, but because he has something else that does for him what eyes do; and someone who has no feet is said to have feet because he has something else that does for him what feet do.

It seems to me that whenever a name or verb is attributed improperly* to some thing, the thing to which it is attributed is related to the thing of which that name or verb is properly said as similar, or as cause, or as effect, or as genus, or as species, or as whole, or as part, or as equivalent, or as representation, or as what is represented (for although every representation bears some similarity to the thing it represents, not everything that is similar is a representation or something represented), or (as I was about to say) as signifying in some way other than representation the thing whose name or verb it receives, or as signified by it, or as being in it; or, conversely, that of which it is properly said is in that of which it is predicated improperly; or else the two are related as someone who makes use of something and the thing of which he makes use, in a case in which 'to do' is predicated.

Now all these modes that I identified in the verb 'to do' are sometimes found in other verbs as well—at least one or more of them, even if not all of them are found in each verb. After all, every verb is said according to the first mode if it is said properly of some thing that does what the verb expresses: for example, "he throws" or "he sits" or "he runs" (when he does this with his feet) or "he builds a house" (when he does this with his hands) or "daylight exists" or "the sun shines" and so forth.

By contrast, if what is expressed by the verb is not done by the subject, it is said according to some mode other than the first: for example, if someone is said to build a house who does not actually do anything but merely gives orders, or when we say "The horseman gallops" when the horseman doesn't gallop but makes the horse gallop. So whenever we hear a verb applied to some thing that does not do what is expressed by the verb, careful examination will find that the verb is said in one of the five modes, following the first, that I have described.

So when someone tells me, "I ought to be loved by you," he is speaking improperly. For if he ought, he is obligated to be loved by me; and so he ought to demand from himself that he be loved by me, since he is the one under an obligation, and if he does not carry out what he ought to do, he is sinning. But that's not how he understands what he is saying, even though that's the way he puts it. He says he ought to be loved by me because he makes it the case that I ought to love him. After all, if he has done something to deserve it, he has made it the case that I ought to love him; and if he has not done anything to deserve it, by the mere fact that he is a human being he has in himself a reason why I ought to love him. Thus, 'ought' is said of someone who is not under an obligation but somehow makes it the case that someone else is under an obligation, because he is a cause of the other person's being under an obligation—just as I showed earlier that 'do' is said of someone who does not do anything but is the cause, in one of the ways described earlier, of someone else's doing something. In this same way it is said that the poor ought to receive help from the rich. The poor are not under the obligation; rather, they are in need of this help, and their need is the cause by which the poor make the rich obligated to give them that help.

We also say that we are not obligated to sin instead of saying that we are obligated not to sin.[11] For if one examines this properly, not everyone who does what he is not obligated to do sins. For just as 'to be obligated' is the same as 'to be under an obligation,' so too 'not to be obligated' is the same as 'not to be under an obligation.' And human beings do not always sin when they do something they are not under an obligation to do. For example, a man is not under an obligation to get married, since it is permissible for him to remain a virgin. It follows from this that he is not obligated to get married; yet if he does get married, he does not sin. Therefore, a man does not always sin when he does something he is not obligated to do, if 'not to be obligated' is understood properly. Yet no one denies that a man ought to get married.[12] Therefore, he is both obligated and not obligated. But if we are mindful of what was said earlier, then just as we say 'not bring about being' for 'bring about non-being,' we also say 'is not obligated to do' for 'is obligated not to do.' And so wherever we find 'is not obligated to sin,' it is said for 'is obligated not to sin.' This usage is so common that no one takes it to mean anything other than 'is obligated not to sin.' Now as for saying that a man ought to get married if he wants to, "He ought to get married" is said for "He is not obligated not to get married," just as I showed earlier that 'bring about being' is said for 'not bring about non-being.' In exactly the same way, then, just as we say 'is not obligated to do' for 'is obligated not to do,' we also say 'ought to do' for 'is not obligated not to do.' Granted, 'ought to do' can also be understood in the sense it has when we say that God ought to rule over all things. After all, God is not obligated to do anything, but all things ought to be subject to him. So it is said that God ought to rule over all things because he is the cause of the fact that all things ought to be subject to him, just as I said the poor ought to receive help from the rich because

---

11. This paragraph is largely dedicated to sorting out an ambiguity that does not arise in English. Latin sometimes uses *non debere* for *debere non*. The English equivalent for *non debere* is 'it is not the case that one ought' or 'one need not'; the English for *debere non* is 'one ought not.' Obviously we do not mix up these expressions in English—no one is tempted to say "It is not the case that one ought to sin" or "One need not sin" to mean "One ought not to sin," and it would never occur to anyone to suppose that it is always a sin to do something we need not do. Since the point will be lost in English anyway, translation is hopeless; but I've done my best by using 'is obligated' and 'ought' to translate *debere*, 'is not obligated' to translate *non debere*, 'is obligated not to . . .' to translate *debere non*, and 'is [not] under an obligation' to translate *debitor [non] esse*.

12. That is, no one says that a man is obligated not to get married.

what causes the rich to be obligated to give them that help is in the poor. So it can be said in this sense that a man ought to get married, since everything that is up to a given person ought to be subject to that person's will. And it is up to every man who has not taken a vow of celibacy whether he gets married or not. Therefore, since getting married or not ought to be up to his will, it is said that he ought to get married if he wants to and he is not obligated to get married if he does not want to.[13]

But when we pray that God will forgive[14] us our sins, it would not actually help us if God did for us exactly what our words express. For if God forgives us our sins, he does not remove them or take them away from us. Rather, when we pray for our sins to be forgiven, we are not praying that our sins themselves will be forgiven, but that what we owe on account of our sins will be forgiven. For sins cause it to be the case that we owe these debts, which we need to have forgiven; that is why we pray for our sins to be forgiven when we ought to pray for our debts to be forgiven. What we are praying for in this case is not that our sins will be forgiven but that the debts caused by our sins will be forgiven. This is made clear in the Lord's Prayer when we say "forgive us our debts."[15] This accounts for the fact that in the usual way of speaking, someone says to a man who has burned down his house or inflicted some other sort of harm on him, "Make good the damage you have caused," and the one who burned down his house says, "Forgive me the damage that I caused you." This is not taken to mean that the *damage* should be restored or forgiven, but that what was destroyed by the damage should be made good, and that what ought to be given in restitution for the damage should be forgiven. Along these same lines, the Lord says that those whom we mercifully forgive, and to whom we mercifully give, "will give into your bosom a good measure, pressed down, shaken together, and running over,"[16] because those to whom mercy is shown are the cause that a reward is given to those who show mercy, and so they are said to give the reward.

[8. On will and willing]

We say 'to will' in the same six modes in which we say 'to bring about being.' Similarly, we say 'to will non-being' in the same variety of ways in which we say 'to bring about non-being.'

Notice that we sometimes will in such a way that, if we are able, we bring it about [*facere*] that what we will is the case: for example, when a sick person wills

---

13. Cf. *Cur Deus Homo*, Book 2, Chapter 18.

14. It helps to think of 'forgive' in the sense in which we speak of 'forgiving a debt'—that is, canceling the debt without requiring repayment.

15. Matthew 6:12.

16. Luke 6:38.

health. For he brings it about that he is healthy, if he can; and if he cannot, he would bring it about if he could. This will can be called "efficient," since, so far as it is in the will's power, it brings it about [*efficit*] that what it wills is the case.

Sometimes, however, we will something that we can bring about but don't; and yet, if it is brought about, it pleases us, and we approve. Suppose someone were to say to me that some naked pauper whom I do not will to clothe is naked because I want[17] him to be naked or because I do not want him to be clothed. I respond that I want him to be clothed and not to be naked, and I approve of his being clothed more than his being naked, even though I do not bring it about that he is clothed. We can call this will, by which I will in this way that he be clothed, an "approving" will.

We also will in another way, if, for example, a creditor, by way of accommodating his debtor, wills to accept barley in place of the wheat that the debtor cannot repay. We can call this a merely "concessive" will. For the creditor would prefer the wheat, but because of his debtor's neediness he makes a concession and allows the debtor to pay back barley.

It is also a common way of speaking to say that someone wills what he neither approves nor concedes, but merely permits, although he could prevent it. For example, when a ruler does not will to crack down on robbers and plunderers within his domain, we complain that he wills the evil things that they do, even though they displease him, because he wills to permit them.

Now it seems to me that every will is included in this fourfold division. Of these four different sorts of will, the one that I have called "efficient will" brings about, so far as it can, what it wills; it also approves, concedes, and permits it. The approving will, by contrast, does not bring about what it wills, but merely approves, concedes, and permits it. The concessive will, however, neither brings about nor approves what it wills, except for the sake of something else, but merely concedes and permits it. And the permissive will neither brings about nor approves nor concedes what it wills, but merely permits it, though deploring it.

Holy Scripture makes use of all these different sorts of willing. I shall offer a few examples of this. When it is said of God that "all things whatsoever that he willed, he made,"[18] and "he has mercy on whom he wills,"[19] this is efficient will, and it belongs to the first mode of willing to be, after the likeness of causing to be, since God wills the very thing that he is said to will.

But when we read that "he hardens whom he wills,"[20] this is permissive will, and it is in the second mode of willing to be, since God is said to will someone

---

17. Keep in mind that 'will' and 'want' are the same verb in Latin.

18. Psalm 115:3 (113:11).

19. Romans 9:18.

20. Ibid.

to be hardened on the grounds that he does not will by an efficient will that the person not be hardened; that is, God does not will to bring it about that he is not hardened. Now if we say that God wills to harden him because he does not will to soften him, the meaning will be the same, and it will likewise be a case of permissive will, but in the fourth mode of willing to be. For God is said to will to harden him on the grounds that he does not will something else, namely, that he be softened. For someone who softens brings it about that someone is soft and that he is not hardened.

But when we hear that "God wills that every human being be saved,"[21] this is an approving will, and like God's willing to harden, it will be in the second mode of willing to be, since he does not will to bring it about that anyone is not saved, and in the fourth mode, since he does not will something else, namely, he does not will by an efficient will that a human being be damned, that is, he does not will to bring about that on account of which a human being is damned. This was said as a response to those who say that God's will is the cause of their being not just but unjust, and of their not being saved. For the injustice on account of which they are damned is from them; it does not come from God's will.

If we say that "God wills that virginity be preserved," this is an efficient will in the first mode of willing to be in the case of those in whom God brings it about that they preserve virginity. But in others it is an approving will, either because he does not will by an efficient will that it not be preserved (which is in the second mode) or because he does not will that it be violated (which is in the fourth mode).[22]

[9. On causes]

Now some causes are called efficient—for example, an artisan (for he makes his product) and wisdom (which makes someone wise)—whereas others by contrast with them are not called efficient—for example, the matter from which something is made, and place and time, in which placed and temporal things are made. Nevertheless, *every* cause is said, in its own way, to bring about [something]; and everything that is said to bring about [something] is named a cause.[23]

---

21. 1 Timothy 2:4.

22. There are two additional fragmentary remarks on the subject of will that Schmitt omits from his edition: (1) "Sometimes we will something for its own sake, as when we will health, and sometimes for the sake of something else, as when we will to drink something bitter for the sake of health." (2) "'Will' is said equivocally. . . . A permitting will is when we permit something to be done that nevertheless displeases us."

23. Throughout this section as well I have translated *facere* as both 'do' and 'bring about.'

Every cause brings about something. But one sort brings it about, and is the cause, that that which it is said to bring about—whether being or non-being—is the case; another sort does not bring it about that that which it is said to bring about is the case, but merely that it is said [to be the case]. Thus, both the executioner and Herod are equally said to have killed John [the Baptist], since each brought it about, and was the cause, that what they are said to have brought about was the case.

An example: the fact that the Lord Jesus in his infancy and boyhood interacted with Joseph as though he were Joseph's son brought it about, and was the cause, not that he *was* Joseph's son, but that he was *called* Joseph's son. Now I shall first say something, as God grants me, about the cause that brings it about that what it is said to bring about is the case, and then about the other sort.

Now some of the former sort are proximate causes, which by themselves bring about what they are said to bring about, with no other intermediate cause existing between them and the effect that they bring about; others are remote causes, which do not bring about by themselves what they are said to bring about, without one or more other intermediate causes. For a fire, the one who kindles the fire, and the one who orders that the fire be kindled all bring about the burning, but the fire brings about the burning by itself, without any intermediate cause between it and its effect. By contrast, the one who kindles the fire brings about the burning with the fire alone as an intermediate; and the one who commands that the fire be kindled brings about the burning by means of two other intermediate causes: the fire and the one who kindles it. And so some causes bring about by themselves that which they are said to bring about, whereas others bring about something that is then adequate to produce that same effect, in which case the cause is remote.

It does sometimes happen, however, that an effect is primarily attributed to the cause that brings about something else rather than to the cause that brings about that same effect by itself. For example, we attribute to a ruler that which is done by his command and authority; and we say of someone who does something because of which he is killed that he was killed by himself rather than by someone else.

Now just as some efficient causes are proximate causes that bring about by themselves what they are said to bring about, whereas others are remote causes that bring it about through an intermediary, the same is true in non-efficient causes. For the iron of a sword is a proximate cause and in its way brings about the sword through itself, without there being any other cause as an intermediate; and earth, from which iron is made, is a remote cause of the sword, bringing it about through something else, that is, through an intermediate, which is the iron. For every cause has causes, all the way up to God, the supreme cause of all, who, because he is the cause of all things that are anything, has no cause. Also, every effect has many causes, and causes of different kinds, except for the first effect, when the supreme cause alone created all things. Indeed, in the killing of one human being the one who kills is a cause, as is the one who commands the killing, as is that on account of which he is killed, as well as the place and the time apart from which the killing is not done, as well as many others.

Also, some causes are said to bring about [*facere*] by acting [*faciendo*], but others by not acting—and sometimes not merely by not acting but by not even existing. For in this way someone who does not prevent bad things is said to bring it about that they exist, and someone who does not bring about good things is said to bring it about that they do not exist. And in the same way, just as when teaching is present it brings it about that good things exist and bad things do not exist, so too when it is absent, we affirm that through its absence it brings it about that bad things exist and good things do not exist. But these sorts of causes are included among those that are said to bring about by not acting.

Now although causes are quite commonly said to bring something about not through themselves but through another, that is, through an intermediate—for which reason they can be called remote causes in such a case—nonetheless, every cause has its own proximate effect that it brings about through itself and of which it is the proximate cause. For example, someone who lights a fire is the proximate cause of the fire, and through the fire as an intermediate he brings about burning, of which he is the remote cause. So when something is a proximate cause it is said properly to bring about, because it brings about through itself; whereas when something is a remote cause, it is said to bring about [the remote effect] on the grounds that it brings about something else [that in turn brings about the remote effect].

Every cause is either being or non-being, and similarly, every effect is either being or non-being, since every cause either brings about being or brings about non-being. Now by 'being' I mean everything that is expressed without a negation, whether in one word or in more than one, and by 'non-being' I mean what is said by means of a negation. When the sun is named, a being is said, but it is not yet signified to be a cause. Likewise, when I say 'shines,' I say something, but I do not yet signify that it is an effect of something. But when I say "The sun shines," 'sun' is the cause and 'shines' the effect, and each of them is something and a being, since the sun has its being and brings it about that light has being. So in this case the cause is a being and the effect is a being. On the other hand, if I say "The sun brings it about that it is not night," in this case the cause is a being and the effect a non-being. Similarly, I can express a being using a plurality of words. For example, the sun's being over the earth is something, and it brings it about that it is day and that it is not night. Here a being brings about both a being and a non-being. The sun's not being over the earth brings it about that it is night and that it is not day. In that sentence a non-being brings about both a being and a non-being. Just as that which is said to bring about is clearly a cause, so too that which in any way is signified to be a cause brings about the thing whose cause it is said to be. For example, if one says, "It is day, and it is not night, on account of the presence of the sun," or "It is night and it is not day, on account of the absence of the sun," that is the same as saying, "The presence of the sun brings it about that it is day and that it is not night" and "The absence of the sun brings it about that it is night and that it is not day." And so someone who says, "My knees are weak from fasting and my flesh has been transformed because of oil,"[24] is saying the same as this: "Fasting has weakened my knees and oil has transformed my flesh"; but fasting did this because it was present and oil because it was absent, that is, because it was not present. For often some cause is said to bring about being and non-being by means of its presence and absence, even though 'presence' and 'absence' are not said explicitly—as, for example, in "The sun makes day exist and not exist, and it makes night exist and not exist." But it brings about some things by means of its presence and others by means of its absence.

[10. On the senses of 'something']

We say 'something' in four ways:

1. What we properly call 'something' is what is uttered by means of its name and is conceived in the mind and exists in reality, such as a stone or a log. For these things are named by means of their own terms and are conceived in the mind and exist in reality.

2. What has a name and a mental conception but does not exist in reality, such as a chimera, is also called 'something.' For a certain mental conception in the likeness of an animal is signified by this name; nevertheless, a chimera does not exist in reality.

3. We are also accustomed to call 'something' that which has only a name, without any conception of that name in the mind, and which is without any being at all, such as injustice and nothing. For we say that injustice is something when we claim that someone who is punished for injustice is punished for something. And we say that nothing is something if we say something like "Something is nothing" or "Something is not nothing," since whether the statement is true or false, we are saying that 'something' is affirmed of something or that 'something' is denied of something. Nonetheless, 'injustice' and 'nothing' have no conception in the mind, although they do constitute an understanding in the way that indefinite names do. You see, to constitute an understanding is not the same as to constitute something in the understanding. 'Not-man'[25] constitutes an understanding because it makes someone who hears it understand that man is not contained in, but rather is excluded from, the signification of this word. It does not, however, constitute something in the understanding that is the significate of this word, in the way that 'man' constitutes a certain conception of that which this name signifies. In this

---

24. Psalm 109:24 (108:24).

25. 'Not-man' is offered as an example of an indefinite name.

way 'injustice' excludes required justice and does not posit anything else in the understanding, and 'nothing' excludes something and does not posit anything in the understanding.

4. We even call 'something' that which does not have its own name or any conception or any existence, as when we say that a non-being is something and a non-being exists. For when we say that the sun's not being above the earth makes it not be day, if every cause is called 'something' and every effect is called 'something,' we will not deny that the sun's not being above the earth and its not being day are something, since one is a cause and the other an effect. Now we say that a non-being exists when someone denies that something exists and we reply by asserting that it is just as he says it is—when in fact, if we were speaking properly, we ought rather to say that it is not just as he says it is not.

Therefore, although 'something' is predicated in four ways, in only one of them is 'something' predicated properly; the others are not something but quasi-something (because we speak of them as if [*quasi*] they were something).

SELECTED LETTERS

Letters concerning the *Monologion*

Letter 72 (i.63), To Lanfranc, Archbishop of Canterbury (1075–1077)

1   To his master, a servant; to his father, a son; to the reverend Archbishop Lanfranc, brother Anselm.

2   Concerning the little work that I have sent for your fatherly judgment, I would have preferred to read it aloud myself to have it tested by that judgment in your presence, if only there had been an opportunity. Since that cannot now take place, I would earnestly plead that your fatherly prudence, so dear to me, not disdain to listen to whoever else might read it, and to give instructions about what should be done with it—except that I fear I would be indiscriminately troublesome to Your Worthiness, who I do not doubt are continually engaged in many important deliberations regarding more important matters. Hence, since I do not want any satisfaction for myself at the cost of your displeasure, just as it is a matter for your experience to judge how far you approve of what I acknowledge I want very much, so too it is a matter for your judgment to decide whether it pleases you. Nevertheless, I will not give up imploring, even with persistence, that your authority determine what should be done with this work, whether you hear it read or not.

I have not, however, given it a title; I did not at all think the work was important enough for me to dignify it with a name of its own. So if it meets with your approval that "what I have written, I have written,"[1] let the one who gives

---

1. John 19:22.

authority to the work also give it its name. And let the name be given by you to your servant, my beloved brother and fellow servant Dom Maurice, who is one of those at whose particular urging the work was written. But if your scrutiny should determine otherwise, then let the copy that I am sending to you not be returned to me or to the aforementioned brother; rather, let it be banished by one of the elements: buried, sunk, burned up, or scattered. But whatever you decide should be done with it, I ask you most earnestly to command that it be made known to me in some way, so that the copy I have kept will receive exactly the same verdict as the one I sent.

3   Concerning my dearly beloved one, your nephew, I plead with all my might, by heart and voice and letter, that as soon as you find he has recovered his former health, you will by no means deprive me any longer of his companionship, which I dearly love. For indeed I must tell you that when he was present, he so conducted himself with me and all our brethren who love good behavior that we cannot help longing for him when he is absent, if he can be returned to us without any inconvenience to himself, which we do not at all want.

Letter 77 (i. 68), To Lanfranc, Archbishop of Canterbury (late 1075–early 1078)

1   To his lord and father, Archbishop Lanfranc, worthy of the love and reverence of the sons and daughters of the Catholic Church, Brother Anselm, in obedience his servant, in affection his son, in learning his student, sends all his best wishes.

2   My heart is immeasurably grateful to Your Highness that in the midst of so many duties of such great importance you did not regard it as burdensome or beneath your dignity to attend to my ramblings with fatherly indulgence and correct them with kindly wisdom. For you ask that my love for you not grow cold because of these corrections, which you offer—as God and his saints are your witnesses—with love; and indeed I too am a witness to your inmost thoughts on this matter. Far be it from me, therefore, to be annoyed by receiving advice that I request with great longing, and you send with pure affection, from across the sea. And so I accept your fatherly admonition with gratitude, and I offer my reply with humility.

3   Concerning certain things I said in that little work, you admonish me, with wise and salutary advice, to weigh them more carefully in the balance of my mind and discuss them with those who are learned in the sacred books, and, where reason fails, to give them the support of divine authorities. This I have done both after your fatherly and loving admonition and before it, to the best of my ability. For my intention through that whole disputation, whatever its quality, was not to

assert anything at all except what I thought could be defended directly from the words of Scripture or of Saint Augustine. And now, however many times I go back over what I have said, I cannot see that I have asserted anything else. No reasoning of my own, however compelling it might have seemed, would have persuaded me to presume to be the first to say any of the things from that little work that you mentioned in your letter, or other things that you did not mention. For in his book *On the Trinity* Saint Augustine so proves those very things by extensive arguments that I could rely on his authority in saying them as if I were discovering them for myself in my more abbreviated reasoning. I say this, not to defend to you any of the things I said, but to show that I did not presume to say them on my own, but took them from someone else.

4   Be that as it may, the writing awaits your command, to be kept or destroyed by your authority. Even so, some of the things I said in it could have been said better, and some are so badly expressed that they can be more easily misunderstood than understood correctly. I so distrust my own ignorance that I do not deny this; I have such confidence in your wisdom that I hope these things can be corrected by it. Therefore, may God's merciful will grant us the opportunity to discuss everything in this little work that you say requires discussion with you, as well as everything I wish to discuss myself.

Letters concerning Roscelin

Letter 129 (i. 112), To John, a monk of Bec (1090–spring 1092)

1 To his beloved lord and brother John,[1] Brother Anselm: may you ever be making progress toward better things.

2 I have delayed so long in replying to the letter that you sent to me, beloved brother, concerning that man who says that in God the three persons are three things, or else the Father and the Holy Spirit were incarnate along with the Son, because I wanted to speak more fully on this matter. But since I received your letter, I have been unable to do so, owing to the many matters of business that have stood in my way; so, for the time being, I will offer a brief reply. In the future, however, if God sees fit to grant me the opportunity, I intend to deal with the matter at greater length.

3 In saying that the three persons are three things, he means this to be understood either in terms of the three relations—that is, as God is called "Father" and "Son" and "Spirit proceeding from the Father and the Son"—or else in terms of what is called "God." But if he is saying that those three relations are three things, there is no point in saying that: no one denies that in this sense the three persons are three things, provided that we are careful in understanding how those relations are called things, and what sort of things they are, and whether those relations affect the substance (as many accidents do) or not. It seems, however, that he does not understand the three persons to be three things in this way, because he adds that there is one will or power of the three persons. For the three persons do not have will or power in virtue of the relations, but in virtue of the fact that each person is God. But if he is saying that the three persons are three things insofar as each person is God, either he means to set up three gods, or else he does not understand what he is saying. Let these words suffice, for the time being, to show you what I think about the view in question, my beloved brother.

4 As for your request to spend some time with me before you go on to Rome: know that as far as my love for your worthiness is concerned, I would gladly consent. But, to my way of thinking, it would be of little use to you because of my busy schedule, and it would even be a hindrance to you. For I am entirely convinced

---

1. John was an Italian papal clerk who became a monk at Bec. In 1098, during Anselm's first exile, John provided Anselm with a place to stay at a villa at Sclavia, where he finished *Cur Deus Homo*. By 1100 John was cardinal bishop of Tusculum.

that unless you remain with the bishop[2] until you set out, he will be of little or no help to you in what you ought to do, and I cannot do anything that would be of service to you for the journey you have to undertake.[3]

Letter 136 (i. 118), To Fulk, Bishop of Beauvais (1090–summer 1092)

1   To his most dear lord and friend Fulk, reverend bishop of Beauvais, Brother Anselm, called abbot of Bec, sends greetings.

2   I hear—though I cannot entirely believe it—that the clergyman Roscelin says that in God the three persons are three things, distinct from each other in the way that three angels are, yet such that there is one will and power, or else that the Father and the Holy Spirit were incarnate; and he says that it would be correct to call them three gods if usage allowed. He claims that Archbishop Lanfranc of blessed memory held the same view, and that I hold it myself. I have been told that a council is to be convened shortly by Rainaldus, the venerable archbishop of Rheims, to deal with this matter. So, since I understand that Your Reverence will be in attendance there, I want you to be informed about how you ought to reply on my behalf if the occasion requires it.

3   Certainly his life, so well-known to many wise and religious men, clears Archbishop Lanfranc of this charge, since no such thing was ever said of him; and his absence and death bar any new accusation. Concerning me, however, I want everyone to have this true judgment: I uphold the things we profess in the Creed when we say, "I believe in God, the Father Almighty, Creator of heaven and earth," and "I believe in one God, the Father Almighty, Maker of heaven and earth," and "Whoever wills to be saved, before all things it is necessary that he uphold the Catholic faith,"[4] and the things that follow. The three foundations of our Christian profession that I have set forth here, I so believe in my heart and profess with my mouth[5] that I am confident that if anyone—be he mortal or angel—should wish to deny any part of them, and especially if someone should assert as true the blasphemous claim that (as I said earlier) I have been told Roscelin made, he is

---

2. Fulk of Beauvais, to whom the next letter is addressed.

3. Instead of this final paragraph, some MSS end the letter simply with "May you remain always in good health."

4. These are the opening words of the Apostles' Creed, the Nicene Creed, and the Creed of Saint Athanasius, respectively.

5. Cf. Romans 10:10: "For one believes with the heart and so is justified, and one professes with the mouth and so is saved."

anathema.[6] And I affirm further: as long as he persists in this obstinacy, let him be anathema, for he is in no way a Christian. If he was baptized and brought up among Christians, he should not be listened to at all; no defense of his error should be demanded from him, and no defense of our truth should be offered to him. No: as soon as his faithlessness becomes known beyond any doubt, either he must anathematize the poison that he has spewed forth in his speech, or he must be anathematized by all Catholics unless he returns to his right mind.

For it is utterly foolish and silly to fall into wavering and doubt about what has been most firmly established on the solid rock, simply on account of one person who does not understand it. Our faith should be defended by reason against the impious, not against those who profess to rejoice in the name of Christian. From them it is just to demand that they hold unshaken the pledge made in baptism, whereas the impious should be shown by reason how unreasonable they are in scorning us. For Christians ought to progress through faith to understanding, not reach faith through understanding—or, if they cannot understand, leave faith behind. Now if they can achieve understanding, they rejoice; but if they cannot, they stand in awe of what they cannot grasp.

4   I earnestly request that Your Holiness will take this letter of ours to the afore-mentioned council, or, if perhaps you do not go, that you will send it by one of your scholars. If the defense of my name requires it, let the letter be read in the hearing of the whole assembly; but if not, there will be no need for anyone to see it. Farewell.

On the Incarnation of the Word (prior recension)

To all lords and fathers and brothers who are devoted to the catholic and apostolic faith who will see fit to read this letter, Brother Anselm, though unworthy, yet by divine appointment called abbot of Bec: greetings in the Lord.

1   If I, a trivial and inconsiderable fellow, should try to write something to add strength and support to the Christian faith, when there are so many holy and wise people all over the world, I would indeed be judged arrogant and could appear worthy of ridicule. For if other people were to see me well-supplied with stakes and ropes, and the other usual equipment for trying to secure and steady things that are wavering, working to strengthen Mount Olympus so that no force would shake it or cause it to fall, it would be amazing if they could contain their laughter and derision. How much more so, then, with that "stone" that was "cut out of the mountain without hands and struck and crushed the statue" that Nebuchadnezzar

---

6. Cf. Galatians 1:8: "But even if we, or an angel from heaven, should preach to you a gospel contrary to that which we preached to you, let him be anathema."

saw in his dream, which has now "become a great mountain that filled the whole earth."[7] If I should try to support it with my arguments and steady it, as if it were wavering, so many holy and wise people who rejoice that they are secure upon its eternal steadfastness could grow angry with me and attribute my efforts not to sober-minded diligence but to frivolous self-aggrandizement. So if in this letter I have engaged in disputation concerning the steadfastness of our faith, let anyone who sees fit to read it understand that I have not done so in order to strengthen that faith, but to defend myself: for the more someone knows what I understand of its truth, the less he will believe that I would set down something contrary to it.

2   For I have recently been informed by letter that a clergyman in France has raised a question along these lines: "If the three persons are just one thing and not three things (each person a thing in himself taken separately, like three angels or three souls, but such that they are altogether the same in will and power), then the Father and the Holy Spirit were incarnate along with the Son." He says that Dom Lanfranc of blessed memory, the archbishop of Canterbury, conceded his view, and that I would concede it if he were to engage in disputation with me. I had also been told something similar even before that: a certain Frenchman (though him I knew, because he is a friend of mine) claimed that he heard me say that 'Father' and 'Son' and 'Spirit proceeding from the Father and the Son' are said of God in the way that 'white' and 'just' and 'expert' and similar things are said of a given individual human being.

3   On the archbishop's behalf it is surely enough for me to reply that just as the witness of his life and his wisdom, which has spread for so many years and in so many places, exonerates him of this crime, so too the fact that his accuser aims this libel at someone who is dead and gone undermines his claim.

But on my own behalf I reply that I do not know that I have ever, even in infancy, thought that God is a Trinity like three angels or three souls, or that the Father is incarnate; and I do not in the slightest believe this or want anyone else to believe it; and inasmuch as anyone—I or anyone else—willingly asserts this, he is anathema and should be anathema. And as for his claim that if he were to engage in disputation with me, I would concede his point, I do not know and do not believe that anyone could entrap me in this claim through dialectical sophisms, but I am certain that no one could persuade me of it through rhetorical dazzlement.

4   But I deny and anathematize the claim that 'Father' and 'Son' and 'proceeding' are said of God in the same way that 'white' and 'just' and similar things are said of a particular human being, if this is understood as meaning that fatherhood and filiation and procession cause some change to the divine substance by approaching

---

7. Daniel 2:34 ff.

or withdrawing, as whiteness and justice cause a change in a human being. And I deny and anathematize the claim that the Father can be called 'Son' and 'proceeding' because the Father and the Son and the Holy Spirit are one God, in the way that an expert is called both 'white' and 'just' because these three things are said of one human being. But as for the claim that just as when 'white' and 'just' and 'expert' are said of a particular human being, for example of Paul, they do not make it the case that there is more than one Paul, so too 'Father' and 'Son' and 'Holy Spirit,' which are said of God, do not make it the case that there is more than one God: this I accept, this I believe, this I do not deny having said.

For I believe with my heart and profess with my mouth[8] that the Father alone or the Son alone or the Holy Spirit alone is the one and only God; that any two of them—the Father and the Son, or the Father and the Holy Spirit, or the Son and the Holy Spirit—are the one and only God; and that the three together—the Father and the Son and the Holy Spirit—are the one and only God. Without any reservation and without any doubt, I believe, and affirm that it is incumbent on us to believe, whatever is said in the Creed in which we say "I believe in God" and the things that follow; and in the one in which we say "I believe in one God" and the things that follow; and as we proclaim daily when we sing "whoever wills to be saved" and so forth.[9] This is the rock on which Christ built his Church, against which the gates of hell will not prevail.[10] This is the solid rock on which the wise man built his house,[11] which was not buffeted by the force of the waves or the blowing of the winds. I will try to build my house upon this rock. One who builds on the solidity of this faith builds upon Christ; and one who does not build upon this faith does not build upon Christ—and besides him no other foundation can be laid.[12] Under God's protection I will never engage in disputation about how this faith is not true; by God's gift, in what I believe and love and in how I live, I will always engage in disputation about how it is true. If I succeed in understanding, I will give thanks; if I do not, I will not brandish my horns to scatter,[13] but instead bow my head in reverent submission.

---

8. Cf. Romans 10:10: "For one believes with the heart and so is justified, and one professes with the mouth and so is saved."

9. These creeds are, respectively, the Apostles', the Nicene, and the Athanasian.

10. Cf. Matthew 16:18: "And I [Jesus] say to you that you are Peter, and upon this rock (*petra*) I will build my church, and the gates of hell will not prevail against it."

11. Matthew 7:24.

12. Cf. 1 Corinthians 3:11: "For no one can lay any other foundation besides the one that has been laid, which is Christ Jesus."

13. In the Old Testament the horn is regularly a symbol of power and aggression. The nearest parallels to Anselm's usage in the Latin Vulgate are in Psalm 43:6 (44:5), "In you we will scatter our enemies with the horn"; Ezekiel 34:21, "And with your horns you have scattered all the weak sheep"; and Zechariah 1:19, "These are the horns that have scattered

For human wisdom trusting in itself can more quickly tear out its own horns by brandishing them than it can roll this stone by pushing. For as soon as some people have begun to produce, as it were, horns of self-confident knowledge—not realizing that "if someone thinks he knows something, he does not yet know it as he ought to know it"[14]—they often presume to rise to the very loftiest questions of the faith before they have spiritual wings. This is how it comes about that they absurdly attempt to climb up through the understanding to those things that first require the ladder of faith—as Scripture says, "Unless you believe, you will not understand"[15]—and are compelled by the failure of their understanding to fall into all sorts of errors. For it is obvious that they do not have the firmness of faith, given that they raise objections against the truth of that faith, which has been made firm by the holy fathers, simply because they cannot themselves understand what they believe. It is as if bats and owls, which see the sky only at night, should dispute about the midday sun with eagles, who behold the sun itself with unflinching eyes.

So first our heart must be cleansed by faith; Scripture describes God as "cleansing their hearts by faith."[16] And first our eyes must be enlightened by our keeping the Lord's commandments, since "the command of the Lord is bright, enlightening the eyes."[17] And first we ought to become little children through our humble obedience to the testimonies of God, in order that we might learn the wisdom that the testimony of the Lord gives, for "the testimony of the Lord is sure, giving wisdom to little children."[18] This is why the Lord says, "I thank you, Father, that you have hidden these things from the learned and wise, and have revealed them to little children."[19] First, I say, we must set aside the things of the flesh and live according to the Spirit. Only then can we investigate perceptively the deep things of faith. For someone who lives according to the flesh is carnal or sensual. Of such a person Scripture says that "the sensual man does not perceive the things that are of God";[20] but one who "by the Spirit puts to death the deeds of the flesh"[21] is made spiritual, and of him we read that "the spiritual man judges all things."[22] For it is

---

Judah and Israel and Jerusalem." The close parallel with Ezekiel suggests that by "scattering" Anselm is talking about the disturbing effect that undisciplined skepticism has on those whose faith is weak.

14. 1 Corinthians 8:2.
15. Isaiah 7:9 in the Old Latin text.
16. Acts 15:9.
17. Psalm 19:8 (18:9).
18. Psalm 19:8 (18:7).
19. Matthew 11:25.
20. 1 Corinthians 2:14.
21. Romans 8:13.
22. 1 Corinthians 2:15.

true that the more abundantly we take nourishment in Holy Scripture from those things that feed us through obedience, the more acutely we are brought to those things that satisfy us through understanding. Indeed, someone who ventures to say, "I have more understanding than all my teachers," is speaking in vain unless he is bold to add, "because your testimonies are my meditation."[23] And someone who proclaims, "I have more understanding than my elders," is lying unless he is well-acquainted with what follows: "because I have sought out your commandments."[24] There is no room for doubt about what I say: one who has not believed will not understand. For one who has not believed will not experience, and one who has not experienced will not know. For as much as experiencing a thing is superior to hearing about it, so much does the knowledge of someone who has experience surpass that of someone who merely hears. Let no one, therefore, be in a hurry to plunge into a thicket of questions unless he has first sought in firmness of faith the weight of good character and wisdom, lest he should run carelessly and frivolously along the many side-roads of sophistries and be snared by some obstinate falsehood.

And since everyone ought to be admonished to approach questions concerning Holy Scripture as cautiously as possible, those dialecticians who suppose that universal substances are nothing but empty air,[25] who cannot understand color to be anything but body or human wisdom anything but the soul, ought to be blown far away from any engagement with spiritual questions. Indeed, in their souls, reason—which ought to be the ruler and judge of everything in a human being—is so wrapped up in bodily imaginations that it cannot extricate itself from them; their reason cannot discriminate between those images and the things that ought to be contemplated by reason itself, alone and unmixed. For they do not yet even understand how the plurality of cows in the species are one cow. How, then, will they comprehend how the plurality of persons in that most hidden and most exalted nature—each of whom individually is perfect God—are one God? Their minds are too dark to distinguish between a donkey and its color. How, then, will they distinguish between the one God and his threefold relation?

I have said these things so that no one will venture to investigate the most exalted questions before he is ready—or so that, if he does venture to do so, the difficulty or impossibility of understanding them will not dislodge him from the truth to which he has held fast by faith. Now we must come to the matter on account of which I have undertaken to write this.

---

23. Psalm 119:99 (118:99).

24. Psalm 119:100 (118:100).

25. "empty air": *flatus vocis*, literally, "the breathing of a voice." The expression is associated in particular with Roscelin.

5   This fellow who is said to claim that the three persons are like three angels says this (so I hear): "The pagans defend their law, the Jews defend their law, so we Christians ought also to defend our faith." Let us hear how this Christian defends his faith. He says, "If the three persons are just one thing and not three things (each person a thing in himself, like three angels or three souls, but such that they are altogether the same in will and power), then the Father and the Holy Spirit were incarnate along with the Son."

Look at what this fellow says, at how this Christian defends his faith. Surely he either intends to acknowledge three gods or else does not understand what he is saying. But if he acknowledges three gods, he is not a Christian; and if he does not understand what he is saying, he is a fool. Now in order to make my exposition easier and briefer, I will speak only of the Father and the Son, since these two persons are clearly distinguished from one another by their own proper designations. (The name 'Holy Spirit,' after all, is not foreign to the Father and the Son, since both of them are spirit and both are holy.) But what we will find in the case of the Father and the Son regarding the unity or plurality of the thing or things that he is talking about, we will recognize in the case of all three persons, without any room for doubt.

So let him say, "If the two persons, the Father and the Son, are not two things, like two angels." Let us ask first what he means by "two things." We do after all believe that each person is that which is common to all and is also that which is proper to himself. The person of the Father is God, which is common to him and the Son, and is also Father, which is proper to himself. Similarly, the person of the Son is God, which is common to him and the Father, and is also Son, which is said only of this person. So in these two persons one feature is common, namely God, and two are proper, namely Father and Son. For all those features that are common to them—for example, omnipotent, eternal*—are understood in the meaning of the one common term 'God.' And the features that are proper to the individual persons—as begetter or begetting is proper to the Father, and Word or begotten to the Son—are signified by these two names, 'Father' and 'Son.' So when he says that these two persons are two things, I want to know what he is calling two things: what is common to them, or the individual characteristics that are proper to the individual persons. Now if he is saying that the two proper characteristics (namely, Father and Son) are two things, but in such a way that what is common is just one thing and not more than one, there was no point in saying this, because no one says that these two proper characteristics are one thing. For everyone knows that the Father is not the Son and the Son is not the Father, because being a father is different from being a son, and being a son is different from being a father. After all, we typically apply the word 'thing' to whatever we say is something in any way, and when we say 'Father' or 'Son' of God, we are saying something of God.

So in this way there is nothing to prevent our saying that the two persons, the Father and the Son, are two things. But the words he says next make it clear that this is not the way he understands the two persons to be two things. For he goes on to say, "like

461

two angels or two souls, but such that they are altogether the same in will and power." Of course we do not predicate 'two angels' of any substance that is numerically one or 'numerically one substance' of two angels, in the way that 'one and only God' is said of the Father and the Son and 'Father' and 'Son' are said of God. But neither is there any will or power of the proper characteristics in their own right; rather, the substance of which they are predicated has will and power in its own right. So if he means that the two persons under discussion are two things, like two angels, according to their proper characteristics, it is clear both how unnecessary and how pointless his words are.

So if he is saying that the two persons are two things according to what is common to them—that is, as each of them individually and the two of them at once are one perfect God—then I must first ask whether he is a Christian. I believe he will reply that he is. So then he believes that there is one God, and that this one God is three persons, Father, Son, and Holy Spirit, and that only the person of the Son was incarnate, although with the cooperation of the other two persons. But someone who believes these things also affirms that someone who sets out to make any claims that contradict them is not a Christian. So when he says (I will continue to speak of two persons, meaning what I say to be understood of all three), "If the two persons are one thing and not two, like two angels, it follows that the Father too was incarnate along with the Son," I take it that his reasoning goes like this:

> 6   If God is numerically one and the same thing, and that very thing is the Father and is also the Son, how can it be that the Father was not incarnate as well, given that the Son was incarnate? Clearly an affirmation and its negation are not both true of one and the same thing at one and the same time. But it is perfectly fine to affirm something of one thing and deny it of another thing at one and the same time. For it is not the case that one and the same Peter both is an apostle and is not an apostle. Even if we speak of that one person by two different names, and say of him under one name that he is an apostle and under another that he is not—for example, "Peter is an apostle" and "Simon is not an apostle"—it is not the case that both statements are true; one of them is false. By contrast, it is possible for "Peter is an apostle" and "Stephen is not an apostle" both to be true, since Peter and Stephen are two different people. So if the Father and the Son are one and the same thing and not two distinct things, whatever the Son is, the Father is also. Now the Son was incarnate; therefore, the Father also was incarnate.

7   But if this reasoning is sound, the heresy of Sabellius[26] is true. For if whatever is said of one person is also said of another, on the grounds that the two persons are

---

26. Sabellius taught that Father, Son, and Holy Spirit are not distinct persons in God but merely different ways in which an utterly unitary God relates to his creation. He was excommunicated by Pope Calixtus I in 220.

one thing, it follows that just as 'Son' is said of the Son, 'Son' will also be said of the Father and likewise 'Father' will be said of the Son. And if that is the case, the Father is not distinct from the Son nor the Son from the Father. Therefore, they are not two persons, but one. After all, the reason they are said to be two persons is that the Father and the Son are believed to be distinct from each other, assuming that God is both Father and Son. For a father is always the father *of* someone, and a son is always the son *of* someone; but a father is never his own father, and a son is never his own son. Rather, a father is distinct from the one whose father he is, and similarly a son is distinct from the one whose son he is. Hence, if, in God, the Father and the one whose Father he is are not distinct, and the Son and the one whose Son he is are not distinct, it is false to say of God that he is Father or Son. And from that it will follow that there is no basis for speaking of two persons in God: for we speak of two persons on the grounds that God is a Father and God is a Son, and a father is distinct from a son.

8   So do you see how our faith is destroyed by the opinion of this fellow who supposes that if the plurality of persons in God are one thing and not a plurality of things, it follows that the Father was incarnate along with the Son? If this inference of his is correct, then what follows is not only what I have already said about the Father and the Son, but such extensive confounding of all three persons that whatever is said properly of any one of them must be said of all three in common. Consequently there will be no basis for distinguishing from one another the Father, the Son, and the Holy Spirit who proceeds from the Father and the Son, as I have shown in the case of the Father and the Son. Nor will there be any relation in God, since only items that are distinct can be related to each other. Therefore, there will not be a plurality of persons. For on the supposition that one thing is three persons, either the conclusion he draws does not follow, or else all the conclusions I have drawn follow at once: for the strength of the inference is similar in each case.

But if he says that the plurality of persons can be one thing, but one cannot be incarnate without the other because of the unity of the thing, surely he agrees that they are a plurality precisely because one is distinct from the other. So how is it astonishing or impossible for the Son to have assumed human being into the unity of his person, in which he is distinct from the Father, whereas the Father did not assume that same human being into the unity of his person, in which he is distinct from the Son? It is in fact more impossible for distinct persons, each and in common, to assume one and the same human being into their own unity. For if one human being is one person with each of a plurality of persons, it must be the case that a plurality of persons is one person, which is impossible. Hence, if he believes that it is possible, independently of the Incarnation, for one thing to be three persons, he has to admit that either none of the three persons, or only one, is incarnate. But if he thinks that everything I have said does follow if we affirm that the three persons are one thing, why does he go straight to the Incarnation, as if that alone raised a question? Why does he not instead say, "If the three persons are one thing, they are not three persons"? For he can raise this question both independently of the Incarnation and on the basis of the Incarnation. On the other hand, if he means to assert outright that the persons, insofar as each is God, are not one thing, but three things, each person in himself a thing as three angels are, then it is unmistakably clear that he is setting up three gods.

9   Perhaps, though, he was not the one who said, "like three angels," but merely affirmed that the three persons are three things, without adding any comparison, and the man who sent me his question offered this comparison on his own. Why, then, is he fooled—or why does he fool others—by this name 'thing,' given that the name 'God' signifies this very thing? Surely either he will deny that God is a thing, or else he will likewise affirm that the three persons are not one God, but three gods. I leave it to Christians to judge how impious this claim is.

10   But he will reply, "My saying 'three things' does not compel me to acknowledge three gods, since these three things are one God." To this we say: Therefore, each of these three things—that is, each person—is not God; instead, God is composed of three things. Therefore, the Father is not God, the Son is not God, and the Holy Spirit is not God, since 'God' must not be said of any one person or of two, but only of all three persons named together. And that likewise is impious. For if that is the case, God is not a simple nature but a composite one. Yet anyone who has a simple understanding, one that is not overloaded by a surfeit of phantasms, understands that simple things as such are superior to composites as such, since necessarily every composite can be divided either in reality or in the understanding. Such division is unintelligible in the case of simple things, since no intellect can divide up into parts something that cannot be conceived to have parts. Therefore, if God is composed of three things, either no nature is simple, or there is some nature that is in one respect superior to God's nature—and it is no great mystery just how false both of those alternatives are. Even if he belongs to those modern dialecticians who believe that nothing exists apart from what they can grasp through their imagination, and he does not think there is anything that has no parts, he will at least not deny that he understands that if there *were* something that could not be dissolved either in reality or in the understanding, it would be greater than what could be dissolved, even if only in the understanding. And so if God is a composite nature and every composite can be dissolved, at least in thought, when he says that God is composite, he is saying that he can understand something greater than God. So his understanding passes beyond God.

11   But let us see what he adds as if to drive away the absurdity that seems to result if these three persons are three things: "but such that there is one will and power of these three things." Here we must ask whether these three things are of divine nature insofar as they are understood separately from each other, or in

accordance with their common will and power, or neither only in accordance with what they possess individually nor only in accordance with what is common to them, but in accordance with both at once. Clearly if they possess deity in accordance with what they are separately, they are three gods, and they can be understood to be the same apart from their will and power, since proper characteristics are always understood as distinct from common characteristics and vice versa. So the three will be distinct, and they can be understood to be God—indeed to be three gods—apart from will and power.

Now if the persons taken singly or two at a time or all three at once are God in accordance with their one will and power, what are these three separate things doing there? For some other thing would have to bring them together into unity, and they would not be sufficient for perfection or for any contribution to God's existence. After all, if one will and power is sufficient for God's perfection, what are these three things that God needs, and for what purpose does he need them? For we believe that God needs nothing. So it is pointless to conceive of those three things in God.

And if it is not just these three things, and not just the one will and power, but all these taken together that make up God, I will note again that God is a composite, and that things that are not themselves God make up God. Or if he says that these three things bear the name 'gods' or 'God' in virtue of their power or will, in the way that a human being is called 'king,' then 'God' is not the name of a substance; rather, those whatever-they-ares are called 'gods' accidentally.*

I would need to fill a sizeable volume if I undertook to write out all the absurdities and impieties that follow if we were to say that the Father and the Holy Spirit are incarnate, on the grounds that the three persons are one thing; or if we were to agree that the three persons are three things according to what they are in common as God, rather than according to their individuating characteristics. Perhaps this fellow who makes such claims about an incarnation of the Father and the Holy Spirit, or about the three things in God, understands what follows from them; perhaps he does not. Either way, it is clear that he lacks understanding, and that he ought not to be eager to engage in disputes about the most profound matters, and especially about those in which error is dangerous.

12   But perhaps he will say, "You think the conclusions you draw follow necessarily if the Father and the Holy Spirit were incarnate, or if the three persons are three things according to what is common to the three persons. But I think the inferences I make in the reasoning that you yourself expounded above are no less necessary: if indeed those three persons are something, either the three persons are three things, or, if they are one thing, the Father and the Holy Spirit were incarnate."

Letters on the Sacraments

Letter 415, To Walram, Bishop of Naumburg (before December 1105), On the Sacrifice of Unleavened and Leavened Bread

Anselm, servant of the Church of Canterbury, to Walram, bishop of Naumburg.

To a knowledgeable man I speak briefly. If I had some assurance that Your Wisdom does not favor the successor of Julius Caesar and Nero and Julian the Apostate[1] over the successor and vicar of Peter the Apostle, I would most willingly greet you as "reverend and most beloved bishop." Still, since we ought to do everything in our power not to fail anyone in the defense of the truth, which you are seeking as a rebuttal to the Greeks who have approached you, I have sent you the short work I wrote against them *On the Procession of the Holy Spirit*.

1   Now as for the sacrifice concerning which those same Greeks do not agree with us, it seems to many reasonable Catholics that the Greeks are not doing anything contrary to the Christian faith. For the faith consecrates (*sacrificat*) both unleavened and leavened bread. And neither 'unleavened' nor 'leavened' is added in the text where we read that the Lord "took bread and blessed it"[2] when he made bread his body. Nonetheless, there is no doubt that he blessed unleavened bread—not, perhaps, because what he was doing required it, but because the meal in which this was done provided it. And elsewhere, when he called both himself and his flesh "bread"—because just as human beings live temporally by ordinary bread, so too by this bread they live for ever[3]—he does not specify unleavened or leavened, because both are equally bread. For unleavened and leavened bread do not differ substantially,* as some think, just as a new man prior to sin in no way differs substantially from a man grown old in the leaven of sin. So it seems that the only reason the Lord called himself and his flesh "bread" and made bread his body is that just as earthly bread—whether unleavened or leavened—gives transitory life, so too his body gives eternal life, not because the bread is unleavened or leavened. Nevertheless, in the Law, in which nearly everything was done with a symbolic meaning, the eating of unleavened bread at Passover was commanded in order to show that Christ, whom they were awaiting, would be untainted and pure, and

---

1. The Holy Roman Emperor, Henry IV, who was frequently in conflict with the pope.

2. Matthew 26:26.

3. Cf. John 6:51–52: "I am the living bread that came down from heaven. If any eat of this bread, they will live forever, and the bread that I will give is my flesh for the life of the world."

that we who would eat his body would be admonished to be pure in the same way from all "leaven of malice and wickedness."[4] But now that we have moved on from the old symbol to the new reality and have eaten the unleavened flesh of Christ, we no longer need the old symbol in the bread out of which we confect that very flesh.

2   Nevertheless, it is altogether clear that it is better to consecrate unleavened bread than leavened bread, both[5] because doing so is much more fitting, pure, and faithful, and because the Lord did so. Hence, we must not keep silent about the fact that when the Greeks anathematize the "azimites"[6] (that is what they call us), they are anathematizing Christ. Now if they say that we are Judaizing, let them say that Christ likewise was Judaizing. And if they dare to claim that Christ made his body from unleavened bread on account of Judaism, in order to keep the commandment concerning unleavened bread, their error is absurd in the extreme, because they suppose that he spoiled what was so pure and new with the old leaven. So it is clear that when he used unleavened bread for that act, he did not do so in order to keep the commandment about unleavened bread, but to express his approval of the azimites, who he foresaw would be criticized by the fermentarians,[7] or else, surely, if he also approved of the fermentarians, to express his approval of the azimites as well.

3   As for their claim that we are Judaizing, it is not true, because we do not consecrate unleavened bread in order to keep the old law, but in order to imitate more faithfully what the Lord, who was not Judaizing, did. For when we do something that the Jews did in order to observe Judaism, we are not Judaizing if we do not do it for the sake of Judaism, but for some other purpose. Suppose someone eats unleavened bread during the days of Passover—maybe because that is the only bread he has, maybe because he likes the taste better than that of leavened bread. Or suppose someone is compelled because of an illness to circumcise his foreskin, or someone does not muzzle his ox when it is threshing grain, so that it will not go hungry.[8] Only a fool would judge that those who do these things are Judaizing. Therefore, when we consecrate unleavened bread, not in order to signify through the symbol of unleavened bread that the Lord Jesus will come, but in order to consecrate that very bread as his body by the working of divine power, just as he

---

4. 1 Corinthians 5:8.

5. Reading *tum* for *cum*.

6. "azimites": *azimitas*, formed from *azymus*, a Latin word borrowed from Greek, meaning unleavened bread. "Unleavenders" or "unleavenedites" would be a comparable English coinage, but it doesn't sound quite harsh enough.

7. "fermentarians": *fermentarii*, formed from *fermentatus*, meaning leavened (bread). Hence, the partisans of leavened bread.

8. Cf. Deuteronomy 25:4 (quoted at 1 Corinthians 9:9 and 1 Timothy 5:18): "You shall not muzzle an ox when it treads out the grain."

did himself, we are in no way keeping the old Law; we are celebrating the truth of the Gospel.

Furthermore, when he himself did this, and said to his disciples, "Do this in remembrance of me,"[9] if he had not wanted us (to whom he gave this commandment through the apostles) to do this with unleavened bread, he would have warned us through them and said, "Do not do this with unleavened bread." Hence, given that when he said "Do this," he did not exclude unleavened bread, is there anyone whose understanding would dare to take exception to what he himself did, and to prohibit what he himself not only did not prohibit by any words, but actually commanded by his act? Only someone, I say, who "thinks more highly of himself than he ought to think"[10] and has such great confidence in his own wisdom that he presumes even to utter this claim: that when the Lord says, "Do this," just as we rightly understand this to mean "Do what I am doing," so too we must unhesitatingly understand it to mean "Do this, but not with the material with which I am doing it."

Moreover, if we ought to carry out the divine mysteries using what we recognize as worthier, since we are agreed that the sacrifice of which we are speaking should be celebrated using the substance of either unleavened or leavened bread, which kind of bread do we regard as worthier in bringing about the true body of the Lord, if not that which the old Law chose for signifying, and the Gospel chose for presenting, that very truth? So if we reply to the Greeks that we do this with unleavened bread, not for the sake of symbol, but for the reasons I have stated, there is no conceivable justification for the Greeks to anathematize us, or even to criticize us.

4   Suppose they say that we cannot do this with unleavened bread without understanding a symbolic meaning, and on that basis they argue that we are Judaizing. Then they likewise cannot use leavened bread without a symbolic meaning, because in the Old Testament leaven stands for sin—hence the prohibition of consuming leaven during their Passover—and the New enjoins us to celebrate our Passover[11] "not with the old leaven, neither with the leaven of malice and wickedness."[12]

---

9. Luke 22:19.

10. Romans 12:3. The word for "think" is *sapere*, from which we get *sapientia*, "wisdom," in the next clause.

11. "our Passover": Easter. Both Passover and Easter are called *Pascha* in Latin. The phrase translated "celebrate our Passover" can also be translated as "keep the feast in our Passover," and then "Passover" means Christ (see the next note).

12. 1 Corinthians 5:8: "Christ our Passover is sacrificed for us. Therefore, let us keep the feast, not with the old leaven, neither with the leaven of malice and wickedness, but with the unleavened bread of purity and truth."

We also say that even if we do maintain a symbol in the unleavened bread, we are not Judaizing, because we are not signifying (as the Jews did) that Christ will come without the leaven of sin. No, we are showing, as Christians, that he has in fact come as one without the leaven of sin; and by this we are admonished to present ourselves as ones like our Passover whom we eat. But in this respect the Greeks do not profess to be either Jews or Christians, because by the symbol of their leavened bread they signify neither that God will come without sin, as the Jews did, nor that he has come without sin, as Christians do. Instead they seem to be more inclined toward the pagans, who suppose that Christ was leavened with sin just as other human beings are.

But if they say that Christians ought not to use symbols because "the old things" in which symbols were necessary "have passed away,"[13] let them deny (to take just one example) that baptism is a symbol of a certain death and burial—contrary to the Apostle, who says, "All of us who have been baptized into Christ Jesus have been baptized into his death. For we are buried together with him by baptism into death."[14] Perhaps they will concede that we do use symbols, just not in the same things in which the old Law used them, and for that reason unleavened bread should not be used for any symbolic meaning because it was used symbolically in the old Law. In that case, let them not baptize in water, because "our fathers . . . all were baptized in Moses in the cloud and in the sea,"[15] which they cannot deny was done with symbolic meaning, and to avoid the appearance that they are baptizing with the baptism of John, who baptized in water. So if we are blameless in baptizing with symbolic meaning in water, even though the old baptism that was a symbol of the new baptism was in water, what in the world is this "wisdom" on the part of the Greeks? On the grounds that the old Passover, which symbolized ours, was celebrated using unleavened bread, they abhor our consecrating the body of Christ, who is our Passover, using unleavened bread, with its symbolic meaning: whether to call to mind that he whose body we are offering was without any taint of sin, or to admonish us, who eat his body, that we should be as the Apostle describes: "Cleanse out the old leaven that you may be a new lump, as you really are unleavened; for Christ, our Passover, bas been sacrificed for us. Therefore, let us keep the feast, not with the old leaven, neither with the leaven of malice and wickedness, but with the unleavened bread of purity and truth."[16]

5   And so whether we consecrate unleavened bread with a symbolic meaning or without any symbolism, the Greeks can in no way show that we are worthy of reproach. Instead, either we alone are acting well and they are not, or else, if they

---

13. 2 Corinthians 5:17.

14. Romans 6:3.

15. 1 Corinthians 10:1–2.

16. 1 Corinthians 5:7–8.

are acting well, we are acting better and more faithfully. Indeed, they give sufficient evidence that they have no argument to support their side and undermine ours when it is seen that the objections they raise against us are in no way against us or for them. For as I read in your letter, they raise as an objection against us what the Apostle says: "The letter kills, but the spirit gives life";[17] and what the prophet Amos says: "Offer a sacrifice of praise from that which is leavened."[18] On this basis they attempt to show that the "letter," which commands that the old Passover be celebrated with unleavened bread, kills us when we observe it by consecrating unleavened bread. They do not rightly understand the words of the Apostle. For he says that the letter kills when, in commanding him to abstain from sin, it reveals sin, because unless grace helps him to do what is commanded, the letter makes him disobedient and dishonest. The Apostle shows this explicitly in the epistle to the Romans when he says:

> If it had not been for the Law, I would not have known sin. For I would not have known what it is to covet if the Law had not said, "You shall not covet." But sin, finding opportunity through the commandment, worked in me all kinds of covetousness. For apart from the Law, sin was dead; but I was once alive apart from the Law. But when the commandment came, sin revived, but I died, and the very commandment that promised life proved to be death to me. For sin, finding opportunity in the commandment, led me astray and thereby killed me.[19]

It is in this way that "the letter kills" apart from the help of grace, "but the spirit gives life."[20] As the same Apostle says to Titus, "But when the kindness and humanity of God our Savior appeared, he saved us, not because of works of righteousness that we ourselves did, but according to his mercy, by the washing of regeneration and of the renewal of the Holy Spirit, whom he poured out upon us richly through Jesus Christ our Savior, so that, being justified by his grace, we might be heirs through hope of eternal life."[21]

For that reason, when he said, "Our sufficiency is from God, who has made us able ministers of the new covenant, not by the letter, but by the spirit,"[22] he added, "for the letter kills, but the spirit gives life."[23] In other words, God made

---

17. 2 Corinthians 3:6.
18. Amos 4:5.
19. Romans 7:7–11.
20. 2 Corinthians 3:6.
21. Titus 3:4–7.
22. 2 Corinthians 3:5–6.
23. 2 Corinthians 3:6.

us ministers of the new covenant, which is not in the letter that kills, like the old covenant, but in the spirit that gives life. But what he went on to say applies to both—that is, both to the letter that kills and to the spirit that gives life:

> Now if the ministration of death, carved in letters on stone, came with such splendor that the children of Israel could not look upon the face of Moses because of its splendor, fading though it was, will not the ministration of the spirit come with yet greater splendor? For if the ministration of condemnation comes in splendor, the ministry of righteousness will overflow with much greater splendor. For what once shone with glory has come to have no splendor at all because of the splendor that surpasses it. For if what faded away had splendor, what endures has much greater splendor.
>
> Therefore, having this hope, we are very bold, not like Moses, who put a veil over his face so that the children of Israel might not look upon its fading splendor. But their minds were dulled. For to this very day that veil remains unlifted when they read the Old Testament, because in Christ it fades away. Yes, to this very day whenever Moses is read, a veil lies over their hearts. But when someone turns to the Lord, the veil is taken away. For the Lord is the Spirit, and where the Spirit of the Lord is, there is freedom. And we all, with unveiled face, beholding the splendor of the Lord, are being transformed into his image from glory to glory, as by the Spirit of the Lord. Therefore, having this ministry, as we have received mercy, we do not falter.[24]

I think it is unnecessary to add anything to this about the letter that kills and the spirit that gives life. So it is quite clear that the Greeks' objection concerning the letter that kills neither helps their case nor hurts ours.

6   Now as for the passage they quote from the prophet—"Come to Gilgal and act wickedly . . . offer a sacrifice of praise from that which is leavened"[25]—we must understand that this was said either with approval of such a sacrifice or with disapproval. But if the prophet commands this—here I am speaking as they do—"the letter kills" those who follow the letter and sacrifice from that which is leavened. And if those words express reproach, how impudent they are in offering a sacrifice that the prophet abhors! How unreasonable they are in quoting this passage as an authority in their favor! In any event, it is perfectly clear that the prophet said this as a reproach, not as a command, because he associates it with a wicked action. After all, he had said, "Come to Bethel and act wickedly," and then a little later, continuing his denunciation, he says, "and offer a sacrifice of praise from that which is leavened." Therefore, either let the fermentarians defend their side with

---

24. 2 Corinthians 3:7–4:1.

25. Amos 4:4–5.

reasons as compelling as the azimites have to strengthen theirs, or else let them cast away their own leaven and become azimites. Or, if they cannot do the former and refuse to do the latter, let them at least not reproach the azimites.

7   On the third point of dispute, as I understand it, you wrote that the Greeks denounce our marriages in which blood relatives are joined with blood relatives from another clan. I see no basis in reason or authority for them to do so. For if they forbid this from being done in their marriages, either they do not extend relationships to the seventh generation as we do, or it seems impossible for their requirement to be kept. After all, in a given clan there are often more than a hundred men and women needing to get married. So it would be necessary to find that many clans from which men and women would be selected, to whom those of a single clan would get married, each to a member of a different clan. And so either their marriages are undoubtedly detestable, if they are within seven generations, and ours should not be reproached when blood relatives are joined with blood relatives from another clan—which no authority and no argument forbids—or else, as I have said, it is impossible to keep their requirement that as many clans must be sought out for the marriages of one clan as there are men and women in that clan seeking marriage. But what is done without any basis in authority or reason, indeed contrary to reason, is unhesitatingly judged to be worthy of rejection by reason.

Letter 416, From Bishop Walram to Anselm (before August 1106)

To the most serene Lord Anselm, most reverend archbishop of the holy Church of Canterbury, Walram, by the grace of God bishop of Naumburg, offers a servant's homage, earnest prayers, and himself, utterly devoted in all things.

In the company of Minerva it is extraordinarily foolish to put oneself forward as having something to say on matters of learning, and among distinguished practitioners of the learned arts it is beyond my power to inspire confidence by the force of my argumentation. But in the company of the prophet I sigh, "Open my eyes, and I will examine the wonders of your law."[26] With supreme devotion I lift up my eyes to the hill of your loftiness, that from there my help might come.[27] Your help is help "from the Lord, the maker of heaven and earth."[28] "He who is united to the Lord is one spirit with him,"[29] and hence it is clear that from his fullness you search

---

26. Psalm 119:19 (118:18).
27. Cf. Psalm 121:1 (120:1): "I have lifted up my eyes to the hills, from where my help is to come."
28. Psalm 121:2 (120:2).
29. 1 Corinthians 6:17.

even the deep things of God,[30] whereas I, in my smallness, hear his voice but do not at all know "where he comes from or where he is going."[31]

1   God is an indivisible Trinity, and whatever is in God is one in God. Diversity in the Church is wholly contrary to oneness. Something that attacks itself through strife among its parts cannot long endure. As for the sacraments of the Church, Palestine holds one view, Armenia another, and our Rome and three-parted Gaul still another. And the Roman Church performs the mystery of the Lord's body in one way, the Gallican Church in another way, and our Germany in quite a different way. We have our Eucharistic liturgy[32] from the ancient fathers, and I very much wonder from what source this novelty has crept into the house of the Lord. "Jesus Christ, yesterday and today, and forever"[33] is always one, always the same, undergoing no change. Those who bend their course toward diversity part ways with Christ. Christ is the bread of angels, who came down from heaven and became the bread of mortals, nourishment for the poor, repletion for those who reign with him, in order that those who eat him worthily might live forever and ever. "We who are many are one bread, one body" in Christ, "all of us who share in the one bread."[34] Christ is the way[35] on which we should walk, the one whom we should imitate. Those who stray from the path of Christ are walking dangerously. When we offer sacrifice, let us do what Christ did when he said, "Do this, as often as you"[36] receive it.

2   The Armenians indeed suppose that they are offering a sacrifice of praise from what is leavened:[37] but they are not "walking with Christ in newness of life."[38] Imitators of Christ should keep the feast, "not with the old leaven . . . but with the unleavened bread of purity and truth."[39] "A little leaven corrupts the whole lump."[40] So far as is possible, let not the incorruptible body of Christ be tainted with corruption; let all such corruption be purged from the sacrifice of purity.

---

30. Cf. 1 Corinthians 2:10: "God has revealed to us through his Spirit, for the Spirit searches all things, even the deep things of God."

31. Cf. John 3:8: "The Spirit blows where he wills, and you hear his voice, but you do not know where he comes from or where he is going."

32. "Eucharistic liturgy": literally, "order of sacrificing."

33. Hebrews 13:8.

34. 1 Corinthians 10:17.

35. John 14:6.

36. 1 Corinthians 11:25.

37. Amos 4:5.

38. Romans 6:4.

39. 1 Corinthians 5:8.

40. 1 Corinthians 5:6, Galatians 5:9.

Those who aspire to put on the incorruption of Christ's body[41] should "put off the old nature"[42] by the purity of the new sacrifice. In confecting the body of Christ, only the substance that Christ himself sacrificed is acceptable. And, if I may venture to say so, the rule for sacrificing that he himself gave must be kept.

3 We bless the bread and the cup separately. The canons require, and the Roman Ordo requires, that from the beginning, in the canon of the mass, we make individual signs of the cross over each. We maintain this everywhere as a universal and time-honored custom "from generation to generation,"[43] and we are astonished at your diversity of practice. This is what Christ did; this is what Christ commanded us to do. He said, "Do this, as often as you" receive it.[44] Taking bread, he blessed it separately, and likewise the cup. As indeed our Roman Ordo prescribes, he made a separate sign of the cross over each; and thus our custom has sprung from him who is the same yesterday, and today, and forever.[45] The authority of Christ gives its approval to us on the matter of individual signs of the cross. I very much wonder, then, for what reason such diversity in offering sacrifice has arisen. "There is one faith, one baptism,"[46] one friend, bride, and dove of Christ. It is a great barrier to the unity of the Church when there is inconsistency about the sacraments, and one is allowed to do whatever one likes.

4 Furthermore, during the consecration many keep the chalice covered from the beginning: some with a corporal, some with a folded cloth, an image of the cloth that had been on Jesus' head, which, as we read, was found in the tomb "not lying with the linen wrappings, but rolled up in a place by itself."[47] Christ is "the way, the truth, and the life."[48] He is the way by which we must walk so that we might come to him. "Those who say they abide in Christ ought to walk just as he walked."[49] Only those who are imitators of life come to life. The Paschal victim was sacrificed naked on the altar of the cross. He who made known to his own disciples all that he heard from the Father[50] was willing to be offered naked. In his sacrifice he manifested himself "as he is,"[51] and we will behold his glory "with

---

41. 1 Corinthians 15:53.
42. Colossians 3:9.
43. Luke 1:50.
44. 1 Corinthians 11:25.
45. Hebrews 13:8.
46. Ephesians 4:5.
47. John 20:7.
48. John 14:6.
49. 1 John 2:6.
50. John 15:15.
51. 1 John 3:2.

unveiled face," so that we might be conformed to him in all things,[52] fashioned according to the likeness of his glorious body,[53] that he might be all things to us in eternal blessedness.[54] And to use his own words, "It is finished."[55] This he said so that we might have no doubt that the old things have passed away and all things are new.[56] "The veil of the temple was torn from top to bottom"[57]—the veil that "to this very day lies over the hearts"[58] of the Jews, so that "having eyes, they may not see, and having ears, they may not understand."[59] But we, to whom "God has given revelation through his Spirit,"[60] should not conceal the mysteries of sacrifice, but reveal them, following the example of the Lord Jesus. Let us not join with Moses in covering up with a veil, as the Jews do, but instead let us take care to make our offering with the Lord Jesus and "be changed from glory to glory."[61] Jesus was naked on the altar of the cross; let him appear naked on the altar of our sacrifice. What we proclaim in our words, let us carry out in our deeds. That bread is truly the body of Christ, and it ought to be sacrificed as the sacrifice of Christ's body. Christ's body, naked on the altar of the cross, was wrapped in linen in the tomb. Naked in his suffering, he was wrapped for his burial by the devotion of his disciples. By burying him according to the burial customs of the Jews, they showed their devoted care for their master, but they did not yet know the reality of the sacrament. They buried him as a Jew, like other Jews, because they had not yet come to grips with the mystery of the Cross. "The Spirit searches all things, even the deep things of God."[62] But the Spirit had not yet been given to them, for Jesus, who in his weakness had been crucified, had not yet been glorified. But once he had been glorified, Jesus cast off the garments of corruption. He took off corruptible things; clothed in incorruption, he left the tomb and manifested his glory to those who loved him. Why, then, do we in effect proclaim the weakness of Christ, and his concealment in darkness, by wrapping him in a corruptible cloth, in the moment at which we most truly proclaim that he is the power of God[63] and

---

52. 2 Corinthians 3:18.

53. Philippians 3:21.

54. Cf. 1 Corinthians 15:28: "that God might be all in all."

55. John 19:30.

56. Cf. 2 Corinthians 5:17: "Therefore, if there is in Christ a new creation, the old things have passed away; behold, all things have become new."

57. Matthew 27:51, Mark 15:38.

58. 2 Corinthians 3:15.

59. Cf. Isaiah 6:10, Matthew 13:15, Mark 4:12, Luke 8:10, John 12:40.

60. 1 Corinthians 2:10.

61. 2 Corinthians 3:18.

62. 2 Corinthians 3:18.

63. 1 Corinthians 1:24.

the light of the world?[64] The Light from Light,[65] which enlightens every human being,[66] must on no account be hidden under the bushel-basket[67] of a cloth. No: just as the Priest and Victim offered himself, so too we must offer our sacrifice to him. Set forth in the open, let it light the way to life in Christ for all in the house.[68] Our sacrifice will be most acceptable if it is just like Christ's sacrifice.

Granted, even we wrap the life-giving Victim, not from the beginning, as is your custom, but at the end, with Joseph and Nicodemus.[69] What is offered not only in appearance but in very truth should not diverge in the manner of its sacrifice. One who diverges in offering sacrifice is not walking as Christ walked.[70] If, however, the purity of the sacrifice is urged as a reason for your practice, it is very easy to do as we do and safeguard the cleanness of the pure sacrifice with a lid, without straying from a most ancient rite of the Church from the very beginning of the sacrifice.

5   May your eyes look upon what is imperfect in me,[71] and as you have been built up, as though by the hands of the virtues, into all the fullness of discernment, have compassion on the errors of our imperfection. The Catholic Church glorifies God in me, because the grace of divine goodness is apparent in our transformation. "By the grace of God I am what I am":[72] from Saul I have become Paul, from an enemy of the Roman Church I have become her intimate friend, in highest favor with Pope Paschal, a sharer in the secrets of the cardinals, and in this regard I have hopes for favorable results in all things. Joseph was in the house of Pharaoh; I was in the palace of Emperor Henry. "It was no iniquity or sin of mine"[73] if—God forbid!—I was like Nero the Incestuous or Julian the Apostate. Thanks be to God that under the governance of Your Holiness the wolf and the lamb pasture together, the lion and the kid lie down together, and a little child leads them.[74] And because the scepter of justice is the scepter of your kingdom,[75] we praise the power of God that the wild beasts have grown tame for fear of the Church, and they will not harm anyone on the mount of the Lord of hosts. "The lion will roar: who will

---

64. John 8:12.

65. Nicene Creed.

66. John 1:9.

67. Matthew 5:15.

68. Matthew 5:15.

69. John 19:3–41.

70. 1 John 2:6.

71. Psalm 59:3 (58:5).

72. 1 Corinthians 15:10.

73. Psalm 59:3 (58:5).

74. Isaiah 11:6.

75. Hebrews 1:8, quoting Psalm 45:6 (44:7).

not fear?"[76] But because the righteous are as bold as a lion,[77] your heart, like the heart of strong-handed David, does not tremble before such things, but triumphs in all things in the power of God. May the Lord, who has anointed you with the oil of gladness above your fellows,[78] crown you with mercy and loving-kindness[79] in the kingdom of blessedness.

Letter 417, To Walram, Bishop of Naumburg (c. 1107), On the Sacraments of the Church

To my lord and friend Walram, by the grace of God venerable bishop of Naumburg, Anselm, servant of the Church of Canterbury: greetings, service, prayers, and affectionate love.

I rejoice and give thanks to God that, as you write, the Catholic Church glorifies God in you, because the grace of divine goodness is apparent in your transformation, and you enjoy friendship and close acquaintanceship with Lord Pope Paschal, so that I can greet Your Holiness on friendly terms. But that Your Sublime Humility compares me with Minerva and calls me "the hill": this I do not take for my own, because I know there is nothing in me that would justify such words. Yet I should not be ungrateful to Your Benevolence, because the abundance of your good will toward me causes you to say these things. For we often think better of those whom we love than they deserve. So my heart does not glory in the praise, which does not belong to me; but it rejoices with gratitude in the affection, which is always worthy of love.

1   Your Reverence asks about the sacraments of the Church, because they are not performed in the same way everywhere, but are celebrated in different ways in different places. Certainly, if they were celebrated in one way and uniformly throughout the whole Church, this would be a good and praiseworthy thing. Since in fact, however, there are many differences that do not conflict with the supreme sacrament or its power, or with the faith, and it is not possible for everyone to be brought together into a single usage, I judge that they should be harmoniously tolerated in peace, rather than disharmoniously condemned with scandal. For we have it on the authority of the ancient fathers that so long as the unity of charity is preserved in the Catholic faith, a diversity of customs is not detrimental at all. If, however, you are asking from what source the variety of customs has arisen, I think the answer is simply the diversity of human judgment. For although people

---

76. Amos 3:8.

77. Proverbs 28:1.

78. Hebrews 1:9, quoting Psalm 45:7 (44:8).

79. Psalm 103:4 (102:4).

do not disagree about the power or the reality of the sacrament, they do not have the same opinion about how it is fitting and seemly to administer it. Often, what one person judges to be more fitting, another regards as less fitting. And I do not think that failure to agree on these sorts of differences means straying from the truth of the thing itself.

2   Yes, in consecrating the body and blood of the Lord, some make one sign of the cross over each from the beginning of the canon of the mass. Others make only one sign of the cross over each when the bread or body is named by itself and the cup or blood is named by itself; but when the victim or the offering is named, they make one sign of the cross over both, because just as there is one Christ who offered himself for us, so too there is one offering and one victim in the bread and wine that we offer. I do not see that in doing this the latter are more out of harmony with Christ, who blessed each individually, than are all who do not consecrate the cup after supper, as Christ did, and always at night, as Christ did, and who call both together by one name—'offering' or 'victim'—which Christ did not do. From this we can conclude that we can differ from each other in such actions without being blameworthy, provided that the truth of the thing itself is preserved, since we diverge from the very Author of that sacrifice without offense.

But where we say "these gifts, these offerings, these holy sacrifices," whether the bread and wine are signed separately with the cross or both are consecrated together with a single cross, I find no disharmony worthy of reproach in this divergence—except perhaps that it is more suitable for both to be designated with a single cross, just as they are consecrated with a single formula of blessing. For when we bless several people or a number of different things at the same time, we do not make the sign of the cross on each of them individually; we believe that one sign of the cross is sufficient for all of them.

3   As for the fact that many people cover the chalice from the beginning—some with a corporal, some with a folded cloth—in order to keep it clean, and do not leave it bare as Christ was crucified naked in order (as you understand the sign) to show himself revealed to the world, I do not think they ought to be criticized on the grounds that they fail to signify in their sacrificing the nakedness of Christ, any more than they should be criticized because in that same sacrifice they do not show that he was crucified outside the city, outdoors, and under open skies. And yet these things do have great significance. For "Christ, who suffered for us, leaving us an example that we might follow in his footsteps,"[80] also gave us an example in these things of bearing up for righteousness' sake under incomparable contempt and poverty. For he was held in such contempt, judged to be so accursed, that he was not held worthy to die in the midst of any human habitation, or among any

---

80. 1 Peter 2:21.

men but the accursed, or under any roof but the sky—for he could not be cast out from under the sky—so that, as the prophet wrote, he would be regarded as "the scorn of men and an object of contempt to the people."[81] Indeed, he was so poor that when he came into the world, he was born, not in his own home, but in another's; when he was born, so lowly was the place that he was put into a manger belonging to witless animals; living in the world, he had no place to lay his head;[82] dying, he had nothing to cover his nakedness; and when he had died, he had no shroud to be wrapped in, and no tomb or place where his dead body could be laid.

We should take care to imitate all these things by living out their meaning as reason demands, rather than requiring that the nakedness of Christ be signified by the nakedness of the sacrifice. Nor can I conjure up any reason why we ought to care more that the sacrifice not be covered by a cloth, on the grounds that Christ suffered naked, than that it not be offered under a roof or inside the city, on the grounds that Christ suffered under open skies outside the city. And given that custom does not allow the celebration to take place out of doors because of disturbances in the air, there seems to be a similar reason for the chalice not to be uncovered during the sacrifice [even indoors], because of unseemly things that might occur. And so I think it is safer and more faithful for the chalice to be covered, lest a fly or something unseemly fall into it, which we know has often happened, rather than to leave it uncovered and expose it to possible contamination.

This is my response to Your Wisdom according to my own judgment; I do not reject anyone's better reasoning. As for those who offer the sacrifice using leavened bread, I sent you a letter some time ago.

---

81. Psalm 22:6 (21:7).
82. Matthew 8:20, Luke 9:58.

Letters of Friendship and Spiritual Counsel

Letter 5 (i. 5), To Henry, a monk of Bec (September 1070–spring 1073)

1   To his dearest lord and brother Henry,[1] Brother Anselm sends greetings.

2   As much as your reputation, most beloved, testifies to me that your manner of life toward all is growing day by day toward nobility of conduct along with devout holiness, so much is the heart of your friend enkindled with a longing to see what he hears of with love, and to enjoy what he loves to hear of. But because I have no doubt that your love for me is like mine for you, I am also certain that you long for me as I long for you. For those whose minds are fused into one by the fire of love are right to grieve if their bodies are separated by the places where they live. Yet because "whether we live or die, we belong to the Lord"[2] and not to ourselves, we must be more concerned with what the Lord, to whom we belong, is making of us than with what we, who are not our own, want. Let us therefore serve the longing of brotherly charity in such a way that we serve the dominion of his heavenly will. And let us so display the obedience of subjection demanded by his almighty governance that we preserve the affection of love lavished upon us by divine gift. For we will not be able to unite God's ordering with our own well-being any better than by willingly obeying his will in the arrangement of our own affairs. Furthermore, since both of us have brothers present with us whom we love and who love us in return, as we enjoy them with delight governed by reason, let us fit ourselves to enjoy them with reason filled with delight, and let us pray earnestly that someday we will be together with friends both present and absent to enjoy God himself in their company. For when by heavenly mercy we arrive by our various roads at the homeland for which we now sigh, we will rejoice all the more that we have been called back from our diverse places of exile and now come together. I am urging this effort on your part, dearest one, not as if I feared that you are not already making it, but in the desire that you persevere unfailingly in what you are already doing well.

---

1. Henry was an Italian-born monk who took his vows at Bec in the first half of the 1060s. He followed Lanfranc to Caen and then to Canterbury; his later career as prior and abbot was marked by discord.

2. Romans 14:8.

3   I commend to you Dom Herluin,[3] whom we love and who loves us, as you will learn from his companionship. He will be able to tell you more about my affairs and the matters for which I ask for your kindness than I can do in a brief letter.

4   Consider the letter I sent to Dom Gundulf,[4] changing only the name, to be yours, and yours his. For whatever our love writes to you or to him—whether in declaring itself or in making a request—it says exactly the same to you and to him. But because I can never pray to God or implore men enough for the most beloved soul of Osbern,[5] our departed brother, I again impress upon you that whatever I write to Dom Gundulf on behalf of Osbern's soul, I say it also to you.

Dom Abbot and the whole congregation of our brethren greet you and Dom Gundulf, offering great thanks for your gifts, but much greater thanks for your conduct and good endeavors. Farewell, and lift up the soul of Osbern, my other self, not as his, but as mine.

Letter 17 (i. 15), To Henry, a monk of Bec (late 1070–c. 1075)

1   To his most beloved lord and brother Henry, Brother Anselm sends greetings.

2   Because, as my own conscience bears witness, I am unwilling to love you less than myself, I am very much at odds with myself if I am willing to advise you any differently than myself. But I find no advice that is more useful, or more universally applicable, than the advice wisdom gives us: we should do everything with advice, lest our acts be followed by regret.[6] This advice was most wisely given and so is most truly reliable: so much so that to whatever extent someone ignores it, to that extent he is choosing not to rejoice in his acts, but to regret them. Therefore, if anyone advises you to heed this advice, you should listen to his advice no less attentively than to that very advice that should be obeyed by all people and in all matters.[7]

---

3. Herluin was a monk of Bec transferred to Canterbury (not to be confused with the Herluin who founded Bec and was its abbot until his death in 1078).

4. Gundulf was Norman-born and educated at Rouen Cathedral. In 1057 he became the sixty-seventh monk to make his profession at Bec; Anselm was sixty-eighth. Gundulf was bishop of Rochester from 1077 until his death in 1108.

5. Osbern was professed at Bec at a very early age, in about 1070. Anselm treated him with gentleness and forbearance until he was ready for stricter discipline. Osbern died in about 1071, and Anselm grieved him deeply.

6. Cf. Sirach 32:24: "Son, do nothing without counsel, and after you act you will have nothing to regret."

7. That is, you should treat that human advice as a directive from Scripture itself, since it is.

3   Your friend is speaking with you about advice, most beloved, because I hear you are preparing to take up a certain business against the advice of your friends. You want—so I am told—to leave England for Italy to rescue your sister, who you hear has been pressed into unjust servitude by the wiles of a certain rich man. I beg you, dearest one, through our mutual friendship, if there be any in you, through my joy in you, if you want me to have such joy, not to do this. What does it matter to monks, most beloved, what does it matter to those who profess the will to flee from the world, who is a servant in this world, or whom they serve, or under what title they serve? Are not "all human beings born to toil as birds are born to fly?"[8] Do not all human beings, or nearly all, serve, whether under the title of superior or under the title of servant? Is not "one who is called a servant in the Lord a freedman of the Lord, and one who is called free" in the Lord "is a servant of Christ"?[9] If, therefore, all toil and all serve, and servants are freedmen of the Lord and the free are servants of Christ, what does it matter—apart from pride—whether someone is called servant or free in the eyes of the world or before God? The Apostle says, "if you are called a servant, let it be no concern of yours,"[10] and will we be so gravely concerned on others' behalf about something that we are forbidden, or have no need, to be concerned about for ourselves?

4   Good though it may be to want to free someone bound under duress, what you are planning is certainly not good enough to justify someone who holds the plow of Christ in looking so far back,[11] to justify a monk in breaking his vow with such a hiatus, in exposing himself to so many toilsome dangers and dangerous toils of body and soul on account of a great desire that no one else shares, and—here I rebuke, as charity demands, a friend whom I know I love, and who knows I love him—in resisting the advice of all his friends—inferiors, equals, superiors, and prelates—with such solitary, such inflexible determination. These many and great troubles—or, rather, evils—are so certain, that if that one good—so inopportune, so uncertain, and so harmful—is set against them, would not any intelligent man say that it is not in fact good, but instead evil?

4b   Oh, most beloved friend, put more trust in the advice of your friends than in your own deliberation, unless you regard yourself alone as wiser than all of them together.

5b   I do understand, my brother, that you do not see things this way. For because your mind weighs its great desire along with that very little good, it deceives itself

---

8. Job 5:7.

9. 1 Corinthians 7:22.

10. 1 Corinthians 7:21.

11. Cf. Luke 9:62: "Jesus said to him, 'No one who puts his hand to the plow and looks back is fit for the kingdom of God.'"

by not weighing on a fair scale the only things that really deserve to be weighed. For that reason, whenever we set out to choose from a number of possibilities the one that we ought to, we should set aside every desire of our own and consider only the weight of the things themselves. If we join the weight of love to the weight of the thing loved, our judgment in distinguishing things will inevitably go astray. So if your prudence does not want to deceive itself, it should not add its desire to the thing desired when it deliberates about its choice; it should weigh only the thing itself against the considerations that we bring against it. But if you insist on having your own way—which, under God's protection, will not happen—you will oppose the judgment of every one of your friends, and so you will not have the approval of any of them in this matter, which is so harmful to you.[12]

6   Dom Abbot greets you as a most beloved son; he means for everything I have said here to be understood as his own words. Yield, then, to his admonitions and to mine, and by obeying a kindly father and agreeing with a friendly brother make the father and the brother happy, if you love them. Greet on our behalf our beloved brothers Dom Herluin and Dom Osbern. Farewell, and if there is anything I can do for you, send word to me as quickly as possible whether you are leaning on the will of someone who loves another according to the flesh—your own will, I mean—or instead are bending to the judgment of those who love you according to the spirit.

Letter 61 (i. 52), To Fulk, Abbot-elect (late January–August 1078)

1   To the reverend lord and father, his dearest friend Fulk,[13] Brother Anselm, praying that he may be so ordered by divine grace in this life that he may be worthy to be enrolled among the saints in the life to come.

2   Your Holiness, so dear to me, compels me by your pleas to promise that I will be of service to you; but this I am always eager to do to the best of my ability, without the need for any promise. I know that my prayers are so dragged down by their trifling value in the eyes of God that I am embarrassed to offer them on anyone else's behalf, and yet I have so dedicated myself to you that I strive to pray for you every day with all my might. Know, therefore, my loving brother, that you are never deprived of our prayers (such as they are), not only in the business about which you recently wrote to us, but in all things that concern you. As for

---

12. The MSS diverge significantly beginning at 4b; I have translated the more expansive text.

13. Fulk was abbot-elect of Saint-Pierre-sur-Dives.

our advice, your good judgment does not really need it; yet, because you insist on it, let this page set it forth briefly.

3   We know, of course, that it is safer for someone to escape so great a burden as far as it is up to him, being always fearful of his own weakness, than to take it lightly upon his shoulders, trusting in his own strength. But because, as it is written, "None of us lives to himself, and none of us dies to himself," but "whether we live or die, we belong to the Lord,"[14] we must so tread the path of discernment between fear of our own weakness and obedience to the Lord's will that it is evident that we are not renouncing either of them. First, then, entrust yourself to God's mercy with a pure affection of mind, that he might order your life as he sees fit. Then, with an undivided mind and humble effort, resist taking up this burden in every way you can, so long as you do not sin. If you cannot refuse it without sinning, take it up obediently and bear it conscientiously.[15]

4   May Almighty God allow nothing to be done by you or to you but what pleases him and is of benefit to you.

Letter 96 (i. 84), To Richard and other brethren at St Neots (1086–mid-1087)

1   Brother Anselm, called abbot of Bec, to his most dearly beloved brothers and sons, Richard and others from the congregation of Bec living in England, greetings and fatherly blessings, with love.

2   If you are in good health, and prosperous, and—above all—living in harmony and in accordance with God's will, my soul congratulates your loving hearts with all the affection of a brother and father. For my conscience bears witness to me that nothing brings me as much happiness as the prosperity and uprightness of those who, by some divine judgment I do not profess to understand, have been entrusted to my lowliness; nothing grieves me as much as their misfortune and wickedness. I therefore beseech you as brethren, I admonish you as most dearly beloved sons, always to keep your monastic profession persistently in mind, so that you may show in your life and conduct what the habit of your profession publicly declares.

Truly, neither place nor time exempts anyone from being able to live well, since no one anywhere can ever banish a good will from the hearts of human beings against their will, and a system of conduct ordered according to the harmony of

---

14. Romans 14:7–8.

15. A few months later, when Anselm was weighing whether to accept his election as abbot of Bec, Fulk wrote to him, quoting this paragraph in full and urging Anselm to "take up submissively the yoke of the Lord."

things can stand firm in any disorder. For God never demands deeds beyond our ability when he perceives the integrity of our good will and good conduct. Accordingly, I want you—in all circumstances, and without exception—so to conduct yourselves that you show you are not lovers of the world, or of the things that are in the world, but of God and of the things that belong to God.[16] As others praise God for your good life, you can rejoice in God in this life and the next, and I can truly rejoice with you, my brothers and sons.

3   As for Dom Henry, who was cellarer, I hear that he is behaving in a disorderly fashion in many respects, and particularly in drinking, so much so that he goes drinking in taverns with drunkards and gets drunk with them. If that is true, I cannot express how much my heart grieves over my brother's great fall. This misery will not be his only one for long: unless he quickly amends his life under the chastisement of God, this wretched behavior will drag him toward others, to the very cliff edge of death. Therefore, insofar as an abbot ought to forbid a monk, I, sinner though I am, forbid him by the authority of God and of his saints, and by our own authority, to dare to drink any more in taverns or in the company of those who get together only to get drunk, from the time he learns that I have forbidden it. This, too, I command: he must not fail to do penance for his past disorderly conduct (if he cannot deny it) according to the judgment of our lord Archbishop Lanfranc, or of Dom Bishop Gundulf, or your own; and thereafter he must take care, with God's help, to keep himself from drunkenness and foul language. But if he refuses to amend his life, I altogether prefer that he be returned to us so that he can be kept under discipline—never mind the service we ought to have from him in England—instead of remaining for long without discipline, to his own ruin.

4   But I gently ask Dom Henry of Gournay to endure patiently and calmly what he asked about so urgently in his letter, until Dom Richard (who, as I have heard from the king, is to come to us very soon) arrives; and then that he will bear with gentle patience and patient gentleness whatever is decided by our advice and that of our brethren concerning him and all of you who were sent to England for Dom Richard's sake.

Letter 134 (i. 117), To Lady Ermengarda (22 February 1079–6 March 1093)

1   To Lady Ermengarda, beloved in God, Brother Anselm, abbot of Bec, sends greetings and faithful prayers.

---

16. Cf. 1 John 2:15a: "Do not love the world, or the things that are in the world."

2   Although I do not know you by sight, it should not surprise anyone—for I belong to an order that is obligated to wish everyone well and to offer salutary advice to all—if I impress upon your reverence what is expedient according to what I hear. I have heard, most dearly beloved lady, how things stand between your husband and you, because your nobility does not allow the matter to be kept private, but instead makes it known far and wide. In this matter I first give thanks to God, from whom every good thing comes, that he has given your husband such great steadfastness of purpose to scorn temporal glory for the sake of eternal glory, and has granted you to endure manfully so many trials in order to safeguard your chastity, and yet in such a way that in scorning the world your husband does not love himself more than he loves you, and nothing in this world is dearer to you than he is. Truly, in this both of you are worthy to be loved by God and by good human beings; both of you are worthy of praise. It must be believed that in your great and genuine mutual love you do not love each other's bodies as much as your souls. For you cannot rescue your body from temporal death by any endeavor, by any mutual love; but if you know how to govern your love, you can attain eternal life for your souls.

3   What is it, then, admirable lady, lady of proven chastity, what is it that compels you to hinder your husband from seeking unreservedly the salvation of his soul, which you love no less than your own? For it cannot be supposed, not even for a moment, that you are doing this for the sake of base physical pleasure, which you have so scorned since your husband left you that you have suffered many trials and resisted many advances to avoid taking another husband when you could not keep this one. If you are restraining his soul from making progress toward its salvation for the sake of reputation and temporal advantages that you love and hope to retain through him, how are you loving the soul to whose certain and eternal welfare you prefer your own doubtful, contemptible, and transitory advantages? Or by what justification can you demand that he defer the eternal goods of his soul to the temporal goods of your body, if you prefer the goods of his soul to the goods of your body? See, then, most beloved lady, see, strong and prudent wife,[17] see how, if you do this, you are not governing your love well, how you are failing to love rightly the husband who loves you. What if you compel him to abandon the counsel of his soul for your will and then, because one of you dies or some other misfortune strikes (as so often happens), he cannot help you, and you harm him? Indeed, if you harm his soul, you harm your own.

4   Oh, how much better, admirable lady, how much more laudably you show that you love your husband if you do not merely allow him, but indeed advise him and assist him to strive to bring to completion, with God's help, what he has already

---

17. Cf. Proverbs 31:10.

undertaken by God's inspiration; if, in loving his good, you make it your own; if you trust with complete assurance that the more firmly you reject human help for the sake of love of God and love of neighbor, the more intimately and confidently you entrust yourself to God's protection. Let your wise courage and courageous wisdom trust therefore in God. If your husband were dead, you would suffer his absence unwillingly, and with no benefit to him or to you; so while he is still alive, endure it willingly, for the sake of great reward, both for him and for you. Allow him the freedom to do what he longs to do, so that you may share the reward with him. If God takes care of widows who are not widows for his sake, how much more tenderly will he show favor to one who he sees is a widow willingly, for the sake of love for him! If it should happen (as perhaps it will not) that you lose earthly honor, do not be sorrowful: you will receive greater honor in heaven. And certainly what is much scorned by those who are greater and wiser is not worth much sorrow if it is lost.

5   I would like to counsel you further, but I dare not; yet I am not afraid to pray. May almighty and merciful God grant you, as he has granted your husband, such scorn for the world that you, sister and lady beloved in God, may be your husband's equal in the kingdom of heaven.

Letter 231, To the monks of St Werburgh at Chester (c. 1102)

Archbishop Anselm, to his most dearly beloved brothers and sons, the monks entrusted to the monastery of St Werburgh in Chester,[18] sends greeting and blessings, both God's and his own.

Blessed be God in his gifts, and "holy in all his works,"[19] who causes you both to grow in number and to make progress in increasing devotion. For although I rejoice in the progress of all the servants of God, I have a particular reason why I ought to be happy about your progress, for it was through me that God saw fit to found your congregation and to give you your first abbot, Dom Richard, our most dearly beloved son. I therefore thank God for the grace that he shows in you, and I pray that, as that grace has seen fit to precede you, so too it will follow you without ceasing, so that it may never permit you to fall away from the progress you have made, but grant that you will always move ahead to better things.[20]

---

18. The monastery was founded in 1093 by Anselm, as abbot of Bec, and Hugh, earl of Chester.

19. Psalm 145:17 (144:17).

20. Anselm is alluding to a prayer in the Gregorian sacramentary that begins, "Lord, we pray that your grace may always precede and follow us, that we may be continually given to good works."

This he will certainly do if you take care to preserve the good things you have already attained. For since it is for God always to precede us with his grace, it is for us, by his aid, to be zealous in safeguarding what we have received. For although we can neither have nor preserve anything except through him, it is only by our own negligence that we lose it and fall away. This begins so very often with the smallest things: our crafty enemy[21] is accustomed to deceive us by persuading us that nothing much hangs on them. From this follows that abominable harm of which we read: "One who disregards small things falls little by little."[22] It is a matter of complete certainty, as we have learned from experience in many churches, that in a monastery in which the smallest things are strictly observed, the rigor of the order of monks remains inviolable, there is peace among the brethren, and angry outcries fall silent in chapter. But where the smallest things are overlooked, little by little all order falls to pieces and is ruined. If, then, you want to rise from strength to strength,[23] from success to success, always be afraid to offend God in every single thing, even the smallest.

You should not consider how small the matter is in which you act contrary to a prohibition, but how great an evil it is to commit disobedience for some small thing. For it was obedience alone that could keep human beings in paradise, from which they were banished because of disobedience; and no one can be brought into the kingdom of heaven except through obedience. Ponder this: if, because of just one act of disobedience, human beings have been cast into such great wretchedness as we suffer in this world, how much ought we to shrink in horror from disobedience and bend our efforts toward the good of obedience! All the strength for living rightly is built up by obedience; it is destroyed when obedience is neglected. Therefore, offer obedience to your abbot in all things, not only in deeds, but also in will, and have peace and harmony one with another through your mutual love. And you can nourish and maintain that love if each of you will seek, not to have others do what you want, but to do what others want.

Banish idleness from your midst as an enemy of your souls, and let each of you consider that we are to give an account to God of every moment of our lives. Therefore, when God gives someone grace for some useful purpose, let him put that grace to good use insofar as he has an opportunity. For someone who does not make use of a power for good action that he has will be judged in the Day of Judgment as if he does not have it, and the very thing that he seems to have will be taken away from him;[24] for not only will he lack the reward he could have earned, but from then on, in his punishment, he will have no power for any good work.

---

21. Genesis 3:1.
22. Ecclesiasticus 19:1.
23. Psalm 84:7 (83:8).
24. Cf. Matthew 25:29.

Instead, it will be as if what is taken away from him is given to another[25] when the reward of one who acted well according to the gift he received is increased, because he did not fail in good works despite the example of the other's careless life.

I thank you because you pray for me, and I pray that you will not desist from this work of charity.

Letter 232, To Hugh the monk (c. 1102)

Archbishop Anselm, to his most dearly beloved brother and son Hugh: greetings and blessings.[26]

I have learned from Dom Abbot's words that you have such great love toward me that when you hear of my successes, you rejoice greatly, and when you know of my troubles, you are deeply grieved; that your heart is stirred up against those who you know are causing me any trouble; and that you do not cease to pray for me to the best of your ability. Since, therefore, your love for me is so great, if I do not love you, I must account myself unjust. And because true love desires that the beloved always be making progress, I exhort and admonish you that your mind should always make an effort to strain forward to better things.[27]

If you seek counsel as to how you can do this: always love your monastic vow above all things. You can safeguard it well if you never will to conceal or defend your guilt. For as foxes have their dens, where, hidden away, they bear their kits and bring them up, and as birds have their nests out in the open,[28] in which they shelter their chicks, so the demons make dens and multiply sins in the heart of one who conceals them, and they openly build nests in which sins likewise accumulate in the mind of one who defends them. Be alert, then, if you do not want to be a den or a nest for a demon, never to conceal or defend your guilt. Let your heart be always open to your abbot, and wherever you may be, reckon that not only your body but also your thoughts are before his eyes: and then do and think what you would not be embarrassed to do and think in his presence. If you so act, the devil will flee from the dwelling place of your inmost being as a thief avoids the house of someone who will not conceal him or defend him. For a thief will bring his stolen goods into the house of someone he trusts will either hide him or defend him. But if you put into practice what I am telling you, the Holy Spirit will make his

---

25. Matthew 25:28.

26. Hugh was a monk of St Werburgh at Chester; this letter appears to have been sent along with the previous one.

27. Cf. Philippians 3:13b: "forgetting those things that lie behind, and straining forward to what lies ahead."

28. Cf. Matthew 8:20.

dwelling in you,[29] and he will not be carried off or driven away by any wickedness that comes upon you; no, your good practice, through him, will keep all wickedness away. And this will be turned into such delight for you that you can never imagine anything sweeter, anything more joyful. But you cannot understand what I am talking about except insofar as you will to experience it in your actions.

Dom Abbot recounted many good things to me concerning your growing into maturity, but he added one thing that I could not approve of: you prefer what your own opinion decides, rather than what obedience demands. For although you have skill in writing, you prefer to do anything else that seems better to you, rather than write and thereby be obedient. Know, then, that a single prayer from one who obeys is better than ten thousand prayers from someone who scorns obedience. And so I admonish you as a most dearly beloved son, as one whom I love and who loves me, to put obedience first in every act of yours, to keep constantly in mind the advice I gave above, and to make every effort to carry it out effectively in your deeds.

Almighty God, by the blessing of his grace, direct you always and in all things, and guard you from every evil. Amen.

Letter 403, To Eulalia, Abbess of Shaftesbury, and her nuns (1106)

Archbishop Anselm, to the reverend abbess Eulalia and her daughters, greetings.[30]

I give thanks for your devout love because you prayed for me the whole time I was in exile from England, as you longed for my return; now, however, I ask you to pray with still greater longing that my return will be fruitful. I want you to know that my love toward you, from the time I first came to know you, is alive and endures; and as long as I am alive, it will endure, by God's gift. So, while this love abides, I want to write something to you—though you do not need it—so that you might know that I love you and am concerned for you.

I exhort and admonish you, my beloved sisters and daughters, to be subordinate and obedient to your mother, not only before human eyes, but in the eyes of God, from whom nothing is hidden. For there is genuine obedience when a subordinate's will so obeys a prelate's will that, wherever the subordinate is, she wills what she understands the prelate wills, provided that it is not contrary to the will of God. Your congregation ought to be a temple of God, and "the temple of God is holy."[31] If, then, you are leading holy lives, as I hope, you are a temple of God. And you are leading holy lives if you are diligently safeguarding your order and your resolution; and you are doing this diligently if you do not scorn the very smallest things. Your

---

29. Cf. 2 Timothy 1:14.

30. Eulalia was abbess of St Edward, Shaftesbury, from 1074 until August 1106.

31. 1 Corinthians 3:7.

resolution should always be to aim for progress and to fear falling away with all your heart. Now as it is written, "One who disregards small things falls little by little."[32] And one who falls does not make progress. Accordingly, if you want to make progress and you fear falling away, do not despise small things. Indeed, just as it is true that one who disregards small things falls little by little, so too it is true that one who does not disregard small things makes progress little by little.

Do not think any sin is small, although some sins are greater than others. For nothing that is done out of disobedience—which by itself banished human beings from paradise—can be called small. What sin, indeed, will turn out to be small if, as Truth bears witness, "One who is angry with his brother will be liable to judgment, and one who says 'racha' will be liable to the council, and one who says 'you fool' will be liable to the hell of fire"?[33] I beseech you, therefore, most dearly beloved daughters, not to be careless about anything, but always to make every effort to guard your deeds and your hearts as being in the sight of God.

Be at peace among yourselves, since God's "dwelling has been established in peace";[34] and "great peace there is for those who love God's law, and for them there is no stumbling block."[35] With heart and voice I pray God's blessing and absolution for you; and, if it is worth anything, I give and send my own, to the best of my ability. Farewell.

Letter 414, To Robert and his nuns (Fall 1106)

Archbishop Anselm, to his most dearly beloved friend and son Robert, and to his most beloved sisters and daughters Seit, Edit, Thydit, Lwerun, Dirgit, and Godit, sends greetings, and God's blessing—and his own, if it avails for anything.[36]

I rejoice and give thanks to God for the holy resolution and holy conduct that you enjoy among one another in love of God and holiness of life, as I have learned from our brother and son William. In your love, which I so cherish, most dearly beloved, you request that I write to you some words of instruction to teach you and enkindle you to lead good lives, although you have our beloved son Robert with you, whom God has inspired to care for you in accordance with God's will, and who teaches you thoroughly every day, by word and example, how you ought to live. Nonetheless, because I ought to comply with your holy request if I have anything to offer, I shall attempt to write a few words that bear on what you are asking.

---

32. Ecclesiasticus 19:1.

33. Matthew 5:22.

34. Psalm 76:2 (75:3).

35. Psalm 119:165 (118:165).

36. Robert was a Norman monk with authority over a small community of Anglo-Saxon nuns.

Most dearly beloved daughters, every praiseworthy or blameworthy action derives its praise or blame from the will. For the root and source of all actions that are in our power is in the will; and if we cannot carry out what we will, we are each of us nonetheless judged by God on the basis of our own will. So pay attention not only to what you do, but to what you will; not only to what your deeds are, but to what your wills are. For every action that is done by a righteous (that is, a just) will is righteous; and what is done by a will that is not righteous is not righteous. It is on the basis of a just will that human beings are called just, and on the basis of an unjust will that they are called unjust. If, therefore, you want to live rightly, keep an unceasing watch over your wills, in great matters and in small, in those that are within your power and in those that are beyond your control, lest you fall away from righteousness in any way.

And if you want to know what will of yours is righteous, a will that is subject to the will of God is unquestionably righteous. So when you are planning or thinking about doing anything, great or small, speak thus within your hearts: "Does God will that I will this, or not?" If your conscience answers, "God truly wills that I will this, and such a will is pleasing to him," then love that will of yours, no matter whether you can carry it out or not. But if your conscience bears witness to you that God does not will that you have that will, then turn your heart away from it with all your might; and if you truly want to drive that will away from you, banish from your heart, insofar as you can, even the thought and the memory of it.

As for how you banish a wayward will and wayward thoughts from yourselves, understand and remember this modest advice I give you: do not struggle with perverse thoughts or a perverse will; instead, when they disturb you, forcefully occupy your mind with some beneficial thought and will until the perverse ones fade away. For a thought or a will is never banished from the heart except by another thought or another will that is incompatible with it. Therefore, so act toward harmful thoughts and wills that by focusing with all your energy on beneficial ones, your mind will scorn even to remember or look upon the harmful. But when you want to pray or to focus on some good meditation, if you have thoughts clamoring for your attention that you ought not to entertain, never allow their relentlessness to cause you to leave behind the good thing you have begun, lest the devil, the instigator of those thoughts, rejoice because he has made you fail in the good you had undertaken. Instead, vanquish him by scorning those thoughts in the way I have explained. Do not grieve or sorrow that these thoughts are disturbing you, as long as you give no assent to them, scorning them in the way I have explained, lest in a moment of sadness they come back to mind and resume their relentless attack. For it is the way of the human mind that what brings it pleasure or sadness comes back to mind more often than what it feels or thinks is not worth attention.

A person who is zealous in her holy resolution should behave in the same way toward any unseemly impulse in body or soul, such as an "incitement in the flesh"[37] to anger or envy or vainglory. They will be quite easily destroyed when we refuse to pay attention to them, to think about them, or to do anything under their influence. And do not fear that any such impulses or thoughts will be imputed to you as sin if your will in no way consorts with them: for there is "no condemnation for those who are in Christ Jesus, who do not walk according to the flesh."[38] Walking according to the flesh means willingly agreeing with the flesh. Now the Apostle calls every vicious impulse in the body or the soul "flesh" when he says "The flesh lusts against the spirit, and the spirit against the flesh."[39] We destroy such temptations easily indeed if we crush them from the beginning, in accordance with the advice given above—but only with difficulty once we allow their first stirrings into our mind.

I thank you, most dearly beloved friend and son Robert, as much as I can for the care and love that you have toward these handmaids of God, for God's sake, and I pray with all my fervor that you will persevere in this holy and devout will. For you can be certain that a great reward for this holy endeavor of yours awaits you in the presence of God.

May almighty God ever be the guardian of your whole life. Amen. May the almighty and merciful Lord grant you absolution and remission of all your sins and cause you always to progress with humility toward better things and never to fall away.

Letter 420, To Basilia (c. 1099)

Archbishop Anselm to Basilia,[40] his most dearly beloved friend and daughter in the Lord, sends greetings, and God's blessing—and his own, if it avails for anything.

I have learned from your messengers that you ardently desire a letter from us. In this I recognize your good will and Christian intention, since I see no reason why you might desire a letter other than to receive from it some salutary counsel for your soul. Therefore, although all of Holy Scripture teaches you how you ought

---

37. 2 Corinthians 12:7.

38. Romans 8:1.

39. Galatians 5:17.

40. Basilia was the widow of Hugh of Gournay, who had been an important donor to the Abbey of Bec. Hugh became a monk of Bec, and Basilia apparently entered the abbey when he did, sometime around 1080, and lived there until her death in 1099. Sally Vaughn comments, "Why Anselm placed this letter at the end of the archiepiscopal collection is a mystery, unless the nearness of his own death made his memory of her death seem to suggest its relevance there" (*St Anselm and the Handmaidens of God* [Turnhout: Brepols, 2002], 94).

to live, if you have it explained to you, I ought not to be grudging or unmoved by your devout request.

I will therefore tell you something, most dearly beloved daughter, that will be able to enkindle your heart fiercely toward fear of God and love of a good life if you will meditate on it again and again with all your attention. Let it be always before the eyes of your mind that this present life comes to an end, and no one knows when its last day, to which we grow ever nearer, day and night, will come. This present life is a journey, and as long as we human beings are alive, we are doing nothing but walking that path. We are always either going up or going down: going up into heaven, or else going down into hell. When someone does a good deed, he takes one step upward; but when someone sins in any way, he takes one step downward. This upward or downward path becomes known to each soul when it departs the body. Someone who zealously strives, so long as he is living here, to go upward by means of good conduct and good works will be welcomed to his place in heaven alongside the good angels; but one who goes downward through bad conduct and bad deeds will be cast into hell with the fallen angels. It should indeed be kept in mind that one goes downward much more quickly and much more easily than upward. Hence, in all their wills and in all their actions Christian men and women ought to consider attentively whether they are going upward or downward, and to embrace wholeheartedly those in which they see they are going upward, and to flee and abhor like hell itself those in which they recognize the downward path. And so I admonish and counsel you, dearest friend and daughter in Christ, to recoil from any sin, great or small, and to employ yourself in holy acts, as much as you can with God's help.

I pray to almighty God that he will protect, guide, and guard you, always and everywhere. Amen.

Selected Prayers

Prologue

The prayers and meditations that follow were written to arouse the minds of readers to love or fear God, or to examine themselves. So they should not be read in the midst of commotion, but in tranquility; not quickly and in a hurry, but a little bit at a time, with attentive and deliberate meditation. Nor should readers set out to read any of them all the way through, but only as much as they feel will serve, with God's help, to kindle their affections for prayer, or as much as pleases them. And there is no need always to start one from the beginning; readers should start wherever it suits them. For this very purpose they are divided into paragraphs, so that readers can begin and end wherever they choose; in this way the abundance of words and frequent repetition of the same theme will not grow annoying, and instead readers can derive from them something of the spirit of devotion for the sake of which they were written.

Prayer to Christ When the Mind Desires to Burn with Love for Him

Lord Jesus Christ,
    my redemption, my mercy, my salvation:
    I praise you; I give you thanks.
Although my thanks fall far short of your gifts,
    although they are so destitute of worthy devotion,
    although they are barren of the fullness of your sweetest affection,
        for which I long,
    yet such praises as I have, such thanks as I can give—

not such as I know I owe you, but such as I can offer—
   such my soul sets before you.

Hope of my heart, strength of my soul, help in my weakness,
   let your kindness, so full of power, bring to completion
      what my weakness, so lukewarm, has undertaken.
My life, goal of my striving,
   although I have not yet attained the merit to love you
      as much as I ought to love you,
   I do at least long to love you as much as I ought.
My light, you see my inmost thoughts:
   for "all my longing is before you, O Lord,"[1]
   and if my soul wants any good thing,
      that longing is your gift.
Lord, if it is good—
no, because it is good—
   that you inspire me to want to love you,
   grant what you cause me to want;
   grant me the merit to love you as much as you command.
I give you praise and thanks for the longing that you have inspired;
   I offer praises and prayers,
   lest the gift you have given me of your own accord should prove unfruitful.
Bring to completion what you have begun;
   by kindly coming first to me, unworthy though I am,
      you have caused my longing;
   grant what I long for.
O most merciful,
   turn my lukewarm affection into a burning love for you.
O most compassionate, this is the aim of my prayer,
   for this purpose I call to mind your gifts and meditate on them:
   that I might enkindle love for you in myself.

Your goodness, Lord, created me;
   your mercy cleansed from original sin what you had created;
   and since, after that cleansing in baptism,
   I became filthy by wallowing in other sins,
   your longsuffering has borne with me, nourished me, and waited for me,
      even to this day.
   You wait, good Lord, for my amendment:

---

1. Psalm 38:9 (37:10).

my soul waits for full repentance,

    for the inspiration of your grace to lead a good life.

My Lord, you have created me, borne with me, and nourished me:

    help me.

I thirst for you; I hunger for you; I long for you; I sigh for you; I yearn for you.

    As an orphan bereft of a most loving father weeps and cries out,

    and embraces his father's beloved countenance with his whole heart,

      and will not let go,

  even so do I—

      not as much as I ought, but as much as I can—

    even so do I call to mind your passion,

        I call to mind your beatings,

        I call to mind your scourging,

        I call to mind your Cross,

        I call to mind your wounds;

    I call to mind how you were killed for my sake,

        how you were anointed for burial,

        how you were laid in the tomb;

    and at the same time I call to mind your glorious resurrection

      and wondrous ascension.

I hold on to all these things with unwavering faith;

    I weep over the bitterness of my exile;

    I put my hope in the one consolation of your coming;

    I burn for the glorious vision of your countenance.

Alas for me,

    that I was not able to see the Lord of angels

    humbled to dwell among human beings,

    so that he might exalt human beings to dwell among angels!

Alas that I was not counted worthy

    to stand amazed in the presence of such wondrous,

      such immeasurable mercy,

    when God willingly died

      so that the sinner who had dishonored him might live.

Why, O my soul, were you not there to be pierced by the sword of bitterest sorrow,

    since you could not bear to be wounded by the spear in your Savior's side?[2]

Why were you unable to behold the hands and feet of your Creator

    being profaned by the nails?

Why did you not shudder in horror when the blood of your Redeemer was shed?

---

2. John 19:34.

Why were you not drunk with bitter tears when he was given bitter gall to drink?[3]
Why did you not share in the sufferings of the Virgin most pure,
    his Mother most worthy,
    your Lady most kind?

My most merciful Lady,
    how can I speak of the streams that poured forth from your most modest eyes,
        when you saw your only Son, your innocent Son, before you,
        bound, scourged, and offered as a sacrifice?
    What can I know of the floods that drenched your most devoted face,
        when you looked upon your guiltless Son, your God and your Lord,
        stretched out upon the Cross,
        and saw the flesh from your own flesh cruelly torn apart by wicked men?
    How can I rightly value the sobs that convulsed your most pure heart,
        when you heard, "Woman, behold your Son,"
        and the disciple heard, "Behold your mother,"[4]
        when you received as your son a disciple in place of the Master,
        a servant in place of the Lord?

Would that I, with happy Joseph,[5]
    might have taken my Lord down from the Cross,
        anointed him with fragrant spices,
        and laid him in the tomb;
    or at least that I had followed,
    so that so great a burial would not have been without some mourning from me.
Would that I, with the blessed women,
    had been overcome with fear by a glittering vision of angels,
    that I had heard the news of the Lord's resurrection,
        the news of my consolation,
        news so long expected,
        news so earnestly desired.
Would that I might have heard from the angel's lips,
    "Fear not! Jesus, who was crucified,
        Jesus, whom you are seeking:
        he is not here."[6]

---

3. Matthew 27:34.
4. John 19:27.
5. Joseph of Arimathea: cf. Matthew 27:57 ff.
6. Matthew 28:5; Mark 16:6.

O most kind, most gentle, most joyous Lord,
>when will you make it up to me
>>that I did not see the blessed incorruption of your flesh,
>>that I did not kiss the places of your wounds, the marks of the nails,[7]
>>that I did not sprinkle with tears of joy
>>>the scars that testify to the true body?

Wonderful, inestimable, incomparable Lord,
>"when will you comfort me"[8] and restrain me from my sorrow?
>For my sorrow cannot be contained within me
>>so long as I am absent from my Lord.[9]

Alas for me, Lord; alas for my soul!
>You, the comfort of my life, have departed,
>and you have not said farewell.

You blessed your servants when you went your own way,
>and I was not there.

"With hands uplifted"[10] you were taken up to heaven in a cloud.[11]
>and I did not see it.

Angels promised that you would return,[12]
>and I did not hear it.

What shall I say? What shall I do? Where shall I go?
>Where shall I seek him? Where or when shall I find him?
>Whom shall I ask?

Who will give me news of my beloved, "for I am sick with love"?[13]
>"The joy of my heart has failed; my laughter has been turned to mourning."[14]
>"My heart and my flesh have failed me;
>>but God is the strength of my heart and my portion forever."[15]

"My soul has refused to be comforted"[16] except by you, my sweetness.

"For what have I in heaven, and what have I desired upon earth besides you?"[17]

---

7. Cf. John 20:25.

8. Psalm 119:82 (118:82).

9. Cf. 2 Corinthians 5:6: "while we are at home in the body, we are absent from the Lord."

10. Luke 24:50.

11. Acts 1:7.

12. Acts 1:11.

13. Song of Solomon 2:5.

14. Cf. Lamentations 5:15.

15. Psalm 73:26 (72:26).

16. Psalm 77:2 (76:3).

17. Psalm 73:25 (72:25).

It is you whom I desire,
> you in whom I hope,
> you whom I seek.

"To you my heart has said, 'I have sought your face;
> your face, Lord, will I seek.'
> Turn not your face from me."[18]

Most kindly lover of mortals,
> "the poor have been left in your hands;
> you will help the orphan."[19]

My most secure defender,
> have mercy on this orphan who has been left in your hands.

I have become an orphan without a father;
> my soul is like a widow.[20]

Look upon my tears of bereavement and widowhood,
> which I will bring before you until you return.

Come now, Lord: show yourself to me, and I will be comforted.
> Show me your face, and I will be saved.[21]
> Manifest your presence, and my desire will be fulfilled.
> Reveal your glory, and my joy will be complete.

"My soul thirsts for you, my flesh longs for you."[22]
> "My soul is athirst for God, the living stream:
> when will I come and appear before the face of my God?"[23]

When will you come, my comforter, whom I await?

O that the day will come when I see my joy, for which I long!
> O that I might be satisfied when your glory appears,[24]
> > for which I hunger!
> O that you might give me to drink from the rushing water of your delights,
> > for which I thirst![25]

---

18. Psalm 27:8 (26:8).
19. Psalm 10:14 (9:35).
20. Cf. Lamentations 5:3.
21. Cf. Psalm 80:3, 7, 19 (79:4, 8, 20).
22. Psalm 63:1 (62:2).
23. Psalm 42:2 (41:3).
24. Psalm 17:15 (16:15).
25. Psalm 36:8 (35:9).

Until then, O Lord, let my tears be my food day and night,[26]
    until they say to me, "Behold your God,"
    until I hear, "Soul, behold your bridegroom."
Until then, feed me with my sobs;
    until then, give me to drink from my tears;
    revive me by my sorrows.
And perhaps in the meantime my Redeemer will come, because he is good;
    nor will he tarry,[27] for he is kind.
"To him be glory forever and ever. Amen."[28]

---

26. Psalm 42:3 (41:4).
27. Hebrews 10:37.
28. Romans 11:36.

Prayer before Receiving the Body and Blood of Christ

Lord Jesus Christ,
    who in accordance with the Father's plan,
    and with the cooperation of the Holy Spirit,
    by your death redeemed the world—
    mercifully and by your own free will—
    from sin and eternal death:
    Though my affections are weak and my devotion lowly,
        with all my might I worship and adore this, your holy Body,
        this, your holy Blood,
        giving thanks for so great a gift.
    I long to receive them,
    that I might be cleansed and defended from sins.[1]

I confess, Lord, that I am altogether unworthy[2] to approach them,
    to touch them;
    yet because I have confidence in your mercy toward sinners—
        the mercy by which you gave your Body and Blood,
            laying down your life[3] for sinners, that they might be made righteous,
        the mercy by which you were willing to be offered
            as a pure sacrifice to the Father—
    I make bold to receive them, sinner though I am,
        that by them I may be made righteous.

Therefore, kneeling before you, who are kind and merciful to mortals,
    I beg you that what you have given for the forgiveness of sins
        will not cause my sins to increase;
        no, let it bring pardon and protection.
O Lord, make me so perceive them on my lips and in my heart,
make me so discern them by faith and love,
    that by their power I will be made worthy
        to be planted together in the likeness of your death and resurrection,[4]

---

1. Cf. 1 John 1:7.
2. Luke 7:6.
3. John 10:15, 17, 18.
4. Romans 6:5.

by the putting to death of the old man and the newness of righteous life,[5]

so that I may be fit to be incorporated into your Body, which is the Church,[6]

that I may be a member of you, and you my Head,

that I may abide in you, and you in me:[7]

until in the resurrection you refashion my lowly body

to be like your glorious body,[8]

as your Apostle has promised,

and I rejoice in you forever in your glory,

who with the Father and the Holy Spirit live and reign,

God, forever and ever, Amen.

---

5. Romans 6:6, 4.

6. Colossians 1:24.

7. John 15:4 ff.

8. Philippians 3:21.

Prayer to the Holy Cross

O holy cross,
>which recalls to us that Cross on which our Lord Jesus Christ, by his death,
>brought us back from the eternal death
>>for which we were most wretchedly destined,
>and led us into the eternal life that we had lost through sin:

In you I worship, venerate, and glorify that Cross
>which you represent for us,
>and in that Cross I glorify our Lord, the Merciful One,
>and the acts that he accomplished there by his great mercy.

O Cross worthy of love,
>in which is our salvation, our life, our resurrection![1]

O precious wood,
>through which we have been saved and set free![2]

O admirable sign,
>by which we are signed for God!

O glorious Cross,
>in which alone we ought to glory![3]

It is not because of the mad blasphemy of those cruel men who made you ready for
the Most Gentle One that we are to meditate upon you,
>but because of the One who in supremely wise obedience willingly took you up.

For they could do nothing to him but what he wisely permitted,
>and he bore nothing but what he mercifully willed.

They chose you in order to carry out their wicked designs;
>he chose you to fulfill his righteous work;

they, that by you they might hand over the righteous one to death;
>he, that through you he might rescue sinners from death;

they, that they might kill life;
>he, that he might destroy death;

they, in order to condemn the Savior;
>he, in order to save the condemned;

they, to bring death to the living;

---

1. Cf. Introit for the Mass of the Holy Cross.
2. Ibid.
3. Cf. Galatians 6:14 and the Introit for the Mass of the Holy Cross.

he, to bring life to the dead.
They acted foolishly and cruelly;
> he acted wisely and mercifully.
Therefore, O wondrous Cross,
> we do not value you according to the cruelty and madness they intended,
> but according to the mercy and wisdom he accomplished.

How, then, shall I praise you?
> How shall I exalt you?
> With what love shall I pray to you?
> And with what joy shall I glory in you?
Through you hell is despoiled,
> and it is emptied of all those who have been redeemed through you.
Through you the demons are filled with terror and held in check,
> conquered and trampled underfoot.
Through you the world is renewed;
> it is made lovely by the light of truth and the rule of righteousness.
Through you sinful humanity is justified,
> the condemned are saved,
> the slaves of sin and hell are set free,
> and the dead are raised to life.
Through you the blessed heavenly city is restored and made complete.
Through you God, the Son of God, willed for our sakes
> to become obedient to the Father, even unto death;
> therefore he was highly exalted,
> and received the Name that is above every name.[4]
Through you he made ready his throne[5] and inaugurated his reign.

O Cross,
> chosen and prepared for the sake of such unutterable goods,
> not human minds and tongues alone, but angelic ones, too,
> praise and exalt the great works that have been done through you.
O Cross,
> in which and through which is my salvation and my life,
> in which and through which is all my good,
> far be it from me to glory, except in you![6]
For what profit is it to me if I am conceived and born,

---

4. Cf. Philippians 2:8–9.
5. Cf. Psalm 9:7 (9:8).
6. Cf. Galatians 6:14.

if I live and enjoy all the good things of this life,
    but afterwards descend into hell?
Truly, if it were to be thus with me,
    it would be better had I never been conceived.[7]
And it would indeed be thus with me,
    if I had not been redeemed through you.

With what great joy, then, shall I glory in you,
    without which there would be no glory for me,
    but indeed only the eternal misery and grief of hell!
With what great delight shall I rejoice in you,
    through which, instead of the enslavement of hell,
    I am made an inheritor of the kingdom of heaven!
With what great joy shall I exult in you,
    since without you I should be terrified to exist even for a moment,
    and with you I can rejoice that I shall live forever!
For although as yet I am halfway between fear and hope in serving God,
    still, I know with assurance that through you I will attain such great joys
    if I glory in you by giving thanks, in how I love you, and in how I live.

Through you, therefore, and in you be my glory,
    through you and in you be my true hope.
Through you let my sins be wiped away;
    through you let my soul die to its old life
    and be made alive to the new life of righteousness.
As in baptism you cleansed me from the sins in which I was conceived[8] and born,
    cleanse me anew, I pray, from the sins
        that I have committed since I was reborn,
    that through you I might attain those good things
        for which human beings were created,
    which are offered to us by our Lord Jesus Christ,
    who is blessed forever. Amen.[9]

---

7. Cf. Matthew 26:24.
8. Cf. Psalm 51:5 (50:7).
9. Cf. Romans 1:25.

Prayer to Saint Paul

Holy Paul, great Paul,
one of the great apostles of God,
following all the others in time,[1]
    but leading all the others in your work[2] and efficacy in God's field;[3]
who, when still weighed down by mortality,
    were caught up into the third heaven,[4]
who, caught up into paradise, heard things of which mortals dare not speak;[5]
who among Christians were not merely like a nurse caring for her children,[6]
    but in your wondrous and deeply felt concern
        were in travail with your children a second time;[7]
who became all things to all people in order that you might win them all:[8]
to you, sir, even to you,
    who are known to the world by these and many other words and deeds
    to have great power in the sight of God,
    and immeasurable tenderness toward mortals,
to you comes one who is most certainly a sinner,
    one who stands accused before God,
    a mighty and exacting judge.

He is accused, not of one, not of a few, but of countless crimes.
He is accused not only of small sins, but of immense sins.
The charges are not doubtful; they are certain.
The indictment is not short, but as long as his life is.
He has not one accuser, but as many as know his sins.
For the Judge himself is my stern accuser, and I am openly a sinner against him,
    and all the good and evil spirits in the presence of God
        accuse me along with him:

---

1. Cf. 1 Corinthians 15:8.
2. Cf. 1 Corinthians 15:10.
3. Cf. 1 Corinthians 3:9.
4. Cf. 2 Corinthians 12:2.
5. Cf. 2 Corinthians 12:4.
6. Cf. 1 Thessalonians 2:7.
7. Cf. Galatians 4:19.
8. Cf. 1 Corinthians 9:22.

the good, because they owe their righteousness to God;

the evil, because they serve my unrighteousness;

the good, because they bear witness to the truth they discern;

the evil, because they seek my punishment, which they desire.

Even the good pronounce judgment upon my wickedness,

in that they know I deserve to be damned in accordance with justice.

Alas, how many judges, how many accusers there are against one wretched man!

How stern they are toward one who is weak,

how strict toward one whose guilt is palpable!

Alas, who will defend someone who has God as his accuser?

Is there even one who will intercede for him if all accuse him, if all judge him?

And yet I, too—I myself am my own accuser, my own judge,

for my conscience compels me.

I know that I have done great wrong, and so I have deserved grave damnation.

Even creatures lacking reason, creatures lacking sense, confound me with shame,

if I have any sense myself.

I understand that I ought to blush before all creatures,

because I have sinned against one

who was so powerful that he was able to create them,

and so good that he willed to create them.

I am confounded with shame even by myself,

because I, too, was made by him.

Alas, from what source do so many and such great evils

rush in to attack and overwhelm this wretch?

From you, my wicked sins: it is from you that all these evils flood over me.

It is you who draw my accusers, you who repel my defenders.

You bring forward those who would condemn me;

you cast out anyone who might intercede for me.

You call forth the punisher;

you banish the pardoner.

You lead into fear and shame the one whom you have seduced;

you hide from him hope and comfort.

You drive him into eternal destruction;

you drive away all help.

And to make every wretched thing you do to me more wretched still,

you add this to the pile of misery upon misery:

though this is truly how things are,

I am in such a state that it does not seem so to me.

Truth reveals my condition to me,

and yet my emotions do not feel it.

Reason teaches it,
 and yet my heart does not grieve.
I see that it is so,
 and alas, I cannot melt into tears because it is so.
If I could, perhaps I would have hope;
 having hope, I would pray;
 and praying, I would obtain what I prayed for.
But instead there is no feeling, no grief, in me to match my woes.
How, then, will I have hope?
 Without hope, how will I pray?
 Without prayer, what will I obtain?

Unhappy, insignificant man, what has become of your prayer?
 Where have your hope and trust gone?
I had begun to pray out of presumptuous hope,
 but I fell into despair when I began to understand my true state,
 and my prayer withered because I lost all hope
  that anyone would be good to me.
For if everything is justly against me,
 whose goodness will be with me?
If everything that exists has rightly turned its back on me,
 whose compassion will be turned toward me?
If Creator and creature rightly have contempt for me,
 who will look upon me and have regard for me?
Wretched sinner,
 if all this is so, what is left for you?
Nothing but this:
 your hope must grow listless and your prayer fall silent,
 and you must remain always as you are,
  wretched and ruined.
Truly, you have made yourself wretched of your own accord,
 and so it is just for you to be wretched always.

Wretched sins, truly this—this—is how you repay your promises.
When you are leading us on, you promise such sweet things;
 as soon as you have seduced us, you flood your victim with bitterness.
When you are wooing us, you are as smooth as silk;
 once you win us over, you pierce the soul even unto death.
When you call us into your lair,
 you pretend that it will be so easy for us to return—
 we need only sorrow and repent—
 but when we have fallen into your clutches, you bury us,

blind us,

harden us,

and close off all means of escape.

And so you make your wretched victim—

deceived, ensnared, bound—

lose hope, fall silent, and lie stunned,

as one who is lost to God, who has forgotten God,

until you sell him to the merchants of hell,

who carry off their ill-gotten gains to the lake of death.

All this you have done to me,

all these things I have experienced,

except that I have not yet been handed over to the merchants of death.

Yet that is what I must await in my wretched fear;

that is what they look forward to in their malicious joy.

Alas, how bad it is to be thus without hope;

how bad it is to fall silent.

Alas, also, how futile it is to cry out without hope;

how futile it is to struggle when hope is lost.

O God,

whose goodness is never spent,

whose mercy never runs out,

whose knowledge never fails,

whose power accomplishes whatever it wills:

how will I come to breathe freely again,

when my sins compel me to despair?

Yes, you are angry against those who sin,

but you are also accustomed, kind Lord,

to give counsel to those who seek you.

Teach me, Lord, where I should look for hope,

so that I may be able to pray.

For I do want to pray to you,

but in my ignorance I do not know how,

and in my hardness of heart I cannot,

and despair over my wickedness constrains me.

I look for anything to acquit me,

but there is nothing that does not accuse me.

I look for someone to pray for me,

but I find that everything is against me.

I look for someone to have mercy on a miserable wretch,

but everything that exists has turned its back on him.

Jesus, good Lord,

    why did you come down from heaven,

    what did you do in the world,

    to what end did you give yourself over to death,

    if not to save sinners?[9]

Holy Paul,

    what else did you teach as you made your way through the world?

It is to this faith that Jesus and his apostles, and you most of all, invite us;

    this alone is the secure refuge that you show us.

How, then, can I fail to hope,

    if I believe this, and in that faith make my prayer?

And how will this hope go unfulfilled,

    if the faith from which it is born does not deceive me?

Jesus, my God, and you, his apostle:

    sinner though I am, at your urging I put my trust in this faith,

    I throw myself upon it—

    indeed, I threw myself upon it long ago.

Clothed in this faith,

    I have come before you to pray.

In this faith I ask,

    in this faith I seek,

    in this faith I knock,[10]

    that you might have mercy on a sinner:

        you, Jesus, by sparing me; you, Paul, by interceding for me;

        you, Jesus, by saving me; you, Paul, by praying for me.

Before you both I wrap myself in this faith,

    to hide myself from those who would pry into my sins and exact their penalty—

    and to hide myself from your punishment, O God, my stern Judge.

By your counsel a sinner asks for this concealment;

    I beg you: do not, by your judgment, expose him to damnation.

But alas, another grave evil comes forth to meet me!

    I hoped to attain hope through faith,

    and behold! I see that I do not even have faith.

I thought I was wrapped in this faith,

    and I know that I have been stripped bare of it.

I was confident that I was hidden in this faith,

    and I perceive that I am far away from it.

---

9. Cf. Matthew 9:13.

10. Cf. Matthew 7:8.

For faith without works is dead,[11]

    and dead faith is no faith at all:

    someone who has dead faith has no faith.

Woe is me!

    The fecundity of my bad deeds forbade me to have hope,

    and the sterility of my good deeds proves that I lack faith.

Woe to one who does what is evil!

    Woe to one who fails to do what is good!

For just as evil deeds must displease God,

    without faith it is impossible to please God,[12]

    and apart from good deeds there is no faith.

Truly, if the righteous live by faith,[13]

    those who do not have faith are dead.

And if those who are barren of good things are dead,

    how much more dead are those who are fruitful in bad things?

For if a tree that does not bear good fruit[14] is cut down as something lifeless,

    one that bears bad fruit will surely be rooted up as something harmful.

This is the death, not of the flesh, but of the soul.

How much greater, how much worse, is this death for the one who suffers it

    than the death of the flesh!

For all human flesh that has died will someday rise again,

    but not every human soul that has died will rise again.

And the death that destroys life that may never come back

    is worse than the death that destroys life that will inevitably return one day.

Those who lose the life of righteousness,

    and thereby lose the happy life,

    die a worse death than those who lose this wretched life.

Oh, how much worse, how much more wretchedly, are they lost

    who abandon the life of righteousness—

        for such a life, if kept, restores to the flesh an even better life than it had lost,

        and without such a life it would be better that they had never been born—

    than those who leave behind the life of the flesh—

        for the soul can still be happy apart from the flesh.

I live in this wretched life,

    and I am dead to that happy life.

---

11. James 2:20, 26.

12. Hebrews 11:6.

13. Romans 1:17.

14. Matthew 3:10, 7:19.

I am alive to what is basest in me;
    I am dead to what is best.
So I am more dead than alive,
    and this death of mine is worse than the death of my flesh will be,
    for the death of my flesh will be an evil for me
        only because the death of my soul has already come first.

Holy Paul,
    I have come to you as a sinner to be reconciled,
        and behold! I have appeared before you as a dead man to be raised.
    I have come as a guilty man in need of someone to intercede for him,
        and I have appeared as one who has died a terrible death
            and is in need of someone to revive him.
I have come as a wretch,
    and I have found myself to be wretched beyond description.
I have approached you as a living man under accusation,
    and behold! in your presence I am a dead man under damnation.
For though I have not yet been delivered to the torment of eternal death,
I have already been consigned to the spiritual death
    that brings eternal death in its wake.
Though I have not yet been thrust down into the prison of torments,
    I have already been confined in the pit of sins.
Though I have not yet been buried in hell,
    I am already shrouded for burial, wrapped in my sins.
This, certainly, is why I could not pray, why I did not know how to pray.
    This, truly, is why I understood that I was abhorrent to all things
        and yet was not sorrowful, as if I had lost all feeling.
    By my rational nature I understood it,
        but in the insensibility of death I could not feel it.
Truly, I had died, and I have come to you as a dead man,
    and I have only now discovered that I am dead.

O God,
    who will pray for this dead man?
Holy Paul,
    I have brought him to you:
    do not turn him away;
    pray for him.
Sir,

to revive the dead, Elijah[15] and Elisha[16] stretched themselves out on the dead,
    joining limbs to limbs, living to dead.

Sir,

    they who were alive brought back to life the dead whom they touched,
    and the dead imparted nothing to them but glory.

Sir,

    you, too, say that you have become all things to all people,
    in order that you might win them all.[17]

Friend of God,

    the examples of others make me bold;
    your words bid me to have confidence.

Therefore will I speak, sir:

    I will say,
    "Sir, O sir, come down to this dead man;
    stretch yourself out upon this dead man;
    make yourself, not dead, but like this dead man.
    Let this dead man grow warm again by the warm touch of your compassion;
    let this dead man come to life again by the working of your power;
    let this dead man as a living man give glory to God and to you."

Sir,

    you are not powerless to revive this dead man,
    for God bears witness that his grace is sufficient for you.[18]

For if it was sufficient for you when you were in pilgrimage on earth,
    it will certainly not fail you now that you are at home in heaven.

Why, sir, should this dead man, offered to you, lie any longer without life,
    when God bears witness to your power,
    and you bear witness to your piety?

Lord God, you say to Paul, "My grace is sufficient for you";[19]
    holy Paul, you say to us, "I have become all things to all people."[20]

Look, therefore: this dead man awaits the fulfillment of your words,
    drawn to you by this hope.

You speak, and the dead man hears and hopes;
    you promise, and the dead man prays and awaits.

---

15. 1 Kings 17:21.
16. 2 Kings 4:34.
17. Cf. 1 Corinthians 9:22.
18. 2 Corinthians 12:9.
19. Ibid.
20. 1 Corinthians 9:22.

You speak, and by you it is done:
> I beg you, let me experience the powerful work
>> that has been openly shown to a rejoicing world.

If you do not deny your words,
> why do you withhold their fulfillment from one who asks for it?

If one who is brought before you dead is carried away dead,
> to whom can a dead man be brought with greater assurance to be restored to life?

Where will you send him if you send him away?

Where will he go if he leaves you?

O God, who will bring him back to life if you do not?

In whom is there hope if there is no hope in God?

By whom will his lost life be restored if not by the one from whom he first received it?

Holy Paul,
> who will be good to the needy and sorrowful
> if he who promises to make himself weak among those who are weak[21]
>> proves unyielding?

> Who will deign to pray for the wretched
> if he who declares that he has made himself all things to all people[22]
>> disdains to pray?

> Who will even hear, if the one for whom God's grace is sufficient[23]
>> does not listen?

> Can the one for whom God's grace is sufficient
>> fail in goodness or be lacking in power?

I appeal to you both:
> what will move you if these pleas do not move you?

If not from you, from what source can I acquire something to lay before
> you to arouse your mercy?

What of its own does a dead soul have to lay before you
> but its sinfulness and wretchedness?

Yet still it prays, in penitence and sorrow.

Oh, if he who came from heaven to call sinners to repentance,[24]
> and he who after him worked harder than all others[25] to that same end,
> should scorn a penitent soul because it is sinful;

---

21. 2 Corinthians 11:29.

22. 1 Corinthians 9:22.

23. 2 Corinthians 12:9.

24. Luke 5:32.

25. 1 Corinthians 15:10.

if he who left the Father's bosom[26] to carry our sorrows,[27]

and he who says he made himself weak among those who are weak,[28]

should despise a sorrowful soul because it is wretched;

if he who died that he might bring life to the dead,

and he who shows himself to have become all things to all people,[29]

should spurn a prayerful soul because it is dead!

Not so, God: let it not be so!

It must not be, cannot be so!

If it is so, compassion has perished;

if it is so, mercy is dead.

O soul cast down and cast away—

cast down because you have sinned,

cast away when you make your appeal—

where will you turn?

Turn yourself to persistent prayer.

They seek after the sorrowful one who persists in prayer;

they choose the tenacious wretch;

they love one who never ceases to lament.

Go, then, and continue to seek from them

what you never tire of offering them.

O holy Paul,

where is the one who was called the nurse of the faithful,

taking care of her children?[30]

Who is that affectionate mother,

who preaches everywhere that she is in travail once again with her children?[31]

Sweet nurse, sweet mother,

who are these children whom you bear, whom you suckle,

if not those whom you beget and rear by teaching them in the faith of Christ?

What Christian after you has not been born and strengthened in the faith

because of your teaching?

---

26. John 1:18.

27. Isaiah 53:4.

28. 2 Corinthians 11:29.

29. 1 Corinthians 9:22.

30. 1 Thessalonians 2:7.

31. Galatians 4:19.

For even if this blessed faith was born and nourished in us by other apostles too,
> it was even more by you,
>> because in this you worked harder and accomplished more than all of them.[32]

So although they are mothers to us,
> you are even more our mother.

Therefore, holy Paul,
> this dead man is your son.

Mother, this dead man is most assuredly your son.

Sweet mother, know your son by the voice of his confession;[33]
> let him know his mother by the warmth of her compassion.

Know your son by his confession of the Christian faith;
> let him know his mother by the sweetness of your mercy.

Come, mother—
> you who were once again in travail with your children[34]—
> offer your dead son to be restored to life by him
>> who by his death restored his servants to life.

Come, mother,
> offer your son to the one who, by a death he did not owe,
> recalled his guilty servants from the death that was their due;
> offer your son to him, that he might recall him to the life he has lost.

For by baptism he was drawn out of death;
> by his sterility and wickedness he was drawn back to death.

O mother of celebrated kindness,
> let your son experience the deep compassion of your motherly goodness.

Present him before the one who restored you to life
> and upheld you as long as you lived.

Pray to him for your son, because he is his servant;
> pray to him for his servant, because he is your son.

And you, Jesus, good Lord:
> are not you also a mother?

Is one not a mother who like a hen gathers her brood under her wings?[35]

Truly, Lord, you too are a mother.

For the very fact that others have been in labor and given birth
> is something they received from you.

---

32. 1 Corinthians 15:10.
33. Psalm 42:4 (41:5).
34. 1 Thessalonians 2:7.
35. Matthew 23:37.

You first, before them, died in labor with those whom they bore,
     and in dying you gave birth to them.
If you had not given birth to them, you would not have suffered death;
     and if you had not died, you would not have given birth.
For in your longing to bring children into life, you tasted death,
     and in dying you brought them to life.
You did this by your own power, they at your command and with your help;
     you as author, they as your ministers.
Therefore, you, Lord God, are even more a mother.

Therefore, you are both mothers.
Yes, you are fathers, but you are nonetheless also mothers.
For you have brought it about—
     you, Jesus, through yourself; you, Paul, through him—
     that we who are born into death are reborn into life.
So you are fathers in the power of your effect,
     mothers in the tenderness of your affection;
     fathers in authority, mothers in gentleness;
     fathers in protecting us, mothers in pitying us.
Therefore, you are both mothers.
Though you are not equals in the greatness of your affection,
     you are not much different in the character of your affection.
Though you not evenly matched in the extent of your kindness,
     you are harmonious in your wills.
Though the full scope of your mercy is not the same,
     your intentions are in full agreement.

Why should I keep quiet about what you are saying?
To what end should I hide what you are openly showing?
Why should I conceal what you are doing?
You make it known far and wide that you are mothers;
     I acknowledge that I am your son.
I give thanks that you have begotten me as your son,
     because you have made me a Christian:
     you, Jesus, through yourself;
          you, Paul, through him;
     you, Jesus, through the teaching you gave;
          you, Paul, through the teaching he inspired in you;
     you, Jesus, through the grace you bestowed on me;
          you, Paul, through the grace you received from him.

Mother Paul,
>   he gave birth to you too.

Set down your dead son at the feet of Christ, your mother,
>   because he is Christ's son.

No, indeed: throw him upon the bosom of his kindness,
>   because he is even more a mother.

Pray that he will restore life to this dead son,
>   who is his own son even more than he is yours.

Pray for your son, because you are a mother:
>   pray that he will bring him back to life, because he is a mother.

Mother of my soul,
>   do what the mother of my flesh would do.

Truly, if she had hope, she would pray as much as she could;
>   nor would she cease to pray until she received what she asked for,
>>   if it were possible.

Assuredly, if you are willing, you cannot lack hope;
>   and if you pray, you can receive what you ask for.

Pray earnestly, then, that the dead soul whom you bore alive
>   will be restored to life,
>   and do not cease until it is returned to you alive.

You too, my soul,
>   who are dead by your own doing,
>   run to shelter beneath the wings[36] of Jesus your mother,
>   and bewail your sorrows beneath his pinions.[37]
>   Ask him to tend to your wounds,
>   so that they can be healed, and you restored to life.

Mother Christ,
>   who gather your brood beneath your wings,[38]
>   this dead chick of yours takes shelter under your wings.

For by your gentleness the terrified are comforted;
>   by your sweet smell the hopeless are restored.

Your warmth revives the dead;
>   your touch justifies sinners.

---

36. Matthew 23:27.
37. Psalm 91:4 (90:4).
38. Matthew 23:27.

Mother, recognize your dead son at least by the sign of your Cross,
    and by the voice of your confession.[39]
Restore your chick,
    raise your dead,
    justify your sinner.
Let your terrified child receive your consolation;
    let one who despairs of himself receive comfort from you;
    restore him to the fullness of your indivisible grace.
For the comfort of the wretched flows from you,
    who are blessed forever. Amen.[40]

---

39. Psalm 42:4 (41:5).
40. Romans 1:25.

Meditation on Human Redemption

Christian soul,
    soul brought back to life from burdensome death,
    soul redeemed and set free from slavery by the blood of God:[1]
    arouse your mind,
    remember your resurrection,
    ponder once again your redemption and liberation.
Consider once again the power of your salvation,
    what it is and where it is found;
    take time in meditating on it;
    take pleasure in contemplating it.
Cast off your weariness,
    put vigor in your heart,
    and firmly direct your mind to this.
Taste the goodness of your Redeemer,
    burn with love for your Savior.
Chew the honeycomb of his words;
    savor their taste, which is better than honey;
    drink deeply of their healthful sweetness.
Chew by pondering,
    savor by understanding,
    drink by loving and rejoicing.
Rejoice in your chewing,
    be glad in your savoring,
    delight in your drinking.

---

1. Cf. Ephesians 1:7.

What, then, is the power and strength of your salvation,
> and where is it to be found?

Truly, Christ has brought you back to life.
> He is the good Samaritan who has restored your health;[2]
> he is the good friend who by his own life has redeemed you and set you free.

Yes, it is Christ.

The power of your salvation, then, is the power of Christ.[3]

Where is this power of Christ to be found?

Surely "horns are in his hands;
> his strength is hidden there."[4]

Horns indeed are in his hands,
> because his hands were nailed to the arms of the Cross.

But what strength is there in such great weakness?[5]
> What loftiness is there is such great humility?
> What is worthy of reverence in such great scorn?

Ah, but truly it is hidden, because it is in weakness;
> it is concealed, because it is in humility;
> it is veiled, because it is in scorn.

O hidden strength:
> a human being hanging on the Cross
>> lifts the burden of eternal death that weighs heavily upon the human race;
> a human being bound to a tree
>> looses the bonds of a world held fast by everlasting death.

O concealed power:
> a human being condemned in the company of thieves[6]
>> saves human beings condemned in the company of demons;
> a human being stretched out on the gallows
>> draws all people to himself.[7]

---

2. Cf. Luke 10:33 ff.

3. Cf. 2 Corinthians 12:9.

4. Cf. Habakkuk 3:4.

5. Cf. 2 Corinthians 12:9.

6. Cf. Mark 15:27 ff.

7. John 12:32.

O veiled might:
> one single soul sent forth in torment
>> rescues countless souls from hell;
> a human being accepts the death of the body
>> and utterly destroys the death of souls.

Why, good Lord, kind Redeemer, mighty Savior:
> why did you conceal such great power in such great humility?
Was it in order to deceive the devil,
> who by deceiving human beings expelled them from paradise?
But surely Truth does not deceive anyone.
Those who do not know the truth,
> who do not believe the truth—
> they deceive themselves.
Those who see the truth,
> and hate it or scorn it—
> they deceive themselves.
And so Truth does not deceive anyone.
Was it, then, in order for the devil to deceive himself?
Certainly not: just as Truth does not deceive anyone,
> he does not mean for any to deceive themselves,
> although we might say that Truth does this when Truth permits it.
For you did not assume human nature in order to conceal what was known of you,
> but to reveal what was unknown.
You proclaimed yourself truly God and truly human,
> and in your works you proved yourself to be so.[8]
The matter itself was a mystery,
> but it was not deliberately made mysterious.
It was not done in this way in order to be hidden,
> but so that it might be accomplished in due order;
> not to deceive anyone,
> but to be carried out in a fitting way.
If we say that it was mysterious,
> this means simply that it has not been revealed to everyone.
For even if Truth does not show himself openly to everyone,
> he does not deny himself to anyone.
Therefore, Lord, you did not act in this way to deceive anyone,
> or so that any might deceive themselves:

---

8. Cf. John 5:36.

no, you acted so as to do what had to be done,
> in the way it had to be done;
> in all things you remained steadfast in truth.[9]
Those, therefore, who have deceived themselves concerning your truth
> must lament, not your falsehood, but their own.

Did the devil have some just claim against God or against human beings,
> on account of which God was obligated to act against the devil
>> on our behalf in this way,
> rather than by an open show of strength,
> so that when the devil unjustly slew that just human being,
> he justly lost the power he had had over the unjust?
No, surely God owed the devil nothing but punishment,
> and human beings owed him nothing but requital:
> as human beings by sinning let themselves be easily vanquished by the devil,
> they were now to vanquish him by preserving justice whole and sound,
>> even up to the torment of death.
But even that, human beings owed only to God,
> for they did not sin against the devil,
>> but against God;
> human beings did not belong to the devil;
>> no, both human beings and the devil belonged to God.
The devil was not tormenting human beings from a zeal for justice,
> but from sheer wickedness;
> not at God's command, but by God's permission;
> not because the devil's rights gave sanction,
> but because God's justice demanded it.
So there was nothing in the devil that required God to conceal or curtail his power
> in acting against the devil to save the human race.

Did any necessity compel the Most High to stoop to such lowliness,[10]
> the Almighty to labor so hard to accomplish his work?
No: all necessity, all impossibility, is subject to his will.
Indeed, what God wills, must be;
> what God does not will, cannot be.
So he did all this by his will alone:
> and since his will is always good,
> he did all this by his goodness alone.

---

9. Cf. John 8:44.
10. Philippians 2:8.

For God did not need to save human beings in this way;

no, human nature needed to make recompense to God in this way.

God did not need to suffer such labors and pains,

but human beings needed to be reconciled in this way.

God did not need to be brought so low,

but human beings needed to be rescued in this way from the depths of hell.

The divine nature did not need to be brought low or to labor so hard;

it was not even capable of lowliness or labor.

But it was necessary for human nature to do all these things

so that it might be restored to the state for which it was created;

yet neither human nature, nor anything that is not God,

could be sufficient for this.

For human beings are not restored to the condition for which they were created,

unless they are exalted to be like the angels[11] in whom there is no sin.

And that cannot be done unless they have received forgiveness of all their sins,

which cannot be given until they have first made a complete recompense.

The recompense must be like this:

the sinner, or someone on his behalf, must give God something of his own,

something he does not owe God,

that is of greater value than everything that is not God.

For if sinning is dishonoring God,

and it was not right for human beings to dishonor God,

even if that should mean that everything that is not God

would inevitably perish,

surely unchangeable truth and evident reason demand

that a sinner repay God for the honor he has taken away,

by giving something greater

than that for the sake of which he ought not to have dishonored God.

And because human nature by itself had no such thing to give,

and it could not be reconciled without the recompense that was owed—

lest God's justice allow the disorder of sin to remain in his kingdom—

the goodness of God came to our help:

the Son of God took human nature into his own person,

so that in that person there would be a God-man,

who would have something of greater value

not only than every being that is not God,

but greater even than every debt that sinners are bound to pay;

---

11. Cf. Matthew 22:30, Mark 12:25, Luke 20:36.

and because he owed nothing for himself,

    he could give it as payment of the debt for others,

    who did not have what they needed to pay back the debt they owed.

For the life of that one human being is more precious than all that is not God;

    its worth surpasses every debt that sinners owe in order to make recompense.

For if killing him is worse than all the many and great sins

    that can be conceived outside the person of God,

    it is clear that his life is a greater good than all sins outside the person of God are evils.

This human being did not owe the debt of death, for he was not a sinner;

    yet of his own accord he gave his life, something of his own,

        for the honor of the Father,

    when he allowed his life to be taken from him for the sake of justice,

    to give an example to all that they should not abandon the justice of God

        on account of death—

    a death they owed, and would of necessity someday pay—

    when he, who did not owe death,

        and could have avoided death while preserving justice,

    accepted of his own accord, for justice' sake, the death inflicted on him.

And so in that human being human nature gave God something of its own—

    gave it of its own accord, and not in payment of a debt—

    in order to redeem itself in other human beings,

    in whom it did not have the wherewithal to repay what the debt demanded.

In all this the divine nature is not humbled;

    instead, human nature is exalted.

Divine nature is not diminished;

    human nature is mercifully helped.

Human nature in that human being did not undergo anything by necessity,

    but only by free will.

It was not crushed by any violence;

    no, by its own spontaneous goodness,

    for the honor of God and the benefit of other human beings,

    it bore, laudably and mercifully, what was inflicted on it by evil will.

No obedience compelled this;

    mighty wisdom ordained this.

For the Father did not command and compel this human being to die;

    he understood what would please the Father and benefit human beings,

    and that he did of his own accord.

The Father indeed could not compel him to do this,

    because it would be wrong for him to demand it of him.

And such great honor, which the Son offered by so good a will,
> could not but please the Father.

And so in this way he offered free obedience to the Father,
> by willing to do of his own accord what he knew would please the Father.

Because the Father gave him this good will—free though it was—
> it is not inappropriate to say that he received it as a command from the Father.

It is in this way that he was "obedient" to the Father "even unto death,"[12]
> that he "did as the Father commanded" him,[13]
> that he "drank the cup that the Father gave" him.[14]

For this is perfect, and perfectly free, obedience on the part of human nature:
> to subject its free will to God's will of its own accord,
> and, when it has received a good will,
> to carry it out in action spontaneously, freely, and without compulsion.

Thus this human being redeemed all the others,
> because what he gave to God of his own accord
> is reckoned as payment of the debt they owed.

By this price human beings are not merely redeemed once from their faults;
> they are welcomed back again and again,
> whenever they return with worthy repentance,
> though such repentance is not promised to sinners.

Because all this was done on the Cross,
> our Christ has redeemed us by the Cross.

Those who will to approach this grace with the love it deserves are saved,[15]
> but those who scorn it are justly damned,
> because they do not pay the debt they owe.

Behold, Christian soul,
> this is the power of your salvation,
> this is the cause of your liberation,
> this is the price of your redemption.

You were a captive,
> but by this you have been redeemed.

You were a slave,
> and by this you have been set free.[16]

---

12. Cf. Philippians 2:8.
13. Cf. John 14:31.
14. Cf. John 18:11.
15. Hebrews 7:25.
16. Cf. Galatians 4:31.

By this the exiled soul has been brought back home,

    the lost soul restored,

    the dead soul brought back to life.

O mortal,

    let your heart bite down upon this, chew it, savor it, drink of it deeply,

    when your mouth receives the Body and Blood of your Redeemer.

Make this your daily bread[17] in this life,

    your sustenance,

    your food for the journey,

    because by this, and this alone,

    you will abide in Christ, and Christ in you,[18]

    and in the life to come your joy will be full.[19]

But you, O Lord, who accepted death that I might have life:

How am I to rejoice in my liberation,

    which is simply to rejoice in your bonds?

How am I to exult in my salvation,

    which is simply to exult in your sufferings?

How am I to take joy in my life,

    which is simply to take joy in your death?

Shall I rejoice in the things you suffered,

    shall I rejoice in the cruelty of those who did those things to you,

    because if they had not done them, you would not have suffered,

    and if you had not suffered, these good things would not have been mine?

But if I sorrow over them,

    how shall I rejoice over the good things for the sake of which they were done,

    good things that would not exist if those sufferings had not existed?

Truly, their wickedness could do nothing except because you freely permitted it,

    and you suffered only because you mercifully willed it.

And so I ought to curse their cruelty;

    I ought to imitate your death and your labors by suffering along with you;

    I ought to love your merciful will by giving thanks.

This is how I may safely exult in the good things you have bestowed upon me.

Therefore, insignificant mortal,

    leave their cruelty to the judgment of God,

    and turn your thoughts instead to what you owe to your Savior.

---

17. Cf. Matthew 6:11, Luke 11:3.

18. Cf. John 6:57.

19. Cf. John 16:24, 1 John 1:4 and *passim*.

Ponder what he was for you, what was done for you,

    and consider what great love the one who did this for you deserves.

Look upon your need and upon his goodness,

    and see what thanks you should render him,

      how much you owe to his love.

You were in darkness,

    on slippery ground,

      falling into the boundless void of hell,

      from which there is no return.

An immeasurable weight as of lead hung from your neck

    and was dragging you down;

      a heavy load beyond bearing was pressing upon you;

      unseen enemies[20] were fighting against you with all their power.

Such was your state, with nothing to help you;

    and you did not know it,

      for you were conceived and born in such a condition.[21]

Oh, what troubles beset you,

    and to what misery they were bearing you away!

Call them to mind and be terrified;

    ponder them and tremble.

O good Lord Christ Jesus,

    so I was, not seeking your help, not even imagining it,

    when you shed your light on me and showed me my true state.

You threw away the leaden weight that was dragging me down;

    you lifted the burden that was pressing down on me;

    you drove away those who were attacking me

      and fought against them yourself on my behalf.

You called me by a new name[22] that you gave me from your own name;

    I was bent double, but you stood me upright so that I could look upon your face.

You said to me:

    "Be of good cheer![23]

      I have redeemed you;[24]

      I have given my life for you.[25]

---

20. Cf. Ephesians 6:12.

21. Cf. Psalm 51:5 (50:5).

22. Cf. Revelation 2:17.

23. Cf. Matthew 9:2, 22.

24. Cf. Isaiah 43:1.

25. Cf. John 10:15.

If you cling to me,

    you will escape the evils that used to beset you,

    and you will not fall into the pit where you were heading.

    Instead I will lead you into my kingdom,

    and I will make you an heir of God and joint-heir with me."[26]

From then on you took me into your care,

    so that nothing would harm my soul against its will.

And behold! although I have not yet clung to you as you counseled me to do,

    you have not allowed me to fall into hell;

    you are still looking for the day when I cling to you

        and you do what you have promised.

Truly, Lord, that was my state,

    and you have done these things for me.

I was in darkness,

    for I knew nothing—not even myself.

I was on slippery ground,

    for I was weak and frail,

    prone to fall into sin.

I was falling into the boundless void of hell,

    because in our first parents I had fallen from righteousness into unrighteousness,

        by which one falls into hell,

    and from happiness to wretchedness in this world,

        from which one falls into eternal wretchedness in the next.

The weight of original sin was dragging me down,

    and the unbearable load of God's judgment was pressing down on me.

My enemies, the demons, were attacking me furiously,

    trying as hard as they could

    to make me worthy of yet greater condemnation

    because of other sins.

So I was, bereft of all help.

You shed your light on me and showed me my true condition,

    for when I was still unable to recognize it,

    you taught it to others who came before me,

    and then you taught it to me,

        even before I asked.

You threw off the leaden weight that was dragging me down,

    the burden that was oppressing me,

---

26. Cf. Romans 8:17.

the enemies that were attacking me,

because you took away the sin in which I was conceived and born,[27]

canceled its condemnation,

and forbade the malicious spirits to attack my soul.

You caused me to be called a Christian, called by your own name;

in that name I profess my faith,

and by that name you know me

to be in the company of those whom you have redeemed.

You have set me upright and lifted me up, so that I may know you and love you.

You have made me trust in the salvation of my soul,

for which you gave your life;

and you have promised me your glory,

if I but follow you.

And behold! even when I no longer follow you in the way you have counseled me,

but go on committing many sins that you have forbidden,

you still look for the day when I will follow you

and you will give what you have promised.

Ponder, my soul,

pay heed, all my innermost being,

how much my whole substance owes him.

Truly, Lord, because you made me,

I owe my whole self to your love.

Because you redeemed me,

I owe my whole self to your love.

Because you promise me such great things,

I owe my whole self to your love.

Indeed, I owe to your love as much more than myself

as you are greater than I,

for whom you gave yourself,

and to whom you promise yourself.

I beseech you, Lord:

grant me to taste through love what I taste through knowledge;

let me perceive through my affection what I perceive through my understanding.

I owe more than my whole self,

but I do not have more to give,

and I cannot, of my own strength, give even all I have.

---

27. Psalm 51:5 (50:5).

O Lord, draw all I have into your love.
All that I am is yours by creation;
    make all that I am yours through love.

Behold, Lord, my heart is before you.
It tries, but it has no power of itself;
    do what it cannot.
Grant me entrance into the inner chamber[28] of your love.
I ask, I seek, I knock.[29]
You who cause me to ask: cause me to receive.
You grant me to seek: grant that I find.
You teach me to knock: open the door to me.
To whom will you give,
    if you deny one who asks?
Who will find,
    if the seeker seeks in vain?
To whom will you open the door,
    if you shut it against one who knocks?
What will you give to one who does not pray,
    if you deny your love to one who prays?
It is from you that I have this longing;
    from you let me have its fulfillment.
Cling to him, my soul;
    cling to him with persistence.
O good, good Lord,
    do not reject my soul.
It is fainting from hunger for your love:[30]
    revive it.[31]
Let your love satisfy it,
    your affection strengthen it,
    your love fill it.
Take control of everything I am,
    seize possession of it all,
    for with the Father and the Holy Spirit you are one God,
    "blessed forever and ever. Amen."[32]

---

28. Cf. Matthew 6:6.
29. Cf. Matthew 7:7 ff.
30. Cf. Song of Solomon 2:5.
31. Cf. Lamentations 1:11.
32. Cf. Romans 1:25, 9:5; 2 Corinthians 11:31.

Glossary

ACCIDENT: An accident is a feature something has that does not belong to its essence* (sense 3).

ACCIDENTAL (NATURE): An accidental nature is simply an accident.*

ACCIDENTALLY: (1) "differ accidentally": If two things have the same essence but differ from each other in some way, they are said to differ accidentally. For example, two human beings differ accidentally, since they have the same essence but differ in their accidents;* a human being and a cat differ substantially,* since they have different essences. (2) "said (or predicated) accidentally": see SUBSTANTIALLY/ESSENTIALLY.*

BODY: The word 'body' is used more broadly in philosophy than in ordinary language. Any material object at all is a body in the philosophical sense. (Similarly, in scientific language we might speak of "a body in motion.") So chairs and tables are bodies, as are the bodies of human beings and other living creatures.

CONSUBSTANTIAL: The Nicene Creed says that God the Son is consubstantial with the Father; that is, God the Son is one in being with the Father.

It might be helpful for the reader to have the relevant portions of the Nicene Creed. The italicized phrases are those that Anselm deals with explicitly in the *Monologion*. Following each phrase is the number of the chapter in which he argues for the truth of that phrase.

> I believe in one Lord, Jesus Christ, the only-begotten *Son* (42) of God, begotten of the *Father* (42) *before all worlds* (32), God from God, Light from Light, true God from true God, *begotten* (40–41), *not made* (29), *consubstantial with the Father* (29). *Through him all things were made* (29). . . . I believe in the Holy Spirit, the Lord and Giver of life, *who proceeds from the Father and the Son* (50, 54).

DENOMINATIVE: In Anselm's usage, a denominative is a name* derived from a cognate noun. For example, *grammaticus* (noun: "grammarian"; adjective: "grammatical") is a denominative derived from the noun *grammatica* ("grammar").

DIFFERENCE: In a definition, the difference is what sets apart one sort of thing from others in the same genus.* For example, in the definition of human being as "rational animal," *rational* is the difference that sets human beings apart from other things in the genus *animal.*

EFFICIENT CAUSE: In Chapter 6 of the *Monologion* Anselm distinguishes three sorts of causes. The efficient cause is the one that more or less corresponds to our ordinary usage of the word 'cause' (though note the broader characterization of efficient causes in Lambeth Fragments 9). The efficient cause of *x* is whatever brings about or produces *x*. The material cause of a thing is the matter out of which it is made; the instrumental cause of a thing is any tool that was used in bringing it about. To use a standard example, the material cause of a marble statue is the marble it is made of, the instrumental cause is the sculptor's chisel or other tools, and the efficient cause is the sculptor.

In Chapter 6 of the *Monologion* Anselm is generally careful to use different prepositions for each of the three causes. A thing is said to come about "by the agency of" an efficient cause, "from" a material cause, and "by means of" an instrumental cause.

ESSENCE (LATIN, *ESSENTIA*): Anselm uses the word *essentia* in a variety of ways: (1) It signifies the individual thing that exists. In this usage "an essence" is synonymous with "an existent being." (2) Sometimes it is used to indicate what a present-day philosopher might call "ontological status." In this sense one might say that darkness, for example, has no essence, because it is nothing more than the absence of light, whereas light has essence because it is something in its own right. To say that darkness has no essence, in this sense, is therefore equivalent to saying that it is nothing and that it is not something. (3) It sometimes signifies the nature of a thing. For example, the essence of a human being is to be rational and animal. Such other features as being tall or short, dark or fair, male or female are accidents.* (4) Sometimes (particularly in *On Truth*, Chapter 7) Anselm uses it strictly as the abstract noun corresponding to *esse*, "to be," where that verb includes the meanings "exists" and "is a certain way." In such cases I translate *essentia* as 'being,' and 'being' should be understood to include the meanings 'existence' and 'being a certain way.' (5) Occasionally it simply means 'existence.'

ESSENTIALLY: See SUBSTANTIALLY/ESSENTIALLY.

ETERNAL: To say that God is eternal is *not* to say that he exists at all times. Rather, it is to say that God exists outside time altogether. That is, he exists in such a way that he has no past, present, or future; all of his existence is simultaneous.

GENUS: In a definition, the genus is the general classification to which the thing defined belongs. For example, in the definition of human being as "rational animal," *animal* is the genus to which human beings belong. (See also DIFFERENCE.*)

IMPASSIBLE: This word comes from the Latin *pati*, "to undergo or suffer," which is contrasted with *agere*, "to do or act." To say that God is impassible therefore means that he cannot suffer or undergo anything. He cannot be acted upon by anything else; he simply acts.

IMPROPERLY: A word is used improperly when it is used in a way that is misleading or not philosophically precise. Anselm is concerned in particular about expressions that, if taken literally, seem to attribute a power, obligation, or characteristic to something that does not actually have that power, obligation, or characteristic. For example, if I say "Elderly parents ought to be supported by their children," I seem to be attributing an obligation to the parents. But in fact it is the children who have an obligation, the obligation to support their parents; so Anselm would say that I am using the word 'ought' improperly. See also PROPERLY.*

IMPUTED: An act is imputed to an agent whenever the agent is held to be both causally and morally responsible for the act.

NAME: A name (*nomen*) is a noun or adjective.

NATURAL/NATURALLY: An act is natural (or someone acts naturally) when the act can be fully explained by the nature God gave the agent.

NATURE: 'Nature' is interchangeable with essence* in senses 1, 2, and 3.

NECESSARY: A proposition is necessary (or necessarily true) if it is not possible for that proposition to be false. An action is necessary if it is not spontaneous.*

NECESSITY: An action is said to happen out of necessity if it is not done spontaneously.*

POSTERIOR TO: There are a number of different ways in which something can be posterior to something else. For example, x is posterior to y if (1) x is later in time than y, or (2) x is caused by y, or (3) the existence or truth of x is explained by the existence or truth of y, but not vice versa.

PRIOR (IN NATURE): x is prior in nature to y if and only if x explains, accounts for, or causes y. Priority in nature does not imply priority in time, as Anselm argues in Chapter 22 of *On Truth*.

PROPERLY: A word is used properly when it is used strictly and literally, not loosely or in a way that is apt to be misleading or violates precise philosophical usage.

QUALITY/QUANTITY/QUIDDITY: These three terms are associated with three different kinds of questions one can ask about a thing. One can ask "*Quid est?*" or "What is it?" The answer to that question will tell you a thing's quiddity—in other words, its essence* (sense 3). One can ask "*Qualis est?*" or "What sort of thing is it?" (more colloquially, "What's it like?"). The answer to that question will tell you some quality a thing has, such as justice or goodness. Finally, one can ask "*Quantum est?*" or "How great is it?" The answer to that question will tell you something about the quantity of the thing, as for example whether it is great or small. Anselm argues in Chapter 16 of the *Monologion* that when we apply words like 'just' and 'great' to God, they do not signify some quality or quantity of God's. Rather, they signify his essence. For example, justice is not a quality God *has*, as if God were one thing and his justice some other thing. Rather, justice is what God *is*.

RELATIVE(S): 'Daughter,' for example, is a relative (or "relative term"), since it implies a relation to a parent. Someone is called a daughter, not because of what she is in herself, but because of the relation she has to someone else.

RELATIVELY: Anselm claims that relatives* are not said substantially* of things. In the sentence "Mary is a daughter," 'daughter' is not said substantially of Mary, since it does not signify her essence or substance. Instead, it is said relatively of Mary. If instead one said "Mary is rational," 'rational' would be said substantially of Mary, since being rational is part of the essence of being human.

SEVERAL: I sometimes use 'several' to translate the Latin word *plures*, which means "more than one." The reader should therefore keep in mind that 'several' need not imply a large number; it simply implies more than one.

SIMPLE: To say that God is simple is to say that he has no parts. More specifically, Anselm argues that God has no spatial parts, no temporal parts, and no metaphysical parts.

SIMPLY: See UNQUALIFIED/IN AN UNQUALIFIED SENSE/SIMPLY.*

SPONTANEOUS(LY): 'Spontaneous' and 'spontaneously' are used in this translation to represent the Latin *spontaneus* and *sponte* in contexts in which the usual English equivalents (such as 'willingly,' 'freely,' or 'of one's own accord') could be misleading; they do not connote impulsiveness or lack of premeditation, as they do in ordinary usage. An act is spontaneous (or an agent acts spontaneously) when the act can be fully explained only by reference to something that originates within the agent. For example, Anselm argues in *On the Fall of the Devil* that the sin of the angels was spontaneous, because it was up to them whether to sin or not; the powers and the knowledge they had received from God were not enough to explain either their sinning or their remaining just. If an act is not spontaneous, it is natural.*

SUBSIST: 'Subsist' means "to exist (as a substance)." In other words, saying that a substance subsists is exactly the same as saying that it exists. But accidents* do not subsist; they can only exist *in* a substance, not *as* a substance.

SUBSISTENT: An individual existent being; a thing that subsists.

SUBSTANCE: The word 'substance' is used in a variety of ways: (1) It can be used interchangeably with essence* (senses 1 or 3). (2) It can be used to signify the individual thing that underlies accidents.* In Chapter 79 of the *Monologion* Anselm argues that individual things are properly called substances because they "stand under" (*substant*) accidents. He argues in Chapter 26 of the *Monologion* that God cannot be called a substance in sense (2), because he does not, strictly speaking, have any accidents. (3) It has a technical usage in Trinitarian theology. Anselm explains his use of the term in the Prologue to the *Monologion* and in Chapter 16 of *On the Incarnation of the Word* with reference to a terminological difference between the Eastern Church ("the Greeks") and the Western Church ("the Latins").

SUBSTANTIAL (NATURE): A substantial nature is simply a substance.

SUBSTANTIALLY/ESSENTIALLY: (1) "differ substantially": Two things differ substantially when they have a different essence* (sense 3). For example, a dog and a horse differ substantially, whereas two horses differ only accidentally.* (2) "said (or predicated) substantially": In the sentence "Socrates is human," 'human' is said substantially (or essentially) of Socrates. That is, 'human' signifies something belonging to Socrates' substance* or essence* (sense 3). Contrast this with 'pale' in "Socrates is pale." Being pale is not part of Socrates' substance or essence, and so in that sentence 'pale' is not said of Socrates substantially, but instead accidentally.* When Anselm asks what can be said of God substantially, he is asking what terms (if any) signify God's essence.

SUSTAINER: Recently the practice has arisen of speaking of the Trinity as "Creator, Redeemer, and Sustainer" rather than as "Father, Son, and Holy Spirit." It is therefore important for me to point out that when Anselm uses the word 'Sustainer' he is not referring exclusively to the Holy Spirit. When the word is first introduced in Chapter 14 of the *Monologion*, it refers to God the Father. Later, after Anselm has argued that all three persons of the Trinity are Creator, we can assume that all three are also Sustainer, since he argues in Chapter 14 of the *Monologion* that the same agency both creates and sustains all things.

UNQUALIFIED/IN AN UNQUALIFIED SENSE/SIMPLY (LATIN, *SIMPLEX/SIMPLICITER*): The colloquial English equivalent is "period" (or in British English, "full stop"). For example, "God is an unqualified good" or "God is good in an unqualified sense" or "God is simply good" means that God is good, period; no qualification of the statement is necessary (or even possible). A creature, by contrast, can only be good *in a certain respect* or *for a certain purpose* or *to a certain degree*. Similarly, Anselm says that God *exists* in an unqualified sense, or "simply exists." Creatures exist *for a time* or *in a certain way* or *to a certain extent*; God just exists, period.

WORD: The Prologue to the Gospel according to John states, "In the beginning was the Word. And the Word was with God; and the Word was God. All things were made through him, and without him was nothing made." As Anselm explains it, 'Word' is a particularly apt name for God the Son, since he is God's *utterance* of himself and of creation. In keeping with these words from Scripture as well as the Nicene Creed (see CONSUBSTANTIAL*), Anselm argues that this utterance or Word existed *in the beginning* (that is, eternally: see Chapter 32, *Monologion*); that he *is God* (Chapter 29); and that *all things were made through him* (Chapter 29).

Index